PRINCIPLES AND METHODS OF SOCIAL RESEARCH

Used to train generations of social scientists, this thoroughly updated classic text covers the latest research techniques and designs. Applauded for its comprehensive coverage, the breadth and depth of content is unparalleled. Through a multi-methodology approach, the text guides readers toward the design and conduct of social research from the ground up. Explained with applied examples useful to the social, behavioral, educational, and organizational sciences, the methods described are intended to be relevant to contemporary researchers.

The underlying logic and mechanics of experimental, quasi-experimental, and nonexperimental research strategies are discussed in detail. Introductory chapters covering topics such as validity and reliability furnish readers with a firm understanding of foundational concepts. Chapters dedicated to sampling, interviewing, questionnaire design, stimulus scaling, observational methods, content analysis, implicit measures, dyadic and group methods, and meta-analysis provide coverage of these essential methodologies.

The book is noted for its:

- Emphasis on understanding the principles that govern the use of a method to facilitate the researcher's choice of the best technique for a given situation.
- Use of the laboratory experiment as a touchstone to describe and evaluate field experiments, correlational designs, quasi experiments, evaluation studies, and survey designs.
- Coverage of the ethics of social research, including the power a researcher wields and tips on how to use it responsibly.

The new edition features:

- A new co-author, Andrew Lac, instrumental in fine-tuning the book's accessible approach and highlighting the most recent developments at the intersection of design and statistics.
- More learning tools, including more explanation of the basic concepts, more research examples, tables, and figures, and the addition of boldfaced terms, chapter conclusions, discussion questions, and a glossary.
- Extensive revision of Chapter 3 on measurement reliability theory that examines test theory, latent factors, factor analysis, and item response theory.
- Expanded coverage of cutting-edge methodologies, including mediation and moderation, reliability and validity, missing data, and more physiological approaches such as neuroimaging and fMRIs.
- A new web-based resource package that features PowerPoint presentations and discussion and exam questions for each chapter and, for students, chapter outlines and summaries, key terms, and suggested readings.

Intended as a text for graduate or advanced undergraduate courses in research methods (design) in psychology, communication, sociology, education, public health, and marketing, an introductory undergraduate course on research methods is recommended.

William D. Crano is the Oskamp Distinguished Chair and Head of the Department of Psychology at Claremont Graduate University.

Marilynn B. Brewer is Professor Emeritus at The Ohio State University and a Visiting Professor of Psychology at the University of New South Wales.

Andrew Lac is Research Professor of Psychology at Claremont Graduate University.

PRINCIPLES AND METHODS OF SOCIAL RESEARCH

Third Edition

William D. Crano, Marilynn B. Brewer, and Andrew Lac

NEW YORK AND LONDON

Third edition published 2015
by Routledge
711 Third Avenue, New York, NY 10017

and by Routledge
27 Church Road, Hove, East Sussex BN3 2FA

Routledge is an imprint of the Taylor & Francis Group, an informa business

© 2015 Taylor & Francis

The right of William D. Crano, Marilynn B. Brewer, and Andrew Lac to be identified as the authors of this work has been asserted by them in accordance with sections 77 and 78 of the Copyright, Designs and Patents Act 1988.

All rights reserved. No part of this book may be reprinted or reproduced or utilised in any form or by any electronic, mechanical, or other means, now known or hereafter invented, including photocopying and recording, or in any information storage or retrieval system, without permission in writing from the publishers.

Trademark notice: Product or corporate names may be trademarks or registered trademarks, and are used only for identification and explanation without intent to infringe.

First edition published by Allyn & Bacon 1986
Second edition published by Lawrence Erlbaum Associates, Inc. 2002

Library of Congress Cataloging-in-Publication Data
Crano, William D., 1942–
Principles and methods of social research / William D. Crano, Marilynn B. Brewer,
  Andrew Lac. — Third edition.
    pages cm
  1. Social sciences—Research. 2. Social sciences—Methodology. I. Brewer, Marilynn B.,
1942– II. Lac, Andrew. III. Title.
  H62.C692 2014
  300.72—dc23
  2014012586

ISBN: 978-0-415-63855-5 (hbk)
ISBN: 978-0-415-63856-2 (pbk)
ISBN: 978-1-315-76831-1 (ebk)

Typeset in Bembo
by Apex CoVantage, LLC

CONTENTS

Preface xi
Acknowledgements xvii
About the Authors xix

PART I
Introduction to Social Research Methods 1

1 Basic Concepts 3
  Science and Daily Life 4
  Theories and Hypotheses 5
  From Theory, Concept, or Idea to Operation 6
  Role of Theory in Scientific Inquiry 15
  Conclusion and Overview 18
  Questions for Discussion 19
  References 19

2 Internal and External Validity 22
  Causation 23
  Phases of Research 25
  Distinguishing Internal and External Validity 27
  Basic Issues of Internal Validity 31
  Basic Issues of External Validity 39
  Conclusion 41
  Questions for Discussion 42
  References 43

3 Measurement Reliability 45
  Classical Test Theory 45
  Contemporary Test Theory 53
  Conclusion 61

Questions for Discussion	62
References	62

4 Measurement Validity — 64
Types of Measurement Validity	65
Threats to Measurement Validity	74
Conclusion	78
Questions for Discussion	78
References	78

PART II
Research Design Strategies: Experiments, Quasi-Experiments, and Nonexperiments — 81

5 Designing Experiments: Variations on the Basics — 83
Basic Variations in Experimental Design	83
Expanding the Number of Experimental Treatments	86
Blocked Designs: Incorporating a Nonexperimental Factor	94
Repeated-Measures Designs and Counterbalancing	96
Conclusion	98
Questions for Discussion	99
References	99

6 Constructing Laboratory Experiments — 101
Steps for Constructing an Experiment	101
Types of Experimental Manipulations	104
Manipulation Checks	109
Assignment of Participants to Conditions: Randomization Procedures	110
Realism in an Experiment	111
Social Simulations and Analogue Experiments	112
Conclusion	120
Questions for Discussion	120
References	121

7 External Validity of Laboratory Experiments — 125
Generalizability Across Participants	126
Experimenter Expectancy and Bias	131
Three Faces of External Validity	135
Conclusion	138
Questions for Discussion	138
References	139

8 Conducting Experiments Outside the Laboratory — 141
Research Settings and Issues of Validity	142
Constructing a Field Experiment	143
The Internet as a Site for Experimental Research	149
Conclusion	155
Questions for Discussion	155
References	156

9 Nonexperimental Research: Correlational Design and Analyses	159
Analyzing and Interpreting Nonexperimental Research	160
Multiple Regression	166
Uses and Misuses of Correlational Analysis	167
Multi-Level Models	170
Structural Equation Models	172
Conclusion	181
Questions for Discussion	182
References	183
10 Quasi-Experiments and Evaluation Research	185
Program Evaluation Research	186
Quasi-Experimental Methods	189
Use of Archival Data in Longitudinal Research	211
Conclusion	213
Questions for Discussion	213
References	213

PART III
Data Collecting Methods — 217

11 Survey Studies: Design and Sampling	219
Selection vs. Assignment	219
Random Sampling	224
Nonrandom Sampling	233
More Sampling Issues	236
Types of Survey Studies	241
Missing Data	244
Conclusion	246
Questions for Discussion	246
References	247
12 Systematic Observational Methods	250
Three Aspects of Naturalism	250
Observer Involvement in the Naturalistic Setting: The Participatory–Nonparticipatory Distinction	253
Coding Observations	260
Conclusion	274
Questions for Discussion	275
References	276
13 Interviewing	280
Modes of Administration: Face-to-Face and Telephone	280
Developing the Interview	281
Interview Structure	286
Conducting the Interview	290
Interviewer Characteristics: Establishing Rapport	293
Group Interviews and Focus Groups	296
Conclusion	298

Questions for Discussion	298
References	299

14 Content Analysis — 303
- Conducting a Content Analysis — 304
- Representative Examples — 314
- Conclusion — 319
- Questions for Discussion — 319
- References — 320

15 Questionnaire Design and Scale Construction — 323
- Questionnaires — 323
- Constructing Rating Scales — 326
- Conclusion — 338
- Questions for Discussion — 338
- References — 339

16 Indirect and Implicit Measures of Cognition and Affect — 342
- Indirect Measures — 343
- Information Processing: Attention and Memory — 344
- Priming: Processing Without Awareness or Intent — 350
- Social Psychophysiology: Physiological Traces of Affect and Cognitive Processing — 358
- Conclusion — 363
- Questions for Discussion — 364
- References — 366

17 Scaling Stimuli: Social Psychophysics — 370
- Scaling Stimuli — 371
- Techniques for Stimulus Scaling — 372
- Multidimensional Scaling Models — 377
- Conclusion — 382
- Questions for Discussion — 382
- References — 383

18 Methods for Assessing Dyads and Groups — 385
- Dyadic Designs — 385
- Deriving Dyadic and Group Level Variables — 387
- Designs to Study Group Structures — 391
- Designs to Study Multiple Groups — 396
- Measuring Group Process and Outcomes — 398
- Conclusion — 402
- Questions for Discussion — 402
- References — 403

PART IV
Concluding Perspectives   407

19   Synthesizing Research Results: Meta-Analysis   409
    Stages in the Meta-Analysis Process   411
    Interpreting the Meta-Analysis   422
    Conclusion   424
    Questions for Discussion   424
    References   425

20   Social Responsibility and Ethics in Social Research   428
    Ethics of Research Practices   428
    The Regulatory Context of Research Involving Human Participants   435
    Ethics of Data Reporting   438
    Ethical Issues Related to the Products of Scientific Research   440
    Conclusion   441
    Questions for Discussion   441
    References   442

Glossary   445
Suggested Additional Readings   459
Author Index   467
Subject Index   477

PREFACE

When this book's "great-grandfather" first saw the light of day, William Crano and Marilynn Brewer were fresh out of graduate school, former students of Donald T. Campbell, one of social science's preeminent research methodologists. Then and now we recognized the need for a clear understanding of the proper application of the scientific method to the study of human social behavior. As before, many people today still contend that science has nothing to say about the beliefs, values, and behavioral characteristics that define us as human. From this ultimately pessimistic point of view, love, hate, identity, alienation, prejudice, reason, discrimination, altruism, attitudes, intergroup relations, and a host of other distinctly human characteristics and properties are defined as beyond the reach of science. The argument goes, "Such things are better left to poets or priests or philosophers—they are not appropriate subjects of scientific study." We disagree.

We disagree because we are convinced that in the short space of this book's life, good social research has added immensely to our store of knowledge about all of these difficult-to-research but ultimately understandable issues. Complex aspects of human social life are subject to good scientific analysis, which when applied properly produces knowledge that leads to a better understanding of the human condition. This book is designed to help lay the necessary foundation for this quest. It is firmly grounded in the scientific method, and provides the background knowledge necessary to design and implement good research. It is crucial, however, that the rigorous application of the scientific method is accompanied by creativity and dedication if real progress is to be made in social research. Although we believe this book can supply the necessary grounding, you will need to bring your own creativity and motivation.

In our earliest rendition of this book, we focused strongly on the experimental method as a touchstone against which other research methodologies were to be judged. We still view the experiment as the preeminent means of developing strong causal inferences, but even in the original volume we recognized that the environment of the laboratory was quite restrictive, and so we expanded the field of play to include topics like interviewing and content analysis, topics that at the time were deemed "esoteric" inclusions in a book on research design. In the book's later version, we expanded our consideration of the more traditional experimental models and extended our discussion to include new topics, including analogue experiments, meta-analysis, regression-based causal modeling, survey sampling, evaluation research, dyadic analysis, and considerations of experimenter expectancy effects. Emerging methods in social cognition also made the chapter list, along with an augmented emphasis on external validity and generalizability, the use of field research accompanied by relatively novel techniques like propensity analysis, and other methods of intervention and evaluation that fit with our growing realization that good science owes a debt to the society that nurtured it, a concern Campbell advanced insistently in his later years.

The basic structure of our book has been designed to build logically from fundamental research strategies (experimental and quasi-experimental methods, correlational designs, etc.) to the tactics of data collection and the logistics of proper research procedures. We have presented this material as clearly as we could, and believe a conscientious student should not have problems understanding the concepts and advice included across the various chapters. To facilitate comprehension, important terms throughout the chapters are printed in boldface type, indicating a word or concept that has been defined and included in the glossary at the end of the book. We have been relatively selective in our use of citations throughout the book. The works that have been cited represent the best and most relevant work we could find. For conscientious students, then, we suggest that it might be wise to spend some time reflecting on these key contributions to methodological understanding.

A unique feature of this book is its comprehensiveness. We do not know of a book of this type that considers such a broad range of experimental, nonexperimental, correlational, quasi-experimental, and evaluation research designs, and that has combined these with data collection methods ranging from survey sampling to interviewing to content analysis, scale development, and methods for assessing dyads and groups. There is much to do in developing a working understanding of the intricacies of good methodological design, and we believe that this presentation will facilitate its readers in doing so.

Content Overview

The volume is broken into four major, multi-chapter sections. Part I is focused on the basics, the fundamental introductory concepts that must be well in hand if the rest of the material is to be properly learned and profitably employed. Crucial issues of reliability and validity occupy the initial section, as it should occupy the initial considerations of any research method. We emphasize the basics in the first chapter, the nature of the scientific method, operationalization, the place of theory in a developing science, and ideas of causation, moderation, and mediation. The second chapter leans heavily on Campbell's and Stanley's classic exposition of threats to internal and external validity in experimentation. Chapter 3 is a major reworking of measurement reliability theory. It includes discussion of classic and contemporary test theory, latent factors, exploratory and confirmatory factor analysis, and item response theory. In Chapter 4 we draw heavily on our earlier discussion of measurement validity. Here, we discuss the many faces of validity, the multi-trait multi-method matrix, and the various threats to validity that must be considered when developing trustworthy measures.

Part II is concerned with important features of experimental design. Experimentation is a fundamental feature of the book, as it provides a disciplined way of thinking about research that we believe is productive and generative. This mindset infuses our discussion of research methods that do not involve the strict control and behavioral constriction of the experiment. Chapter 5 is focused on true experimental designs, factorialization, and interpreting interaction effects. Chapter 6 is concerned with the nuts and bolts of actually designing and conducting an experiment. It deals with various forms of manipulations and manipulation checks, analogue and simulation studies, and mundane and experimental realism. Chapter 7 develops this latter theme; it highlights generalizability, or external validity, with a special emphasis on the nature of the individuals who serve as the participants in our studies, the possibly distorting effects of experimenter expectancies on the research results, and ways to avoid them.

In the later sections of Part II, we expand the canvas to consider research outside the friendly confines of the laboratory. Chapter 8 deals with the special issues involved in field experimentation, including research that makes use of the Internet as a source of both information and research participants. We discuss the types of replications that are most likely to advance progress, and come down firmly on the side of conceptual rather than exact replications. Chapter 9 moves from experimentation to correlational designs, including considerations of multiple regression, path analysis, and latent structural equation approaches, which are used to specify and evaluate the adequacy of complex multivariate models of causation.

Chapter 10 rounds out Part II with a discussion of quasi-experimental designs and evaluation research. This chapter is a unique entry not often included in many introductions to research design in the social sciences. However, these methods add value to the social scientist's arsenal of tools and should be well understood, as they greatly expand the range of phenomena that can be investigated in a rigorous manner. We noted in an earlier volume that there was never a single, *right* way to support a position. That being the case, it is important to have a command of a variety of methods beyond the experiment that allow different features of a phenomenon to be investigated in different ways. To hold out for the experiment over all other design alternatives suggests a shallow understanding of the research process, because some questions are *not* ideally studied with experimental methods, just as some almost demand them. To manipulate a research question so that it "fits" an experimental approach is backwards. It is far better to fit the appropriate method to the question at issue, and often that method is not an experiment.

Part III of the book is concerned with data collection methods used to supply the raw material for the design possibilities discussed in Parts I and II. Here we learn about the many techniques in which grist for the social scientist's mill can be collected as reliably and validly as possible. Chapter 11 concerns the survey in all its various forms, with a focus on sampling methodologies. In addition, we consider various forms of missing data and their implications for interpretation of results. Chapter 12 provides an overview of systematic observational methods and ways to develop systems to code the often unruly data of field observations. Chapter 13 is focused on the various forms of interviewing, ranging from the unsystematic exploratory interview to the highly structured, scheduled interview, and the interviewing tactics designed to capture the most useful, reliable, and valid data from this method. Chapter 14 deals with content analysis and factors that must be considered when contemplating either a deductive or inductive form of communication analysis. In Chapter 15, we focus on the proper design of items and responses for questionnaires and scales, using Thurstone's, Guttman's, Likert's, or Osgood's measurement approaches.

Chapter 16 is an exposition of techniques used to measure implicit thoughts and feelings. It describes the use of implicit approaches, ranging from the thematic apperception test to the implicit associations test. The chapter also considers more physiologically oriented approaches, including event-related potential (brain waves), neuroimaging (positron emission tomography, or PET scans), and functional magnetic resonance imaging (fMRI). Chapter 17 discusses psychophysical methods that have been in use in psychology since the 1800s. Psychophysical scales were among the earliest contributions of the pioneers of psychology, and include measures derived from pair comparison and rank order scaling. These techniques are valuable in and of themselves, and serve as a lead into the more modern techniques of multidimensional scaling analysis.

Data describing dyadic and group interactions are the special focus of Chapter 18. This chapter outlines some of the ways in which this inherently social form of data can be understood and the designs that can be used to capture this understanding. Round-robin designs, sociometric assessments, and social network analysis are considered in this final chapter of Part III.

Part IV of the text consists of only two chapters, but both of them are crucial to the research enterprise. The first of these, Chapter 19, deals not with a specific research design method or technique, but rather with meta-analysis, a means of quantitatively synthesizing data across a host of studies that have all focused on the same relationship. As a way of summarizing the collected knowledge of a phenomenon or variable relation, meta-analysis has a clear advantage over simple vote counting methods and narrative reviews in coming to conclusions about conceptual relationships. Fixed-effect and random-effects models of meta-analysis are discussed, as are the potential effects of publication bias, the file-drawer problem and how to assess it, and the various search strategies that are useful in any comprehensive literature search.

The final chapter of the book is devoted to a comprehensive consideration of the ethics of research. We considered a possible alternative approach, which involved spreading various ethical caveats thinly throughout the chapters, but judged this to be a less useful strategy than a concentrated discussion of the ethics of social research in a dedicated chapter. There is no doubt that the rights of human research participants must be protected, and strict guidelines have been laid down to ensure that this happens. We applaud the increasing sensitivity to the rights of human research participants, and are reasonably confident that increasing sensitivity to this issue will result in a more secure research environment that protects both the research participants and its originator.

In addition to discussing the rights of human participants, this chapter also considers the responsibilities of ethical methodologists in dealing not only with their research participants but also with their peers when judging the merits of their research. It is not enough for the methodologist to raise an issue that might signal a potential methodological problem with another's study; to make a cogent and fair evaluation of research, the critic must also suggest an alternative explanation that logically might account for the reported research results, and this alternative must be *at least* as plausible as the one offered by the scientist whose work is being questioned.

Intended Audience

We believe this is one of the few books that are comprehensive enough to provide the necessary depth to prepare graduate and upper-level undergraduate students to design, execute, critically evaluate, interpret, and describe various methodological approaches used in social research. This book is ideal for graduate or advanced undergraduate courses in research methods (design) in psychology, particularly social psychology, as well as in communication, sociology, education, social work, and public health. A previous course in research methods at the undergraduate level is useful in taking full advantage of this work, but with sufficient motivation, conscientious students who did not have this "prerequisite" in past years have been able to fare well.

New to This Edition

This brings us to the current version of *Principles*. As is evident, the original lineup has been augmented by a talented new author, Andrew Lac, a second-generation Campbellian, having studied under both of the initial authors. His unique contribution to the book, in addition to shining a strong light on the most recent developments at the intersection of design and statistics, was to insist that in addition to presenting information as clearly as possible, we do so without watering down the coverage at the expense of accuracy. We believe the earlier editions of our text fit this bill and that the current one does as well, despite the ever-increasing complexity of the material with which today's good methodologists must contend. We strove to make even the most complex ideas understandable, and hope we have succeeded—but in the end, a complex idea is still complex.

From the start, we set out to produce a book that focused almost exclusively on design issues, without digging into the minutia of statistical computations. We have maintained this focus, but the development of increasingly sophisticated methods of statistical analysis has opened the door to increasingly sophisticated research design strategies, and we have taken advantage of both in this latest edition. The work is most evident in sections devoted to reliability analysis, scale construction, causal models, and measures of implicit cognitions, but in fact it has colored all that is presented. The growth of statistical sophistication in today's practicing social scientists must be matched by an equally sophisticated vision of research design, the seeds of which we have tried to impart in the book's current rendition.

As might be expected given the explosion of interest in new and better ways of doing research, the list of additions to earlier editions of this text is large, making this a major revision of our earlier book, even though the chapter titles have not changed much. However, the text now contains new material on a host of important issues in social research methodology, including a more intensive consideration of missing data and how this issue may be addressed in maintaining the integrity of research. We have added sections on contemporary test theory, which involves latent scores and their effect on measurement reliability, a major reworking of measurement validity, and an extended discussion of the external validity of laboratory experiments. New sections on multi-level models, latent structural equation modeling, and growth curve models also have been added. We discuss, too, the utility of archival data in social research, the growing use of social network research and online experimentation, and computer-mediated group interaction We have added to our earlier discussion of various neuroscience-based measures of brain activity and their relevance to social scientists. Finally, the issue of data falsification, the role of exact vs. conceptual replication in social research and its effect on data integrity, and some recent safeguards suggested to secure the validity of research results also have found a place in this text. This is a small sampling of the changes that we have made in this book while attempting to maintain the strength of earlier editions.

The new edition also includes more learning tools—more explanation of the basic concepts when first introduced, more research examples, tables and figures, the addition of chapter conclusions, discussion questions, boldfaced terms, a glossary, suggested readings, and new web resources at www.routledge.com/9780415638562. All of these are meant to provide the student with a more usable and user-friendly means of developing the skills necessary to understand and conduct sophisticated social research.

ACKNOWLEDGEMENTS

This book is dedicated to the memory of our mentor, Donald T. Campbell, as have been all prior versions of this work. It is made in acknowledgement of his contributions to the social sciences, and of the debt we owe to him personally for fostering the development of our ideas about the right way to think about research. In his classes on research methods, Campbell never tried to teach what to do, or even how to do it, but rather how to think about questions and problems and how to approach their solutions in as a rigorous and scientifically sound manner as possible. The continued evolution of research methods, designs, and statistics over the years attests to the astuteness of his teaching strategy. By focusing on the fundamentals that lie at the base of all research methods, the student is capable of absorbing new approaches as variations of what is already known. This allows continual updating of techniques and approaches without major dislocations. Following new developments is more a question of generalizing what is known to new contexts, rather than starting from scratch with each advance.

In addition to Don Campbell, many other colleagues have contributed to the development of this book. We are happy to acknowledge Wen-Pin Chang, Creighton University, Gene Gloeckner, Colorado State University, Gwen M. Wittenbaum, Michigan State University, Tiffany Yip, Fordham University, and an anonymous reviewer who read the prospectus for this edition of the book and provided many suggestions for improvement that we found exceedingly helpful. Their views challenged ours and encouraged us to embark on the thoroughgoing revision that this book is. We also acknowledge the help of our students Nicole Gray, Chris Lamb, Cody Packard, and Vanessa Romero for invaluable commentary on all the chapters. We also are grateful to Debra Riegert, our editor, for encouraging us to embark on this journey and for making room for a new edition of this book.

Finally, we thank the members of our respective families, Suellen, Christine, and Igor for their encouragement and patience, indisputable requisites for almost any author's close relationships.

ABOUT THE AUTHORS

William D. Crano earned his doctoral degree from Northwestern University in 1968. He has taught at Michigan State University, Texas A&M University, the University of Arizona (Chair of Communication), and Claremont Graduate University, where he is the Oskamp Distinguished Chair and Head of the Department of Psychology. His primary areas of research involve the study of persuasion and social influence, including the effects of minority groups on the majority, the effects of vested interest on attitudes, and the application of principles of persuasion to drug misuse in youth. He has published more than 100 research articles and authored 14 books, including *The Rules of Influence,* in which he explored the application of social psychological research on minority influence to issues of social change. His professional honors and contributions include being a NATO Senior Scientist in Europe, a Fulbright Senior Fellow to Brazil, a liaison scientist in the behavioral sciences for the U.S. Office of Naval Research, and Program Director in Social Psychology at the National Science Foundation.

Marilynn B. Brewer received her doctoral degree from Northwestern University in the U.S. in 1968, and over the course of her academic career has been a member of the faculty of Psychology at the University of California, Santa Barbara, the University of California, Los Angeles, and The Ohio State University. She is now Professor Emeritus at The Ohio State University and currently a Visiting Professor of Psychology at the University of New South Wales. Her primary areas of research are the study of social identity, collective decision-making, and intergroup relations, and she is the author of numerous research articles and books in these areas. Among other honors she has received for her research contributions, Dr. Brewer was recipient of the 1996 Lewin Award from Society for the Psychological Study of Social Issues, the 1993 Donald T. Campbell Award for Distinguished Contributions to Social Psychology from the Society for Personality and Social Psychology, and the 2003 Distinguished Scientist Award from the Society of Experimental Social Psychology. In 2004 she was elected as a Fellow of the American Academy of Arts and Sciences, and in 2007 she received the Distinguished Scientific Contribution Award from the American Psychological Association.

Andrew Lac received his PhD in Psychology from Claremont Graduate University in 2011. He served as Visiting Professor in the Psychology Department at Loyola Marymount University, and is currently Research Professor of Psychology at Claremont Graduate University. In addition to his expertise in methodology and statistics, his primary research interests include scale development and validation as well as social norms and interpersonal relationships in the prevention of substance misuse. He has more than 50 publications in peer-reviewed journals. He is a recipient of the Peter M. Bentler Multivariate Award and the Robert L. Solso Research Award from the Western Psychological Association.

PART I
Introduction to Social Research Methods

1
BASIC CONCEPTS

When American astronauts landed on the moon in the summer of 1971, their activities included an interesting and, for some, surprising demonstration. They showed that when the effects of atmospheric air friction are eliminated, a light object (a feather) and a heavy object (a hammer) will reach the ground at the same time if dropped simultaneously from the same height. This verification of a basic principle of high school physics delighted many viewers of the live televised broadcast, but probably few of them considered the fact that for hundreds of years before Galileo (who is thought to have originally proposed this process), Western scholars had accepted Aristotle's hypothesis that heavy objects would always fall faster than lighter ones. For most of us, Aristotle's assumption seems intuitively correct, even though we now know that it is contrary to scientific theory and demonstrated fact. Not all scientifically demonstrated phenomena contradict "common sense" intuitions in this way, but this case serves to illustrate the difference between science and intuition as bases of understanding the physical and social world.

The emphasis on subjecting all theoretical concepts, hypotheses, and expectations to empirical demonstration—that is, of testing our ideas and observing the outcomes of these tests—is basically what distinguishes the scientific method from other forms of inquiry. The **scientific method** is a general approach for acquiring knowledge using systematic and objective methods to understand a phenomenon. The scientific method provides an overarching methodological blueprint that outlines the steps useful in conducting such investigations. Its goal is to control for extraneous conditions and variables that might call into question the results of our observation.

In attempting to control the simultaneous release of the feather and hammer, for example, the astronaut was employing a very rough form of the scientific method. Although probably not discernible to the naked eye, both objects were unlikely released at precisely the same the time, so a more carefully controlled and systematic study might drop both objects concurrently by a mechanical claw in a vacuum devoid of air resistance. Observation requires that the outcomes of experimentation be discernible and measurable. If a question is to be addressed using the scientific method, the results of the methods used to answer the question must be *observable*. The requirement that science deals with observables plays a role in continued scientific advance, as it prods us to continually develop ever more sensitive instruments, methods, and techniques to make observable the formerly invisible. Another advantage is that recorded observational data can be verified by others and at times even witnessed by those who might benefit from the results without having to replicate this study. The astronaut as well as the television audience observed the same outcome of the feather and hammer study, and therefore likely arrived at a similar conclusion, that objects fall at a rate independent of their mass once air friction is eliminated.

Outlining the principles of the scientific method, which lend structure to the procedures used to conduct systematic inquiries into human behavior, is what this book is all about. The book is intended to present the research methods and designs that have been derived from basic principles of the scientific method, and to show how these techniques can be applied appropriately and effectively to the study of human cognition, affect, and behavior in social contexts.

Science and Daily Life

It is important to understand that the research principles and techniques presented throughout this text are not reserved solely for the investigation of major scientific theories. At issue in many instances are questions of purely personal interest—the consensus surrounding one's beliefs, the relative quality of one's performance, the wisdom of one's decisions—and in these circumstances, too, the application of the scientific method can prove useful. At first glance, using scientific methods to guide one's own decision-making processes (or to judge the quality of their outcome) might appear somewhat extreme; however, in light of much current research on human judgment, which demonstrates the frailty of our decision-making powers, this is a fitting application of research methods, especially when issues of personal consequence have the potential to benefit many others.

For example, the susceptibility of people's judgmental processes to a host of biasing influences is well documented (e.g., Kahneman, Slovic, & Tversky, 1982; Sanna & Schwarz, 2006; Wegener, Silva, Petty, & Garcia-Marques, 2012; West & Kenny, 2011). Research suggests that it is risky to depend solely upon one's own opinions or intuitions in evaluating the quality of a judgment or an attitudinal position. If Aristotle could be fooled, imagine how much more likely it is that *we* can be mistaken, especially in situations in which we are highly involved. To develop an intuitive grasp of the difficulties that can affect the quality of even simple decisions, consider the following scenario (adapted from Ross, Greene, & House, 1977):

> Suppose that while driving through a rural area near your home, you are stopped by a county police officer who informs you that you have been clocked (with radar) at 38 miles per hour in a 25-mph zone. You believe this information to be accurate. After the policeman leaves, you inspect your citation and find that the details on the summons regarding weather, visibility, time, and location of violation are inaccurate. The citation informs you that you must either pay a $200 fine by mail without appearing in court or appear in municipal court within the next two weeks to contest the charge.
>
> Q1. What would you do? Would you pay the fine or contest the charge? ___Pay ___Contest
> Q2. What would most of your peers do? Do you estimate most of them would pay the fine or contest the charge? ___Pay ___Contest

Now let's consider your estimates of your peers' behavior in light of your decision to pay or contest the fine. Did your own personal decision influence your estimate of other people's decisions? Although you might not think so, considerable research suggests that it probably did (e.g., Askoy & Weesie, 2012; Fabrigar & Krosnick, 1995; Marks & Miller, 1987). In a variation of this study, for example, approximately half of those posed with the speeding scenario said they would opt to pay the fine, whereas the remainder opted to contest it (Ross et al., 1977). However, if you would have paid the $200, there is a good chance that you assumed more of your peers would have done the same. On the other hand, if you would have gone to court, you are more likely to have assumed that your peers would have done so to "beat the rap." The "false consensus" effect, as this phenomenon has been termed, is an apparently common and relatively ubiquitous judgmental heuristic. In the absence of direct factual information, people tend to use their own personal perspectives to estimate what others would do or think. Such a heuristic, of course, can have a substantial influence on the quality of our assumptions and subsequent behaviors.

Clearly, our decision-making apparatus is far from foolproof. Like Aristotle, we are inclined to rely heavily, perhaps too heavily, on our own insights, feelings, and interpretations, and to assume that other reasonable people would think, feel, and act just as we do. There is no simple solution to such problems, but there is an available alternative, namely, to test our intuitions, opinions, and decisions rather than merely to assume that they are valid or commonly accepted. The means by which we make such decisions are based on learning and understanding how to conduct valid research.

The specific purpose of this first chapter is to acquaint readers with the fundamentals of research using the scientific method, and to introduce several important themes that run throughout the text. There are a number of controversial issues in the philosophy of science—such as the status of induction or the logical framework for theory verification (e.g., Bhaskar, 1978, 1982; Kuhn, 1970; Manicas & Secord, 1983; Popper, 1959, 1963)—but these concerns will be avoided in favor of a more descriptive and explanatory presentation of the "ground rules" of scientific inquiry as agreed to by most social scientists.

Theories and Hypotheses

A **theory** is formulated based on observations and insights, and consists of a series of tentative premises about ideas and concepts that lay the foundation for empirical research about a phenomenon. It serves as an overarching foundation and worldview for explaining a process. A "good" theory serves as a fountain of possibilities from which researchers may generate a wealth of hypotheses to be tested via the scientific method. Theories provide an inspirational framework to guide research. Usually, in any area of research, competing theories vie to explain the same phenomenon, using different conceptual perspectives. Take for instance the theories striving to understand engagement in health behaviors, which include the Health Belief Model, Social Cognitive Theory, the Theory of Planned Behavior, and Protection Motivation Theory. Although there are distinctions across these theories, some common themes also arise: Three of the theories contain a self-efficacy construct, but how self-efficacy is conceptualized varies considerably among the competing theories (Lippke & Ziegelmann, 2008).

Drawn from implications of a theory, a **conceptual hypothesis** is a prediction about relationships involving the theoretical constructs, and therefore guides the purpose of a research study. It may be viewed as a prediction about what should happen in a research study. At a finer level of specificity is a **research hypothesis**, which is an empirical specification of the conceptual hypothesis and is therefore a testable directional prediction about specific relationships in a study. A **research question** is a non-directional statement about specific relationships in a study that ends with a question mark ("Are people with higher pain management skills more likely to survive after major surgery?"), but the hypothesis is expressed as a directional, but still tentative, statement regarding the anticipated direction of the results ("People with higher pain management skills will be more likely to survive after major surgery"). Although not all hypotheses are drawn from some formally established theory, ideally this should be the case, as doing so may contribute to the accumulation of established scientific knowledge. A theory operates at a relatively abstract level, and therefore is tested only indirectly via the observed data of studies testing research hypotheses generated from the same theory.

The common feature of all approaches making use of the scientific method, regardless of discipline, is the emphasis on the study of observable phenomena. No matter how abstract the generalization or explanatory conceptualization at the theoretical level, the concepts or ideas under investigation must be reduced to, or translated into, observable manifestations. So, for example, the very rich and complicated concept of aggression as a psychological state might be translated in the research laboratory to participants deciding whether to push a button that delivers an electric shock to another. After "translation" into a form conducive for observation, the very powerful methods of scientific inquiry can be applied to the phenomena of interest. Often, results obtained from these methods suggest that our understanding of the phenomenon was not entirely correct and that we should go back to the drawing board and develop alternative hypotheses. These alternative hypotheses, in turn, are "translated" into a new set of measureable "observables" and the process is repeated, often many times and by many different researchers, for the goal of offering successively better understanding of the topic under investigation. From this perspective, the conduct of scientific inquiry can be viewed as a cyclical process, which progresses from explanation to observation to explanation. From a theory regarding the nature of a phenomenon come deductions (hypotheses), which guide observations, which facilitate refinement of the theory, which in turn fosters the development of new hypotheses, and so forth. We explore the phases of this cyclical progression for scientific inquiry in this first chapter.

From Theory, Concept, or Idea to Operation

Figure 1.1 represents pictorially the translation of theoretical concepts into research operations. In the first phase of the translation process, the researcher's general theory, concept, or idea is stated specifically in the form of a conceptual hypothesis. There are many ways that such hypotheses are formed, and we consider some of these in the following section.

Generating a Hypothesis

Many factors prompt us to emphasize the importance of theory in the social sciences, and one of the most crucial of these is the role of theory in the development of hypotheses, a process that allows for the continued advancement, refinement, and accumulation of scientifically based knowledge. The development of hypotheses is one of science's most complex creative processes. As McGuire (1973, 1997) and others (e.g., Jaccard & Jacoby, 2010) have observed, instructors and researchers alike have been reluctant to attempt to teach their students this art, believing it to be so complex as to be beyond instruction. However, by following the lead of some of the field's most creative researchers, we can learn something about the means that they employ in developing hypotheses.

The most important, straightforward, and certainly the most widely used technique of hypothesis generation involves the logical deduction of expectations from some established theory. The general form of hypothesis deduction from a theory is as follows:

Theory X implies that A results in B.

Therefore, if the assumptions in theory X are true, a conceptual hypothesis might be generated to anticipate that producing A will result in the occurrence of B. These hypothetical deductions are based on the tentative premises, assumptions, and implications advanced in the theory. Keep in mind that many hypotheses could be creatively generated to test any single theory. Thus, this very same theory might enable the inference of a hypothesis statement for another study proposing that A also produces C.

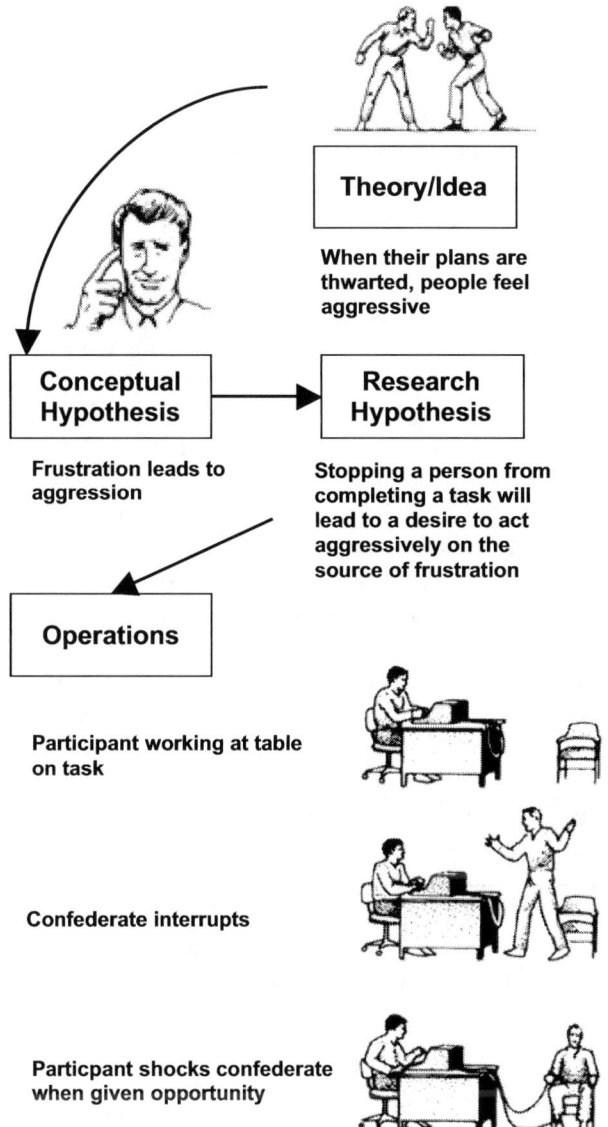

FIGURE 1.1 Translating a theory or idea into research operations.

A second source of generating a hypothesis arises from conflicting findings in the published research. Typically in this approach, the researcher searches for a condition or observation whose presence or absence helps to explain observed variations or conflicts in findings in an area of investigation. This approach helps to refine theory by testing hypotheses that provide a more strict specification of the conditions under which a particular outcome can be expected to occur (or not to occur).

An example of the use of the "conflicting findings" technique can be seen in research that examined the relationship between ambient temperature and the tendency of people to act aggressively. Experimental research conducted in laboratory settings by Baron and colleagues (e.g., Bell & Baron, 1990) consistently demonstrated that high temperatures *inhibited* the influence of aggressive models. Under normal room temperature, a **confederate**, or actor or accomplice hired by the researcher to pretend to be another participant in the study, could induce considerable aggression on the part of naive participants; however, when the ambient temperature of the laboratory was raised, participants' aggressive tendencies diminished. These findings from the laboratory were in marked contrast to those observed by Anderson and his colleagues (e.g., Anderson, 1989; DeWall & Anderson, 2011) outside the laboratory, when they examined the average temperatures of the days on which major riots took place in the United States. They found a positive relationship between these two measures—riots were *more* likely to occur when temperatures were high, suggesting that heat provokes rather than inhibits the spread of aggressive behavior in naturalistic contexts outside the laboratory.

One possible means of reconciling these apparently conflicting results involves an explanation based upon the uniqueness, or prominence, of the temperature in the two research settings. In naturalistic settings (as reviewed by Anderson & DeNeve, 1992), we adjust to the temperature. Although a heat wave is obviously uncomfortable, it is consistent, or constant. We experience the discomfort more as a dull ache than as a searing pain, but because this irritation is relatively constant; we do not consciously identify our discomfort as being caused by the heat. Under these conditions, an extraneous event in the environment—such as a confrontation between a policeman and a minor traffic offender—might be misinterpreted as the source of discomfort. Thus, the reactions of a crowd of people are likely to escalate when temperatures are high and have been for some time.

In the case of the laboratory research of Baron and his colleagues, however, the high ambient temperature of the laboratory typically comes on very abruptly. Participants walk into the laboratory from a relatively normal environment and find themselves in the middle of a heat wave. Under this circumstance, participants readily identify the source of their discomfort, and this discomfort is unlikely to "transfer" to (or be identified with) other stimuli. This explanation of an apparent contradiction of findings from two different programs of laboratory and naturalistic research gave rise to a new theory, known as "excitation transfer," which has been used to explain interesting behaviors ranging from violent anger to intense attraction in various contexts (Zillman, 1979, 1996). Based on the premises of this theoretical perspective, a multitude of hypotheses have been subsequently developed to help further this line of investigation and to provide a clearer understanding of the link between external excitatory factors and later behavior (Wang & Lang, 2012). Field research using a novel application of excitation transfer theory discovered that participants who recently exited a rollercoaster ride were more likely to find a photograph of an opposite-sex person to be highly attractive than participants waiting to get onto the ride (Meston & Frohlich, 2003).

A third source of hypothesis generation comes from observation of seemingly paradoxical behavior. For example, in a classic study, Festinger, Riecken, and Schachter (1956) found that an extremely reclusive "doomsday" cult became much more publicity conscious and much more active in pushing their beliefs *after* their prophecy concerning the end of the world had been shown to be obviously incorrect. This was in stark contrast to their typical behavior before the disconfirmation. The researchers' attempts to make sense of this apparently paradoxical behavior helped to lay the foundations of Festinger's (1957) theory of cognitive dissonance. This classic theory, originating from preliminary observations, has continued to spur countless hypothesized studies more than 50 years after its inception, usually designed to determine the conditions under which dissonance occurs; interestingly, the basic structure of the original theoretical postulates have remained largely intact (Kenworthy, Miller, Collins, Read, & Earleywine, 2011; Zentall, 2010).

A fourth method of hypothesis development in social research requires that we attend closely to the common, everyday behavioral tactics that people employ in dealing with others. For example, how can some used-car salespersons promise a car at an impossibly low price, later rescind their offer, and still succeed in selling an automobile that is considerably more expensive than that which was agreed upon originally? Why is it that we are much more likely to agree to a rather major imposition if we have recently "given in" to a much smaller request? Social scientists attuned to issues of this sort have been able to develop some interesting and potentially valuable ideas on the basis of their observations, and to apply these insights to hypothesized topics ranging from inducing charitable donations to AIDS prevention to fostering organ donations (e.g., Burger, 1999; Cialdini, 1988; Dillard, 1991; Eisenberg, 1991; Siegel et al., 2010).

The case study is yet a fifth useful source of hypothesis generation. By concentrating intensively on observing a specific person or interaction, we sometimes can discern systematic or regular relationships among observations, and these in turn can provide the impetus necessary for developing a testable proposition. Sometimes this particular approach to developing a hypothesis is used because insufficient prior research or knowledge exists in this area, and thus a special case of this situation is sought for vigilant scrutiny. These observations are then used to inform later hypotheses to test whether the systematic patterns or regularities that were observed are consistent across other people, situations, and interactions. Some of the most noteworthy examples of the use of the case study in the development of theory are provided by Freud and Piaget, both of whom used this approach extensively (some would say exclusively) in developing their theories. These theories have also guided the development of subsequent hypotheses.

Although the list is far from complete, we hope it provides some idea of the range of possibilities available to the social scientist in developing testable hypotheses (see McGuire, 1973, 1997, or Campbell, Daft, & Hulin, 1982, for a more complete set of suggestions). After the hypotheses have been developed, we move to the perhaps less "artistic" but nonetheless creative phase of operationalization.

Operationalization

Historically, the social sciences are still quite close to the speculative stages of their initial development. It was not much more than 100 years ago that psychology as a discipline was tied to a pseudo-scientific approach known as *introspectionism*. In studies of the introspective variety, research participants were exposed to some stimulus presented by the investigator and then asked to describe their internal elemental sensations and reactions to it. In this way, the early psychologists attempted to enter directly into the "black box" of the mind and thereby gain insight into the nature of the human organism. It was common that the investigator's own students would play the role of participant in these types of studies, and often the same participants would be used in repeated experiments. Unfortunately, different participants exposed to the same stimuli often provided entirely different "observational" reports of their internal mental states, making these results difficult to replicate across people.

Today's social researchers, possessing information unavailable to their predecessors, consider the introspective approach risky. For one thing, we have learned that people do not always have access to subjective experience in a way that can be verbalized (Nisbett & Wilson, 1977). We also have learned that participants involved in a scientific study may be overly willing to "please" the investigator by helping to confirm the research hypotheses (Chapter 7). In the early days of introspectionism, participants often were well aware of the particular theoretical position under investigation, and there was probably a great deal of informal pressure on these students to "confirm" the hypotheses of their teachers. Thus, introspectionism left a lot to be desired as a method of objective scientific inquiry. Nevertheless, the era of introspectionism was a valuable phase in the development of scientific methods for psychology in particular and the social sciences in general, because it presented a bridge between the purely speculative, philosophical explanations of human behavior and the more rigorous scientific approach (see Crano & Lac, 2012).

Operational Definitions

The transition to objectivity in social research was marked by a strong emphasis on **operationalization**—translating an abstract theoretical construct or concept into a concrete specification of procedure and measure, so that it may be observed, recorded, and replicated. The requirement for explicit description of research procedures did much to clarify theoretical issues and to place the social sciences on firmer ground as scientific disciplines.

Operationalization requires that we specify the variables that are critical in empirically assessing the phenomenon of interest. A **variable** is any characteristic or attribute that may differ, and is the basic unit of observation and measurement in a study. Variables may include differences among individuals (e.g., gender, aggressive tendencies, ability to ride a unicycle, level of enthusiasm while reading the textbook), situations (e.g., room temperature, number of people present) or information (e.g., instruction complexity, message content, task difficulty). Although this textbook will largely describe studies involving psychological and behavioral variables among humans, variables may also refer to an array of differences in animals (e.g., level of salivation in dogs) as well as inanimate objects (e.g., type of car driven). Scientists make use of variables for the purpose of understanding and addressing how gradations or differences in a variable (or a set of variables) might predict or correspond to gradations or differences in another variable (or set of variables): For instance, whether social influence plays a role in the type of car an individual drives (foreign or domestic), or whether students who spend more time and effort in critically reading this textbook will receive a higher grade in their research methodology course. Contrast the definition of a variable with that of a *constant*, an attribute on which the value is fixed (or identical) across individuals, and therefore is conceptually uninteresting and cannot be used to explain differences that might be observed among them. It would be wasteful of resources, for instance, to conduct a study at an all-boys high school testing the effects of sex on academic achievement. The predictive value of sex in this context is precisely zero. However, in contexts in which sex is not a constant, asking this same question may produce a useful and interesting result.

The translation of conceptual variables to scientifically researchable—and thus observable and measurable—variables generally takes place in two steps. The first involves the redefinition of the abstraction of a conceptual variable into an empirical definition; that is, the variable is specified in such a way so that it could be manipulated or observed. Of course, what can be observed is inevitably a function of perceptual skills and available instrumentation—what can be seen with the naked eye is different from what can be observed with the aid of a high-powered electron microscope. Thus, what is "objective" or observable must be defined in terms of the current limitations of our senses and technology. (See Chapter 16 for methods that allow scientists to "read" the implicit content of the human mind—content that previously was not available for scientific investigation.) In general, an observation is considered sufficiently objective if independent researchers with similar training and available technical aids can agree upon its evaluation or assessment.

The second step of concept translation involves a specification of the procedures and instruments required to make the actual observations, detailed sufficiently so that other scientists could duplicate the observation for purposes of replication or validation. This translation is referred to as the *operationalization* of the conceptual variable, and requires close attention as the most rigorous aspect of scientific methodology. For purposes of empirical testing, it is essential that very specific and precise delineation of the empirical definitions be provided, as suggested in the first step. However, it should be made clear that this specification of research operations is not the end product of the scientific investigation, but merely a necessary step in the research process.

Imperfection of Operationalizations

The operationalization phase is not the end of investigative efforts. Operationalized constructs are put to use in testing hypotheses and refining theory. As we emphasized, the operational definition is the result of a specification of the research processes employed in the investigation of a given phenomenon in such a way as to make it directly observable, which lends itself to measurement. One's measurement instrument, for example, might be labeled an attitude test, but what is being observed, and hence what constitutes the operationalization of "attitude," are the directly observable pencil marks that an individual has made on the questionnaire we have provided. Most theories in the social sciences, however, are concerned with processes that are somewhat removed from what is directly observed. (We are not especially interested in pencil marking behavior.) Whether attempting to examine anxiety, communication skill, or attitude change, for example, we are dealing with internal cognitive processes that are only indirectly and imperfectly *inferred from* an individual's observable actions. It thus becomes extremely important to note whether the operationalization has any psychological reality: Do the processes that constitute the operations meaningfully reflect the underlying processes that give rise to the observable responses? Put another way, researchers should be concerned with the degree of overlap between the operation and the internal processes it is purported to represent.

In the social sciences, theoretical concepts are generally of a high level of abstraction, but they must be defined through operations that can be carried out with available technological aids. We move, for example, from the conceptual definition of a construct like "attitude" (e.g., a consistent internal evaluation of an attitude object) to the more empirical realm of endorsements of positively or negatively evaluative statements regarding the attitude object, and finally to the specification of a set of instructions and verbatim items that provide the actual measure of attitude in a particular research study (see Chapter 15).

Specific operations are always imperfect definitions of any given theoretical construct because the product of any particular observation is a function of multiple sources—including observer errors, **instrumentation errors**, and environmental and contextual conditions—many of which may be totally unrelated to the conceptual variable of interest. In the physical sciences many of the factors that affect instrument readings have been identified and can be minimized or corrected, but even so, some slight variations in measurements, which do not correspond to variations in the attribute being measured, do occur. In social science research these unidentified sources of variation are considerably more profound, and even those factors that can be identified can seldom be successfully eliminated or controlled. Campbell (1969) represented this state of affairs well when he observed:

> Measurements involve processes which must be specified in terms of many theoretical parameters. For any specific measurement process, we know on theoretical grounds that it is a joint function of many scientific laws. Thus, we know on scientific grounds that the measurements resulting cannot purely reflect a single parameter of our scientific theory . . . Let us consider in detail . . . a single meter, the galvanometer. The amount of needle displacement is certainly a strong function of the electrical current in the attached wire. But, it is also a function of the friction in the needle bearings, of inertia due to the weight of the needle, of fluctuations in the earth's and other magnetic and electrical fields, of the strong and weak nuclear interactions in adjacent matter, of photon bombardment, etc. We know on theoretical grounds that the needle pointer movements cannot be independent of all of these, i.e., that the pointer movements cannot be definitional of a single parameter . . . Analogously, for a tally mark on a census-taker's protocol indicating family income, or rent paid, or number of children, we know on theoretical grounds that it is only in part a function of the state of the referents of the question. It is also a function of the social interaction of the interview,

of the interviewer's appearance, of the respondent's fear of similar strangers, such as bill collectors, welfare investigators, and the law, etc., etc. A manifest anxiety questionnaire response may in part be a function of anxiety, but it is also a function of vocabulary comprehension, or individual and social class differences in the use of euphoric and dysphoric adjectives, or idiosyncratic definitions of key terms frequently repeated, of respondent expectations as to the personal consequences of describing himself sick or well, etc.

(pp. 14–15)

Given these considerations, it is of critical importance that social researchers recognize that their abstract theoretical concepts are never perfectly embodied in any single measured observation.

Multiple Operationalization

Because of the imperfect correspondence between conceptual variables and their observable manifestations, we subscribe to defining a variable using multiple operationalization or multiple operational definitions. **Multiple operationalization** recognizes that no single operation or measurement provides enough information to adequately define a concept a theoretical concept, so the construct is measured through several techniques or operations. Ideally, these techniques should be as different as possible *on irrelevant dimensions*. Any single operationalization of a concept is in error to the extent that it does not completely overlap with the internal physical or psychological state it is purported to represent. However, if many diverse measures of a phenomenon are employed, it is probable that they will have non-overlapping sources of error. They will each miss the mark to some extent, but will miss it in different ways. Multiple, diverse measures with non-overlapping sources of error allow the researcher to "triangulate" on the concept. This methodological triangulation is the logical outcome, and central advantage, of multiple operationalization. Researchers aggregate the data obtained from these multiple operations to create a more representative, but still imperfect, overall composite, index, or factor. The common variations among heterogeneous observations, all of which focus on the same construct, provide the information necessary to adequately identify, or define, the component of interest (Crano, 1981, 2000).

To gain an intuitive feel for multiple operationalization, consider an individual just waking from a night's sleep and wondering exactly what time of day it is. Our usual procedure for assessing time is to consult a clock, but clocks vary as instruments of timekeeping. Some are based on electrical power impulses, some are battery operated, some run on mechanical spring loading, etc. The interesting thing about these variations in power source for our various timepieces is that the clocks are each subject to different kinds of potential inaccuracy, or error. Electric clocks are affected by power failures or temporary disconnection from a central power source; batteries die; and springs can be over- or under-wound or fatigued by long use. Consequently, consulting any single clock, whatever its type, leaves some room for doubt about the accuracy of its time assessment. When three different clocks all agree on the time, our confidence is increased, although just how confident we can be depends on whether the three timepieces share a common source of inaccuracy or bias. If all three clocks are electrically powered, they could have been simultaneously affected by the same 20-minute power outage during the middle of the night, and hence all would be reporting the same inaccurate reading. When three clocks with three different sources of power all agree, however, our confidence is enhanced considerably. When the three do not agree, the nature of their disagreement and our knowledge of the different types of inaccuracy to which each clock is subject can help us to track down the sources of error and to zero in on the correct time.

Visualizing the process of triangulation via multiple operationalization is helpful. In Figure 1.2, the black box corresponds to the "phantom" construct or concept—for example, the stress

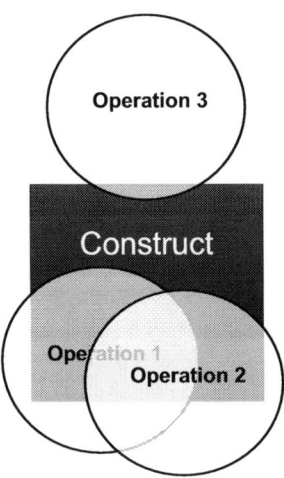

FIGURE 1.2 Triangulating on a construct via multiple operationalization.

experienced by college students in taking an advanced research methods course. Each circle represents a different operational indicator designed to capture underlying stress levels—but what are the conceptual properties that constitute the very abstract idea of being "stressed out"? Imagine that operation 1 is defined using a psychological measure asking you to estimate, from 0 to 10, "What is the level of stress you are experiencing?"; operation 2 is a biological measure of cortisol concentration in your blood; and operation 3 is a behavioral measure of the number of times you awaken in the middle of the night in a cold sweat. Diverse operations should be sought, as they may help us measure different features of the construct. As depicted in how much of the black box is covered by the circles, a single operation is sorely inadequate in capturing the conceptual breadth of the construct, but a set of operations increases the likelihood that a greater percentage of the construct will be represented in the study. As might be the case if different quality measures are undertaken, operations 1 and 2 are better manifestations of the underlying construct than operation 3. Also notice that within the construct operation 1 partially overlaps with operation 2, indicating that portions of these measures tap the construct in the same way.

From Operation to Measurement Scales

The product of most scientific observations is expressed in terms of some scale of *measurement* (Stevens, 1951). Measurement scales refer to the assignment of numbers to specific observations in such a way as to reflect variations among those observations. The level of measurement, or the degree of correspondence between number assignment and extent of variation in the attribute being observed, depends upon the rules of the measurement scale assignment. The simplest level of correspondence is represented by the **nominal scale**, a measure requiring only that different numbers be assigned to observations that can be differentiated on some specified construct. Values assigned to nominal scales are arbitrary and therefore not meaningful, as higher and lower values do not signify more or less of that variable. Examples include coding of participants into qualitative variables representing gender (male or female), racial or ethnic identification (White, Black, Latino, or Asian), or political partial affiliation (Republican, Democrat, or Independent).

Somewhat more complex than the requirements for the application of the nominal rule are those measurements that apply to the **ordinal scale**, a measure requiring higher scores to represent greater levels of the construct (the ordering of number labels corresponds to the ordering of observations) and therefore ranks on the construct. Ordinal scales are commonly employed to rank situations along such dimensions as degree of anxiety arousal (high, medium, low), socioeconomic status (upper, upper middle, middle, lower middle, etc.), or finish in a hot chili pepper eating contest (1st place, 2nd place, 3rd place, etc.).

Even more measurement sophistication is achieved using an **interval scale**, a measure requiring higher scores to represent greater levels of a construct, and equal distances in numbers reflect equal gradations in different observations. The Fahrenheit scale is an instance of interval scale, as a 10-point difference between 70 and 80 degrees indicates the same change in heat as a the difference between 90 and 100 degrees. A Fahrenheit reading of zero, however, does not signify the absence of heat, as this temperature scale may assume negative values. Measures of social attitudes derived from Thurstone scaling techniques (Chapter 15) provide examples of interval scales in social research.

A fourth type of measurement scale requires the application of number assignment using the **ratio scale**, a measure requiring higher scores to represent greater levels of a construct, equal distances in numbers to reflect equal gradations in different observations, and a meaningful absolute zero–point. In ratio scaling, the zero-point meaningfully reflects the absence of the attribute being measured. For interval scaling, it is sufficient that the different distances reflect comparative values of differences in observations rather than measurements against some absolute zero–point, but both criteria are required for ratio scales. The requirements of a ratio scale are satisfied in some measurement techniques, such as the amount of time taken to make a response, the amount of pressure exerted on a hand-press device, and the number of inches of rainfall. A decision tree that illustrates the level of measurement scale we are using (or contemplating) is presented in Figure 1.3.

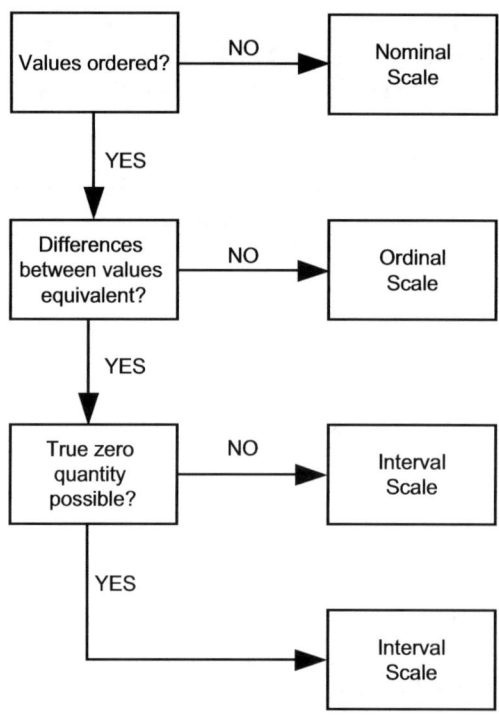

FIGURE 1.3 Decision tree to determine level of measurement.

For practical purposes, the essential distinction among these four levels of measurement is the extent of correspondence between the numbers recorded by the researcher and the subtle variations in the attribute or construct being measured, that is, in the "fit" between assignment of numbers and observations. The higher the level of measurement, the greater the number of gradations in the data are represented in the numbers given by the researcher. We do not always aim for the highest level of measurement, however, because they make increasingly greater demands on data quality and on respondents' abilities to successfully differentiate the levels. Higher levels of measurement also make available more sensitive statistical techniques to detect more subtle nuances in observations and responses. Thus, the ability to interpret observations in terms of higher order measurements adds considerable precision to the research process, but the assignment of numbers does not automatically create precision in measurement if the rules of number assignment have been violated.

Role of Theory in Scientific Inquiry

It is traditional to think of scientific theories as convenient data-summarizing generalizations that are helpful in guiding decisions about the content and interpretation of future observations, but which are discarded when obtained observations do not fit the conceptual framework. The actual role of theory in most scientific endeavors, however, differs from this ideal. In our view, a formal theory is a template, or a pattern, against which various data sets, obtained from studies testing hypotheses, are compared. The extent of the "match" between theory pattern and data pattern provides an indication of the usefulness of the theory. Of course, the match is rarely, if ever, perfect, but with the continual modification of the theoretical template, an increasingly better fit can be obtained. Even when the fit between data and theory is unsatisfactory, the theory is rarely discarded until an alternative theory that provides a better match with the data is available.

As suggested in the preceding paragraph, the interplay between theory and data is not entirely an "objective" process. Kuhn's (1970) still stimulating and controversial analysis of scientific "revolutions" has produced increased awareness of the influence of social factors on the process of scientific advance (Bird, 2000; Horwich, 1993). The acceptance of particular theoretical positions is partly determined by the prevailing social climate, and frequently in large part by the personalities of the advocates of competing theoretical perspectives. Furthermore, vigorous and valuable research is not necessarily inspired by formal theoretical considerations. Some active areas of research have been derived from essentially exploratory investigations, inspired more by hunches and guesswork than by formal theory.

For example, following much speculation on the inevitable conservatism of group decision-making, Stoner (1961, 1968) compared responses made by individuals on a test of their willingness to advocate risky decisions with the responses of six-person groups. He found (to the surprise of many) that the average group decision was significantly more risky than the average individual decision. This finding, which was labeled the group "shift-to-risk" phenomenon, or the "risky shift," generated much further research. However, the extensive program of research evident in this area was not stimulated simply by an interest in risk taking per se, but by the controversy that developed over theory-based explanations that were advanced to account for the group effect on the riskiness of decisions. The outcome of this collective research effort has demonstrated that under some circumstances groups do indeed make riskier decisions than the individuals who constitute the group, whereas in other circumstances the opposite is true (Blumberg, 1994; Isenberg, 1986). As is often the case with social sciences in general, the most active, visible, and extended areas of research are those that are inspired by the theory-testing process and the competition of alternative theoretical explanations.

Ideally, the theory-testing process begins with the derivation (from the theoretical structure) of implications that can be stated in the form of hypotheses regarding the existence of relationships among observable variables. Most of these derived hypotheses are of the general form, "If theory U is true, then, with irrelevant factors eliminated, the occurrence of variable A should be related to the occurrence (or condition) of variable B." Comparisons between these predicted relationships and the actual outcomes of controlled observations comprise the testing process, through which the original theory is subjected to continuous potential disconfirmation (although the failure to obtain the predicted results *in any particular case* can always be attributed to the inadequacy of the empirical statement or the research operations to reflect the theoretical position). Successive failures of empirical investigations to *dis*confirm the derived hypotheses create incremental acceptance of the theoretical position. This process continues until some outcome is encountered that cannot be explained by the current theory at a time when some alternative theory accounts for all the previous findings *and* the otherwise inexplicable result.

This continuous process of theory purification can be illustrated with the following example: A gunslinger of the Old West rides into a town, and the terrified inhabitants form the impression (i.e., hypothesis) that "Joe is the fastest gun in the territory." The clear implication of this position is that in a contest against any other gunman, Joe's gun will be fired first. The expectation can be "proved" only one way—that is, by showing that alternative hypotheses (i.e., that other gunmen are faster) are empirically incorrect. Each time Joe's skill is pitted against that of someone else and the hypothesized outcome is attained, the theoretical allegation gains credibility. The more challenging the rival, the more encouraging is Joe's victory. If Joe were to shoot the local unarmed schoolmarm, for example, he would generate little enthusiasm for his claim. Conversely, if he were to meet and outshoot an internationally famous desperado, confidence in the hypothesis would increase appreciably. However, if on just one occasion Joe's gun fires second (or not at all) in such a contest, a logical alternative—which can account for all the outcomes—suggests itself, namely, that "Joe was fast, but Irving is faster." To the extent that the critical result actually reflected relative ability (rather than some extraneous factor such as Joe's gun jamming or his having been shot from behind), the new theoretical position is likely to replace the old. However, even if the critical case did not occur and Joe were to knock off the top 200 on the "hit parade," the original hypothesis would still not be completely secure, because there would always be the nagging realization that sometime, somewhere, the disconfirming case might come along.

This analogy might at first seem silly, but parallels can be drawn between the Old West and the new social science. Today, a scientist rides into town and proposes the hypothesis that X causes Y. Others dispute this, claiming that A causes Y, or B causes Y, or C causes Y. Some of these alternatives will be clearly implausible, and the scientist will have little trouble discrediting them. If our researcher's explanation holds up against a number of highly plausible alternative explanations, he or she will have strengthened the theoretical case considerably. Like the gunman, unfortunately, the scientist can never be completely sure that the competitive (theory testing) process has eliminated *all* rivals.

There are, of course, degrees of uncertainty. A scientist whose theory has been tested only once or twice should be more concerned about its validity than one whose theory has been shown to be consistently successful in the face of strong, plausible challenges. Thus, the general approach to be emphasized throughout this text will consist of various strategies whose major function is the *falsification* of as many competing hypotheses as possible. Through this continuous process, the gradual purification of theory can be accomplished, though certainty is never assured. Again, however, it must be stressed that even long-term success and widespread acceptance is no guarantee that a theory is true or valid or even optimally useful.

In the case of successive gun battles, one disconfirming result can eliminate the possibility of further testing of the original theory. In the case of scientific theory, a position rarely stands or falls as a result of a single observation. Every individual study is subject to a number of potential explanations. Only the total pattern of multiple test outcomes determines the goodness of fit between theory and

Basic Concepts   17

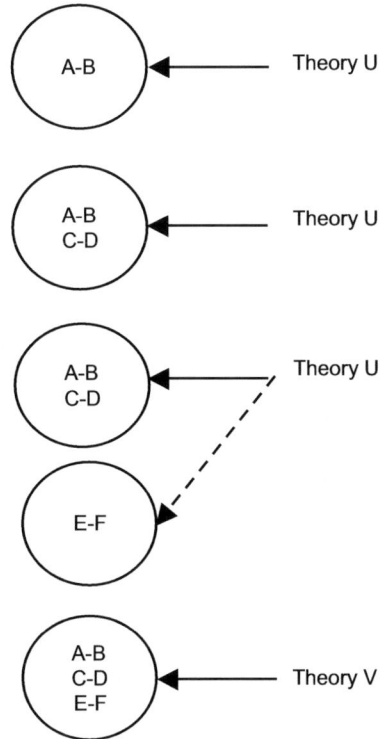

FIGURE 1.4 Euler diagrams illustrating process of theory development.

data. Thus, the process of theory testing via the measurement of observations is best viewed in terms of multiple operationalization across many studies. A theory frequently stands in the absence of perfect fit between its implications and every data outcome *until* some alternative theory that accounts for more of the actual observations becomes available. The more convergence there is between the hypothesized outcomes of successive heterogeneous investigations and the implications of a particular theoretical position, the less likely it becomes that some alternative explanation will become available to replace it, although the possibility of such an alternative can never be ruled out entirely.

The process of theory testing described here is represented in the series of Euler diagrams of Figure 1.4.

1. A hypothesized relationship (A-B) between two variables is supported by the observed outcome, which is consistent with Theory U, although several rival theories explaining the same relationship (not shown here) are available.
2. Another hypothesized relationship (C-D) is supported in a second study, and the outcome is consistent with Theory U, but not the other rival theories that related A and B. This new relationship rules out alternative theoretical explanations of A-B that are not also consistent with the C-D findings. Theory U is bolstered.
3. A third hypothesized relationship (E-F) is not supported by observed outcomes, which is *in*consistent with the implications of Theory U. The status of Theory U is now tentative.
4. The explanations of Theory U are replaced by those of Theory V (which may be a modification of U or an entirely different theoretical statement), because the latter is consistent with the formerly observed outcomes of A-B and C-D, and also with the new findings (E-F).

Within this framework of theory testing, the purpose of good research design is to conduct each empirical investigation in such a way as to minimize rival alternative explanations for the theoretical relationships under investigation, and to plan programs of research in such a way as to represent the theory being tested under a maximum number of heterogeneous conditions in order to successively rule out potential alternative theoretical positions.

Conclusion and Overview

The preceding section on the role of theory in social research presents a view of research as an iterative, cumulative process extended across time and persons. Any single research study should be regarded as a part of this larger scientific enterprise—like an individual piece in a giant jigsaw puzzle. No single study will be sufficient in and of itself to prove or disprove a theory or hypothesis (Greenwald, 1975), but each study contributes in some unique way to piece together the total picture. For the individual researcher, however, the major focus of attention will be the design and conduct of one research project at a time. It is the purpose of this book to introduce students of social research to the basic tools needed for that purpose.

The stages of any individual research study are diagrammed in Figure 1.5. We have already discussed briefly the principles involved in translating conceptual variables into empirical definitions and then operational definitions. The discussion of research ideas further may be divided into two basic steps. The first is the selection of an overall research design—the master plan that defines the systematic procedures we are conducting. Research design includes decisions as to the setting in which the research is to be undertaken, the relevant variables to be included, and whether or not the researcher controls or manipulates critical features of the situation. The second step is that of choosing the specific methods of data collection to be used in the study. How are the selected variables of interest to be assessed, and what are the respective roles of the researcher and the participants in the data collection process?

The combination of research design and data collection methods helps to define the research study. When the design and methods have been carried out, the final stages of the study involve analysis and interpretation of the resulting data. Correct interpretation of the results of such analyses must take into account the design and methods by which the data were obtained, and these are the features of the research process that we will focus on throughout this text. It is of utmost importance to craft a well-designed study with methods appropriate to the topic of investigation, as failing to do so will produce a host of problems that subsequently compromise observed outcomes, making these results susceptible to interpretation problems that cannot be remedied by statistical analyses.

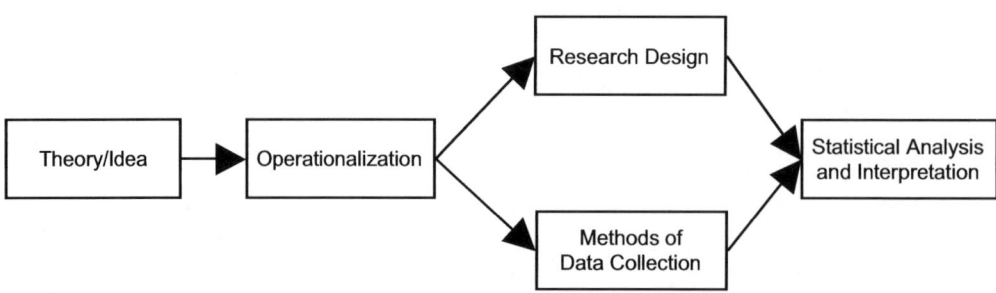

FIGURE 1.5 Stages of research.

Chapters 2 to 4 are devoted to general issues in the operationalization of theoretical concepts and the selection of research design and methods of measurement. Chapters 5 to 10 present more detailed discussion of specific research designs that may be employed, elaborating on a basic distinction between experimental and non-experimental research approaches. Chapters 11 to 18 discuss procedures of specific data collection methods, with attention to the relative strengths and weaknesses of each. Specific issues of analysis and interpretation are raised as they are relevant to materials covered in these two sections. Finally, Chapters 19 to 20 addresses more general issues that crosscut all methods of research in the social sciences. These general issues include the social and ethical responsibilities associated with the conduct of social research and advancing the cumulative knowledge base through combining and synthesizing findings from different primary studies. In these final chapters we hope to make clear that science is a collective enterprise undertaken in the context of societal values.

Questions for Discussion

1. What does it mean for a theory to be "falsifiable?" Why is falsifiability an important aspect of the scientific method?
2. What is the conceptual relationship between theory purification and the falsification of hypotheses?
3. Define "operationalization." Provide an example by operationalizing the research question: "Does attraction increase liking?" Be sure to explain why your example is an appropriate operationalization of this research question.
4. How would you operationalize the six phenomena below? Provide two or three unique *operationalizations* per phenomenon.
   a. Aggression
   b. Discrimination (i.e., as result of gender expression, age, race/ethnicity, etc.)
   c. Intoxication (i.e., as result of substance abuse)
   d. Happiness
   e. Love
   f. Creativity

References

Aksoy, O., & Weesie, J. (2012). Beliefs about the social orientations of others: A parametric test of the triangle, false consensus, and cone hypotheses. *Journal of Experimental Social Psychology, 48*, 45–54.

Anderson, C. A. (1989). Temperature and aggression: Ubiquitous effects of heat on occurrence of human violence. *Psychological Bulletin, 106*, 74–96.

Anderson, C. A., & DeNeve, K. M. (1992). Temperature, aggression, and the negative affect escape model. *Psychological Bulletin, 111*, 347–351.

Bell, P. A., & Baron, R. A. (1990). Affect and aggression. In B. S. Moore & A. M. Isen (Eds.), *Affect and social behavior* (pp. 64–88). Cambridge, UK: Cambridge University Press, and Paris: Editions de la Maison des Sciences de l'Homme.

Bhaskar, R. (1978). On the possibility of social scientific knowledge and the limits of behaviorism. *Journal for the Theory of Social Behavior, 8*, 1–28.

Bhaskar, R. (1982). Emergence, explanation, and emancipation. In P. F. Secord (Ed.), *Explaining social behavior: Consciousness, behavior, and social structure*. Beverly Hills, CA: Sage.

Bird, A. (2000). *Thomas Kuhn*. Chesham, UK: Acumen, and Princeton, NJ: Princeton University Press.

Blumberg, H. H. (1994). Group decision making and choice shift. In P. Hare & H. H. Blumberg (Eds.), *Small group research: A handbook* (pp. 195–210). Norwood, NJ: Ablex.

Burger, G. (1999). The foot-in-the-door compliance procedure: A multiple-process analysis and review. *Personality and Social Psychology Review, 3*, 303–325.

Campbell, D. T. (1969). Definitional versus multiple operationism. *Et al., 2,* 14–17.
Campbell, J. P., Daft, R. L., & Hulin, C. L. (1982). *What to study: Generating and developing research questions.* Beverly Hills, CA: Sage.
Cialdini, R. B. (1988). *Influence: Science and practice* (2nd ed.). Glenview, IL: Scott, Foresman.
Crano, W. D. (1981). Triangulation and cross-cultural research. In M. B. Brewer & B. E. Collins (Eds.), *Scientific inquiry and the social sciences: A volume in honor of Donald T. Campbell* (pp. 317–344). San Francisco: Jossey-Bass.
Crano, W. D. (2000). The multitrait-multimethod matrix as synopsis and recapitulation of Campbell's views on the proper conduct of social inquiry. In L. Bickman (ed.), *Research design: Donald Campbell's legacy* (Ch. 3, pp. 37–61). Beverly Hills, CA: Sage.
Crano, W. D., & Lac, A. (2012). The evolution of research methodologies in (social) psychology. In A. Kruglanski & W. Stroebe (Eds.), *Handbook of the history of social psychology* (pp. 159–174). New York: Psychology Press.
DeWall, C. N., & Anderson, C. A. (2011). The general aggression model. In P. R. Shaver & M. Mikulincer (Eds.), *Human aggression and violence: Causes, manifestations, and consequences.* (pp. 15–33). Washington, DC: American Psychological Association.
Dillard, J. P. (1991). The current status of research on sequential-request compliance techniques. *Personality and Social Psychology Bulletin, 17,* 283–288.
Eisenberg, N. (1991). Meta-analytic contributions to the literature on prosocial behavior. *Personality and Social Psychology Bulletin, 17,* 273–282.
Fabrigar, L. R., & Krosnick, J. A. (1995). Attitude importance and the false consensus effect. *Personality and Social Psychology Bulletin, 21,* 468–479.
Festinger, L. (1957). *A theory of cognitive dissonance.* Stanford, CA.: University of California Press.
Festinger, L., Riecken, H. W., & Schachter, S. (1956). *When prophecy fails.* Minneapolis, MN: University of Minnesota Press.
Greenwald, A. G. (1975). Consequences of prejudice against the null hypothesis. *Psychological Bulletin, 82,* 1–20.
Horwich, P. (Ed.). (1993). *World changes: Thomas Kuhn and the nature of science.* Cambridge, MA: MIT Press.
Isenberg, D. J. (1986). Group polarization: A critical review and meta-analysis. *Journal of Personality and Social Psychology, 50,* 1141–1151.
Jaccard, J., & Jacoby, J. (2010). *Theory construction and model-building skills: A practical guide for social scientists.* New York: Guilford Press.
Kahneman, D., Slovic, P., & Tversky, A. (1982). *Judgment under uncertainty: Heuristics and biases.* Cambridge, UK: Cambridge University Press.
Kenworthy, J. B., Miller, N., Collins, B. E., Read, S. J., & Earleywine, M. (2011). A trans-paradigm theoretical synthesis of cognitive dissonance theory: Illuminating the nature of discomfort. *European Review of Social Psychology, 22,* 36–113.
Kuhn, T. S. (1970). *The structure of scientific revolutions* (2nd ed.). Chicago: University of Chicago Press. (1st ed. 1962).
Lippke, S., & Ziegelman, J. P. (2008). Theory-based health behavior change: Developing, testing, and applying theories for evidence-based interventions. *Applied Psychology: An International Review, 57,* 698–716.
Manicas, P. T., & Secord, P. F. (1983). Implications for psychology of the new philosophy of science. *American Psychologist, 38,* 399–413.
Marks, G., & Miller, N. (1987). Ten years of research on the false-consensus effect: An empirical and theoretical review. *Psychological Bulletin 102,* 72–90.
McGuire, W. J. (1973). The yin and yang of progress in social psychology. *Journal of Personality and Social Psychology, 26,* 446–456.
McGuire, W. J. (1997). Creative hypothesis generating in psychology: Some useful heuristics. *Annual Review of Psychology, 48,* 1–30.
Meston, C. M., & Frohlich, P. F. (2003). Love at first fright: Partner salience moderates roller-coaster-induced excitation transfer. *Archives of Sexual Behavior, 32,* 537–544.
Nisbett, R. E., & Wilson, T. D. (1977). Telling more than we can know: Verbal reports on mental processes. *Psychological Review, 84,* 231–259.
Popper, K. R. (1959). *The logic of scientific discovery.* New York: Basic Books.

Popper, K. R. (1963). *Conjectures and refutations: The growth of scientific knowledge*. London: Routledge.
Ross, L., Greene, D., & House, P. (1977). The "false consensus" effect: An egocentric bias in social perception and attribution processes. *Journal of Experimental Social Psychology, 13*, 279–301.
Sanna, L. J., & Schwarz, N. (2006). Metacognitive experiences and human judgment: The case of hindsight bias and its debiasing. *Current Directions in Psychological Science, 15*, 172–176.
Siegel, J. T., Alvaro, E. M., Crano, W. D., Gonzalez, A. V., Tang, J. C., & Jones, S. P. (2010). Passive-positive organ donor registration behavior: A mixed method assessment of the IIFF model. *Psychology, Health & Medicine, 15*, 198–209.
Stevens, S. S. (1951). Mathematics, measurement, and psychophysics. In S. S. Stevens (Ed.), *Handbook of experimental psychology* (pp. 28–42). New York: Wiley.
Stoner, J. A. (1961). *A comparison of individual and group decisions involving risk* (Unpublished master's thesis). Massachusetts Institute of Technology, Cambridge, MA.
Stoner, J. A. (1968). Risky and cautious shifts in group decisions: The influence of widely held values. *Journal of Experimental Social Psychology, 4*, 442–459.
Wang, Z., & Lang, A. (2012). Reconceptualizing excitation transfer as motivational activation changes and a test of the television program context effects. *Media Psychology, 15*, 68–92.
Wegener, D. T., Silva, P. P., Petty, R. E., & Garcia-Marques, T. (2012). The metacognition of bias regulation. In P. Briñol & K. DeMarree (Eds.), *Social metacognition* (pp. 81–99). New York: Psychology Press.
West, T. V., & Kenny, D. A. (2011). The truth and bias model of judgment. *Psychological Review, 118*, 357–378.
Zentall, T. R. (2010). Justification of effort by humans and pigeons: Cognitive dissonance or contrast? *Current Directions in Psychological Science, 19*, 296–300.
Zillman, D. (1979). *Hostility and aggression*. Hillsdale, NJ: Earlbaum.
Zillman, D. (1996). Sequential dependencies in emotional experience and behavior. In R. Kavanaugh & B. Zimmerberg, (Eds.). *Emotion: Interdisciplinary perspectives* (pp. 243–272). Mahwah, NJ: Erlbaum.

2
INTERNAL AND EXTERNAL VALIDITY

A wide range of potential research designs will be covered in the chapters that follow. They can be categorized roughly into either experimental or nonexperimental strategies. **Experimental methods** involve research in which participant actions are limited or in some way constrained by the controlled manipulation of variables determined by the researcher. Ideally, experiments should be characterized by random assignment, a procedure used to place participants by chance alone into the different conditions, which enables strong inferences of causality. **Quasi-experimental methods** are a variant of experimental methods lacking in random assignment, but as in experiments, participants are exposed to some form of variable manipulation imposed by the researcher. For example, we might be interested in the effects of National Merit Scholarships on college performance. Obviously, a researcher cannot randomly assign high school seniors to receive a Merit scholarship or not because of ethical concerns and the fact that receipt of the award is determined by scores on a test. Quasi-experimental methods (Chapter 10) are an attempt to make inferences about possible variables responsible for the outcome differences between recipients and non-recipients of the scholarship, and to disentangle the effects of the scholarship from other variables such as intelligence or work ethic.

In **nonexperimental methods**, no variables are manipulated. Instead, the relationships of naturally occurring variables are measured by the researcher. Generally, nonexperimental studies are characterized by a focus on associations or correlations among concepts that the researcher is unable to manipulate—sex, race, religiosity, social status, political party affiliation, intelligent design beliefs, and so on—as they involve variables over which the researcher has little, if any, control. In nonexperimental studies, correlational techniques could be used to reveal the strength of association among non-manipulated variables, as the researcher does not interfere with respondents' characteristics and normal behavior. In experimental studies, the researcher is an "active observer," systematically manipulating variables and observing the outcome of these interventions. In nonexperimental studies, however, the researcher can be characterized as a "passive observer" of naturally occurring variables. In nonexperimental studies, the researcher does not actively intrude on the environment of the investigation. Rather, the associations of naturally occurring variations, or of individual factors the participants bring to the research, are the focus of study. These distinctions are consistent with those advanced by Campbell and Stanley (1963) in their classic discussion of research design. These different research design strategies should not be regarded as discrete and mutually exclusive, but rather as points on a continuum about the extent that the researcher has controlled or constrained the context of participant experiencing, and the manner in which their reports of this experience is restricted by the study's arrangements.

The advantages and limitations of experimental and nonexperimental research strategies tend to be complementary, so effective programs of research should make use of both in different stages of the research process.[1] Experiments are deemed the "gold standard" of research because of their methodological rigor and their consequent capacity to foster causal inferences. Experimental studies are usually undertaken in the laboratory because the laboratory provides the conditions allowing the researcher to carefully regulate the context in which controlled variations are implemented and their effects observed. However, this control and precision come at a cost. In research on human behavior, the very control that marks the advantage of experimental techniques places limitations on the representativeness of the phenomena they are used to study and the generalizations that may be advanced.

Nonexperimental (or correlational) strategies, on the other hand, are more likely to have the value of "real world" context and the availability of mass data in developing information about human actions. However, these advantages are bought at the cost of a lack of control over nonsystematic variation in the variables of interest. The inability to exert control over critical variables can result in interesting but scientifically inconclusive findings. The relative value of experimental versus nonexperimental research methods depends to a large extent on the importance placed by the researcher on being able to make causal inferences about the relationships among the variables being studied (Brewer, 2000).

Nonexperimental studies are typically found in field research, but sometimes are employed in laboratory settings as well. For example, if we invite both male and female participants to come to a laboratory to complete questionnaires regarding their need for affiliation and then assess the difference between the men and women in their questionnaire responses, this is still a nonexperimental (correlational) study. Both participant sex and level of affiliation need are individual difference variables, not systematically controlled or manipulated by the researcher. The fact that the measures were obtained in a lab and that there are two groups being compared does not make this an experiment or quasi-experiment.

Causation

The purpose of most research studies is to investigate a hypothesized relationship between the occurrence of variation or change in one variable, A, and the occurrence of variation or change in another variable, B. Variables may be states of the physical or social environment (e.g., weather conditions, the number of people present in the situation), properties of a stimulus (e.g., the facial expression in a photograph, the content of a message), or characteristics of a person or a person's behavior (e.g., mood state, degree of aggression), to name a few possibilities. Hypothesized and observed relationships can involve two environmental variables (e.g., the relationship between variations in barometric pressure and rain), an environmental or stimulus variable and an individual characteristic or trait (e.g., the relationship between the state of the weather and the average mood of people exposed to it), or characteristics of individuals (e.g., the relationship between mood and aggressiveness). To say that there is a relationship between two such variables means that if the value or state of one variable differs or changes, we can expect that the value or state of the other will also change or differ. So for example, if we measure people's mood on a sunny day and then again on a cloudy day, with the result showing that mood is more negative on the second occasion, we can say that the data suggest a relationship between the state of the weather and people's mood.

The more precise the theoretical specification of a predicted relationship, the more closely the obtained data can be matched against the prediction. The nature of the relationship may be specified in terms of the *form* it will take, that is, what kind of changes in variable A will accompany particular changes in variable B, and what the *causal direction* of the relationship will be. Directionality of relationships may be classified into three types.[2]

1. **Unidirectional causation**, a relationship in which changes in A produce subsequent changes in B, but changes in B do not influence A (e.g., increases in the temperature-humidity index produces an increase in aggressive responses of rats, but the degree of aggressiveness of rats does not affect weather conditions).
2. **Bidirectional causation**, a relationship in which changes in A produces changes in B and, in addition, changes in B produce changes in A (e.g., perceiving threat produces feelings of anxiety, and increasing anxiety enhances the perception of threat).
3. **Noncausal covariation** (or correlation, or third-variable causation), a relationship in which changes in A are indirectly accompanied by changes in B, because both A and B are determined by changes in another variable, C. For example, increases or decreases in the cost of living, C, results in the rise or fall of birth rate, A, and consumption of beefsteak, B.

Causation vs. Covariation

The simple observation that when A varies, B also varies, is not sufficient to demonstrate which of these three possibilities is correct. To determine that any particular causal direction exists, alternative explanations for the observed relationship must be ruled out. Both types 1 and 2 must be distinguished from type 3 by demonstrating that when A (or B) changes in isolation from changes in any other variable (C), subsequent changes are observed in B (or A). When an observed relationship is found to have been mistakenly interpreted as a causal relationship of type 1 or 2, when it is actually a case of type 3, the relationship is said to be *spurious*.

Type 1, unidirectional causation, can be distinguished from type 2, bidirectional, by observing whether modifications in A produce changes in B, and vice versa. Finally, the validity of the predicted third variable in a case of type 3 can be determined by noting whether the relationship between A and B can be eliminated if C (and only C) is held constant (that is, not permitted to vary). All of these differentiations are possible only under conditions in which variations in the relevant variables can be observed uncontaminated by related variations that are not relevant to the theoretical relationship.

Moderators and Mediators of Relationships

In addition to specifying the nature and direction of a relationship under study, it also is important to distinguish between two different types of "third variables" that can influence predictive relationships—moderators and mediators (Baron & Kenny, 1986; Hayes, 2013). A **moderator** is a third variable that can either augment or block the presence of a predictive relationship. To take another weather-related illustration, consider the relationship between exposure to sun and sunburn. Although there is a well-established cause-effect link here, it can be moderated by a number of other variables. For instance, the sun to sunburn relationship is much stronger for fair-skinned than for dark-skinned persons. Thus, fair skin is a moderator variable that enhances the relationship between sun exposure and burning. However, this does not mean that the sun to sunburn relationship is spurious. The moderator variable (skin pigmentation) does not produce the effect in the absence of the predictor (sun exposure). Other moderator variables can reduce or block a causal sequence. For instance, the use of effective sunscreen lotions literally "blocks" (or at least retards) the link between the sun's ultraviolet rays and burning. Thus, a researcher who assesses the correlation between sun exposure and sunburn among a sample of fair-skinned people who never venture outdoors without a thick coat of 90 SPF sunblock would be ill-advised to conclude that there is a complete absence of the relationship across all groups. Moderator relationships can be represented notationally as follows:

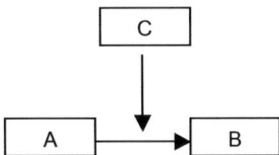

Like Baron and Kenny, we think it is important here to distinguish between third variables that serve as moderators (as in the illustration) and those that serve as mediators of a relationship. A **mediator** is a third variable that serves as intermediary to help explicate the chain of processes of a predictive relationship. With moderator effects, there is a link from A to B, but the observed relationship between these two variables is qualified by levels of moderator variable "C" which either enhances or blocks the causal process. A mediational relation, on the other hand, is represented as follows:

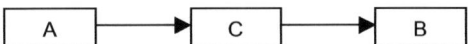

In this case, the presence of "C" is necessary to complete the directional process that links A to B. In effect, varying A results in variations in C, which in turn results in changes in B. To return to our weather examples, the effect of rain on depression may be mediated by social factors. Rain causes people to stay indoors or to hide behind big umbrellas, hence reducing social contact. Social isolation, in turn, may produce depression. However, rain may not be the only determinant of social isolation. In this case, rain as a predictor variable is a sufficient, but not necessary, cause in its link to depression. To demonstrate that A results in B only if C occurs does not invalidate the claim that A and B have a relationship; it only helps to explicate the relationship in terms of a chain of causation.

Moderator variables are determined by testing the interaction of a predictor variable and moderator variable on an outcome, as will be discussed more fully in Chapter 5. Mediational hypotheses will be covered in Chapter 9. The role of moderating and mediating variables in predictive relationships can be evaluated for both experimental and nonexperimental research strategies.

Phases of Research

Much of the preceding discussion characterized research as a venture in hypothesis testing. Such a preoccupation with the *verification* (theory testing) phase of scientific investigation is typical of social research in general. The total research process, however, does not begin with testing hypotheses and verifying theory, but rather with the naturalistic observation of human behavior. Scientific observation is quite often an informal activity of researchers who are interested in the people and things around them. There is probably no way to describe adequately the skill that enables one to decipher the interrelationships that exist in the environment, but without this skill, the chances of generating useful social research ideas, or even developing the building blocks for a theory, are slim.

Given sufficient observation of natural phenomena, the social scientist is in the position to enter into the second phase of the research process, namely, that of *classification*. Observations are ordered according to a system of categorization, or taxonomy. At this stage of the research cycle, there is greater stress on the accuracy of observation. At the same time, the validity of the classificatory rules employed in ordering observations is continually reassessed, particularly if the observational data are not amenable to easy classification.

With the completion of the classificatory phase, the researcher is in a position to initiate the verification process. At this point different sciences diverge, depending upon the nature and source of their data. Although all scientific methods are empirical, not all are experimental. Some areas of investigation—for example, astronomy—involve phenomena that cannot be brought under the manipulative control of the researcher, and can only be observed naturally using nonexperimental strategies. However, where experimentation is possible, it is the most powerful research strategy available for determining the source and direction of relations between variables. Essentially, the purpose of the hypothesis-testing experiment is to clarify the relationship between two (or more) variables by bringing the variation of at least one of the elements in the relationship under the control of the researcher; that is, in experiments the researcher determines when and how changes in this variable occur.

The **independent variable** is a characteristic manipulated independently of its natural sources of covariation to produce different conditions in an experimental study. We refer to its conditions or variations as experimental *treatments*, or manipulations, or levels. The experimenter manipulates or controls participants' exposure to one of the variations in the independent variable in some systematic way. This is done to ensure that effects from other natural sources of covariation (or other variables related to this predictor) would not obscure the impact on the outcome of interest. The **dependent variable** is the measured outcome or consequence not manipulated by the researcher, and expected to be influenced by (or dependent upon) manipulation of the independent variable in an experimental study. If the experiment is adequately controlled (see Chapters 5, 6, and 7), the observed variations in scores of the dependent variable will be attributable to the effects of the independent variable. Thus, the experiment provides a critical setting for demonstrating the nature of the A to B predictive relationship between theoretically relevant variables, but it is only one phase in the theory-building process.[3]

For the most technically correct usage, the terms independent variable and dependent variable are typically reserved for experimental methods. Many researchers and methodologists, out of convenience, have adopted this same terminology for nonexperimental strategies as well, although this is not entirely consistent with the original intended meaning of these terms. The terms *predictor variable* and *criterion variable* (or outcome), used in both experimental or nonexperimental designs, are more encompassing language to describe the A to B relationship. The independent variable represents a specific type of a predictor variable, and the dependent variable is a special case of a criterion variable or outcome.

The quality of the earlier efforts of the observation and classification phases usually determines the value of the verification process. If, during these earlier phases, the interrelationships between the independent and dependent variables are accurately assessed, then the probability is high that the experimental investigation will confirm earlier intuitions and add to our store of trustworthy social knowledge. A trial-and-error approach to experimentation sometimes opens up new and meaningful lines of investigation, but premature emphasis on the verification phase also can lead to a misdirection of attention to interrelationships among variables having no real or important connection. If real progress is to be made, investigators must realize that research does not involve a discrete, one-shot investigation of a hypothesis, but rather is a process whose earlier phases are as critical as the more prestigious verification stage.

The successful verification of a suspected relationship within the limited conditions of the laboratory, where the majority of experimental studies usually occurs, does not complete the research process. The artificially controlled nature of the laboratory experiment introduces the possibility that an observed relationship exists only under the restricted conditions of a specific research setting. To rule out this threat to the validity of a theoretical proposition, the relationship must be empirically demonstrated under a variety of controlled *and* natural conditions. If it turns out that the predicted relationship exists under some conditions, but not under others (e.g., increasing monetary incentives increases work output in large manufacturing companies, but not in small ones), the theory must be modified to account for these limiting circumstances or risk being supplanted by one that does. To insure that our theoretical concepts and hypotheses have been adequately tested, our research repertoire must contain a number of heterogeneous methods and techniques.

Distinguishing Internal and External Validity

The stage of research at which a particular investigation falls should dictate the research strategy the investigator adopts. This choice, in turn, should be guided by considerations of two types of validity—internal and external validity (Campbell & Stanley, 1963). These forms of validity reflect upon the quality of different, but critically important, aspects of the research process. **Internal validity** is the extent that inferences of causality could be made about the obtained relationship between the independent variable and the dependent variable. Confidence in causal inferences is enhanced when the treatment or manipulation is under the systematic control of the researcher. **External validity** is the extent of generalizability or certainty that results can be applied to other respondent groups, different settings, and different ways of operationalizing the conceptual variables.

Typically, discussion of internal validity is reserved for research that involves experimental methods, and this is proper because the issue of internal validity is concerned with the appropriate interpretation of the causal relationship between an independent and a dependent variable, the central feature of all experimentation. Considerations of internal validity, however, also may be applied when evaluating relationships observed in nonexperimental contexts, but because such studies do not manipulate variables, causal inferences about their naturally observed relationships generally are regarded as being lower in internal validity. Considerations of external validity or generalizability of results are equally important in evaluating the worth of experimental and nonexperimental research, and as such should be considered in both research contexts. Internal validity and external validity, as well as other types of validities, should not be evaluated in black-and-white terms—of whether a study possesses one or the other or both—but rather as points on a continuum. Before discussing the internal-external validity distinction further, however, we will consider three closely related issues—the role of statistics, the field/laboratory distinction, and the distinction between basic and applied research.

Role of Statistics (Statistical Conclusion Validity)

Just as the choice of research method must depend upon considerations of the nature of the phenomenon of interest, so too must the role of statistical techniques be evaluated with respect to the general goal of eliminating or reducing the plausibility of rival alternative hypotheses for the events under investigation. One potential rival explanation that plagues social research at all stages of investigation is *chance*. The phenomena of interest in the social sciences are generally subject to considerable nonsystematic variation—variations from individual to individual, for example, and from one time to another within individuals. Given such uncontrolled (and unexplained) variability among observations, the occurrence of any observed relationship or effect is always potentially attributable to the operation of chance, or random happenstance. Statistical analyses assess the possibility that chance is a reasonable alternative explanation of any relational finding. When investigating a phenomenon, studies almost always collect data from a limited sample of participants (Hallahan & Rosenthal, 1996). We do so because it would be prohibitively difficult and expensive to collect data from all individuals in a target population. Thus, a study's sample is always susceptible to *sampling error*, because the outcome observed in a particular sample by chance is not perfectly consistent with what would be found if the entire population was used. This uncertainty due to sampling error is partly responsible for the heavy use of probabilistic language and triple negatives (e.g., "The failure to reject the null hypothesis …") that serves to terrify so many students of elementary statistics.

The purpose of inferential statistical tests (e.g., t-tests, analyses of variance, multiple regression) is to assess the likelihood that an obtained effect could have occurred by chance, given that the null hypothesis is true. Statistical inference allows us to assign a probability of the operation of chance due to sampling error as a possible explanation of any relationship discovered. Results of a statistical inference test tell us the probability of a *Type I error* of inference—the probability that the observed effect would have been obtained by chance if the *null hypothesis* (no true relationship between the predictor and outcome variables) was true. **Statistical significance** is achieved if the probability of obtaining the observed effect by chance is so low as to render the chance explanation implausible. Usually, a Type I probability value of .05 or less (i.e., an outcome that could have occurred by chance no more than 5 times in 100) is chosen as the cutoff value in determining whether or not the observed relationship is defined as statistically significant.[4] Suppose you thought that high school boys' participation in contact sports (football, hockey, etc.) was associated with their scoring higher on a test of aggressiveness, and that the more sports they participated in, the higher their aggressiveness scores would be. You gather data on extent of boys' participation, administer a good test of aggressiveness, and find a statistically significant association (at $p = .05$) between predictor and criterion variables. You are happy that your hypothesis was supported, but remember, there is a 5% chance that you might have obtained this result by chance, even if there was no actual relationship. If 100 researchers replicated your study, it is possible that 5 of them would find results similar to yours—by chance. Tests of statistical significance provide insight into the likelihood that chance is a viable alternative explanation of our findings.

When the probability of a Type I error is not low enough (e.g., not below $p < .05$) to rule out the null hypothesis, we should be concerned with a *Type II error* of inference—the probability of failing to reject the null hypothesis if it is false (i.e., there really *is* a relationship between the predictor and outcome variables, but our study failed to detect it at above chance level). Reducing the probability of Type II error requires that we design studies with sufficient power (see Cohen, 2003) to detect an effect above and beyond random variation. **Statistical power** is the probability of obtaining a statistical significant effect, if indeed that effect truly exists. It is desirable to make sure that your study has high statistical power, because if it does not, valuable resources may be wasted in conducting a study that fails to obtain adequate evidence for statistical significance of results. The power of a study depends in part on a number of properties of the study (Cohen, 2003): (a) number of participants that are measured (power increases as the number of participants in the study increases), (b) the reliability of the measures that are used (power increases when reliable measures are used; see Chapter 3), (c) the strength (effect size) of the relationship, because as the strength of the observed effect increases, so does the power to detect it, and (d) the Type I critical value that is used for the statistical test (tests using a critical rejection region of $p < .05$ have more power than those using a lower probability of $p < .001$, for example). Ideally, our studies should be designed to have sufficient statistical power to attain statistical significance, allowing us to identify real relationships when they exist.

Figure 2.1 describes the four possible outcomes that can be found when testing whether a study's outcome corresponds with reality. To give an applied example using this figure, suppose that during a short break from reading this textbook, you tune in to an episode of a daytime talk show in which a woman has accused a man of being the biological father of the child she recently gave birth to. The man adamantly denies this claim, arguing that he could not be the baby's daddy as he was out of

		Actuality/Reality	
		Effect	No Effect
Test/Outcome	Effect	Correct Decision (Power)	Type I Error
	No Effect	Type II Error	Correct Decision

FIGURE 2.1 Possible scenarios involving a test result and correspondence with reality.

town during the months in which conception had occurred. After allowing for incivility to increase viewership, the host then dramatically announces the outcome of the DNA test, but before doing so, alerts the audience that that there is some uncertainty about the accuracy of paternity tests.

We know that four outcomes are possible in this example: (a) the test indicates he is the father—and he actually is (correct decision); (b) the test indicates he is the father—but he actually is not (Type I error); (c) the test indicates he is not the father—but he is actually is (Type II error); (d) the test indicates he is not the father—and he actually is not (correct decision). If the test outcome correctly corresponds to the underlying reality, either scenario (a) or scenario (d) should occur. In the first case, there is empirical evidence necessary to support the mother's hypothesis. This cell of the table corresponds to a researcher's directional hypothesis—A is related to B. It represents the usually sought-for outcome of researchers' efforts. Statistical analyses are powerful and necessary research tools. However, the time and effort required to master the theory and calculations essential for the proper use of statistical significance testing techniques have led many students of social science to confuse statistical sophistication with expertise in research design. Statistical considerations are not the beginning and end of our research design concerns. Indeed, in our view, proper research design almost invariably simplifies the statistical analyses that we require (Smith, 2000). The statistical analyses that are chosen should depend upon their relevance to the theoretical issues being addressed and the nature of the design that is used. Complicated statistics cannot compensate for poor design. Learning to avoid the pitfall of equating current tools of analysis with the *purpose* of research methodology is a major aim of this text. Our sentiments lie with those of Agnew and Pike (1969, p. 142) who observed:

> It is our view that the researcher who works outside the laboratory should, if anything, be more sophisticated about the principles of measurement, research design, statistics, and rules of evidence than the laboratory researcher. Note that we are talking about principles of research design, not about rituals. Though more difficult to teach, it would be preferable to provide the student with an appreciation of the main rules of evidence used in science. Hopefully, the student would then be able to select research tools that fit his research interests, rather than looking for a research problem that will fit his research tools.

Field vs. Laboratory Research

For a long time in social research, a controversy existed between the proponents of field research and those who favored laboratory studies. Field researchers claimed that only in real-life settings could we discover anything of value—that the responses of participants who were studied in the cold, antiseptic environment of the laboratory could not be viewed as valid representations of the behavior they would have emitted in more normal, everyday, circumstances. Basically, they were arguing that laboratory stories have no external validity (generalizability). Laboratory researchers, on the other hand, argued that so many theoretically extraneous events occurred in the natural environment—the field—that one could never be certain about the true relationship that existed among any given set of variables.

As is the case with most arguments of this type, both sides were partly correct—and both were partly wrong. To be sure, there are numerous examples of laboratory studies that are so devoid of reality that their practical or scientific utility must be seriously questioned. It is just as obvious, however, that not all laboratory research is psychologically, behaviorally, and socially "unreal" (Aronson, Wilson, & Brewer, 1998). In many areas of investigation—communication, persuasion, group interaction—we have gained much valuable information about the complicated nature of human social interaction. To argue that nothing of generalizable value can come out of the social laboratory is to deny the obvious.

On the other side of the argument are the laboratory researchers who contend that because so many uncontrolled events occur in the relatively free-form field environment, no clear specification of relationships between or among theoretically implicated measures is possible. As before, there are plenty of examples that would serve to "prove" the contentions of the critics of field research. The inability of these researchers to control for powerful factors that could have major influences on critical behaviors is one of the more telling problems mentioned by critics. The problems introduced by this lack of control are real, and are part of the standard set of difficulties the field researcher faces whenever studies of this type are attempted. With the increasing sophistication evident in much contemporary field research, however, it is becoming ever more apparent that these difficulties can be surmounted—or, if not completely offset, their effects at least identified. Many recent research methodology texts have focused specifically on the complete or partial solution of the many problems encountered in field research settings (Donaldson & Crano, 2011).

There is a place in the social sciences for both field and laboratory research. Each reinforces the value of the other. The findings of the laboratory are retested in the field, where their robustness is put to a severe test. If the findings hold, then we may gain a potentially important addition to our knowledge base. Likewise, the less-than-completely-controlled observations of the field researcher can be brought to the laboratory for more rigorous examination. If these observations prove valid within the more strict confines of the laboratory, their value is already established, given their initial development in the "real world." Thus, field and laboratory research not only do not compete, they complement each other in real and important ways. Many of today's leading social researchers are in agreement with this assessment. Many of our most precise research endeavors are, in fact, field experiments (Chapter 8); and, some of our most powerful generalizations were born in the sterile confines of the laboratory (Mook, 1983). The integration of field and laboratory research methodologies using experimental and nonexperimental strategies will be examined in the forthcoming chapters.

Basic vs. Applied Research

Viewing the research process as the accumulative reduction of plausible alternatives to a particular theoretical account provides a context for consideration of the traditional distinction between "basic" and "applied" research. Essentially, the difference between the two lies in whether relatively long-term or short-term gains are expected from the outcomes of the research. The "applied" label refers to those research efforts that are directed toward affecting a particular phenomenon in some preconceived way (e.g., which of several advertising campaigns will produce the greater number of product sales; which serum formula will terminate the symptoms of skin cancer most effectively; which remedial program will reduce illiteracy in the urban ghetto). Because the goals of applied research are relatively concrete, feedback on any observed outcomes is immediate. For basic research, the goal of each research project is to contribute to that ephemeral universe of knowledge, or, in more specific terms, to add to the accumulative pattern of data that will ultimately determine the survival value of alternative theoretical interpretations of the phenomena under investigation (e.g., *which* theory of consumer motivation; *which* etiology of skin cancer; *which* explanation of the nature of mass illiteracy). In this enterprise, the value of any particular research contribution can only be judged from a historical perspective.

The differential value of applied and basic research does not lie in any major differences in rigor of research methodology or clarity of results (Bickman & Rog, 1998). Rather, from the perspective provided in this chapter, the essential difference lies in the relative probability that results of research programs will contribute to the development of a broadly based explanatory theory or to a limited exploration of some causal relationship. To the extent that applied research is restricted to the examination of variations in a particular A-B relationship, it is unlikely to uncover an explanatory principle that accounts for C-D and E-F, *along with* A-B. The applied social researcher is likely to limit the research explorations, for example, to sources of tension between Blacks and Whites in contemporary American society. A basic research program, on the other hand, would more likely be concerned with the general phenomenon of ethnocentrism in intergroup relations, thus involving the investigation of Black-White relations *as well as* inter-ethnic relations, international relations, and many other manifestations of the phenomenon (probably including interactions among lower animals within an evolutionary framework).

Many of those who are committed to basic social research contend that its long-run benefits, in terms of the alleviation of social problems, will be greater than those of applied research. However, just as the distinction between long-term and short-term is a relative one, the difference between applied and basic research is a matter of degree. To the extent that applied researchers are open to creative variations in their research problems, it becomes probable that they will serendipitously arrive at findings that will have broad theoretical impact. On the other hand, the more the basic researcher becomes involved in the permutations or combinations of a particular A-B relationship, or the more committed he or she becomes to a minor theoretical point (that is, the closer one comes to the stereotypic version of the "ivory tower" scholar), the less likely it is that the research will contribute to a meaningful expansion of the explanatory power of the discipline, no matter how *in*applicable the results of the research may be!

Basic Issues of Internal Validity

As we have indicated, the purpose of the design of experiments is oriented toward eliminating possible alternative explanations of research results (variations in scores on the dependent variable) that are unrelated to the effects of the treatment (independent variable) of interest. When an experiment is adequately designed, changes in the dependent variable can be attributed to variations in the treatment, which is systematically controlled and manipulated by the investigator. That is, response differences on the dependent variable can be accounted for by differences in degree of exposure (or lack of exposure) to the experimental treatment. These differences may occur between measures on the same persons taken before and after exposure (the *pretest-posttest design*) or between measures on different groups that have been exposed to different conditions (*the comparison-group design*). In either case, if obtained outcome differences can be attributed directly to and caused by the independent variable, the study is said to have internal validity. If factors other than the experimental treatment could plausibly account for the obtained differences, then the internal validity of the study is uncertain. A **confound** is a type of extraneous variable in which its effect and the effect of the independent variable on the dependent variable cannot be separated; thereby it poses a threat to internal validity. A research study is said to be confounded, or internally invalid, when there is reason to believe that obtained differences in the dependent variable would have occurred *even if exposure to the independent variable had not been manipulated*. Potential sources of such invalidity that could affect almost any research program have been identified and discussed by Campbell and Stanley (1963). The eight major *threats to internal validity* that they discussed may be summarized as follows:

1. *History*. Differences in scores are attributed to differential events (unrelated to the experimental treatment) that occurred during the passage of time.
2. *Maturation*. Scores are caused by changes in the internal or physical characteristics of the participants (e.g., growing older, becoming more tired, less interested). These are termed maturation effects, even though some representatives of this class (e.g., growing tired) are not typically thought of as being related to physical maturation.
3. *Testing*. Scores obtained in a second administration of the measure are caused by participants having been exposed to the same measure previously.
4. *Instrumentation error*. Scores are caused by changes in the properties of the measurement instrument, rather than by changes in the participants being measured. Examples include the instrument being damaged or the measurement device failing.
5. *Statistical regression* (toward the mean). Outcome scores are subject to misinterpretation if participants are selected on the basis of extreme scores at their initial measurement session. Owing to unreliability of repeated measures, at the later round scores will tend toward the mean score of the participants. (This threat to internal validity will be discussed more fully in Chapter 10).
6. *Selection error*. If scores for two or more groups of participants are being compared, differences are caused by selection (e.g., nonrandom) procedures employed when participants were assigned to the groups.
7. *Mortality*. Selection procedures, treatment differences, or issues that yield different proportions of participants dropping out of the study may cause the observed differences between the groups in the final measurement.
8. *Selection-based interactions*. If participants were differentially (nonrandomly) selected to serve in comparison groups, these specially selected groups may experience differences in history, maturation, testing, etc., which may produce differences in the final measurement.

An example of a simple research study may help to clarify how these threats to internal validity operate to make it impossible to determine whether the independent variable is actually responsible for producing changes in the dependent measure. In this hypothetical study, the attitudes of a group of college students toward their school's administrators are measured. One week after the initial measurement, the same group of students is exposed to an administrator's speech (the experimental treatment), which advocates stricter discipline for students. The student group is then measured again on the attitude test. In this simple pretest-posttest design involving only one group, the researcher is interested in whether the speech communication changed attitudes expressed on the test. However, with this design, attitude changes (or lack of change) in the group occurring between pretest and posttest cannot be directly and unambiguously attributed to the effects of the communication because of the many uncontrolled extraneous variables that could provide rival alternative explanations.

For instance, during the passage of time between pretest and posttest, some event might have occurred on campus (*history*) that altered attitudes instead of the communication. The school authorities, for example, might have voted for a major tuition reduction. It should be noted here that although individual histories may cause individual changes in test scores, only commonly experienced events, which affect most of the group in the same way, will produce *systematic* changes between pretest and posttest scores. That is, individuals may have different (historical) experiences, some of which tend to increase attitude scores and some of which tend to decrease scores. Across all individuals, however, the effects of these different experiences will cancel out, unless most of the individuals have the *same* experience, which exerts a consistent effect in one direction on all of their scores, thereby producing a discernible overall change in the total group's mean test score.

Similarly, the class of variables categorized as *maturation* effects could account for changes in attitude scores. It is possible, for instance, that as students become older and more experienced, they generally become more tolerant or accepting of authority figures. The longer the time period between pretest and posttest, the more likely it is that maturation or intervening historical events will provide plausible rival explanations for obtained attitude change.

A third rival explanation or threat to internal validity concerns *testing*, and could arise from the possibility that pretesting produces sensitivity to the issue, which causes changes in responses to the second test. For some kinds of dependent variables, particularly achievement tests, test-taking practice effects usually lead to improved performance on a second measure, even if different questions are used. Unlike history or maturation, these *pretest sensitivity* or *practice effects* are more likely to provide plausible alternative explanations of results with *shorter* intervals between pretest and posttest.

Another type of internal validity threat, *instrumentation*, could occur if there were possible differences in scoring procedures employed between the pretest and the posttest. This would be especially likely if the attitude test was in the form of an essay exam (where scorers could shift standards between tests) rather than an objectively scored (e.g., multiple choice) test. Whenever measurements are in any way dependent on subjective judgments of scorers or observers, as is often the case with many social variables, biases of the measure may produce instrumentation effects. For instance, in the above study the researcher's assistants may have presented the pro-authority speech. If they were strongly personally committed to influencing the participants, and if they were scoring an essay-type attitude test under these circumstances, they would be more likely to detect pro-authority statements in the essays after the speech than during the pretest, thereby introducing scoring differences in favor of their own biases. Even with well-trained objective scorers, subtle differences in attitudes or conscientiousness over time may produce systematic instrumentation effects.

Instrumentation effects can be controlled by requiring several unbiased scorers to agree in their judgments or by scoring pretests and posttests at the same time without letting the scorers know which is which. Unfortunately, other rival factors cannot be so readily eliminated within the simple pretest-posttest design. Ideally, the factors of history, maturation, and testing could be controlled if we could measure each participant at the same time both with and without the experimental treatment. Then any differences between the two measures could be interpreted as due to the effect of the treatment, and nothing else. As long as we are bound by the restrictions of Aristotelian logic, however, the best we can do is to measure two *different* groups of participants that are *equivalent* in terms of the effects of the rival factors. If one of these groups is then exposed to the experimental treatment and the other is not, then any changes in the "experimental" (or treatment) group above and beyond those that occur in the "control" group (the one receiving no treatment) can be attributed to the experimental variable. Even though history, maturation, etc., may produce changes *within* the two groups, any difference *between* the groups can be accounted for by the experimental treatment that was administered to one group but not to the other.

Random Assignment and Experimental Control

As noted, the design of experiments is intended to eliminate threats to internal validity. The prototype of a good experimental design is one in which groups of people who are initially equivalent

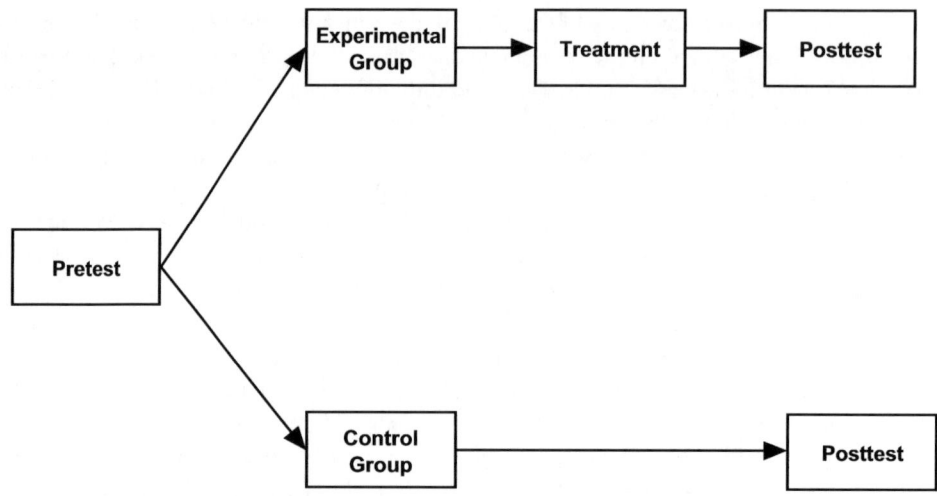

FIGURE 2.2 Diagram of a pretest–posttest control group design.

(at the pretest phase) are randomly assigned to receive the experimental treatment or a control condition and then assessed again after this differential experience (posttest phase). A graphic depiction of this *pretest-posttest control group design* is presented in Figure 2.2.

The success of the two-group experimental design depends primarily on the assumption that experimental and control groups are equivalent on all factors except exposure to *different levels* of the independent variable. The ideal of comparability between two groups with respect to all variables other than the ones under experimental investigation may be met in either of two ways. Some variables may literally be "held constant," that is, be maintained at the same level for all participants in all groups (e.g., testing everyone at the same time of day, using the same experimenter for all participants, etc.). Other *unmeasured* variables may be allowed to vary randomly with the assumption that there will be no systematic differences between the sets of participants in the two comparison groups on these extraneous sources of variation. This is accomplished through the technique of random assignment of participants to groups.

Random assignment requires that all persons available for a particular research study be able to participate in either the experimental or the control group, and that only chance determines the group to which any individual is assigned. A coin (if there are only two groups) or random number generator may be used to assist in randomly assigning participant units to groups. The faith in statistical chance to place participants into groups equally is bolstered as the number of participants in a study increases. The "law of large numbers" is crucial if randomization is to accomplish its goal. Without large numbers of participants available for assignment to conditions, randomization cannot deliver on its promise to produce equivalent groups. When enough participants are available, chance assignment assures that there will be no preexisting systematic differences (e.g., average age, birth order, sex, educational background, intelligence) between the groups at the onset of the study, and also that there is no reason to believe that they will experience any systematic differences during the research period other than the treatment, whose delivery is controlled by the experimenter.

Without random assignment, myriad preexisting group differences would obscure the relation of the independent variable to the dependent variable relationship under investigation. Random assignment represents the strictest form of experimenter control that can imposed, as doing so rules out many, if not all, threats to internal validity. For this reason, random assignment is required for any design is to be considered a *true experiment*. If any basis other than chance is used to assign participants to groups, then another threat to internal validity, *selection*, may account for differences on the dependent variable. Particularly hazardous is any selection procedure that permits participants themselves to determine to which treatment they will be exposed. Such *self-selection* on the part of the research participants makes it impossible to tell whether the treatment affected the dependent variable scores or whether differences in scores were determined by the personal characteristics of the individuals who chose to expose themselves to, or avoid, the experimental treatment. For example, in educational research dealing with remedial teaching programs, it is unwise to expose volunteers to the program and then to compare their progress with that of a "control" group of students who declined to take part in the program. If any differences in achievement do show up, it is not possible to determine whether they were brought about by the remedial program or whether characteristics of the volunteer participants, such as a greater motivation to improve, were responsible for performance differences. Only volunteer participants who were randomly assigned to a no-remedial-treatment condition could provide an equivalent control group for comparison with the experimental group.

The self-selection of participants to experimental or control conditions can cloud the interpretability of a study, but other forms of selection artifacts also can arise when randomization is not employed, and these sometimes can prove even more difficult to recognize than simple self-selection. Unfortunately in some research circumstances, nonrandom selection is nearly impossible to avoid. Under such circumstances, extreme caution must be exercised in the interpretation of research findings. Let us expand our example of an experimental testing program to illustrate this point.

Suppose that the government developed a program designed to offset the academic deficiencies of children whose parents fell below federal poverty guidelines. Only poor children, in other words, were eligible for this program. How would the researcher determine whether the educational program was succeeding? A pretest-posttest control group experimental design would seem ideal for the investigator's purposes. But who would constitute the control group? From our earlier discussion, it is clear that one would not compare the academic achievement of treatment group participants with that of children who were eligible for the program, but who had failed to volunteer for it. Too many differences already exist between volunteers and non-volunteers to trust such a comparison (Rosenthal & Rosnow, 1975).

Alternatively, one could sample from a group of children who were not eligible for the program. However, these "control" group children likely would be from a higher economic stratum than that of the experimental group, and we already know from years of educational research that there is a positive relationship between socioeconomic status and academic achievement. Thus, a comparison of this type would almost surely show large initial (pretest) differences between the groups, in favor of the (wealthier) control group participants. Such a difference would reflect the selection problem that is operating here.

Another possibility would be to systematically search for children in the control group whose pretest scores exactly matched those of children in the experimental condition. If a suitable one-to-one match could be found for every participant in the experimental group, then by definition the average pretest scores of the two groups would be identical. Whereas this might seem an appealing solution to some, it is fraught with difficulties because it implicitly assumes that the histories, maturation rates, etc., of the two samples will be identical over the course of the study. This is a risky assumption at best, and in light of considerable research (Cronbach & Snow, 1977; Trochim, 1984, 1986), palpably unlikely in the present circumstances. We know that children of higher socioeconomic status are academically advantaged relative to their poorer peers, and that this "achievement gap" widens as time goes by. This *selection x maturation interaction* threat to internal validity often is difficult to recognize and even more difficult to offset. Likewise, if the histories of the two groups differed systematically over the course of the experiment (a likely possibility if the treatment is extended for any period), we will encounter an interaction of selection x history—effects that can bias our ability to infer causation just as surely as would a simple selection bias.

Solutions to the problems introduced by selection artifacts are not simple. Generally, complex statistical techniques are employed in the attempt to assess, if not offset, the biases that can occur when the assignment of participants to conditions is not random (see Chapter 10 for a discussion of quasi-experiments). It should be kept in mind that these statistical "fixes" are not ideal, but rather akin to a salvage operation. Clearly, if random assignment can be accomplished, it should be.

Participant Loss

The advantages of random assignment for internal validity are assured as long as the initial equivalence of the experimental and control groups can be maintained throughout the study. Unfortunately, research involving human participants is never free of the possibility that at some time between random assignment to groups and the posttest, some participants may drop out of the experiment and become unavailable for final testing. If the groups are initially equivalent, and if this dropout rate (referred to by the more morbid as participant mortality) occurs randomly across groups, then the loss of participants should not be any different for the experimental and control groups, and so does not pose a threat to internal validity. If we have pretested all participants at the beginning of the experiment, we can check the pretest scores for those participants who have dropped out. If those scores are essentially the same for dropouts from both the experimental and the control groups, we may have some confidence that the two groups are still equivalent except for effects of the experimental treatment.[5]

If there is something about the experimental treatment that enhances or otherwise affects the chances of participants dropping out of the study, a serious problem is introduced because the initially equivalent groups may become differentially selected groups by the time of final testing. For instance, if after random assignment to research groups participants in the experimental treatment group learn that they are going to be faced with a task that involves a lot of hard work or effort as part of their participation, many of them may find excuses for discontinuing their involvement in the experiment. Thus, at the time of post-treatment testing, the experimental group would be composed largely of unusually hard-working or unusually compliant participants, unlike the control group, which had not been exposed to the same selective pressures.

The researcher must be aware that participant selection is a potential problem not only at the initial stage of assigning participants to groups but also throughout the study, and should attempt to design the experiment so that differences between the treatments received by experimental and control groups will not introduce differential tendencies to drop out of the experiment. In the example given here, for instance, the experimenter could see to it that both experimental and control groups were led to expect that they might all have to work hard (even though only the experimental group would actually do so). This procedure would not prevent participants from dropping out of the study, but it would help assure that such dropouts were equally distributed between experimental and control conditions.

Sometimes participants are dropped from an experiment by the researcher, either during the course of the experiment or at the time of data analysis. For instance, upon identifying one or two participants who show unusual performance after the experimental treatment, the researcher might examine the background information for these participants, conclude that they were highly atypical, and thereby justify the removal of their data from the final analysis. If the participants in the control group are not also examined for similar atypical cases, the researcher has applied a selection rule which may result in an apparent "treatment effect" that would not have appeared if all the data had been included. In general, it is not permissible for a researcher to eliminate participants at any point after assignment to groups has occurred, although weeding out the participant pool *prior* to random assignment is sometimes acceptable.

To summarize these eight threats to internal validity, consider examples using a common scenario, as presented in Table 2.1. Setting up this study, suppose that using a pretest-posttest control group design, a therapist creates a treatment plan to help a people who are habitually unable to enjoy the antics and delights of clowns and who have been diagnosed with clown phobia. This clinical problem is called coulrophobia (Flora, 2006). To measure level of fear and anxiety toward clowns, both the experimental and control groups complete a clown phobia questionnaire at pretest and also at posttest. Between both test administrations, only the experimental group receives the treatment of exposure therapy, involving desensitization to clown paraphernalia and activities, which is designed to reduce their unrealistic terror of these circus professionals. Table 2.1 shows how the various threats to internal validity could operate in this research context.

TABLE 2.1 Threats to internal validity as illustrated with a clown phobia study.

Threat to Internal Validity	Example
1. History	While all experimental group participants are sitting in the waiting room for the intervention to begin, the television in that room airs breaking news that a disgruntled clown was just convicted of arson in burning down a circus tent. As the control group did not view the news, higher scores are found on the posttest for the experimental group.
2. Maturation	The control group is administered the clown phobia posttest immediately, but the experimental group receives it 1 year after the therapy. As participants in the experimental group became older and wiser, and thus outgrew their fear of clowns, lower posttest scores were reported than control participants.
3. Testing	Participants in the experimental group were more likely to have answered a clown phobia questionnaire as part of a previous study by another researcher. Encountering the same questions again, experimental group participants rush through the questionnaire very quickly without paying attention.
4. Instrumentation	For the control condition, the researcher administers the full 100-item posttest. For the experimental condition, the researcher fails to make photocopies of the last page of the questionnaire and accidentally administers an 80-item version. Consequently, the total posttest score in the experimental group appears to be lower than in the control group.
5. Statistical Regression	As the researcher is interested in only the most severe clinical cases, only participants with the highest clown phobia scores on the pretest are selected to receive the therapy. Thus, an overall pretest to posttest reduction in clown phobia is observed among treated participants.
6. Selection	Participants are allowed to choose which group they wish to participate in, with those most motivated to reduce their fear of clowns tending to select the experimental group. Results show that the experimental group, in comparison to the control group, showed lower posttest scores.
7. Mortality	As part of the exposure treatment requires putting on aesthetically questionable clown makeup, participants in the experimental group are more likely than those in the control group to drop out before completing the posttest.
8. Selection-history interactions	Allowed to select the group, more motivated participants request to serve in the experimental group. Also because of this motivation, they are more likely to watch online videos of friendly clowns making animal balloons in their spare time, prior to returning for the posttest.

Other Sources of Invalidity

Complete control over experimental treatments is necessitated by the fact that inferences drawn from studies using a control group are acceptable only when the treatments to which the experimental and control groups are exposed differ *only* on the variable under consideration (i.e., all other conditions are "held constant"). For example, in physiological research dealing with the effects of surgical ablation of the parts of the brain, some animals are subjected to the full surgery (the experimental group) while others go through a "sham operation," in which they undergo all of the phases of the surgery *except* the actual removal of the brain section. The sham operation control is used to assure that differences between experimental and control animals are attributable to effects of the surgical ablation and not to experiences associated with general operative procedures, such as anesthesia or post-operative shock. Similarly, a researcher interested in the effects of anxiety-producing situations must be sure that the conditions to which the experimental and control groups are exposed differ only in induced anxiousness and not in such extraneous variables as the relationship between participant and experimenter.

The Fallible Observer

One source of internal invalidity that can threaten an experiment even when random assignment has been used is derived from the researcher's *expectations* about how the experiment will (or should) turn out. In Chapter 7, we will discuss research indicating how such expectations can influence in relatively complex and subtle ways the nature of the experimenter-participant interaction. But more direct experimenter effects may influence the outcome of a study independent of any effects upon participant responses. Such effects are generated by *unintentional* differences in criteria applied by observers to participants in different groups, *unintentional* misinterpretation of participants' responses, *unintentional* errors of data recording and analysis, and the like.[6] (Such factors would be considered "instrumentation" effects in our earlier discussion of threats to internal validity.)

A valuable example of the effects of observer bias on the (mis)recording of participants' responses was provided by Kennedy and Uphoff (1939). These experimenters asked individuals who were classified on the basis of their belief or lack of belief in extrasensory perception (ESP) to take part in a test of ESP ability. Using a standard card-guessing task, the participant-observers were to "transmit" one of four symbols portrayed on each of a set of cards to another individual and to record the guesses made by this "receiver." The persons whose ESP was being tested were, in fact, experimental accomplices, and the "guesses" they made were pre-recorded. The principal dependent measure of this investigation was the number of times the participant-observers erred in recording the accomplice's responses. Of 11,125 guesses, only 126 (1.1%) were misrecorded. Given the magnitude of the recording task, an *error rate* of 1.1% would not seem overly bothersome. However, closer examination of the *direction* of these errors as a function of the individual student-observer's beliefs in ESP proved revealing. Of the 57 errors tending to increased telepathy scores, 36 (63%) were committed by believers in ESP. Conversely, 18 of the 27 errors (67%) lowering telepathy scores were made by the nonbelievers. These errors, then, were definitely influenced by observers' prior beliefs. They clearly were not random, though they were admittedly small, as is typical of findings in this area of research.

Controlling Variables

The ideal of *ceteris paribus*, that there be no differences in conditions to which comparison groups are exposed except the experimental variable under consideration, is seldom perfectly met in practice. The experimental and control groups can never be treated precisely alike in every detail;

some minor variation can be ignored as irrelevant. However, it pays to be aware of details—today's irrelevancy may become tomorrow's major breakthrough.[7] The need for careful control over experimental variables has driven some social researchers to limit themselves to laboratory research and ritualized research techniques. However, it is our hope that greater awareness of the principles that underlie research methods will encourage investigators to apply their ingenuity to achieving controlled variations in a variety of potential research settings.

Basic Issues of External Validity

The design issues we have been discussing thus far in the chapter have been concerned almost exclusively with the internal validity of a research study. In many ways, internal validity is the *sine qua non* of good experimental research. The essence of experimental design is to control the assignment of participants to treatment groups and the conditions of treatment delivery in such a way as to rule out or minimize threats to the internal validity of the study, so that any differences observed in the dependent measures can be traced directly to the variations in independent variables introduced by the experimenter. For experimental as well as nonexperimental strategies, there may arise questions about the validity of interpretations of relationships obtained in any given study, particularly their applicability or generalizability beyond the results of the specific study. These concerns constitute issues of external validity, which can be further divided into questions of (a) generalizability of operationalizations, and (b) generalizability of results to other places and participant populations (Cook & Campbell, 1979; Shadish, Cook, & Campbell, 2002).

Generalizability of Operationalizations

Concerns over the validity of operations refer to the correct identification of the nature of the predictor and outcome variables and the underlying relationship between them, that is, the extent to which the operations and measures embodied in the procedures of a particular study reflect the theoretical concepts that gave rise to the study in the first place. Threats to this form of validity arise from errors of measurement, misspecification of research operations, and, in general, the complexity of stimulus features that constitute our variables.

The complex constructs characteristic of social research are marked by what Aronson et al. (1998) called "multiple meaning;" that is, their impact on participants may be due to any of several factors inherent in the research situation, many of which may be completely irrelevant to the conceptual variables of interest. In such cases, researchers cannot be sure that any effects obtained actually reflect the influence of the one construct they were attempting to represent in their experimental operations. Confidence in interpretation is enhanced if a series of experiments is conducted in which the conceptual variable is represented by a number of *different* operations which vary as much as possible, having in common only the one basic factor of (theoretical) interest. When different techniques produce the same result, attributing the effect to the common conceptual variable is substantiated.

As an illustration of this process of identifying the "active ingredient" of our manipulation, consider an experiment undertaken by Aronson and Mills (1959) to test the hypothesis that undergoing a severe initiation to join a social group enhances the attractiveness of that group to the initiate. In their original experiment, Aronson and Mills convinced female college students that they needed to pass an "embarrassment test" to qualify to participate in a series of group discussions on various sensitive topics. In one version of the experimental procedures, the initiation test was relatively mild; but the severe initiation condition required that the participant read aloud (in front of a male experimenter) a considerable amount of sexually explicit material and a list of obscene words. As predicted, those participants who underwent the severe initiation were more favorable in their later evaluations of the group discussion (which was actually quite dull) than were the participants in the mild initiation condition.

Aronson and Mills (1959) designed their study as an operational representation of "effort justification," a concept derived from dissonance theory. The basic idea being tested was that the participant needed to justify effort expended in qualifying for the group discussion, and they could do so by evaluating the goal of their effort—the group discussion—as worth that effort. The greater the effort involved, the greater the need for justification and hence, the greater the need to value the group experience positively. When the experiment was published, however, a number of alternative explanations for the effect of initiation severity on attraction ratings were proposed. Most of these alternatives revolved around the fact that the Aronson and Mills' procedures for manipulating "effort" involved a potentially sexually arousing experience. If that were the case, then the carryover of sexual excitement to evaluations of the group discussion, rather than effort justification, may have accounted for the positive effects of the severe initiation condition (Bryant & Miron, 2003).

To rule out this alternative interpretation, Gerard and Mathewson (1966) designed a replication experiment with a different operationalization of effort expenditure. In this second experiment, electric shock, rather than reading obscene materials, was used as the severe initiation experience, and the shocks were represented as a test of "emotionality" rather than as an "embarrassment test." Having thus removed sexual arousal as a component of the experimental manipulations, Gerard and Mathewson obtained results consistent with the original findings: participants who underwent painful shocks to join a dull group evaluated that group more positively than did participants who underwent very mild shocks. This replication of the basic effect with different experimental operations confirms, at least indirectly, the effort-justification interpretation of the original study and provides support for the external validity of the initial experimental manipulations. The Gerard and Mathewson experiment represents a conceptual replication of the earlier Aronson and Mills (1959) study. The role of such replication studies in the validation of social science theory will be discussed in more detail in Chapter 8.

Generalizability of Results to Other Places and Populations

Once a research study has been completed, the investigator is usually interested in reaching conclusions that are generalizable across people and settings. Results that are applicable only to particular persons at a particular time or place are of little value to a scientific endeavor that aims at achieving general principles of human behavior. Generalizability refers to the robustness of a phenomenon— the extent to which a relationship, once identified, can be expected to recur at other times, places, and populations under different environmental conditions. Threats to this form of external validity arise from possible *interaction* effects between the treatment variable of interest and the context in which it is delivered, or the type of participant population that is involved. A finding lacks external validity if the nature of the effect of the predictor variable would be reduced or altered if the setting or the participant population were changed. Because so many of the laboratory studies in social sciences are conducted with college students as participants, it has been suggested that the truth of the relationships we observe may be limited to that particular population. If it happens that college students—with their youth, above-average intelligence, health, and socioeconomic background— respond differently to our variables than do other types of people, then the external (but not internal) validity of our findings would be suspect. But this hypothesis about population differences is subject to the same rules of evidence as any other hypothesis (Sears, 1986).

Just as the validity of measurement depends upon an adequate representation of variation in the theoretical concept, participant generalizability depends upon the extent to which the participants included in a study represent the potential variability of the human organism. We have already discussed the principle of random assignment of participants to treatment conditions, but **random selection** requires that chance determines selection of participants for a study, and is used to assure generalizability of results from the sample to the entire population of relevant persons (In Chapter 11 we consider a number of different forms of respondent selection). Avoid confusing random selection and random assignment, as the only similarity is that chance is used as an ally. The ground rule of random selection is that all persons in the population of interest are equally likely to be included in the research sample, whereas random assignment requires that persons in the research sample are equally like to participate in the different groups within a study. Another critical distinction is that the purpose of random selection is to increase a study's external validity, whereas random assignment is to increase a study's internal validity.

Random selection to yield a representative sample is a rarely realized ideal in social research. Limited resources and participant availability make it impossible, and in many cases the necessity for keeping experimental and control groups equivalent further limits the participant pool. Under the typical volunteer participant conditions, the usual procedure is to randomly sample from some readily available population and then to generalize to those persons who cannot be assumed to be systematically different from those who took part in the research study. This still places severe limitations on generalizability of findings—research results obtained from college sophomores can hardly be automatically assumed to apply to a population that includes grade school dropouts and people over 60—but the cost and impracticality of true random sampling usually make this limitation a necessity. Crowdsourcing approaches (e.g., Amazon's Mechanical Turk) are becoming popular ways of gathering samples of participants who are not necessarily college students (We discuss these approaches in Chapter 8).

One way to overcome the lack of generalizability of most research studies is to repeat essentially the same design with different populations of persons as they become available. To the extent that research results are reproduced with different types of persons, generalization across all persons becomes more convincing. Even a *failure* to replicate findings with different populations adds to our understanding of the phenomenon being investigated, by identifying the limitations of the effects of the variables under study.

Apart from generalizability of the sampled participants to the population of interest, the reproducibility of any research findings may be limited to the conditions under which the phenomenon was studied. *Condition replicability* involves two aspects: the internal conditions of the research participants across time, and the external physical and social environment in which the research is carried out. Too often, replication of research studies is conducted with the aim of reproducing, in precise detail, the exact conditions of the original research. Apart from the inevitable futility of such an approach to replication, it is not consistent with the aim of identifying principles and relationships that have some survival value across heterogeneous circumstances. Conclusions are of limited value if they cannot satisfy this criterion of robustness in the face of altered research conditions.

Conclusion

Enhancing the internal validity of research operations generally involves the use of highly controlled experiments, in which participants from a restricted group (e.g., introductory psychology students) are assigned randomly to study conditions. This tactic helps enhance internal validity, but is possibly the most serious limitation to generalizability of research results. The laboratory setting represents a unique and isolated social experience, in which the researcher exercises unusual control over the environmental conditions to which the participant is exposed and which limit the participant's available choices of behavior. In many respects this is the strength of the scientific approach to understanding social phenomena, for until simple principles are isolated and identified, the complex gamut of social relations will remain unfathomable. However, the unusual relationship that occurs between researcher and participant, and the participant's awareness of being an object of scientific investigation, may produce phenomena that are unique to the laboratory setting. Until the implications of such research are examined under broader social conditions, any generalized conclusions drawn are at best tentative.

Questions for Discussion

1. Why does the success of random assignment at combating threats to internal validity depend on a sufficiently large sample size?
2. Distinguish random assignment from random selection. What are their implications for internal and external validity?
3. Briefly describe and compare internal and external validity. In your answer, be sure to consider for each validity type: (a) a reasonable definition, (b) the critical issue it addresses, and (c) whether it is higher or lower in experimental versus nonexperimental (field) research.
4. Hermione and Luna conducted a study on the effects of marijuana on academic performance, and the effect of school on marijuana usage. They recruited 50 people from a well-known group of marijuana users at school, and 50 people from a well-known group of abstainers. At the beginning of the school year, they administered three measurements of key variables: (a) marijuana use—"how often do you smoke marijuana?" (b) grade point average (GPA)—"what were your grades for the previous semester?"; and (c) relationship with their teachers—"in general, how good is your relationship with your teachers?" At the end of the school year, the researchers reassessed the three key variables. They found that by the end of the school year, 25% of the users had dropped out of school (and thus were out of the study), whereas none of the abstainers had dropped out. They also found that students in the "users" group had significantly poorer GPAs and poorer relationships with their teachers than those in the "non-user" group. However, they also found that marijuana users decreased their usage by the end of the school year, whereas a significant percentage of abstainers started using marijuana by the end of the school year. Thus, they concluded that marijuana negatively affects students' scholastic achievements, that school helps habitual users stop using marijuana but simultaneously causes people who never used marijuana to start using. Obviously, this study has many problems, particularly with internal validity. Please describe how *four* of the eight threats to internal validity may have influenced the results of this study, and offer solutions for how to deal with these internal validity threats. In your answer, be sure to describe each threat, identify how each threat is present in the study, explain how the threat would *specifically* impact the results of the study, and offer one suggestion for how to solve or prevent each threat.

Notes

1. The word "program" is used loosely here to refer to accumulated evidence relevant to a particular theoretical position, whether planned and executed by a single researcher or research team or derived from the uncoordinated efforts of independent researchers working in the same area.
2. This discussion of causal-noncausal relationships is not affected by the possibility of multiple "levels" of causation. The relationship between any stimulus-response pairing may be examined in terms of organism-environment interactions, sense receptor-effector sequences, or changes in biochemical structure. It is our view that accounts of phenomena at each of these levels of explanation are equally legitimate, provided that the implications of explanations at one level are not contradictory to the implications of those at other levels. For behavioral scientists, causal links are usually described in terms of changes in the overt behavior of an organism

relative to changes in the external environment or stimulus features. To be acceptable, however, explanations of these links must be compatible with known limitations of the neurophysiological capacities of the organism and with conditions determined by the requirements of physical survival and social organization.
3. Lachenmeyer (1970) makes a strong argument for the role of experimental methodology in all phases of theory construction, including the development of observational techniques and measurements, fact-finding exploratory research, and the verification of the existence of hypothesized relationships. In our view, however, the unique features of the experiment make it most useful as a hypothesis-testing device.
4. In the social research literature, the use of statistical significance testing has come under challenge (Hunter, 1997), but for many reasons it still represents current practice (Abelson, 1997; Estes, 1997).
5. The problem with this technique is that it relies on *accepting* the null hypothesis of no difference between the dropouts and those who remained in the experimental groups. A more thorough approach would compare groups on a host of theory-relevant variables to ensure that the dropouts are not in some ways systematically different from the remainers on important, theory-relevant variables.
6. The word *unintentional* is stressed here because such effects can occur even when the experimenter makes an honest effort to avoid them.
7. At one time, for example, researchers paid little attention to the correspondence between a persuasive source's group membership and that of the group being influenced. Now, group identity is recognized as an important factor in a source's power to influence others.

References

Abelson, R. P. (1997). On the surprising longevity of flogged horses: Why there is a case for the significance test. *Psychological Science, 8*, 12–15.

Agnew, N. M., & Pike, S. W. (1969). *The science game: An introduction to research in the behavioral sciences.* Englewood Cliffs, NJ: Prentice-Hall.

Aronson, E., & Mills, J. (1959). The effect of severity of initiation on liking for a group. *Journal of Abnormal and Social Psychology, 59*, 177–181.

Aronson, E., Wilson, T., & Brewer, M. B. (1998). Experimentation in social psychology. In D. Gilbert, S. Fiske, & G. Lindsey (Eds.), *The handbook of social psychology* (4th ed., vol. 1, pp. 99–142). Boston: McGraw-Hill.

Baron, R. M., & Kenny, D. A. (1986). The moderator-mediator variable distinction in social psychological research: Conceptual, strategic, and statistical considerations. *Journal of Personality and Social Psychology, 51*, 1173–1182.

Bickman, L., & Rog, D. J. (Eds.). (1998). *Handbook of applied social research methods.* Thousand Oaks, CA: Sage.

Brewer, M. B. (2000). Research design and issues of validity. In H. Reis & C. Judd (Eds.), *Handbook of research methods in social and personality psychology* (pp. 3–16). New York: Cambridge University Press.

Bryant, J., & Miron, D. (2003). Excitation-transfer theory and three-factor theory of emotion. In J. Bryant, D. Roskos-Ewoldsen, & J. Cantor (Eds.), *Communication and emotion: Essays in honor of Dolf Zillmann.* (pp. 31–59). Mahwah, NJ: Erlbaum.

Campbell, D. T., & Stanley, J. C. (1963). Experimental and quasi-experimental designs for research on teaching. In N. L. Gage (Ed.), *Handbook of research on teaching* (pp. 171–246). Chicago: Rand-McNally. Reprinted as *Experimental and quasi-experimental designs for research*. Chicago: Rand-McNally, 1966.

Cohen, J. (2003). A power primer. In A. E. Kazdin (Ed.), *Methodological issues & strategies in clinical research* (3rd ed., pp. 427–436). Washington, DC: American Psychological Association.

Cook, T. D., & Campbell, D. T. (1979). *Quasi-experimentation: Design and analysis issues for field settings.* Chicago: Rand-McNally.

Cronbach, L. J., & Snow, R. (1977). *Aptitude and instructional methods.* New York: Irvington.

Donaldson, S. I., & Crano, W. D. (2011). Theory-driven evaluation science and applied social psychology: Exploring the intersection. In M. M. Mark, S. I. Donaldson, & B. Campbell (Eds.), *Social psychology and evaluation* (pp. 140–161). New York: Guilford Press.

Estes, W. K. (1997). Significance testing in psychological research: Some persisting issues. *Psychological Science, 8*, 18–20.

Flora, C. (2006). No laughing matter. *Psychology Today, 39*, 10–11.

Gerard, H. B., & Mathewson, G. (1966). The effects of severity of initiation on liking for a group: A replication. *Journal of Experimental Social Psychology, 2*, 278–287.

Hallahan, M., & Rosenthal, R. (1996). Statistical power: Concepts, procedures, and applications. *Behaviour Research and Therapy, 34*, 489–499.

Hayes, A. F. (2013). *Introduction to mediation, moderation, and conditional process analysis: A regression-based approach.* New York: Guilford Press.

Hunter, J. E. (1997). Needed: A ban on the significance test. *Psychological Science, 8,* 3–7.

Kennedy, J. L., & Uphoff, H. F. (1939). Experiments on the nature of extrasensory perception: III. The recording error criticism of extrachance scores. *Journal of Parapsychology, 3,* 226–245.

Lachenmeyer, C. W. (1970). Experimentation—a misunderstood methodology in psychology and social psychological research. *American Psychologist, 25,* 617–624.

Mook, D. G. (1983). In defense of external invalidity. *American Psychologist, 38,* 379–387.

Rosenthal, R., & Rosnow, R. W. (1975). *The volunteer subject.* New York: Wiley-Interscience.

Sears, D. O. (1986). College sophomores in the laboratory: Influences of a narrow data base on social psychology's view of human nature. *Journal of Personality and Social Psychology, 51,* 515–530.

Shadish, W. R., Cook, T. D., & Campbell, D. T. (2002). *Experimental and quasi-experimental designs for generalized causal inference.* Boston, MA: Houghton, Mifflin and Company.

Smith, E. R. (2000). Research design. In H. Reis & C. Judd (Eds.), *Handbook of research methods in social and personality psychology* (pp. 17–39). New York: Cambridge University Press.

Trochim, W. (1984). *Research design for program evaluation: The regression-discontinuity approach.* Beverly Hills, CA: Sage.

Trochim, W. (1986). *Advances in quasi-experimental design and analysis.* San Francisco: Jossey-Bass.

3
MEASUREMENT RELIABILITY

Measurement is a form of operationalization in which abstract concepts are *translated* into observable and quantifiable information or data. In the social sciences, various measurement techniques are used to assess differences among the people or units being studied. The objects of measurement can be individuals reporting on themselves, observations of behaviors, characteristics of situations, or records of past events. For the purposes of this chapter, we adopt a classic measurement theory orientation, also known as psychometric theory, which is focused primarily on self-reports by respondents of internal states or behaviors. The classic test theory approach assumes that there is a consistent, stable underlying state that reflects the construct we are attempting to quantify. In later chapters, we will expand this orientation to include other measurement models.

Although all translations (that is, measures) are imperfect, individual measures vary in the adequacy with which they characterize the underlying conceptual variable of interest. Some measures come closer than others to representing the true value of the concept, in part because they are less susceptible to sources of systematic error or random fluctuation. The quality of a given measure is expressed in terms of its reliability and validity. Briefly, **reliability** is the consistency that a measurement instrument assesses a given construct; **validity** is the degree of relationship, or the overlap, between a measurement instrument and the construct it is intended to assess. In this chapter we will review methods for assessing the reliability of psychological measures; evaluation of measurement validity will be addressed in Chapter 4.

Classical Test Theory

The concept of reliability derives from classical measurement theory, which assumes that the score obtained on any single measurement occasion represents a combination of the *true score* of the object being measured and random *errors* that lead to fluctuations in the measure obtained on the same object at different occasions (Gullicksen, 1950). The standard classical test theory formula, modified slightly to fit our particular position on reliability, is expressed as follows:

$$O = T + \Sigma E_{r+s}$$

where O = **observed score** or score obtained on a measurement instrument (e.g. math test, behavioral checklist, or attitude scale),

T = true score,
ΣE_{r+s} = sum of random and systematic errors that combine with true score to produce the observed score.

The standard formula usually lists only random error; it does not take account of systematic error, or it combines it with random error. Combining random and systematic error is misleading because both forms of error affect observed scores, but they do so in different ways. Hence we have modified the more standard formula to incorporate both types of error.

The **true score** is the replicable feature of the concept being measured. It is not "true" in the sense that it is a necessarily perfect or valid representation of the underlying construct. "True" in the present context signifies replicability, the component part of the observed score that would recur across different measurement occasions in the absence of error. In this sense, the true score actually represents the reliable portion of the observed measurement across infinite potential measurements, which at its heart has to do with measurement consistency or repeatability of observations (Raykov & Marcoulides, 2011). On any single measurement occasion, only a participant's observed score obtained from the measure is known, but the formula contains two unknown elements—the true score and error—making this equation unsolvable. To estimate the error component, we must have replication of measurement.

A common example may help clarify the meaning of true score. Often, when using a standard bathroom scale, we will notice our observed weight fluctuating. In fact, weighing ourselves twice, almost simultaneously, often results in different readings. Has our weight changed? Probably not, but factors extraneous to "true" weight have varied from the first to the second weighing (the tension of the scale's spring, the placement of our feet on the scale, etc.). These extraneous factors are error. They really do not have anything to do with how much we actually weigh. They degrade the relationship between true and observed scores. The greater the proportion of error, the less the observed score reflects the underlying true score, and the more unreliable the measure is said to be.

To understand the relationship of reliability and measurement error, it is important to distinguish between random and systematic sources of error. **Random error** is attributed to unexpected events that tend to artificially widen the variability or spread of observed scores in a *nonsystematic* way. Examples include inadvertent misrecording (coder misrecords values—sometimes they are too high, at other times too low) a faulty spring on a bathroom scale (the scale sometimes overestimates and other times underestimates people's weight) or the mood induced by communicating with one's parent earlier that day (depending on one's attachment security, some will have a more positive mood, while others might have a more negative mood than usual). Chance events, by definition, are nondirectional on average, that is, across a large number of replications negative and positive errors would cancel each out. According to classical test theory, if the group is large enough, random errors across participants will sum to zero. This is not to suggest that random error is harmless, however, because such errors not only reduce the accuracy of measurement, but they also affect the measure's sensitivity to detecting differences in observed score between different groups of participants. Random error increases variability of scores, and increased variability reduces the power of tests of statistical significance. Obscured by random error, larger mean differences between groups are needed before the true differences between groups can be judged real or trustworthy (or statistically significant above random chance).

In contrast to random error, **systematic error** is attributed to unexpected events that tend to artificially inflate or deflate observed scores in a *systematic* way. Examples of systematic error include misrecording by a coder who is high on methamphetamines (recorded scores are typically higher than actual numbers due to an overactive nervous system), forgetting to ask participants to take off their shoes prior to getting on a scale (weight is overestimated across all participants), or a heavy snowstorm on the day of the study (consistently inducing more negative mood states than usual across participants). Systematic error should shift most, if not all, scores in the same direction. Because systematic error (bias) is not random, it does not cancel between groups; rather, it either exacerbates or mitigates differences that actually exist. The situation that results depends on the direction of the bias. If the difference between groups becomes smaller, it will be judged incorrectly as being less likely to be statistically significant. If the difference between groups becomes larger, it will be judged incorrectly as being more likely to be statistically significant.

An example of a hypothetical experiment will help to clarify this conceptual differentiation between random and systematic error. Suppose an experimental treatment (e.g., positive compliments) is designed to increase the likelihood that people will succumb to a persuasive communication. In the experimental group, participants are told privately by a confederate that their performance on a task indicates that they are highly intelligent. The controls are given no feedback on their performance. Both groups then read a persuasive message that argues for future enrollment increases at their university. The critical dependent measure is an attitude scale that assesses the extent of their agreement with this message. Scores can range from 0 to 20, with higher scores indicating greater agreement with the message.

The true scores of the treatment (complimented) and control (not complimented) groups are presented in the first two columns of Table 3.1. The values in these columns depict idealized results from a hypothetical scenario, as the true scores and the sources and degree of error are unknowns. A statistical test of the difference between mean true scores of these two groups discloses a significant difference, with the treatment participants (column 2) demonstrating greater agreement with the message than the control participants (column 1).

Suppose, however, that our attitude-measuring device contained random error, which either raised or lowered actual test scores for each participant. Overall, however, being random (or unbiased), the error averaged out to 0 for each group. Then the observed scores that we obtained would be those derived through an addition of columns 1 and 3 (true score + error component) for the control group, and columns 2 and 4 for the treatment group. Notice that the same degree of "error" was added to each group's scores. Thus, the respective column sums remain the same.

TABLE 3.1 Results of a hypothetical experiment with true scores and error components.

Participant #	(1) Control Group True Score	(2) Treatment Group True Score	(3) Control Group (Random Error)	(4) Treatment Group (Random Error)	(5) Control Group True Score + (Random Error)	(6) Treatment Group True Score + (Random Error)	(7) Treatment Group True Score − (Systematic Error)	(8) Treatment Group True Score + (Systematic Error)
1	8	12	2	6	10	18	6	18
2	6	10	−1	−6	5	4	4	16
3	7	9	4	−1	11	8	8	10
4	9	10	−4	4	5	14	6	14
5	9	11	8	2	17	13	9	13
6	12	14	−6	−7	6	7	7	21
7	6	12	4	1	10	13	11	13
8	10	13	−8	5	2	18	8	18
9	4	12	−2	1	2	13	11	13
10	3	10	3	−5	6	5	5	15
Sum =	74	113	0	0	74	113	75	151

Yet upon reanalysis, the same statistical test that had disclosed a significant difference between columns 1 and 2 would now disclose no significant difference between the groups (when comparing columns 5 and 6). This reversal of fortune is attributable to the increased within group variability of scores when the random error components are added to each column. With these results, we would be forced to conclude, incorrectly, that our manipulation had no effect on persuasion. This form of erroneous conclusion is termed a Type II error.

To complete the example, suppose instead that all participants in the experimental condition were given the attitude test in an uncomfortably hot room, putting them in a negative mood. This influenced their responses in such a way that the error scores of the treatment group were all negative, i.e., systematic error *decreased* all the scores of this group only (all of the error terms in column 4 are in now the negative direction). The ratings of the control group participants remained unaffected. This systematic deflation of the observed treatment group (column 7) scores in the direction of the observed control group scores (column 2) reduces the between-group difference, even though the true scores were higher for the experimental group. The results would lead the researcher to conclude that no relationship exists between the independent and dependent variables (another instance of a Type II error).

Now, suppose instead that the conditions of testing for the experimental group biased the results in a *positive* direction, confirming the study's hypothesis. To show how this would change the conclusions drawn from the study, the systematic error score (column 4) is now added to each treatment participant's true score (column 2), but the control group participants are unaffected by the bias. Results now reveal a larger difference in scores between the control group (column 1) and the treatment group (column 8), yielding a *more* statistically significant finding (from $p < .05$ to $p < .001$). Had the original difference in true scores between the control group (column 1) and the treatment group (column 2) not been statistically significant in the first place, this direction of systematic error would have increased the likelihood that results would have achieved statistical significance. Recall (Chapter 2) that erroneously finding a statistically significant result that is not truly attributable to the treatment is termed a *Type I error*.

Assessing Reliability

Systematic errors in measurement become part of an individual's "true score" on that observed measure and hence affect its validity as a measure of the conceptual variable of interest. As we have illustrated above, systematic error (bias) can result in either Type I or Type II errors. Depending on the direction of the bias, it fosters conclusions of a stronger or weaker difference between groups. Random errors, on the other hand, affect the measure's reliability. Random error lessens the chances of finding a true difference between groups when, in fact, a true difference may exist. As such, random error fosters Type II errors. When measures are taken on a large group of individuals with a given instrument, the variability in obtained scores is due partly to differences among those individuals in their true scores on the measure, and partly to random and systematic fluctuations. Technically, the reliability of a measure is defined as the proportion of the total variance in observed scores that is due to true score variability. A perfectly reliable instrument would be one in which this proportion was equal to 1.00, or in which true score equaled observed score (Observed = True + 0.00). A perfectly unreliable score, on the other hand, would be one in which the observed score equaled the sum of the error components, and true score contributed nothing to the observed score (Observed = 0.00 + Error). It is hard to imagine a measure this bad, but it could exist theoretically. The important take-home message of the formula for classical test theory is that instruments are fallible in practice because they are susceptible to the incidental sources of random and systematic error.

Although the technical definition of reliability presented in the prior paragraph is standard, the actual meaning of the term reliability varies, depending upon how it is assessed and when the definition was made. Reliability has referred to the degree to which participants' scores on a given administration of a measure resembled their scores on the same instrument administered at some later point in time—or the extent to which two judges, observing the same behavior, produced the same ratings of the behavior. If the test-retest scores tended to be very similar (i.e., highly interrelated), the measure (or the judges) was said to be reliable. Or, if parallel forms of a test—two forms of the test that are thought to measure the same construct—were highly correlated, the test was said to be reliable. However, reliability also has come to indicate the degree to which the set of items or questions *within* a particular multiple-item scale are interrelated. The three types of reliability are *internal consistency*, *temporal stability*, and *interrater*, with the latter being discussed in Chapter 12. These features of reliability are important and should be considered when evaluating the quality of an instrument.

Internal Consistency

The question of internal consistency is concerned with the extent to which the components (e.g., individual items, observations) of a measuring instrument are interrelated. The idea of internal consistency is usually applied to a measure—such as an ability test or attitude scale—that consists of a set of individual items. It is assumed that all the items of the scale measure the same underlying construct. The same logic is applied when the "measuring instruments" are human observers, or judges. In this case, the question is, "Have the judges seen the same thing (as inferred from their giving more or less identical scores to the observations)?" The answer to the question is assessed by the extent to which the observers' observations overlap or correlate. If the items that purportedly constitute a scale assess a variety of different constructs (i.e., if the scale is *multidimensional*), then there is little to justify their being combined as a representation of a single construct (i.e., as being *unidimensional*). Similarly, if observers are judging the same phenomenon (say, a group interaction) using different criteria, then combining their individual observations into an overall summary score is logically indefensible. As Nunnally (1967, p. 251) has observed, "a test should 'hang together' in the sense that the items all correlate with one another. Otherwise, it makes little sense to add scores over items and speak of total scores as measuring any attribute." To justify the combination of items in deriving an individual's overall score on such a test, the internal consistency of the item set must be established.

One of the earliest techniques to assess the internal consistency of a scale is a technique known as split-half reliability. **Split-half reliability** is assessed by randomly dividing a scale into two sets containing an equal number of items, both administered to the same respondents, with a test of relatedness calculated between these two summed scores.[1]

If there is a high degree of interrelatedness among items, then the relation between total scores from the two halves of the scale should be strong, thus indicating that the items are focused on the same underlying attitude or aptitude. If the two halves of the measure do not "hang together," this suggests that the scale items might not all be measuring the same underlying construct.

An alternative to the once common split-half technique is now more commonly employed to determine a scale's internal consistency. This approach, called **Cronbach's alpha**, is an index of the hypothetical value that would be obtained if all of the items that could constitute a given scale were available and randomly put together into a very large number of tests of equal size (Cronbach, 1951). The average correlation between all possible pairs of these "split-half" tests is approximated by coefficient alpha.

Determining the alpha coefficient of a scale is relatively simple, if one has a computer available (or if a relatively short test is being used). Computationally, we determine coefficient alpha as follows:

$$r_{tt} = \frac{k}{k-1}\left(1 - \frac{\Sigma \sigma_i^2}{\sigma_T^2}\right)$$

where r_{tt} = coefficient alpha (α), the estimate of whole-scale reliability,
 k = the number of items in the scale,
 $\Sigma \sigma_i^2$ = the sum of the variances of each of the individual items,
 σ_T^2 = the variance of the total scale.

Cronbach's alpha can range from .00 to 1.00, with the degree of internal consistency usually considered acceptable if this coefficient is .75 or better, though the actual value depends on the extent of error that the investigator is willing to tolerate.[2]

From the internal consistency computational formula presented, we can infer that the *number* of items in a scale plays an important role in the scale's (internal consistency) reliability, as do the interrelationships that obtain among the items. If the items are highly interrelated, alpha will be high. In addition, the formula suggests that, all other things being equal, the more items, the greater the scale's coefficient alpha will be. Thus, one simple tactic of enhancing alpha is to "lengthen" the scale—that is, to add items to it. *If* participants' responses to the new items are similar to their responses on the original set (that is, if the correlations between new and old items are high), the addition will enhance the coefficient of internal consistency. The qualification presented at the beginning of the previous sentence suggests that considerable care should be exercised when developing new items to add to an established set. Of course, this method of enhancing reliability is subject to the law of diminishing returns. Adding a good item to a 5-item scale will have a much greater effect on internal consistency than adding a good item to a 15-item scale. If the average correlation between items is reasonable (say, greater than .25), adding an item to a scale already containing 9 or 10 items will have relatively little effect on coefficient alpha. Furthermore, the higher the existing inter-item correlations, the less the effect of added items.

It sometimes happens that the coefficient of internal consistency is unsatisfactory even with relatively lengthy tests. One possible solution in situations such as these is to inspect relations among pairs of items and to eliminate those items that do not relate well with the majority of other items. Another simpler method is to assess all item-total relations, that is, the correlation between participants' scores on each item and their total score over all items.[3]

If a specific item is measuring something very different from that of the others in the item set, its relation with the total score will be weak. This information will alert the scale developer that this particular item can be deleted and substituted with one that (hopefully) better represents the concept under investigation.

Our emphasis on internal consistency should not be taken to mean that all of the items on a scale should be mere clones of one another. Ideally, the items of a scale should share a common focus—but they should be entirely different in all other aspects that are irrelevant to this focus. For example, consider these two items, developed for a scale of attitudes toward ecological issues:

- The federal government should rule that automobiles must be constructed so that hydrocarbon emissions are completely reduced.
- All communities must employ both primary and secondary sewage treatment facilities before pumping wastes into public waters.

An individual's response to either of these items will be determined by a number of factors. The first item will be affected not only by the respondent's concern for the protection of the environment, but also by attitudes toward governmental intervention in private business, beliefs regarding the feasibility of complete elimination of hydrocarbon emissions, etc. Similarly, agreement with the second item will be affected by beliefs about the effectiveness of primary and secondary sewage treatment, the ecological integrity of the water supply, etc., *in addition to* attitudes regarding the environment, the central issue of the scale.

Thus, both items potentially tap factors that are irrelevant to the issue of concern for the researcher, but these irrelevancies are *different* across items. Such heterogeneity of item content will produce some inconsistency of response (and hence, lower alpha), but as long as many such items are used, all focused on one common construct (though, perhaps, numerous non-common determinants as well), the total set of items will provide a better measure of the central attitude than any single item. In this context, using the method of item-total correlations to examine relationships is useful in determining whether an item is a good representative of the construct under study.

It is possible for items on a test to be too closely related (Cattell, 1972; Dawson, Crano, & Burgoon, 1996). Consider the following example:

- Today's Volkswagen is a wonderful automobile.
- The new Volkswagen Beetle is a terrific car.

Clearly, we would expect the degree of relationship between responses to these two items to be high. However, because they provide little, if any, nonredundant information, their consistency does not contribute much to the overall quality of the measure.

Temporal Stability

The development of measurement scales possessing a high degree of interrelatedness among the items is one of the primary tasks of the test constructor. However, there is a second feature of reliability, called temporal stability, which also merits consideration in our discussion of test construction. Questions pertaining to this aspect of scale quality are concerned with the degree to which the observations obtained in a given test administration resemble those obtained in a second testing, which employs the same measure and the same respondent sample.

In considerations of temporal stability, researchers generally make use of one of two techniques. The most common is called **test-retest reliability**, which is assessed by administering a scale to participants, and at a later time re-administering to the same participants, with the degree of relatedness calculated between two administrations. Respondents' scores on the first administration are compared to the scores they obtain on the second; a large positive correlation is taken as evidence of (temporal stability) reliability.

The major problem with the test-retest method is that the information it provides can prove ambiguous. Consider a few extreme examples: suppose an investigator employs a test-retest procedure with a delay of only three minutes between test administrations. Chances are good that the correlation between participants' scores on the tests would be nearly perfect. This would not, however, necessarily indicate that the scale would be reliable (i.e., replicable) across a longer period of time. There is a delicate balance that must be struck when deciding upon the appropriate interval between test administrations. Apparent temporal reliability will be enhanced artificially if participants can remember their previous responses and wish to appear consistent. Conversely, a very long delay between administrations can diminish temporal stability, because people *do* change over time. Thus, even a very good test can appear unreliable if the temporal separation between administrations is extreme.

It is difficult to specify the "ideal" temporal lag between scales when using the test-retest method. Sometimes even a modest time lag will artificially reduce the test-retest relationship. For example, suppose that we constructed a scale to measure attitudes toward a well-known politician and administered this scale to a sample of 500 respondents. Two days later, we readministered the same scale to the same respondents. A two-day lag would not seem overly long. However, what if, during that interval, the politician had been implicated in a juicy, well-publicized public scandal. These things have been known to happen in US politics. In this case, we could have little hope that the scale would prove temporally stable. The attitudes of those who originally were favorably disposed toward the now-discredited public servant would be expected to change drastically, whereas those of people who had always hated the fallen politico would remain substantially the same. Such a change pattern would adversely affect the obtained test-retest correlation. In this case, changes in the observed score would suggest unreliability, even if the error components of the measure were minimal. "History," rather than "instrumentation," would be the cause of the apparent lack of temporal stability of the scale.

A procedure was developed to circumvent some of the problems introduced by a temporal separation between test administrations and encountering identical items twice. Known as **parallel forms** (or alternate, or equivalent forms) **reliability**, it is assessed by devising two separate item sets intended to assess the same underlying construct, administered to the same participants at the same time with degree of relatedness calculated. If a high relationship is obtained between scores on the two tests, it is interpreted as an indication of the reliability of the instrument(s). One way to verify if parallel scales were obtained is to show that the means and standard deviations of the two tests are very similar, if not identical. The rationale here is the same as that of the split-half approach, except that the two ("equivalent") forms are considered whole tests.

The major difficulty encountered in this situation is that a weak relationship between equivalent forms is not completely informative. Possibly, this result indicates that the scales are indeed unreliable. However, it might also be the case that the parallel forms simply are not equivalent. In attempting to determine the reasons underlying a lack of interrelatedness between two theoretically identical measures, the investigator sometimes must devote more time than would be demanded in the development of an entirely new set of scales.

As can be seen, questions of temporal stability can cause some difficulty for the test constructor. What's more, the information that a test is temporally stable usually is not considered sufficient evidence of a scale's reliability because it is possible that a scale could elicit stable responses across time and still not be internally consistent. To satisfy the full set of criteria of scale reliability, it is desirable that the scale demonstrate both temporal stability and internal consistency. Nonetheless, though temporal stability does not provide a complete estimate of a scale's reliability, it is important because it furnishes a comparison against which the effects of agents of change can be assessed. Thus if a test is known to be temporally stable, then the explanation of changes between test administrations can be directed at external agents—e.g., a social intervention, a historical event, maturation, etc.

Cronbach and his colleagues proposed a more ambitious approach to reliability estimation, which they termed generalizability theory (Cronbach, Gleser, Nanda, & Rajaratnam, 1972). This approach recognizes that irrelevancies (error) can be introduced into a test by many different factors, or *facets*, to use their terminology. These irrelevancies can reside in observers, items, contexts, occasions for measurements, respondents, etc. The more generalizable the instrument—that is, the more consistent it is across occasions, respondents, contexts, etc., the better or more trustworthy the instrument is. Cronbach and associates provided a framework for conceptualizing these different error sources and for determining their individual impact on the measure under consideration. The generalizability approach has won adherents among psychologists (e.g., see American Psychological Association, 1985), but has yet to be widely adopted in practice. At a minimum, it provides a more comprehensive outline of the multitude of factors that may affect a score, and alerts the researcher to the wide variety of factors that may affect the utility of an instrument.

Contemporary Test Theory

To this point, we have discussed the psychometrics of scale construction and assessment strictly using classical test theory. The "classical" modifier is used to distinguish this traditional measurement framework from methods taking advantage of advances in contemporary or modern test theory. Contemporary approaches to testing extend the fundamental ideas of classical test theory (Embretson, 1996; Zicakr & Broadfoot, 2009; Zimmerman, 2011). Seminal concepts of contemporary testing have been around for quite some time, but the measurement framework has gained ground thanks to the advent of modern computer processing. To evaluate the various psychometric properties (e.g., central tendency, dispersion, reliability) of a scale employing classical test theory, researchers could choose to perform calculations by hand (e.g., mean, standard deviation or variance, Cronbach's alpha), but modern test approaches require sophisticated mathematical procedures too complex to be conducted by the impatient without the aid of computing power.

Although no consensus exists regarding the features that constitute a contemporary test theory, one definition is that it is characterized by the search for a **latent factor** (Borsboom, Mellenbergh, & van Heerden, 2003), a characteristic or construct that is not directly measured or observed but that underlies responses on a measurement scale. Latent factors are analogous to the "true" score component of classical test analysis. Measurement error becomes part of the scale score in classical testing, but its distorting effect is explicitly estimated and removed from a latent factor (DeShon, 1998). Latent approaches may be divided into two general varieties (Borsboom et al., 2003). The first type includes factor analysis and structural equation modeling (the latter is elaborated on in Chapter 9). The second type is based on item response theory and is discussed later in this chapter.

Contemporary testing approaches were developed to address limitations of classical testing (Embretson, 1996). A major distinction in practice between the two approaches is the focus in the scale construction and evaluation process (Fan, 1998). Classical testing places greater emphasis on the total scale; for example, the mean and reliability are calculated and reported to provide information about properties of the total scale. Contemporary testing, however, focuses on individual items, offering greater information into how each item functions in the context of the total scale. Additional insights about item features help to evaluate each item's appropriateness for inclusion into the final test.

Latent Factors and Correction for Unreliability

In classical testing, as discussed, the observed score will contain not only the underlying true score but also measurement error. A scenario will help illustrate the measurement disadvantages of a scale score contaminated by error. Before summing 10 items to yield a summary score of altruism, we compute the internal consistency of the scale. Let's say this resultant composite is shown to yield a relatively reliable result (Cronbach's alpha = .85). Keep in mind, however, that the remaining .15 represents the unreliable remaining part of the scale variance. This error is a part of the summary score. Unfortunately, our inability to remove measurement error variance from the observed total score is the cost of using traditional classical testing. This contamination of an observed score is problematic when using the measure for hypothesis testing. When the altruism score is correlated to any criterion of interest, such as a score obtained from a volunteerism behaviors scale, this statistical relationship will be attenuated, its magnitude diluted because a proportion of each factor contains random error due to imperfect measurements. This obscures the detection of the real association between the two variables. A technique proposed to remedy this problem of random error when performing statistical analyses using classic test theory is the *correction for attenuation* (Spearman, 1904), the formula for which is:

$$\text{Corrected } r = \frac{r_{xy}}{\sqrt{(r_{xx})(r_{yy})}}$$

where r_{xy} = uncorrected correlation between scale X and scale Y,
r_{xx} = reliability of scale X,
r_{yy} = reliability of scale Y.

The correction for attenuation is an estimate of the correlation between the two variables *if* the measures were perfectly reliable. As the reliability coefficients are input into the denominator, a scale lower in reliability will show a larger improvement after the correction, as it contains a greater portion of random error. For example, suppose our results showed that the altruism and volunteerism scales correlated at .40, and that reliability for altruism is .70 and for volunteerism is .80. After accounting for the unreliability in the scale scores (i.e., correcting for attenuation), the disattenuated correlation jumps to .53. However, if the scales were perfectly reliable (i.e., $r_{xx} = r_{yy} =$ 1.0), the "correction" for attenuation would not change the original result.

A larger correlation to account for the effect of unreliability is obtained because the correction now represents the correlation between two perfectly reliable factors (Bedian, Day, & Kelloway, 1997; Schmidt & Hunter, 1999). Despite being an important attempt to clean out random error, however, the correction for attenuation formula has not been widely adopted due to several criticisms (Charles, 2005). First, in some instances it is possible to obtain out-of-bounds correlation coefficients ($r > 1.0$) after the adjustment. In other words, it is possible for the attenuation formula to *over*correct and inflate the estimate of the true relationship. A second issue concerns the most appropriate type of reliability to be entered into the formula. Although parallel form reliability has been suggested as the best estimator, others have argued for internal consistency and test-test approaches (Muchinsky, 1996).

To skirt these limitations, an alternative for isolating the replicable true score variance is to conduct analyses using latent factors (Bedian et al., 1997, DeShon, 1998). Latent approaches statistically remove error—through iterative estimation procedures—by keeping the statistical variance consistent across items in the factor. Applying the concept of latent factors to our established understanding of classical test theory, only the part of the variance reflecting the true score component remains, manifesting itself as the observed score. Again, true score exclusively pertains to replicability of scores and implies absolutely nothing about whether the construct was validly assessed. To fully appreciate the methodological appeal and usefulness of a latent factor, imagine calculating Cronbach's alpha on just the isolated latent factor. Theoretically, the alpha of the latent factor will be 1.00. Most accurately, to stipulate that the factor is perfectly reliable (or "error-free," to use latent factor terminology) presumes that a representative sampling of items from the world of content was used to tap the all aspects of the construct. It is prudent to avoid stating that the scale itself is perfectly reliable, instead saying that the latent factor has been corrected for unreliability for the items that were administered, and as applicable only to that sample.

Factor Analysis

The earliest and best-known application of a latent technique is factor analysis. When scales are constructed with an emphasis on item variability, it can happen that participants' responses are so inconsistent over the entire set of items that few items correlate strongly with the total score, the summation of all the items in the scale. In this circumstance, it is important to determine whether the items, in fact, do focus upon a single central, underlying construct (*unidimensional*), or if the scale is *multidimensional*, that is, if it taps a number of different constructs. Using Cronbach's alpha or simply inspecting the pattern of item-total correlations is usually insufficient for evaluating the properties of a newly developed scale, especially if multiple dimensions or factors underlie the structure. To evaluate the possibility that the scale is multidimensional, the entire matrix of item intercorrelations can be entered into a factor analysis. This type of statistical analysis provides the researcher with information regarding the actual number of constructs or "subscales" that may exist in the instrument under construction, as evidenced by the respondent sample. Based on this information, the investigator may decide to retain only a subset of the original items (e.g., those that form the most internally consistent subset, as indicated by a reliability analysis on the various subcomponents of the overall instrument) and to develop additional items to add to this subset in constructing an improved scale. The other items would be discarded or used to create a separate scale or scales, with their own internal consistency coefficients, etc.

For example, suppose we developed and administered a number of items that we believed tapped people's feelings about the preservation of the environment. If we were to perform factor analysis on the item set, we might find that one group of items that "hang together" (i.e., have high internal consistency) all have to do with participants' feelings of obligation to future generations. Another set of items that hang together might all have to do with the financial implications of environmental depredations. These items do not relate much with the "future generations" items. In this case, we have two possible scales, which measure different aspects of environmentalism worthy of study. We could add more items to each to create two revised, more reliable measures (recall that adding good items increases coefficient alpha), and re-administer both to a new sample. This procedure will enable us to determine the extent to which the new items hang together with the original set(s) of items. Eventually, an iterative process of factor analysis and reliability analysis will enable the investigator to generate a scale—or subscales—of acceptable internal consistency. The skill and insight of the scale constructor, the complexity of the issue under consideration, and the investigator's understanding of the issue and the respondent sample used all play a role in the ultimate success of the measurement process.

An important and useful tool, factor analysis, may be divided into two categories (Bollen, 2002; Brown, 2006). Also known as common factor analysis, **exploratory factor analysis** is a technique to determine the underlying factor structure if the researcher does not have hypotheses regarding the number of underlying factors and the items that might constitute each factor. The technique is data driven, as the analysis offers a factor solution that optimally represents the underlying interrelations among items (exploratory factor analysis is discussed more fully in Chapter 15). **Confirmatory factor analysis** is a technique to determine the underlying factor structure, if the researcher starts with hypotheses precisely stipulating the number of potential factors, which items should load on (or correlate with) which factors, and how the factors should be correlated. As the features of the factor structure are defined by the hypotheses, the resulting analysis reveals the degree to which items load on the prespecified factors. In exploratory and confirmatory factor analysis, the user interprets the pattern and strength of the relationships revealed in the analysis.

Figure 3.1 depicts a confirmatory factor analysis in which two latent factors are assessed by their respective items. Partitioned out of each measured item are two sources: the latent factor that produces or causes the variance of each item, and its measurement error (E1, E2, E3, etc.) that explains the remaining variance of each item (Bedian et al., 1997). The factor loading or weight (interpreted

56 Introduction to Social Research Methods

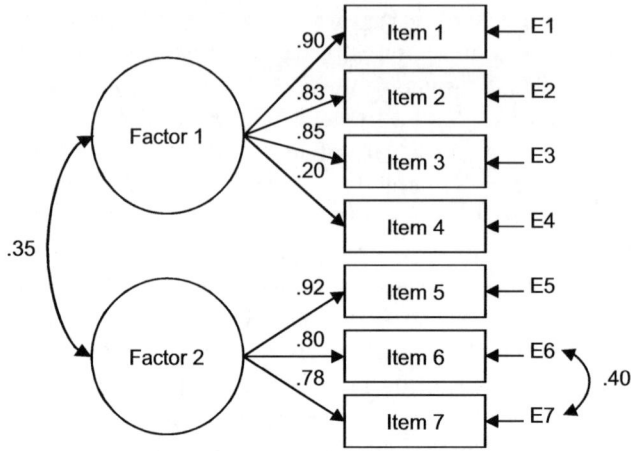

FIGURE 3.1 Confirmatory factor analysis.

like correlations) between each item and the factor it was hypothesized to load on is also shown in the diagram. Item 4 yields a poor factoring loading that suggests inadequate representation of the factor. You could allow the item to load on the other factor and then redo the analysis, or delete the item if the modification does not yield a higher loading. The arrowheads of factor loadings always point from factor to items, because the unobservable phantom construct is thought to drive these various observable manifestations (items). This seemingly backwards logic makes sense in theory and in practice: A factor loading indicates the extent that that latent factor, statistically derived from the item commonalities, in turn explains or causes each item. An item sharing more of its variability with other items in the same factor is granted a larger factor weight, and is correspondingly contaminated by less measurement error.

To compute an overall score in classical test theory, the researcher usually sums the items, a procedure that suggests item scores are additive (DeVellis, 2012). Doing so always assumes that items must have equal importance. Factor analysis allows computation of "factor scores," in which items are given different weights (based on their factor loading) before being summed.

Also diagrammed in Figure 3.1, each measurement error term (E1 through E7) contains the variance portion of an item that is not explained by the latent factor. Measurement error may be decomposed into two elements (Bedian et al., 1997). Random error of each item has been separated from the latent factor, and therefore the factor has been corrected for unreliability attenuation. Furthermore, systematic error also has been estimated for each measurement error term—but only in instances when an extraneous bias affects a single item (Brown, 2006). For example, if *only* item 2 was confusingly worded, and so the question was difficult for participants to comprehend, this source of systematic error would be extracted as part of E2. Because the bias was not shared among other items, it was statistically removed from the latent factor. Also in confirmatory factor analysis, it is possible to determine if systematic error is influencing more than a single item by testing whether two or more error terms show a non-negligible correlation (Shevlin, Miles, Davies, & Walker, 2000). The estimated correlation between E6 and E7, for example, yields a value of .40, indicating that some source of systematic error that was not caused by the second latent factor is causing the unexplained variability of these two items in the same manner. If all items in a factor are being affected by the same source of bias, results would fail to extract systematic error from the latent factor. Finally, the figure shows the correlation obtained between the two factors, demonstrating that although latent factors are not directly observable (they are observed through their items), they can be estimated and subjected to hypothesis testing.

Item Response Theory

Item response theory (IRT) is a technique to determine how each item operates in terms of difficulty, discrimination, and guessing with respect to the overall scale. Research applying IRT is dominated by scale development applications in educational testing and assessment. For this reason, the terminology of item response analysis makes use of language common in standardized testing, for the purpose of evaluating the appropriateness of items for inclusion into test banks (e.g., SAT and GRE). In the most widely used variety of IRT, the technique requires items that use a binary response format (de Champlain, 2010). In educational testing, for example, responses to each item may be scored as either correct or incorrect. In other social sciences, attitudinal and behavioral questions might involve a yes/no or agree/disagree response. Although performing a mean or median split on quantitative items generally is not advised, it might be necessary to dichotomize responses into meaningful groupings—for example, recoding values so that all the levels of agreement are lumped together as the correctly endorsed response, and all levels of disagreement are recoded as incorrect (unendorsed).[4]

The basic logic of IRT is to estimate how item responses in a test are related to performance on the test as a whole. The relationship between the probability of item endorsement and performance or skill on its latent factor is evaluated. This is represented by an *item characteristic curve* or item response function, an S-shaped probabilistic curve that best approximates a model of the data. Figure 3.2a plots the levels of each of three hypothetical items in comparison to gradations in its latent factor, which in IRT is known as *ability* or theta. Theta ranges on a continuum from low to high, ranking participants in terms of overall performance (or attitude or behavior) on the latent factor. On this metric, participants who performed at the average level relative to others on the scale have a theta of zero; those who performed better are represented by positive values, and those who performed worse have negative values at the left half of the ability continuum. Notice that the resulting characteristic curves are not straight lines, as would be in the item–total correlation analysis of classical testing.

A response probability, ranging from 0.00 to 1.00, reflects the likelihood that an item will be correctly answered (endorsed), given any person's location on the latent factor. Probabilistic language is used in IRT, as there is no guarantee that a particular person will respond a predetermined way, but across participants, an item characteristic curve estimates the probability of giving an affirmative response depending on where participants are situated on the underlying attribute. The concept of probability might be more intuitively grasped by thinking of the proportion or percentage of people in support of an item. An item with a .25 probability suggests that 25% of participants at that point on the latent factor endorsed or correctly answered this particular item.

To perform an item response analysis, it is crucial to satisfy two major assumptions about the data (Henard, 2000; DeMars, 2010); otherwise, results will produce inaccurate and uninformative estimates. The *assumption of unidimensionality* requires that the factor be represented by items assessing no more than a single construct. Unlike factor analysis, IRT is inappropriate for analyzing a multidimensional scale. Only a single ability factor may be modeled in item response theory. If the scale is multidimensional, an imperfect solution is to select the dominant factor, usually the subscale containing the largest number of items in the inventory. Another possibility is to evaluate each subscale separately, but this fails to account for relations among the factors. The *assumption of local independence* requires that all items be statistically independent. That is, a participant's response to an item should not depend on responses to any other items. The assumption is violated, for example, if the content of one question offers vital clues to answering another question. The idea is that the factor should be the sole determinant of each item response on the test. This is the same assumption in other latent techniques: Only the underlying construct should drive responses to the manifest items.

Parameters of Item Characteristic Curves

The relation between the ability factor and the probability of an item response is described using up to three parameters or characteristics (Coaley, 2010; de Ayala, 2009; DeMars, 2010). The three parameters are presented in Figure 3.2.

The *difficulty parameter* is the first property of an item characteristic curve, and provides information on how likely people are to endorse or correctly answer an item relative to the other items. An item response analysis containing the difficulty parameter only is known as a Rasch model (Reid, Kolakowsky-Hayner, Lewis, & Armstong, 2007). An item deemed to be easy, or one that has a high likelihood of a correct or positive response is represented by an item characteristic curve situated in a location more to the left of the latent continuum. As shown in Figure 3.2a, a comparison of the three response curves reveals that item 1 is the easiest (or most endorsed), but item 3 is the most difficult (or least endorsed). Specifically, for a person with a relatively low ability level, say theta of -1, item 1 indicates a .40 probability, item 2 indicates a .15 probability, and item 3 indicates a .05 probability of endorsement. Conversely, for better performers, say theta of 1, the probability of positive endorsement for item 1 is .95, for item 2 is .85, and for item 3 is .60. Higher ability on the factor tends to correspond to an equal or higher rate of item endorsement. On either extreme of the latent factor, we find individuals who scored the lowest or highest on the total test, where each item has near 0 or 1.00 probability of being endorsed. In classical test theory, estimating the difficulty parameter is analogous to computing the proportion of participants endorsing each item and then comparing these proportions across items (Coaley, 2010; Sharkness & DeAngelo, 2011).

The *discrimination parameter* is the second property of the item characteristic curve and offers information on how well an item successfully separates people of a particular ability on the construct. Discrimination is gauged by inspecting the slope for the item characteristic curve. An item possessing a steep slope that points more vertically is more effective in distinguishing participants' performance on the factor. An item possessing a slope resembling a horizontal line, however, is uninformative in discerning performance levels on the construct. As shown in Figure 3.2b, item 1 possesses the flattest slope and item 3 has the steepest slope. From a relatively low ability theta (-1) to a high ability theta (1), the curve for item 1 shows a respectable increase in proportion of endorsement from about .30 to .65, but item 3 shows a more substantial discrimination of abilities from .03 to .95. This underscores that item 1 feebly differentiates the ability of respondents and might be a lackluster candidate for inclusion into the scale. A psychometrically sound scale or test should be able to show that each item successfully discriminates among its range of scores in terms of attitudes or ability. In classical test theory, discrimination is conceptualized as the degree of item-total correlation, with the magnitude of the correlation reflecting the steepness of the slope (Coaley, 2010).

The *guessing parameter* is the third and final property of an item characteristic curve, and offers information about the likelihood that an item is vulnerable to being endorsed or answered correctly. Guessing may be understood as the probability of endorsing a particular item for people who had the lowest total performance on the scale. Imagine that students in your class received a surprise exam, but some students did not spend any time hitting the books. By estimating the guessing parameter, the item characteristic curves will take into account the fact that among students with

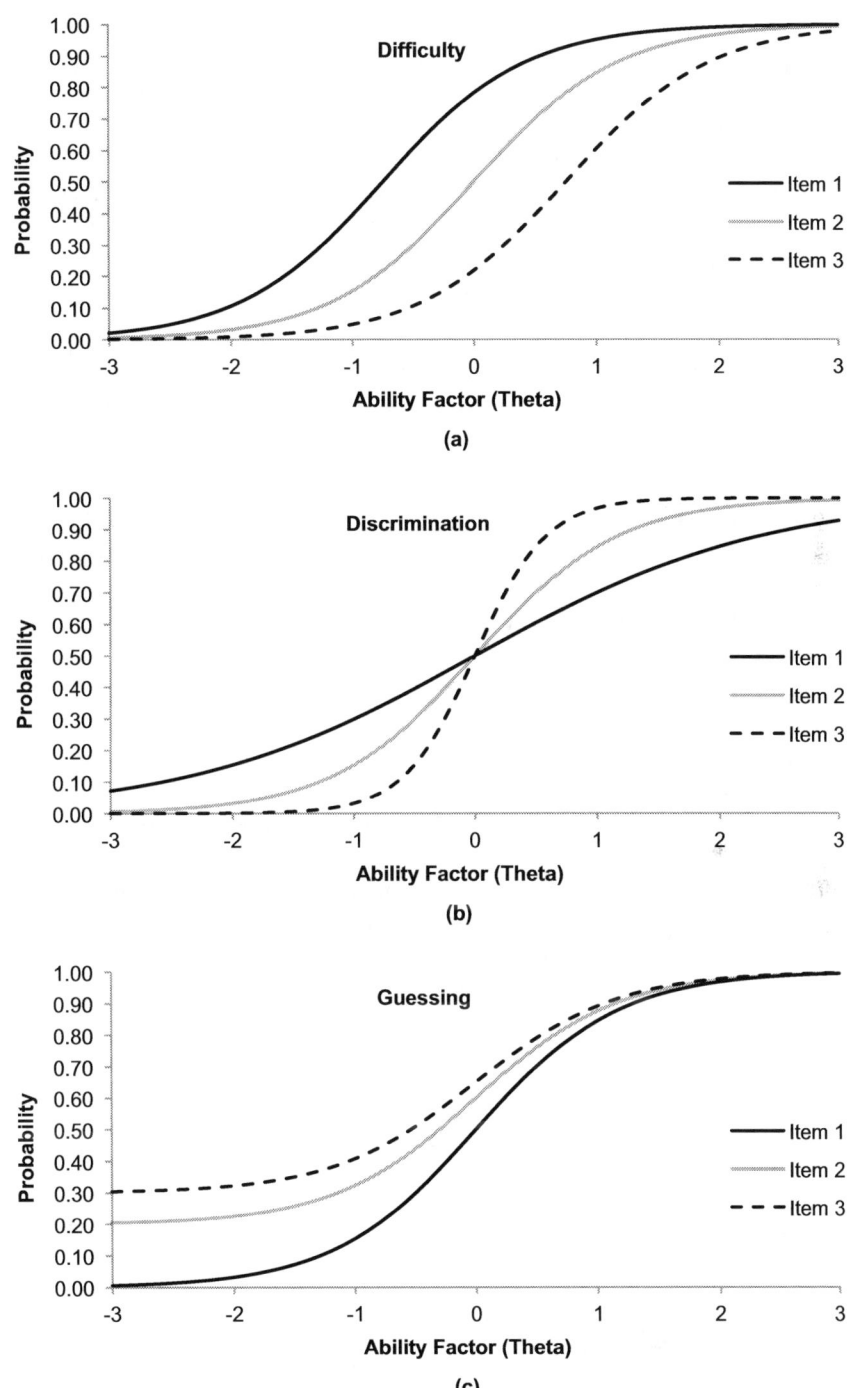

FIGURE 3.2 The three parameters of item characteristic curves in item response theory.

the poorest total exam score, the responses of some items will tend to be correctly deduced. To evaluate the guessing parameter, identify the probability of endorsement for an item characteristic curve located near the leftmost end of the factor (e.g., theta −3). As diagrammed in Figure 3.2c, for people scoring poorest on the overall factor, item 1 has a near 0 probability of being guessed correctly, but the vulnerability for guessing correctly increases to .20 for item 2, and .30 for item 3. Applying this situation to our previous example, students who did not study at all (and performed worst on the exam) are expected to show a 30% likelihood of correctly answering item 3. Guessing plays virtually no role in obtaining a correct response for item 1. It is practical to eliminate items showing a high probability of being guessed correctly by respondents.

Simultaneously Estimating All Three Parameters

The collective interpretation of these three parameters, using an item response theory, is illustrated using a large sample of alcohol users. Respondents answered yes/no to questions regarding whether they usually drink alcohol on each of the five weekdays (e.g., "typical Monday"). The five items were subjected to an item response analysis, with results shown in Figure 3.3. In this scenario, the ability factor represents a continuum of the total number of weekdays that respondents usually consumed alcohol. That is, lower ability denotes people who infrequently engage in weekday drinking, and higher ability denotes those who drink on more of these days. Examining the difficulty parameter, the item response curve for Friday is positioned near the left end of the factor and is therefore the most common drinking day. For people light in drinking ability (e.g., theta = −1), they are most likely to drink on Friday. The implication is that for those who are least likely to drink alcohol across the weekdays, there is a small, near zero probability of consumption Monday to Thursday, but these same individuals have a greater likelihood of consuming on Friday, the start of the weekend. In contrast, heavier daily drinkers (e.g., theta = 1) have a higher probability of alcohol use *not only* on Friday, but also on the other weekdays, with the lowest probability on Tuesday.

The success of each particular weekday in discriminating along the continuum of overall weekday drinking is evaluated next. Among people lower on daily drinking, Friday posses the steepest slope in effectively discriminating such participants, but Friday does not offer as much discernment

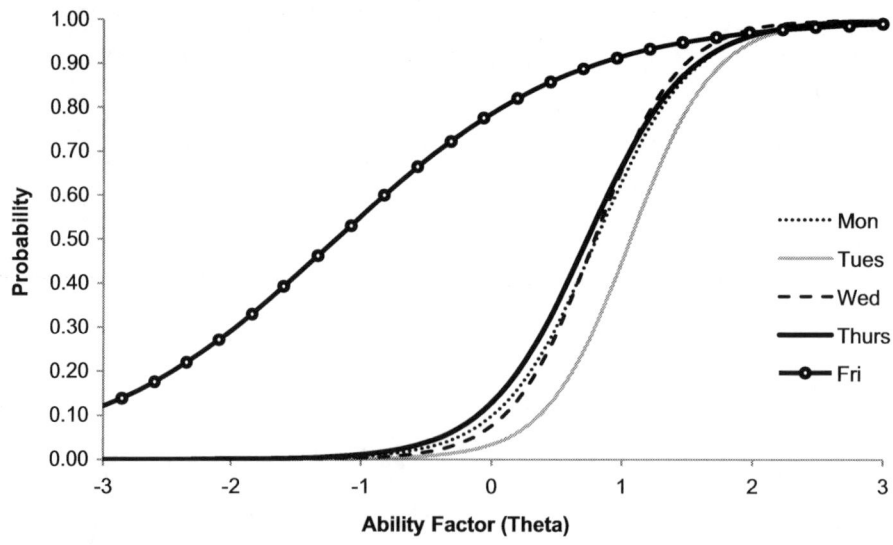

FIGURE 3.3 Item response analysis of weekday alcohol consumption.

compared to the other weekdays among higher daily drinkers. The slopes of Monday to Thursday items are almost flat at the low ability range, signifying that these days offer very little information for discriminating individuals who do not drink much. In contrast, Mondays to Thursdays are more able to differentiate among those who are relatively higher on latent daily consumption.

Finally, consider the guessing parameter: The probability of drinking on each of the five days for respondents who drink the least or very minimally. For a person at the lowest end of drinking ability, the probability of guessing is near .00 for Monday to Thursday, but approximately .13 for Friday. In other words, even among infrequent weekday drinkers, 13% of them will succumb to temptation when Friday arrives.

Information obtained in item response theory could be used in various ways, depending on the purpose of the study. It appears that Friday and Tuesday drinking least resemble the response patterns for the other days; consequently, a summary score using only items representing the other three weekdays would produce the most reliable scale. For a different purpose, the response curves of Monday, Wednesday, and Thursday were found to be very similar and provide highly redundant information. Thus, any of those days, along with Tuesday and Friday, could be used as three separate, but sufficient, indicators of weekday drinking.

A practical advantage of item response analysis is that test developers are able to estimate the ability level of participants who have completed only a few items selected from the entire inventory (Reid et al., 2007). This time-saving application is found in computerized adaptive testing, whereby new test takers are administered only a small subset from a large pool of questions (Hol, Vorst, & Mellenbergh, 2008). The sequence of items received by a participant is a function of the test taker's competence on the previous items. Thus, the test adapts to how well a person is performing at any point during the examination. A person deemed to possess low ability, due to poor performance early on the test, will continue to receive "easy" questions determined in previous test administrations to have a high rate of being answered correctly by most people. A person showing high ability early on will continue receiving more "difficult" questions that have a low probability of being answered correctly by most people. Because adaptive testing does not require the administration of the entire pool of items, it is an efficient approach for isolating and narrowing any person's performance during the exam. A person's overall score is calculated by locating or linking where he or she falls on the ability continuum in comparison to others tested, whose scores were used to establish the response curve norms. Conversely, just from knowing a person's theta level, it is possible to make inferences about the probability of correctly answering an item a respondent never received.

Conclusion

Our conceptualization of a phenomenon or entity consists of diverse operations caused by unobservable underlying factors. When you are asked to describe "love," this abstract concept may conjure up love of your romantic partner, love of your parents, or even love of your pets. You do not go around thinking that your gut feeling of love is impure and contaminated by measurement noise. Latent factors also allow items to possess appropriate weights in relation to their adequacy in tapping the aspects of the attribute. In a sample of newlywed participants, a factor analysis of the data might show that the largest factor loading or weight arises from the item of "romantic love," as it more quintessentially captures how this cohort perceives the emergent quality of love. Equal weights used in non-latent approaches presume that the different operations reflecting love (e.g., intimacy, passion, commitment) are equally sufficient in capturing the replicable and unobservable essence of love.

Some clear benefits emerge from the use of latent variables, but this is not to imply that there are no advantages to classical test analysis, as the primary benefits include ease of learning, estimation, and interpretation. Thus, classical test analysis remains a popular method for evaluating the quality of measures. Comparative studies have discovered that when both non-latent and latent techniques are undertaken and contrasted on the same scale or test, they produce highly parallel results (Fan, 1998; Sharkness & DeAngelo, 2011). These psychometric theories should be viewed as complementary rather than entirely different ways of conducting research. If possible, the researcher may report results of classical test analyses (e.g., item-total correlations and overall mean) as well as latent analyses (e.g., item characteristic curves showing relations between each item and the latent factor) in the same study, to allow the audience to make better informed conclusions about the utility of the measures to be used in examining the substantive research.

Questions for Discussion

1. Explain the relationships among true score, observed score, and random error.
2. What are the two main assumptions that need to be satisfied when conducting an item response analysis?
3. In terms of reliability, describe how analyses with latent factors are different from classical test theory techniques like Cronbach's alpha or test-retest. Are they better or worse, and why?
4. William Smythe wanted to create a scale that measured the likelihood that people will burst into laughter in a movie theater. So far, he has four items written. These three items yielded a Cronbach's alpha of .50 and the following output:

Item-Total Correlations	
Item 1	.76
Item 2	.62
Item 3	.10
Item 4	.52

Given what you know about Cronbach's alpha and improving internal consistency, describe the ways in which Will could increase the internal consistency of his scale. (Hint—there may be more than one way.)

Notes

1. Various means are used to split the total item set in half: even-numbered items are contrasted with odd-numbered items, the first half compared with the second half (probably a poor choice because of possible fatigue effects on the part of participants), the total item set is randomly split into two groups, etc.
2. Cronbach's alpha is actually a generalization of the KR-20, an index of internal consistency for scales using dichotomous items (Kuder & Richardson, 1937). For scales using binary items, the formulas for Cronbach's alpha and the KR-20 yield the same value.
3. It is good practice to adjust these "item-total correlations" statistically, so as to remove the influence of the particular item under consideration on the total score. This adjustment becomes especially important when the scale is composed of relatively few items, because in such cases the contribution of any given item to the total score is great.
4. Advances allow nominal responses with more than two categories, called polytomous item response theory, but rather stringent assumptions make it the purview of books dedicated to the topic (DeMars, 2010).

References

American Psychological Association. (1985). *Standards for educational and psychological testing.* Washington, DC: APA Press.

Bedian, A. G., Day, D. V., & Kelloway, E. K. (1997). Correcting for measurement error attenuation in structural equation models: Some important reminders. *Educational and Psychological Measurement, 57,* 785–799.

Bollen, K. A. (2002). Latent variables in psychology and the social sciences. *Annual Review of Psychology, 53*, 605–634.

Borsboom, D., Mellenbergh, G. J., & van Heerden, J. (2003). The theoretical status of latent variables. *Psychological Review, 110*, 203–219.

Brown, T. A. (2006). Confirmatory factor analysis for applied research. New York: Guilford Press.

Cattell, R. B. (1972). *Personality and mood by questionnaire.* San Francisco: Jossey-Bass.

Charles, E. P. (2005). The correction for attenuation due to measurement error: Clarifying concepts and creating confidence sets. *Psychological Methods, 10*, 206.

Coaley, K. (2010). *An introduction to psychological assessment and psychometrics.* Thousand Oaks, CA: Sage.

Cronbach, L. J. (1951). Coefficient alpha and the internal structure of tests. *Psychometrika, 16*, 297–334.

Cronbach, L. J., Gleser, G. C., Nanda, H., & Rajaratnam, N. (1972). *The dependability of behavioral measurements: Theory of generalizability for scores and profiles.* New York: Wiley.

Dawson, E. J., Crano, W. D., & Burgoon, M. (1996). Refining the meaning and measurement of acculturation: Revisiting a novel methodological approach. *International Journal of Intercultural Relations, 20*, 97–114.

de Ayala, R. J. (2009). Theory and practice of item response theory. New York: Guilford.

de Champlain, A. F. (2010). A primer on classical test theory and item response theory for assessments in medical education. *Medical Education, 44*, 109–117.

DeMars, C. (2010). *Item response theory.* New York: Oxford Press.

DeShon. R. P. (1998). A cautionary note on measurement error corrections in structural equation models, *Psychological Methods, 4*, 412–423.

DeVellis, R. B. (2012). *Scale development: Theory and applications* (3rd ed.). Thousand Oaks, CA: Sage.

Embretson, S. E. (1996). The new rules of measurement. *Psychological Assessment, 4*, 341–349.

Fan, X. (1998). Item response theory and classical test theory: An empirical comparison of their item/person statistics. *Educational and Psychological Measurement, 58*, 357–381.

Gulliksen, H. (1950). *Theory of mental tests.* New York: Wiley.

Henard, D. J. (2000). Item response theory. In L. W. Grimm & P. R Yarnold (Eds.), *Reading and understanding more multivariate statistics* (pp. 67–97). Washington, DC: American Psychological Association.

Hol, A. M., Vorst, H.C.M., & Mellenbergh, G. J. (2008). Computerized adaptive testing of personality traits. *Journal of Psychology, 216*, 12–21.

Kuder, G. F., & Richardson, M. W. (1937). The theory of the estimation of test reliability. *Psychometrika, 2*, 151–160.

Muchinsky, P. M. (1996). The correction for attenuation. *Educational and Psychological Measurement, 56*, 63–75.

Nunnally, J. C. (1967). *Psychometric theory.* New York: McGraw-Hill.

Raykov, T., & Marcoulides, G. A. (2011). *Introduction to psychometric theory.* New York: Routledge.

Reid, C. A., Kolakowsky-Hayner, S. A., Lewis, A. N., & Armstrong, A. J. (2007). Modern psychometric methodology: Applications of item response theory. *Rehabilitation Counseling Bulletin, 50*, 177–188.

Schmidt, F. L., & Hunter, J. E. (1999). Theory testing and measurement error. *Intelligence, 27*, 183–198.

Sharkness, J., & DeAngelo, L. (2011). Measuring student involvement: A comparison of classical test theory and item response theory in the construction of scales from student surveys. *Research in Higher Education, 52*, 480–507.

Shevlin, M., Miles, J.N.V., Davies, M.N.O., & Walker, D. S. (2000). Coefficient alpha: a useful indicator of reliability? *Personality and Individual Differences, 28*, 229–237.

Spearman, C. (1904). Proof and measurement of the association between two things. *American Journal of Psychology, 15*, 72–101.

Zickar, M. J., & Broadfoot, A. A. (2009). The partial revival of a dead horse? Comparing classical test theory and item response theory. In C. E. Lance & R. J. Vandenberg (Eds.), *Statistical and methodological myths and urban legends: Doctrine, verity and fable in the organizational and social sciences* (pp. 37–59). New York: Routledge/Taylor & Francis Group.

Zimmerman, D. W. (2011). Sampling variability and axioms of classical test theory. *Journal of Educational and Behavioral Statistics, 36*, 586–615.

4

MEASUREMENT VALIDITY

Developing measures that meet the criteria of reliability in terms of internal consistency and temporal stability, or inter-observer agreement, satisfies a basic requirement for the operationalization phase of a scientific investigation. In the first chapter of this text, however, we made a distinction between the adequacy of an operation in terms of objectivity and replicability and its adequacy as a manifestation of a theoretical construct. This distinction marks the difference between the reliability of a measuring device and its validity. Whereas reliability has to do with the internal qualities of measurement, the validation of operations relative to the hypothetical concepts under investigation is crucial from the standpoint of theory development. It is easily conceivable that the procedures usually followed to generate a reliable scale of individual differences could lead to an internally consistent, temporally stable instrument that had no relationship whatever to the theoretical attributes that motivated the research in the first place. Consistency of responses, from item to item or from time to time or from observer to observer, although necessary, does not sufficiently establish a scale's validity. Although some degree of response consistency is essential in diagnosing any underlying attribute, the validity of a measuring instrument must be studied through the use of operations beyond those applied to assess reliability.

Basically, the validity of a scale refers to the extent of correspondence between variations in the scores on the instrument and variation among respondents (or other objects of measurement) on the underlying construct being studied. In classical test theory, the true score represents a measure of the replicable "shared variation," or the "common factor" that underlies participants' responses to all items. Whether this response factor adequately reflects the particular conceptualization that the investigator wants to measure, however, is still a matter for investigation. It is important to keep this point in mind when validating any measure. Validation *always* requires empirical research beyond that used in the scale construction (reliability) phase of instrument development and refinement. This validation process will invariably focus on the relationship of the scale with some other indicators of the construct under investigation.

Nunnally (1967) noted that validity is a relative, descriptive term, not an all-or-none property, and his view accords with Messick's (1989, p. 13) definition of validity as a "judgment of the degree to which evidence and theoretical rationales support the *adequacy* and *appropriateness*" of a construct. This definition suggests that validity is not a thing or a feature of a measure, but rather an aspect of the interpretation of a measure. As such, validity is always open to question, review, and revision—it is never a closed issue, but rather a continuous process. It is "the best available approximation to the truth or falsity of propositions" (Cook & Campbell, 1979, p. 37); but the judgment must always be tempered by recognition that the best available evidence may change, and thus the evaluation of validity of a construct also may change.

This view suggests that the researcher always attempt to determine the extent to which the scale is valid in the particular application in which it is employed. The fact that previous research demonstrated the validity of a scale does not necessarily imply that it will be valid in another setting, with different respondents, at different times, and so on. Too often, validity is conceptualized as a static, enduring property; thus, once a scale is validated, it is viewed as valid for all time. This interpretation is inconsistent with the more realistic view of validity as a relativistic, descriptive quality. Because validity changes from time to time and from sample to sample, it should be reevaluated periodically to ensure that what once was a valid indicator of some theoretical construct (e.g., attitude) remains so (see Campbell, 1950, for an extensive discussion of the concept of validity).

As an example of the instability of scale validity, consider the changing "validities" of an attitude scale developed to tap opinions regarding the justification of war. Would this scale, developed in the Cold War climate of the 1950s to measure relatively broad, general feelings about war, be likely to provide valid information when used in the context of an investigation of participants' feelings about the government's intervention in political strife in the Middle East today? Probably not. A person who might feel that war was indeed justified under certain circumstances might answer this scale very differently if it were used to assess governmental actions in regions where he or she felt that the United States had no business meddling. In other words, our hypothetical scale, which might provide a valid indicator of people's *general* attitudes toward the justification of a defensive war in which the survival of the country was at stake, could prove to be invalid as an indicator of participants' specific attitudes toward a particular war or war-related governmental policy at a particular point in time.

Types of Measurement Validity

With this general introduction to what the concept of validity is, and what it is not, let us consider some specific subcategories of validity that are of central concern to social scientists. An appreciation of these more specific features of validity provides a more complete understanding of the concept of validity as it is applied in the scaling of people or stimuli, which are considered in Chapters 15 and 17 respectively. In discussing these various forms of validity, it is important to keep in mind that they all are component parts of what is generally termed **measurement construct validity**, which is concerned with the validity of the measure with respect to the theoretical construct of interest. The various components of construct validity, presented in the following paragraphs, are important insofar as they reflect the underlying theoretical construct that the measure is intended to assess.

Face Validity

Face validity is based on superficial impressions regarding the extent that a measure appears to capture a construct. A scale designed to assess interpersonal satisfaction probably should not contain the question, "Do you enjoy the company of cats?", but it might include "Are you happy with your interpersonal relationships?" Unlike face validity, claims stemming from other forms of validity are examined using systematic established procedures (deVellis, 2012). For this reason, many do not embrace it as a form of validity. Face validity poses the dilemma: If the item does not appear to tap the attribute, then why was such an item generated in the first place? A central issue with face validity is that sometimes it might be good thing to avoid, especially if the goal is to conceal the purpose of the question from respondents. Measures that have high face value in tapping socially unacceptable behaviors or social stigmas might deter honest responses. The Minnesota Multiphasic Personality Inventory (MMPI), designed to assess psychopathology, contains questions purposely designed to possess poor face validity (Gynther, Buckhart, & Hovanitz, 1979). An example item requiring a true/false response is "I prefer a shower to a bath" (Ben-Porath, 2012). The question appears to innocuously assess hygiene preferences, but people who would rather sit than stand in warm water tend to score lower on empathy and compassion for others. Although initially selected on the basis of low face validity, inclusion into the final version of the MMPI occurred only after other types of validity established the item as an acceptable indicator of the construct. Thus, the mere fact that a scale's items appear to tap the construct under study (i.e., have "face validity") is simply not sufficient.

Content Validity

Content validity is the extent that measure adequately represents (or samples) the complete range or breadth of the construct under consideration. In establishing the content validity of a test of eighth-grade mathematics, for example, we would be concerned with whether or not the scale adequately sampled the range of mathematical skills that an eighth grader should know. If the test focused exclusively on addition and subtraction, it is obvious that it would not have sampled enough of the hypothetical domain of interest, so some modifications to include a greater variety of items would be indicated.

With factual materials (i.e., when developing tests of knowledge or ability), constructing scales with adequate content validity is not overly difficult. The domain of interest is relatively well specified, and a representative sample of items can be drawn from this pool of potential questions. When the researcher is dealing with other psychological or social variables, however, the situation typically is not so clear-cut. In such cases assessment of content validity often is a subjective operation. To help ensure content validity, many researchers begin the scale construction process by generating large numbers of diverse items. Whether this represents an adequate sampling of content is based almost solely on the subjective judgment of the researcher who constructed the scale, and as such is subject to bias. Three more systematic procedures offer alternative ways to evaluate content validity.

The first approach is to perform a thorough literature review of the topic to acquire insights about the appropriate types of items or factors that would ensure representative coverage of the construct. Examining concepts and definitions commonly employed in that area of research will help with decisions of not only defining content breadth but also how best to phrase these items. A second means of promoting content validity is through the use of experts, perhaps assembled in focus groups. Expert opinions regarding the adequacy of coverage of a particular scale, although far from infallible, provide more trustworthy information than that of an investigator working independently. The most empirical way to evaluate content validity is to use factor analysis to assess the adequacy with which various features of the construct are represented in the measure as a whole (Bryant, 2000). Doing so will reveal not only the number of factors or content areas emerging from the scale, but also the number of items that tap each factor. Factors showing inadequate coverage will be represented with fewer items relative to the other factors. Based on this information, the researcher might revise the scale by devising additional questions for these under-focused domains.

Criterion Validity

The procedures designed to assess the validity of a scale should vary according to the purposes for which the instrument is devised. **Criterion validity** is concerned with the extent that a measure is related to, or explains, a target outcome or criterion, usually a behavior. For example, a scale constructed to tap attitudes toward exercising should show that it is related to frequency of gym attendance or the number of exercise behaviors indicated in a checklist. Depending on the distance in time between administration of the scale and the outcome, criterion validity may be divided into two types (Bryant, 2000). **Concurrent validity** is the extent that a measure is related to, or explains, a relevant criterion behavior, with both variables assessed at the same occasion. The problem with concurrent validity is that it is impossible to unravel the temporal precedence of events. Did positive attitudes about exercising explain frequent exercising behaviors, or do the variables flow the other way? **Predictive validity** is the extent that a measure is related to, or explains, a relevant criterion behavior assessed at a subsequent occasion. It is considered the more desirable and rigorous of the two forms of criterion validity.

Predictive validity is of major concern when the purpose of a measure is to anticipate either the likelihood, or the extremity, of some behavior or outcome of interest at a later point in time. The behavior itself serves as the criterion, and the strength in which the scale predicts the level of the criterion is taken as an indication of the scale's predictive validity. A test of reading readiness, for example, should enable an investigator to discriminate the "ready" from the "unready," to predict which children are most likely to succeed (or fail) in grasping the fundamentals of this essential skill. To assess the degree that the test is able to successfully discriminate this behavior, a researcher could administer the test to a sample of preschoolers on the first day of school and correlate these results with the scores received on a standardized test of reading achievement after their first year of formal schooling. The strength of the relationship would suggest the predictive validity or invalidity of the readiness test.

In judging the utility of prediction to establish the validity of a measure, three important limitations should be kept in mind. First, as other variables may influence the magnitude of a relationship, predictive validity in and of itself is not sufficient to confirm or refute the validity of a measure. A failure to obtain a strong relationship in the foregoing example might have been due to a massive failure of the instructional system to teach reading effectively to any of the children in the sample. Or, it might have indicated that the standardized test was not appropriate for the sample.

A second difficulty with this validation approach is that it can be relatively uninformative, even if scale scores are strongly related to the criterion scores. Whereas a strong predictive relationship is certainly encouraging, it does not explain *why* such a relationship occurred. In the absence of theory relating the measure to children's performance, the validation process is much less informative, and much less useful, than it needs to be.

A third, more practical limitation on the usefulness of prediction in establishing the validity of a scale has to do with the relative absence of useful criteria in social science. Few of the variables of our field are as easily quantified as standardized first-grade reading achievement. Typically, our investigations, and consequently our measures, are constructed to assess complex, abstract qualities. In these instances, predictive validation approaches often are not fully useful, because appropriate criteria against which predictions might be compared do not exist and must be inferred. For example, suppose we wanted to develop a measure of religiousness. In this instance, predictive validity would be difficult to assess. What would be the criterion measure? Attending religious services? Helping those in need? Both of these possibilities might characterize people of high or low religiousness. For reasons like these, predictive validation approaches are most widely used when dealing with scales of fact—that is, for issues on which there are consensually agreed-upon answers. In these instances, useful criteria often do exist (or can be constructed), and the full power of the predictive validation approach can be realized. Predictive validation approaches are less useful, but still may be informative when constructing measures of opinion, on which the answers reflect matters of preference or choice, which vary from person to person, and on which there is no necessarily, consensually correct answer; but these circumstances are less common than those involving scales of fact.

Convergent Validity

If a measure is a valid indicator of a construct, then it should be positively correlated with other types of measures of the same or similar constructs. Testing whether this is the case is termed **convergent validity**, or the extent that measures of constructs that are theoretically related are actually related. This term should not be confused with concurrent validity, described earlier. These other measures used to assess convergent validity may be scales of theoretically similar types of constructs, but could also involve measures of the same construct employing different methods, such as peer reports, coded observational records, or other types measurement formats.

Convergent validation subsumes other, more specific validity forms—predictive validity, concurrent validity, and so on. "In the ideal case, indicators that are as dissimilar as possible are used to estimate of the convergent validity of a measure. This view distinguishes the search for convergent validity from the assessment of reliability, in which maximally similar measures are sought. In the quest for convergent validity, measures as dissimilar as possible are developed and used so as to increase the likelihood that they share different sources of error. The more similar the measures, the greater the probability that they are prone to the same irrelevancies, thereby compounding error" (Crano, 2000, p. 40).

Let's return to our earlier example, in which we are developing a measure of religiousness. One might expect this measure to be theoretically related to other measures with which religiousness is thought to covary. For example, we might expect this measure, if it is valid, to relate to similar constructs, such as measures of compassionate beliefs or conservative ideology. If these expected relationships do not materialize, two possibilities arise: The most obvious is that our scale does not adequately assess the construct (it is assumed that the instruments measuring the related constructs, compassion and conservative ideology, are relatively valid). The second possibility is that the scale is valid, but that the theory on which the hypothesized relationships are based is incorrect, and thus no relation between the constructs should be expected.[1] However, if another scale of religiosity does exhibit the hypothesized pattern of interrelationships with the external validating scales (compassionate beliefs and conservative ideology), the investigator is left with the first alternative—the new measure is probably invalid and in need of reconceptualization.

Of the many ways in which convergent validity is assessed, perhaps the most common is called the *known groups method*. In this validation approach, a measure designed to assess a proposed construct is given to different groups of people who are known to differ on an attribute that is related to the focus of the instrument. If the scale actually measures what it purports to, then these groups should have different scores, and these differences should be known in advance of the test's administration. For example, if an investigator has devised a scale to measure prejudice against African-Americans, then the overall scale score of a mob of Ku Klux Klan members should be different from that of that of a group of members of the American Civil Liberties Union. If no differences are found, or if the differences are in a direction opposite to that expected, then it is clear that the validation process has failed—either the theory on which the expected relations are based is in error, or the test itself is not a good indicator of racial attitudes.

The known groups method has been used in a number of different situations and generally proves a convincing technique in establishing the case for validity. For example, Wheeler and Austin (2000) were interested in validating a scale to assess adolescent women's grief responses. They assembled a sample of young adolescent women, 13–19 years of age, some of whom had recently suffered a perinatal loss. As indicated by the authors' "Loss Response List," those women who had lost their babies exhibited significantly more grief and depression than the women who had not endured such a loss. These score differences were as might be expected on the basis of theory and common sense, and supported the validity of the measure.

Although the known groups method is useful, there are some contexts that preclude its use for practical purposes. Sometimes, for example, the appropriate groups will not cooperate. At other times, the quality under consideration does not suggest identifiable groups who would be expected to differ greatly on the construct. An investigator studying trait self-esteem, for example, might have a hard time finding established, identifiable groups known to differ on this quality. As such, the application of the known groups technique is limited by the nature of the underlying construct the instrument is designed to measure. Thus in some areas of social research, alternative procedures must be employed to establish convergent validity by relying on correlations among related measures.

Discriminant Validity

In the convergent validation process, we generate a series of hypotheses regarding probable interrelationships expected between the measure of the construct under development and other, perhaps more established, scales of related constructs, independent of extraneous factors (e.g., similar methods of measurement). In an opposite approach, we also can assess validity by examining the extent to which the construct of interest is distinct from other measures with which it should be *unrelated*. **Discriminant validity** is the extent that measures of constructs that are theoretically unrelated are actually unrelated. The religiousness scale should not overlap highly with measures of patriotism, kindness, or intelligence.

To illustrate the various forms of validity that we have considered thus far, Table 4.1 describes the procedures associated with different types of measurement validity using a hypothetical example that involves developing a scale of Student Research Potential. As shown, content validity is

TABLE 4.1 Developing and validating a "Student Research Potential Scale." Examining the major forms of measurement validity.

Measurement Validity	*Example Process*
Content Validity	The published literature is scoured to review the characteristics and profiles of students who are productive with research. Professors prolific in research are interviewed to identify the most common beliefs and views about why they enjoy research. Two common themes are identified: (a) Creativity in generating novel research ideas, and (b) Passion for learning about research methods. Diverse items are generated based on these domains.
Criterion Validity	After administering the scale of items to college students, behavioral outcomes are completed by the same sample one year later to assess predictive validity. These criterion indicators include involvement in a number of research projects with faculty and the number of research conferences attended during the one-year span. The Student Research Potential Scale should longitudinally predict or explain variability in the behavioral measures.
Convergent Validity	Similar, but established, measures in the literature are administered along with our scale: The Need for Achievement Scale, Academic Aspirations Scale, and Workaholic Measure. The Research Potential Scale should reveal relations to these other measures: All stem from a strong work ethic. To demonstrate why this new scale offers nonredundant information from these other similar scales, relations should not be strong.
Discriminant Validity	Scales unrelated to our new construct are also administered alongside our scale: Need for Security Inventory, College Partying Scale, and Clown Phobia Scale. Relations should be negligible, if not zero, to show that the Student Research Potential Scale is tapping a phenomenon different from these other assessments.

enhanced through a thorough review of the literature and intensive interviews of prolific researchers to isolate attitudes and behaviors that seem to be associated with students' research productivity. After developing a number of items designed to tap this trait, the researcher administers these items to a large sample of college students, and one year later assesses their research performance through measures of the number and quality of research projects in which they have been involved, the number of scientific conferences they have attended, the number and grades on research-based courses they have taken, and so on. If students' scores on our new scale are correlated with these indicators of potential research productivity, the scale will be judged to have good predictive validity, a component of criterion validity.

At the same time that indicators of criterion validity are collected, the researcher also could administer established tests of features that *theoretically* should be associated with research potential. If these measures relate to (or converge with) our measure in expected ways, the new scale is said to have convergent validity. Finally, the researcher also might have administered scales with which our new measure would *not* be expected to relate. This is done to ensure that the new measure actually discriminates among constructs—that is, it relates to measures with which it should theoretically relate, and that it does not relate to measures with which it should not. If this latter criterion is satisfied, the Student Research Potential scale is said to have discriminant validity.

Combining Convergent and Discriminant Validity: The Multitrait-Multimethod Matrix

In general, construct validation is an approach whose aim is to establish the reality of a psychological concept—it is a test of whether or not the hypothesized construction plausibly exists. If it does, then it should enter into predictable patterns of relationships with other constructs. When attempting to validate a construct, investigators must develop a set of hypotheses regarding other constructs with which their particular conceptualization should be (or should not be) related. If a measure is to be judged a valid indicator of the construct, then the hypothesized relationships should exist, and measures purportedly assessing these associated constructs should be interrelated.

Operations that assess the relationships between a new measure and other established measures with which the new test was thought to relate were termed *convergent validation techniques* by Campbell and Fiske (1959), because in essence the measures converge upon, or define, a hypothesized network of interconnected traits, processes, dispositions, and/or behaviors. A successful convergent validation operation not only suggests that the critical scale is an adequate measure of the construct in question, but also bolsters the theoretical position that was used to develop the hypothesized interrelationships that formed the basis of the validation process.

Furthermore, *discriminant validation techniques* also can be used in conjunction with studies of convergent validity to assess scale quality. Both convergent and discriminant validity are subclasses of the more general concept of construct validity, and are investigated simultaneously in the multitrait-multimethod matrix approach developed by Campbell and Fiske (1959). Each of these two validity forms provides different and useful information about the quality of an instrument.

In the **multitrait-multimethod matrix** (MTMMM), multiple measures are used to assess the extent of association of theoretically related but different constructs, over and above the association that might come about simply from having shared the same method of measurement. The MTMMM is a logical extension of the complementary principles of multiple operationalization and triangulation introduced in the first chapter of this text. The technique involves computing a correlation matrix that reveals the relationships among a set of carefully selected measures. The measures are chosen to represent a combination of several different (theoretically relevant) constructs, each assessed by several different methods of measurement. Each construct is measured by *each and every* measurement technique. Analysis focuses on the interrelationships among measures theorized to assess the *same* construct. These relationships are compared with those involving measures of *different* constructs that happen to be measured by the same measurement technique. The pattern of interrelationships among traits sharing the same and similar and different methods of measurement helps us determine the construct validity of the measures under study.

A concrete example may help elucidate this approach. Suppose a social developmentalist was interested in creating a new self-esteem scale for young children using the method of behavioral observation. On the basis of theory, the researcher believes that self-esteem should be related to, but distinct, from sociability, and even less related to intelligence. To use the multitrait-multimethod matrix (MTMMM) approach, the researcher finds two previously established measures of self-esteem shown in the research to possess desirable psychometric properties. The first of these scales uses the method of self-ratings to measure self-esteem, whereby each child participant completes this scale individually. The second scale employs the method of peer ratings, in which the best friend of each child is asked to rate the respective child's self-esteem. The new measure, remember, uses the method of behavioral observations, in which the researcher observes the playground interactions of each child for 10 minutes and uses a checklist to quantify their self-esteem. Then, the researcher finds *established* scales of sociability and intelligence that are assessed by the same three different methods used to assess self-esteem (self-ratings, peer ratings, and behavioral observations). Thus, nine different measurements are obtained: Three different psychological tests are administered to a sample of 200 first-graders, three assessments are obtained from their corresponding best friends, and three different behavior observations are obtained for each child by the researcher. The resulting correlation matrix of (hypothetically) obtained relationships among the nine measures is presented in Table 4.2.

Four Critical Entries in the Matrix

In examining this set of results, Campbell and Fiske (1959) recommend that we consider four important components of the matrix before attempting to form an assessment of convergent and discriminant validity. These critical components are:

1. The *reliabilities* of the three methods of measurement, contained in the main diagonal of the matrix (parenthesized values), are considered first. The reliabilities (either internal consistency or test-retest) of the measures must be strong enough to encourage further consideration of the data. If they are not, there is not much point to inquire about validity. However, as shown, the reliabilities of our hypothetical measures are reasonably strong.
2. Adjacent to the reliability diagonals, enclosed in solid lines, are the *heterotrait-monomethod* triangles. These entries reflect the correlation between two *different* traits that are assessed by the *same* measurement method. Thus, in the topmost data triangle of Table 4.2, we find the correlations between self-esteem and sociability, self-esteem and intelligence, and sociability and intelligence when all of these traits are measured by self-report ($r = .50, .40,$ and $.30$ respectively).
3. Next, we consider the *heterotrait-heteromethod* triangles, which are enclosed in broken lines. These values reflect the relationship between *different* traits assessed by *different* methods of measurement. In Table 4.2, the correlation between sociability as measured by peer checklist and self-esteem as measured by self-report is of moderate magnitude (i.e., $r = .25$).
4. The final entries to be considered are the *monotrait-heteromethod* values, which lie on the diagonal that separates the heterotrait-heteromethod triangles. These *validity diagonals*, as they are termed, reflect the association of presumably *identical* traits assessed by *different* methods of measurement. They are presented in bold type in Table 4.2.

TABLE 4.2 (Methods: A, B, C) × 3 (Traits: 1, 2, 3) Multitrait-multimethod matrix.

Traits	Method A (Self-Rating)			Method B (Peer Rating)			Method C (Behavioral)		
	1 (Self-Esteem)	2 (Sociability)	3 (Intelligence)	1 (Self-Esteem)	2 (Sociability)	3 (Intelligence)	1 (Self-Esteem)	2 (Sociability)	3 (Intelligence)
Method A (Self-Rating)									
1 (Self-Esteem)	(.90)								
2 (Sociability)	.50	(.88)							
3 (Intelligence)	.40	.30	(.75)						
Method B (Peer Rating)									
1 (Self-Esteem)	**.58**	.20	.18	(.92)					
2 (Sociability)	.25	**.56**	.11	.70	(.91)				
3 (Intelligence)	.17	.09	**.48**	.60	.51	(.83)			
Method C (Behavioral)									
1 (Self-Esteem)	**.57**	.20	.19	**.69**	.41	.30	(.93)		
2 (Sociability)	.23	**.59**	.16	.44	**.68**	.29	.71	(.89)	
3 (Intelligence)	.18	.12	**.48**	.34	.28	**.61**	.82	.66	(.82)

Note: Reliabilities are the parenthesized values on the main diagonals. Validity values are in bold type. Heterotrait-monomethod values are enclosed in solid lines. Heterotrait-heteromethod values are enclosed by broken lines.

Evaluating Results of the MTMM Matrix

We use these various entries to assess construct validity. Practical tips should help in deciphering the mechanics of the matrix. The idea of the MTMMM originated during a period when personality trait theory dominated scale validation research (Campbell & Fiske, 1959). It is helpful to think of "traits" as what today's researchers more broadly and intuitively refer to as "constructs." "Method" does not refer to a research method or design in the strictest sense, but essentially a "modality of administration" or "method of measurement." Possibilities for additional measurement methods in this example, given today's technology, could include a web-based survey, a cell phone interview, physiological and hormonal assessments, or even brain scans. Of course, the same sample of participants would be required to complete all of these methods to build a MTMMM. Although not limited exclusively to three trait factors assessed with three method factors, extending the matrix makes it unwieldy, as each new trait must be measured by every method. For this reason, MTMMM studies generally do not go beyond this limit (Chang, Connelly, & Geeza, 2012; Marsh, 1989).

In terms of classical test theory, the underlying theoretical traits represent true scores, and different assessment methods represent different sources of measurement error that influence the observed scores (Eid & Nussbeck, 2009; Höfling, Schermellel-Engel, & Moosbrugger, 2009; Scullen, 1999). In practice, almost all research studies assess constructs using only a single measurement method (e.g., paper and pencil surveys, behavioral observations), and thus the contribution of the method itself cannot be disentangled from trait variance in the scores obtained by researchers. The MTMMM is an important theoretical device to help visualize and remind us to be mindful of the many methodological artifacts that can affect the validity of obtained scores.

In their classic paper, Campbell and Fiske (1959) suggest that four important requirements be met before we conclude that our measures are valid indicators of a construct. The first is that the correlations in the validity diagonals (the monotrait-heteromethod values) be statistically and practically significant. This requirement is concerned with convergent validity. It is reasonable to require these values be strong because they are meant to express the association between different measures of the (presumably) identical trait. For most theoretical purposes, measurement method is considered incidental, or theoretically vacuous, and as such should not affect the values of the traits or constructs of interest. We have convergent validity when there is a strong overlap among the various assessments of traits that are considered identical (and which differ, presumably, only in the manner in which they were measured). Thus in our example, all three of our measures of self-esteem should correlate strongly—this is a reasonable requirement if we are to infer that they measure the same underlying construct. If they do not, it is possible that the *measurement method* we used to assess self-esteem, which plays no role in our theory, is impinging on our results. In Table 4.2, the correlational results satisfy this requirement.

The second (critical) requirement of the MTMMM is that the validity values exceed the entries in relevant heterotrait-monomethod triangles (which are bound by solid lines). This "common sense desideratum" (Campbell & Fiske, 1959, p. 83) requires that the relationship between different measures of the same trait should exceed the correlation between different traits that merely happen to share the same method of measurement. If this requirement is not met, we are left to conclude that systematic (but theoretically irrelevant) measurement error may be controlling outcomes to an unacceptable degree. As illustrated, the results of our hypothetical study are not completely in accord with this second critical requirement. For example, consider the correlation ($r = .58$) of Trait 1 (Self-esteem) measured by Method A (self-ratings) and Method B (peer-ratings). This monotrait-heteromethod (validity) entry exceeds some, but not all, correlations involving different traits that happen to be measured by the same method; for example, the correlation between Traits 1 and 2 (sociability and intelligence respectively) measured by Method B (peer ratings) is higher ($r = .70$).

As Campbell and Fiske observed, failing this requirement is "probably typical" of research on individual differences. Method factors contribute substantially to obtained scores, so different traits assessed by the same method will often be significantly correlated.

A third requirement, which like the earlier one is concerned with discriminant validity, is that each validity value exceeds the correlations of the entries of the row and column in which it is located within its respective heterotrait-heteromethod triangle. So, returning to the comparison of correlations using Methods A and B, we see that the first validity ($r = .58$) exceeds the values in its relevant row ($r = .20$ and .18) and column ($r = .25$ and .17). In the language of the MTMMM, the monotrait-heteromethod values should exceed associated heterotrait-heteromethod associations. This too, is a reasonable requirement. It means that the relationship between different measures of the (presumably) same trait should be stronger than correlations between different traits assessed with different measures. Discriminant validity is called into question if the association of different traits determined by disparate measures exceeds that involving identical traits (also measured by means of dissimilar methods). In the example provided in Table 4.2, discriminant validity is supported in every case.

The final requisite of the MTMMM technique is that the same patterns of trait interrelations be observed in the heterotrait triangles irrespective of measurement overlap; that is, the pattern of trait interrelations should be the same in the monomethod and the heteromethod blocks. Such a requirement would be met if method were truly incidental, as required. The patterning of traits should be maintained whether the traits are measured by the same method (as in the monomethod triangles) or by different methods (the heteromethod triangles).

Over the years, researchers have used these "rules of thumb" to interpret the outcome of MTMMM research. Since its introduction, the technique has stimulated more than 2,000 published studies. Even so, considerable controversy still surrounds the question of the proper statistical method to decompose the matrix, but these issues will not concern us here (for discussion of some of the issues involved in the analysis of the MTMMM, see Crano, 2000; Marsh & Bailey, 1991; Schmitt, Coyle, & Saari, 1977; Schmitt & Stults, 1986). In a reprise of their technique more than 30 years after its publication, Fiske and Campbell (1992) avoided the statistical slugfest surrounding the technique and instead observed that the "criteria proposed in the original article seems like a sound first step, especially when one has an extended research program and sees the particular matrix as only a step toward constructing an improved set of measuring procedures" (p. 394). This is sound advice. It reemphasizes the procedural nature of validity, the need for continual assessment and refinement of instruments, and the fact that validity ultimately is a data-informed judgment, not a state of being.

Threats to Measurement Validity

The different validation operations we have presented should not be viewed as mutually exclusive. Each of these approaches provides valuable and necessary information, and they should be employed concurrently whenever possible. The aim of each is to supply information that enables construction of more and more refined measures of some psychological or behavioral attribute. It is through such operations that valid measures of theoretically relevant concepts ultimately emerge.

If, as we hold, validity is not an all-or-none property, but rather a relativistic, descriptive quality that indicates the extent to which theoretically expected variations on the attribute of interest are reflected in the obtained measurements, then the more valid the scale, the greater should be this correspondence. We must acknowledge that the score a person receives on a measurement scale is never a pure, totally accurate picture completely determined by the attribute or construct in question, but rather is the product of a complex interaction of many factors, only one of which is the attribute or construct of theoretical interest. Methodologists have identified a number of irrelevant factors that (more or less) systematically influence responses to questionnaires and other self-report measures. It is important that these threats to measurement validity (known variously as *response sets* or *response biases*) be understood and controlled, because they can systematically influence participants' responses and thus lower validity.

Response bias exists to the extent that the measurement operations themselves influence the obtained results. The degree to which data are affected by these measurement artifacts, or by factors that are independent of the construct under consideration, partially determines the scale's validity. At the most extreme level, we could envision a situation of complete invalidity, in which the way that questions are worded totally determines participants' responses, independent of the content or meaning of the items themselves. Under ideal conditions, the opposite is sought: format and question wording are designed so as to be irrelevant, and only the content of the questions determines responses. This ideal is never met, but an understanding of some of the potential threats to attaining this ideal can enhance the degree to which it will be approximated.

Mood

Perhaps not surprisingly, a respondent's mood may have a strong impact on the responses he or she gives to a social query. An interesting example of mood effects is provided by Schwarz and Clore (1983), who asked people to tell them about the quality of their lives. The telephone survey was conducted over a wide geographic area, and some of the respondents were enjoying a bright sunny day when they answered. Others were in a part of the country where it was raining when the survey was done. Quality of life responses were quite different depending on the weather. The more pleasant the weather, the higher the reports of quality of life. Obviously, the quality of one's life may be affected somewhat by weather, but it is enlightening to see how strongly such transitory effects can influence answers to questions that are meant to tap more stable states. In an interesting extension of their research, Schwarz and Clore (1983) asked some of their respondents what the weather was like before beginning their questionnaire. Among these respondents, weather had no effect on quality of life responses. Why? Presumably because when the source of their transitory mood state was brought to mind, they were able to discount it when answering the survey. This same result has been replicated in many different studies. When German respondents were asked to report on the quality of their lives, for example, they reported much higher quality of life scores if the German national soccer team had won their games in the World Cup Playoffs than if they had lost (Schwarz, Strack, Kommer, & Wagner, 1987).

Social Desirability

In many measures of social variables, the respondent is asked to present a self-report concerning some more-or-less important belief, value, attitude, or behavior. There are some situations in which an individual's actual beliefs, values, attitudes, and/or behaviors are not aligned with those approved by common social norms. Under such conditions, the respondent might be tempted to respond in a "socially desirable" way by misrepresenting true feelings and responding in a manner that is consistent with social mores. Variations in respondents' sensitivity to the demands of social desirability, or differences in people's perceptions of what is and is not socially desirable, can invalidate a scale. The findings of many early surveys of adolescent sexual behavior offer a good illustration of this point. In many of these reports, we discovered that a high proportion of adolescent men had engaged in sexual intercourse, whereas relatively few women of this age had done so. Such findings suggest a number of interesting possibilities: It could be that a small number of dedicated women were indeed picking up the slack for their less-active sisters. It is more likely, however, that the cultural values approving sexually experienced males and virginal females were well learned by the time a person reached adolescence, and respondents' reports of their activities were at least in part a function of these learned values, rather than of actual behavior.

In attempting to solve the problems that a bias of this type can generate, it is useful to speculate on the factors that cause it. The social desirability response bias occurs because of a lack of self-knowledge on the part of the respondent, his or her refusal to be completely frank or honest, or both. There is little that can be done when an individual simply does not know himself or herself well enough to give answers based on fact and reality rather than some idealization formed in part by the demands of the society. On the other hand, administering scales anonymously can combat problems attributable to a lack of candor. If respondents can be assured anonymity, it would seem more likely that they would be willing to supply honest answers, even if these answers were contrary to established social beliefs or practices.

Language Difficulty

A more tractable problem arises when a verbal measure uses language that is different from that characteristically employed by the respondent sample. In Wilson and Patterson's (1968) scale of conservative attitudes, for example, the word *apartheid* appears. The definition of this word probably was quite apparent for Wilson's sample of British respondents. Personal experience in attempting to employ this scale in the United States has shown that a widespread understanding of this term cannot be assumed. Because most scales of opinion are intended to be fairly general instruments, capable of being administered to a variety of respondents, it is advisable to determine in advance whether the meaning of the items that constitute the scale is the same as that originally intended. A preliminary interview of respondents drawn from the test population can supply a relatively inexpensive, rapid, and usually accurate determination of the "understandability" of the items on a scale. If the language used is too difficult, or is misinterpreted, an alternate wording should be adopted. In brief, the language of the scale should be adapted so as to fit the language of the respondent group.

Extreme-Response Sets

There is some evidence in the attitude scaling literature suggesting that reliable differences exist among people in terms of their tendency to employ (or to avoid) the extreme response options of rating scales. Some people, it seems, characteristically select the middle parts of scales, whereas others characteristically employ the extremes. Researchers have correlated these response tendencies with intelligence, conservatism, dogmatism, and other personality attributes, but the results of such investigations are not clear-cut. There seems to be no way to design a scale that is impervious to this potential bias; however, we do have available statistical methods to determine the degree to which "extreme-response sets" occur on any given administration (see Nunnally, 1967, pp. 612–613). Research generally suggests that the extreme-response tendency does not greatly affect validity, but it is conceivable that on some issues this bias could have an impact on results. Remember, a bias that skews the responses of only 5–10% of the sample could have a powerful effect on the outcome of a statistical analysis (Crano, 1997).

Acquiescence

People's tendency to acquiesce to, or to agree with, positively worded statements is the final stylistic response trait to be considered. A positively worded statement is one on which agreement indicates a position favorable to the attitude object under investigation. Research indicates that some people characteristically acquiesce or agree with positively worded statements. Known variously as the tendency to "guess true," "acquiesce," "agree," or "yeasay," this variable has generated more research on stylistic biases than any other. This interest was probably stimulated by the development of Adorno's, Frenkel-Brunswik's, Levinson's, and Sanford's (1950) theory of the "authoritarian personality." The California F (for fascism) Scale was one of the principal measurement devices employed in the assessment of authoritarianism, and over time became a very popular scale, being used in hundreds of investigations. Indeed, more than 50 years after the publication of the classic work of Adorno et al. (1950), research interest on authoritarianism and its measurement is still active (Altemeyer, 1988, 1996; Duckitt, Bizumic, Krauss, & Heled, 2010).

All the items on the original F scale were worded positively, and thus higher levels of agreement with the items resulted in high authoritarianism scores. Some researchers hypothesized that the characteristic to agree with positively worded statements, rather than the content of the statements per se, might be responsible for some respondents' authoritarianism scores. Thus, the scale was not measuring authoritarianism so much as it was the tendency to agree with positively worded statements. To test such suspicions, F scales consisting of positively worded items that were designed to be opposite in meaning to the original items were constructed. If item content was the major determinant of respondents' scores, a strong negative correlation between the original and the derivative F scale items would be expected. Instead, substantial *positive* correlations were obtained, thus supporting those who hypothesized the existence of an acquiescence response set.

Results of this type stimulated considerable research, which was focused not only on the F scale but also upon response sets in general (see, for example, Altemeyer, 1988; Block, 1965; Chapman & Campbell, 1957, 1959; Forsman, 1993; Jackson & Messick, 1962; van Herk, Poortinga, & Verhallen, 2004). Much of this research employed item-reversal techniques of the type discussed above. A major conceptual difficulty with this approach is that it is sometimes impossible to know when an item has truly been reversed. Consider the following item:

Capitalism Represents the Most Equitable Economic System.

One might reverse this item by substituting the word socialism or communism for capitalism; another possibility would change the word "equitable" to "inequitable." Still other reversals of the original item are possible, and unfortunately an individual might logically agree or disagree with both the original and its reversal. In the present example, for instance, a respondent might feel that neither capitalism nor socialism nor communism is an equitable economic system. The predicted negative correlation between apparently reversed scales might well not occur given a sufficient number of reversals of this type. In light of the difficulties discussed, such a finding would not necessarily indicate the presence of an acquiescence response bias, but rather the failure to develop good reversals.

Interpretational problems of this type led Rorer (1965) to question the very existence of response sets. In an influential paper, Rorer argued that the response style question was a pseudo-issue and need not be considered a real danger to the validity of scales. This reaction to the complexities and interpretational difficulties of this research area is understandable, but probably too extreme. Campbell, Siegman, and Rees (1967), following Rorer, were able to demonstrate convincingly the presence of response biases in both the F scale and selected subscales of the Minnesota Multiphasic Personality Inventory (MMPI). The effects of these stylistic biases were not great, but this is different from saying that they did not exist (Ferrando, Condon, & Chuico, 2004; Richardson, 2012).

Like all the other set or stylistic biases, that of acquiescence has been shown to be a real phenomenon whose potential effect on the validity of an instrument is not great; however, their impact on the outcome of an analysis could be sufficient to substantially alter the conclusions we might draw from it (Weijters, Geuens, & Schillewaert, 2010). If one is committed to the development of increasingly sensitive, reliable, and valid measurement instruments, even minor distortions should be eliminated. Procedures for reducing acquiescence biases are discussed in Chapter 15.

Conclusion

To construct a measure that can be used to assess people's attitudes, attributes, thought processes, or behavioral predispositions reliably and validly requires substantive knowledge, technical competence, and a certain intuitive feel for the ways that people think and feel and act. Knowledge of correlational statistical techniques is also helpful, and with increasingly sophisticated computer programs available at most research installations today, the computational work involved in these analyses is not technically daunting. Even more so than most areas of measurement research, "learning by doing" is crucial here. One learns how to write good items for an instrument by writing items. One learns how to create good items from practice in developing and phrasing items. Coupled with strong theoretical knowledge of the phenomenon of interest, these experiences in scale construction (see Chapters 15 and 17) contribute to desirable psychometric properties of the new scale.

Questions for Discussion

1. You conducted a laboratory experiment investigating the effects of a perspective taking intervention on participants' attitudes toward outgroup members (e.g., if participants were Democrats, outgroup members would be Republicans). You created a new measure of prejudice because you did not like the established scales. Your results indicated that at Time 1, prejudice scores were similar for the treatment and control groups; however, at Time 2, prejudice scores were slightly, but significantly, lower in the *control* group. How could that be? Could there be something wrong with the way you measured prejudice? How might your knowledge of measurement validity explain these results? What other possibilities can you generate? Discuss the different aspects of measurement validity and how they could have affected your results.
2. Of all the various kinds of validity (predictive, convergent, face, content, discriminant, etc.) are there some forms of validity that are more important than others? Are they all equally important?
3. Describe what is meant by *heterotrait-monomethod, monotrait-heteromethod,* and *heterotrait-heteromethod* in the multitrait-multimethod matrix approach. Explain what these concepts are supposed to assess.

Note

1. One might argue, for example, that compassion is not necessarily indicative of religiousness. That is, non-religious people can be compassionate or not, just as religious people can.

References

Adorno, T. W., Frenkel-Brunswik, E., Levinson, D. J., & Sanford, R. N. (1950). *The authoritarian personality.* New York: Harper.
Altemeyer, B. (1988). *Enemies of freedom: Understanding right-wing authoritarianism.* San Francisco: Jossey-Bass.
Altemeyer, B. (1996). *The authoritarian specter.* Cambridge, MA: Harvard University Press.
Ben-Porath, Y. S. (2012). *Interpreting the MMPI-2-RF.* Minneapolis, MN: University of Minnesota Press.
Block, J. (1965). *The challenge of response sets.* New York: Appleton-Century-Crofts.

Bryant, F. B. (2000). Assessing the validity of measurement. In L. G. Grimm & P. R. Yarnold (Eds.), *Reading and understanding more multivariate statistics* (pp. 99–146). Washington, DC: American Psychological Association.

Campbell, D. T. (1950). The indirect assessment of social attitudes. *Psychological Bulletin, 47*, 15–38.

Campbell, D. T., & Fiske, D. W. (1959). Convergent and discriminant validation by the multitrait-multimethod matrix. *Psychological Bulletin, 56*, 81–105.

Campbell, D. T., Siegman, C. R., & Rees, M. B. (1967). Direction of wording effects in the relationships between scales. *Psychological Bulletin, 68*, 293–303.

Chang, L., Connelly, B. S., & Geeza, A. A. (2012). Separating method factors and higher order traits of the Big Five: A meta-analytic multitrait–multimethod approach. *Journal of Personality and Social Psychology, 102*. 408–426.

Chapman, L. J., & Campbell, D. T. (1957). Response set in the F scale. *Journal of Abnormal and Social Psychology, 54*, 129–132.

Chapman, L. J., & Campbell, D. T. (1959). The effect of acquiescence response-set upon relationships among F scale, ethnocentrism, and intelligence. *Sociometry, 22*, 153–161.

Cook T. D., & Campbell, D. T. (1979). *Quasi-experimentation: Design and analysis issues for field settings*. Chicago: Rand-McNally.

Crano, W. D. (1997). Vested interest, symbolic politics, and attitude-behavior consistency. *Journal of Personality and Social Psychology, 72*, 485–491.

Crano, W. D. (2000). The multitrait-multimethod matrix as synopsis and recapitulation of Campbell's views on the proper conduct of social inquiry. In L. Bickman (Ed.), *Research design: Donald Campbell's legacy* (Ch. 3, pp. 37–61). Beverly Hills, CA: Sage.

DeVellis, R. B. (2012). *Scale development: Theory and applications*. Thousand Oaks, CA: Sage.

Duckitt, J., Bizumic, B., Krauss, S. W., & Heled, E. (2010). A tripartite approach to right-wing authoritarianism: The authoritarianism-conservatism-traditionalism model. *Political Psychology, 31*, 685–715.

Eid, M., & Nussbeck, F. W. (2009). The multitrait-multimethod matrix at 50! *Methodology: European Journal of Research Methods for the Behavioral and Social Sciences, 5*(3), 71.

Ferrando, P. J., Condon, L., & Chico, E. (2004). The convergent validity of acquiescence: An empirical study relating balanced scales and separate acquiescence scales. *Personality and Individual Differences, 37*, 1331–1340.

Fiske, D. W., & Campbell, D. T. (1992). Citations do not solve problems. *Psychological Bulletin, 112*, 393–395.

Forsman, L. (1993). Giving extreme responses to items in self-esteem scales: Response set or personality trait? *European Journal of Psychological Assessment, 9*, 33–40.

Gynther, M. D., Buckhart, B. R., & Hovanitz, C. (1979). Do face-valid items have more predictive validity than subtle items? The case of the MMPI Pd Scale. *Journal of Consulting and Clinical Psychology, 47*, 295–300.

Höfling, V., Schermelleh-Engel, K., & Moosbrugger, H. (2009). Analyzing multitrait-multimethod data: A comparison of three approaches. *Methodology: European Journal of Research Methods for the Behavioral and Social Sciences, 5*, 99–111.

Jackson, D. N., & Messick, S. (1962). Response styles on the MMPI: Comparison of clinical and normal samples. *Journal of Abnormal and Social Psychology, 65*, 285–299.

Marsh, H. W. (1989). Confirmatory factor analyses of multitrait-multimethod data: Many problems and a few solutions. *Applied Psychological Measurement, 13*, 335–361.

Marsh, H. W., & Bailey, M. (1991). Confirmatory factory analyses of multitrait-multimethod data: A comparison of alternative models. *Applied Psychological Measurement, 15*, 47–70.

Messick, S. (1989). Validity. In R. L. Linn (Ed.), *Educational measurement* (3rd ed., pp. 13–103). New York: Macmillan.

Nunnally, J. C. (1967). *Psychometric theory*. New York: McGraw-Hill.

Richardson, J. T. (2012). The role of response biases in the relationship between students' perceptions of their courses and their approaches to studying in higher education. *British Educational Research Journal, 38*, 399–418.

Rorer, L. G. (1965). The great response style myth. *Psychological Bulletin, 63*, 129–156.

Schmitt, N., Coyle, B. W., & Saari, B. B. (1977). A review and critique of analyses of multitrait-multimethod matrices. *Multivariate Behavioral Research, 13*, 447–478.

Schmitt, N., & Stults, D. M. (1986). Methodology review: Analysis of multitrait-multimethod matrices. *Applied Psychological Measurement, 10*, 1–22.

Schwarz, N., & Clore, G. L. (1983). Mood, misattribution, and judgments of well-being: Information and directive functions of affective states. *Journal of Personality and Social Psychology, 45*, 513–523.

Schwarz, N., Strack, F., Kommer, D., & Wagner, D. (1987). Soccer, rooms, and the qualify of your life: Mood effects on judgments of satisfaction with life in general and with specific domains. *European Journal of Social Psychology, 17*, 69–79.

Scullen, S. E. (1999). Using confirmatory factor analysis of correlated uniqueness to estimate method variance in multitrait-multimethod matrices. *Organizational Research Methods, 2*, 275–292.

van Herk, H., Poortinga, Y. H., & Verhallen, T.M.M. (2004). Response styles in rating scales: Evidence of method bias in data from six EU countries. *Journal of Cross-Cultural Psychology, 35*, 346–360.

Weijters, B., Geuens, M., & Schillewaert, N. (2010). The individual consistency of acquiescence and extreme response style in self-report questionnaires. *Applied Psychological Measurement, 34*, 105–121.

Wheeler, S. R., & Austin, J. (2000). The loss response list: A tool for measuring adolescent grief responses. *Death Studies, 24*, 21–34.

Wilson, G. D., & Patterson, J. R. (1968). A new measure of conservatism. *British Journal of Social and Clinical Psychology,* 264–269.

PART II
Research Design Strategies
Experiments, Quasi-Experiments, and Nonexperiments

5
DESIGNING EXPERIMENTS
Variations on the Basics

In Chapter 2 we introduced the concepts of internal and external validity, two important forms of validity to be considered in experiments, and provided some information on the basic structure of an experiment. Here, we expand on this basic structure to consider variations in the ways in which experiments can be designed, set up, and executed.

Basic Variations in Experimental Design

To summarize our earlier discussion, the classic "true experimental design" (Campbell & Stanley, 1963) involves the following steps:

1. Obtaining a pool of participants,
2. Pretesting participants on the dependent variable of interest,
3. Randomly assigning each participant to experimental or control groups,[1]
4. Carefully controlling for differences in the application of the experimental treatment between the two groups, and
5. Remeasuring both groups on the dependent variable at some time following the experimental manipulation.

These steps are diagrammed in Figure 5.1. Variations on this basic structure include elimination of the pretest, the addition of multiple experimental treatments, and the repeated use of the same participants in all conditions of the experiment. In this chapter, we will discuss each of these modifications.

Pretest-Posttest Control Group Design

In the just described **pretest-posttest control group design**, both pretest and posttest are given to participants in control and experimental groups. Pretesting makes it possible to determine that participants assigned to different conditions of the study are initially equivalent in their response to the dependent variable at the outset. Ideally, after random assignment the two groups should be largely the same, on average, in their pretest scores within the limits of chance variation. Random assignment also helps to ensure that both conditions are similar on virtually all unmeasured

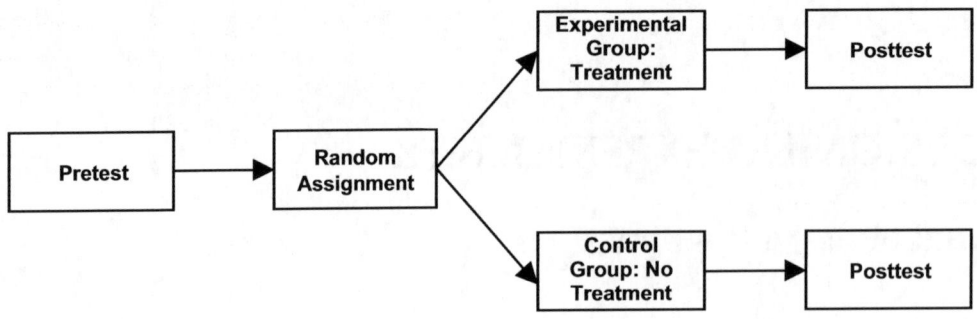

FIGURE 5.1 Pretest–posttest control group design.

extraneous variables. Pretests also serve other purposes in controlling for individual differences, as will be discussed in this chapter and in the quasi-experimental methods of Chapter 10.

Although pretesting has a number of benefits, this design often is altered to offset a potential problem that can be introduced by the pretest itself. This problem is termed **pretest sensitization**, or the possibility that the pretest can make participants in the experimental group unduly reactive to the treatment to which they are exposed. Under these circumstances, the effect of the treatment may be artificially enhanced—the treatment appears stronger, or more effective, than it would be when applied to people who were not exposed to the pretest. It also is possible that the pretest can dampen the effectiveness of a treatment if, for example, it alerts participants to the fact that the experimenter is trying to change their position on an issue and arouses their resistance to such change. Either pretesting effect is especially likely if the pretest is administered in the same session as the experiment itself, just prior to the introduction of the manipulation.

An example may help to clarify the sensitizing bias. Suppose that we administered a pretest of racial attitudes to a large sample of research participants. The treatment is a communication that we hope will influence participants to be less biased in their attitudes toward other racial groups. We administer the treatment and find it to be successful: Participants in the experimental group are much less biased on the posttest measure than are those in the control group (who did not receive the communication), though both groups were identical on pretest attitudes.

From these results we cannot be sure that the experimental communication alone would be an effective means of changing people's racial attitudes. It is possible that the pretest might have sensitized the experimental participants to the treatment and thereby altered its effectiveness as reflected on the posttest. As a result of the pretesting, participants were unintentionally led to ponder the legitimacy of their racial beliefs. Those in the experimental group—already sensitized to the subject—were especially susceptible to the communication when they received it. Participants in the control group might also have been induced to think about their racial attitudes due to the pretest, but because they were not exposed to the communication, they did not show as much attitude change at posttest assessment.

One way to reduce this problem would be to administer the pretest measure some time in advance of the treatment—at least a few days or weeks prior to participation in the experiment itself. Assuming that the participants do not make a strong connection between the earlier testing and the experiment, the passage of time may reduce any sensitization stemming from the pretest measure. However, this does not always work. If the pretest involves an important or emotionally loaded issue (such as the racial attitudes example above, or a measure of self-esteem or self-concept), respondents may ruminate about their responses after they have taken the test. Under these circumstances, it is possible that exposure to the pretest itself leads to a *change* in attitudes over time. Thus, when participants later enter the experiment, the pretest no longer reflects their current attitude or position. Even when this kind of sensitization is unlikely, it is not always possible to administer the pretest at a much earlier time. Participants may only be available for one measurement session.

Posttest-Only Control Group Design

To solve the problem of pretest sensitization, researchers usually eliminate the pretest as part of the experimental design. This is especially likely in experimental contexts in which a pretest would have to be administered in the same session as the experimental treatments and may bias results by sensitizing participants, thereby making them more (or less) susceptible to the treatment. The design solution to this problem is diagrammed in Figure 5.2. In the **posttest-only control group design**, only a posttest but no pretest is given to participants in control and experimental groups. Pretesting is used to determine that participants assigned to conditions were initially "equivalent" on the dependent variable, but random assignment allows the presumption of initial equivalence, by chance, of experimental and control groups. So there is no need for pretesting to establish that the groups are the same prior to the introduction of the experimental treatment. Of course, this assumption rests on the use of a relatively large number of participants. Random assignment of a small pool of participants to the conditions of an experiment is not likely to produce initially equivalent groups on the variable of interest. As a general rule of thumb, we recommend that the pool of participants be large enough to randomly assign at least 25–30 individuals per condition if we wish to take advantage of randomization as a method for achieving initial equivalence of the experimental groups.

Solomon Four-Group Design

The posttest-only control group design has several advantages in reduced cost and effort, along with the avoidance of the pretest sensitization bias. However, it has one disadvantage in that it prevents the researcher from assessing the potential effect of pretesting on the experimental treatment under study. This disadvantage can be overcome by combining both the pretest-posttest and posttest-only control group designs. This is known as the **Solomon four-group design** (Solomon, 1949), used to determine treatment effect of experimental and control groups and the effect of pretest sensitization on the dependent variable. In this variation, participants are randomly assigned to one of four

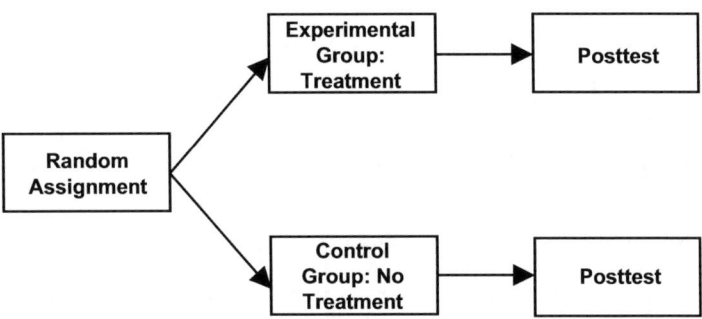

FIGURE 5.2 Posttest–only control group design.

86 Research Design Strategies

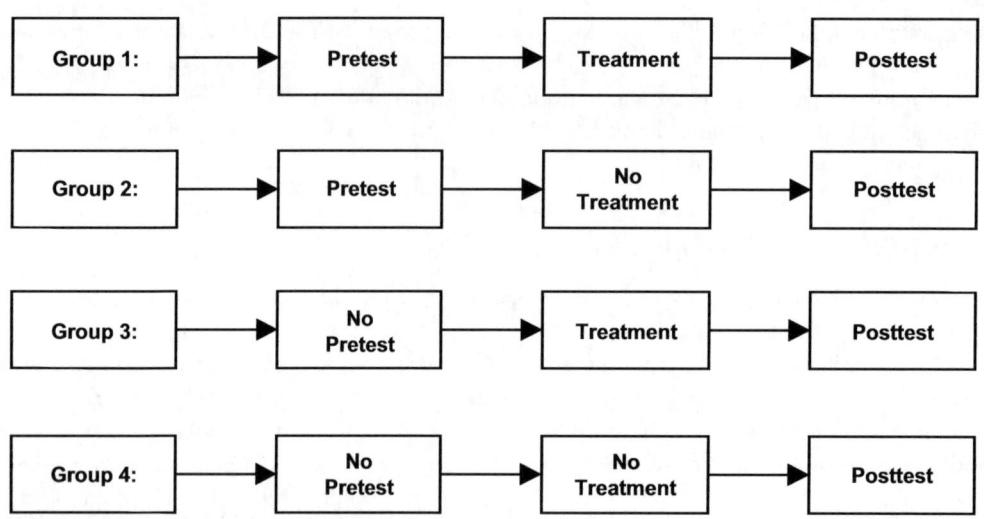

FIGURE 5.3 Solomon four-group design.

groups, two of which are pretested and two of which are not. One of the pretested groups and one of the non-pretested groups are then exposed to the treatment; the other two groups are not, and this produces the division of participants represented in Figure 5.3.

The use of this design permits several effects to be evaluated in the same experiment. Equivalence of groups 1 and 2 on the pretest suggests that the randomization procedure has been effective, and posttest results across all four groups can then be used to assess the effects of both the treatment variable and of pretesting. Any effect of the experimental treatment above and beyond testing and other rival factors can be determined by comparing the posttest results of the two experimental groups (1 and 3) with those of the control groups (2 and 4). Effects of pretesting alone can be obtained by comparing the posttest scores of groups 2 and 4, whereas any effects of pretesting on sensitivity to the experimental treatment can be detected in differences between groups 1 and 3, who have received the same treatment but differ in their prior exposure to a pretest measure.[2]

A good example of the use of the Solomon four-group design is provided by Rau et al. (2010), who investigated the effectiveness of a sexual assault prevention program. The researchers were concerned that the preexisting attitudes of their participants (more than 1,000 Navy men at the completion of their basic training) might influence the results of the program, so they decided to measure these attitudes before the program. However, they also realized that the pretest might sensitize the men to the treatment. To assess both issues, they pretested approximately half the participants before the program began; the remaining participants were not pretested. The prevention program enhanced the subjects' rape knowledge and empathy for rape victims and reduced rape myth acceptance. These results held up even for the non-pretested subjects.

Expanding the Number of Experimental Treatments

So far we have been considering experimental designs in which the independent variable consists of the presence or absence of a single experimental treatment (the treatment-control group design). However, there is no reason that more than one variation of an experimental treatment cannot be made within the same experiment so long as certain rules for enlarging the number of treatments are followed. First, instead of presence vs. absence of the experimental treatment as the basic comparison, we can also perform comparisons with two types of treatment conditions that do not involve a control group. For instance, we might wish to know whether drug A is more effective than drug B in curing infections. This is a legitimate question, and a "no drug" control group need not be used.[3] Furthermore, we may compare groups that have been exposed to different *amounts* or *kinds* of the independent variable. Then, in addition to determining whether the existence (presence or absence) of the treatment makes any difference in the posttest dependent variable, the researcher can determine whether variations in the treatment also make a difference. These variations may be quantitative—different amounts of the variable (e.g., 0 vs. 0.3 cc. vs. 0.6 cc. of a drug, or high vs. medium vs. low payment for an action)—or qualitative—different ways of producing the independent variable (e.g., anxiety induced by social conditions vs. anxiety induced by physical danger). The number of variations of a given experimental treatment (including its absence as represented in a control group) is referred to as the number of *levels* of that variable. Thus, the basic treatment-control group design is a two-level experiment; introducing additional variations of the same experimental treatment (independent variable) expands the design to three, four, or more levels.

Factorial Designs

In addition to adding levels of an experimental treatment, an experiment can also be expanded to include more than one treatment factor. In a **factorial design**, levels of one independent variable or factor are combined with levels of other independent variable(s), to further expand the number of conditions in an experimental design. For complete interpretability of results, these variables should be conjoined so that the levels of each independent variable are combined with all levels of the other(s) to yield the various conditions.

Creating the Design

With a factorial design, we can assess the effects of variation in one independent variable while systematically varying one or more other independent variables as well. Each independent variable manipulated in a factorial design is a "factor," and the number of conditions (or "cells") in the design is equal to the product of the number of levels of all its factors. For a two-factor design, for example, the combined treatments might be as shown in Table 5.1. In this illustration, variable 1 has 5 levels, and variable 2 has 4 levels. This would be designated a 5 × 4 factorial design. It consists of 20 (5 × 4) separate conditions, formed by the factorial combination of the two independent variables.

TABLE 5.1 Two independent variable (5 × 4) factorial design.

		Factor 2			
		Level 1	*Level 2*	*Level 3*	*Level 4*
	Level 1	Condition 1-1	Condition 1-2	Condition 1-3	Condition 1-4
	Level 2	Condition 2-1	Condition 2-2	Condition 2-3	Condition 2-4
Factor 1	*Level 3*	Condition 3-1	Condition 3-2	Condition 3-3	Condition 3-4
	Level 4	Condition 4-1	Condition 4-2	Condition 4-3	Condition 4-4
	Level 5	Condition 5-1	Condition 5-2	Condition 5-3	Condition 5-4

TABLE 5.2 Three independent variable (3 × 2 × 3) factorial design.

			Factor 3		
		Factor 2	Level 1	Level 2	Level 3
Factor 1	Level 1	Level 1	Condition 1-1-1	Condition 1-1-2	Condition 1-1-3
		Level 2	Condition 1-2-1	Condition 1-2-2	Condition 1-2-3
	Level 2	Level 1	Condition 2-1-1	Condition 2-1-2	Condition 2-1-3
		Level 2	Condition 2-2-1	Condition 2-2-2	Condition 2-2-3
	Level 3	Level 1	Condition 3-1-1	Condition 3-1-2	Condition 3-1-3
		Level 2	Condition 3-2-1	Condition 3-2-2	Condition 3-2-3

For a three-factor design, the two-factor case is repeated for each level of the third factor, as in Table 5.2. Theoretically, the number of variables that can be combined in one experiment is limitless. Note, however, that the number of treatment groups, and therefore the number of participants required, increases multiplicatively as independent variables are added to the design. This fact automatically places some practical limits on the number of independent variables that can be included in any single study. Table 5.2, for example, presents a 3 × 2 × 3 factorial design. Randomly assigning 25 participants to each cell of the design would require 450 participants, the product of 25 × 3 × 2 × 3. If we wished to add another factor involving 3 levels to the design and still maintain the same number (25) of participants per cell, we would need exactly 3 times as many participants, as in the 3-way (3 × 2 × 3) design of the table. Obviously, then, there are practical constraints on the number of conditions that can be run in a factorial design, so both the number of factors and the number of levels of each factor must be limited by available resources.

It is preferable, but not mandatory, that the same number of participants be used in each of the cells of the design, which represent the various combinations of levels of independent variables. Then the effect of any single independent variable can be obtained by comparing dependent variable scores of all participants who were exposed to the first level of that independent variable with those exposed to the second level, the third level, and so on. A **main effect** is evidenced if overall mean differences are observed on a dependent measure as a function of one independent variable while holding constant all levels of the other independent variable(s). Thus, equivalence of groups is maintained because an equal number of participants in all levels of the independent variable have been exposed to each of the levels of the other independent variables.[4]

Factor Independence

Just as random assignment to experimental conditions presumes control over exposure to the independent variable, factorial designs presume that two or more experimental factors can be manipulated *independently*. Sometimes, however, the nature of two variables is such that the levels of one cannot be independent of the other. Suppose, for example, that one wanted to study the effects of high or low anxiety-producing conditions in combination with the physical attractiveness of an experimenter on the dependent measure, the complexity of children's speech. Suppose further that our experiment required that anxiety be induced by the behavior of the experimenter. In such a design, it is unlikely that the two "independent" variables could be independently manipulated, because it is not reasonable to expect that participants would find a person who was practically scaring them to death as physically attractive. This example indicates the importance of going beyond the mere mechanics of factorializing. Some thought is required in combining independent variables to ensure that meaningful experimental conditions have been created. Although almost any set of independent variables can be combined on paper, the way they are perceived by our participants is critical.

Treatment Interaction Effects

There are a number of reasons why we might want to expand an experiment beyond a single independent variable. One of the most important of these is to allow for the identification of interaction effects, which are discussed later in this chapter. Conceptually, interaction effects are relatively easy to illustrate. For example, suppose we are interested in manipulating both information about group consensus and the self-relevance of an issue to observe their combined effects on personal opinions and beliefs. We believe that high consensus will shape group members' opinions rather strongly, but only when the issue at hand is not highly self-relevant to the participant. When the issue is highly self-relevant, group members will resist the apparent consensus, and may even go so far as to adopt a more radical anti-group opinion than they held before the consensus became known. They might respond in this way because they resent the apparent restriction on their personal freedom that the consensus estimate implies (Burgoon, Alvaro, Grandpre, & Voloudakis, 2002). Low group consensus, on the other hand, is not expected to have much impact, no matter the self-relevance of the issue. We could not test this hypothesis by manipulating only one independent variable, so we combine two of them in a factorial design. The patterns of mean differences found in the dependent variable that occur in the high self-relevance condition as a consequence of high or low consensus would be contrasted with those that occur when self-relevance is low.

A second important reason to combine factors is to enhance the power of our designs to detect theoretically meaningful differences. The variance of a factor on a dependent variable is controlled, or accounted for, when that factor is a part of the experimental design. If the factor is not a part of the design (i.e., not systematically manipulated by the researcher), its variation is unexplained and must be classed as error or "unaccounted for" variance in the dependent variable This unaccounted error variance lowers the power of our design to detect differences between groups, and hence may lead to Type II error, mistakenly failing to reject the null hypothesis (Chapter 2). To return to our example, suppose that we did not consider self-relevance but rather hypothesized that high group consensus would have a strong persuasive effect on group members' beliefs. Our prediction would be confirmed if we happened to use issues that participants did not find highly self-relevant. However, if we had stumbled on highly self-relevant issues for our participants, our hypothesis would be disconfirmed. By adding self-relevance to the experimental design, we have controlled and explained the variation of this factor on the outcome, and created a more comprehensive and fine-grained theoretical view of the effects of consensus on group members' expressed beliefs. Moreover, the overall Type II error rate of our experiment has been lowered, and our consequent statistical power to detect real differences has been enhanced.

Solomon Four-Group Design: An Example

We have already considered one 2 × 2 factorial design in our discussion of the use of pretesting in experiments. In the Solomon four-group design, discussed earlier, two factors are systematically manipulated—presence or absence of a pretest, and presence or absence of the experimental treatment—each with two levels. Thus, the Solomon four-group design depicted in Figure 5.3 can be rewritten in factorial form, as in Table 5.3. Using this design, the overall main effect of having received the experimental treatment versus not receiving it (ignoring pretesting conditions) is obtained by comparing posttest mean scores of participants in row 1 (groups 1 and 3) with those

TABLE 5.3 Solomon four-group design as a 2 × 2 factorial of treatement levels and pretest levels.

		Pretest Main Effect	
		Pretest	No Pretest
Treatment	Treatment	Group 1	Group 3
Main Effect	No Treatment	Group 2	Group 4

in row 2 (groups 2 and 4) of the table. The overall main effect of pretesting on posttest scores is obtained by comparing participants in column 1 (groups 1 and 2) with those in column 2 (groups 3 and 4). In obtaining the treatment effect, we can ignore the effect of the pretesting factor because both treatment and control groups have equal numbers of randomly assigned participants who have been pretested or not pretested. Thus, pretesting effects have been "held constant" across the two treatment conditions. The same logic holds when we wish to consider the main effect of the pretesting factor independent of the treatment factor. As can be seen among the pretested group, an equal number of participants served in the treatment and control conditions, and this equality is found in the non-pretested group as well. Thus, treatment variations "cancel out" when assessing the main effects of pretesting. Finally, the pretest-sensitization effect can be assessed by examining the *interaction* between the pretest factor and the treatment factor, as discussed in the following section.

Interaction Effects

We have shown how a factorial design allows us to examine the effect of each independent variable with the effects of all other independent variables controlled, or held constant. The overall effect of each variable is called the main effect of that factor (i.e., the effect of variations in the levels of that factor, when variations in the other factor have been systematically controlled). As noted, the main effect of each variable can be detected with greater power and efficiency when other influential variables have been systematically controlled or manipulated in a factorial design, rather than being allowed to vary naturally. However, the primary advantage of the use of factorial designs in which two or more experimental factors are combined lies in the opportunity to detect an **interaction effect**, evidenced if the effect of an independent variable on a dependent variable is altered or moderated by variations in the level of other independent variable(s), while controlling for the main effects.

The combination of the pretest sensitization factor and treatment factor, discussed earlier in this chapter, is an example of a type of interaction effect. In the four-group design depicted in Table 5.3, sensitization might potentially produce differences in the effect of the treatment depending on whether the pretest had been present or not. In this case, the mean difference between group 1 and group 2 (pretest present) might be *greater* than the mean difference between group 3 and group 4 (no pretest). That would indicate that the pretest sensitized participants in such a way as to enhance the effect of the treatment manipulation. Thus, the effect of the treatment or no treatment is altered by the presence or absence of pretesting.

To return to an earlier example, suppose we wanted to test the effects of a sexual assault prevention program on Navy enlistees. We wanted to pretest all participants to ensure that those who received the program did not differ initially from those who did not. However, we were afraid that the pretest might sensitize the enlistees to the intervention. To test this possibility, along with the central question—the treatment's efficacy—we factorially combine administration (or

TABLE 5.4 Mean "Empathy for Rape Victim" scores as a function of pretest administration and participation in the sexual assault prevention program.

		Pretest Main Effect		
		Pretest	No Pretest	
Treatment	Prevention Treatment	20	5	12.5
Main Effect	No Treatment	5	5	
		12.5	5	5

non-administration) of the pretest with either participation in the prevention program or some other (control) activity. The dependent measure consists of a scale of empathy for rape victims, whose score can range from 0 to 30.

We analyze these scores and find two statistically significant main effects: As shown in Table 5.4, we see that those who received the sexual assault prevention program were significantly more empathic toward rape victims than those who did not. This main effect suggests that the treatment worked as we had hoped. However, in addition to the statistically significant treatment main effect, we also find a main effect of pretest. On inspecting the means, we see that those who received the pretest were significantly more empathic than those who did not. However, looking carefully at results in Table 5.4, we notice something interesting, namely that three of the four groups had identical mean scores. Empathy scores were enhanced by the treatment only if the participants had received the pretest. The main effect of the prevention was qualified by the level of another variable, in this case the presence or absence of the pretest. This "qualification" of one variable's effect by another is called an interaction effect, which supplies considerably more valid insights into the efficacy of the prevention treatment program than either of the two independent variables considered in isolation.

In this example, the interaction effect obtained in our Solomon four-group example is important for both theoretical and methodological reasons. For methodological reasons, it was important to know that the pretest apparently sensitized participants to the treatment. For theoretical reasons, it was important to learn whether the treatment had an effect when administered without a measure that sensitized participants to it.

The Solomon design is not used often in social science research, in part because the issue of pretest sensitization often does not arise. However, understanding how levels of one manipulated variable affect participants' reactions to different levels of other independent variables is an almost constant feature of experimental research. Predicting and understanding interactions between and among variables is crucial to enlarging our understanding. Almost always, study of the interactions among variables of theoretical interest enhances our understanding of the phenomena we are investigating. For example, suppose we were interested in the effects of various styles of leadership on the productivity of small work groups, and further theorized that the stress of outside competition influenced these leadership effects. To address this issue, we might design an experiment in which four-person groups were assembled, given tools, materials, and instructions, and tasked with producing widgets.

The groups could be set up so that each group's leader was trained to act in either a democratic or an authoritarian manner. Leadership style thus becomes an experimental treatment, or factor, with two levels. The second factor, which we label competitive stress, has three levels. This factor is created by informing participants that they are competing with an outside company, whose production figures are made available to them. The sales information the groups receive is the second

TABLE 5.5 Mean number of widgets produced as a function of leadership style and competitive stress: Example of a cross-over interaction.

		Competitive Stress			
		Low	Medium	High	
Leadership Style	Democratic	25	35	45	35
	Authoritarian	45	35	25	35
		35	35	35	

independent variable. It indicates that the "other" company always seemed much more productive, about as productive as, or much less productive than the participants' own work group. To enliven the proceedings, we could promise a $500 prize to the most productive group. Notice that all participants are promised this reward, so it is a constant across groups, and thus it is not an experimental treatment (or independent variable).

By combining these two independent variables factorially, the experiment takes the form of a 2 (democratic vs. authoritarian leadership) × 3 (low, medium, or high competitive stress) factorial design. In this setup, instead of using individual participants, the productivity of each 4-person work group is the unit of analysis. The number of widgets produced by each work group in each of the 6 groups formed by the factorial combination of the 2 independent variables is the study's index of group productivity, the dependent measure. Suppose that we randomly assigned 15 groups (of 4 workers each) to each of the 6 conditions formed by the factorial combination of our 2 experimental factors. The average group's productivity in each condition is depicted in Table 5.5. A quick scan of the results indicates that neither the leadership nor the stress factors alone produced a substantial main effect: Across the 2 levels of leadership style, the groups exposed to high competitive stress produced 35 pieces of widgets on average, just as did each of the groups exposed to medium and low stress. Similarly, the democratically run groups produced 35 widgets on average, neither more nor less than the authoritarian groups.

Although there is no evidence of a main effect for either independent variable on the dependent variable, by simply looking at the data pattern (always a good idea) it becomes clear that the manipulations did influence widget productivity. Leadership style per se had no differential impact on productivity, but *in combination with* levels of competitive stress, its influence on productivity was qualified. The interaction of these two independent variables on the dependent variable suggests that under the condition of low stress, a democratically structured group will out-produce groups led in a more authoritarian fashion. However, as the stress of competition increases, the authoritarian group increased productivity, whereas the democratic group became less productive. Because of this interaction effect, we cannot specify the nature of the effect of leadership style on production without knowing the competitive stress conditions under which the work group is operating.

Common Forms of Interaction Effects

Interactions can take many different forms. The most common interaction forms are *divergent* interactions and *crossover* interactions. The productivity data of Table 5.5 provide an illustration of a crossover form of interaction. The basis for this terminology is evident from the graphic portrayal of the results in Figure 5.4. As shown in this figure, the productivity levels of the authoritarian and democratic groups cross over, in this case at the medium level of competitive stress.

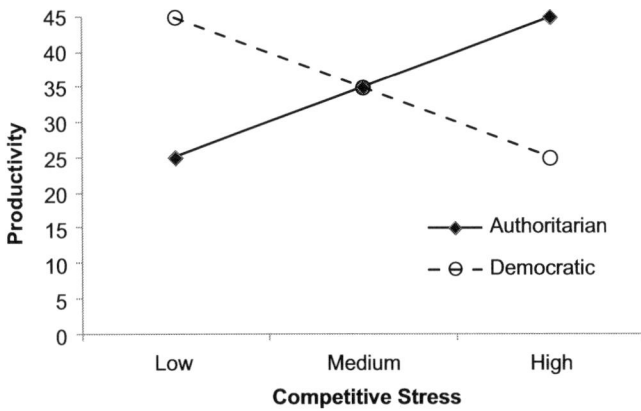

FIGURE 5.4 Effects of competitive stress and leadership style on productivity (see Table 5.5).

TABLE 5.6 Mean number of widgets produced as a function of leadership style and competitive stress: Example of a divergent interaction.

		Competitive Stress			
		Low	Medium	High	
Leadership Style	Authoritarian	25	35	45	35
	Democratic	25	15	5	15
		25	25	25	

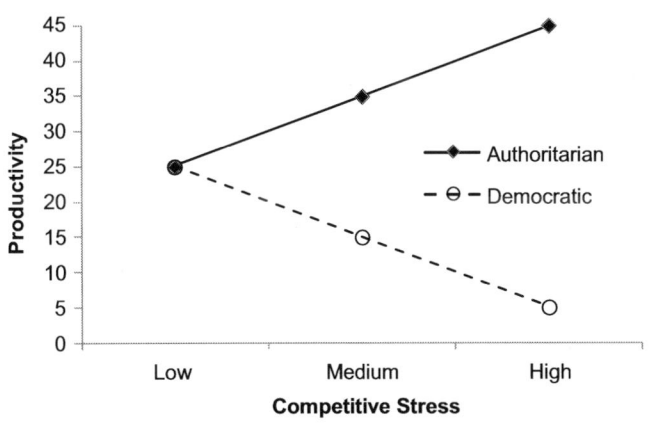

FIGURE 5.5 Effects of competitive stress and leadership style on productivity (see Table 5.6).

A divergent interaction effect is illustrated in the data of Table 5.6, which is depicted graphically in Figure 5.5. Note that the divergent effect could just as well take on the appearance of a *convergent* interaction if the levels of competitive stress were reversed—that is, if the high level was presented first and the low level last on the horizontal axis. Convergent and divergent interactions are simply alternative forms of the same interaction effect.

As shown in this illustration, democratic and authoritarian groups are equally productive under low levels of stress, but as stress increases, the production rates of the groups diverge: The democratic groups become less productive, the authoritarian groups more productive. A main effect of leadership style also becomes evident in this example—across stress conditions, the authoritarian groups produced more widgets overall than did the democratic groups. However, interpretation of this main effect has to be tempered in light of the interaction effect obtained. Authoritarian groups did not outproduce democratic groups under all conditions, only when competitive stress was medium or high.

Moderator Variables as Interaction Effects

In our discussion of causal relationships in Chapter 2, we discussed the role of moderator variables. Recall that a moderator is a factor that alters (inhibits or enhances) the effects of a particular independent variable on a dependent variable. That is, the causal relationship between A and B is modified by the presence or absence of a third variable, C. When both A and C are included in an experimental design as factorially combined independent variables, we can test whether A and C interact in determining the outcome on the dependent measure. The presence of an interaction, in effect, is a test of the moderator variable hypothesis. Thus, in our productivity example, we can say that the causal effect of authoritarian vs. democratic leadership style was *moderated by* competitive stress. That is, the level of stress influences whether or not leadership style has a positive effect on group productivity.

In this example, the moderator variable is an environmental condition that can be manipulated by the experimenter and is subject to random assignment. In many cases, however, a hypothesized moderator variable is a trait or characteristic of individuals that cannot be manipulated or controlled by an experimenter. For example, the effectiveness of democratic leadership may be influenced by group members' high or low need for structure. Those who are low in need for structure may perform better under a democratic leader than under authoritarian leadership, whereas those high in need for structure may not do as well under democratic leadership. Because need for structure is a personal characteristic that is not under experimenter control, it cannot be manipulated as an independent variable. But the possibility of an interaction between leadership style and the need for structure can still be tested by measuring participants' need for structure and then using level of need as a *blocking variable*, as discussed in the next section.

Blocked Designs: Incorporating a Nonexperimental Factor

As was mentioned, the effectiveness of random assignment in creating initial equivalence among our various experimental conditions depends upon the "law of large numbers." Only when a large pool of participants is available can random placement guarantee a "cancelling out" of uncontrolled sources of variations across cells of the experimental design. If the initial pool of participants is relatively small and diverse, the researcher may be concerned that randomization may not distribute participants evenly among groups. When only a small initial pool is available, and particularly when this pool includes a few extreme cases, random assignment may not produce the desired equivalence between conditions. Another scenario preventing random assignment occurs when a factor cannot be manipulated because it is difficult to do so, or when doing so violates ethical guidelines. Generally, researchers are unable to manipulate subject variables such as participant intelligence, sex, height, or country of birth. When this is the case, or when it is desirable to gain greater control over these non-manipulated sources of variation, participants may be sorted into categories *before* assignment to experimental groups. This variation in the procedure of random assignment is called a "blocked" design.

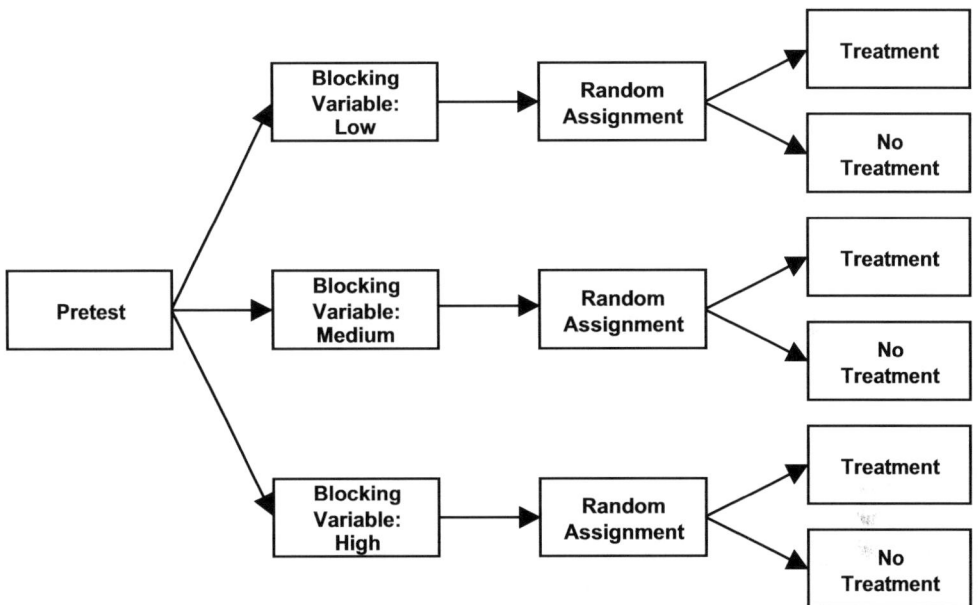

FIGURE 5.6 3 × 2 design of blocked variable and experimental variable.

In blocked designs, the participant pool is first "blocked" or ordered according to levels on some relevant variable (for example, dividing participants into groups of high, medium, or low on some measure of intelligence, or sorting participants by sex). Then, *from within each of these groupings*, participants are randomly assigned to experimental and control groups so that each group is intended to have an equal number of members for each level of the blocked variable. As long as this assignment of pre-classified participants is determined by chance, the assumption of random assignment is not violated and the initial equivalence of experimental groups is assured. One form of a blocked design makes use of a pretest on the dependent variable (usually a pretest that has been administered sometime prior to the experimental session). All participants in the pool are first categorized into groups based on pretest scores. Then participants within each of the groups, or blocks, are randomly assigned to experimental and control conditions, as diagrammed in Figure 5.6.

A blocked design is a form of factorial design. The blocking factor is crossed with the experimental factor (or factors, if there is more than one independent variable). A design consisting of a mixture of manipulated and non-manipulated variables is known as a "mixed" factorial design. Experimental factors are those that can be manipulated by the researcher, or randomly assigned to participants. Blocking variables are not manipulated or randomly assigned—they are characteristics with which the participant comes to the experiment. Blocking increases experimental control by assuring that differences among participants on the blocked variable are approximately equalized across experimental conditions. In terms of interpretation of main effects, causal inferences could be made regarding the effect of the experimental factor, but not the blocked factor, on the dependent variable. Systematic differences related to the blocked factor are said to be associated with the dependent measure, but not necessarily in a causal fashion.

Blocking also permits testing interactions between the experimental variable and participant characteristics. For instance, it may be that the effectiveness of a particular persuasive communication depends on the level of intelligence of those who hear it. A complex argument may be processed, understood, and accepted by recipients who are high in intelligence but misunderstood or rejected by those with lower levels of intellectual capacity or cognitive skills (see McGuire, 1997; Rhodes & Wood, 1992). A simplistic argument, on the other hand, may appeal to people of average intelligence but be dismissed by high IQ individuals. If intelligence of the audience is ignored, it may appear that across all participants no difference is found in the effectiveness of complex or simple arguments. However, if participant intelligence is measured before the experimental communication is delivered, and participants are then divided into high, medium, and low IQ blocks prior to random assignment, differences in effectiveness of the two types of communication could be observed between the different IQ groups. Using a blocked variable may enable us to learn more about the intelligence conditions under which different types of communication are effective. In this example, intelligence can be recognized as a *moderator variable*, as discussed earlier. The presence of an interaction between IQ level and message complexity means that the effect of complexity on attitude change is altered by whether the recipient is high or low in intelligence

It also is possible to conduct a fully blocked design using a variant of the experimental designs discussed in this chapter. Due to ethical and practical restrictions on the capacity to manipulate some types of variables and attributes, (e.g., participant demographic characteristics), the research might involve only blocked variables, which technically reduces it to a nonexperimental design. Such a study might involve, for example, a 2 × 2 factorial combination of participants' gender and intelligence level as factors affecting performance on a verbal ability test. Neither of these factors are "independent" of co-occurring extraneous variables that may be responsible for confounding the observed differences in verbal ability between gender groups. For example, because women may tend to be better listeners or more attentive in speech acquisition, these unmeasured confounds, rather than gender, may be responsible for higher verbal ability in women over men. Although blocked variables may be used as factors in an experimental design, such designs do not have the internal validity of a "true" experiment because participants are not randomly assigned to levels of the factors. Thus, the ability to make cause-and-effect conclusions about the relationship between the design factors and the dependent variables is limited.

Repeated-Measures Designs and Counterbalancing

In most experimental designs, each participant is exposed to one and only one condition. Although a condition may represent the factorial combination of a number of experimental treatments, it is still true that each participant is assigned to only one cell of the experimental design, in which the independent variable is known as a *between-subjects factor*. However, the same participants may be exposed to more than one level of an independent variable or combination of treatment conditions. This is known as a **repeated-measures design**, as the same participants are repeatedly measured on the dependent variable, usually after each treatment exposure in each level of the independent variable(s). An independent variable manipulated in this way is called a *within-subjects factor*.

The pretest-posttest control group design is an example of a repeated-measures design. In this design, all participants are measured on the dependent variable, once prior to the treatment and then again after they have been exposed to the independent (treatment) variable. Thus, the pretest can be used as a no-treatment base of comparison for assessing the treatment effect as reflected in the posttest. In other types of repeated-measures experiments, all participants are exposed to a series of different treatment conditions, one after another, and the dependent variable is administered after each exposure. Every participant may be exposed to all possible treatments in a predetermined order, or better yet, to minimize carryover effects of any single order, they may be randomly assigned to different sequences of treatment orderings.

Just as pretest sensitization effects can influence the results of a pretest-posttest experiment, the effects of one level of a treatment may carry over in some way to influence the effects of succeeding treatments. Thus, the order in which treatments in a repeated-measures study are administered may have a major effect on its results. There is no way that order effects can be eliminated from the pretest-posttest design because, by definition, the pretest measure has to be taken first, before any other experimental treatment is administered. With successive treatments, however, varying the order in which different participants receive the various treatments can control for the impact of treatment order effects. For maximum interpretability of results not confounded by a particular treatment sequence, the same set of treatments should be presented to different participants in *counterbalanced* order.

In **complete counterbalancing**, to control for treatment order effects sequences involving every combination of treatment orderings are determined, with each participant randomly assigned to one of the sequences. If a study involves only two conditions, complete counterbalancing is manageable. Half the sample could be assigned to receive the first treatment, followed by the second treatment. The remaining half of the sample would receive the treatments in reversed order. Participants are measured on the dependent variable after receipt of each treatment. Repeated-measures designs may entail more than two treatment levels from an independent variable, but counterbalancing then becomes more complex and rather unwieldy. To control for order effects in such cases, **partial counterbalancing** is a compromise to complete counterbalancing that uses a *Latin square* design to take into account the fact that it may be cumbersome to assign participants to every possible sequence of treatment orderings.

For instance, if each participant is to be exposed to four different messages—one from a pleasant communicator (treatment A), one from a neutral source (B), one from an unpleasant communicator (C), and one for whom no source is identified (D)—a counterbalanced ordering could be achieved by varying the order (or sequence of presentation) as in Table 5.7. In this particular scenario, after exposure to each treatment message, participants are immediately measured on the dependent variable four times. The dependent variable is used to determine if there are changes in mean scores from treatment to treatment.

Notice that partial counterbalancing does not involve using every possible order of all conditions (for designs with four or more treatments, this would run into a nearly unmanageable number of combinations). The requirements of partial counterbalancing are met if: (1) Each treatment occurs once and only once in each position, and (2) Each treatment is immediately preceded by every other treatment once and only once across the presentation orderings. In our four-condition example, treatment A is the first treatment (in sequence 1), preceded once by B (sequence 4), once

TABLE 5.7 A partially counterbalanced design.

		Order of Communication Treatment			
		1st	2nd	3rd	4th
	1	A	B	C	D
Sequence	2	B	D	A	C
	3	C	A	D	B
	4	D	C	B	A

by C (sequence 3), and once by D (sequence 2). The only other requirement for partial counterbalancing is that the number of participants randomly assigned to each sequence be equal, so that each ordering is used an equal number of times. Using this procedure, each sequence of participants receives one of the different orderings, and sequence becomes a type of blocking variable in the overall experimental design. When counterbalancing is used in a repeated-measures design, researchers are not interested in whether the four sequences yield different mean scores, but rather are interested in the mean differences obtained among the four treatments, after collapsing results across the different sequences.

Repeated-measures designs with counterbalancing have the advantage of assuring the equivalence of groups exposed to different treatments because each participant, in effect, serves as his or her own "control group." Because participants are exposed to all possible conditions, participant differences in characteristics and attributes across conditions are held constant, and if counterbalancing is successful, any observed differences across conditions should be attributable to receipt of the different treatments. However, repeated use of the same participants is just not possible for all types of experimental variables. In many cases, one level or combination of variables would severely interfere with, or preclude, administering any other treatment combinations. For some variables, effects are cumulative. In studies involving intake of different amounts of drugs or alcohol, for instance, the experimenter could not administer a second dosage level to the same participant until all traces of the first dose were eliminated from that participant's system; otherwise the repeated doses would accumulate and obliterate any differences in the effects of dose level. Other experimental treatments are such that once participants have been exposed to one of them, their fatigue, level of awareness of experimental purposes or procedures, or lack of naiveté may make them unsuited for use in further experimental conditions. However, there are some types of experimental manipulations that lend themselves to repeated-measures designs more readily. For instance, people in real life often are exposed to information about several different persons or to multiple news stories in succession on a particular topic. So in experiments where the independent variable involves different content of information about persons or events, exposing the same participant to different levels of the manipulation may be reasonable. Even in these cases, however, the order in which a particular condition is received may make a difference, but counterbalanced design makes it possible to assess such order effects and take them into account in interpreting the effects of the experimental treatment(s).

Conclusion

In this chapter we have started with the basic two-group pretest-posttest experimental design and demonstrated how elements can be added to or subtracted from that basic design to create useful variations in the structure of an experiment. The levels of an independent variable can be expanded from two conditions to multiple variations. More than one independent variable can be manipulated in an experiment using factorial designs. Pretesting can be excluded or included, and used either as a blocking variable or in a repeated-measures design. Deciding among these different design features must be done on the basis of the purposes of the experiment (including theories about potential interaction effects among different variables) and one's knowledge or intuitions about factors such as sensitization, carryover, and order effects.

Whichever form the experimental design takes, the design stage is still just the blueprint of the experiment itself. The design tells us what variables are being manipulated, at how many different levels, and in what combinations. Once this blueprint has been put into place, the real task is constructing the conditions and procedures through which the intended design will be implemented—i.e., the *operations* of the experiment. As with any construction, building each experiment always involves some unique features, decisions to be made, and problems to solve. However, there are some general principles and guidelines for constructing experimental procedures that can help maximize the internal validity of the results of the experiment and contribute to external validity as well. The following chapter covers some of these general principles in a step-by-step approach to conducting a laboratory experiment.

Questions for Discussion

1. Your advisor conducted a study on decision-making using a 2 (mood prime: negative, positive) × 2 (physiological arousal: adrenaline injection, saline solution injection) factorial design, and had a final sample of 80 participants. However, upon further investigation, you realized that half of participants, randomly chosen, were administered a questionnaire about their attitudes toward authority figures before the primary dependent measure, and half completed the attitudinal questionnaire after the primary dependent measure. How would you describe this design? Is it possible in this study to obtain a statistically significant 3-way interaction, even if there are no significant main effects or 2-way interactions? Do you have sufficient power to obtain a significant 3-way interaction? Is it ever appropriate to divide participants into additional groups or categories after all data have been collected? Why?
2. Using a modified pretest-posttest control group design, you investigated the effects of participants' gender and an experimental intervention on reducing prejudice toward people who are obese. Could this study use a Solomon four-group design? How?
3. What advantages and disadvantages should you consider when considering use of a Solomon four-group design in your research?

Notes

1. In much of our discussion, we assume that experiments are conducted with individual persons as the unit of analysis. However, in some cases, experimental treatments are delivered not to individuals independently assigned to groups, but to groups of persons (e.g., small work groups or even whole classrooms) randomly assigned to one or another condition of the experiment. In this case, the group, rather than the component individuals within the group, becomes the unit of analysis. More discussion of the issue of randomizing individuals or groups will be provided in Chapters 6 and 17.
2. A review of research (Lana, 1959) making use of this four-group design indicated that loss of generalizability of findings because of pretesting effects was minimal. However, Rosnow and Suls (1970) found that the pretesting effect operates differentially in groups of volunteer and nonvolunteer subjects. Because this issue remains unresolved, investigators are urged to exercise caution when interpreting studies that make use of pretests, especially in contexts in which pretest sensitization is a reasonable possibility.
3. However, by not having a control group, it is impossible to determine whether either drug is more effective than nothing at all.
4. Strictly speaking, we can employ different numbers of subjects in the various treatment combinations of a factorial design, and at times this may be desirable. If certain assumptions of proportionality are met, common statistical techniques (e.g., Winer, 1971) will allow us to estimate treatment effects. However, both analysis and interpretation are simplified when an equal number of participants are employed in each condition.

References

Burgoon, M., Alvaro, E. M., Grandpre, J., & Voloudakis, M. (2002). Revisiting the theory of psychological reactance: Communicating threats to attitudinal freedom. In J. Dillard & M. Pfau (Eds.), *Handbook of persuasion* (pp. 213–232). Beverly Hills, CA: Sage.
Campbell, D. T., & Stanley, J. C. (1963). Experimental and quasi-experimental designs for research on teaching. In N. L. Gage (Ed.), *Handbook of research on teaching* (171–246). Boston: Houghton Mifflin.

Lana, R. E. (1959). Pretest-treatment interaction effects in attitude studies. *Psychological Bulletin, 56*, 293–300.

McGuire, W. J. (1997). Creative hypothesis generating in psychology: Some useful heuristics. *Annual Review of Psychology, 48*, 1–30.

Rau, T. J., Merrill, L. L., McWhorter, S. K., Stander, V. A., Thomsen, C. J., Dyslin, C. W., ... & Milner, J. S. (2010). Evaluation of a sexual assault education/prevention program for male U.S. Navy personnel. *Military Medicine, 175*, 429–434.

Rhodes, N., & Wood, W. (1992). Self-esteem and intelligence affect influenceability: The mediating role of message reception. *Psychological Bulletin, 111*, 156–171.

Rosnow, R. L., & Suls, J. M. (1970). Reactive effects of pretesting in attitude research. *Journal of Personality and Social Psychology, 15*, 338–343.

Solomon, R. L. (1949). An extension of control group design. *Psychological Bulletin, 46*, 137–150.

Winer, B. J. (1971). *Statistical principles in experimental design* (2nd ed.). New York: McGraw-Hill.

6
CONSTRUCTING LABORATORY EXPERIMENTS

In the preceding chapter, we discussed the design of experimental studies at a relatively abstract level to introduce basic principles of planning and constructing a laboratory experiment. In the present chapter, we will become somewhat more concrete and consider how to *implement* an experimental design in terms of the basic construction of a laboratory experiment, and consider the different forms of experimental treatments used in contemporary social research. Along the way, we also will reflect on aspects of the experiment that, while not formal features of the design, can nevertheless have a powerful impact on a study's outcome. Although this text is not meant to be a nuts and bolts "how to do it" book, this chapter contains details and information that should provide a useful guide to the conduct of experimental research.

Steps for Constructing an Experiment

Figure 6.1 presents a skeletal framework for constructing a laboratory experiment, outlining the elements that comprise any experimental study. In developing an experiment, the researcher in effect creates an "alternate universe"—a small but self-contained environment in which the main "action" of the study takes place. Each step in the construction has to be defined and controlled by the experimenter, and this control constitutes an important feature—both the strength and the weakness—of the experimental method.

Select Participant Pool

The first step in developing any study is arranging for the availability of a pool of eligible participants. This is the essential first step because it will control many of the later decisions the experimenter must make—the particular form of treatment manipulation, the types of measures to be used, the extent that the researcher will play a role in the experimental context, and so on. This step also may be one of the most difficult for the experimenter to control. We will discuss some of the ways in which participants may be recruited for participation in experiments later in this chapter. At this point, let us assume that a pool of participants is potentially available for the study. It is the researcher's role to define which participants are eligible to take part in the investigation. For some purposes, or for practical or theoretical reasons, researchers may wish to limit their investigations to individuals with particular characteristics, such as only male participants or only those of a specific age range, race, or religion. In such cases, experimenter control over variables in the study may be purchased at some cost to external validity (see Chapter 7).

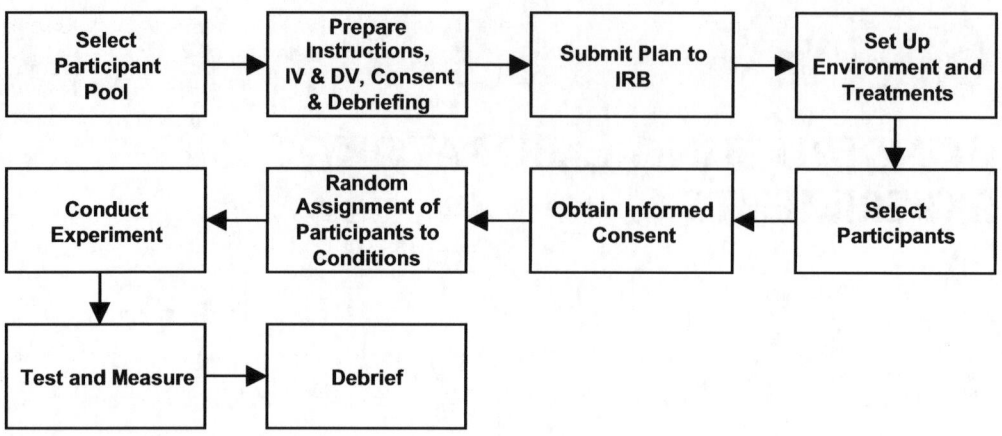

FIGURE 6.1 Framework for constructing the experiment.

Deciding on Sample Size

Having identified a pool of eligible participants, the next decision to be made concerns the *number* of participants that will be actually included in the experiment itself. The issue here is one of statistical power. It is important to ensure that a sufficient number of participants have been included to detect meaningful differences between experimental conditions above and beyond random variation. If the number of participants is too low, statistical inference will have low power—that is, we will fail to detect a significant difference, even though one might actually be present (a Type II error—see Chapter 2).

How do we know how many participants will be sufficient? The most widely accepted method is to perform a power analysis prior to conducting the experiment. Cohen (1992) provided a useful table for estimating necessary sample sizes for the most common statistical tests used in social research. The formula depends on choosing the size of the effect that one would like to be able to detect.[1] A popular computer application, GPower, provides researchers a quick and easy calculator to determine power. It is easy to use and applicable to a host of different statistical designs. For practical purposes, in social research we generally aim to design treatments that have at least medium effect sizes. In a two-group experiment, this would require 64 participants to have sufficient statistical power to detect a medium difference at the $p < .05$ level of statistical significance (two-tailed). To detect a much smaller effect, the sample would have to increase exponentially—the same two-group experiment would require 393 participants to have sufficient power to detect a small effect. Practical constraints usually limit the statistical power of our research endeavors. In Chapter 2, we discussed methods of increasing power in addition to simply increasing the number of participants. Effect size as the indicator of practical significance will be discussed further in Chapter 19.

Prepare Materials

Once the participant pool has been identified and the selected sample is defined as eligible for participation, the experimenter can organize the various features that will constitute the experiment itself. Instructions must be prepared, independent variables and dependent measures planned and constructed, and the informed consent and debriefings written. Immediately upon arriving at the experimental setting, participants should be asked to provide their informed consent, a process in which the researcher notifies potential research subjects of the potential benefits and risks they might experience as a result of their participation, so that they may make a reasonable decision about engaging in the study. After participants have served in the research, debriefing is the experimenter's honest explanation of what the study is about and represents an indispensable part of the study, especially if voluntary participants are used in the research.[2] Many experimental treatments can be developed in such a way that it is unnecessary to deceive participants, and we consider this important issue in detail in the final chapter. However, if deception is planned, the experimenter must develop a strategy to offset its effects in a careful post-experimental debriefing. A good general rule is that participants should leave the study feeling as good about themselves as they did when they entered it. If the experimental treatments put participants at risk, or if they were misinformed in any way, this potential damage must be offset at the study's completion.

Submit Plan to IRB

Before an experimental study can be conducted, the central features of the experimental design—the instructions, independent and dependent variables, and consent and debriefing messages must be submitted for approval to a committee specifically constituted to protect the welfare of research participants. In most universities, this body is called the Institutional Review Board (IRB) or, less formally, the "human participants committee." It is imperative that no research involving human participation ever be conducted without prior approval of the IRB. Failure to meet this requirement can have serious consequences for an investigator, and result in sanctions on the entire institution.

Set Up Laboratory Environment

Assuming that the IRB has reviewed the study and allowed it to go forward, the researcher then must set up the experimental context. In considering all of the elements of an experimental setting, we need to distinguish between those features of the context that are to be *held constant*, and those that are to be *systematically manipulated*. Experimental contexts are characterized by both a physical and a social environment. Because social experiments involve the use of mindful and cognizant persons, participants must be given some kind of information or instructions regarding the experiment—what it is about and what they are supposed to do. Apart from the specific features that are to be manipulated as the independent variable (or variables) and the outcome measures constituting the dependent variable(s), it is critical to good experimental design that potential extraneous features of the study be identified and controlled by the experimenter in a systematic way. This is to prevent potential extraneous variables from interfering with or confounding the effect of the intended independent variable on the dependent variable.

Most environmental features other than the independent variable of interest should be controlled or held constant by assuring that they are kept the same for all participants in all conditions in the experiment. This makes it possible to draw conclusions that the independent variable is solely responsible for differences across groups, as observed on the dependent variable. Ideally, the same laboratory or research space should be used for all conditions, the same set of instructions should be recorded and played for all participants, the same experimenter should run every session, etc. Some features cannot be held constant in this way. It is difficult, for instance, to run all sessions of an experiment at the same time of day, and the same experimenter may not be available for every session. In these cases, the researcher should control the situation so that contextual variations are evenly distributed across the conditions. Some experimental sessions may be run at 10:00 a.m. and others at 5:00 p.m., but every condition must be as likely to occur at the early sessions as the later ones.

For example, suppose we create a simple experiment with one treatment and one control condition. It would be a mistake to conduct all the treatment runs in the morning sessions, and to test all control participants in the evening sessions, because differences might ensue as a result of factors associated with the time of day that participants were studied (e.g., fatigue, hunger, etc.), rather than the effect of the independent variable itself. In our example, the manipulation is perfectly confounded with time of day, rendering an interpretation of results ambiguous. Similarly, it would be a mistake to have one experimenter conduct all the experimental treatment sessions, and another experimenter all the control sessions. To do so would create an uninterpretable outcome because the treatment and control conditions would be perfectly confounded with experimenter, and thus we could not be certain if differences on the dependent variable occurred because of the experimenters, or because of the particular condition to which participants were assigned.

Features of the physical environment are usually considered background factors that must be controlled to avoid confounding with the experimental treatment of interest. Sometimes, however, an environmental intervention is an integral part of the experimental set-up. Consider, for example, an experiment by Latané and Darley (1968) conducted as part of their investigation of diffusion of responsibility in groups. They hypothesized that an individual's reaction to an emergency would be determined by the presence or absence of other people in the setting. A lone individual was expected to react promptly to signs of an emergency, but when others were present, the responsibility for action was expected to diffuse throughout the group, thereby reducing the probability that anyone would respond. To test this hypothesis, the experimenters arranged a situation in which a participant arrived at the laboratory and was directed to a waiting room, either alone or in the company of other participants. In the room was a sign instructing the participant(s) to begin work on a questionnaire. Soon after participants began the questionnaire, thick, dark smoke began to pour into the room through a ventilator. The time participants stayed in the room after the smoke appeared constituted the dependent variable of the study. As predicted, the more people in the room, the longer it took anyone to respond.

In this example, the environmental intervention (smoke pumped through the ventilator) constituted a part of the setup or staging of the experiment. It was held constant for all levels of the independent variable—in other words, although the smoke was a pivotal feature of the experimental context, it was not a manipulation—all participants experienced it. The independent (manipulated) variable was the number of people present, not the physical context. However, the physical environment was part of the staging of the experiment, arranged by the researcher, to create the situation needed to address the hypothesis.

Types of Experimental Manipulations

We classify experimental manipulations into five broad types. An **environmental manipulation** entails the systematic manipulation of some aspect of the physical setting. A **stimulus manipulation** involves modification of visual or verbal material. The use of a **social manipulation** is based on the scripted action of another human being, usually a confederate working for the experimenter, on the participant in an experimental situation. An **instructional manipulation** involves modification of the description of the purposes and procedures that participants encounter in the study. A **priming manipulation** involves a task that induces a particular mindset or mental state of readiness in participants. These manipulation varieties may be combined in same study, but for illustrative purposes we will discuss them separately as "pure" types.

Environmental Manipulations

Some experiments require some intervention or manipulation of the properties of the physical environment. In these types of manipulations, features of the environment, such as lighting, background noise, or room temperature, are systematically varied by the experimenter to determine whether the differences introduced in the context lead to differences in how participants respond on the dependent variable. In a noteworthy study, Berkowitz and LePage (1967) exposed their participants to either one or seven electric shocks in the first part of the experiment. In the second part, the participants were given the opportunity to administer shocks to the person who had shocked them. In some conditions, a 12-gauge shotgun and a .38 revolver had been placed on a table near the shock key; in other conditions, the table contained either nothing or two badminton racquets and shuttlecocks. Analysis indicated that participants in the weapons conditions delivered significantly more electric shocks to their partner than those in the badminton or control groups if they had been in the maximal shock condition. The mere presence of the aggression-arousing environmental cue, the researchers suggested, had "elicited strong aggressive responses" from the angered subjects (p. 202).

Stimulus Manipulations

Sometimes even subtle variations can have powerful effects, even if participants assume they would not. For example, prior to the 2008 presidential election, Carter, Ferguson, and Hassin (2011) assessed participants' attitudes toward the candidates (Barack Obama and John McCain), along with their voting intentions. Printed on the first page of the questionnaires of *some* participants was a small American flag. The remaining participants received identical questionnaires, except the flag was not included on theirs. In a demonstration of the effects of an apparently minor environmental manipulation, the researchers found that the independent variable (the flag's presence or absence) was associated with "a significant increase in participants' Republican voting intentions, voting behavior . . . and explicit attitudes, with some effects lasting 8 months after exposure to the (flag) prime" (p. 1011).[3]

The example of an environmental manipulation involved a manipulation of the context in which participants responded to a communication. Another form of environmental manipulation is used in experiments in which participants are given some visual or verbal materials and asked to make a judgment or decision about the content of those materials. In such judgment experiments (Aronson, Wilson, & Brewer, 1998), the independent variable consists of variations in aspects of the stimulus materials that are presented. For instance, in much of the experimental research on impression formation, or person perception, participants are given a verbal description of some individual person (sometimes with a photograph accompanying the description) and are asked to judge how much they would like this person, or what traits or personality the individual might have. In these studies, specific pieces of information about the individual stimulus person are varied (e.g., age, ethnicity, physical or psychological traits, specific behaviors) to determine how those particular features influence judgments of the person as a whole.

Judgment experiments, in which the independent variable involves features of the stimulus or information given to the participant to respond to, are used across a wide array of social research topics, including, for example, descriptions of criminal cases to vary factors that might influence judgments of guilt or innocence, variations in the physical features of stimulus materials (such as font, color, contrast) to study the effects of the ease or difficulty of viewing the materials on subsequent judgments of quality or validity, or variations of whether information is presented by visual or auditory means to assess the effects of different types of nonverbal cues on judgments.

Social Manipulations

Social features of the experimental environment include the presence or absence of other people and their behavior in the experiment. The use of a social manipulation is exemplified in Asch's (1948, 1951) classic studies of conformity, in which a naïve participant was paired with varying

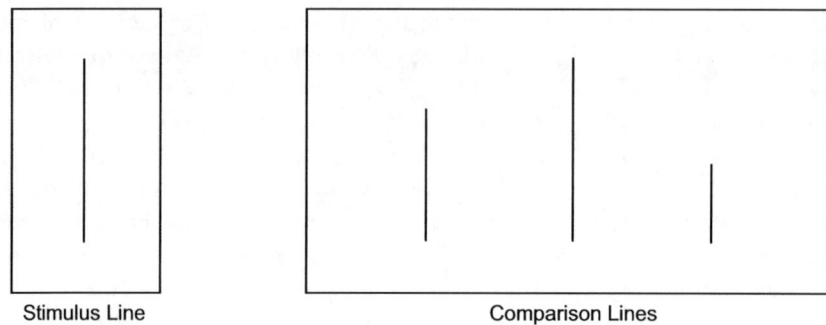

FIGURE 6.2 Example of stimulus and comparison lines used by Asch (1948).

numbers of experimental confederates. The study was introduced as an investigation of perceptual processes. On each trial of the experimental session, a stimulus line was presented, along with three comparison lines. The participant's task was to judge which of the comparison lines most closely matched the stimulus line in length. The stimuli were designed so that the correct choice was obvious and did not demand a fine discrimination (see the illustration in Figure 6.2). The experimental session was set up so that on each trial the naïve participant responded after the confederates; the judgments given by the confederates were preprogrammed so that on some of the judgment trials they unanimously chose the clearly incorrect alternative.

Asch's experiments were conducted to determine how behavior on the part of other people in the setting would influence the overt choices made by the naive participant. Results indicated that participants could best resist the group's influence of making an incorrect judgment in this seemingly easy perceptual task when only one or two confederates were present; the addition of a third confederate dramatically increased the degree of conformity to the incorrect answer, but further increases in group size had no substantial additional effect. An independent variable involving manipulation of the number of other people present in a group is conceptually simple, but when experimental confederates are involved, the cost can be high. In some of Asch's experimental conditions, as many as 15 confederates were employed for 1 participant! Assuming even a minimal rate of pay for accomplices, this can prove very expensive.

To circumvent the excessive cost entailed in an Asch-type conformity experiment, Crutchfield (1955) designed an electrical apparatus that he used to simulate the responses of confederates. The general trend of social research has been in the direction of such mechanization in the manipulation of the social environment (though today computer terminals and video displays often replace devices such as those used by Crutchfield). Such mechanization has advantages in creating a more homogeneous, carefully controlled treatment, avoiding potential biasing effects introduced by overzealous confederates. However, some researchers (e.g., Levy, 1960) have indicated that "electrical confederates" generally do not have as powerful an impact as human accomplices on participants' responses.

An intermediate solution to the issue of human versus artificial social manipulations involves the use of people who may be inferred by way of an audio or video recording. This approach has the advantage of presenting the participant with an apparently human interactant, while at the same time maintaining strict comparability in what is offered to participants in the same experimental condition. With current technology, these simulated interactions can be made to appear quite realistic. For instance, in experiments conducted by Lord and Saenz (1985), the researchers wanted to place participants into a social situation in which they believed they were "solos"— e.g., the only woman (man) in a group of men (women). Actually, all the other members of the participant's "group" were videotaped actors whose responses were pre-recorded. The real participants were placed in a small room facing a video camera, and were led to believe that they were interacting with other participants via "live" video broadcasting. To make the experience as real as possible, the participants were recorded and saw themselves on a video monitor whenever it was their turn to speak. This feedback made the manipulated interaction quite compelling, and no participants reported being suspicious about the presence of other participants at the time they were debriefed about the actual purposes of the study. Similar elements of realism have been used in simulated interactions on computer "chat rooms," where some of the participants are actually simulated group members pre-scripted by the experimenter (Gardner, Pickett, & Brewer, 2000).

Instructional Manipulations

Probably the most common form of experimental manipulation is one that makes use of differences in instructions provided by the experimenter to the participants in the study. In the typical form of this type of treatment, the instructions provided to the different groups are identical except for the substitution of a few words or sentences. Thus, it is extremely important that participants are paying attention so they "receive" the experimental treatment.

If participants are alert and motivated, even small differences in wording can prove to have powerful effects. Consider, for example, an ingenious study by Zanna and Cooper (1974), who were studying the effects of misattribution of arousal on people's judgments. Zanna and Cooper gave participants a pill, which actually consisted solely of milk powder, but participants were instructed in ways that produced different expectations about the pill's supposed effects. Participants in the "arousal" treatment condition were told:

"This M.C. 5771 capsule contains chemical elements that are more soluble than other parts of the compound. In this form of the drug these elements may produce a reaction of tenseness prior to the total absorption of the drug, 5 minutes after the ingestion. This side effect will disappear within 30 minutes" (Zanna & Cooper, 1974, p. 705).

Participants who were randomly assigned to the "relaxation" condition were given the same pill and the identical instructions, except that the word "tenseness" was replaced by "relaxation." This simple variation in wording established different participant expectations and interpretations of their own bodily reactions after ingestion, which, in turn, altered their response on the dependent variable.

Instructional manipulations are not always presented in the initial "instruction" phase of an experimental session. For example, in one investigation of the effects of monetary payment on people's intrinsic interest in a task, Crano and Sivacek (1984) developed the following scenario: Participants were brought individually to the laboratory and asked to write an essay in favor of the legalization of marijuana, a position that pretesting indicated most participants already favored. Some were merely asked to do this to "help out" the experimenter in the first condition, whereas others were offered $5 to do so in the second condition. A third condition provided an alternative basis for paying participants. In this condition, as the experimenter was asking the participant to help out, there was a knock on the door as planned, and a colleague asked the experimenter to step into the hallway for a moment. There, the colleague explained (loudly enough so that the participant could be sure to overhear) that he or she had completed a survey research project and still had $15 remaining in the participant payment fund. The colleague then asked the experimenter if he or she would award $5 to three of the experimenter's participants, as this would "save considerable bookwork" with the agency that had funded the study. The experimenter agreed, returned to the participant, and now offered $5 to write the pro-marijuana essay. This manipulation allowed the researchers to investigate the effects of three different payment conditions.

Apparently "accidental" instructional treatments of this type are common in social psychological research, and probably constitute one of the social scientist's most powerful tools. Indeed, it is not without justification that Aronson and Carlsmith (1968, p. 45) observed that "it might be said that part of being a good experimental social psychologist involves learning to say 'whoops' convincingly."

Instructional treatments do not necessarily involve deception of experimental participants. For example, in research on prevention of inhalant abuse in young adolescents, Crano, Siegel, Alvaro, and Patel (2007) played a persuasive anti-drug video to sixth- and seventh-grade school children. For one group, the video began with a speaker who said, "Parents, do you have a young teen at home?" It then went on to discuss the dangers of inhalant use. The other video was almost identical, except that it began with "Are you in the sixth, seventh, or eighth grade?" The predicted "indirect influence" differences were obtained: Students who apparently did not feel the need to defend themselves against a persuasive message designed for their parents were considerably more persuaded by the message than those who were the obvious direct targets of the message.

Priming Manipulations

A variation on instructional manipulations used frequently in implicit measures research (discussed in Chapter 16) involves administering a task that has been designed to activate or "prime" a particular idea or mental state. Priming refers to the unintended influence that recent experiences have on subsequent thoughts, feelings, and behavior (Bargh & Chartrand, 2000). That is, the thoughts or goals activated by participating in one task are expected to carry over, and affect, how later information or experience is interpreted or judged. An example of a priming manipulation is a task used by Brewer and Gardner (1996) to activate thoughts about the self as an individual, or the self as a part of a group. In the first stage of this experiment, in the guise of a proofreading exercise, participants were given the task of circling all the pronouns in an extended passage of a paragraph they were to read. Two different versions of the passage had been created by the experimenter. Half the participants read a version in which almost all of the pronouns were the words "I," "me," or "my." The other participants read a version of the passage that was exactly the same except that the pronouns were all "we," "us," or "our." In a second part of the experiment that ostensibly was unrelated to the first, participants completed a "who am I" task, in which they were to generate up to 20 aspects that described themselves. Responses to the self-description task were analyzed to determine whether the previous activity had influenced whether participants thought of themselves in terms of personal traits or social relationships.

A particularly interesting type of priming manipulation involves tasks that are designed to create specific bodily experiences that are hypothesized to influence (or prime) related mental content. The ideas underlying such manipulations come from theories of *embodiment* —the idea that certain bodily states or physical actions are closely associated with particular psychological states such as evaluative orientation or emotions (Niedenthal, Barsilou, Winkielman, Krauth-Gruber, & Ric, 2005). As a consequence, engaging the bodily state can prime or activate the associated psychological state. In an early example of such physical priming, Wells and Petty (1980) demonstrated that inducing participants to either nod or shake their heads while listening to a persuasive communication influenced the extent to which the participants changed their attitudes in line with the message. In a more subtle priming manipulation, Strack, Martin, and Strepper (1988) had participants hold a pen in their mouths in a manner that either facilitated contraction of the zygomaticus muscle (i.e., the mouth was in a smiling position) or inhibited the zygomaticus (i.e., prevented smiling). Participants then evaluated a series of cartoons while holding the pen; in general, the cartoons were rated as funnier when participants were induced to smile than when they were not smiling.

Other illustrations of the use of embodied primes include experiments showing that arm flexing (an approach action) results in more positive evaluations of Chinese characters compared to arm extension (Cacioppo, Priester, & Berntson, 1993), that manipulating postural positions influences reported emotional states (Duclos et al., 1989) or feelings of power (Carney, Cuddy, & Yap, 2010), and that inducing an approach reaction (by pulling a joystick toward the self) improves White participants' implicit attitudes towards Black people compared with an avoidance response (pushing the joystick away from the self) (Phills, Kawakami, Tabi, Inzlicht, & Nadolny, 2011, Experiment 1). Like other priming tasks, these manipulations are very subtle, and the influence of the prime occurs without conscious awareness on the part of the participant.

Manipulation Checks

Regardless of whether our manipulation comes in the form of subtle cues in the experimental context, behavior of others in the situation, or experimental instructions, participants' level of engagement in the study is a critical factor. The reason for this is obvious. We need to know that our treatments have been perceived or interpreted as we intended them to be. To help ensure this, a **manipulation check** is a question or series of questions to ask participants whether they noticed the manipulation that they received in the experiment.

To illustrate the use of a manipulation check, suppose we are interested in determining the effects of fear-arousing anti-HIV advertisements on the at-risk sexual behavior of adolescents. After exposing a cohort of participants to a series of such ads, we monitor their reported behavior over the next six months. If no differences in reported behavior were found between those exposed to the ad campaign and those who were not, we might be tempted to conclude that fear arousal does not affect behavior—at least, not the at-risk sexual behavior of adolescents. We might be correct in this interpretation, but it might rather be the case that the ads failed to generate sufficient fear to affect behavior. Our theory about fear arousal and behavior might be perfectly predictive, but our results found no relationship because the fear-arousal manipulation failed miserably in generating differences in fear arousal between the groups. If we had been clever enough to administer manipulation checks at the conclusion of our treatment ("How frightening are these ads?" "Were you more worried about HIV after the presentation than before?" etc.), the proper interpretation of our results would be more certain. Most often, such manipulation check questions are administered in addition to and *after* the main dependent measure that is the central focus of the study.

Manipulation check information also helps us determine if our treatments are operating as we think they did. Suppose, continuing our example, we find that our ad campaign had a powerful effect. That is, adolescents who received a very frightening series of advertisements about HIV and AIDS later indicated much less risky behaviors than those who did not. We could stop here, write up our results, and send them off to the nearest newspaper or scientific journal. But it would be much more informative if we had manipulation check data that indicated that the participants who were most afraid after our presentation were also the most likely to avoid risky sexual encounters. This information would bolster our theoretical interpretation and lend weight to our explanation.

It should be obvious that manipulation check information can be of enormous advantage to the experimenter. Such data can be helpful even when the experimental treatment has apparently failed. The information that manipulation checks can provide, no matter the apparent success of our experiment, is so important that they should be used whenever possible. Nonetheless, we need to caution that such checks—while potentially informative—are not necessarily perfect indicators of whether our experimental manipulations have been received as intended. Participants may not always be able to state explicitly what they have experienced or understood, particularly when a self-report measure is used for the manipulation check (Nisbett & Wilson, 1977). Thus, manipulation checks can be used in conjunction with the results on the dependent variables in an experiment to help understand the findings, but they should be used only as an aid in the process of interpretation.

Assignment of Participants to Conditions: Randomization Procedures

We have spoken at length about the importance of random assignment in developing true experimental designs that allow for causal inference. True random assignment requires that any person in our sample be equally likely to participate in any of the experimental conditions. This is the central requirement of random assignment, and without it we cannot claim that our assignment was random. There are many different ways to implement random assignment once experimental conditions have been designed and constructed, and we cannot go into extensive detail about all of those methods here. However, we can present a few basic principles about the mechanics of random assignment at this point.

In general, there are two different ways to accomplish random assignment of individual participants to experimental conditions. One involves using some process of randomization (e.g., a coin toss, roll of a die, or a table of random numbers) one by one for each participant as he or she arrives at the experimental session. For instance, if we have a 2 × 2 factorial design, resulting in four different experimental conditions, we would label the various conditions 1, 2, 3, and 4. Then as each participant showed up, we would consult a table of random numbers, place a finger on an arbitrary starting point, and then run down (or up) the column on the page until either a 1, 2, 3, or 4 were encountered. Whichever number comes up first will be the condition to which the participant would be assigned.

Randomly assigning participants on a one-by-one basis is one ideal form of random assignment procedure. However, it has a disadvantage: we must run a large number of participants in a short period of time to be sure that the resulting randomization will spread participants evenly across all our conditions. With randomization, we can by chance run into a long string of 1's all in a row, so that participants get "bunched up" into one treatment until chance evens things out. This is not particularly problematic if we have large numbers of participants in our study. In that case, this random process will work quite well in distributing approximately equal numbers of participants across the conditions. However, if our procedures require running individuals one or two or three at a time, or if the study does not have many participants available, this random assignment procedure may not work so well. The alternative is a form of *block randomization*, in which conditions are randomly ordered in advance before participants arrive at sessions. All possible conditions are numbered and then randomly ordered, and then this random ordering is repeated in blocks until the total number of intended participants is reached. For example, using our previous 2 × 2 design, the 4 conditions would be ordered (via a table of random numbers) from 1 to 4. Then, the (random) number that came up first would indicate the condition administered to the first participant, the number coming up next would be the condition administered to the second participant, etc. Once all 4 conditions had been included, the process would be repeated for the next block of participants, and so on. If we were planning to run 25 participants per condition, for a total of 100 participants, this process of randomly ordering the 4 conditions would be done 25 times. This process of blocked randomization assures that participants are both randomly assigned *and* evenly distributed across the 4 conditions.

Technically, random assignment should be implemented in such a way that each *individual* participant in the experiment has an equal chance (at the outset) of being assigned to any of the conditions, independently of any other individual's assignment. Both one-at-a-time and blocked randomization procedures meet this criterion, as long as participants are allocated separately to their randomly determined conditions. However, it sometimes is case that a particular experimental treatment is delivered to all of the participants who show up at a particular session at the same time. This is called *group randomization*. For instance, perhaps we have one independent variable in which an instructional manipulation is to be delivered verbally by the researcher. At the same time, we have a second independent variable involving a stimulus manipulation that is contained in written materials distributed individually to each participant. Now say that we are conducting experimental sessions in which five participants are studied at the same time in the same room. We can still randomly assign each of these five participants to different levels of the written stimulus materials because each participant does not see what the others have received. However, everyone hears the same verbal instructions read aloud by the experimenter, so only one version can be delivered. In this case, the levels of the instructional treatment are randomly assigned to whole sessions, with all five participants in the same session getting the same version.

This process of group random assignment is implemented *across* sessions, but not *within* sessions. Technically, group randomization is a violation of the principles of random assignment at the individual level because there may be non-independence among participants in the same session, which must be statistically controlled for (see Chapter 18 for discussion of how this affects statistical analyses). Non-independence in each session occurs because those who choose to appear at the same session may possess similar background characteristics or preferences (e.g., naturally preferring the morning session), or the room conditions at the time of the session may affect all participants in the same way.

If we run many sessions across the course of an experimental study, this violation of random assigned is not particularly problematic, but it can lead to loss of data at times. For example, suppose we want to study the effects of discomfort on people's judgments of various governmental policies (e.g., welfare, job training, universal health insurance). We have a laboratory that holds 20 participants at a time and seek to administer the same treatment to everyone in the room. We want to make some of them uncomfortable to determine whether discomfort will make them less likely to support government-funded welfare, job training, and health insurance. To do this, we play loud white noise during the "discomfort" condition. The controls are studied under normal circumstances. If we wanted to randomly assign 120 participants (60 into each of the 2 conditions), we would need to conduct 6 sessions—3 treatment sessions and 3 control sessions. We want the sessions to be identical in all respects *except* in the presence or absence of the treatment. However, suppose that during one of the sessions one of the participants became very ill and suffered a seizure. This disruption probably would render the data of this session noncomparable with that of the other sessions, and we would probably have to drop the data from that session, losing all 20 participants. For this reason, it is a good general rule that if experimental treatments are assigned to sessions, one should conduct a large number of sessions with only a few participants (e.g., no more than 5) in any one session.

Realism in an Experiment

The experiment is the sum total of all that we have discussed to this point. It is the combination of our experimental manipulations and measures, enmeshed within a well-considered physical context (usually this context is a laboratory, but it need not be). Once participants have experienced the treatment(s) in the experimental conditions to which they have been assigned, the final step of conducting an experiment involves measuring effects on the dependent variable(s). In addition to deciding how to control the independent variable, the researcher also determines the types of participant behaviors that will be observed and measured. Dependent variables include a wide range of response types. They may involve overt behaviors, questionnaire responses, or cognitive and physiological measures. The methodological issues that guide developing and using these different types of response measures are covered in detail in Chapters 12 to 18.

The frequent use of subtle manipulations as independent variables in experiments highlights the importance of participant involvement and attention as a critical factor in good research. In this connection, Aronson, Wilson, and Brewer (1998) drew an important distinction between experimental and mundane realism, concepts that are closely tied to the manner in which experiments are set up and the types of manipulations used. **Experimental realism** is the degree that an experiment has real impact on participants: The experimental arrangements literally forced participants to attend carefully to the task requirements. In other words, experimental realism is achieved if participants are unable to intellectualize and be self-conscious about their reactions, and rather are responding to the experimental situation in a way that approximates their natural, spontaneous behavior outside the laboratory.

Mundane realism is the degree to which various features of the experiment—instructions, treatments, and measurement operations—mirror real-world, non-laboratory events that participants might encounter in their day-to-day experiences. For instance, some experiments involve asking college students to write essays or take tests, events that are quite usual in the daily life experiences of the average student. Note, however, that this same experimental task would have considerably less mundane realism for participants who were middle-aged truck drivers, for whom such tasks might be considerably more exotic.

Mundane and experimental realism are not mutually exclusive. Whenever possible, a good research design will establish both. However, of the two, experimental realism is the more important for creating a meaningful and engaging situation for research participants. The mere fact that an event occurs in real life does not endow it with importance, and an experimental situation that mirrors a dull real-world experience will probably prove to be dull and uninvolving. Research participants in this type of setting will tend to become apathetic and may fail to respond to the manipulation simply because they did not attend to it. Some of the treatments employed by social researchers are so subtle that the participant must be closely attuned to the research situation if the manipulation is to have any impact. If respondents are bored or apathetic, this needed degree of attention cannot be assumed. It is clearly worth the time and effort that it takes for researchers to keep their participants interested and involved.

Social Simulations and Analogue Experiments

The techniques for conducting laboratory experiments discussed in the preceding sections of this chapter emphasize achieving experimental realism within the laboratory setting. A major concern is that the experimental procedures create an environment that is involving and impactful for the research participants, even if the situation is peculiar to the laboratory setting and bears no direct resemblance to events the participant is likely to encounter in life outside the laboratory. Where but in the laboratory, for instance, would individuals engage in a dull and boring task and then be asked to describe that task to another person as fun and interesting, as were participants in Festinger and Carlsmith's (1959) classic dissonance research experiment? In that study, the investigators deliberately used the research context as an excuse to induce participants to engage in a behavior contrary to their ordinary experience. The fact that the requested behavior had no structural similarity to events outside the laboratory was irrelevant to the purposes of this investigation.

Now we will shift attention to laboratory studies in which there is an explicit intention to emulate events that occur in the "real world." In such studies, the degree of correspondence between the situation created in the laboratory and the real-life situation it is intended to represent becomes a major concern. There are two different types of laboratory experiments that share this concern for real-world correspondence. The first is the **role-playing simulation**, in which participants are instructed to actively imagine that they are actors in a specified real-world situation and to respond as they believe they would in that context.[4] The other is a type of research that we refer to as the **analogue experiment**, in which participants are responding directly to a specially constructed situation that has been designed to reproduce or mimic selected features of a real-world situation. An analogue differs from a simulation in that participants are not asked to play an explicitly defined role.

Role-Playing Simulations

When used for research purposes, simulations are intended to preserve many of the advantages of controlled laboratory experiments while approaching conditions that are more generalizable to the real world. A well-designed simulation has the potential to isolate the social phenomenon of interest without destroying its natural contextual meaning, because participants can "actively imagine that all the normal constitutive relations of a social situation are satisfied" (Greenwood, 1983, p. 243). Because of these added "imaginative" elements, the treatment conditions of a simulation study are inevitably more complex and multidimensional than those of the basic laboratory experiment. Hence, the potential increase in generalizability is attained with some sacrifice of precision in the specification of the independent and dependent variables.

Passive Role-Playing Simulations

Various types of simulation research differ in the extent of active role-playing that is involved. At one end of the spectrum are studies employing what Greenwood (1983) calls "passive-interpretive role-playing," which might also be described as "mental simulations." In such studies participants are provided with a written or verbal description of a situation or scenario and their role in it, and are asked to estimate or predict how they (or others) would behave in that situation.

Such role-playing studies have been used for theory-testing purposes on occasion. Rosenberg and Abelson (1960), for example, placed participants in a role-playing situation to test some hypotheses derived from balance theories of attitudes and attitude change. In their study, participants were asked to imagine themselves in the role of a department store manager. As part of the context of their role-playing, participants were "given" a set of attitudes toward a particular employee (Mr. Fenwick) and his plans to mount a modern art display in the rug department of the store. The affective relationships assigned to different participants were varied to produce different states of psychological inconsistency or imbalance. Participants were then given three different communications to read, each of which was designed to change their attitude toward some aspect of the situation. A dependent measure of final attitudes was used to determine which communication was accepted by the role-playing participants and the extent that this corresponded with researcher predictions derived from formal balance models. Although the results confirmed balance theory predictions to some extent, they also indicated that acceptance of communications was affected by motives other than restoration of cognitive balance (such as avoiding negative interpersonal affect). Thus, even though it did not involve a "real" interpersonal situation, this role-playing study did prove capable of testing the theory in the sense of subjecting it to potential disconfirmation.

Some forms of passive role-playing have been suggested as possible alternatives to the use of deception in experimental social psychology (e.g., Carlson, 1971; Kelman, 1967; Mixon, 1972; Schultz, 1969). The argument here is that if role-playing participants can be given a complete subjective understanding of the experimental conditions that would be used in a real study, their estimates of how they would behave in that situation can substitute for actual participation in such situations. During the 1960s and 1970s, a number of role-playing studies were conducted to determine whether the results obtained would match or reproduce the findings from previously conducted deception experiments. Horowitz and Rothschild (1970), for example, compared reports from two forms of simulation against the data from an earlier Asch-type conformity study conducted by Gerard, Wilhelmy, and Conolly (1968). Darryl Bem (1965, 1967) conducted a series of "interpersonal simulations" of classic dissonance experiments (Brehm & Cohen, 1959, 1962; Festinger & Carlsmith, 1959), and the outcomes of Milgram's (1965) studies of obedience have also been subjected to role-playing simulation (Freedman, 1969). In terms of their ability to reproduce findings in which participants are to be themselves rather than playing an assigned role, the results have been mixed (see Miller, 1972). Even when the findings are parallel, it remains ambiguous whether the results of a passive role-playing simulation can be interpreted in the same way as those obtained under the real experimental conditions (see Cronkite, 1980).

Active Role-Playing Simulations

While passive role-playing has some potential value for theory-testing, the more widely used forms of simulation involve active role-playing efforts, in which participants are allowed to act out their natural responses based on their interpretation of their assigned role in the simulated social situation. The primary version of this research method is the so-called role-playing game. In this form, participants are given roles to play within a specified social system. The parameters of the system are under the control of the experimenter, and within this context the participants make choices and decisions befitting their perception of the roles they have been given. The behavior choices of each participant and their consequences for the behaviors of other participants in the system constitute the major dependent variables in this research design. Participation in such games is usually extended over a considerable period of time, and experience indicates that motivation and involvement among role players run quite high. Elaborate simulation exercises have been developed, ranging from simulations of small decision-making groups, such as jury deliberations (Breau & Brook, 2007; Cox, Clark, Edens, Smith, & Magyar, 2013), management and production teams (Adobor & Daneshfar, 2006; Xu & Bernard, 2013), business organizations, and market economies (Galtier, Bousquet, Antona, & Bommel, 2012; Klein & Fleck, 1990), to whole societies (SIMSOC: Gamson, 1969; Gamson & Stambaugh, 1978) and intercultural relations (Fowler & Pusch, 2010; Hofstede & Murff, 2012).

Probably the most dramatic simulation of a social subsystem is represented by the prison simulation designed and conducted by Philip Zimbardo and his colleagues at Stanford University (Zimbardo, Haney, Banks, & Jaffe, 1973). Zimbardo created a mock prison in the basement of a college building and recruited college student participants who were randomly assigned to play the roles of "guards" and "prisoners" in the simulated setting. Zimbardo was attempting to demonstrate the powerful effects of institutionalization and de-individuation on interpersonal behavior. As with Milgram's (1963) earlier studies of obedience, however, the results of the simulation were more extreme than expected as the participants became fully immersed in their respective roles. Although the simulation had been intended to extend across a two-week period, Zimbardo felt forced to cancel the study at the end of six days because of the escalating cruelty on the part of the guards toward the prisoners, who were showing signs of progressive apathy and depression (Zimbardo, 2007).

Bargaining and Negotiation Games

There is considerable social research on the decisions and behavior of individuals in two-person bargaining games. While the format of most of this research resembles the usual laboratory experiment rather than simulation designs, some background information on the paradigm of experimental games research will be useful to a discussion of the extension of these games into simulation settings.

Most experimental games research to date revolves around the use of the "prisoner's dilemma" situation, which receives its name from the following analogy.

> Two suspects are taken into custody and separated. The district attorney is certain that they are guilty of a specific crime, but does not have adequate evidence to convict them at a trial. He points out to each prisoner that each has two alternatives: to confess to the crime the police are sure they have committed, or not confess. If they both do not confess, then the district attorney states he will book them on some very minor trumped-up charge, such as petty larceny and illegal possession of a weapon, and they will both receive minor punishment; if they both confess they will be prosecuted but he will recommend less than the most severe sentence. If one confesses and the other does not, then the confessor will receive lenient treatment for turning state's evidence whereas the latter will get the book slapped at him.
>
> (Luce & Raiffa, 1958, p. 95)

The maximal joint outcome for both prisoners is attained if neither confesses. However, each of the individuals has to face the risk that if he or she refuses to confess while the other does confess, his or her own outcome will be very bad. Thus, each is motivated to attempt to maximize his or her own personal gain by confessing. If both act on this motivation, as the district attorney wants and expects them to do, their joint outcome will be less than optimal. The prisoner's dilemma is represented in the social psychological laboratory in the form of a "non-zero sum" or "mixed-motive" two-person game. On each trial of such a game, each of the two players makes a choice between two alternatives, and the outcome or payoff from his or her choice is determined by the nature of the choice made (simultaneously) by the other player. The potential choices and outcomes are represented by the joint payoff matrix, shown in Figure 6.3, which is one of many examples of payoff matrices that could be constructed in developing prisoners' dilemma games.

Depending on the joint choices of the two participants, the first value in each cell represents player A's payoff (in coins or chips) and the second represents player B's payoff. In this type of matrix, choice 2 is the low-risk, "rational" choice for each player; however, if both players make this choice on each trial, their joint payoff will be only 1 coin each. The maximum joint payoff of 3 coins each can be achieved only when both players choose choice 1, but if one player chooses choice 1 while the other sticks to choice 2, the resulting payoffs will be highly uneven. Thus, the optimization of income for both players collectively can be achieved only through joint cooperation, in which each player can choose choice 1 with some degree of confidence that the other player will do so too. In the typical experimental games study, the dependent measure is the total number of competitive (choice 2) and cooperative (choice 1) choices made by each player, along with the related measure of total joint payoffs achieved by each dyad.

		Player B's choice	
		1	2
Player A's Choice	1	3, 3	0, 5
	2	5, 0	1, 1

FIGURE 6.3 Prisoner's Dilemma Game matrix.

As a paradigm for studying interpersonal decision-making, the Prisoner's Dilemma Game (PDG) can be considered a "minimalist" situation. To preserve the dilemma aspects of the situation, players are not allowed to communicate with each other or directly negotiate the choices that they make. The basic structure of the dilemma situation is built into more realistic, dynamic, role-playing simulations in the bargaining and negotiation literature (see McDonald, 1998).

International Relations Simulation

Some of the richest outcomes of role-playing research are from the area of simulated international relations (Boyer, 2011). It is not surprising, perhaps, that this area of research should have been the first to lend itself to simulation research, as the real-world political arena provides so few opportunities for testing relevant social science theories.

One of the earliest examples of simulation in this area is the Inter-Nation Simulation (INS) developed at Northwestern University (Guetzkow, Alger, Brody, Noel, & Sidney, 1963). In the INS, individual participants (decision-makers) play roles of government representatives of imaginary nations participating in an international government organization. Variations in inputs and outcomes are possible at three levels of operation—characteristics of the decision-makers and their role definitions, characteristics of the participant nations, and the nature of the supranational alliance structure. Some examples of the use of INS include a study by Brody (1963) of the impact of changing nuclear power relationships on communication and alliance patterns; Raser and Crow's (1968) study of relationships among power levels, threat intensity, group cohesion, goal-seeking, and resorting to violence; Druckman's (1968) investigation of the development of ethnocentrism; and a study by Zinnes (1966) of the relationship between hostile perceptions and hostile communications among nations. Other research (Starkey & Blake, 2001) has extended the use of INS to studies of the UN Security Council (Strand & Rapkin, 2011) and the dynamics of civil wars (Stoll, 2011).

Because of the real-world analogies built into INS studies, it is a temptation to generalize the findings to predict outcomes in the real international arena. Some findings encourage this extrapolation, such as indications that the use of role-experienced participants (State Department employees and diplomatic representatives at the U.N.) does not seem to alter results obtained from college student participants. However, other findings suggest caution. The study by Zinnes (1966) compared outcomes of an INS with results from an analysis of World War I documents, and found that the predicted relationship between hostile perceptions and hostile messages was borne out in the simulation but not in the historical data; a similar result was found in Stoll's (2011) study of civil wars. Even so, any time such comparisons can be made, an opportunity is created for exploring the limitations of relevant theories.

Outcomes of explorations with the INS structure have led to the development of further simulation models. Increased complexity, for example, has been introduced in an expansion called International Processes Simulation (IPS: Smoker, 1968), the Balance of Power game (Chapin, 1998), and EARTH (Exploring Alternative Realpolitik Theses: Bremer & Mihalka, 1977).

Role-Playing Simulations as Research

All active role-playing simulations involve a combination of programmed relationships among variables specified by the researcher and un-programmed activity on the part of the human decision-makers. The increased complexity of many simulations has necessitated the use of computers to provide programmed input as well as to store running records of all output variables. Many simulations have been developed as educational or training tools rather than for research purposes. As a consequence, each simulation has many different components and considerable room for planned or unplanned variations. Using simulations as experiments involves systematically varying one or more aspects of the input or design across different "runs" of the simulation. Each run (no matter how many participants are involved) amounts to a single replication, so it takes 10 or 20 simulation sessions to conduct even a simple 2-condition experiment. Because simulations are time and effort intensive (some International Simulations, for example, run over a period of days or even weeks), this amounts to a very costly way of doing experimental research. More often, experimental variations will be introduced *within* sessions of a simulation, as a type of pretest-posttest or repeated measures design. An earlier study (Raser & Crow, 1968, reported by Raser, 1972) investigated the effects of the development of an invulnerable retaliatory force by one nation in the international system. In the real world, development of such a force would inevitably occur with many other changes, any of which could account for subsequent events, but within the INS this development could be systematically introduced or removed by experimental intervention in a way that eliminated other plausible explanations of its effects. Thus, simulations can be adapted to test specific research hypotheses when time and resources are available.

Analogue Experiments

In simulation research, the "real world" is represented in the laboratory through the researchers' instructions to role-playing participants and the players' ability to imagine themselves in the situation portrayed. The logic of an analogue experiment is quite different. In this type of research, participants are not asked to act out a role in an "as-if" context. Rather, they are presented with a *real* situation to respond to directly. The difference between an analogue experiment and other basic laboratory experiments is in the design of the stimulus situation and its relationship to some specified event or problem existing outside the laboratory. An analogue is designed to preserve an explicit relationship between the laboratory setting and some real-world situation of interest; for every feature of the external situation that is considered theoretically relevant, there is a corresponding feature contained in the laboratory situation. In this sense, an analogue is like a roadmap of a particular geographical region, where there is a one-to-one correspondence between features on the map and essential features of the actual terrain (e.g., highways, rivers, mountains, etc.), but where less relevant features that exist in the real setting (e.g., trees, houses) are not represented on the map. If the important features represented in the analogue situation have been appropriately selected, participants' responses to that situation should provide an accurate "mapping" of their responses to the corresponding situation in real life.

Analogue experiments have been used for some time. Animal models, for instance, are regarded as analogues to human physiology in much medical research, and experimenter-participant roles are treated as analogues to the doctor-patient relationship in both medical and clinical research. The use of analogue experimentation in social science research, however, has been relatively rare, despite its potential role in closing the gap between research in the laboratory and in the real world. This may partly be because such experiments are not easy to design, as they require concern for both experimental realism and accurate simulation of mundane events. Analogues have been successfully employed in a number of areas, however. By calling attention to specific examples of such applications, we hope to increase awareness of the analogue experiment as a potentially valuable research tool.

Analogue experiments vary in the level of social organization that is being represented in the laboratory setting. Some experiments focus on events or problems faced by single individuals, with emphasis on the intra-individual processes that mediate responses to such experiences. Others attempt to structure whole social groups in the laboratory situation, with an emphasis on the interpersonal processes operative within that social structure.

Analogue Experiments of Individuals

One example of the use of analogue experiments to assess intrapersonal decision processes was prompted by a specific real-world event—the killing of Kitty Genovese outside a New York apartment complex in 1963. In the middle of the night, Ms. Genovese was pursued and murdered by her assailant on the streets over a period of 30 minutes, despite the fact that her cries for help could be heard by as many as 38 people in nearby apartments. This event, and the extensive newspaper coverage it generated, led researchers Latané and Darley (1968, 1970) to speculate about the psychological processes involved in an individual's decision whether or not to intervene in such emergency situations, and how those processes might be affected by the actual or inferred presence of other people who fail to help. Their theorizing led to a series of experiments on bystander intervention, in which individuals in the laboratory were faced with various decision crises parallel to those in real-world emergency situations.

Among the studies of bystander intervention, the experiment most closely analogous to the original news event was that conducted by Darley and Latané (1968). In this experiment, each participant was led to believe that this was a communication study that required them to sit in a separate small room to communicate via intercom with the other "participants." Only one real participant was tested in each trial. The other "participants" were actually tape recordings of the other subjects. After a brief warm-up introduction, each person was asked to speak, one at a time, about their college experiences. Midway through his presentation, in which he had mentioned his history of epileptic seizures, one of the apparent subjects (actually a tape recording prepared by the experimenters) said he felt lightheaded. His speech became blurred and disoriented, and he eventually was heard audibly gasping for help. After this, a thud was heard over the intercom, and then silence.

The independent variable in this experiment was the number of passive bystanders in the study at the time of the emergency. In one condition, participants believed that they and the "victim" were the only two participants in the session, while in the other two conditions each participant believed that in addition to the victim, there was either one or four others present in the experiment. As in the real-world event, the actual participant was visually isolated from the potential victim and from other "bystanders," and, as in the real emergency, the participant had to decide whether to respond to the emergency and whether he or she was personally responsible for making such a response. The results confirmed Darley and Latané's predictions about the effects of other bystanders. When participants believed they were the sole potential helper in the situation, 85% responded within less than a minute by seeking the assistance of the nearby experimenter. When participants believed there were others present, the probability of responding within a short interval dropped dramatically as the number of passive others increased, with only 31% responding when they believed there were four other bystanders available. Known as the "bystander effect," this phenomenon of being less inclined to offer help when passive others are present is attributed to diffusion of personal responsibility.

Analogue Experiments of Collective Decisions

Like the Kitty Genovese case, many contemporary real-world problems reflect situations in which individuals have to make decisions under conflict between their own interests and that of others. Dwindling fuel supplies, electrical brownouts, depletion of fresh water supplies, and air pollution are all cases in which individuals acting in their own self-interest can lead to collective disaster. One solution to the negative consequences of social dilemmas requires that individuals restrain their own self-interested behavior (take shorter showers, carpool to work, reduce heat or cooling in their homes) in the interest of the collective good. Unilateral restraint on the part of any single individual is useless, however, unless a large proportion of other individuals exercise the same restraint. Yet if many others exercise such constraint, a single individual doesn't need to, and hence the dilemma.

Because it is difficult to experiment with large-scale social problems such as the conservation of energy and other scarce resources, various stripped-down versions of social dilemmas have been designed for the laboratory to study individual and group decision-making processes (see Balliet, Mulder, & Van Lange, 2011; Messick & Brewer, 1983). In a sense, the Prisoner's Dilemma Game (PDG) described earlier is a two-person version of such collective choice analogues. However, research using the PDG came under heavy criticism for losing sight of any parallels between decision-making in the PDG setting and real-world decision-making contexts. To avoid falling into the same trap, analogues of collective decision problems have been designed with careful attention to their real-world counterparts.

Of the collective dilemmas that have been designed for laboratory investigations, the most clearly analogous to conservation situations is the replenishable resource task, versions of which have been used in a number of group studies (Allison & Messick, 1985; Kramer & Brewer, 1984; Messick et al., 1983; Milinski, Sommerfeld, Krambeck, Reed, & Marotzke, 2008). The basic structure of this task involves the existence of a common pool of points (worth something of value such as money or experimental credits) to which each of the participants in an experimental session has access. On each trial or round of the task, every participant is permitted to draw from the common resource pool a selected number of points (which becomes theirs to keep) up to some maximum limit. After each round, the pool is replenished by some proportion of the pool size remaining after participants have drawn off their portions. The replenishment rate is set in such a way that *if* the participants as a group restrain their total take on each trial to a level below the maximum possible, the resource pool size can be maintained at its original level indefinitely. However, if the total take on each trial exceeds the rate of replenishment, the pool will be depleted gradually until the common resource is completely exhausted.

The participants in this resource dilemma situation are not being asked to *act as if* they were making decisions about conservation of energy or some other simulated experience. Rather, they are making actual decisions about real scarce resources in the scaled-down laboratory setting. Researchers hope that the task has been structured so that the basic elements of the decision to be made are the same as those operative in the dilemma situations that exist outside the lab. As in real large-scale collective problems, participants must make their individual decisions about resource use in the absence of knowledge about what other participants are doing and without coordination of choices. If these structural elements accurately parallel those in the real-world situation, then researchers can use the laboratory analogue to determine how variations in contextual features (e.g., availability of feedback about the state of the resource pool, forms of communication among participants, identity of the group members, etc.) can alter the decisions that are made on the collective level. Such research can be used simultaneously to test hypotheses about basic psychological or group processes and about the effectiveness of potential interventions that might be implemented in the real world to influence the conservation of scarce resources (Messick & Brewer, 1983; Torres & Macedo, 2000).

Analogue experiments also have been designed to mimic other real-world social issues, such as intergroup cooperation (Gaertner, Mann, Murrell, & Dovidio, 1989), school desegregation (Brewer & Miller, 1984), and bribery (Cameron, Chaudhuri, Erkal, & Gangadharan, 2009). Even with a number of structural embellishments, it should be noted that the laboratory analogue will always be a "stripped-down" representation of the corresponding situations in the real world. It is practically impossible to capture the historical and cultural context of social issues in society at large and to fully translate these issues into an analogue experiment. Nonetheless, experience with the analogue paradigm indicates that it can engage—at least temporarily—much of the emotional significance attached to real decision-making. Given this level of involvement, the analogue experiment can provide a low-cost method for testing the potential effectiveness of various intervention strategies designed to reduce social problems such as intergroup discrimination, destruction of the environment, or organizational corruption. By utilizing analogue experiments in this way, promising avenues of policy research can be identified and potentially costly mistakes avoided in the social arena.

Conclusion

Laboratory experiments can take many forms, but their basic requirements are similar across different types of studies. At the most basic level, a participant pool must be selected, the sample size must be decided upon, and materials must be prepared and vetted by the appropriate review body. The type and combination of treatments or manipulations to be used—environmental, stimulus, social, instructional, or prime—will depend upon the issue under investigation. In planning any experiment, issues of mundane and experimental realism must be considered carefully, and treatments should be designed to maximize both of these essential features.

Sometimes the laboratory experiment can take the form of a role-playing simulation, in which the participants adopt different "roles" that might otherwise not be easily or ethically studied. Role-playing research can involve active or passive role players, and can provide important insights into factors that are otherwise difficult to manipulate. Analogue studies are also a common research form, in which specific features of a real-world social context are represented by analogous features in the experimental setting. In this sense, they are not role-playing but responding to a stripped-down parallel of the social environment, allowing the researcher to study very specific responses to equally specifically controlled stimuli. The Prisoner's Dilemma Game is one of the most common analogue designs, and research on social and replenishable resources dilemmas are important outgrowths of the original game. These approaches extend the reach of the laboratory and are designed to lend elements of realism to participants' behaviors, thus enhancing the applicability of experimental results to the issue under investigation.

Questions for Discussion

1. Explain the difference between experimental and mundane realism. Although establishing both is desirable, why might one be more important than the other?
2. Sometimes using a manipulation check to verify that your experimental treatment had its intended effect only undermines the efficacy of your treatment. For example, when people are primed to feel self-uncertainty, having participants report how uncertain they feel may undo the effect of the uncertainty prime. In other words, given the same manipulation, we see effects in the hypothesized direction when a manipulation check for uncertainty is *not* used, but when it is used these effects disappear. If this is the case, how do we know that our manipulation is actually manipulating *uncertainty*, rather than some other construct entirely? How might we be able to assess the degree of people's uncertainty caused by our manipulation without explicitly asking them how uncertain they feel?
3. To what extent do you think social simulations and role-playing scenarios risk inducing participants' idealizations or normative beliefs regarding the types of people they *would like* to be, or what they expect others to be like, rather than accurate representations of how participants would behave if the same situation occurred in real life? That is, in simulations and role-playing scenarios, are participants more likely to base their behavior on subjective (what others think you should do) and injunctive norms (what you think you ought to do), rather than descriptive norms (what you and other people actually do)? Since simulations obviously occur in a

controlled laboratory setting, are participants more likely to alter their behaviors, even slightly, to improve the self-image they present to the experimenter or to conform to certain group norms? How problematic is this possibility? How likely is it? How can you lessen this possibility?

Notes

1. Following recommendations by Cohen (1988), differences between two groups of 0.20, 0.50, and 0.80 standard deviation units are defined as small, moderate, and large effect sizes respectively.
2. In some research, participants are not aware of their being under investigation, and in some instances, as will be seen later in this chapter, it is impractical or impossible to debrief.
3. Earlier research had shown that respondents thought Republican candidates were more likely to brandish the American flag, but they did not believe this would affect their voting behavior. Carter's research suggests the respondents were incorrect.
4. In some types of simulation research, the human participant is replaced by a computer model of the processes under investigation. Such computer simulations are very valuable tools for theory development (cf. Abelson, 1968; Hastie & Stasser, 2000). Their status as empirical research, however, is ambiguous, and such forms of simulation are not covered here.

References

Abelson, R. P. (1968). Simulation of social behavior. In G. Lindzey and E. Aronson (Eds.), *The handbook of social psychology*, (2nd ed., vol. 2, pp. 274–356). Reading, MA: Addison-Wesley.

Adobor, H., & Daneshfar, A. (2006). Management simulations: Determining their effectiveness. *Journal of Management Development, 25*, 151–168.

Allison, S. T., & Messick, D. M. (1985). Effects of experience on performance in a replenishable resource trap. *Journal of Personality and Social Psychology, 49*, 943–948.

Aronson, E., & Carlsmith, J. M. (1968). Experimentation in social psychology. In G. Lindzey & E. Aronson (Eds.), *The handbook of social psychology*, (2nd ed., vol. 2, pp. 1–79). Reading, MA: Addison-Wesley.

Aronson, E., Wilson, T., & Brewer, M. B. (1998). Experimentation in social psychology. In D. Gilbert, S. Fiske, & G. Lindsey (Eds.), *The handbook of social psychology* (4th ed., vol. 1, pp. 99–142). Boston: McGraw-Hill.

Asch, S. E. (1948). The doctrine of suggestion, prestige, and imitation in social psychology. *Psychological Review, 55*, 250–277.

Asch, S. E. (1951). Effects of group pressure upon the modification and distortion of judgment. In H. Guetzkow (Ed.), *Groups, leadership, and men* (pp. 222–236). Pittsburgh: Carnegie Press.

Balliet, D., Mulder, L. B., & Van Lange, P. A. M. (2011). Reward, punishment, and cooperation: A meta-analysis. *Psychological Bulletin, 137*(4), 594–615.

Bargh, J. A., & Chartrand, T. L. (2000). Studying the mind in the middle: A practical guide to priming and automaticity research. In H. Reis & C. Judd (Eds.), *Handbook of research methods in social and personality psychology* (pp. 253–285). New York: Cambridge University Press.

Bem, D. J. (1965). An experimental analysis of self-persuasion. *Journal of Experimental Social Psychology, 1*, 199–218.

Bem, D. J. (1967). Self-perception: An alternative interpretation of cognitive dissonance phenomena. *Psychological Review, 74*, 183–200.

Berkowitz, L., & LePage, A. (1967). Weapons as aggression-eliciting stimuli. *Journal of Personality and Social Psychology, 7*(2, pt.1), 202–207.

Boyer, R. (2011). Are there laws of motion of capitalism? *Socio-Economic Review, 9*, 59–81.

Breau, D. L., & Brook, B. (2007). 'Mock' mock juries: A field experiment on the ecological validity of jury simulations. *Law & Psychology Review, 31*, 77–92.

Brehm, J. W., & Cohen, A. R. (1959). Re-evaluation of choice-alternatives as a function of their number and qualitative similarity. *Journal of Abnormal and Social Psychology, 58*, 373–378.

Brehm, J. W., & Cohen, A. R. (1962). *Explorations in cognitive dissonance*. New York: Wiley.

Bremer, S., & Mihalka, M. (1977). Machiavelli in machina: Or politics among hexagons. In K. Deutsch, B. Fritsch, H. Jaguaribe, & S. Markovits (Eds.), *Problems of real-world modeling: Political and social implications* (pp. 303–338). Cambridge, MA: Ballinger.

Brewer, M. B., & Gardner, W. (1996). Who is this "we"? Levels of collective identity and self- representations. *Journal of Personality and Social Psychology, 71,* 83–93.

Brewer, M. B., & Miller, N. (1984). Beyond the contact hypothesis: Theoretical perspectives on desegregation. In N. Miller & M. B. Brewer (Eds.), *Groups in contact: The psychology of desegregation.* Orlando, FL: Academic Press.

Brody, R. A. (1963). Some systematic effects of nuclear weapons technology: A study through simulation of a multi-nuclear future. *Journal of Conflict Resolution, 7,* 663–753.

Cacioppo, J., Priester, J., & Berntston, G. (1993). Rudimentary determination of attitudes. II: Arm flexion and extension have differential effects on attitudes. *Journal of Personality and Social Psychology, 65,* 5–17.

Cameron, L., Chaudhuri, A., Erkal, N., & Gangadharan, L. (2009). Propensities to engage in and punish corrupt behavior: Experimental evidence from Australia, India, Indonesia, and Singapore. *Journal of Public Economics, 93,* 843–851.

Carlson, R. (1971). Where is the person in personality research? *Psychological Bulletin, 75,* 203–219.

Carney, D. R., Cuddy, A., & Yap, A. (2010). Power posing: Brief nonverbal displays affect neuroendocrine levels and risk tolerance. *Psychological Science, 21,* 1362–1368.

Carter, T. J., Ferguson, M. J., & Hassin, R. R. (2011). A single exposure to the American flag shifts support toward Republicanism up to 8 months later. *Psychological Science, 22,* 1011–1018.

Chapin, W. D. (1998). The Balance of Power game. *Simulation and Gaming, 29,* 105–112.

Cohen, J. A. (1988). *Statistical power analysis for the behavioral sciences* (2nd ed.). Hillsdale, NJ: Erlbaum

Cohen, J. A. (1992). A power primer. *Psychological Bulletin, 112,* 155–159.

Cox, J., Clark, J. C., Edens, J. F., Smith, S. T., & Magyar, M. S. (2013). Jury panel member perceptions of interpersonal-affective traits of psychopathy predict support for execution in a capital murder trial simulation. *Behavioral Sciences & the Law, 31*(4), 411–428.

Crano, W. D., Siegel, J. T., Alvaro, E. M., & Patel, N. (2007). Overcoming adolescents' resistance to anti-inhalant appeals. *Psychology of Addictive Behaviors, 21,* 516–524.

Crano, W. D., & Sivacek, J. M. (1984). The influence of incentive-aroused ambivalence on overjustification effects in attitude change. *Journal of Experimental Social Psychology, 20,* 137–158.

Cronkite, R. C. (1980). Social psychological simulations: An alternative to experiments? *Social Psychology Quarterly, 43,* 199–216.

Crutchfield, R. F. (1955). Conformity and character. *American Psychologist, 10,* 191–198.

Darley, J. M., & Latané, B. (1968). Bystander intervention in emergencies: Diffusion of responsibility. *Journal of Personality and Social Psychology, 10,* 202–214.

Druckman, D. (1968). Ethnocentrism in the Inter-nation Simulation. *Journal of Conflict Resolution, 12,* 45–68.

Duclos, S., Laird, J., Schneider, E., Sexter, M., Stern, L., & van Lighten, O. (1989). Emotion-specific effects of facial expressions and postures on emotional experience. *Journal of Personality and Social Psychology, 57,* 100–108.

Festinger, L., & Carlsmith, J. M. (1959). Cognitive consequences of forced compliance. *Journal of Personality and Social Psychology, 58,* 203–210.

Fowler, S. M., & Pusch, M. D. (2010). Intercultural simulation games: A review (of the United States and beyond). *Simulation & Gaming, 41,* 94–115.

Freedman, J. L. (1969). Role playing: Psychology by consensus. *Journal of Personality and Social Psychology, 13,* 107–114.

Gaertner, S. L., Mann, J., Murrell, A., & Dovidio, J. (1989). Reducing intergroup bias: the benefits of recategorization. *Journal of Personality and Social Psychology, 57,* 239–249.

Galtier, F., Bousquet, F., Antona, M., & Bommel, P. (2012). Markets as communication systems: Simulating and assessing the performance of market networks. *Journal of Evolutionary Economics, 22,* 161–201.

Gamson, W. A. (1969). *SIMSOC, simulated society: Participant's manual with selected readings.* New York: MACM.

Gamson, W. A., & Stambaugh, R. J. (1978). The model underlying SIMSOC. *Simulation & Games, 9,* 131–157.

Gardner, W. L., Pickett, C. L., & Brewer, M. B. (2000). Social exclusion and selective memory: How the need to belong influences memory for social events. Personality and Social *Psychology Bulletin, 26,* 486–496.

Gerard, H. B., Wilhelmy, R. A., & Conolley, E. S. (1968). Conformity and group size. *Journal of Personality and Social Psychology, 8,* 79–82.

Greenwood, J. D. (1983). Role-playing as an experimental strategy in social psychology. *European Journal of Social Psychology, 13,* 235–254.

Guetzkow, H., Alger, C., Brody, R., Noel, R., & Sidney, R. (1963). *Simulation in international relations: Developments for research and teaching.* Englewood Cliffs, NJ: Prentice-Hall.

Hastie, R., & Stasser, G. (2000). Computer simulation methods for social psychology. In H. Reis & C. Judd (Eds.), *Handbook of research methods in social and personality psychology* (pp. 85–114). New York: Cambridge University Press.

Hofstede, G. J., & Murff, E. J. T. (2012). Repurposing an old game for an international world. *Simulation & Gaming, 43*, 34–50.

Horowitz, I. L., & Rothschild, B. H. (1970). Conformity as a function of deception and role playing. *Journal of Personality and Social Psychology, 14*, 224–226.

Kelman, H. C. (1967). Human use of human subjects: The problem of deception in social psychological experiments. *Psychological Bulletin, 67*, 1–11.

Klein, R. D., & Fleck, R. A. (1990). International business simulation/gaming: An assessment and review. *Simulation and Gaming, 21*, 147–165.

Kramer, R. M., & Brewer, M. B. (1984). Effects of group identity on resource use in a simulated commons dilemma. *Journal of Personality and Social Psychology, 46*, 1044–1057.

Latané, B., & Darley, J. M. (1968). Group inhibition of bystander intervention. *Journal of Personality and Social Psychology, 10*, 215–221.

Latané, B., & Darley, J. M. (1970). *The unresponsive bystander: Why doesn't he help?.* New York: Appleton-Century Crofts.

Levy, L. (1960). Studies in conformity behavior: A methodological note. *Journal of Psychology, 50*, 39–41.

Lord, C. G., & Saenz, D. S. (1985). Memory deficits and memory surfeits: Differential cognitive consequences of tokenism for tokens and observers. *Journal of Personality and Social Psychology, 49*, 918–926.

Luce, R. D., & Raiffa, N. (1958). *Games and decisions.* New York: Wiley.

McDonald, D. (1998). The art of negotiating. *Simulation and Gaming, 29*, 475–479.

Messick, D. M., & Brewer, M. B. (1983). Solving social dilemmas: A review. In L. Wheeler & P. Shaver (Eds.), *Review of personality and social psychology* (vol. 4). Beverly Hills, CA: Sage.

Messick, D. M., Wilke, H., Brewer, M. B., Kramer, R. M., Zemke, P., & Lui, L. (1983). Individual adaptations and structural change as solutions to social dilemmas. *Journal of Personality and Social Psychology, 44*, 294–309.

Milgram, S. (1963). Behavioral study of obedience. *The Journal of Abnormal and Social Psychology, 67*, 371–378.

Milgram, S. (1965). Some conditions of obedience and disobedience to authority. *Human Relations, 18*, 57–75.

Milinski, M., Sommerfeld, R. D., Krambeck, H.-J., Reed, F. A., & Marotzke, J. (2008). The collective-risk social dilemma and the prevention of simulated dangerous climate change. *PNAS Proceedings of the National Academy of Sciences of the United States of America, 105*, 2291–2294.

Miller, A. G. (1972). Role playing: An alternative to deception? A review of the evidence. *American Psychologist, 27*, 623–636.

Mixon, D. (1972). Instead of deception. *Journal for the Theory of Social Behavior, 2*, 145–177.

Niedenthal, P. M., Barsilou, L., Winkielman, P., Krauth-Gruber, S., & Ric, F. (2005). Embodiment in attitudes, social perception, and emotion. *Personality and Social Psychology Review, 9*, 184–211.

Nisbett, R. E., & Wilson, T. D. (1977). Telling more than we can know: Verbal reports on mental processes. *Psychological Review, 84*, 231–259.

Phills, C., Kawakami, K., Tabi, E., Inzlicht, M., & Nadolny, D. (2011). Mind the gap: Increasing associations between the self and Blacks with approach behaviours. *Journal of Personality and Social Psychology, 100*, 197–210.

Raser, J. R. (1972). *Simulation and society. An exploration of scientific gaming.* Boston, MA: Allyn and Bacon.

Raser, J. R., & Crow, W. J. (1968). A simulation study of deterrence theories. In L. Kriesberg (Ed.), *Social processes in international relations.* New York: Wiley.

Rosenberg, M. J., & Abelson, R. P. (1960). An analysis of cognitive balancing. In C. I. Hovland & M. J. Rosenberg (Eds.), *Attitude organization and change: An analysis of consistency among attitude components* (pp. 112–163). New Haven, CT: Yale University Press.

Schultz, D. (1969). The human subject in psychological research. *Psychological Bulletin, 72*, 214–228.

Smoker, P. (1968). International processes simulation: A man-computer model. Accession Number: AD0737741: Defense Technical Information Center. Evanston, Ill.: Northwestern University [mimeographed].

Starkey, B. A., & Blake, E. L. (2001). Simulation in international relations education. *Simulation & Gaming, 32*, 537–551.

Stoll, R. J. (2011). Civil engineering: Does a realist world influence the onset of civil wars? *Simulation & Gaming, 42,* 748–771.

Strack, F., Martin, L., & Stepper, S. (1988). Inhibiting or facilitating conditions of the human smile: A nonobtrusive test of the facial feedback hypothesis. *Journal of Personality and Social Psychology, 54,* 768–777.

Strand, J. R., & Rapkin, D. P. (2011). Weighted voting in the United Nations security council: A simulation. *Simulation & Gaming, 42,* 772–802.

Torres, M., & Macedo, J. (2000). Learning sustainable development with a new simulation game. *Simulation and Gaming, 31,* 119–126.

Wells, G. L., & Petty, R. E. (1980). The effects of overt head movements on persuasion: Compatibility and incompatibility of responses. *Basic and Applied Social Psychology, 1*(3), 219–230.

Xu, Y., & Bernard, A. (2013). A quantitative model on knowledge management for team cooperation. *Knowledge-Based Systems, 45,* 41–46.

Zanna, M. P., & Cooper, J. (1974). Dissonance and the pill. An attribution approach to studying the arousal properties of dissonance. *Journal of Personality and Social Psychology, 29,* 703–709.

Zimbardo, P. (2007). *The Lucifer effect: Understanding how good people turn evil.* New York: Random House.

Zimbardo, P. G., Haney, C., Banks, W. C., & Jaffe, D. A. (1973, April). Pirandellian prison: The mind is a formidable jailer. *New York Times Magazine, 8,* 38–60.

Zinnes, D. A. (1966). A comparison of hostile state behavior in simulate and historical data. *World Politics, 18,* 474–502.

7
EXTERNAL VALIDITY OF LABORATORY EXPERIMENTS

It often is thought that the use of laboratory experiments in social research involves achieving internal validity at the cost of external validity, or generalization of results to the world outside the laboratory. This view betrays a misunderstanding of the logic and meaning of internal and external validity, but it is common, and because of this critics within and outside the social sciences have argued that the experimental approach that structures so many of our research endeavors is inadequate or inappropriate for the study of social beings.

A commonplace criticism of the social laboratory experiment concerns its artificiality, or reactivity, and the consequent impossibility of determining the adequacy of generalizations based upon experimental data. After reviewing nearly 20 years of research in his field, for example, Cronbach (1975, p. 116) appeared to have despaired even of the possibility of developing lasting and useful generalizations from social research when he stated, "it [is] unlikely that social scientists will be able to establish generalizations applicable beyond the laboratory or that generalizations established in the field work will be maintained. Social research should be less concerned with hypothesis testing and more concerned with interpreting findings in local contexts." A similar theme was sounded by Gergen (1973, 1976; but see Schlenker, 1974; Wallach & Wallach, 1993), who argued that social science research was more a historical than a scientific enterprise. Our theories, he argued, are little more than post hoc descriptions restricted by the particular set of historical circumstances in which they are developed. As circumstances change, so too must these time-bound descriptions. These critiques were discomforting, but they were valuable because they motivated social researchers to become more conscious of the factors that could compromise the ultimate contribution of their work. As a result, the field now is much more concerned with issues of generalizability and applicability than it was a short time ago.

Even so, the question of the generalizability of our research findings is never definitively settled. Although the certainty of generalizations can never be attained, it can be approximated, or approached, and the approximations can become progressively more exact if we are sensitive to the forces that influence behavior within and outside the experimental laboratory. So for the remainder of this chapter we will consider aspects of the laboratory experiment that affect the trustworthiness of experimentally based generalizations. Although our observations cannot answer all of the objections that have been raised by the critics of experimentation in social research, it is clear that our recommendations will provide much firmer grounds for generalization if followed than if ignored. It also will become clear that the issues of generalization that have been raised in the context of the controlled experiment apply also to alternate non-experimental research tactics, to be discussed in the upcoming chapters.

Generalizability Across Participants

The principal components of all social experiments include participants, experimenters, measures, and the manipulations employed to influence participants' behavior. In the first part of this chapter, we concentrate on aspects of the participant sample and the manipulations to which participants are exposed. In the last part, questions and findings concerning the actions of the experimenter— and the potential impact of these behaviors on the internal as well as external validity of an experiment—will be discussed.

Restriction of Participant Populations

Many critics of social experimentation have argued that from the viewpoint of generalization of findings, the individual typically used in research, the college undergraduate, is perhaps not the most ideal choice. In fact, it has been stated in the past that there is possibly nothing more dissimilar to the average "man in the street" than the college undergraduate. The average college student is more intelligent than the typical person on the street; is usually healthier; is more concerned with the social forces operating on the physical and social environment; is sensitive to the various communication media and thus better informed; is less likely to hold strongly fixed attitudes; and plays a greater and more active role in exerting control over the factors influencing daily life (Sears, 1986). Furthermore, the college students that we do study are drawn almost exclusively from Western, educated, industrialized, rich, and democratic societies (WEIRD: Henrich, Heine, & Norenzayan, 2010).

The impact of these differences in some investigations is probably great. In many areas of psychological research, however, the use of college students as participants could be expected to have only a minor, if any, influence. In a great proportion of investigations, the processes under study represent processes so basic that the special peculiarities of the college student could not reasonably confine the generalizability of results to just this cohort. One such fundamental process is people's judgment of attractiveness and the stereotypes that arise. Countless experimental investigations have demonstrated that regardless of the sample being studied, participants almost always tend to ascribe more favorable stereotypes and attributes, such as social and intellectual competence, to a person perceived to be attractive rather than unattractive (Eagly, Ashmore, Makhijani, & Longo, 1991; Lemay, Clark, & Greenberg, 2010). In a situation in which basic human processes are under study (and it is in precisely this type of situation that the experiment is most advantageously employed), it seems reasonable to assume that the particular idiosyncrasies of the individuals sampled should have relatively little effect upon the results obtained. Even if this were not the case, the sampling of unusual populations still might be encouraged, if the experimenter cannot find other, more nearly "average" groups. Consistent with the general orientation of Campbell and Stanley (1963), we would argue that the development of social theory based on research using the college student (or of any other esoteric or conveniently sampled group) is better than no research at all. Once results are determined from a restricted population, principles of behavior can then be investigated systematically in other demographic groups to test whether participant characteristics limit the generalizability of the original findings.

Participant Awareness

Arguments about the representativeness of college student participants deal with only one aspect of the "participant" issue. Many critics of laboratory experimentation object not simply because a sample is drawn from an unusual population, but also because the responses of any individual conscious of the fact that he or she is under observation could be quite different from those of persons not under such experimenter scrutiny. This argument is an important one, but we need to consider the degree to which this "self-consciousness effect" might operate within any given experiment. In some cases, the participant's awareness of being observed may be the most salient feature of the total experimental situation. If this is so, then the obtained results of such a study should be viewed with caution—but certainly not dismissed from consideration. In more ideal instances, however, because the situation engages the attention of the participant, it seems likely that the participant's awareness of being studied would be greatly diminished, and thus would have negligible or no impact on the results. In most cases, the experimenter should attempt to construct situations that reduce the self-consciousness of participants as much as possible.

One characteristic that can be expected to influence participants' awareness of being under study, and how they respond to that awareness, is the degree of freedom that they had in agreeing to commit themselves to the research. Depending on how participants are recruited to the investigation, they can be generally classified into one of three categories, which we have termed voluntary, involuntary, and nonvoluntary participants.

Voluntary Participants

Individuals considered to be **voluntary participants** are aware that they are under investigation, but have made a conscious decision that the potential benefits outweigh the costs (measured in terms of time spent, privacy invaded, etc.) of being in the study. This decision can be prompted by many factors: monetary incentives, altruism, attainment of greater personal insight, possibly contributing to human science, etc. If this positive mindset is maintained during the experiment (i.e., if the design and procedures do not force participants to revise their estimates of benefits and costs), then it is doubtful that such participants would willfully attempt to subvert the experiment. This is not to suggest that participants all of a sudden become unaware of the fact that they are being studied, but rather that they consider this potential invasion of privacy to be part of the social contract with the experimenter, and are willing, as long as the benefit-to-cost ratio remains positive, to respond in an honest and authentic manner.

It sometimes happens that the voluntary participant proves to be too willing to cooperate, too eager to help the experimenter confirm the research hypotheses. Rosenthal and Rosnow (1975), in an extensive review of the volunteer participant literature, found volunteers to be better educated than non-volunteers and to have higher occupational status, a higher need for approval, higher intelligence, and better adjustment than non-volunteers. If these factors contribute to an overly cooperative volunteer, that is, a participant intent to help confirm the research hypotheses, the generalizability of the study could be impacted.

Involuntary Participants

Individuals who are **involuntary participants** feel that they have been coerced to spend their time in an experimental investigation and consider it unjustifiable, and therefore vent their displeasure by actively attempting to ruin the study. They have proven to be the bane of experiments. The feeling of coercion on the part of participants can be stimulated in a number of different ways. In many universities in the United States, for example, introductory psychology students are expected to serve in some minimum number of research studies as part of course requirements. In earlier times in the armed forces, draftees were commonly tested and sometimes experimented upon without their consent. Individuals of minority groups, because of their relative rarity, often find themselves the targets of unwanted scientific scrutiny. Persons forced to comply with the demands of some higher authority can generate considerable resentment, which can seriously affect the outcome of the study. Dissatisfaction with "guinea pig" status in many situations is both understandable and justified. Unless the experimenter can demonstrate that participation in the study is not a one-sided proposition, but rather a cooperative venture in which both parties can gain something of value, there is no reason to expect willing acquiescence to the participant role. Sometimes payment can be used to help the participant justify participation in the study. More satisfactory is the experimenter's explanation of the reasons for and the importance of the investigation prior to the experiment. Participants' willingness to serve in studies they perceive to be of scientific importance is gratifying and surprising.

Whether participants are more accurately described as voluntary or involuntary, some rationale for their participation always should be provided at the beginning of the experiment. No one likes to waste time, even if paid to do so. By informing participants of the importance of the research project and of the importance of their role in the research process, the experimenter can instill a sense of positive commitment in participants. In many circumstances, informing participants of their role is a prerequisite for their participation. Most ethics review committees require at the beginning of the study that participants be apprised of their rights, which includes information regarding the time involved, the potential risks their work might entail, and the potential contribution of their efforts.

Nonvoluntary Participants

Those considered **nonvoluntary participants** unknowingly enter into an experimental situation and are unaware that they are part of a study until after the completion of the study. After their responses are recorded, the investigator may (or may not) explain the nature of the study to the "participants." Because they are unaware of their participation in a study, it is obvious that the reactions of nonvoluntary participants cannot be described as artificial or laboratory dependent. Results based on the reactions of such individuals should enjoy a high degree of external validity, or generalizability. A discussion of the ethical considerations involved in the use of nonvoluntary participants will be deferred until the final chapter, but because our argument will be that this practice is sometimes defensible, some description of the ways in which these participants can be employed will be presented here.

Many issues can be investigated experimentally in naturalistic surroundings with nonvoluntary participants, if one is attentive to the investigative possibilities offered by contemporary events. For example, Sivacek and Crano (1982) polled students on a number of issues of concern, including an upcoming referendum on the drinking age. Participants were divided into three groups according to whether their own age group would be affected by the change in the law. Two weeks later, the same subjects were recontacted and asked if they wished to work for an organization (that was fictitious) to help defeat the referendum. At this point, the participants did not realize they were still a part of a psychological study. As expected, even though students of all ages had the same negative attitude toward the law change, younger participants, who were most vested in the issue, were more willing to pledge more of their time.

Nonvoluntary participants are typically used in field research situations outside the laboratory, where participants do not know they are taking part in an experiment. However, even within the context of laboratory experiments, some studies have been designed so that the participants entering (or leaving) an experimental laboratory are treated and tested before they realize the experiment has begun (or after they think it has ended). Bargh, Chen, and Burrows (1996) provide an interesting example of the use of nonvoluntary participants in their intriguing study on the effects of priming (which is discussed as an implicit measure in Chapter 16). In their experiment, they activated the stereotype of the elderly to determine its effects on subsequent behavior in a sample of college students. Researchers gave the participants 30 sets of 5 words. In an apparent test of language proficiency, they were instructed to rearrange and unscramble each set of words so they made grammatical sense. In the "elderly prime" condition, the sentences contained words associated with old age, such as *old, lonely, grey, forgetful, retired, wrinkle, ancient, Florida,* and *bingo,* among others. For the control group, these words were replaced by words that were unrelated to age (thirsty, clean, etc.).

After participants individually completed the task, they were partially debriefed and dismissed. They were told the elevator to leave the building was down the hall, and when they left the office, a confederate activated a hidden stopwatch and timed their journey from the doorway to the carpet in front of the elevator. At this point, the experimenter intercepted the participant and fully explained the study. The results showed that participants who had been randomly assigned to the elderly prime took significantly longer to walk to the elevator (as would the elderly) than those in the control group.

This study provides an interesting examination and extension of the nonvoluntary participant concept. Obviously, participants in Bargh's and associates' experiment knew they were the subjects in a psychological experiment. However, the critical behavior was assessed after they thought the experiment was completed and were on their way out of the building, so it is unlikely that their speed of walking to the elevator was affected by their awareness of being the subject of psychological study.

Participant Roles

In an interesting discussion of the effects of participant characteristics on research outcomes, Webber and Cook (1972) attempted to characterize the roles that participants most frequently choose to adopt in experimental settings. In their system, they identified four general participant types: **good participants**, who attempt to determine the experimenter's hypotheses and to confirm them; **negative participants**, who also are interested in determining the experimenter's hypotheses, but only in order to sabotage the study (Masling, 1966, referred to this type of reaction as the "screw you" effect); **faithful participants**, who are willing to cooperate fully with almost any demand by the experimenter, and who follow instructions scrupulously and ignore any suspicions they might have regarding the true purpose of the study; and finally, **apprehensive participants**, who worry that the experimenter will use their performance to evaluate their abilities, personality, social adjustment, etc., and react accordingly in the study.

This categorization is compatible with, and amplifies, the voluntary-involuntary-nonvoluntary participant distinction that we drew earlier. We assume that almost all participants are at least partly apprehensive about taking part in an experiment, although this apprehension probably diminishes with experience. Involuntary participants are most likely to be negativistic, as are voluntary participants who learn that the cost-to-benefit ratio of their participation is not as favorable as they thought it would be when they originally signed up for the study. The good and the faithful participant roles are most likely to be assumed by voluntary participants. Nonvoluntary participants, being unaware that they are being studied, are unlikely to assume any of the roles that Webber and Cook defined. Although some experimenters find little support for these role distinctions (e.g., Carlston & Cohen, 1980), some very careful and thoughtful research (Carlopio, Adair, Lindsay, & Spinner, 1983) has produced evidence in essential agreement with the participant role categories we have discussed (see Strohmetz, 2008).

In studies of participants' motivation in experiments, it has been found that many would go to great lengths to "please" the experimenter, that is, to help confirm the perceived research hypotheses. Although Orne (1962) was not the first to investigate this issue (e.g., Pierce, 1908), he was able to demonstrate quite clearly the almost incredible degree to which participants were willing to help the experimenter. Presenting participants with approximately *2,000* pages of random numbers, instructing them to sum adjacent numbers for a total of 224 additions performed on each page, and to continue to work at this task until his return, Orne found almost no one who was willing to quit this ridiculous task even after 5 hours had elapsed. Adding a final step to this process—asking participants to tear the completed pages into "a minimum of *32* pieces," to throw the pieces into the wastebasket, and to begin again—had almost no effect on the participants' persistence. Participants continued other similarly self-defeating tasks beyond reasonable limits. When questioned about their unusual perseverance, they often responded with a guess that the research hypothesis was concerned with endurance, and thus their actions were quite appropriate. Respondent performances of this type have alerted researchers to the tremendous degree of behavioral control the experimenter can intentionally and unintentionally exert in the laboratory.

Nowhere was this fact more evident than in the studies of Stanley Milgram (1963, 1965). While investigating the effects of a range of variables on "obedience" behavior, Milgram's basic experimental procedure took the guise of a two-person (teacher-learner) verbal memory and learning study. In these studies, the naive participant was asked to serve as the "teacher," whose task was to shock the "leaner" (confederate) each time the leaner committed a recall error from a list of words. In fact, a confederate played the role of the learner and received no shocks.

The shock generator was a rather formidable-looking apparatus, with 30 switches and voltage levels in 15-volt increments, ranging from 15 to 450 volts, and written descriptions of these voltages ranged from "Slight Shock" to "Danger: Severe Shock." The confederate was placed in an adjacent room and purposely gave many wrong answers based on a predetermined script to standardize the study across participants. In response to each incorrect answer, the teacher was to increase the level of punishment.

The dependent measure of this study was the voltage level at which the naive participant refused to administer further punishment to the "learner." When the 150-volt level was reached, the learner audibly demanded to be set free, to terminate the experiment. Though the learner was unseen, his protestations, amplified from the adjacent room, were truly heartrending. At this point in the investigation, almost all the participants requested to end the study. The researcher, however, always responded, "You have no other choice, you must go on!" A substantial percentage of the participants obeyed all of the researcher's commands. In one of these studies, for example, 61% of the individuals tested continued to the very end of the shock series (Milgram, 1965), and across the entire study series, the mean compliance rate was in the 60% range!

When questioned about their actions afterward, Milgram's participants' responses were similar to those of Orne's. The most common rationale offered by participants was that they viewed themselves as an integral part of a scientific investigation, and they were determined to fulfill their commitment to the study, even though this might entail some discomfort. It should be stressed that these participants did not enjoy themselves in this study. Milgram's filmed records indicate that many naive participants vehemently protested the demands to continue the experiment and demonstrated clear signs of nervousness, stress, and tension. Even so, most continued to the bitter end of the shock generator. It would appear that under the auspices of a "scientific investigation" people were willing to obey the commands of the authority figure and to commit themselves to boring, tedious, meaningless, and even blatantly immoral actions, which they very well might have refused to perform outside of the laboratory setting.

Apart from the moral and ethical implications of this investigation, we must also consider findings of this type from the standpoint of generalizability. Were the participants willing to perform their questionable behaviors only when asked to do so for the sake of science? If so, we must question whether the relationships discovered would hold outside the laboratory setting. But suppose the participants *were* willing to assume these roles outside the laboratory and to perform as told whenever an important authority (duty, allegiance to a higher law, etc.) was involved. In that case, Milgram's research would be applicable in a variety of contexts.

Experimenter Expectancy and Bias

To this point, we have shown how decisions regarding the basic features of the experiment can influence the internal and external validity of the investigation. Should we use voluntary, involuntary, or nonvoluntary participants? Should we be concerned with experimental realism or mundane realism (discussed in the previous chapter)? Recall that *mundane realism* refers to the extent to which the research setting and operations resemble events in normal, everyday life. *Experimental realism* is concerned with the impact of the experimental treatment. Do participants notice the treatment and feel psychologically involved in the experimental situation? These decisions, under the control of the experimenter, have great bearing on the quality and ultimate contribution of the research enterprise. However, in addition to these deliberate choices, there are aspects of the setting that generally are not consciously controlled, but which also can have considerable influence on the quality and generalizability of the results of an investigation. These influences originate in the experimenter or the experimental setting. For example, we have learned that the mere presence of the experimenter can operate as a subtle but nevertheless potentially powerful "treatment," differentially affecting participants' responses as a result not of the experimental manipulation, but of the experimenter's own expectations about the study.

In an important series of studies initiated in the1960s, Robert Rosenthal and his associates demonstrated that the expectations held by a researcher seemingly can be transmitted to his or her participants, be they elementary school children (Rosenthal & Jacobson, 1968), college sophomores (Rosenthal & Fode, 1963), or Spraugue-Dawley albino rats (Rosenthal & Lawson, 1964). Although controversy still surrounds the medium of communication involved in producing such effects, the process has been demonstrated over a range of experimental contexts (Harris & Rosenthal, 1985, 1986; Rosenthal, 1966).

Research on expectancy effects is not novel. At the turn of the century, Moll (1898) and Jastro (1900) devoted serious attention to this issue. In fact, the "double-blind" method in pharmacological research (in which neither the patient nor the physician knows whether a real drug or a placebo has been administered) was developed specifically to combat expectancy effects on the part of physicians. A **placebo effect** occurs when participants' belief in the efficacy of the treatment, rather than the actual effects of treatment, is responsible for the results found in an experiment. Experimenters test this phenomenon by administering an inert "treatment" superficially resembling the real treatment in order to deliberately mislead participants in the placebo group into believing that they are receiving the treatment. In pharmacological research, participants in the placebo group typically ingest a sugar pill that physically resembles the actual drug. If the experimental and placebo groups exhibit the same outcome scores, this result suggests that the actual treatment itself is not effective, at least not beyond that motivated by participants' beliefs about treatment effectiveness.

In an early investigation of placebo effects, Beecher (1966) compared the effects of morphine, a powerful narcotic, with those of a placebo in the management of moderate pain. Using a double-blind procedure, no differences in pain alleviation were detected between the experimental and control (placebo) groups. Similarly, Reed and Witt (1965) apparently were able to induce hallucinations on the part of a participant who thought he had been given the hallucinogenic drug LSD when, in fact, a placebo had been administered. If effects this profound can be produced through simple manipulations of participants' treatment expectations, imagine how much more intrusive such expectations can be when inadvertently caused by the experimenter.

Rosenthal and Fode (1961, 1963) convincingly demonstrated the presence of experimenter expectancy effects in psychological research. Using a group of students in his experimental psychology course, Rosenthal conducted a laboratory exercise in which selected students were to serve as experimenters. Each experimenter's task was to present a set of 10 full-face photographs to volunteer participants from an introductory psychology course. The participants were asked to rate the "successfulness" of the people depicted in the photographs. Up to this point, the study is completely straightforward. However, before they began, Rosenthal told a cover story to half his experimenters, indicating that previous research had demonstrated that the photos depicted successful people, and thus they could expect relatively high ratings from participants. The other experimenters, although they administered the same photos, were told the opposite. (In fact, the photos were chosen from a larger pool of pictures that had been previously administered to a different group of participants; the photos were chosen because they had been rated essentially neutral with respect to "successfulness.") All experimenters then were told that because the lab exercise was designed to give them practice in "duplicating experimental results," they would be paid twice the usual amount ($2/hour, rather than $1/hour) if their results agreed with these previous findings.

The ratings the two groups of experimenters obtained from their participants were substantially different, in ways consistent with the expectancy hypothesis. Experimenters led to expect positive ratings from the participants recorded and reported significantly more positive ratings from participants than experimenters who expected negative scores. In a variation of this study, in which the biased experimenter was removed to the extent that he or she did not even handle the photographs and was not in direct facial contact with the participants, Fode (1960) obtained results similar to those of the first investigation. Adair and Epstein (1968) removed the biased experimenter even farther from the experimental situation by recording the instructions read by experimenters who had been led to expect either a high or low rating. They played these instructions to a new sample of participants, and obtained expectancy effects in both the face-to-face and the tape-recorded instruction conditions. This result suggests that even unintentional vocal intonation and cues of experimenters may inform participants about the hypothesized and desired direction of results.

As experimenters were offered a monetary incentive to produce findings consistent with "previous research," the question remains as to whether experimenters deliberately misrecorded responses in the confirmatory direction. Rosenthal has argued that although intentional recording errors on the part of the student-experimenters were possible in these studies, they were unlikely to occur. Because the setting allowed participants to observe the experimenter recording their ratings, Rosenthal reasoned that any errors would have been detected and corrected immediately by the participants. Later studies in which the same general approach was employed have resulted in generally confirmatory findings of robust expectancy effects (e.g., Harris, 1991; Harris & Rosenthal, 1985; Rosenthal & Rubin, 1978).

Although the effects of *experimenter bias* due to recording, observation, and computation errors are troublesome, these effects can be detected and avoided (Simonsohn, 2013). More subtle and troublesome is the possibility in which a participant, through some subtle and unintentional cues from the experimenter, decides to perform "correctly," that is, in a manner that he or she thinks will please the researcher (Webber and Cook's (1972) "good" participant role). The interactive nature of the experimenter-participant relationship renders control extremely difficult in such situations. How could such cuing occur? Suppose that each time a "correct" response was made, the experimenter reinforced the participant (either verbally or nonverbally). The reinforcement could be extremely subtle and unintentional. A slight nod of the head, a hardly perceptible smile, a leaning of the body toward the participant, might be all that is needed to trigger a cooperative response. Returning to Rosenthal and Fode's (1963) photo-rating task, consider a participant's relief when, actively attempting to "psych-out" the study, he or she realizes that the experimenter gives a nod of the head, or smiles, or says "good," each time a high photo rating (or a low one, depending upon the experimental condition assigned) is given.

These cues are not limited to ones emitted directly by the experimenter, but could involve artifacts in a laboratory setting—for example, improperly placed equipment (e.g., syringe in a tray) that is unessential to the experiment at hand and that inadvertently provokes participant anxiety. Another example is a "Just Say No to Drugs" poster carelessly posted on the doorway of a laboratory that investigates participants' attitudes and behaviors toward use of illicit substances. **Demand characteristics** are the totality of all social cues communicated in a laboratory not attributable to the manipulation, including those emanating from the experimenter and the laboratory setting, which alter and therefore place a demand on responses of participants. When participants feel constrained by demands that may explicitly or implicitly suggest the preferred response, the study is said to suffer from demand characteristics. Because of the clues transmitted by the experimenter or the laboratory setting, participants believe they have gained insight into the hypothesis and thereby seek to solve the research problem by performing in a way designed to please the investigator.

If this reconstruction is correct, then the majority of expectancy findings can be explained in terms of the behaviors of an experimenter too eager to obtain evidence that will confirm expectations and hypotheses, in combination with research participants who are too eager to please the experimenter. Pseudo-confirmation of expectations can result from experimenters who:

- Systematically err in observation, recording, or analysis of data (whether intentionally or not), and/or
- Cue the participant to the correct response through some form of verbal or nonverbal reinforcement.

Solutions to the Problems of Experimenter Expectancy Bias

The design problem that must be overcome in controlling demand effects is twofold. It consists of controlling both experimenter bias and the intentional or unintentional cuing of the experimental participant. By properly controlling one of these factors we often take care of the other.

Monitoring

From the earlier discussion of observer bias, it would seem that a possible control consideration would entail more careful observation of experimenters to insure that their data transcription and analysis were accurate. This could be accomplished by recording the experimenter-participant interaction and comparing the results found by the experimenter with those obtained through the unbiased observers of this interaction. Unfortunately, this process does not preclude the possibility of subtle, nonverbal cuing of the participant by the experimenter. While a more rigorous observation of the social exchange between experimenter and participant is certainly worthwhile, it does not solve completely the potential expectancy problem.

Blind Procedures

A more effective solution is the use of **double-blind procedures**, in which participants as well as the researcher responsible for administering the study are made unaware which treatment condition participants are in. This is used to control for the effects of both researcher bias and participant cuing, and borrows heavily from pharmacological research. The most obvious way this control can be achieved is through the simple expedient of not informing the researchers who interact directly with participants about the aims of the research hypotheses or the condition to which the participants were assigned. This control is useful and widely used, because if experimenters do not know what is expected, they will be unlikely to pass on any biasing cues to participants.[1] Similarly, any recording or calculation errors that might be made should be unbiased and thus would not systematically influence results.

Unfortunately, experimenters, even hired experimenters specifically shielded from information about the theory under development, have been shown to be hypothesis-forming organisms that over the course of an investigation might evolve their own implicit theory of the meaning and nature of the work they are performing. This possibility can be assessed through an investigation of the variability or spread of scores of the experimental data over the course of the entire study. If in a particular condition, scores tend to become more and more homogeneous as the investigation progresses, it would seem that an implicit hypothesis was formed by the experimenter as the study progressed (with the attendant expectancy problems). Although such an analysis enables us to evaluate the probability of the occurrence of implicit hypothesis formation, it does not suggest any realistic way of correcting for this effect.[2] Thus, the particular application of the experimental blind procedure would not seem to offer a real solution to the experimenter expectancy problem, unless the entire experiment could be completed before a researcher could realistically develop a series of implicit hypotheses. It seems likely that this hypothesis-generation behavior could be impeded if the experimenter was prohibited from discovering the hypothesized direction of results until the completion of the investigation, but often because of information conveyed by the materials and measures used in an experimental situation, this is not possible.

A slight variant of this procedure does not presume to eliminate knowledge of the research hypotheses from the investigators, but rather limits their information about the research condition to which any participant or group of participants has been assigned. Often, in a variant of the double-blind experiment, it is possible to test both treatment and control participants in the same setting, at the same time, without the experimenter's or participants' knowledge of the specific condition into which any individual falls. This is especially likely when (written) instructional manipulations are used. For example, suppose that a market researcher wanted to decide between four spokespersons for a newspaper advertising campaign designed to help sell a new automobile model. Accordingly, the researcher develops four newspaper advertisements with an identical message designed to sell a new car, except that they are attributed to different sources: a noted consumer advocate, a Nobel-prize winning physicist, a trusted TV personality, and a popular sports hero. To avoid problems of experimenter expectancy, the market researcher randomly mixes the four newspaper ads and distributes them to participants whose reactions to the new car model then are assessed. Each participant in the room is presented an envelope containing the advertisement corresponding to one of the four conditions Because the researcher does not know which participant received which source, it is obvious that experimenter expectancies could not influence the results. Thus, even though the researcher might hold a strong expectation that the consumer advocate's endorsement would prove most persuasive, experimenter bias could not operate on participants' responses if the researcher could not distinguish between those who received the ad copy attributed to this source and those whose copy was attributed to other sources.

Mechanized Procedures

Whereas this variant of the blind procedure can be employed in many different experimental settings, it cannot be used in all situations. In some settings the experimental and control conditions cannot be studied simultaneously, in the same location. In such cases, mechanization of the experimental procedures can provide the solution to the problem of experimenter expectancy. Instructions, manipulations, and procedures could be presented to participants via audiotape, videotape, or a computer program, with respondents' answers collected using these electronic devices, and data analyzed by an impartial computer. Procedures where data are collected "untouched by human hands" helps render implausible the alternative hypothesis of experimenter expectancy if these devices are employed intelligently and not subverted by inappropriate actions on the part of the investigator.

As experiments administered via computer technologies usually involve using a mouse (or touchscreen) and a keyboard as a proxy for social interactions, such procedures can prove uninvolving, uninteresting, or unreal to the participant. These reactions in turn can give rise to a host of contaminating features. This need not always be the case. With adequate preparation, a realistic, interesting, and sometimes even educational experimental situation can be devised. And, as recent experience with computer-based experimental administration has demonstrated, the intelligent use of computers to present experimental treatments, or to monitor participants' reactions, can represent a positive and important step in the solution of the problem of experimenter bias.

Clearly, any list of suggestions for controlling or minimizing experimenter expectancy effects will of necessity prove incomplete. Many other approaches to the solution of the expectancy problem are possible but are idiosyncratic to the experimental setting employed. The important consideration that should be kept in mind is that attempts to prevent expectancy effects must be made as part of good experimental design. Blind procedures, especially the double-blind variety, should be used where possible, and mechanization, which often creates a somewhat artificial social experience, should be retained for those situations in which the experimental blind is not possible and where translating the manipulation into an electronic format does not compromise the essence of the treatment.

Three Faces of External Validity

External validity refers to the question of whether an effect (and its underlying processes) that has been demonstrated in one research setting would be obtained in other settings, with different research participants and different research procedures. Actually, external validity is not a single construct but represents a whole set of questions about generalizability, each with somewhat different implications for the interpretation and extension of research findings (Brewer & Crano, 2014). The sections that follow discuss three of the most important forms of external validity—robustness, ecological validity, and relevance. Each of these raises somewhat different questions about where, when, and to whom the results of a particular research study can be generalized.

Robustness: Can It Be Replicated?

A result that is replicable across a variety of settings, persons, and historical contexts is said to be robust. In its most narrow sense, **robustness** is concerned with the external validity issue of the extent an effect obtained in one laboratory can be exactly replicated in another laboratory with different researchers. More broadly, the question has to do with whether the general effect holds up in the face of variations in participant populations and settings. Some findings appear to be fragile, obtainable only under highly controlled conditions in a specific context; other results hold up across significant variations to the contexts under which they were originally established.

Technically, robustness would be demonstrated if a particular research study were conducted using a randomly selected sample of participants from a broadly defined population in a random sampling of settings. This approach to external validity implies that the researcher must have defined the populations and settings to which the effect of interest is to be generalized, and then must compile a listing of the populations and settings from which a sample is drawn. Such sampling designs, however, are usually impractical and can be exceptionally expensive. More often, this form of generalizability is established by repeated replications in systematically sampled settings and types of research participants. For instance, a finding initially demonstrated in a laboratory with college students from an eastern college in the U.S. may later be replicated with high school students in the Midwest and among members of a community organization in New England. Such replication strategies involving disparate samples are not only more practical, but they also have potential advantages for theory-testing purposes. If findings do not replicate in systematically selected samples, we sometimes gain clues as to what demographic factors may be moderators of the effect in question (Petty & Cacioppo, 1996).

Generalizability across multiple populations and settings should be distinguished from generalizability to a particular population. A phenomenon that is robust in the sense that it holds up for the population at large may not be obtained for a specific subpopulation or in a particular context. If the question of generalizability is intended to extend to a specific target population (say, from college students to the elderly), then replications must be undertaken within a sample drawn from that new population of interest.

External validity, or generalizability, is related to settings as well as participant populations. The external validity of a finding is challenged if the relationship found between independent and dependent variables is altered when essentially the same research design and procedures are conducted in a different laboratory or field setting, or by experimenters with different characteristics. For example, Milgram's (1974) initial studies of obedience were conducted in a research laboratory at Yale University, but used participants recruited from the community of New Haven. Even though these experiments were conducted with a nonstudent sample, a legitimate question is the extent to which his findings would generalize to other settings. Because participants were drawn from outside the university and because many had no previous experience with college, the prestige and respect associated with a research laboratory at Yale may have made the participants more susceptible to the demands for compliance that the experiment entailed than they would have been in other settings.

To address this issue, Milgram replicated his experiment in a very different physical setting. Moving the research operation to a "seedy" office in the industrial town of Bridgeport, Connecticut, and adopting a fictitious identity as a psychological research firm, Milgram sought to minimize the reputational factors inherent in the Yale setting. In comparison with data obtained in the original study, the Bridgeport replication resulted in slightly lower but still dramatic rates of compliance to the experimenter. Thus, setting could be identified as a contributing, but not crucial, factor to the basic findings of the research.

Ecological Validity: Is It Representative?

The question of whether an effect holds up across a wide variety of people or settings is somewhat different from asking whether the effect is representative of what happens in everyday life. This is the essence of **ecological validity**, which is concerned with the external validity issue of the extent an effect occurs under conditions that are typical or representative in the population. The concept of ecological validity derives from Brunswik's (1956) advocacy of "representative design," in which research is conducted with probabilistic samplings of people and situations.

Representativeness is not the same as robustness. Robustness asks whether an effect can occur across different settings and people; ecological validity asks whether it does occur in the world as is.

From the Brunswik perspective, findings obtained with atypical populations (e.g., college students) in atypical settings (e.g., the laboratory) never have ecological validity until they are demonstrated to occur naturally in more representative circumstances.

Many researchers (e.g., Berkowitz & Donnerstein, 1982; Mook, 1983; Petty & Cacioppo, 1996) take issue with the idea that the purpose of most research is to demonstrate that events actually do occur in a particular population. They argue that testing a causal hypothesis requires demonstrating only that manipulating a cause can alter an effect. Even most applied researchers are more interested in questions of whether interventions *can* change outcomes rather than what *does* happen under existing conditions. Ecological validity is too restrictive a conceptualization of generalizability for research that is designed to test causal hypotheses. Ecological validity is, however, crucial for research that is undertaken for descriptive or demonstration purposes.

Furthermore, the setting in which a causal principle is demonstrated does not necessarily have to resemble the physical settings in which that principle operates in real life for the demonstration to be valid. As Aronson, Wilson, and Brewer (1998) put it, most social psychology researchers are aiming for "psychological realism" rather than "mundane realism" in their experiments. An experimental setting may not resemble features in the real world, but still may capture processes that are representative of those that underlie events in the real world.

Relevance: Does It Matter?

In a sense, the question of ecological validity is also a question of **relevance**, which concerns the external validity issue of the extent an effect obtained is pertinent to events or phenomena that actually occur in the real world. However, relevance also has a broader meaning of whether findings are potentially useful or applicable to solving problems or improving quality of life. Relevance in this sense does not necessarily depend on the physical resemblance between the research setting in which an effect is demonstrated and the setting in which it is ultimately applied. Perceptual research on eye-hand coordination conducted in tightly controlled, artificial laboratory settings has proved valuable to the design of instrument panels in airplanes, even though the laboratory is usually not mistaken for a cockpit.

Relevance is the ultimate form of generalization, and differences among research studies in attention to relevance is primarily a matter of degree rather than of kind. All social research is motivated ultimately by a desire to understand real and meaningful social behavior. But the connections between basic research findings and their application are often indirect and cumulative rather than immediate. Relevance is a matter of social process—the process of how research results are transmitted and used rather than what the research results are (Brewer, 1997).

Is External Validity Important?

External validity—like other issues of validity—must be evaluated with respect to the purpose for which research is being conducted. When the research agenda is essentially descriptive, ecological validity may be essential. When the purpose is utilitarian, robustness of an effect is particularly critical. The fragility and non-generalizability of a finding may be fatal if one's goal is to design an intervention to solve some applied problem. On the other hand, it may not be so critical if the purpose of the research is testing explanatory cause and effect relationships, in which case internal validity is more important than satisfying the various forms of external validity.

In physics, for example, many phenomena can be demonstrated empirically only in a vacuum or with the aid of supercolliders. Nonetheless, the findings from these methods often are extremely important in developing an understanding of basic principles and ultimate application of the science. Mook (1983) has argued compellingly that the importance of external validity has been exaggerated in the psychological sciences. Most experimental research, he contends, is not intended to generalize directly from the artificial setting of the laboratory to "real life," but to test predictions based on theory. He draws an important distinction between "generality of findings" and "generality of conclusions," and holds that the latter purpose does not require that the conditions of testing resemble those of real life. It is the understanding of the underlying processes themselves, not the trivial nuances of the findings, that has external validity.

In effect, Mook argued that construct validity is more important than other forms of external validity when we are conducting theory-testing research. Nonetheless, the need for conceptual replication to establish construct validity requires robustness across research operations and settings. This requirement is similar to that for establishing external validity. The kind of systematic, programmatic research that accompanies the search for external validity inevitably contributes to the refinement and elaboration of theory as well as generalizability.

Conclusion

Issues surrounding the external validity of laboratory experiments are numerous and varied. We agree with the nearly unanimously accepted contention that the question of external validity, or generalizability, can never be answered definitively. However, this does not preclude experimenters from enhancing generalizability in their studies. For example, simply ensuring that a wide range of individuals are used in research means that replicated findings are not tied to the standard college student sample. Understanding and offsetting, to the extent possible, the constraints that the experimental context places on participants also supports the external validity of research results. Conducting studies in ways that limit experimenter bias and experimental demand helps to ensure the validity—external as well as internal—of experimental findings. And finally, dealing with issues of relevance to the participants, issues that matter and that are studied in realistic contexts, in experiments that produce strong effects all add confidence in the external validity of the research. These requirements are not easily satisfied, but meeting them results in findings that are relevant and that may accurately reflect the relationships that exist in the contexts in which they were investigated.

Questions for Discussion

1. When/how does the use of college student samples in social research affect external validity?
2. Why bother to replicate social research studies?
3. You have developed a new form of behavioral therapy for people with various conduct disorders, and you think it is a relatively robust treatment. Specifically, the therapy has been successful when it was practiced in your private clinical office and in a public park, and it has been successful across various age groups (e.g., children, teens, middle-aged individuals, seniors). However, whenever another researcher tries to replicate your treatment implementation, or when individuals attempt to reproduce what they have seen you do on television, no one seems to be able to achieve the same levels of success that you do (and your argument is that others have less success because "they aren't doing it right"). That is not to say your results are fabricated; indeed, your therapy works, just only when you administer it.

    In this example, how would you classify the validity and generalizability of your behavioral therapy? Is it an externally valid therapeutic technique if only you can implement it successfully? How generalizable is it?

Notes

1. This would involve hiring experimenters or data analysts; the individual responsible for mounting the study could hardly be expected to do so without knowing his or her own hypothesis.
2. This observation illustrates the important conceptual distinction between methodological versus statistical control. A methodological control of expectancy would, through appropriate experimental design procedures, render the contamination of results by "experimenter expectancy" improbable. Conversely, statistical control would not rule out the possibility of the occurrence of experimenter effects, but rather would enable us to gauge their strength.

References

Adair, J. G., & Epstein, J. S. (1968). Verbal cues in the mediation of experimenter bias. *Psychological Reports, 22*(3, pt. 2), 1045–1053.

Aronson, E., Wilson, T., & Brewer, M. B. (1998). Experimentation in social psychology. In D. Gilbert, S. Fiske, & G. Lindsey (Eds.), *The handbook of social psychology* (4th ed., vol. 1, pp. 99–142). Boston: McGraw-Hill.

Bargh, J. A., Chen, M., & Burrows, L. (1996). Automaticity of social behavior: Direct effects of trait construct and stereotype activation on action. *Journal of Personality and Social Psychology, 71,* 230–244.

Beecher, H. K. (1966). Pain: One mystery solved. *Science, 151,* 840–841.

Berkowitz, L., & Donnerstein, E. (1982). External validity is more than skin deep: Some answers to criticisms of laboratory experiments. *American Psychologist, 37,* 245–257.

Brewer, M. B. (1997). The social psychology of intergroup relations: Can research inform practice? *Journal of Social Issues, 53,* 197–211.

Brewer, M. B., & Crano, W. D. (2014). Research design and issues of validity. In H. T. Reis & C. M. Judd (Eds.), *Handbook of research methods in social and personality psychology* (2nd ed., pp. 11–26). Cambridge, UK: Cambridge University Press.

Brunswik, E. (1956). *Perception and the representative design of psychological experiments* (2nd ed.). Berkeley, CA: University of California Press.

Campbell, D. T., & Stanley, J. C. (1963). Experimental and quasi-experimental designs for research on teaching. In N. L. Gage (Ed.), *Handbook of research on teaching.* Houghton Mifflin: Boston.

Carlopio, J., Adair, J. G., Lindsay, R. C. L., & Spinner, B. (1983). Avoiding artifact in the search for bias: The importance of assessing subjects' perceptions of the experiment. *Journal of Personality and Social Psychology, 44,* 693–701.

Carlston, D. E., & Cohen, J. L. (1980). A closer examination of subject roles. *Journal of Personality and Social Psychology, 38,* 857–870.

Cronbach, L. J. (1975). Beyond the two disciplines of scientific psychology. *American Psychologist, 30,* 116–127.

Eagly, A. H., Ashmore, R. D., Makhijani, M. G., & Longo, L. C. (1991). What is beautiful is good, but . . .: A meta-analytic review of research on the physical attractiveness stereotype. *Psychological Bulletin, 110,* 109–128.

Fode, K. L. (1960). *The effect of nonvisual and nonverbal interaction of experimenter bias* (Unpublished master's thesis). University of North Dakota, Grand Forks, ND.

Gergen, K. J. (1973). Social psychology as history. *Journal of Personality and Social Psychology, 26,* 309–320.

Gergen, K. J. (1976). Social psychology, science and history. *Personality and Social Psychology Bulletin, 2,* 373–383.

Harris, M. J. (1991). Controversy and cumulation: Meta-analysis and research on interpersonal expectancy effects. *Personality and Social Psychology Bulletin, 17*(3), 316–322.

Harris, M. J., & Rosenthal, R. (1985). Mediation of interpersonal expectancy effects: 31 meta-analyses. *Psychological Bulletin, 97,* 363–386.

Harris, M. J., & Rosenthal, R. (1986). Four factors in the mediation of teacher expectancy effects. In R. S. Feldman (Ed.), *The social psychology of education: Current research and theory* (pp. 91–114). New York: Cambridge University Press.

Henrich, J., Heine, S. J, & Norenzayan, A. (2010). The weirdest people in the world? *Behavioral and Brain Sciences, 33,* 61–135.

Jastro, J. (1900). *Fact and fable in psychology.* Boston, MA: Houghton Mifflin.

Lemay, E. P., Jr., Clark, M. S., & Greenberg, A. (2010). What is beautiful is good because what is beautiful is desired: Physical attractiveness stereotyping as projection of interpersonal goals. *Personality and Social Psychology Bulletin, 36,* 339–353.

Masling, J. (1966). Role-related behavior of the subject and psychologist and its effects upon psychological data. *Nebraska Symposium on Motivation, 14,* 67–103.

Milgram, S. (1963). Behavioral study of obedience. *Journal of Abnormal and Social Psychology, 67,* 371–378.

Milgram, S. (1965). Some conditions of obedience and disobedience to authority. *Human Relations, 18,* 57–75.

Milgram, S. (1974). *Obedience to authority.* New York: Harper & Row.

Moll, A. (1898). *Hypnotism* (4th ed.). New York: Scribner's.

Mook, D. G. (1983). In defense of external invalidity. *American Psychologist, 38,* 379–387.

Orne, M. (1962). On the social psychology of the psychological experiment. *American Psychologist, 17,* 776–783.

Petty, R. E., & Cacioppo, J. T. (1996). Addressing disturbing and disturbed consumer behavior: Is it necessary to change the way we conduct behavioral science? *Journal of Marketing Research, 33,* 1–8.

Pierce, A. H. (1908). The subconscious again. *Journal of Philosophy, Psychology, and Scientific Methods, 5,* 264–271.

Reed, C. F., & Witt, P. N. (1965). Factors contributing to unexpected reactions in two human drug-placebo experiments. *Confina Psychiatrica, 8,* 57–68.

Rosenthal, R. (1966). *Experimenter effects in behavioral research.* New York: Appleton-Century-Crofts.

Rosenthal, R., & Fode, K. L. (1961). The problem of experimenter outcome-bias. In D. P. Ray (Ed.), *Series research in social psychology. Symposia studies series, No. 8.* Washington, DC: National Institute of Social and Behavioral Science.

Rosenthal, R., & Fode, K. L. (1963). Three experiments in experimenter bias. *Psychological Reports, 12,* 491–511.

Rosenthal, R., & Jacobson, L. (1968) *Pygmalion in the classroom.* New York: Holt, Rinehart & Winston.

Rosenthal, R., & Lawson, R. (1964). A longitudinal study of the effects of experimenter bias on the operant learning of laboratory rats. *Journal of Psychiatric Research, 2,* 61–72.

Rosenthal, R., & Rosnow, R. W. (1975). *The volunteer subject.* New York: Wiley-Interscience.

Rosenthal, R., & Rubin, D. B. (1978). Interpersonal expectancy effects: The first 345 studies. *Behavioral and Brain Sciences, 1,* 377–415.

Schlenker, B. R. (1974). Social psychology and science. *Journal of Personality and Social Psychology, 29,* 1–15.

Sears, D. O. (1986). College sophomores in the laboratory: Influences of a narrow data base on social psychology's view of human nature. *Journal of Personality and Social Psychology, 51,* 515–530.

Simonsohn, U. (2013). Just post it: The lesson from two cases of fabricated data detected by statistics alone. *Psychological Science, 24,* 1875–1888.

Sivacek, J. M., & Crano, W. D. (1982). Vested interest as a moderator of attitude-behavior consistency. *Journal of Personality and Social Psychology, 43,* 210–221.

Strohmetz, D. B. (2008). Research artifacts and the social psychology of psychological experiments. *Social and Personality Psychology Compass, 2,* 861–877.

Wallach, L., & Wallach, M. A. (1993). Gergen versus the mainstream: Are hypotheses in social psychology empirical? *Journal of Personality and Social Psychology, 67,* 233–242.

Webber, S. J., & Cook, T. D. (1972). Subject effects in laboratory research: An examination of subject roles, demand characteristics, and valid inference. *Psychological Bulletin, 77,* 273–295.

8
CONDUCTING EXPERIMENTS OUTSIDE THE LABORATORY

In the preceding chapters, we discussed ways in which experiments conducted in laboratory environments can be made as realistic, involving, and impactful as possible. Even when such methods are used, however, it still is desirable to move outside the laboratory into field contexts to extend the construct, internal, and external validities of the results of any research program. As we have stated throughout this book, research should be viewed as a process in which initial observation of a phenomenon gives rise to theory development, which is followed by empirical research. Discrepancies between hypotheses and research results lead us back to further observations, to theory revision and refinement, and then to additional research, as shown in Figure 8.1. Note that neither laboratory nor field research is accorded primacy in this diagram. Each has its place, and each should be engaged in only after appropriate observation and theory development. In this chapter, we support this view by considering ways that experimental methods can be applied outside the laboratory, and how laboratory and field experiments can be used in conjunction with each other. In later chapters, we will take up non-experimental research methods in field contexts.

Fundamentally, the distinction between laboratory and field is one of setting, the context in which the research is conducted. A laboratory is a designated location where participants must go to take part in the research. A **field study** is research conducted outside the laboratory, in which the researcher administers the study in participants' own naturalistic environment or context. With the advent of the Internet as a venue for research, we move the experiment even farther away from the sterile confines of the laboratory to an electronic location, completed in the convenience of participants' own worlds, often into their homes or offices.

The distinction between lab and field is not always clear-cut. The school classroom, for instance, is sometimes converted into a "laboratory" for research purposes, and many laboratory studies have been conducted under the guise of some other activity, such as job interviews or group discussions. In general, however, the dimension that separates laboratory and field experiments is research participants' awareness that they are involved in a scientific study. In field settings, even when informed in advance that a research study is underway, participants are less likely to be as conscious of their behaviors and the research goals as they are in a laboratory environment. Studies conducted on the Internet can be more like laboratory experiments if respondents log on to a site knowing that they are participating in a scientific investigation, or more like a field study if the research is being conducted using ongoing, naturally occurring forums such as chat rooms or other social media sites.

As a general research strategy, the movement between laboratory and field settings should involve a two-way street. Many phenomena of interest to social scientists are first observed in naturalistic

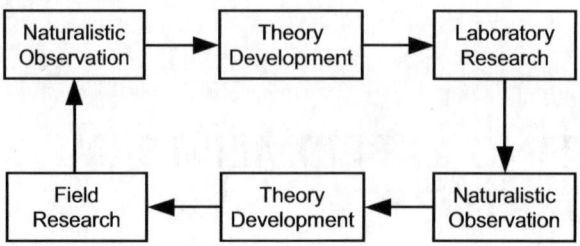

FIGURE 8.1 Research cycle.

settings, but in the complex environment of the real world, it often is difficult to pinpoint the specific effect one variable has on another. To test a particular cause and effect relationship, the independent variable of interest must be dis-embedded from its natural context or causal network and translated into appropriate operations to be studied the laboratory. The laboratory is an ideal setting for the experimenter to take special precautions to control, and therefore prevent, the intrusiveness of extraneous variables from becoming confounds. Once a particular causal relationship has been established in the experimental laboratory or Internet experiment, however, the reasons for moving back into the field as a research site are exactly the reverse of those we have given. It is important to re-embed the causal variable into its natural context, to be certain that its effect is not suppressed or reversed under circumstances in which the phenomenon normally occurs.

Research Settings and Issues of Validity

The interchange between laboratory and field experiments is critical if we are to establish the external and construct validity of a research finding. For the most part, internal validity is inherent in a single study. With sufficient information about how an experiment was conducted, how participants were assigned to treatments, and how treatment conditions were manipulated, we should be able to assess whether the results of that particular study are internally valid. However, issues involving construct validity or external validity can rarely be resolved within the context of a single experiment. These questions require multiple replications of the effect under consideration, ideally across many different research contexts, before meaningful assessments are possible.

Here it is important to distinguish between two types of replication research, where replication refers to the design and conduct of a new study that attempts to repeat the findings of an earlier one. In an **exact replication**, an attempt is made to reproduce the results of a previous study by using the same procedures, particularly the same operationalizations, to represent the same constructs. That is, the operational definitions and conceptual definitions are identical to those of the original study. Only the participants, the time, and the place (and, usually, the experimenter) are changed. The purpose is to determine whether or not a given finding can be reliably repeated under slightly different circumstances. In a **conceptual replication**, an attempt is made to reproduce the results of a previous study by using different operational definitions to represent the same constructs. To establish external validity of a research result, it is sufficient to demonstrate that the same independent variable has a similar effect on the dependent variable in different contexts with different types of participants. To establish construct validity, conceptual replications are required, in which the operationalizations of variables are *dissimilar* from the original study.

In principle, exact replications change the contextual environment of the studies while holding research procedures constant. Conceptual replications change both context and procedures. In reality, variations in context and research operations are neither independent nor mutually exclusive, and both are closely related to alterations in the setting in which an experiment is conducted. In many cases, it is difficult to change the context in which a study takes place without altering the entire experimental setup, and this is particularly true when a replication involves the shift from laboratory to field or Internet settings. The advantages of field experiments are best realized when the operations of the independent and dependent variables are translated to be appropriate to the new context. Such modifications often involve a fundamental rethinking of the theoretical variables and a concern with conceptual, rather than exact, replication of the original study.

Although specific procedures may differ, the basic rationale for the conduct of either field or laboratory experiments is the same. For purposes of the present chapter, however, we will pay particular attention to the ways in which the conduct of a field or Internet experiment is most likely to differ from that of the typical laboratory experiment.

Constructing a Field Experiment

Selection of Participants

Field experiments generally differ from laboratory experiments in the extent to which participants are consciously aware that they are involved in a research project. The two settings (field and laboratory) also differ in the types of people who are usually recruited as participants. A major criticism of laboratory research has been the extent to which it relies on college students as participants (see Krantz & Dalal, 2000; Sears, 1986). Field experiments often provide for a broader, or at least different, representation of participant populations, and these participant variations are even more evident in Internet research. Researchers sometimes select particular field sites specifically to reach participant groups of a particular age or occupation—they go to aged-care homes to study the elderly, to schools to study young children, to circuses to study clowns, and to courtrooms to study lawyers. Other settings (e.g., the city streets) do not permit such selection over a narrowly defined group, but do provide for a wider demographic range of potential participants. It should be emphasized, however, that moving into field settings does not automatically guarantee greater representativeness of participants. Anderson, Lindsay, and Bushman (1999) conducted a comparative review of laboratory and field research in various areas of social psychology. In general, correspondence was high between results from lab- and field-based studies involving conceptually similar independent and dependent variables. The authors concluded that "the psychological laboratory has generally produced psychological truths, rather than trivialities" (p. 3).

Control Over the Independent Variable

Although the essence of experimentation is systematic manipulation by the researcher of variations in treatments or conditions that constitute the independent variable, the extent of experimenter-controlled manipulation in different research settings is a matter of degree. In some instances, the researcher creates experimental conditions from scratch, controlling background context as well as experimental variations (Levine, Cassidy, Brazier, & Reicher, 2002). In other cases, the experimenter controls less of the setting but introduces some systematic variation into the existing conditions, as in the field experiment by Piliavin, Rodin, and Piliavin (1969), where the behavior of an experimental confederate in a subway train was manipulated to study bystander helping in that setting.

In other field research contexts, the experimenter neither manipulates the stimulus conditions directly nor controls participant attention, but instead selects from among naturally occurring stimuli in the field that represent the independent variable of interest. Here the line between experimental and non-experimental research becomes thin indeed, and the distinction depends largely on how well the selected field conditions can be standardized across participants. A good illustration of the use of laboratory research in conjunction with selected field sites comes from the literature on mood and altruism. A number of mood induction manipulations have been developed in laboratory settings. Typically, they require participants to read affectively positive or negative passages or to reminisce about happy or sad experiences in their own past (Forgas, 2000). Following the mood induction, participants are given an opportunity to respond to some form of request—to help a person in need, to exhibit generosity, and so on. Results generally show that positive moods elevate pro-social behavior. Despite multiple replications of this effect in different laboratories with different investigators, however, these findings have been challenged both because of the artificiality of the settings in which the behaviors are induced and because of the potential demand characteristics associated with the rather unusual procedures used to induce moods.

To counter these criticisms, researchers took advantage of a natural mood induction situation based on the emotional impact of selected motion pictures (e.g., Underwood et al., 1977). Following pilot research in which ratings were obtained from moviegoers, a double feature consisting of "Lady Sings the Blues" and "The Sterile Cuckoo" was selected for its negative mood-inducing qualities for use in the experimental condition. Two other double features were selected as the control condition to induce a neutral mood. A commonly occurring event—solicitation of donations to a nationally known charity with collection boxes set up outside the movie theater lobby—was selected as the dependent variable of helping behavior.

Having taken the laboratory mood induction manipulation and translated it into a field manipulation, a major design problem the researchers then encountered was that of participant self-selection to the type of movie preferred. Whereas random assignment of volunteer moviegoers to the two types of movies was a possibility, such a strategy would have recreated many of the elements of artificiality and reactivity that the field setting was designed to avoid. Therefore, the investigators decided to live with self-selection and to alter the research design to take its effect into consideration. For this purpose, timing the collection of charitable donations at the various movie theaters was randomly alternated across different nights, to occur either while most people were entering the theater (prior to seeing the movies) or while leaving it (after seeing the double feature). The rate of donation of arriving moviegoers could be used as a check of preexisting differences between the two samples prior to the mood induction. Fortunately, there were no differences in pre-movie donation rates as a function of the type of movie the participants chose to see, whereas post-movie donations differed significantly in the direction of lowered donation rates after watching the sad, but not neutral, movies.

Two points should be emphasized with respect to this illustration of field research. First, the field version of the basic research paradigm was not and could not be simply a "transplanted" replication of the laboratory operations. Significant alterations were necessary to take full advantage of the naturalistic setting. The researchers had considerably less control in the field setting. They could not control the implementation of the stimulus conditions or extraneous sources of variation. On any given night, a host of irrelevant events may have occurred during the course of the movies (e.g., a break-down of projectors, a disturbance in the audience) that could have interfered with the mood manipulation. The researchers were not only helpless to prevent such events, but might not even have been aware of them if they did occur. In addition, the experimenters were unable to assign participants randomly to conditions in this field setting, and had to rely on luck to establish equivalence in initial donation rates between the two groups.

The second point to be emphasized is that the results of the field experiment as *a single isolated study* would have been difficult to interpret without the results obtained from conceptually related laboratory experiments. This difficulty is partly due to the ambiguities introduced by the alterations in design, and partly to the constraints on measurement inherent in the field situation where random assignment usually is not feasible. The concurrence of results in laboratory and fielding settings greatly enhances our confidence in the findings obtained from both sets of operationalizations of mood in measuring the same underlying concept. Had the field experiment failed to replicate the laboratory results, however, many possible alternative explanations for this discrepancy would have arisen and would have rendered interpretation very difficult.

Random Assignment in Field Settings

Participant self-selection problems plague field experimentation in many different ways. In the field experiment on the relationship between mood and helping behavior, random assignment to conditions was not even attempted. Instead, the effects of potential selection factors were handled in another way, which involved an element of risk-taking. The pre-movie data collection served as a pretest check on the assumption that people who attend sad movies are not inherently different from people attending other movies in their propensity to give to charities. But what if that assumption had proved false and there had been an initial difference in the rate of donations from attendants at the different types of movies? Such prior baseline differences in behavior would have made interpretation of any differences in donations after exposure to the movies hazardous at best. In this case, the researchers were taking a gamble in counting on the absence of pre-movie behavioral differences between conditions. Personal experience, or better yet pilot research, could have led the researchers to expect that the factors determining which type of movie most people saw on a particular night were irrelevant to their propensity to give to charity.

In other settings, too, the research may rely on the essentially haphazard distribution of naturally occurring events as equivalent to controlled experimental design. Parker, Brewer, and Spencer (1980), for instance, studied the outcomes of a natural disaster—a devastating brush fire in a Southern California community—on the premise that the pattern of destruction of private homes in the fire constituted a "natural randomization" process. Among homes in close proximity at the height of the fire, only chance factors, such as shifts in wind direction and velocity, location of firefighting equipment, and traffic congestion, determined which structures were burned to the ground and which remained standing when the fire was brought under control. Thus, homeowners who were victims of the fire and those who were not could be regarded as essentially equivalent prior to the effects of the fire, and differences in their attitudes and perceptions following the fire could be attributed to that particular differential experience. As this "assignment" was made by Mother Nature rather than by the researchers, the study is most properly considered a quasi-experiment (see Chapter 10). Thus, when comparisons are made between such naturally selected groups, the burden of proof rests on the investigator to make a convincing case that the groups were not likely initially to differ systematically in any relevant dimensions other than the naturally arising event of interest.

One should not conclude from these examples that experimenter-controlled random assignment is impossible in field experiments. Often, the nature of the experimental manipulation is such that the researcher can deliver different versions or conditions to potential participants in accord with a random schedule. Consider another study of helping behavior in which the effect of positive, rather than negative, mood was being investigated. As one manipulation of positive mood, Isen and Levin (1972) arranged it so that some users of a public phone booth would find a dime in the coin return slot of the telephone as they started to make their call. Although the researchers had no control over which persons would make use of the targeted phone booths during the course of the experiment, they could control the timing and frequency that dimes were or were not placed in the coin returns. They alternated these conditions on a random basis and then observed the behavior of the next caller who happened to use the selected phone booth. With this kind of random assignment, in which conditions are randomly assigned to participants rather than participants randomly assigned to conditions, the researchers could be relatively confident that no prior-existing participant differences influenced their results.

In some field research efforts, the investigator may be able to assign participants randomly to conditions but, once assigned, some participants may fail to participate or to experience the experimental manipulation. If such self-determined participant attrition occurs differentially across treatment conditions, the experimental design is seriously compromised. One way of preserving the advantages of random assignment in such cases is to include participants in their assigned experimental conditions for purposes of analysis, regardless of whether they were exposed to the treatment or not (assuming, of course, that one is in a position to obtain measures on the dependent variable for these participants). This was the solution applied to the two field experiments conducted by Freedman and Fraser (1966) to test the effectiveness of the "foot-in-the-door" technique for enhancing compliance to a rather large, intrusive request from the researcher (i.e., to permit a five-person market survey team to come into one's home for two hours to classify household products). Of primary interest was the rate of compliance to this large request by participants who had been contacted previously with a small request (e. g., to respond to a very brief market survey over the telephone), in comparison to control participants who were not contacted until the time of the larger request.

The purpose of the manipulation in Freedman and Fraser's study was to test the effect of compliance to the initial small request on responses to the later one. However, nearly one-third of the participants in the experimental group (those who received the initial small request) did not comply. This posed a logical problem for the experimenters. How were they to treat these participants' data? Although the participants had been assigned randomly to the experimental condition, they did not actually perform the action that was thought to be the cause of their responses to a later, larger request. However, if they had removed the participants from the analysis, the random assignment process would have been compromised, and the comparability of the two groups would be in serious doubt. Freedman and Fraser's solution was proper: They included responses from all participants in the originally assigned groups, regardless of their compliance with the initial request. This was a conservative decision, because the full treatment was significantly diluted in the experimental group. As it turned out, the initial compliance effect was powerful enough to generate a significant difference between the two groups (on the order of 50% versus 20% compliance), *despite* the dilution of the experimental condition. If the results had been more equivocal, however, we would have been uncertain whether to attribute the absence of significant differences to lack of treatment effects or to failure to achieve the experimental manipulation.

Assessing Dependent Variables in Field Settings

In many field contexts, the design and evaluation of dependent measures is parallel to that of laboratory experiments. In the guise of a person-on-the-street interview or a market research survey, for example, field researchers may elicit self-reports of the attitudes, perceptions, judgments, or preferences of randomly selected individuals. Or, measures may be designed to assess people's willingness to engage in relevant acts such as signing a petition or committing themselves to some future social or political cause. Finally, situations may be constructed to elicit the type of behavior of interest to the experimenter, such as providing participants with opportunities to donate to charity. One advantage of experimentation in field settings is the potential for assessing *behaviors* that are, in and of themselves, of some significance to the participant. Instead of asking participants to *report* on perceptions or intentions, we observe them engaging in behaviors with real consequences. In such cases, our dependent measures are much less likely to be influenced by experimental demand characteristics or social desirability response biases. In laboratory settings, participants might check a particular point on a liking scale to please the experimenter or to look good; but we think very few people would choose to engage in a difficult, daylong task unless there were more powerful reasons to do so.

Unobtrusive Measures

In some field settings, the kinds of dependent measures typically employed in laboratory studies might be viewed as so intrusive that they would destroy the natural flow of events. For this reason, field experiments often are characterized by the use of concealed or indirect measures of the dependent variable under study.

In a sense, all measures of psychological variables are indirect, in that we have no direct access to the thoughts or perceptions of another person. However, some measures are more indirect than others. Indirect measures are those for which the link to the concept of interest involves a hypothetical intervening process. For example, in an interesting study of the "illusion of control" over chance events, Langer (1975) sold 50-cent lottery tickets to participants under one of two conditions. In one condition, participants were handed a particular ticket by the salesperson (experimenter); in the other, participants were allowed to choose their own tickets manually from the available set. Regardless of condition, each ticket had an equal probability of winning the lottery. Langer was interested in examining the effect of the illusory "control" implied in the "choice" condition on participants' confidence that they might possess the winning ticket. Rather than simply asking the participants how confident they felt, Langer used a less direct measure of this variable. Each participant was approached after obtaining a ticket, but before the lottery, and was told that someone else wanted to purchase a ticket and the seller had run out. Each participant was then asked for how much he or she would be willing to sell back his or her own ticket. The reasoning behind this procedure was that the asking price requested by the participant would reflect the ticket's subjective value, which reflected the perceived probability the participant attached to their ticket winning the lottery. As predicted, those who were allowed to choose their own tickets wanted significantly more money to sell their ticket than participants who had been given their tickets with no choice.

What is interesting about this use of an indirect behavioral measure is the likelihood that participants would have been embarrassed to report on their differential confidence had they been asked directly whether they thought they had a winning ticket; after all, they would know that the "objective" view would be that the probability was quite low and attributable purely to chance. Assuming that the indirect measure used was closely related to true subjective confidence, it may have detected an effect that would not have appeared in the results of direct self-report.

Indirect measures are among a variety of techniques used by field researchers to make *unobtrusive measurements* of the dependent variable of interest (see Webb et al., 1981). Some unobtrusive measures are based on observations of ongoing behavior, using methods of observation that interfere minimally or not at all with the occurrence of the behavior. For instance, voluntary seating aggregation patterns have been used as an index of racial behaviors under varied conditions of classroom desegregation; observational studies of conformity have recorded public behaviors such as pedestrians crossing against traffic lights; and studies of natural language often resort to eavesdropping on conversations in public places. Cialdini and associates (1976) used naturalistic observation of clothing and accessories to study what they call the "Basking in Reflected Glory" phenomenon. They recorded the number of students wearing t-shirts and other apparel bearing the school name or insignia in introductory psychology classes at seven universities each Monday during football season. The proportion of students wearing such apparel at each school proved to be significantly greater on Mondays following a victory by that school's team than on days following defeat.

A simple monitoring of public displays provided quantitative confirmation of the hypothesized tendency to identify with success—or to bask in reflected glory. Alabastro, Rast, Lac, Hogg, and Crano (2013) found a similar tendency after election day, as did Sigelman (1986), who noticed that those who supported the winning candidate tended to keep their political signs and posters up longer that those whose candidates lost. Further research has shown that people tend to assume that electoral victors' policies are more in line with their views than those of losers, even though these beliefs might not have been held *before* the election were held (Alabastro et al., 2013; Quist & Crano, 2003).

Other observational techniques may rely on the use of hidden hardware for audio or video recording of events that are later coded and analyzed, though the ethics of such research have come under heavy criticism. Finally, some techniques make use of the natural recording of events outside the experimenter's control, such as physical traces left after an event. One interesting illustration of the use of unobtrusive physical trace measures is provided in Langer and Rodin's (1976) field experiment testing of whether or not being granted personal control over decisions had a positive effect on the well-being of residents of a nursing home. The major outcome in that study was the general alertness and activity level of the residents following introduction of the experimental treatment. This was assessed not only by the traditional methods of participant self-report and nurses' ratings, but also by various behavioral measures, one of which involved placing two inches of white adhesive tape on the right wheels of patients' wheelchairs. The tape was removed after 24 hours and analyzed for amount of discoloration, which served as an index of patient activity level. Unfortunately, the amount of dirt picked up by the tape turned out to be negligible for patients in all conditions, so the measure proved insensitive to treatment effects. Had the nursing home's cleaning staff been less motivated, the measure might have worked. The results of Langer and Rodin's nursing-home study illustrate some of the problems and pitfalls of reliance on unobtrusive indirect measures in field settings. While creative, the adhesive tape index did not produce any detectable treatment effect, whereas other more direct self-report and behavioral measures demonstrated a significant impact of the experimental treatment. Had the researchers been forced to limit their assessment to the least obtrusive measure, they would have missed a great deal.

These results highlight the importance of pilot testing one's measures before relying on their use in a full study, as well as two potential problems with unobtrusive measures that must be considered. The first of these has to do with reliability. In general, the reliability of unobtrusive measures will not be as great as the more direct measures they are designed to mimic (Webb et al., 1981). As might be expected, therefore, the measurement validity of the dependent variable—the extent to which measures measured what they are supposed to measure—also is likely to be of greater concern with unobtrusive measurements. This concern comes about because the farther removed the actual measure is from the concept of interest, the less likely it is to prove valid. The rationale for this observation can be demonstrated simply. For instance, consider the number of steps involved in going from the dependent variable of patient activity level to the measurement of discoloration of white adhesive tape in Langer and Rodin's (1976) nursing-home study. First, patient activity had to be translated into distance traveled in the wheelchair, which in turn had to be related to the amount of dirt picked up by different sections of the tape, which had to produce measurable differences in discoloration. In such a chain, the correspondence between the intended conceptual variable (activity) and the observed measurement can be influenced by many intervening processes, such as the speed with which the wheelchair traveled, how often the floors were cleaned, whether the patient's movement was self-propelled or passive, whether the patient's movement occurred typically before or after floor cleaning, etc. Reliance on a single dependent measure that could be affected by so many irrelevant factors is hazardous at best. The researchers in this instance did not rely on any single measure, and so had some interesting findings to report at the end of the day. Imagine if their study rested entirely on the analysis of the wheelchair tapes. In that case, they would have had nothing to say. The reason for our continued emphasis on multiple operationalization is nowhere more evident than in studies of this type, which make use of creative unobtrusive measurement approaches.

Field Experimentation and Application

Conceptual replication highlights the advantages of combining laboratory and field experimentation for purposes of theory building, but the interplay between laboratory and field research is critical to the development of effective applications in social science as well. Basic experimental research may isolate important causal processes, but convincing demonstrations that those processes operate in applied settings are essential before theory can be converted into practice. The research literature on people's perceptions of control provides a particularly good example of how a synthesis between field and laboratory experiments can work at its best. This research began with animal research in the laboratory (Brady, 1958), extended to field studies of stress in humans (e.g., Janis, 1958), then moved to laboratory analogues (e.g., Glass & Singer, 1972), and back to the field (e.g., Aspinwall & Taylor, 1992; Johnson & Leventhal, 1974; Mills & Krantz, 1979). Results from both types of settings repeatedly demonstrated the potent effect of the perception of control or responsibility on an organism's ability to cope with stressful events (Moghaddam & Studer, 1998; Taylor & Aspinwall, 1996). Even the illusion that one has personal control over the onset or the consequences of potential stressors is apparently sufficient to increase tolerance for stress and reduce adverse effects. As a result of these findings, procedures that are applicable in medical practice and the administration of health care institutions have been developed for inducing actual or perceived personal control (e.g., Thompson & Collins, 1995). At the same time, the fact that field applications permit testing research hypotheses in the presence of severe, noxious, or potentially life-threatening situations has contributed substantially to our basic theoretical understanding of the role of psychological factors in physiological processes.

The Internet as a Site for Experimental Research

The advent of the Internet, and social networking sites in particular (e.g., Facebook), has created a whole new venue for field research in the social sciences. Although the first studies conducted via the Internet are of recent vintage (some consider the survey study of Kiesler and Sproul, 1986, to be the first Internet study, and research by Krantz, Ballard, and Scher, 1997, to be among the first published web-based experiments), the potential of the Internet as a research venue is enormous. The entire world is increasingly becoming wired, thus the Internet offers an opportunity to tap into it as a source of research participants, as well as a site for observing social activity.[1] The use of the Internet as both a medium for conducting research studies and as a subject of research has grown accordingly. A review by Wilson, Gosling, and Graham (2012) was able to identify 412 research studies on Facebook published between 2005 and 2012, demonstrating that "researchers have discovered the utility of Facebook as a novel tool to observe behavior in a naturalistic setting, test hypotheses, and recruit participants" (p. 3).

At this point we need to make a distinction between research that uses the Internet to recruit respondents for participation in online surveys or experiments, and research designed to study online behavior itself. Research employing online surveys will be covered in Chapter 11. Of more relevance to the present chapter is (a) research that uses the Internet as a site for running experiments and (b) research on how, when, and why people use online social networks as a form of social behavior.

Research on Social Network Activity

The review by Wilson et al. (2012) of research on Facebook illustrates how online activity can itself be studied as a form of social behavior in a naturalistic setting (see Chapter 12). Research has been conducted to address questions about who uses online social networks, why people make use of this form of social communication, the content of information that is disclosed online, and the consequences of online social activity for real-life relationships. Much of this research utilizes surveys (conducted offline) that assess respondents' self reported use of online social networking (and correlated variables), but some research uses online activity as data, including rates of usage of online sites over time, content of user profiles, and demographic statistics on users. For the most part, the research conducted thus far has been descriptive or correlational, similar to observational research methods (see Chapter 12) or content analysis research (see Chapter 14). However, it is possible to introduce experimental interventions into ongoing network activity, such as randomly assigning participants to increase their frequency of status postings on Facebook to assess effects on perceived social connectedness (Deters & Mehl, 2013), or posting experimentally designed messages to online discussion groups to assess effects on emotional content of responses (Gonsalkorale & von Hippel, 2011). Such studies, then, are a special class of field experiments, with practical, methodological, and ethical considerations similar to experimental research in other field sites.

Conducting Experiments Online

Experiments on online behavior are still relatively rare, but the use of the Internet as a venue for conducting online experiments is becoming more and more common as software and specialized sites for such research become available. In many cases, versions of laboratory experiments are created for mounting online in order to determine whether findings from previous lab studies can be replicated in this venue with new participant populations. Research by Williams, Cheung, and Choi (2000) supplies an interesting example of this form of conceptual replication. Williams and his colleagues were interested in studying the effects of ostracism—being ignored and excluded from ongoing social interactions. Considerable research has focused on ostracism, and as might be expected, suggests that experiencing social ostracism is aversive. Williams (1997; Williams & Zadro, 2005) has theorized that ostracism threatens four fundamental needs: belonginess, self-esteem, control, and meaningful existence. From this central axiom, he developed a model that predicts the psychological reactions that ensue in response to ostracism, a model tested in laboratory experiments in which confederates are trained to engage in a ball-tossing exchange while excluding the experimental participant.

To replicate these experiments online, Williams et al. (2000) mounted a web experiment in which participants engaged in an online game (called "cyberball") with two other participants (actually, these others' responses were programmed). Respondents were told that they should envision "throwing and catching a flying disc according to the images that were shown on their screen" (p. 751). The images systematically included the participants in the game or systematically excluded them (where participants received the disk 33%, 20%, or never, after the first throw). Measurements taken immediately afterwards showed that a greater degree of being excluded in this activity had greater aversive impact on participants, as predicted. Perceptions of belonging and self-esteem were most severely threatened by ostracism, even in this online version.

This research supported Williams's (1997) model and provides an interesting and useful model of a web-based experiment. The study made use of more than 1400 participants from 62 different countries, and they ranged from 13 to 55 years of age. The magnitude of the participant sample and its diversity suggest that results on feeling socially rejected when being excluded are probably generalizable beyond the boundaries of the standard college student sample. Perhaps even more important, having open-access sites like this provides researchers with the possibility of obtaining extremely large and diverse samples, sometimes greater than 20,000 respondents, for study (e.g., see www.socialpsychology.org/expts.htm; Johnson et al., in press). Further research comparing data from Internet-delivered experiments conducted on PsychExperiments (a public online psychological laboratory) with comparable data from standard laboratory research indicate that Internet results mirror lab results across a wide range of psychological effects (McGraw, Tew, & Williams, 2000).

Methodological Concerns: Reliability and Validity

Before considering some of the practical issues involved in using the Internet as a research venue, it makes sense to consider whether or not it *should* be used. The net has a number of strong proponents (e.g., see Birnbaum, 2000a; Buhrmester, Kwang, & Gosling, 2011; Reips, 2000), but even these researchers advise caution when mounting or interpreting Internet-based research. The issues that must be considered when using this methodological venue are the same as those we face with the more traditional methods, and can be packaged neatly under the terms measurement reliability and validity. When using the web as a research modality, issues of reliability are the same as those we confront when using conventional laboratory methods. The measures we use in Internet research must be psychometrically sound, which is not different from the requirement of the more standard approaches. In some ways, the Internet offers greater opportunities to develop measures and scales to assess measurement reliability and validity. Buchanan (2000) suggests that with its abundance of available research participants, and their diversity relative to the standard college sample, developing and refining measurement instruments might be facilitated by using the Internet. Developing scales of fact or opinion typically requires large numbers of respondents, and the necessary sample size often is not available in many traditional research settings.

Assessing measurement validity, specifically the construct validity, of measures using the Internet instead of traditional methods is sometimes difficult. One common approach to understand possible differences between the two modalities is to conduct the investigation in the traditional laboratory and also on the web. Investigators point to similarities in research findings between the two methods to suggest the convergent validity of research results. Although this approach is appealing, it rests on a confirmation of the null hypothesis to establish (convergent) validity of different methods. Parallel results from laboratory and the Internet are encouraging, but may be attributable to a host of factors. Confirming the null hypothesis is not a satisfactory approach to establishing validity under any circumstance, and circumstances involving the Internet are not immune to this problem.

Sometimes instead of determining convergent validity of methods, the goal may instead be to determine the topics of investigation or the types of scales that may produce disparate findings between these two modalities of administration. For example, experimental research has found that when either a pencil and paper or an Internet version of the same questionnaire was given to Caucasian participants inside a laboratory, participants managed their impression by offering socially desirable responses in which they favored African-Americans over Caucasians (Evans, Garcia, Garcia, & Baron, 2003). However, when researchers replicated the study outside the laboratory via the Internet, out-group–favoring responses were no longer evident. Removal of the experimenter from the online setting was suggested as producing less deception and therefore prompting greater honesty in participant responses.

Conducting Online Studies

A detailed roadmap on how to make full use of the Internet to facilitate research is beyond the scope of this book. However, there are a number of such books available, and the interested researcher should consult these, or the websites that have been made available to help facilitate social research (e.g., Birnbaum, 2000b; Jones, 1999). Many of the particulars involved in conducting a research project, such as Institutional Review Board approval and the use of incentives, should not be neglected just because it is implemented online. In Table 8.1 are three general steps useful in designing practically any Internet-based study, with a listing of practical websites to assist in this endeavor.

The first step involves designing the treatment materials and stimuli. Experimental factors commonly employed in Internet research include manipulations of instructions, vignettes, messages, photographs, and pictures. Some types of experimental manipulations considered appropriate in laboratory settings lack realism or are impossible to implement when conducted on the Internet. Problematic conversion of treatments to an online format include environmental manipulations, such as having smoke piped into a room to determine participants' reactions to an emergency, as an online equivalent would fail to capture the smell of the smoke or the urgency of the situation. The use of more complex manipulations, such as watching a video of a persuasive health message embedded into a website, is potentially problematic for participants due to technical constraints (Skitka & Sargis, 2006). Be aware that not everyone with Internet access has the sufficient computer requirements or bandwidth to view the multimedia presentations: Participants might be required to wait patiently for the stimuli of a complex treatment to download. These awkward moments of staring at an inactive screen could contribute to higher participant dropout rates. Long download times also may foster skipping over the material

TABLE 8.1 Programs and websites to help design an online study.

Step	Program	Pricing	Website
1) Manipulation of materials and stimuli	Inquisit	Free trial	www.millisecond.com
	WEXTOR	Free	www.wextor.org
	Splashup	Free	www.splashup.com
	FotoFlexer	Free	www.fotoflexer.com
2) Host and administer study (random assignment possible)	Qualtrics	Free and pay versions	www.qualtrics.com
	Survey Gizmo	Free and pay versions	www.surveygizmo.com
	Survey Monkey	Free and pay versions	www.surveymonkey.com
3) Participant recruitment	Mechanical Turk	Pay per participant (set by researcher)	www.mturk.com
	The Web Experiment List	Free	www.exlist.net
	Psychological Research on the Net	Free	psych.hanover.edu/research/exponnet.html
	Lab-United International Online-Research Experiments	Free	www.w-lab.de/lab-united/experiments.php
	Inquisitive Mind	Free	beta.in-mind.org/online-research

and proceeding immediately to answering the dependent variable questions. Although experimenters could design the webpage so that participants will not be able to proceed until fully downloaded, the possibility remains that the participant does not have the necessary software installed to view the complex stimuli.

After designing the materials and stimuli for the treatment conditions, the second step involves finding a website capable of hosting and administering your online study. Given technical advances in freely available online-based programs, researchers no longer need to learn website programming code (HTML) to conduct most types of research designs. Featuring intuitive point-and-click interfaces, many online programs allow researchers to upload manipulated treatment materials, to specify the presentation order of stimuli, to create questions, and to vary the number of available response options, to name a few possibilities. Some websites offer the opportunity to employ random assignment, allowing participants to be assigned to study conditions by chance. A major advantage of using these online programs is that participant responses are automatically recorded into a database or spreadsheet, avoiding data entry errors, and downloaded at the researcher's convenience.

Once the web experiment is designed and placed on a website, the final step involves the participant recruitment. Websites dedicated to cooperating with researchers in mounting a web experiment will, upon request, include a link to the researcher's study to their growing list at no charge. These participants, however, represent a self-selected sample of those who actively pursue being a research participant. Just as in traditional approaches, offering an incentive will yield higher responses rates, given the competition of online studies that are now being conducted.

Crowdsourcing websites that allow the general public to sign up for various tasks for compensation are a potential venue for recruitment of a large and diverse sample. Amazon's Mechanical Turk is one such site popular with social researchers. Once an account is created and the website link to the study is indicated, the researcher offers a set payment amount for each potential participant. Participants make the decision of whether or not to participate based on the research description provided by the investigator and the incentives offered. Evaluation of data using this recruitment source has concluded that measures administered through Mechanical Turk yield responses highly similar to measures involving traditional methods of data collection (Buhrmester et al., 2011).

Using this site, it also is possible to conduct research longitudinally, as previous participants are automatically tracked by a non-identifiable code that might be used to invite these individuals to complete a subsequent round. Researchers could also opt to restrict the study to people from a particular country or make it available internationally. Alternatively, researchers targeting a specific population may recruit participants through other online techniques. Potential members of a targeted group (e.g., people with attention deficit hyperactivity disorder) could be recruited by posting a link to the study on a message board frequented by those with this issue. In addition, e-mails can be sent to various mailing lists that might contain subscribers interested in the topic under investigation. Both recruitment techniques sometimes require establishing the rapport and trust necessary to be gain entry, so that one may then be granted the privilege to post a message to recruit members.

Misconceptions About Internet Research

To determine the veracity of several popular notions about Internet research methods, a large-scale study involving 361,703 Internet participants was compared to the aggregation of participants from 510 published studies that used traditional data collection methods (Gosling, Vazire, Srivastava, & John, 2004). Based on this study, we can dispel four of the most widespread concerns about the use of the Internet for experimental research. First, although Internet samples are not entirely representative of the population, they are markedly more demographically diverse than investigations using traditional methods, such as those employing undergraduate samples. Online participants tend to come from more diverse backgrounds and cultures—after all, the Internet can attract participants from all over the world (Germine et al., 2012). Early research supported the stereotype that online participants were predominantly highly educated White males. Today, the Internet is now available in many public venues—libraries, schools, and coffee shops—and across different electronic devices such as cell phones, making it more accessible to the general populace than ever before. Although the gender gap in Internet use has largely disappeared, a small racial disparity remains with regard to Whites being more likely to have access to this medium than Latinos or Blacks, likely attributed to income differences. Still, the Internet remains impractical for recruiting from certain populations (e.g., the very young, illiterate people, etc.)

A second misconception of Internet users is that they are less well adjusted than those who do not use the Internet. Gosling and colleagues (2004) found that this was not true. Their Internet respondents were not drastically disparate from the usual college sample on indicators of social adjustment or mental health. Kraut and colleagues (1998) found that the view of the typical Internet user as psychologically maladjusted, neglecting interpersonal relationships and social responsibilities for the sake of the sterile computer was largely prompted by early Internet research with convenient samples (Stoll, 1995; Turkle, 1996). The description is not applicable to the majority of online users. Like most of us, Bargh and McKenna (2004) observed that the Internet has evolved into a useful tool to facilitate and maintain social communication and support networks. Consistent with this view, Lebo (2000) reported research indicating that Internet users did not engage in fewer in-person social activities than nonusers.

A third objection to Internet-based research has to do with the lack of correspondence between its results and those derived from standard (paper and pencil) methods of data collection. However, across many areas of investigation, especially those involving survey or scale research, Internet and traditional forms of data collection yield parallel findings. Results obtained from online scales versus paper and pencil versions of the same scales have been found to be highly similar in survey research, although experimental designs, especially ones sensitive to reaction times or requiring attention to subtle stimuli, might be more vulnerable when undertaken on the Internet (Kraut et al., 1998). Nevertheless, the appropriateness of any new research modality should be considered carefully. We should not blindly assume that these different formats produce consistent results across all topics of investigation.

A fourth misconception is that participants completing a study online are not necessarily as motivated as those completing a study in person (Gosling et al., 2004). The misconception that online participants tend to be unmotivated stems from the view that online studies are usually anonymous and could be completed by practically anyone, thus increasing the potential to answer questions carelessly. Because it is convenient to abandon a study in the middle if it appears uninteresting, dropout rate is indeed higher in Internet-based studies (Birnbaum, 2004; Chapter 11). If a study proves boring to Internet participants, they are likely to vote with their feet—or mouse—and leave the study. Do not presume that a lackluster study failing to capture participant attention in the laboratory will somehow magically become exciting if it is instead implemented online.

Motivation to pay attention may be enhanced by the use of financial incentives and lotteries, keeping time demands low (typically, 15 minutes or less), and offering participants automated feedback (e.g., a tailored personality profile resulting from responses reported on a personality inventory) immediately following completion of the online study. These fixes have introduced problems of their own, however. For example, if a monetary award is promised, researchers must be aware of the possibility of participants taking part in the experiment more than once, to gain more money or to enhance their chances of winning a large lottery. Many different solutions to the multiple submission problem have been used (see Musch & Reips, 2000), one of the most common of which prevents duplicate submissions from the same IP address.

Conclusion

A major advantage of Internet-based research is that it removes the physical presence of the experimenter from the research setting. (This is not implying that the online setting is free from artifacts stemming from experimenter expectancies and biases. For example, requiring participants to type their full names into a webpage at the beginning of a study could result in lower rates of self-disclosure and more deceptive responses. Inadvertently providing clues to the research hypothesis also should be avoided in online materials viewed by respondents.) Some research results have suggested that data collected through online studies are largely equivalent to traditional studies, and therefore combining data to yield a larger sample size might be a practical consideration (Beuckelaer & Lievens, 2009). Even though the use of online participants may yield greater external validity due to the potential diversity of respondents, the generalizability of Internet findings is limited to people with Internet access who happen to read and understand the language for the instructions for your study. Nonetheless, using the Internet, in the best of all possible scenarios, we can:

- Conduct experiments outside the laboratory.
- Draw on a much greater demographic range of participants, helping to enhance participant generalizability.
- Minimize experimenter bias and demand.

It remains to be seen if these promises will be fully realized in practice. With sufficient ingenuity, we believe the Internet can be an extraordinarily useful adjunct to social research. To ignore the possible benefits of Internet-based research is foolhardy. However, to fail to recognize and avoid the many potential pitfalls that the Internet user must surmount is equally shortsighted. We are optimistic that the potential difficulties involved with Internet research will be met and solved. It seems a safe bet to assume that the ingenuity the social sciences have brought to bear on other promising but problematic methodological factors on the web, and that the Internet will remain an important part of the researcher's tool kit.

Questions for Discussion

1. What are some practical issues to consider when conducting research on the Internet? What are some of the advantages and disadvantages of conducting studies online?
2. What are your thoughts on the ecological validity of Internet research? Specifically, given the de-individuation and self-presentation bias (e.g., via one's avatar) that can occur on the Internet, would you expect a sample of Internet participants' responses on attitude and behavioral intent measures to reflect the attitudes and intentions of a non-Internet sample? Would you expect Internet responses to differ based on where you recruited participants? For example, would you expect ecological validity to be greatest for a sample recruited from Second Life, Amazon's crowdsourcing website Mechanical Turk, or Facebook? Are all Internet sources created equal when it comes to recruiting participants—why or why not? If we consider the Internet a type of "field setting," is it possible to collect indirect or unobtrusive measures in an Internet sample—what would be an example?

3. Often, the phenomena we are trying to measure involve abstract constructs (e.g., cognitive dissonance) that are captured with written responses or observed behaviors. Developing unobtrusive or indirect measures of already abstract constructs can be difficult, but necessary. In a laboratory setting, how could you use unobtrusive measures to assess the extent to which a person is currently experiencing the discomfort of cognitive dissonance? Would this laboratory-based, unobtrusive measure of dissonance be equally valid in field settings—why or why not? In representative field settings (i.e., contexts with high ecological validity), is there a way you might be able to indirectly or unobtrusively determine whether people were in a dissonant state?

Note

1. In the United States alone, for example, nearly 90 million homes had Internet access in 2012, and of these, in households with annual incomes over $50,000, an incredible 97% were wired.

References

Alabastro, A., Rast, D. E., III, Lac, A., Hogg, M. A., & Crano, W. D. (2013). Intergroup bias and perceived similarity: Effects of successes and failures on support for in- and outgroup political leaders. *Group Processes & Intergroup Relations, 16,* 58–67.

Anderson C. A., Lindsay, J. J., & Bushman, B. J. (1999). Research in the psychological laboratory: Truth or triviality? *Current Directions in Psychological Science, 8,* 3–9.

Aspinwall, L., & Taylor, S. E. (1992). Modeling cognitive adaptation: A longitudinal investigation the impact of individual differences and coping on college adjustment and performance. *Journal of Personality and Social Psychology, 63,* 989–1003.

Bargh, J. A., & McKenna, K. Y. A. (2004). The Internet and social life. *Annual Review of Psychology, 55,* 573–590.

Beuckalaer, A. D., & Lievens, F. (2009). Measurement equivalence of paper-and pencil and Internet organizational surveys: A large scale examination in 16 countries. *Applied Psychology: An International Review, 58,* 336–361.

Birnbaum, M. H. (2000a). Introduction to psychological experimentation on the Internet. In M. H. Birnbaum (Ed.), *Psychological experiments on the Internet* (pp. 3–34). San Diego: Academic Press.

Birnbaum, M. H. (Ed.). (2000b). *Psychological experiments on the Internet.* San Diego: Academic Press.

Birnbaum, M. H. (2004). Human research and data collection via the Internet. *Annual Review of Psychology, 55,* 803–832.

Brady, J. (1958). Ulcers in "executive monkeys." *Scientific American, 199,* 95–100.

Buchanan, T. (2000). Potential of the Internet for personality research. In M. H. Birnbaum (Ed.), *Psychological experiments on the Internet* (pp. 121–140). San Diego: Academic Press.

Buhrmester, M., Kwang, T., & Gosling, S. D. (2011). Amazon's Mechanical Turk: A new source for inexpensive, yet high-quality data? *Perspectives on Psychological Science, 6,* 3–5.

Cialdini, R. B., Borden, R. J., Thorne, A., Walker, M. R., Freeman, S., & Sloan, L. R. (1976). Basking in reflected glory: Three (football) field studies. *Journal of Personality and Social Psychology, 34*(3), 366–375.

Deters, F. G., & Mehl, M. R. (2013). Does posting Facebook status updates increase or decrease loneliness? An online social networking experiment. *Social Psychological and Personality Science, 4,* 579–586.

Evans, D. C., Garcia, D. J., Garcia, D. M., & Baron, R. S. (2003). In the privacy of their own homes. Using the Internet to assess racial bias. *Personality and Social Psychology Bulletin, 29,* 273–284.

Forgas, J. P. (Ed). (2000). *Feeling and thinking: The role of affect in social cognition.* New York: Cambridge University Press.

Freedman, J. L., & Fraser, S. C. (1966). Compliance without pressure: The foot-in-the-door technique. *Journal of Personality and Social Psychology, 4,* 195–202.

Germine, L., Nakayama, K., Duchaine, B. C., Chabris, C. F., Chatterjee, G., & Wilmer, J. B. (2012). Is the Web as good as the lab? Comparable performance from Web and lab in cognitive/perceptual experiments. *Psychonomic Bulletin & Review, 19,* 847–857.

Glass, D., & Singer, J. (1972). *Urban stress.* New York: Academic Press.

Gonsalkorale, K., & von Hippel, W. (2011). Intergroup relations in the 21st century: Ingroup positivity and outgroup negativity among members of an Internet hate group. In R. Kramer, G. Leonardelli, & R. Livingston (Eds.), *Social cognition, social identity, and intergroup relations.* New York: Psychology Press.

Gosling, S. D., Vazire, S., Srivastava, S., & John, O. P. (2004). Should we trust web-based studies? A comparative analysis of six preconceptions about Internet Questionnaires. *American Psychologist, 59,* 93–104.

Isen, A. M., & Levin, P. F. (1972). The effect of feeling good on helping: Cookies and kindness. *Journal of Personality and Social Psychology, 21,* 384–388.

Janis, I. L. (1958). *Psychological stress.* New York: Wiley.

Johnson, J. E., & Leventhal, H. (1974). Effects of accurate expectations and behavioral instructions on reactions during a noxious medical examination. *Journal of Personality and Social Psychology, 29,* 710–718.

Johnson, K. M., Iyer, R., Wojcik, S. P., Vaisey, S., Miles, A., Chu, V., & Graham, J. (in press). Ideology-specific patterns of moral indifference predict intentions not to vote. *Analyses of Social Issues and Public Policy.* doi: 10.1111/asap.12039

Jones, S. (Ed.). (1999). *Doing Internet research: Critical issues and methods for examining the net.* Thousand Oaks, CA: Sage.

Kiesler, S., & Sproull, L. S. (1986). Response effects in the electronic survey. *Public Opinion Quarterly, 50,* 402–413.

Krantz, J. H., Ballard, J., & Scher, J. (1997). Comparing the results of laboratory and World-Wide-Web samples on the determinants of female attractiveness. *Behavioral Research Methods, Instruments, and Computers, 29,* 264–269.

Krantz, J. H., & Dalal, R. (2000). Validity of Web-based psychological research. In M. H. Birnbaum (Ed.), *Psychological experiments on the Internet* (pp. 35–60). San Diego: Academic Press.

Kraut, R., Patterson, V., Lundmark, M., Kiesler, S., Mukophadhyah, T., & Schlerlis, W. (1998). Internet paradox. A social technology that reduces social involvement and psychological well-being? *American Psychologist, 53,* 1017–1031.

Langer, E. J. (1975). The illusion of control. *Journal of Personality and Social Psychology, 32,* 311–328.

Langer, E. J., & Rodin, J. (1976). The effects of choice and enhanced personal responsibility for the aged: A field experiment in an institutional setting. *Journal of Personality and Social Psychology, 34,* 191–198.

Lebo, H. (2000). *The UCLA Internet report: Surveying the digital future.* Retrieved July 6, 2003, from University of California, Los Angeles, Center for Communication Policy website: www.ccp.ucla.edu/UCLA-Internet-Report-2000.pdf

Levine, M., Cassidy, C., Brazier, G., & Reicher, S. (2002). Self categorization and bystander non-intervention: Two experimental studies. *Journal of Applied Social Psychology, 32,* 1452–1463.

McGraw, K. O., Tew, M. D., & Williams, J. E. (2000). The integrity of web-delivered experiments: Can you trust the data? *Psychological Science, 11,* 502–506.

Mills, R. T., & Krantz, D. S. (1979). Information, choice, and reactions to stress: A field experiment in a blood bank with laboratory analogue. *Journal of Personality and Social Psychology, 37,* 608–620.

Moghaddam, F. M., & Studer, C. (1998). *Illusions of control: Striving for control in our personal and professional lives.* Westport, CT: Praeger.

Musch, J., & Reips, U. D. (2000). A brief history of web experimenting. In M. H. Birnbaum (Ed.), *Psychological experiments on the Internet* (pp. 61–87). San Diego, CA: Academic Press.

Parker, S. D., Brewer, M. B., & Spencer, J. R. (1980). Natural disaster, perceived control, and attributions to fate. *Personality and Social Psychology Bulletin, 6,* 454–459.

Piliavin, I. M., Rodin, J., & Piliavin, J. A. (1969). Good Samaritanism: An underground phenomenon? *Journal of Personality and Social Psychology, 13,* 289–299.

Quist, R. M., & Crano, W. D. (2003). Assumed policy similarity and voter preference. *Journal of Social Psychology, 143,* 149–162.

Reips, U. D. (2000). The web experiment method: Advantages, disadvantages, and solutions. In M. H. Birnbaum (Ed.), *Psychological experiments on the Internet* (pp. 89–117). San Diego: Academic Press.

Sears, D. O. (1986). College sophomores in the laboratory: Influences of a narrow data base on social psychology's view of human nature. *Journal of Personality and Social Psychology, 51,* 515–530.

Sigelman, L. (1986). Basking in reflected glory revisited: An attempt at replication. *Social Psychology Quarterly, 49,* 90–92.

Skitka, L. J., & Saris, E. (2006). The Internet as psychological laboratory. *Annual Review of Psychology, 57,* 529–555.

Stoll, C. (1995). *Silicon snake oil*. New York: Doubleday.
Taylor, S. E., & Aspinwall, L. G. (1996). Mediating and moderating processes in psychological stress: Appraisal, coping, resistance, and vulnerability. In H. B. Kaplan (Ed.), *Psychological stress: Perspectives on structure, theory, life-course, and methods* (pp. 71–110). San Diego: Academic Press.
Thompson, S. C., & Collins, M. A. (1995). Applications of perceived control to cancer: An overview of theory and measurement. *Journal of Psychosocial Oncology, 13,* 11–26.
Turkle, S. (1996). Virtuality and its discontents: Searching for community in cyberspace. *The American Prospect, 24,* 50–57.
Underwood, B., Berenson, J., Berenson, R., Cheng, K., Wilson, D., Kulik, J., Moore, B., & Wenzel, G. (1977). Attention, negative affect, and altruism: An ecological validation. *Personality and Social Psychology Bulletin, 3,* 54–58.
Webb, E. J., Campbell, D. T., Schwartz, R. D., Sechrest, L., & Grove, J. (1981). *Nonreactive measures in the social sciences*. Boston, MA: Houghton-Mifflin.
Williams, K. D. (1997). Social ostracism. In R. Kowalski (Ed.), *Aversive interpersonal behaviors* (pp. 133–170). New York: Plenum.
Williams, K. D., Cheung, C., & Choi, W. (2000). Cyberostracism: Effects of being ignored over the Internet. *Journal of Personality and Social Psychology, 79,* 748–762.
Williams, K. D., & Zadro, L. (2005). Ostracism: The indiscriminate early detection system. In K. D. Williams, J. P. Forgas & W. von Hippel (Eds.), *The social outcast: Ostracism, social exclusion, rejection, and bullying* (pp. 19–34). New York: Psychology Press.
Wilson, R., Gosling, S., & Graham, L. (2012). A review of Facebook research in the social sciences. *Perspectives on Psychological Science, 7,* 203–220.

9

NONEXPERIMENTAL RESEARCH

Correlational Design and Analyses

Previous chapters of this book were focused on considerations relevant to the development and use of experimental designs. In these designs, participants' exposure to a treatment or manipulation is totally controlled by the researcher; and the major purpose of such control is to reduce or eliminate the plausibility of confounds or alternative explanations for effects on the dependent variable. In experimental research, a clear distinction is made between the independent (or causal) variable, which is controlled or manipulated by the experimenter, and the dependent (response) variable, which is allowed to vary freely. In many areas of research in social science, however, experimental control over variables is impossible, unethical, or, at the very least completely impractical.

The researcher studying the effects of demographic characteristics such as sex, age, or height, or relatively enduring personal attributes such as religious affiliation, for example, is in no position to manipulate these variables. People arrive at the laboratory with predetermined levels of these characteristics, and these features of the individual are beyond the immediate influence of the researcher. Similarly, if participants' levels of a relevant variable are determined by their responses on a measuring instrument, such as a scale of authoritarianism, extraversion, or need for cognition, the experimenter again is not in a position to manipulate the initial level of this variable. These are intrinsic and generally unmalleable features of the participants. In most investigations of this type, the researcher can no longer determine whether different levels of the independent variable cause differential changes in the dependent variable. Rather, the research question becomes focused on whether the variables are in some way related to or associated with one another. The type of analysis thus becomes nonexperimental or correlational. By correlational, we are not necessarily referring to the use of simple bivariate correlation, but rather a set of analysis techniques such as multiple regression, multi-level modeling, and structural equation modeling, all of which are used to examine relationships among variables in nonexperimental research. Nonexperimental and correlational are terms that are used interchangeably.

In a nonexperimental or correlational research design, the variables are allowed to vary freely, and the researcher observes and records the extent of their covariation—that is, the extent that changes in one variable are associated with (but not necessarily caused by) changes in the other, or vice versa. The most basic correlational study is one in which response to response relationships are investigated, for example, assessing the degree of relationship between responses on two different self-report measures. Scores on a questionnaire to measure religiosity, for instance, might be associated with scores on an instrument designed to measure authoritarianism. Participants' responses on both measures are unconstrained by the researcher—the question is the extent to which scores on one measure are varying together with scores on the other. Does a particular individual's score on one measure give us a clue to, or help us predict, that individual's response to the second measure?

In some experiments, researchers first sort individuals into different groups on the basis of personal characteristics (sex, age, etc.) or responses made on some measuring instrument (e.g., high vs. low extraversion scores), and then introduce an experimental manipulation to study the effects of both variables on the dependent variable. Studies of this type are called a "mixed factorial design," as they investigate both an experimental manipulation of treatment conditions and a nonexperimental variable based on participant characteristics. This "blocked" or "mixed factorial design" was discussed in Chapter 5. The important point to be noted here is that even though the nonmanipulated variable is included in an experimental design, any relationship between that variable and the dependent variable is correlational and should not be interpreted in causal terms.

Analyzing and Interpreting Nonexperimental Research

The major advantage of nonexperimental or correlational research is that it allows both variables of interest to vary freely, so that the degree of relationship between them can be determined. Recall that in experimental research, the levels in the independent variable are limited by controlled manipulation. Likewise, manifestations of the dependent variable are often limited by virtue of the response options made available by the nature of the dependent measure.

Not all nonexperimental research takes advantage of full variations in the measured variables. Consider, for example, a nonexperimental study in which participants with varying degrees of anti-Semitism are assessed. Like most attitudinal variables, anti-Semitic prejudice can be measured on a continuous scale, and this allows the possibility of identifying considerable variation among individuals. However, the researcher may choose to use this measure to divide participants into discrete groups for purposes of comparison. This necessitates redefining variation among individuals according to some categorical scheme, such as "high", "medium", or "low" scores on the variable of interest. Thus, for purposes of the research design, individuals with some variation in degree of anti-Semitic feeling will be considered members of the same grouping. At times, such categorization can result in an unsatisfactory and unnecessarily imprecise use of information. For example, consider the data of Table 9.1. This illustration presents the scores of 10 participants on a scale of anti-Semitism, arranged in order from lowest to highest. Now suppose the researcher wished to categorize these participants into two groups of equal size. One possible decision rule is to use a **median split**, a process in which participants are divided at the "middlemost" score, with 50% of participants above the median termed the "high group," and the 50% below the median the "low group."

As can be seen in the illustration of Table 9.1, dividing participants into discrete classifications on the basis of a continuous measure has some clearly undesirable features. The four participants nearest the median have very similar scores, yet two of them (participants 10 and 4) have been defined (by the median split) as being in the low anti-Semitic group, whereas the other two (participants 2 and 5) have been placed in the high group. This classification holds despite the fact that the scores of participants 10 and 4 on the critical scale are more similar to those of Participants 2 and 5 (who have been classified in a different group) than they are to the other participants in their own group. As Table 9.1 illustrates, participants with scores of 3 and 50 are classified as being identical in terms of their anti-Semitic sentiments—they are both in the "low" group—whereas those with scores of 50 and 51 are defined as different! Problems of this type, in which a continuous variable representing a wide range of scores is forced to be categorical, could be avoided in correlational studies. The correlational approach avoids losing the detailed levels in the variable and enhances the potential for accurately assessing the extent of covariation between measures.[1]

TABLE 9.1 Illustration of a median split categorization into high and low anit-semitic groups in a blocked design.

Participant	Anti-Semitism Score	Blocked Group
6	3	
9	28	
1	30	Low Anti-Semitism
10	49	
4	50	
	Median Split	
2	51	
5	53	
8	67	High Anti-Semitism
3	75	
7	88	

Correlation and Simple Regression

The most commonly computed correlation—the **Pearson product-moment correlation** coefficient—is used to determine the extent of linear relationship between two variables, that is, the extent that variation in one measure is accompanied consistently by unidirectional variation in the other. The scatterplots in Figure 9.1 are provided to illustrate the difference between linear and nonlinear relationships for measures of two variables, designated X and Y.[2] The points on each graph represent the coordinates of test scores on X (horizontal axis) and Y (vertical axis) for a sample of individuals.

In Figure 9.1, Graph (a) illustrates a positive linear relationship. Individuals who have relatively low scores on the X measure also tend to have relatively low scores on the Y measure, and those with high X scores also tend to have high Y scores. An example of two variables that would be expected to exhibit such a relationship would be scores on a statistical methods exam with scores on a research methods exam. Conversely, Graph (b) represents a negative, or inverse, linear relationship in which relatively high X scores are accompanied by relatively low Y scores, and vice versa, such as the relationship that would be expected between scores on a scale of superstitious beliefs and scores on a research methods exam.

Graph (c) in Figure 9.1 illustrates a nonlinear, or curvilinear, relationship, in which increases in scores on X sometimes are accompanied by increases in Y and sometimes by decreases. Such a relationship might be found between measures of anxiety or tension with scores on a complex intellectual task such as a research methods exam. At very low levels of anxiety (the X score), due to lack of motivation, fatigue, or boredom, exam performance (Y score) is poor. As anxiety levels (X scores) rise above this minimal level, performance improves until a point is reached at which anxiety begins to interfere with efficiency of performance. As anxiety increases beyond this level, performance decreases.

The nonlinear relationship of Figure 9.1(c) points out the importance of representing a wide range of variation on *both* variables before drawing any conclusions about the nature of the relationship between them. It also should be noted in the case represented by Graph (c) that despite the orderly relationship between X and Y scores, the Pearson correlation between them would be approximately .00 because the relationship is not well represented by a measure of linear correlation. The assumption of a linear relationship between variables is violated in this figure, and thus the

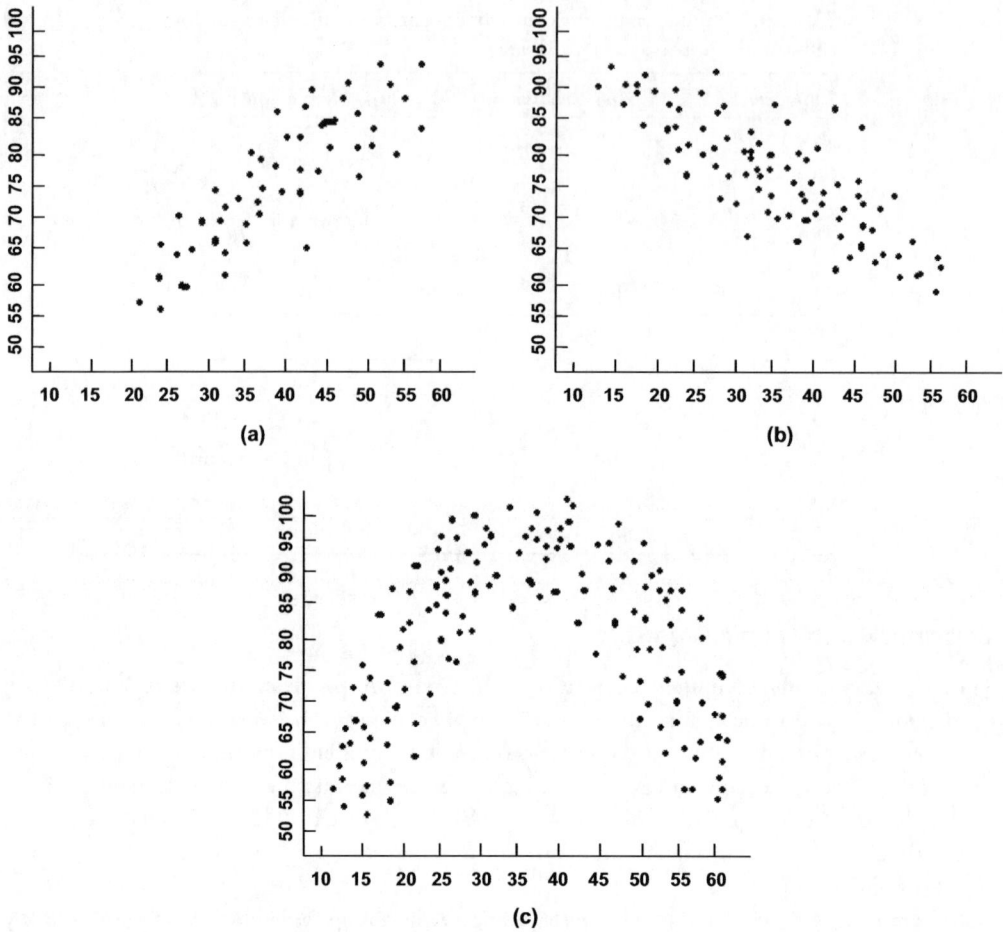

FIGURE 9.1 Examples of relationships between two variables.

Pearson correlation is not an appropriate statistic. This highlights the importance of representing the relationship between two variables graphically before computing the correlation coefficient.

Only when the relationship between two measures is essentially linear does the Pearson correlation coefficient accurately assess the degree of relationship. The correlation coefficient (r) will indicate the magnitude and direction of a linear relationship. The coefficient r may vary from −1.00 to +1.00, with the sign signifying the direction of relationship (positive vs. negative). A coefficient of .00 indicates that no linear relationship exists between these two measures. An r of +1.00 represents a perfect positive linear relationship. In such a case, the scatterplot of X and Y scores forms a straight line, indicating that the relative standing of any person's score on the X measure corresponds exactly to that person's relative position on the Y measure. Such a perfect correspondence between two variables is very rare, but the closeness of the existing relationship to this ideal ($r = +1.00$ or -1.00) is indicated by the size of the r value, which may be interpreted in two ways.

Proportion of Common Variance

The **coefficient of determination**, or squared value of the Pearson correlation (r^2), represents the proportion of variance shared between two variables. The higher this value, the greater the amount of variation in one measure that is accounted for by variation in the other, and vice versa. When $r^2 = 1.00$, the proportion of common variation is 100%. This indicates that if the X variable were "held constant" (i.e., only participants with the same score on the X measure were considered), variation in Y would be eliminated (i.e., they all would have the same Y score).[3] With correlations that are less than perfect, the value of r^2 indicates the proportion by which variation in Y would be reduced if X were held constant, or vice versa. For example, a Pearson $r = .60$ would denote that 36% of the spread in scores of the Y variable could be explained or accounted for by the scores on the X variable, so that if X were held constant, variation in Y scores would be reduced by 36%. It should be emphasized that the existence of shared variance between two variables does not indicate whether one variable causes the other.

Accuracy of Linear Prediction

The nature of the linear relationship can be depicted through the use of a scatterplot, a graphic representation of the set of X and Y scores that are obtained when two measures are taken on a sample of respondents. The best fitting straight line drawn through this set of points is called a *regression line* (see Figure 9.2). The regression line in the scatterplot is derived from a formula for predicting the score on one measure (Y, which is the *criterion variable*) on the basis of a score on another measure (X, which is the *predictor variable*).

The simple linear regression formula is

$$Y' = bX + a.$$

Y': Predicted criterion variable score (upon solving the formula),
b: Slope, which indicates the rate of change on Y scores per unit change in X scores,
X: Score on the predictor variable,
a: The constant (or intercept), which provides baseline information on what the Y' score would be if a person scored a zero on variable X.

For example, suppose we know that number of hours of studying predicts scores on an upcoming research methods exam (scored on a 100-point scale). Based on considerable empirical research from students who took the class last semester, we have developed a formula that attempts to predict a

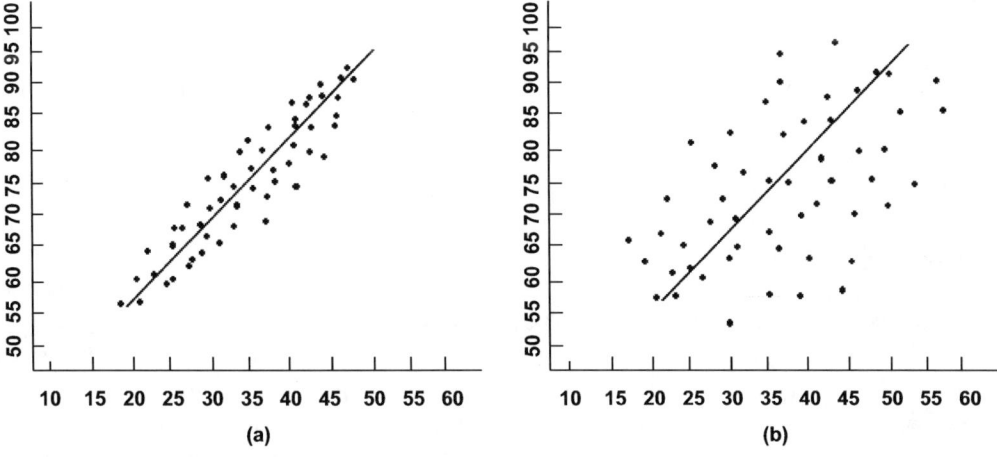

FIGURE 9.2 Scatterplots with regression lines.

person's performance on the exam. This prediction formula takes the following values, $Y' = 1.1X + 35$, where Y' is the predicted research methods exam score, and X is the number of hours spent studying. Plugging in values to solve the formula, a mediocre student who spent only 20 hours studying would be expected to obtain a failing score of 57 on the exam. However, a conscientious student who spent 50 hours studying would be expected to earn the much higher exam score of 90.

The Y' or criterion scores generated on the basis of the regression formula are *predicted* values: They do not always correspond exactly to the actual Y scores for all individuals with a specific X value. This fact is depicted in the discrepancies between the observed points and the plotted regression line as illustrated in Figure 9.2. Perfect prediction of the Y' score stemming from knowledge of a participant's X score only occurs if the correlation is exactly +1.00 or −1.00. The degree of variation, defined as the vertical distances of observed scatterplot points from the linear regression line, is known as the residual or prediction error. The extent of error arising from inaccuracy of prediction of one variable using the other may be computed simply: Error = $1 - r^2$. For example, a relatively strong correlation (e.g., $r = .80$) will have a small amount of error, and participant data points will be closer to the regression line; a weak correlation (e.g., $r = .10$), on the other hand, will have considerable error, and data points will be scattered farther away from the regression line. Thus the higher the correlation coefficient (r), the less variation in observed scores vertically around the regression line (i.e., the tighter the fit between the actual Y values and its predicted Y'), and the greater the accuracy of the linear prediction.

Figure 9.2 illustrates this relationship with a comparison between two scatterplots involving measures that are represented by the same regression line but different correlation values. In the case of Graph (a), with a relatively high correlation, the variation of actual scatterplot points from the regression line is small. Thus for any person, the deviation between his or her actual score on the measure and that predicted (Y') from the X score is potentially quite small. In Graph (b), on the other hand, the deviation is much greater because the relationship (r) is much weaker. The size of the linear correlation reflects the accuracy of prediction.

It should be pointed out that prediction or regression analysis, like correlation, does not imply causation. When prediction equations are based on existing covariation between two measures, the source of covariation is not specified. We have been dealing with the generalized equation for predicting Y' from X, but the procedures could just as well have been used to predict X' from Y. With the Pearson correlation, the choice of "predictor" and "criterion" is often arbitrary, except when the predictor variable is one that temporally precedes the criterion variable.

Interpreting a Zero Correlation

If the results of a Pearson correlation indicate an approximately .00 linear relationship between two measures, there are four potential explanations for this result. First, and most simply, there may be no systematic relationship between the two variables. This would be the expected, for example, if one assessed the correlation between measures of shoe sizes and scores on a research methods exam.

The second possibility, which already has been illustrated, is that there is some systematic relationship between the two variables, but the relationship is essentially nonlinear. Observing a graphic representation of the obtained data in the form of a scatterplot, as recommended earlier, best assesses the plausibility of this explanation. As the linearity assumption for the Pearson correlation is violated, this statistic should not be used to estimate the relation.[4]

The third possibility is that one or both of the measures involved in the correlation is flawed or unreliable. Imperfection in measurement always diminishes the apparent relationship between variables; the greater the imperfection, the more serious its effect on the correlation coefficient. A highly unreliable measure contains items that do not represent the underlying phenomenon. Thus, such a variable contains only a small reliable proportion of the shared variance, and a large proportion of the measurement is contaminated by measurement error (see our discussion of measurement reliability

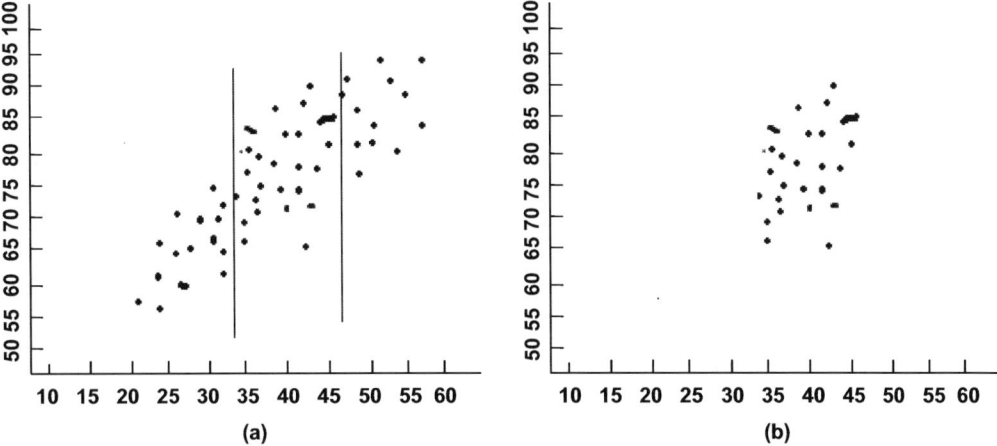

FIGURE 9.3 Example of restriction of range.

in Chapter 3). If a Pearson correlation is computed to assess the association between this unreliable measure and another unreliable measure, we are assessing the relationship between instruments that contain considerable random noise, producing a smaller correlation coefficient.

The fourth possibility is that a very low correlation value may be an artifact of limitations of measurement. The size of the correlation between any two variables will be automatically attenuated (diminished) if the range of scores on either or both measures is restricted or truncated. A truncated measure, for example, might arise if a self-esteem scale is administered to a sample consisting of people suffering from clinical depression. This is problematic because the possible distributional range of self-esteem scores in these psychologically distressed individuals would be much narrower than that found in the general population. A case of attenuation due to limited observations is illustrated in Figure 9.3, in which Graph (a) represents the relationship between measures on X and Y across a wide range of participant scores on both variables. The trend of the relationship is clearly linear and positive, although for every value of X there is some variation in scores on Y (i.e., the relationship is not perfect—the observations do not all fall on a straight line). Graph (b) provides a blowup of the limited range of values represented in the area sectioned off in Graph (a). Within this restricted range of X scores, the previously linear trend in the relationship between X and Y is no longer evidenced with this subsample. If the correlation coefficient were computed between these two measures for a sample with very little variation in their scores on X, the resulting value would be much closer to .00 than that of the relationship involving the entire distribution of respondent scores. Mathematically, there has to be sufficient variation in both measures to compute any meaningful coefficient of correlation.

Figure 9.4 provides an illustration of how the relationship between two variables could be misrepresented if the range of values on one of the variables were unrepresentative of the total range possible. This graph presents, roughly, the relationship obtained between measures of cognitive complexity (see Streufert, 1997; Suedfeld, Tetlock, & Streufert, 1992) and intelligence. In the lower ranges of IQ scores, there is a systematic increase in scores on the complexity variable as intelligence increases. However, as the range of IQ reaches a ceiling, as might be expected in a sample of students from a highly selective university, the variation in complexity scores is no longer systematically related to IQ. This attenuation of relationship among participants at the upper levels of intelligence led early investigators (whose participants were primarily college students from highly selective schools) to conclude that cognitive complexity and intelligence were independent. Only after a wider range of intelligence was represented in this research did the true nature of the relationship become apparent.

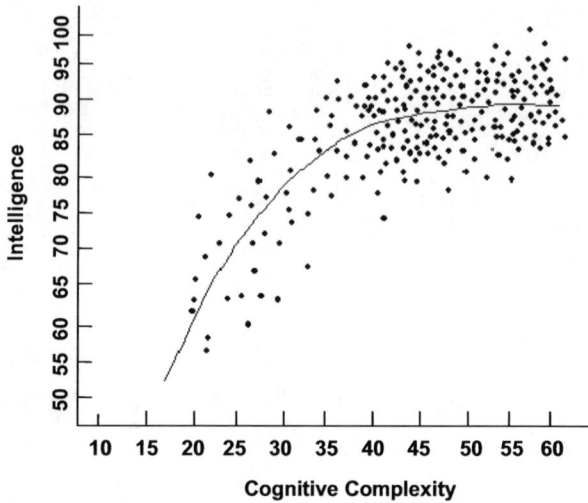

FIGURE 9.4 Curvilinear relation between cognitive complexity and intelligence.

Multiple Regression

Just as the experimental designs discussed in Chapter 5 were not limited to the manipulation of a single independent variable, correlational analyses are not limited to the investigation of a single predictor variable. **Multiple regression** is an extension of the Pearson correlation, to estimate the relationships of multiple predictors to a criterion. A researcher may wish to know in what way the combination of several different predictor variables relates to some particular criterion measure. For example, we may be interested in how well a set of factors such as years of education, socioeconomic status, and openness to experience combine to help explain the number of close friends that come from other racial groups. For such an endeavor, the most commonly used analytic technique is multiple regression, in which a weighted combination of predictor variables is used to estimate predicted outcome values on the criterion variable, which is derived from a multiple regression equation.[5] A multiple regression line may be estimated using the following equation:

$$Y' = bX_1 + cX_2 + dX_3 + a.$$

This is very similar to the regression equation for the Pearson correlation, except that the equation for multiple regression allows for more than one predictor. Let's say X_1 indicates the number of years of education, X_2 is socioeconomic status, X_3 is openness to experience, and Y' is the predicted number of cross-race friends. The constant (a) represents the predicted number of friends if a person scored a zero on all three predictor variables. The remaining parts of the equation are the weights for each predictor variable: b is the weight for X_1, c is the weight for X_2, and d is the weight for X_3. A variable next to a larger weight is given greater weight in prediction than one with a smaller weight. This reflects the degree of change in the criterion variable that can be expected from a change in the specific predictor variable.

A possible regression equation to predict Y' scores might be as follows: $Y' = 4.2X_1 + 1.5X_2 + 2.8X_3 + 2$. To obtain the predicted number of friends for any particular person, we would need his or her scores for years of education (X_1), socioeconomic status (X_2), and openness to experience (X_3). The proportion of variation accounted for by the set of predictors on the criterion is noted by the multiple regression version of the coefficient of determination, otherwise known as multiple R^2. The proportion of variance in the outcome unexplained by the set of predictors is known as predictive error: $E = 1 - R^2$. A larger multiple R^2 is desired because it indicates that the set of predictors collectively explains more of the variability in the criterion.

Because the weights assigned to each predictor in the multiple regression formula are calculated to maximize prediction using data from a *specific* sample of participants, generalizing the resulting equation to a new sample inevitably tends to produce a lower R^2 because the original equation is to some degree less applicable to a different sample. This is so because the regression analysis proceeds on the assumption that the sample data are free from measurement error. As such, any measurement error specific to the sample on which the prediction weights are calculated affects the coefficients in a regression equation. Because error is random, a new analysis employing another sample of respondents would be susceptible to different sources of error (e.g., first sample might be 18-year-olds completing the study at one university, but second sample might involve 20-year-olds completing the survey at a different university), and the regression weights should be expected to change accordingly. Thus R^2 values should be reported with some correction for this expected "shrinkage" (see McNemar, 1969; Yin & Fan, 2001). The extent of shrinkage is affected by the size and composition of the original respondent sample and by the quality of the measures employed in the multiple regression. Higher quality (i.e., more reliable) measures result in less shrinkage. With perfectly reliable measures, no shrinkage would occur.

Another useful means of estimating the extent of "shrinkage" makes use of a cross-validation sample. In this approach, the specific regression weights are determined in an initial sample of participants. These weights then are employed on the data of the second, different sample in calculating a new multiple R^2. If the weights that were determined in the original analysis successfully replicate the multiple R^2 in the second sample of respondents, confidence in the utility of the prediction formula is bolstered.

Uses and Misuses of Correlational Analysis

From a research orientation, the main problem with the evaluation of freely occurring variables is that they usually have natural extraneous covariates; that is, the occurrence of the variable of interest is confounded by the co-occurrence of other (usually unmeasured) factors that naturally accompany it. To take a simple example of a naturally occurring variable, suppose that a researcher is interested in demonstrating a predicted relationship between weather and psychological mood. Specifically, the investigator hypothesizes a positive relationship between rain and depression—the more rain, the greater the score on a depression inventory. However, even if the research confirms the existence of a positive correlation between the occurrence of rain and degree of depression, the investigator is a long way from identifying rain as the underlying causal factor of depression. Frequently co-occurring with rain are other weather conditions such as low barometric pressure, gray skies, and heavy cloud cover, any of which might provide plausible alternative explanations for the occurrence of psychological depression. Only if these other factors were held constant (i.e., if comparisons could be made between rainy days and non-rainy days in which air pressure and cloud conditions could be made the same) could rain be isolated as the determining factor. Unfortunately, until researchers can bring the occurrence of rain under experimental control, they must be aware of the limitations on the interpretation of their nonexperimental data.

Hidden Third Factor

An observed relationship between any two variables may be affected by a third source of variation that is accidentally or causally linked with one of the observed variables (as discussed in Chapter 2). The rain–depression illustration given above is an example of this potential confound in which the natural link between rain and low barometric pressure (or grey skies) may confuse our interpretation of the true nature of the causal relationship. For instance, the actual relationships may be as depicted in Figure 9.5(a).

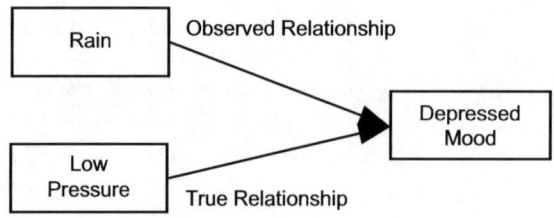

FIGURE 9.5a Illustration of a hidden third variable.

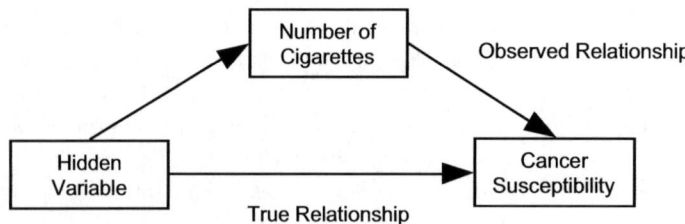

FIGURE 9.5b Hidden variable explanation of the smoking to cancer relationship.

In other cases, the third factor may be a causal variable which accounts for the common variation in both observed variables. Such a "third cause," in the form of some unknown hidden or lurking factor, was at one time proposed as an alternative explanation for the obtained relationship between cigarette smoking and likelihood of developing lung cancer, as depicted in Figure 9.5(b). Tobacco companies long argued that people who smoke do so because they have a higher sensation-seeking personality than the general population. Rather than cigarettes causing cancer, they suggest that such a personality disposition may instead be the culprit in causing these high-risk individuals to not only use nicotine but to also be more susceptible to cancer. As long as studies of the relationship between smoking and disease were limited to the observation of people who are already (through self-selection) smokers or nonsmokers, such third-factor explanations could never be completely eliminated (although the convergence of results from multiple sources of data, especially experiments on animals, has found that nicotine indeed causes cancer).

Because an association between any two (or more) nonexperimental variables can have multiple possible interpretations, students of social research are usually carefully taught to recognize that "correlation does not necessarily imply causation." Just because values on variable A can help predict values on variable B does not necessarily mean that A causes B. Of course, a correlational association *can* reflect a causal relationship, particularly if one variable precedes the other in time (but not always even then). So to be clear, causation implies correlation, but correlation does not (necessarily) imply causation.

Prediction vs. Hypothesis-Testing

Determining the direction and strength of the relationship between a specific predictor and a criterion is particularly difficult if the observed predictor variable is only one of several interrelated factors that contribute to variation in the criterion variable, as in the situation depicted in Figure 9.5(c). In such cases, the relative contribution from only a single source of variation may be misjudged, as many other determinants may also have a role. Determining the extent of the relationship between two variables also is difficult if the effect of one of the variables cannot be extricated from that of the other.

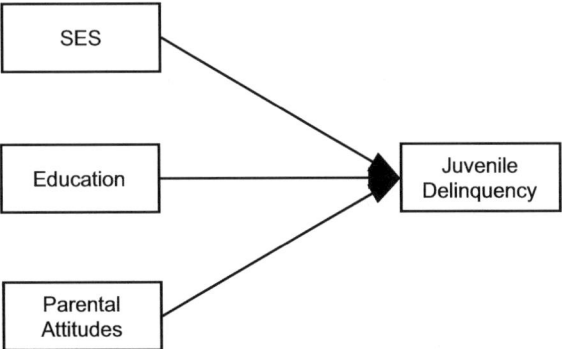

FIGURE 9.5c Three predictors and a criterion.

Because many of the covariates that confound naturally occurring phenomena cannot be extricated or made independent of one another, behavioral scientists have been tempted to substitute correlational strategies for experimental control in attempts to sort out the factors that contribute to variation in measures of interest. Many of these attempts reflect an inadequate understanding of the context of testing and measurement within which most of our commonly used correlational techniques were developed. Measurement theorists are clear that there is a distinction between a measuring instrument and the underlying conceptual variable it is designed to represent, and we emphasized this position in our earlier discussion of validity (Chapter 4). Any single measurement is only a partial and inadequate reflection of the underlying variations on the dimension or construct of interest with regard to a particular sample of participants. As discussed, the score obtained on any measurement consists of both "true score" and "error" components. The true score representing reliable, relatively stable characteristics of the feature or event being measured, and measurement error representing unmeasured factors that affect responses at the time of measurement.

Knowledge of the various sources of true score and error components of any measuring instrument is relatively unimportant if one is interested only in the development of prediction equations. If scores on one measure are consistently related to scores on another, then the former can be used to predict the latter, no matter what the underlying source of covariation may be. Thus, for instance, scores on a high-school achievement test may adequately predict academic performance in college without indicating whether the source of common variation is due to extraneous variables such as basic intelligence, motivation, study habits, parental income, or ability to cheat on tests! Prediction, however, is neither sufficient nor equivalent to theoretical explanation. An appropriate conceptual explanation requires a comprehensive theoretical understanding of the relationships among variables, and failing to distinguish between prediction and theoretical explanation can lead to misinterpretation of the results from correlational studies.

Partial Correlations

One common example of the misuse of multiple regression involves the use of partial correlations to statistically assess and control for multiple predictors of interest on a criterion. *Partial correlations*, also known as standardized weights or beta, are regression weights that have been standardized. Standardization involves converting the original regression weights into the same metric, so that each weight will range from −1.00 to 1.00, for the purpose of comparing the relative contribution of each predictor on a criterion.

To return to our weather research illustration, partialling would involve obtaining three simple Pearson correlations between rain and barometric pressure, between rain and depression, and between barometric pressure and depression. Then the rain to depression relationship would be examined using partial correlation (or, a standardized weight after air pressure has been included in the regression) to determine whether there was any degree of relationship "left over" after the common variation with air pressure had been accounted for. The size of the partial correlation of low pressure to depression could also be compared to that of rain to depression to determine which had a stronger predictive contribution to depression.

Within the context of prediction analysis, in which the partial correlation was developed, there is no problem in interpreting the value of a partial r. The partial correlation between predictor and criterion measure indicates the contribution of that predictor to an improvement in the accuracy of prediction over and beyond other (partialled-out) predictor(s). Thus, to return to our example, if the correlation between rain and depression, with barometric pressure "partialled out," were .00, this result would indicate that rainfall would not improve the prediction beyond the simple correlation between depression and barometric pressure. However, a partial r value significantly greater than .00 for each predictor indicates that the combination of both predictor results in a better prediction of the criterion than if either predictor were used alone.

Because partial correlations (or beta values) indicate how much variable A contributes to prediction of the criterion over and above variable B, researchers are tempted to use partial correlation to test the hypothesis that A is a unique determinant of the criterion—that is, it relates to the criterion in a way that is independent of B. For purposes of hypothesis testing, however, the mere existence of a significant partial correlation can be easily misinterpreted, because such a result does not indicate how or why the improvement in prediction occurs. The partial value may indicate that the two variables under consideration share some theoretical determinant that is not shared by the other, partialled-out variable. On the other hand, it may indicate that the two predictors are both measures of the *same* common underlying construct, but with different sources of error variation. Accepting the former interpretation is equivalent to assuming that the partialled-out variable B has been measured *without error or any other unique sources of variation*—an assumption that may hold with respect to the measurement of rainfall and air pressure, but certainly not for the kinds of conceptual variables common in social science research! Periodic warnings have appeared in the literature against the use of partial correlations to test underlying conceptual variables without regard to the contribution of error variation to the size of the partial correlation (e.g., Brewer, Campbell, & Crano, 1970; Sechrest, 1963; Stouffer, 1936), but the practice continues nonetheless.

Multi-Level Models

As an extension of multiple regression, **multi-level modeling** is used to estimate the relationships of predictor(s) to a criterion, if the design involves a nested hierarchy of units (Kahn, 2011). Multi-level modeling has been used interchangeably with the term *Hierarchical Linear Modeling* (Raudenbush, Bryk, & Congdon, 2004), the most popular software used to specify nested designs. Multiple regression is appropriate if data are collected at only one level, but multi-level modeling is the more sound choice if the design is nested with at least two levels.

To illustrate, suppose you conducted an investigation at a particular bar near the vicinity of your university. You collected predictor measures such as each patron's attitudes toward alcohol and number of hours spent at this local establishment to predict the outcome of number of drinks consumed that night. In this scenario, a multiple regression is entirely appropriate to estimate the contribution of two predictors (attitude and time spent) on the criterion. However, a different approach would be required if you expanded the research geographically to collect measures from

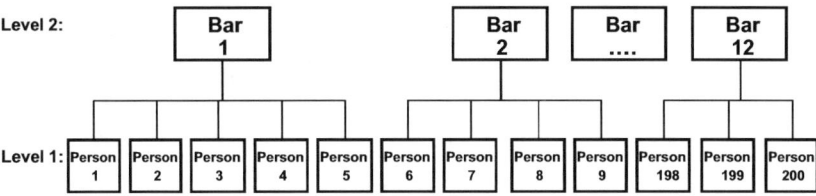

FIGURE 9.6 Multi-level modeling with two levels: 12 bars and 200 customers.

alcohol users at multiple bars in the neighborhood. A multi-level design is illustrated in Figure 9.6, with data from 200 customers (level 1) collected across the 12 neighborhood bars (level 2). Notice that each customer, which is the *nested unit,* is observed in only one of the bars. Phrased differently, the design is hierarchical because participants are nested within each drinking location. If a multiple regression was instead used to assess the relationships of the predictors on the criterion, it would be based on the erroneous assumption that customers were all drinking in the same drinking establishment and affected by this identical environment.

The **intraclass correlation** (ICC) is an index to assess the extent to which participants have more homogeneous scores *within* the higher-order grouping units relative to variability of participant scores *across* all groupings in a multi-level model. It indicates the degree that scores on the criterion variable differ as a function of the grouping units. The ICC ranges from a value of .00 to 1.00, with a value significantly greater than .00 indicating the clustering effect due to the nested design cannot be safely ignored. The important reason to not overlook the ICC is that people clustered in the same nested unit tend to be more similar to one another (demographically, attitudinally, behaviorally) than they are to people who are nested within a different unit.

In Figure 9.6, the greater the variation of the different bars in terms of the criterion of average number of drinks consumed by their respective customers, the higher the ICC. This is because patrons tend to make the decision to consume alcohol at a particular bar over others for various reasons. For example, customers who self-select by choosing to consume their beverage at a country and western bar might be more similar (and their drinking correlated with) customers of the same bar than with those who drink at a karaoke or a hip-hop bar. A country and western bar might tend to have customers who are older, more politically conservative, and who prefer to drink Southern Comfort, to name some possibilities that affect drinking levels. These characteristics may be responsible for confounding the relationship between hypothesized predictors and the outcome variable. Multi-level modeling accounts for, and therefore rules out, the hierarchical design artifact of the ICC, and this enables more accurate estimation of the two predictors to the criterion.

Multi-level research can be undertaken with more than two hierarchical levels. An example of a three-level model is presented in Figure 9.7. Suppose that our research project involved data collected from 10 towns (level 3) involving 100 families (level 2) and 300 children participants (level 1) in California. By using a three-level hierarchical model, the design accounts for the possibility that siblings within the same family are more similar to each other (e.g., genetically, demographically, attitudinally, and behaviorally) than to children from other families. Furthermore, a family tends to be more like other families located in the same town with respect to a variety of unmeasured characteristics (e.g., socioeconomic status and quality of schools) than to families located in different neighborhoods. Aside from allowing the design to estimate the value of the ICC and to account for it, multi-level modeling enables the evaluation of a combination of predictors, even at different levels. For example, the design in Figure 9.7 might involve examining predictors that help account for the outcome of children's scores on a verbal ability test. A level 1 predictor (child level) might be the age of the child and number of books the child typically reads, which could be assessed simultaneously with the level 2 predictors (family

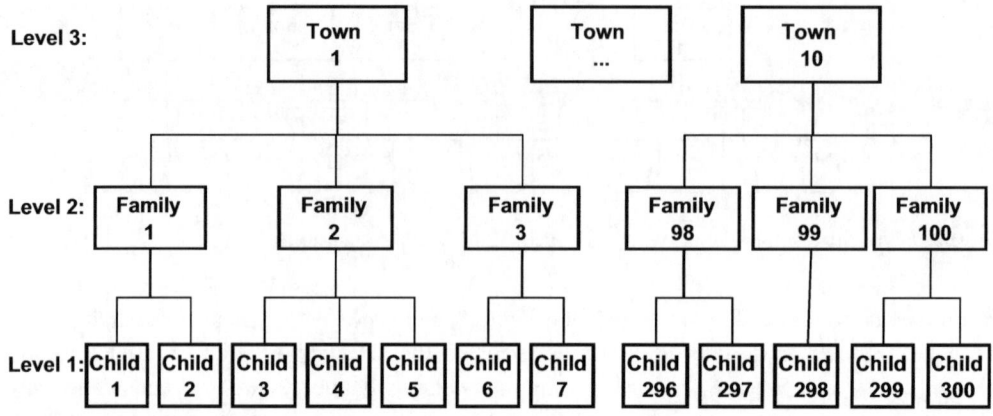

FIGURE 9.7 Multi-level modeling with three levels: 10 towns, 100 families, and 300 children.

level) involving number of books available in each home and each mother's educational attainment. In this multi-level scenario, we have a total of four predictors (from two different levels) to determine the partial correlation weight of each in contributing to children's verbal skills, the criterion variable.

The design of Figure 9.7 could be expanded hierarchically, for example, if we receive additional funding to extend this line of research across states (e.g., California, Michigan, Pennsylvania, etc.). This rather complex model consisting of four hierarchical levels would acknowledge that towns located or clustered within the same state tend to be more similar than to towns located in another state on characteristics such as state policies about reading or educational guidelines. The multi-level modeling approach allows for considerably greater precision in identifying sources of variation in nested research designs. Its development and use across the social sciences has provided the grounds for clearer understanding of the sources of variations.

Structural Equation Models

In recent years more sophisticated multivariate analytic approaches have become available to assist investigators in evaluating the total pattern of intercorrelations among multiple variables in a theory-testing framework. Multiple regression was developed to extend the utility of the Pearson correlation by allowing the inclusion of many predictors, but this extension was restricted to a single criterion outcome. Multi-level modeling extends the linear multiple regression by accounting for the hierarchical design while allowing many predictors (even at different hierarchical levels). Still, only one criterion is allowed. A **structural equation model** overcomes the limitations of a multiple regression analysis by allowing the ability to estimate relationships among multiple predictors and multiple criterion variables. Although advances in structural equation modeling allow for its integration with multi-level modeling, this combined technique is uncommon in the literature due to its complexity and stringent statistical requirements. Thus our elaboration of structural equation modeling focuses on the more widespread non-nested, single-level designs.

Structural equation models are relatively commonplace in those social sciences in which experimental manipulation is difficult (e.g., political science, economics, sociology), and they are becoming more widely used in psychology, communication, and related disciplines (see Hoyle, 1995; McArdle & Kadlec, 2013; Schumacker & Lomax, 1996). Our earlier remarks on multiple regression and partial correlation weights will prove useful here, as these basic correlational techniques were instrumental in the historical development of structural equation models.

Structural equation modeling requires the researcher to hypothesize a set of relations that exist among a set of variables, based on some theoretical framework. These models require specifications of a set of associations that link theory-relevant constructs and typically are closed systems. That is, they assume that the variables presented in the model will involve only a small number of variables and their interrelationships: They are not designed to describe the total universe of all variables in existence that might be related to the variables in the model.

Structural equation models involve understanding diagrammatic terminology, as presented in Figure 9.8. One reason for having a dedicated language is that predictor variables may contribute to other predictor variables, and outcome variables may in turn contribute to other outcomes. The notation system serves to avoid this tangled web of confusion in referring to the variety of possible relationships among variables.

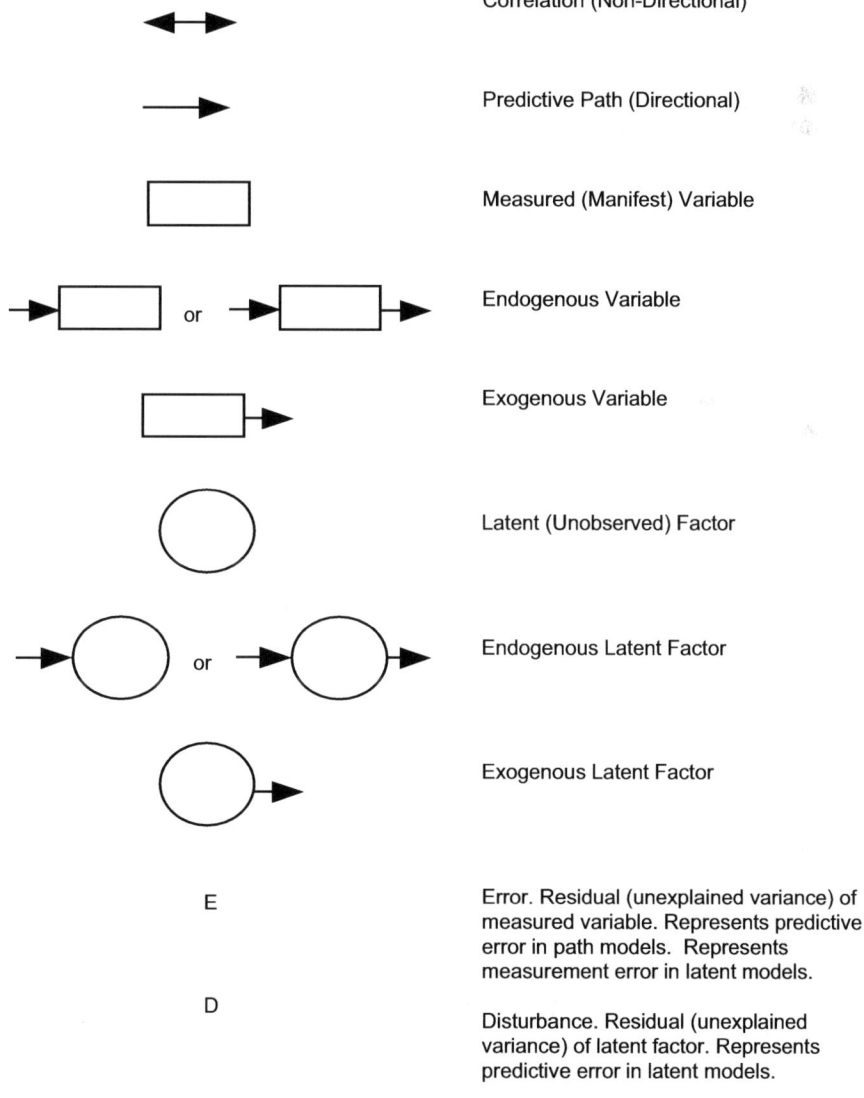

FIGURE 9.8 Notations in a structural equation model.

Research Design Strategies

Structural equation models may be subdivided into two major families: Path models and latent models. Let's start with the discussion of path models, and use this technique to set the groundwork for the subsequent presentation of latent predictive models.

Path Models

A **path model** is a type of structural equation model in which predictive relationships involving only measured variables are estimated. A variable may be represented with a single item or by computing an average or summed composite of a set of highly related items. Items intended to capture a construct should be internally consistent (e.g., Cronbach's alpha) before composites are computed (Cronbach, 1951). These composites are then used as variables in path-analytic models. A one-headed arrow represents a directional relationship of a determinant on a consequent. Keeping in mind the notation system described in Figure 9.8, let's examine the example path models in Figure 9.9.

Similarity is considered an **exogenous variable** (no one-headed arrow is pointing at it), a variable not explained by a determinant or predictor, as postulated in a structural equation model. These models, in other words, do not explicitly specify the variables that cause similarity. Assumed reciprocity and attraction are each considered an **endogenous variable** (a one-headed arrow is pointing at it), a variable explained by a determinant or predictor, as postulated in a structural equation model.

The E in each model indicates predictive error, or the proportion of variance that was not explained by other variables in the model. That is, other variables not measured in the investigation may also play a role in contributing to these endogenous variables. Generally when designing a path model, researchers use the notation of a predictor error to recognize that the model has not specified or measured all of the possible extraneous variables that might determine the endogenous variables. In Figure 9.9b, for example, the model has similarity as the sole predictor of assumed

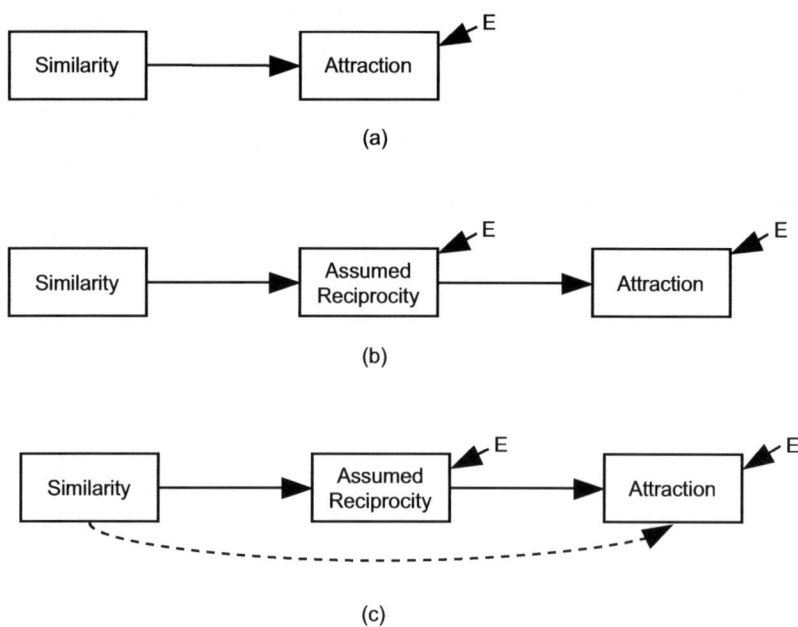

FIGURE 9.9 Path model of hypothesized relations between attitude similarity and attraction.

reciprocity, but we realize that it is probably not the only determinant, because additional variables (outside the model) also may predict this endogenous variable. The error term indicates our explicit recognition of this fact. This term is analogous to the residual or inaccuracy of linear prediction in multiple regression ($E = 1-R^2$) as discussed earlier. Thus, it reflects all of the unmeasured and unspecified determinants of an endogenous variable. Error terms are assumed to be independent of each other and of any other variables in the model. If they are correlated, this suggests the likelihood of model misspecification, that is, that some of the estimated paths should be deleted or added because the hypothesized paths did not correspond well with the data.

Mediation

In most discussions of path analysis or structural equation modeling, a distinction is made between direct and indirect effects. With direct effects, a change in one variable is directly reflected by a subsequent change in another. Conversely, some variables are thought to influence others only indirectly—that is, their influence on a variable is mediated by another variable (or set of variables), as discussed in Chapter 2. Although meditational processes were commonly tested with multiple regression (Baron & Kenny, 1986), today's path models are increasingly being employed to analyze mediation hypotheses (Preacher, Rucker, & Hayes 2007; Zhao, Lynch, & Chen, 2010). Figure 9.9 draws on an example from the literature on interpersonal attraction that will help illustrate the distinction between direct and indirect (mediated) paths.

In his book *The Attraction Paradigm,* D. Byrne (1971) argued that attitude similarity caused attraction—that is, we tend to like those who have attitudes similar to ours. To demonstrate this, Byrne manipulated the extent to which participants' attitudes were shown to be consistent with those of a hypothetical other. When asked whether they thought that they would like to be friends with, and work with, this other person, participants in the high apparent similarity condition were much more likely to report favorable responses than those in the low similarity condition. This finding supported Byrne's hypothesis of a direct effect between similarity and attraction (diagrammatically, this prediction is illustrated in Figure.9.9a).

Later research (Condon & Crano, 1988; Napolitan & Goethals, 1979) suggested that the relationship demonstrated by Byrne was mediated by another variable, namely, the assumption of reciprocity. Diagrammatically, this mediation is summarized as a path model in Figure 9.9b. This proposed mediation was based on the idea that we tend to like others who are similar to us because we assume they will like us back. In other words, although there is a relationship between similarity and attraction, it is not a direct effect, but rather is mediated by the assumption of reciprocated liking. An alternative to a fully mediated model (Figure 9.9b), Figure 9.9c represents a model in which assumed reciprocity acts as a mediator, but in addition, there remains a direct effect of assumed similarity. In Figure 9.9c the *direct effects* are from similarity to assumed reciprocity, from assumed reciprocity to attraction, and from similarity to attraction. An *indirect effect* occurs starting with similarity through the mediator of assumed reciprocity to attraction. The traversal of pathways via indirect effects may be determined by starting the trace (through one-headed arrows) from an initial exogenous variable to a mediator to a final endogenous variable.

To test the models in Figures 9.9b and 9.9c, Condon and Crano (1988) used Byrne's (1971) method for manipulating assumed similarity. Participants then were asked to judge (1) how similar they were to the other person (similarity), (2) the extent to which they believed the other person liked them (assumed reciprocity), and (3) how much they thought they would like the other person (attraction).

The results of path analysis supported both the direct and the mediational hypotheses. Although the Pearson correlation between similarity and attraction was statistically significant ($r = .64$), the assumed reciprocity to attraction relationship was even stronger ($r = .81$). Indeed, when the influence of both assumed reciprocity and similarity was accounted for on the attraction criterion, the resulting partial correlation weight ($r = .18$) of assumed reciprocity to attraction was substantially less than the original correlation of .64 (as shown in Figure 9.9c). Given this attenuation of the similarity to attraction connection after inclusion of assumed reciprocity, it is reasonable to conclude that the mediational model is more plausible than the model without the mediator. Because the partial correlation was not completely reduced to .00 upon controlling for both predictors on attraction, the analysis suggests that both direct and indirect effects from similarity to attraction were plausible. The mediational interpretation is not contradictory to the direct effect idea; rather, it suggests that assumed reciprocity does not fully account for the influence of similarity on attraction. This result encourages us to search for additional potential mediators.

Multiple Mediation

Considerable research demonstrates that we are more attracted to good-looking people (Dion, Berscheid, & Walster, 1972). Some have hypothesized that this relationship is mediated by perceived social competence (i.e., physically attractive people are more socially competent, and therefore more likeable). The path model of Figure 9.10 integrates these two lines of research on attraction, and is an example of a model involving multiple mediators (Preacher & Hayes, 2008). In this model, both similarity and beauty are determinants of likability, but the effects of both predictors are mediated by other factors. Similarity to attraction is thought to be mediated through assumed reciprocity, as was discussed. Beauty to attraction is hypothesized to be mediated through perceived social competence, which in turn is mediated through assumed reciprocity.

The rationale for these mediators is relatively simple. At an early age, good-looking children appear to be more pleasant to interact with than unattractive children (Berry & McArthur, 1986), and as a consequence receive more attention from parents and other adults. As a result, these children learn more social graces and become more socially competent than unattractive children, who usually do not receive such positive attention. We also are more likely to assume that a socially competent person likes us—because he or she is less likely to embarrass us, to criticize us in front of others, etc. As a result of this chain of events, we can hypothesize that people who are physically beautiful are more likely to be liked (attraction), but this effect is mediated through the two variables of social competence and assumed reciprocity of liking. Tracing the pathways, an indirect effect is found from physical beauty to social competence to assumed reciprocity to attraction toward that person. An indirect effect is also shown from similarity to assumed reciprocity to attraction.

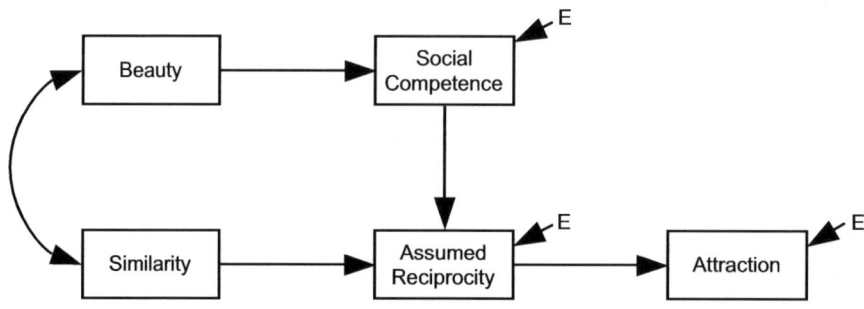

FIGURE 9.10 Path model linking physical beauty and similarity to attraction.

The observant reader will notice that two different types of arrows (single-headed versus double-headed) connect the variables in Figure 9.10. Most common in this diagram are the single-headed arrows, or example, those linking social competence with assumed reciprocity, and assumed reciprocity with attraction. Connections of this type imply directional hypotheses; thus, social competence is hypothesized to be a determinant of assumed reciprocity (though perhaps only one of many), which in turn is thought to be a determinant of attraction. But notice the connection in Figure 9.10 between beauty and similarity. Here, a double-headed arrow connects the variables. Relationships indicated by connections of this type indicate that a non-directional or correlational relationship has been hypothesized between the variables. As noted, both beauty and similarity are exogenous. A third type of relationship also is possible, namely, no relationship. In these instances of variables that are hypothesized to be unrelated, no arrow connects the variables. In Figure 9.10, no direct effect is hypothesized between beauty and assumed reciprocity, and thus no arrow is specified by the researcher to connect these two variables.

Recursive vs. Nonrecursive Models

Notice also that the directional flow of the arrows in Figures 9.9 and 9.10 is consistently from left to right, and furthermore, that no paths ever return to a variable that has already been involved in a relationship. A model of this type is called a *recursive model,* in which circular processes are not involved, and are therefore amenable to relatively straightforward statistical analysis. A *nonrecursive model,* on the other hand, allows for causal paths to "backtrack"—in that a variable can be both a cause and an effect of another. If the recursive model of Figure 9.10 allowed for the possibility that social competence was both a determinant and an outcome of assumed reciprocity, this will resemble the nonrecursive model of Figure 9.11. Given the possibility of reciprocal causation, non-recursive models are considerably more difficult to analyze and necessitate postulating numerous assumptions before they can be assessed statistically (see Kenny, 1979). In practice, because non-recursive models have assumptions that are difficult to satisfy, they are much less common in the literature than recursive models.[6]

Latent Structural Equation Models

A **latent structural equation model** is an integration of confirmatory factor analysis and path analysis. All the path analysis issues discussed up to this point also apply to latent structural equation modeling. A path model uses only measured variables to represent the constructs. This route is taken if the researcher decides, for whatever reason, not to account for measurement error in each factor.

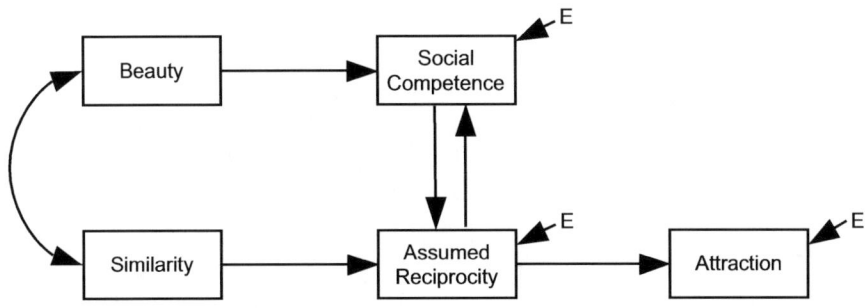

FIGURE 9.11 Example of a nonrecursive path diagram.

A weakness of path analysis is that the measurement error within each factor is not estimated and therefore not partialled out. In latent structural equation modeling, both measurement and predictive error are estimated. Thus, such models contain a *measurement model,* derived from factor loadings in a confirmatory factor analysis, and also a *structural model* representing the predictive relations between factors. Essentially, each variable in the model has been factor-analyzed so that the construct is "free" from measurement error. This pure factor, known as a *latent factor* or *unobserved factor* (not directly observed or measured in the study), is then used to specify predictive relations with other exogenous or endogenous latent factors. The notation system given in Figure 9.8 is necessary to understand latent models.

Suppose you are excited and delighted that the circus is coming to your college town. As this traveling circus will be visiting for an entire month, you take advantage of this important opportunity to investigate a proposed model linking beliefs and behaviors about attending the circus. To help inform specification of the hypothesized relations among constructs, the Theory of Reasoned Action (Ajzen & Fishbein, 1980) serves as the guiding framework. This theory about human motivation postulates that people's personal attitudes about a behavior and the social norms regarding that behavior are correlated, and that both of these constructs simultaneously influence intentions to engage in the behavior. Intentions, in turn, are postulated to predict actual behavioral engagement.

In a study designed to test these relationships, you create a survey containing 11 questions and administer it to a sample of townspeople. Participants rate how much they personally agree or disagree with three attitudinal items regarding whether they believe the circus is fun, exciting, and enjoyable. Norms are measured with three questions regarding participants' beliefs about how much their respective best friend, sibling, and mother like the circus. The intentions construct is also assessed with three items, which ask whether respondents want to, seek to, and plan to visit the circus. Upon departure of the circus a month later, you subsequently ask the same sample two behavioral questions concerning the number of days and number of hours they had spent at the circus.

Taking the path analysis route, our set of predictive relations might resemble the diagram depicted in Figure 9.12. First, the four constructs are indexed by computing the mean of respective items. The path model is then estimated to derive predictive relations among these measured variables.

If instead the decision is to estimate a latent predictive model, the researcher should first estimate the measurement model, essentially a confirmatory factor analysis, indicating the relationship between individual items and the factor they are intended to assess. Figure 9.13 shows a confirmatory factor analysis involving correlations among the four factors, which are tapped by their corresponding measured items. The circles represent latent factor or unobserved factors, called so because these factors are not directly assessed or observed. Rather, the variance of a latent factor is a function of the shared or common variance of its measured items. The E in a latent model

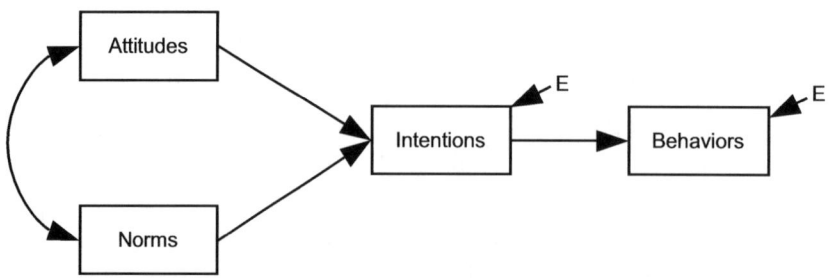

FIGURE 9.12 Path analysis of theory of reasoned action.

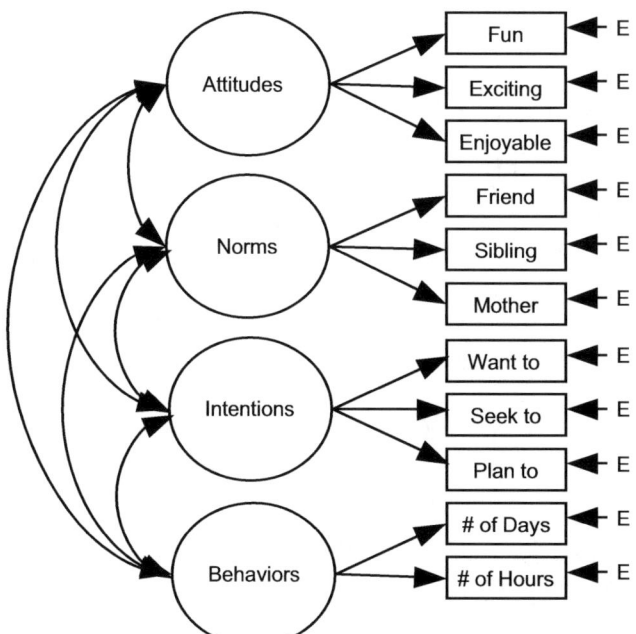

FIGURE 9.13 Confirmatory factor analysis.

represents *measurement error,* but this term in a path model represents *predictive error.* The factor loading, or how representative the item is of its factor, reflects the weight of the measured item on the latent factor. (Recall our discussion of factor analysis in Chapter 3.) The correlation between two latent factors is signified by an arrow with two heads. However, this is no ordinary Pearson correlation (although interpreted similarly), but a correlation in which measurement error has been statistically removed from the factors.

Only upon determining that the measurement model is acceptable, with high factor loadings on latent factors, is it suitable to estimate predictive connections from one factor to another. After all, if the items in a factor are not consistent in measurement, it would be futile to use such a poor factor in any meaningful way in a hypothesized framework. The latent predictive model is presented in Figure 9.14. The loadings between each latent factor and its measured items represent the measurement model, whereas the predictive relations between the various latent factors represent the structural model. The predictive paths between latent factors represent the strength of the relation after the impurity of measurement error is statistically removed from the factors. This is the reason why latent techniques are sometimes said be "free" from measurement error. However, this statement is only true to the extent that the measured items are representative of the underlying phenomenon of interest, but in reality it is impossible to know the entire world of all possible measured items to represent a theoretical construct. Thus, it is advantageous to use a greater variety of related items with the goal of fully capturing the conceptual bandwidth of the construct.

The terminology discussed with regard to path analysis also applies to the latent structural equation model in Figure 9.14 Attitudes and norms serve as the latent exogenous factors, because each only has a predictive role (with no other factor pointing at it) in the model. Intentions and behavior are latent endogenous factors being explicated or determined by other factors in the model. The "D" in the figure indicates the *disturbance* term, essentially the predictive error (i.e., unexplained variance) stemming from an endogenous latent factor not being fully explained by other factors in

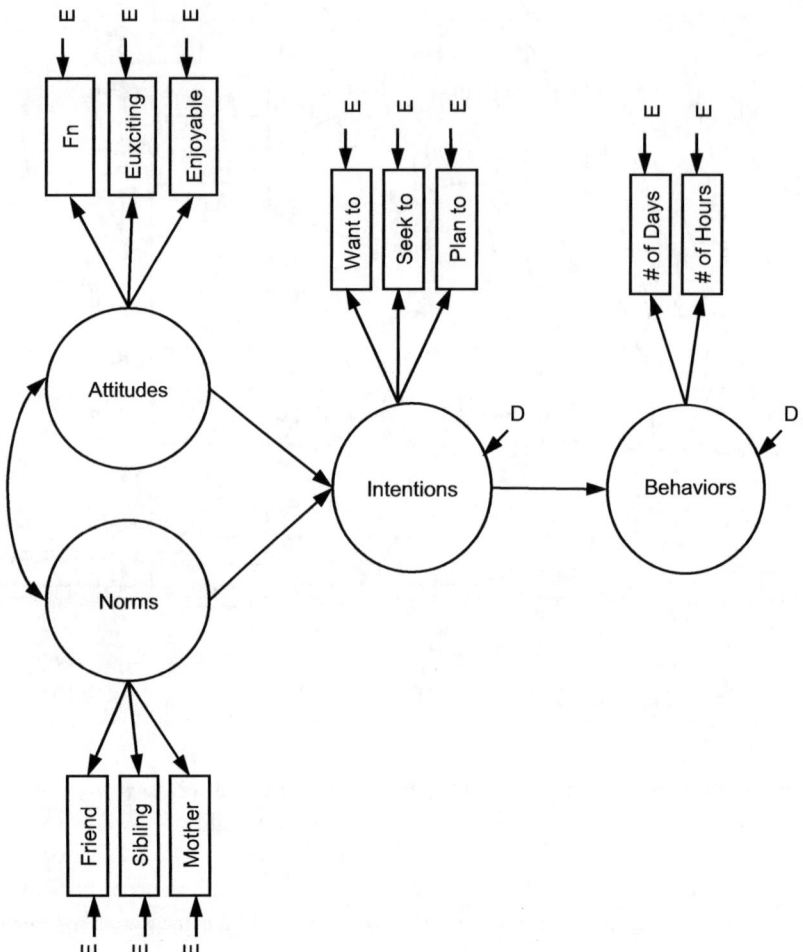

FIGURE 9.14 Latent predictive model.

the model. The disturbance term denotes the fact that other latent factors, outside the contained system shown in the diagram, might also be responsible for explaining these endogenous factors. The direct effects are the estimated one-headed paths in the model: (a) attitudes to norms (b) norms to intentions, and (c) intentions to behavior. Tracing the traversal of directional pathways, two indirect effects are possible: (a) attitudes to intentions to behaviors, and (b) norms to intentions to behaviors. Thus, the pathways from attitudes and social norms to behavior are mediated by intentions.

Fit of Structural Equation Models

Bentler's (2006; see also Mair, Wu, & Bentler, 2010) EQS and Jöreskog and Sörbom's (1993) LISREL are two popular programs used in the statistical analysis of structural equation models (see B. Byrne, 2012). Details of these analyses are beyond the scope of this textbook, but their basic logic is straightforward. The empirical data for testing structural equation models is converted to a matrix of intercorrelations (or covariances) among all of the measured variables used in the model.

From this correlation matrix, analyses derive estimates of path values in the model. Also provided in a structural equation model is a test to evaluate **goodness of fit**, an overall index of how well all the computed estimates of the relationships in the model successfully reproduce the underlying correlation matrix. The better the fit (i.e., less discrepancy between predicted and actual values), the greater is the support for the hypothesized structural model.

Identification

One of the central challenges of structural equation modeling is understanding the issue of identification. Identification is a term that refers to the relative number of knowns to unknowns in a set of equations. A model could be over-identified, just-identified, or under-identified. As you might recall from introductory algebra, it is impossible to solve an equation if it contains more unknown quantities than known quantities. For example, the following is solvable for Y if these two equations are provided: $Y = X + 7$ and $X = 3$. If the X value was not given (becoming an unknown), a solution could not be computed.

This same problem afflicts structural equation models. In an *under-identified model*, in which we have more unknowns (i.e., number of paths and variances estimated) than knowns (number of all possible correlations between variables), the solution of the set of equations that constitute the model becomes impossible.[7] In situations in which we have a greater number of correlations (knowns) in the underlying data than estimated paths or variances (unknowns), the model *is over-identified*. Over-identification of a model is desired, because satisfying this assumption allows the model to yield a viable solution and also permits the testing of different combinations of paths involving the same variables. A final possibility is a model that is *just-identified*—that is, the model has exactly the same number of knowns and unknowns Although such a model can be estimated, such a saturated predictive model is unexciting for model testing because it represents a perfect one-to-one correspondence between the number of hypothesized relations and the number of underlying correlations. An over-identified model is desired because an important goal of structural equation modeling is for the researcher to specify the most parsimonious model possible in an attempt to explain the correlations among the underlying set of variables (knowns) using the fewest number of estimates (unknowns).

Even when a model is over-identified, it should be made clear that goodness of fit of the resulting structural equation model estimates does not "prove" that the hypothesized structural model is correct. Goodness of fit simply indicates that the model is compatible with the obtained data. In fact, there are a great number of paths (and path value estimates) that could be generated from the same empirical data, with varying degrees of fit. For this reason, it is often recommended that structural equation modeling be used to test multiple, competing models (i.e., different sets of structural paths relating the set of variables). The resulting goodness of fit indices cannot establish that one model is the only correct one, but they can be used to determine which of several alternative models is more supported by the data.

Conclusion

Although many new terms have been introduced in this discussion of structural equation models, much of this material builds upon the terms and concepts of the Pearson correlation. In fact, the ideas that underlie correlational modeling are the same as those that lie at the heart of the experimental method. In both research strategies, we begin with a theory or a set of hypotheses regarding the relationships among a set of variables. These relationships should be clearly stated before data are analyzed. For many, a major strength of structural modeling is that it forces us explicitly to detail the relationships that we think exist among our variables. Having specified our model, we *then* collect data to test the hypothesized relationships. In structural equation modeling, we must attend to a number of technical issues regarding the identifiability and recursivity of the model, but such issues are secondary to the theoretical specification of the model itself. If our theory is reasonable, the set of structural equations that we estimate will make sense. And, if our theory has been pitted against other theories, the structural equation approach will enable us to specify each of the different models and then choose the most plausible.

As noted, however, in no case will the structural modeling approach allow us to state with certainty that the model we have constructed provides the complete and true specification of the connections among the variables of interest. One reason for this is that there are a great many possible models that can be constructed from any given set of variables; as the number of variables in the model becomes large, the number of possible combinations of pathways that can be specified and hypothesized becomes astronomical. Thus, many possible alternative models might explain the set of relationships much more persuasively than the model that had been hypothesized originally. However, it would be difficult to make an assessment of this sort even if all possible models were specified, given that more than one type of model involving the same set of variables might be viable. In such instances, it is important to use theory to help inform decisions about selecting the superior framework.

Another reason for caution in interpreting predictive models is implicit in our reference to the size of the predictive error terms. It is possible that a proposed model might involve variables that explain only a miniscule portion of the possible variance in an outcome variable. Such a result would be comparable to a multiple regression study in which our set of predictor variables was only weakly related to the criterion (i.e., with a relatively unsubstantial R^2). In this case, even if the result is statistically significant, it is obvious that the predictors we have chosen to measure are inadequate in providing a complete picture of the factors explicating the criterion.

As in the experimental method, a structural equation model can never be proven correct, no matter how plausible the obtained results. Rather, the approach helps us to consider and render alternative explanations of underlying relationships untenable. Just as in the experimental methods, nonexperimental methods gain credence by a process in which alternative explanations of critical relationships are shown to be less plausible than the theory under examination. It is important to understand, however, that these techniques have to be reserved for circumstances in which considerable information about the phenomenon of interest already exists, so that a model is correctly specified by the researcher. Unless used in an exploratory way for hypothesis development, a possibility suggested by Crano and Mendoza (1987), the structural equation approach usually demands explicit statements of hypothesized relations among variables (derived from some a priori empirical or conceptual framework). This is a different process from completely exploratory research, in which the patterns of associations among variables often are not hypothesized in advance, but observed and interpreted after the data are collected. Interpreting results of analyses based on such post hoc observations under the guise of hypothesis-driven research represents a misuse of an otherwise powerful statistical methodology.

Questions for Discussion

1. Suppose some of your classmates want to use a median split on their data before conducting their analyses. What would you say to them? What issues would you urge them to consider?
2. Define the terms "latent factor," "measurement model," and "disturbance." What role does each play in the structural equation modeling technique?

3. Name some research contexts and questions that might be answered best through the use of multi-level modeling.
4. Given that path analyses and structural equation models are based on correlations among variables, do they mislead readers when they are used to suggest causal relations? How are you less likely to be misled when reading the results of such studies?

Notes

1. The use of median splits is relatively rare in purely correlational research, but it is often used in blocked or mixed experimental designs in order to create a categorical variable for purposes of using analysis of variance statistical techniques. Because this procedure creates the loss of information we are discussing here, it is now recommended that researchers treat the nonexperimental variable as a continuous measure and use regression techniques to analyze effects (MacCallum, Zhang, Preacher, & Rucker, 2002).
2. Scatterplots are common graphic devices for indicating the nature of the relationship between two variables by representing simultaneously the relative standing of all individuals on both measures.
3. Note that r^2 would be equal to 1.00 whether the correlation value (r) equals +1.00 or -1.00. The coefficient of determination indicates degree of linear relationship irrespective of direction.
4. Some correlational statistics—e.g., the correlation ratio (eta)—provide information only on the extent of relationship between the two variables being measured. The correlation ratio, though used rarely, is a coefficient of linear and non-linear association. If the relation between two variables is linear, then eta = r.
5. The combination of predictor variables is usually linear, producing a prediction equation of the general form: $Y' = a + b_1X_1 + b_2X_2 + \ldots + b_iX_i$, where the constant, a, and b-weights, are assigned to maximize the fit with actual Y scores. The prediction equation can also include interactions between predictor variables by entering a new predictor variable, which is the multiplicative product of the relevant variables (see Aiken & West, 1991).
6. In addition to multiple mediators and bidirectional relations, other, more complex relationships can be represented and tested in SEM, including moderated-mediation, mediated-moderation, etc. (e.g., Preacher et al., 2007).
7. To determine the number of "knowns," use the following formula: $k = (n(n-1))/2$, where k = number of knowns, and n = number of measured variables. If the number of paths and variances estimated in the proposed model exceeds this number, the model is not solvable.

References

Aiken, L. S., & West, S. G. (1991). *Multiple regression: Testing and interpreting interactions*. Newbury Park, CA: Sage.
Ajzen, I. & Fishbein, M. (1980). *Understanding attitudes and predicting social behavior*. Englewood Cliffs, NJ: Prentice-Hall.
Baron, R. M., & Kenny, D. A. (1986). The moderator-mediator variable distinction in social psychological research: Conceptual, strategic, and statistical considerations. *Journal of Personality and Social Psychology, 51*, 1173–1182.
Bentler, P. M. (2006). *EQS 6 Structural Equations Program manual*. Encino, CA: Multivariate Software, Inc.
Berry, D. S., & McArthur, L. Z. (1986). Perceiving character in faces: The impact of age-related craniofacial changes on social perception. *Psychological Bulletin, 100*, 3–18.
Brewer, M. B., Campbell, D. T., & Crano, W. D. (1970). Testing a single-factor model as an alternative to the misuse of partial correlations in hypothesis-testing research. *Sociometry, 33*, 1–11.
Byrne, B. M. (2012). Choosing structural equation modeling computer software: Snapshots of LISREL, EQS, AMOS, and Mplus. In R. H. Hoyle (Ed.), *Handbook of structural equation modeling* (pp. 307–324). New York: Guilford Press.
Byrne, D. (1971). *The attraction paradigm*. New York: Academic Press.
Condon, J. W., & Crano, W. D. (1988). Implied evaluation and the relationship between similarity and interpersonal attraction. *Journal of Personality and Social Psychology, 54*, 789–797.
Crano, W. D., & Mendoza, J. L. (1987). Maternal factors that influence children's positive behavior: Demonstration of a structural equation analysis of selected data from the Berkeley Growth Study. *Child Development, 58*, 38–48.

Cronbach, L. J. (1951). Coefficient alpha and the internal structure of tests. *Psychometrika, 16,* 297–334.
Dion, K. K., Berscheid, E., & Walster, E. (1972). What is beautiful is good. *Journal of Personality and Social Psychology, 24,* 285–290.
Hoyle, R. H. (1995). *Structural equation modeling.* Thousand Oaks, CA: Sage.
Jööreskog, K. G., & Sörbom, D. (1993). *LISREL 8: User's reference guide.* Chicago: Scientific Software.
Kahn, J. H. (2011). Multilevel modeling: Overview and applications to research in counseling psychology. *Journal of Counseling Psychology, 58,* 257–271.
Kenny, D. A. (1979). *Correlation and causality.* New York: Wiley.
MacCallum, R. C., Zhang, S., Preacher, K. J., & Rucker, D. D. (2002). On the practice of dichotomization of quantitative variables. *Psychological Methods, 7*(1), 19–40.
Mair, P., Wu, E., & Bentler, P.M. (2010). EQS goes R: Simulations for SEM using the package REQS. *Structural Equation Modeling, 17*(2), 333–349.
McArdle, J. J., & Kadlec, K. M. (2013). Structural equation models. In T. D. Little (Ed.), *The Oxford handbook of quantitative methods (Vol. 2): Statistical analysis.* (pp. 295–337). New York: Oxford University Press.
McNemar, Q. (1969). *Psychological statistics* (4th. ed.). New York: Wiley.
Napolitan, D. A., & Goethals, G. R. (1979). The attribution of friendliness. *Journal of Experimental Social Psychology, 15*(2), 105–113.
Preacher, K. J., & Hayes, A. F. (2008). Asymptotic and resampling strategies for assessing and comparing indirect effects in multiple mediator models. *Behavior Research Methods, 40,* 879–891.
Preacher, K. J., Rucker, D. D., & Hayes, A. F. (2007). Addressing moderated mediation hypotheses: Theory, methods, and prescriptions. *Multivariate Behavioral Research, 42,* 185–227.
Raudenbush, S. W., Bryk, A. S, & Congdon, R. (2004). HLM 6 for Windows [Computer software]. Skokie, IL: Scientific Software International, Inc.
Schumacker, R. E., & Lomax, R. G. (1996). *A beginner's guide to structural equation modeling.* Hillsdale, NJ: Lawrence Erlbaum Associates, Inc.
Sechrest, L. (1963). Incremental validity: A recommendation. *Educational and Psychological Measurement, 23,* 153–158.
Stouffer, S. A. (1936). Evaluating the effects of inadequately measured variables in partial correlation analysis. *Journal of the American Statistical Association. 31,* 348–360.
Streufert, S. (1997) Complexity: An integration of theories. *Journal of Applied Social Psychology, 27,* 2068–2095.
Suedfeld, P., Tetlock, P. E., & Streufert, S. (1992). Conceptual/integrative complexity. In C. P. Smith, J. W. Atkinson, D. C. McClelland & J. Veroff (Eds.), *Motivation and personality: Handbook of thematic content analysis* (pp. 393–400). New York: Cambridge University Press.
Yin, P., & Fan, X. (2001). Estimating R2 shrinkage in multiple regression: A comparison of different analytical models. *Journal of Experimental Education, 69,* 203–224.
Zhao, X., Lynch, J. G., & Chen, Q. (2010). Reconsidering Baron and Kenny: Myths and truths about mediation analysis. *Journal of Consumer Research, 37,* 197–206.

10

QUASI-EXPERIMENTS AND EVALUATION RESEARCH

In the preceding chapters we drew a clear distinction between experimental and correlational (i.e., nonexperimental) research designs. In correlational research, the investigator's role is that of an observer. All variables of interest are permitted to vary freely in their natural context. In a real sense, all the variables in correlational studies are dependent (or response) variables. The researcher's job in these contexts is to assess this natural variation and to tease out the patterns and interrelationships that exist among the critical measures. In experiments, the researcher actively intervenes in the normal pattern of variation, systematically controlling variation in the independent variable (or variables) to assess the causal impact(s) of this variation on some outcome(s). Controlled manipulation of the (presumed) causal variable and random assignment of subjects to the manipulated conditions are the necessary hallmarks of true experiments, which are the backbone of internally valid cause-effect analyses.

In many research contexts, the distinction between experimental and correlational studies may not be all that clear-cut. For example, in our discussion of field experiments, we mentioned studies in which the researcher *selected* rather than *created* the levels of the independent variable. Such studies preserve the logic of experimental design but lack the degree of experimenter control that characterizes "pure" experiments. By the same token, some correlational studies are conducted in the context of interventions into a given social situation (e.g., studies that investigate the natural reactions of an already established group upon arrival of a new member), thus mixing aspects of experimental and correlational design. The distinction, then, between experimental and correlational research should be seen as a continuum rather than a strict dichotomy.

Somewhere between true experiments and pure correlational research are quasi-experimental studies in which some systematic manipulation has been made for the purpose of assessing a causal effect, but random assignment of participants is not employed. This could occur because the intervention involves some pervasive treatment affecting all participants in the social setting at once. Or it could be that some participants are exposed to the treatment while others are not, perhaps because of some other nonrandom assignment process. These situations bear some resemblance to the pretest-posttest control group experimental design, in that a treatment has been introduced at a specifiable point in time or space. Thus, outcomes before the presence of the quasi-experimental treatment can be compared with outcomes occurring after its introduction across times points, but as a research design the structure of the study lacks a critical element necessary for internal validity. In the absence of random assignment, it is much more difficult to separate effects caused by the introduction of the treatment from effects caused by prior group differences, historical events, and other threats to internal validity. Although quasi-experiments often have fewer threats to internal validity than correlational studies, they are generally more susceptible to such threats than randomized experiments. The most recognized applications of quasi-experimental designs are found in evaluation research, in which the quasi-experimental treatment is usually called a program, policy, or intervention.

Program Evaluation Research

One situation in which interventions into a social system (e.g., at the local, city, state, or federal level) may be studied is on the occasion of the introduction of a new social program or policy designed to alleviate a particular social problem or concern. Such interventions may range from the introduction of new tax rates at the national level (e.g., higher income tax rate for the wealthy) to new procedures in the criminal justice system at the state level (e.g., the effects of "three-strikes" laws in deterring crime), to new teaching methods at the classroom level (e.g., the efficacy of Lego blocks to teach geometry). Often determining the effectiveness of such programs or policy changes is largely a political process, derived from stakeholder claims and the vested interests of program managers, beneficiaries, and interested community members.

In many cases, the use of public funding obliges accountability of expenditures, and for this purpose innovators are required to assess the effectiveness of social interventions systematically and scientifically, with empirical observations and quantitative measures of program processes and outcomes. If the results of a program indicate that the intervention is ineffective in achieving the desired results, the information may be used to terminate the social program. Conversely, such results could provide evidence for sustaining a program. **Program evaluation** is the application of social science methodology to the assessment of social programs or interventions by program evaluators. Evaluation research has now developed into a major field of applied social science (Campbell, 1969; Donaldson & Crano, 2011; Donaldson & Scriven, 2003; Struening & Brewer, 1983).

In evaluation research, the scientist is called the **program evaluator**, the person responsible for evaluating and assessing the many aspects and stages of a program or intervention. The information derived from program evaluation is disseminated to other stakeholders as feedback to help revise, understand, and continue or discontinue the intervention as necessary. Assessment of program effects is only one of several ways in which empirical research can and has entered into the design and evaluation of social policy. Among the various functions research may serve in the policy-making process, the following are probably most important and widely recognized in program evaluation research.

Needs Assessment

At early stages of policy formation, there is a need for accurate information about the extent and distribution of a given social problem or need. The purpose of **needs assessment** is to judge the extent of an existing social problem and determine whether a program or intervention is needed at all. At this point personal testimony and experience can be supplemented with quantitative data derived from survey or observational studies. Since 1975, for example, the federal government has supported the *Monitoring the Future* project, an annual study of the attitudes and actions of U.S. students in secondary school, high school, and college, and young adults, focusing particularly on their opinions toward and use of licit and illicit substances. The survey provides an invaluable picture of trends in drug use among adolescents and young adults.

Monitoring the Future was not designed to assess needs in the classic sense, but the information it supplies has been used to infer general trends that may signal the need for intervention. For example, reports of the *Monitoring the Future* group have indicated that adolescents' rates of marijuana use have increased, while their evaluations of its riskiness have decreased (Johnston, O'Malley, Bachman, & Schulenberg, 2013). This information can be used as the starting point for preventive interventions and programs. Indeed, data from the project motivated the federal government to mount a massive media prevention program.

Needs assessment research for developing a program is largely descriptive, with the quality of findings depending primarily on the adequacy of measures and the sampling approaches used in the study. In the case of the *Monitoring the Future* project and the National Survey on Drug Use and Health, for example, the research is trustworthy because it is performed by competent surveying organizations using the best sampling models available (see Chapter 11).

Program Development

Pilot studies of programs at their initial conceptualization or design stage provide a research opportunity for testing concepts in controlled studies on a small scale. The purpose of evaluation research at the stage of **program development** is to provide feedback to program designers that can lead to revisions or alterations in program materials, design, and procedures before the intervention is implemented on a larger and more costly scale. Essentially, this is a pilot study before going forward with implementing the full program. Program design research often is called *formative evaluation* (Scriven, 1967).

Program Feasibility

Once a social program or intervention has been designed, the next step is to determine whether or how the program can be implemented on a large scale through existing agencies or institutions. **Feasibility studies** are conducted on a small scale to determine if the program as planned can be delivered effectively, given the existing constraints. The purpose of this form of small-scale field testing is to decide if the program components can be implemented as intended on a wide-scale basis, and whether services will reach the targeted population. The type of data collected for this kind of study includes administrative records and books, direct observation of service delivery, and interviews with service recipients to ensure that the treatment was delivered as planned.

Program Efficacy

Program efficacy studies also are conducted on a small scale to determine whether the expected effects from the planned intervention occur as planned (Donaldson, 2007; Donaldson, Christie, & Mark, 2009). In efficacy research, the treatment is carefully monitored and implemented in a small sample of the targeted population. The idea is to ensure that the treatment works as planned before devoting additional time and resources to the full-scale intervention. To ensure the best possible outcome, the treatment is delivered under the most ideal circumstances possible. Obviously, if it does not operate as planned under ideal conditions, there is no sense in attempting to deliver it to the larger population in situations that might diminish its effect. The efficacy study presents the "best of all possible worlds," insofar as it is under tighter control than the actual intervention will (or can) be. For example, a national intervention campaign designed to increase exercising behaviors may initially target volunteers at a gym, who may have a greater desire to initiate and maintain this healthy habit. As such, it provides the best chance for treatment effectiveness. Failures at the program efficacy stage can stop the larger intervention in its tracks.

Summative Evaluation

Summative evaluation, which is also known as *impact evaluation* or *outcome evaluation,* is conducted to assess whether a fully implemented program had an effect on the problem it was designed to alleviate. It is perhaps the primary form of evaluation research. Not all evaluation tasks call for research on program efficacy, however, and it is important to distinguish this function from the others. The effectiveness of a program inevitably involves a causal hypothesis, and therefore requires that a number of prior stipulations be met to make the program conducive to such rigorous evaluation. Among the requisite conditions for effectiveness evaluation are the following: (1) The goals or objectives of the program must be sufficiently specified by the designers to allow for definable outcomes; (2) Program features must be defined well enough to determine whether the program is present or absent in a given situation or time; and (3) Some basis for observing or measuring the final outcomes in the presence or absence of the treatment program must be available. These stipulations are not easily met, so many of the problems arising from program evaluation can be traced to instances in which evaluators or policymakers attempted to conduct effectiveness assessments when feasibility, efficacy, or developmental evaluation efforts would have been more appropriate.

Cost-Benefit Analysis

Beyond determining whether a program had any effect at all, analysis of program benefits relative to program costs require that one assess the *degree* of program effect along some quantifiable scale. In other words, the research must determine both the beneficial and negative outcomes that can be attributed to the program. Obviously, benefits should outweigh costs. Relatively few full-fledged cost-benefit evaluations have been done of social programs, partly because of the difficulties of obtaining valid estimates of the size of program effects, and partly because of the absence of a common yardstick for measuring both costs and benefits in the social domain. For example, although we can calculate the financial costs involved in developing and airing an anti-tobacco ad, we cannot precisely determine the costs of the potential annoyance or anxiety associated with its implementation, or the immediate benefit of lessened morbidity associated with people's acceptance of its message. Nonetheless, some research models are available for comparing the size of effects associated with alternative programs that share common goals but different dollar costs (see Andresen & Boyd, 2010; Kuklinski, Briney, Hawkins, & Catalano, 2012; Lee & Aos, 2011).

Special Characteristics of Program Evaluation Research

As a part of the research enterprise, program effectiveness evaluations share much of the same logic and purpose as other hypothesis-testing research. However, the conduct of evaluation research does have some special contextual and functional characteristics that make it a somewhat different form of social research.

Political Context

The primary distinguishing characteristic of evaluation research is its explicitly political character. All social research may have direct or indirect political implications to some extent, but the reason for much evaluation research is political decision-making. The decision of whether to do a systematic evaluation, how it is to be conducted, and how the results are to be used are made largely in the political arena. Because many social programs are controversial to some extent, with supporters and detractors, evaluation studies inevitably become part of the controversy. These contextual factors frequently have an impact on the features and quality of research design that is possible in the particular social setting. Random assignment, for instance, which is a relatively simple matter in the laboratory context, can be a political hot potato when special interests are at stake. For example, imagine attempting to implement random assignment to either a highly sought-after preschool program or a control condition. Parents who want their children to take part in the program are not likely to accept the argument that their child was passed over so that more appropriate causal inferences of program effectiveness could be made.

Separation of Roles

In experimental research, the investigators who plan the study and design the outcome measures also determine how the independent variable is to be operationalized. In evaluation research studies, the program evaluators responsible for research design and measurement often are not the same as the individuals responsible for the program's delivery and implementation. Hence most evaluation projects involve a split between "research people" (program evaluators and methodologists), and "program people" (administrators, social workers, and the like), who sometimes work at cross-purposes. At worst, program personnel may feel threatened and defensive about their program being evaluated (after all, "evaluation" is an emotionally loaded term implying judgment), and may deliberately undermine research efforts. Research personnel, on the other hand, may lack knowledge of the constraints on program personnel, and thus may not understand why their designs are not followed precisely. In the best cases, program and researcher workers feel they are part of a common effort, but even in the ideal case, they will inevitably face differences in priorities because of their different roles. A common source of conflict between program and research staff revolves around the desirability of making changes in the program or program delivery during the course of the implementation process. For experimental purposes, the treatment variable ideally remains constant throughout the study. Program personnel, however, may be inclined to continually alter or improve aspects of the treatment or policy in response to new information (perhaps from the initial evaluation results themselves). A compromise between program rigidity and program flexibility is required in these cases.

Confusion Between Process and Outcome

Another source of difference between program personnel and research staff is their relative concern with process versus outcome. Program implementers tend to want to know how their program is doing (e.g., is it reaching the intended population, are clients happy with the services received, etc.), whereas researchers want to know *what effect* the program is having (i.e., are the clients different or better off when they have received the services). Of course, it is very unlikely that a program will have an impact on outcomes of ultimate interest unless the process of program implementation has been successful, and a good evaluation study will include assessments of many of these intervening or mediating factors to understand the mechanisms that affect the sought-for behavior. However, although it is important, it is not always easy to maintain a distinction between these two levels of program effects.

Quasi-Experimental Methods

Ideally an evaluation research study will employ a true experimental design that includes random assignment of participants to treatment or control conditions, or to different levels of the treatment program. Randomization is possible in many field settings, and good examples of the use of randomized experiments for program evaluation are available in all areas of social policy (see Boruch, 2012; Green et al., 2011), including a large-scale experiment on the implementation of a "negative income tax" program (Kershaw & Fair, 1976), voting behavior (Arceneaux, 2005), a 16-city study of the effects of innovative electric rate structures on energy conservation (Crano & Messé, 1985), and a study of an anti-HIV intervention program in Maryland, Georgia, and New Jersey (O'Leary et al., 1998). In some situations, good arguments can be made for the use of random assignment through lottery as a method of allocating a scarce resource or service in the interests of fairness (e.g., Krueger & Zhu, 2004; Salovey & Williams-Piehota, 2004).

In many cases, such random assignment is not politically or practically feasible. Sometimes it is impossible to control who will make use of available services or programs (e.g., who will choose to watch a public television program or attend an open clinic). At other times, programs can be delivered selectively, but the selection decision is outside the researcher's control and is based upon nonrandom factors such as perceived need, merit, or opportunity. Under these circumstances, the evaluation researcher should look to various quasi-experimental design alternatives to sort out treatment effects from other sources of change. Quasi-experimental designs maintain many of the features of true experiments, but do not have the advantages conferred by random assignment. The absence of random assignment along with the presence of some form of treatment is a defining feature of quasi-experiments and requires researchers to seek factors that help offset the problems that arise because of the lack of random assignment (see Campbell & Stanley, 1963; Shadish, Cook & Campbell, 2002). For the remainder of this chapter, we will be concerned with various quasi-experimental designs and the issues associated with their use in social research.

Regression Artifacts and Assessment of Change

Because new social programs are introduced into ongoing social systems for the purpose of altering or improving some aspect of that system, the ultimate question for evaluation research is whether or not the system or the persons in it have *changed* over time as a result of the program. To understand how the nature of research design affects our ability to assess change meaningfully, we must first consider *regression toward the mean* as a potential artifact in the measurement of change. The concept of regression toward the mean was introduced in Chapter 2 as a potential threat to internal validity. We will elaborate how regression to the mean can operate to undermine the validity of causal interpretations in quasi-experimental research contexts.

A brief history of the origin of the term regression toward the mean provides some insight into this effect. The term was first used by Francis Galton (1885) in a paper titled "Regression towards mediocrity in hereditary stature," in which he reported the results of his study of the relationship between the height of parents and their adult offspring. One finding of this study was that the children of very tall parents were generally not quite so tall as their parents, whereas the children of very short parents were generally not quite so short. Usually the heights of offspring of extreme individuals were closer to the overall population average than their parents were.

The trend observed by Galton is often referred to as the "regression fallacy," because this idea has been frequently misinterpreted as indicating a long-term tendency toward mediocrity. The implication of this erroneous view is that across generations variation in parent-child heights becomes smaller and smaller as the concentration of individuals who are farther away from the mean height of the population diminishes. In fact, the variation does not necessarily change from generation to generation, because even though the offspring of extreme parents tend to be closer to the mean height than their parents were, the offspring of more average parents are equally likely to vary away from the population mean, closer to either end of the two extremes. Phrased differently, very tall parents still tend to have tall offspring (relative to the average of the population), but the offspring tend not to be as extremely tall as the parents. The reverse applies for very short parents and their short offspring. The movement toward the mean in a subsequent measurement is an artifact of the initial selection of extreme cases.

Regression toward the mean is an *inevitable* consequence of examining the association between scores on imperfectly related measures. Whenever the correlation between two measures (like parental height and offspring height) is less than 1.00, there will be some nonsystematic or random deviation between scores on the first variable and corresponding scores on the second. If the first set of scores were selected for its extremity (i.e., to represent the highest or lowest values in the distribution), there is bound to be a bias in what direction subsequent scores using the same measuring instrument will vary. That is, for the tallest parents in a population, any differences between their heights and those of their offspring will usually indicate that their offspring are somewhat shorter, simply because there isn't much room for variation (ceiling effects) in the other direction. Similarly, deviations from the heights of extremely short parents most often will be in the direction of increased height because of a similar selection bias (floor effects).

It is crucial to distinguish between findings that result from artifacts and those that reflect real effects. An **artifact** is an artificial or spurious finding, a "pseudo-effect" that results inevitably from the properties of the measuring instrument or from the method of data collection employed. In Galton's example, regression does not reflect some genetic defect on the part of extreme parents that results in mediocre offspring. Extremely tall parents generally produce tall children and extremely intelligent parents usually have highly intelligent children. However, the relationship between characteristics of parents and offspring is not perfect. Because of this, the selection of parents based on an extreme characteristic biases the direction of differences between parents and children in a way that has nothing to do with the laws of genetics.

Regression Artifact and Reliability

The regression artifact afflicts psychological research most frequently as a result of measurement unreliability, which is responsible for imperfect correlations between repeated tests on the same measure. Test reliability has been referred to in previous chapters, but a detailed consideration is useful here to clarify the role of unreliability in the occurrence of regression effects.

The basic elements of the measurement theory model of test-retest reliability are presented in Table 10.1. Two sets of test scores (pretest and posttest) are obtained on a scale or instrument that is administered twice to the same sample of 20 participants. The data in this table illustrate that each test score is assumed to consist of two components—true score and error (see Chapter 3). The true score component represents stable characteristics of the individual that are tapped by the measure. We assume that the true score for any individual being measured does not change between test administrations unless some basic change has occurred in the individual's underlying response pattern. Thus, in Table 10.1 (which illustrates test-retest relationships under no-change conditions), each of the twenty hypothetical individuals is represented by their underlying true score, which contributes to the obtained score on both testing occasions.

In contrast to the stability of true score variation, the error component of test scores represents all the temporary, chance factors that happen to influence test responses at a particular point in time. The most important assumption of testing theory is that these chance factors operate randomly. That is, some individuals' scores are artificially raised by these chance factors, while others are lowered, so that across individuals the error effects cancel out. This characteristic of error scores is illustrated in column 3 of Table 10.1, where the algebraic sum of the 20 error scores (which represent the extent and direction of random influences on each test score) is equal to 0. The test score obtained by combining the true-score component of column 1 and the error score from

TABLE 10.1 Random error and test-retest reliability.

True Score	Test 1 Random Error	Test 1 Score	Test 2 Random Error	Test 2 Score
95	−5	90	+1	96
93	+2	95	−3	90
92	−6	86	0	92
90	+8	98	−7	83
87	+1	88	+1	88
85	−5	80	+6	91
85	+5	90	+3	88
80	−3	77	+1	81
78	+6	84	−7	71
75	+9	84	+6	81
75	−7	68	+4	79
74	−5	69	+1	75
73	+6	79	−8	65
70	−2	68	−4	66
68	−3	65	−2	66
65	−4	61	+3	68
63	+3	66	+5	68
60	−2	58	+4	64
58	+5	63	−3	55
55	−3	52	−1	54
Sum = 1521	0	1521	0	1521
Mean = 76.05	0	76.05	0	76.05

column 2 for each individual is given in column 3. It represents the observed score, the score an individual would receive on the measure. Because the various error scores cancel each other out, the sum and mean of the obtained test scores are the same as the corresponding values for the true scores. However, the pattern (and variance) of obtained scores is different from that of the corresponding underlying true scores because of the effects of random error.

If error scores are truly random, then the extraneous factors that determine the direction and extent of error on one testing should *not* be the same in a second testing of the same individual. That is, for any individual, the random error component of the score on a first testing should be completely unrelated to the random error score on a second testing. Otherwise, the directional bias affecting scores at both testing administrations would suggest that the measurements were affected by systematic error. In column 4 of Table 10.1, a completely new set of random error scores is shown, affecting participant responses at the second administration. These scores represent the random influences on responses for each individual at the time of retesting. Although the algebraic sum of these test 2 error scores is equal to 0, as on the first testing, the pattern of errors across individuals is entirely different from that of the first testing. The sum of true score and error for the second testing results in the obtained score values for test 2 that are recorded in the final column of Table 10.1.

The combined effect of unrelated error components introduces discrepancies in test results for the same individuals across different testing occasions in repeated measure designs. For any individual, a test score obtained from a second measurement is expected to deviate somewhat from that person's score on the same instrument at the first testing. The extent of deviation in scores between tests reflects the degree of test-retest unreliability of the instrument. The more unreliable the test-retest association, the greater the error, and as such, the greater will be the deviations in scores from the first administration to the next. The degree of *similarity* in patterns of scores across different administrations of the same test is termed the test-retest reliability. Because reliability involves the relationship between two sets of test scores, it is most commonly measured in terms of the Pearson correlation (see Chapter 9). The reliability coefficient is the value of the Pearson correlation between the test results of a set of individuals at time 1 with the results for these *same individuals* on the *same test* at time 2. For the data in Table 10.1, the value of the reliability coefficient is equal to .82, suggesting that those participants who scored high at time 1 also tended to score high at time 2, and those who scored low at time 1 tended correspondingly to score low at time 2.

As mentioned in Chapter 9, the squared value of the correlation coefficient (r^2, the coefficient of determination) measures the extent of common variation between two measurements. In the case of reliability coefficients, the correlation value represents the proportion of true-score variation in the measuring instrument, or the extent that obtained scores at both assessments reflect true-score values rather than chance error. The lower the reliability correlation, the greater the proportional effect of error (defined as $e = 1 - r^2$), and the more that random extraneous factors influence the value of obtained test scores. For our hypothetical data, the value of r indicates that 67% ($.82^2$) of the obtained variation in test scores can be attributed to true score differences, and the remaining 33% is due to random fluctuation. Unreliability in tests is responsible for the internal validity threat of regression toward the mean in test-retest research studies.

The regression toward the mean artifact is most easily understood in the context of a simple pretest-posttest research design, where at least two non-randomized groups are used and the participants in each of the groups are *selected for the extremity* of their pretest results. For instance, suppose that the data in Table 10.1 represent the results of 20 participants who took the same standardized English reading exam on two test sessions (a test-retest design). Assume that the delay in administration of the second test was three months after the first test so that practice or fatigue effects are not likely to affect scores. The instructor decided to select for the study the top 25% of the students, based on the first test. The pairs of scores in Table 10.2 (taken from Table 10.1) illustrate what would happen if only the top students were selected for the study on the basis of English pretest scores.

The overall decrease in mean score is depicted in Table 10.2, which shows what would occur even if there was no treatment after the pretest—that is, the *true* scores did not change from pretest

TABLE 10.2 Selection of participants with a top 5 pretest score from Table 10.1.

Pretest Score	Corresponding Posttest Score
98	83
95	90
90	96
90	88
88	88
Mean = 92.2	90.8

TABLE 10.3 Selection of participants with a bottom pretest score from Table 10.1.

Pretest Score	Corresponding Posttest Score
65	66
63	55
61	68
58	64
52	54
59.8	61.4

to posttest for these top students, whose selection, you will recall, was based on the extremity of their pretest scores. Because of the effects of test unreliability, the top five scores have *regressed toward the mean* at the posttest, giving the appearance of a decrease in performance. Any actual increase in true score performance, if there were any, would be counter to the effect of regression toward the mean.

Regression toward the mean can create an apparent or pseudo improvement effect if scores are selected from the lower extremes of pretest values. For example, if students who scored in the bottom 25% of the test distribution of Table 10.1 are selected, the effect of regression in the absence of any treatment would lead to the *appearance* of change at time 2, as depicted in Table 10.3, but in this case, any improvement in true scores would be artificially enhanced by the regression effect.

In either case, the selection procedure at pretest has the consequence of biasing the direction of scores between pretest and posttest. This occurs because the selection of the top pretest scorers tends to involve overrepresenting participants with positive error scores on the pretest (e. g., in the case of the top five participants from Table 10.1, the obtained scores are based in part on positive errors, which sum to +16, whereas the one negative error score is only −5). Other students might have equally good true scores, but their error scores were not so positive, and so they were not included in the comparison. On the second measurement, when random error scores are unrelated to those of the first, both positive and negative error scores are equally likely to occur, thus producing a posttest score mean for the chosen students that tends to be lower than the pretest mean. Similarly, the selection of the students with the lowest obtained scores on the pretest overrepresents *negative* error components. Thus, the obtained score sum will inevitably increase on the second test (using the same scale), because more positive errors will occur just by the rules of chance.

The size of the regression phenomenon in pretest-posttest comparisons is directly related to the degree of unreliability in the measuring instrument used. A perfectly reliable instrument ($r = 1.00$) would reflect only true-score variation and thus produce no regression effects, because there would be no discrepancies between scores on first and second test administrations in the absence of an intervening event. For all practical purposes, however, perfectly reliable measures of social or psychological variables are impossible to attain. Although the refinement of most tests is aimed at achieving reliability values of .80 or better, the remaining error component could produce considerable regression between tests for scores selected because of their extremity.

Statistical Control of Regression Artifacts

One method of controlling for the effects of regression toward the mean in pretest-posttest research designs involves statistically removing the expected regression toward the mean effect in computing difference scores. This is accomplished by using multiple regression and comparing each individual's actual posttest score (Y) with a "regressed" score, that is, a predicted posttest score (Y′) based on the expected deviation from his or her pretest score.[1] Across all respondents, the average obtained posttest score should not differ from the average of the regressed scores if no true-score change has occurred. If a significant difference between predicted and obtained scores does appear, it indicates that some change has occurred above and beyond that expected on the basis of mere regression toward the mean.

The major difficulty with the statistical adjustment of regression effects is that it requires an accurate assessment of test-retest reliability in the absence of any real change. Computed values of the correlation between pretest and posttest scores suffer from the same sampling fluctuation as any other statistic, and, in addition, the appropriate time period necessary for true test-retest reliability assessment is difficult to determine. Testing must be distant enough in time to assure that for each respondent, the sources of error on the second testing (such as mood, fatigue, misinterpretation of questions, guessing behavior) are unrelated to those of the first test session. The test-retest time period also should be appropriate to provide a base estimate of normal test-score fluctuation against which to compare treatment effects. It is rare that such an estimate of reliability would be available to assure accurate projections of regression effects.

Regression and Matching: Comparison Group Designs

It is fairly obvious how regression effects would influence change scores obtained from a single population with initially extreme test values. Because this effect is so well known, simple pretest-posttest designs comparing groups chosen on the basis of extreme pretest scores are rarely seen in program evaluation or other research contexts. However, the effects of regression artifacts can enter more subtly whenever the research involves two or more respondent groups that are not randomly assigned to treatment and comparison conditions. This possibility arises because when the individuals participating in a social program have been selected nonrandomly, it is likely that they differ from the comparison group in some systematic way on factors that may affect the outcome measures, even prior to the program intervention. This initial nonequivalence attributed to selection biases between groups makes it difficult to interpret any posttreatment differences between them.

Attempts to compensate for pretest inequality between the groups are frequently made through post hoc participant "matching," a procedure that is widely applied despite a history of frequent warnings against its use (Campbell & Stanley, 1963; Hovland, Lumsdaine, & Sheffield, 1949; McNemar, 1940; Thorndike, 1942). Post hoc matching involves making posttreatment comparisons only between the members of the two or more groups who attained similar scores on the pretest (or some related measure). In effect, this procedure amounts to an attempt to apply the blocking design of experimental research (discussed in Chapter 2), but the blocking used in post hoc matching is accomplished *after* assignment to treatments has been determined. A slight variation of this matching technique occurs when an experimental treatment group is composed by some special criteria, and then a "control" group is created on an ex post facto basis by selecting from the general population (i.e., from among those who did not meet the special criteria for inclusion in the experimental group) a group of participants who "match" the predetermined experimental respondents on some specified pretest values. In either case, interpretation of the results of such matched group designs is confounded by the potential effects of differential regression toward the mean.

An extension of the sample data presented in Table 10.1 can illustrate the matched group differential regression problem. Table 10.4 provides a new set of data on pretest scores for 10 hypothetical cases comprising an experimental group, which represent a sample that is randomly drawn from

TABLE 10.4 Pretest scores for experimental group and matched comparison group.

Predetermined Experimental Group			"Matched" Cases from Table 10.1 (Pretest)
True Score	Error	Score	
73	+3	76	77
74	−4	70	69
70	−2	68	68
65	+3	68	68
63	+4	67	66
68	−4	64	65
69	−5	64	63
62	−1	61	61
53	+5	58	58
50	+1	51	52
Mean = 64.70	0.0	64.7	64.7

TABLE 10.5 Posttest scores with no change in true scores.

Experimental Group Posttest Results			"Matched" Cases from Table 10.1 (Posttest)
True Score	Error	Total	
73	1	74	81
74	−2	72	76
70	5	75	66
65	−3	62	79
63	6	69	68
68	2	70	66
69	−3	66	55
62	−5	57	68
53	−3	50	64
50	2	52	54
Mean = 64.7	0.0	64.7	67.7

a special low-scoring population. These cases do not consist only of the extreme scores of the population—the subjects are drawn randomly from it. They are to be compared with 10 cases selected from the pretest (test 1) distribution in Table 10.1 that "match" the experimental participants' pretest scores as closely as possible. By virtue of this selective matching, the initial means of the experimental and control groups appear to be equal. However, Table 10.5 illustrates what would happen on posttest scores in the absence of any treatment effect (i.e., with no change in true scores). The true scores of the experimental group participants are unchanged. Random-error differences introduce some change in the pattern of posttest scores compared with pretest values, but because these errors are random, the overall mean for these cases is unchanged, and no regression occurs.

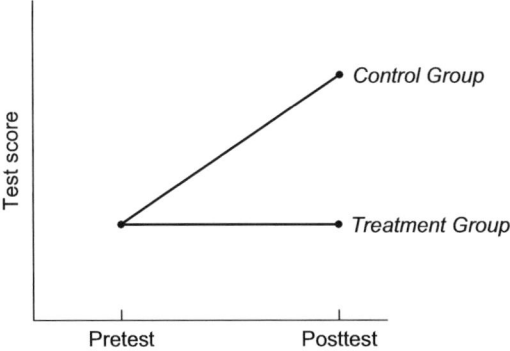

FIGURE 10.1 An illustration of asymmetric regression toward the mean.

The 10 posttest scores from the second group, on the other hand, exhibit a tendency toward increased scores, and their overall mean is almost 3 points higher than the pretest value. Referring to Table 10.1 provides an explanation for this increase. To match the experimental group scores, it was necessary to select the 10 control cases from the bottom extreme of the test 1 score distribution. This selection of extreme cases introduced a bias into the study. Negative error scores were overrepresented among the "matched" (control) cases. On test 2, the random occurrence of some positive error scores would inevitably produce an increase in total score values—that is, a regression toward the original group mean. Figure 10.1 illustrates the mean scores derived from Table 10.3 and Table 10.4. These apparent gains would appear in the absence of any real change.

Figure 10.1 depicts a case in which differential regression (one group exhibiting regression toward a grand mean, while the other does not) causes the experimental treatment to appear to be detrimental: In the absence of any real effect, the final test scores are below those of the control group. Campbell and Erlebacher (1970) provide a detailed discussion of this type of regression artifact, as it affects the interpretation of research on compensatory education programs. Typically, these programs are reserved for particularly disadvantaged populations. Students are not assigned to them randomly. Thus any attempts to evaluate their effectiveness through ex post facto comparison with a matched control group selected from the available general population introduces a regression bias that operates against the apparent value of the treatment. This is the situation represented in Figure 10.1. On the other hand, if matches with a predetermined experimental group are selected from the upper extremes of the available distribution to form a control group, the bias of differential regression would be in the opposite direction—that is, in favor of the experimental group over the control on posttest results.

Differential regression toward the mean for each of the two groups produces even more extreme effects if the matched groups both are drawn as selected cases from initially different populations. In such cases, both groups are likely to exhibit regression effects, but toward different means. This often is the case when comparisons must be made between experimental and control groups composed of previously intact social units, as illustrated in Table 10.6. It is clear from these data that the initial differences between these two groups make the differences obtained on test 2 measure meaningless in an evaluation of the effectiveness of the two-group design. In the absence of any true-score change between pretest and posttest, there is a significant difference between the two groups on the final testing. If there had been some change, it would have been impossible to interpret because it could have been a function of the initial group differences rather than the experimental treatment.

Under such circumstances where the researcher is unable to assign participants randomly to different groups, it is not unusual to attempt to correct for initial differences by selecting participants

TABLE 10.6 Illustration with initial group differences.

	Group 1 (Experimental)					Group 2 (Control)				
True Score	Test 1 Error	Test 1 Score	Test 2 Error	Test 2 Score		True Score	Test 1 Error	Test 1 Score	Test 2 Error	Test 2 Score
75	−5	70	+1	76		53	+3	56	−1	52
73	2	75	−3	70		49	−5	44	+3	52
72	−6	66	0	72		48	−3	45	−5	43
70	8	78	−7	63		45	+5	50	−1	44
67	+1	68	+1	68		45	+2	47	+4	49
65	−5	60	+6	71		42	+7	49	−4	38
65	+5	70	+3	68		42	+3	45	+2	44
60	−3	57	+1	61		38	+4	42	−3	35
58	+6	64	−7	51		36	−8	28	+7	43
55	+9	64	+6	61		35	+2	37	−4	31
55	−7	48	+4	59		32	−2	30	+3	35
54	−5	49	+1	55		30	−5	25	−3	27
53	6	59	−8	45		29	+3	32	+1	30
50	−2	48	−4	46		28	−1	27	−1	27
48	−3	45	−2	46		26	−6	20	+7	33
45	−4	41	+3	48		25	+5	30	−1	24
43	+3	46	+5	48		24	−9	15	−6	18
40	−2	38	+4	44		23	+6	29	0	23
38	+5	43	−3	35		21	+5	26	−6	15
35	−3	32	−1	34		16	−6	10	+8	24
Mean = 56.05	0	56.05	0	56.05		Mean = 34.35	0	34.35	0	34.35

from the original groups in a way that creates two new groups that appear to be equivalent on the initial measure. Table 10.7 illustrates such a selective matching from the groups in Table 10.6. The first two columns represent cases drawn from groups 1 and 2, which are closely matched on the basis of test 1 score results. The resulting means are exactly equal, and so it appears that the selection procedure has been successful in creating initially equivalent subgroups. However, the data in the next two columns, which present the test 2 scores for the pretest-selected participants in the absence of any true-score change, reveal the fallacy of the apparent equivalence.

The matching procedure involved selecting cases from the opposite extremes of the two original pretest distributions—the lower scores from group 1, the upper scores from group 2. As a result, the directional bias in the selected pretest cases had opposite effects for the two sets of posttest scores, causing one group to regress upward and the other downward. In this case the differential regression toward the mean has the effect of artificially enhancing the appearance of effectiveness of one group over the other on the posttest measure, even though no treatment occurred between pretest and the posttest. This effect is pictured in Figure 10.2. Had the initial

TABLE 10.7 Illustration of post hoc matching.

Pretest Matched Scores		Corresponding Posttest Scores	
Group 1	Group 2	Group 1	Group 2
57	56	61	52
49	50	55	44
48	49	59	38
48	47	46	49
46	45	48	43
45	45	46	44
43	44	35	52
41	42	48	35
38	37	44	31
32	32	34	30
Mean = 44.7	44.7	47.6	41.8

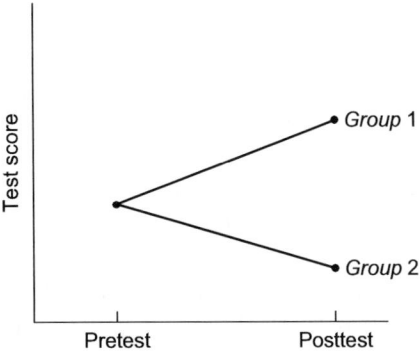

FIGURE 10.2 An illustration of divergent regression to the mean.

group means been reversed, regression would still have led to an erroneous conclusion, but it would be opposite to the conclusion drawn initially.

Post hoc matching on the basis of any extreme score pretreatment variable, or combination of variables (e.g., age, socioeconomic status, intelligence, personality scores), is subject to the same regression phenomenon as long as the matching variables are imperfect (i.e., not perfectly reliable) or imperfectly related to the posttreatment dependent variable measure. Such is the case, for example, with research that attempts to assess racial differences by comparing groups differing in race but "matched" on socioeconomic variables. In a society where race is still inextricably confounded with multiple cultural factors, such post hoc matching can only produce groups that are subject to differential regression effects, resulting ultimately in uninterpretable results.

Propensity Score Matching

In the standard matching design, it would be cumbersome for the researcher to match pairs of respondents on more than a single criterion or pretest measure. Suppose a program evaluator was asked to assess the efficacy of a campaign to promote walking as a form of exercise, with instructional brochures mailed to people living in a targeted community (the experimental group). Because the campaign targeted all residents in that neighborhood, a comparison community would be needed to determine if the campaign was effective in increasing exercising relative to the community that did not receive the mailing (control group). After the campaign, people from each community might be sent a survey asking them about how many minutes they spent walking per day. Because it is possible that participants from disparate communities tend to differ on various characteristics (e.g., age, gender, and race), it is necessary to control for these extraneous covariates so that they do not serve as rival explanations to account for the amount of time spent walking. For example, if men were more likely to engage in physical activity, and one community had many more men than the other, this would confound outcome differences.

As illustrated in Table 10.8, this scenario shows a sample of people who self-selected themselves as residents living in their respective communities. This represents only a sampling of 22 participants from our larger, imaginary dataset who were matched or unmatched. As in standard matching designs, cases that were not successfully matched across groups are discarded. Participants are coupled on the measured covariates of race, gender, and age. Here, this process of sorting participants and matching so that a one-to-one correspondence is attained becomes prohibitively daunting as sample size and the number of matching variables increases. Imagine the challenge in attempting to match 10 pretest variables involving 500 respondents found in 2 groups. One way of overcoming the limitations of matching, which typically involves manually finding optimal one-to-one matches, is to use propensity scoring (Rosenbaum & Rubin, 1983). **Propensity score matching** uses complex statistical procedures to statistically match participants on as many covariates as can be specified by the researcher, to determine differences between comparison groups. Results from propensity score matching reveal differences on an outcome measure between groups after covariates have been accounted for.

A **propensity score** for a participant represents the conditional probability of membership in one group (e.g., the experimental group) over another (e.g., the control group), given the pattern of that person's responses on the covariates. Propensity scores are based on the entire set of pretest measures, and are used to adjust and control for covariates statistically so that groups are initially comparable on the covariate variables. Operationally, responses on the covariates are used to compute a propensity score for each participant. In a randomized two-group design, the propensity score of every participant is expected to be .50 (50% chance of being assigned to either group). In a nonexperimental or quasi-experimental design, because of nonrandomized participant selection into groups (as in our exercise campaign scenario), propensity scores should vary across

TABLE 10.8 Matching two groups on multiple pretest variables.

Matched Pair?	Experimental Group			Control Group		
	Pretest Covariate			Pretest Covariate		
	Race	Gender	Age	Race	Gender	Age
Yes	White	Female	under 40	White	Female	under 40
Yes	Asian	Female	under 40	Asian	Female	under 40
No	Black	Female	under 40	N/A		
No	Latino	Female	under 40	N/A		
No	N/A			Latino	Male	under 40
No	N/A			Latino	Male	under 40
Yes	White	Male	under 40	White	Male	under 40
No	Asian	Male	under 40	N/A		
Yes	White	Female	over 40	White	Female	over 40
Yes	Black	Male	over 40	Black	Male	over 40
No	N/A			Black	Female	over 40
No	N/A			Latino	Female	over 40
Yes	Latino	Female	over 40	Latino	Female	over 40
Yes	Latino	Male	over 40	Latino	Male	over 40
No	Asian	Female	over 40	N/A		

TABLE 10.9 Before propensity score matching (actual posttest scores).

Person	Pretest Covariate			Group	Propensity Score	Posttest	
	Race	Gender	Age			Control Group	Experimental Group
1	White	Female	under 40	Control	0.80	40	
2	Asian	Female	under 40	Control	0.60	30	
3	White	Male	under 40	Control	0.55	40	
4	White	Female	over 40	Control	0.50	20	
5	Black	Male	over 40	Control	0.40	50	
6	Latino	Male	over 40	Control	0.30	65	
7	Latino	Female	over 40	Control	0.20	40	
8	White	Female	under 40	Experimental	0.80		60
9	Asian	Female	under 40	Experimental	0.60		60
10	White	Male	under 40	Experimental	0.55		50
11	White	Female	over 40	Experimental	0.50		45
12	Black	Male	over 40	Experimental	0.40		75
13	Latino	Male	over 40	Experimental	0.30		70
14	Latino	Female	over 40	Experimental	0.20		45

participants. Computed propensity scores are presented in Table 10.9. Notice also that people with the same propensity score have same pattern of responses on the covariates. For example, Person 1 and Person 8 have the same propensity score of .80, a value calculated from the fact that both persons are White, female, and under the age of 40. This statistical property of propensity scores serves as the main criterion to balance the groups to achieve initial comparability.

TABLE 10.10 After propensity score matching (actual and counterfactual posttest scores).

Person	Pretest Covariate			Group	Propensity Score	Posttest	
	Race	Gender	Age			Control Group	Experimental Group
1	White	Female	under 40	Control	0.80	40	≈ 60
2	Asian	Female	under 40	Control	0.60	30	≈ 60
3	White	Male	under 40	Control	0.55	40	≈ 50
4	White	Female	over 40	Control	0.50	20	≈ 45
5	Black	Male	over 40	Control	0.40	50	≈ 75
6	Latino	Male	over 40	Control	0.30	65	≈ 70
7	Latino	Female	over 40	Control	0.20	40	≈ 45
8	White	Female	under 40	Experimental	0.80	≈ 40	60
9	Asian	Female	under 40	Experimental	0.60	≈ 30	60
10	White	Male	under 40	Experimental	0.55	≈ 40	50
11	White	Female	over 40	Experimental	0.50	≈ 20	45
12	Black	Male	over 40	Experimental	0.40	≈ 50	75
13	Latino	Male	over 40	Experimental	0.30	≈ 65	70
14	Latino	Female	over 40	Experimental	0.20	≈ 40	45

Table 10.10 shows the scenario after propensity scores are used to perform the matching. The underlying logic is that if participants from different groups have the same propensity score, then it is possible to deduce what each person's posttest score *would be* if he or she were in the other group, even if he or she was not a participant in that group. The estimated or hypothetical outcome score on the group or condition that a participant was not a member of is known as the *counterfactual score*. After matching, the counterfactual posttest scores have now been estimated in Table 10.10. The posttest score of person 1, who was a participant in the control group, showed that she managed to walk 40 minutes per day. If person 1 were exposed to the campaign (although she was not), she would be expected to exercise for 60 minutes day. The same counterfactual logic could be applied to participants in the experimental group. Person 9, who is a participant in the experimental group, walked for 60 minutes per day. However, based on the propensity analysis, she was projected to walk only 30 minutes per day had she been a member in the control group that did not receive the intervention. This difference is attributed to the treatment. The major implication of propensity score matching is that it is possible to deduce mathematically what someone's hypothetical or counterfactual score would have been in the other group based on their patterns of responses to the measured covariates.

Propensity scoring methods facilitate discovery of the closest matching participant pairs in an available sample. The researcher can also calibrate the matching criteria to decide how close two propensity scores must be before they are considered a matched pair (e.g., should a person with a propensity score of 40 be matched to a person with a propensity score of 39?). Using propensity scores, participants across groups are made statistically equivalent on these initial variables so that any posttest observations would rule out these particular characteristics as confounds.

However, this approach is not without problems (see Crano, Alvaro, & Siegel, in press). Although the technique allows for the matching of as many pretest covariates as possible, the extent and quality of the control is determined by the number of extraneous variables that were identified and measured in the study. For the technique to be most effective, the researcher must consider and assess all the potentially important extraneous variables that come to mind and on which groups may differ initially. Thus, it is important to include as many pretest variables as possible, especially those that prior research and theory suggest. Some highly stringent propensity score studies have controlled for more than 100 pretest covariates. Owing to the number of measures on which participants across groups can potentially be matched and the many combinations of patterns of covariate responses, propensity score approaches often necessitate large sample sizes.

Propensity scoring is the most methodologically acceptable approach when contemplating a matching design. Even after controlling for a wide assortment of variables, however, uncertainty always remains that there are lurking variables the researcher failed to measure, and therefore pretest equivalence was not attained. Propensity scoring is advantageous to other statistical techniques that control for covariates insofar as the assumptions about the data are much more relaxed in propensity analysis. For example, propensity scoring does not require the assumption of linearity between each covariate and the outcome, as required in analysis of covariance, in which effects of pretest differences on the outcome variable are accounted for. Randomization to groups remains the most methodologically rigorous and satisfactory method to ensure the initial comparability of groups that are to be compared. Propensity score matching controls for extraneous variables only if they are measured and entered as part of the propensity score, whereas randomized designs control for both measured and unmeasured extraneous variables.

Time Series Design

Problems associated with differential regression toward the mean and other sources of nonequivalence make many nonrandom comparison group designs inadequate with respect to internal validity. Evaluation researchers have therefore looked for other kinds of baseline information that can replace or supplement comparison groups as a basis for assessing change.

The need for alternatives to the comparison group design is especially acute when a social program that affects an entire population (city, state, nation) is introduced all at once. In this case, the only method for assessing change involves a comparison of observations before and after the treatment is introduced. If the only information available on a pretreatment condition is a single measure taken near the onset of the new program, serious problems of interpreting change are created. Consider, for example, a measure of the incidence of violent crimes in one state for the year before and the year after the introduction of a moratorium on capital punishment. A single pretest-posttest assessment of change is impossible to interpret without some knowledge of the degree of fluctuation expected between two measures in the absence of any true change.

The hypothetical crime statistics represented in Figure 10.3 illustrate the problem. The change in the rate of violent crimes in the two annual surveys may be interpreted in several different ways. It may represent an actual increase in crime rate under conditions where capital punishment is removed as a deterrent. On the other hand, it may simply reflect the normal year-to-year fluctuation in crime rates, which by chance have increased over this particular time period. To make matters worse, social quasi-experiments such as this one often are introduced under exceptional social conditions. Ameliorative efforts are more likely to be undertaken when undesirable circumstances have reached some kind of peak or, in the case of our present example, public opinion may have been particularly amenable to an experiment in eliminating capital punishment following a period of exceptionally low crime. If this is the case, differences in measures taken before and after the quasi-experimental intervention may simply reflect regression back to normal rates.

In an **interrupted time-series design**, the relative degree of change that occurs after a quasi-experimental treatment may be examined by comparing observations of time points prior to the treatment with observations of time points occurring after. Consider how the interpretation of the two-round data from Figure 10.3 may be affected by the different time points recorded in

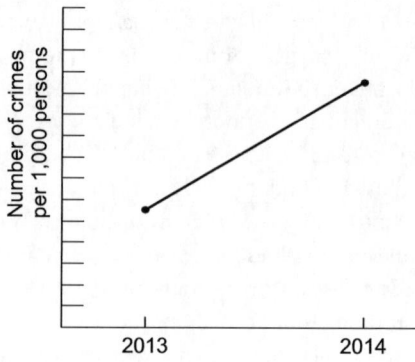

FIGURE 10.3 Data from a change of two time points.

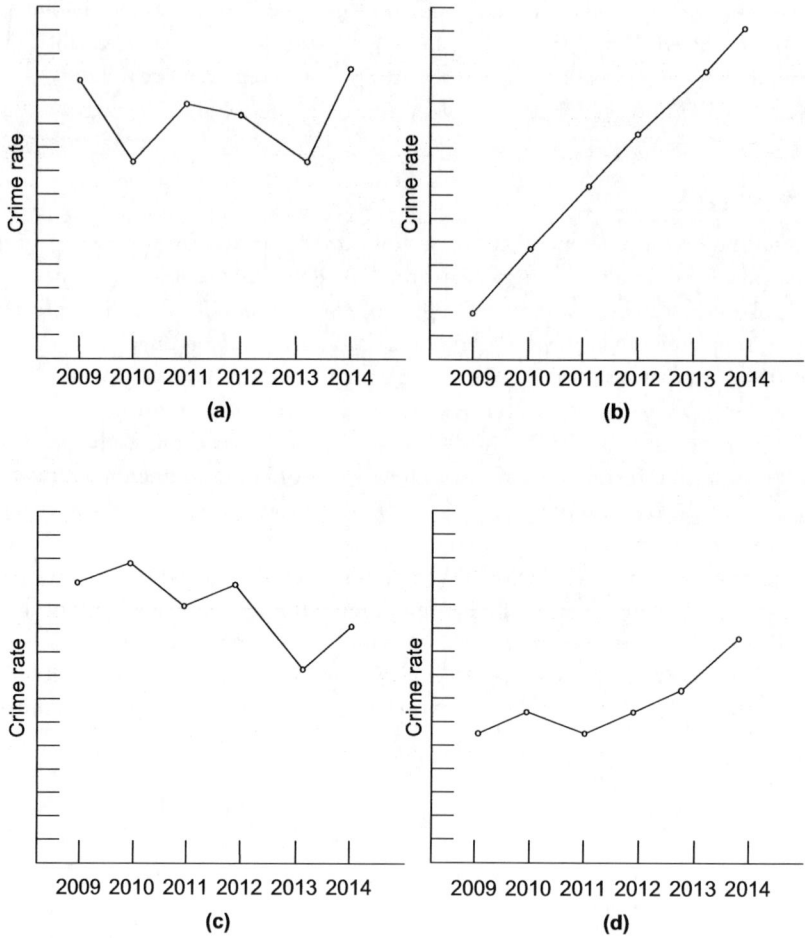

FIGURE 10.4 Time trends by year.

Figure 10.4. To illustrate this point, let's consider some hypothetical crime rates. Figure 10.4(a) suggests that the 2013 to 2014 change in crime rates might represent normal year-to-year fluctuation in the crime index, with no particular rise above previous years. Figure 10.4(b) indicates a rise, but one that is consistent with a general trend toward year-to-year increases established long before the

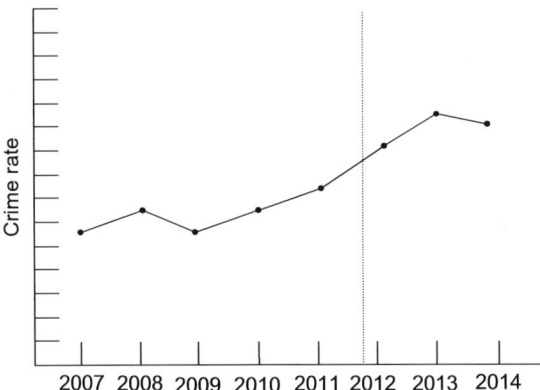

FIGURE 10.5 Interrupted time-series design.

introduction of the treatment. Figure 10.4(c) presents 2013 (pretreatment) as a particularly low year, with 2014 representing a slight regression back toward previous rates. In all of these cases there is reason to believe that the 2013–2014 increase would have taken place even if some major policy change (e.g., a moratorium on capital punishment) had not been introduced.

Figure 10.4(d) provides an example in which the crime rate in 2014 is significantly greater than previous years, suggesting that some real change has occurred. We could be more certain of the meaningfulness of the change if the time series were measured for more years after the quasi-treatment to determine whether the change was stable. Such an interrupted-time series design with extended time points is represented in Figure 10.5 (McCain & McCleary, 1979; McDowell, McCleary, Meidinger, & Hay, 1980; Orwin, 1997).

Of course, knowing that a meaningful and stable change in scores has occurred in a time-series analysis does not rule out sources other than the treatment intervention as possible causes of the change. Alternative explanations might be available, such as an abrupt increase in population density, changes in record-keeping procedures, or other factors related to crime rate that could have occurred simultaneously with the time at which the treatment was implemented. Statistical analyses of changes in time-series data are afflicted by two problems in particular. One is that "errors" (i.e., extraneous unmeasured factors) that influence the data obtained at any one time point tend to be correlated with measurements at adjacent time points. That is, **autocorrelated errors** occur if random events that affect the measurement obtained at one time are more likely to carry over and be correlated with measurements taken at temporally adjacent points than with farther points in time. Such carryover errors make it more difficult to pinpoint a change in the time series at the one specific time of interest to the evaluation researcher. For example, criminal activity and crime patterns in year 2014 are more likely to be autocorrelated with those in 2013 than those in 2000.

The second problem that plagues time-series analyses is the presence of *systematic trends* or *cycles* that affect the pattern of data over a specific time period and are unrelated to the intervention. Changes due to the treatment of interest must be separated from normal changes that occur cyclically across time. When data are obtained on a monthly basis, for instance, regular seasonal fluctuations that may operate across the year must be taken into account. Crime statistics, for example, tend to be influenced by weather conditions. Such patterns introduce complications in the analyses of time-series designs, but they are not impossible to correct. Statistical procedures known as "prewhitening" can be applied to remove regularities in the time series before analyses of experimental effect are begun (Box & Jenkins, 1970).

An applied example of research that made use of an interrupted time series and whose data were affected by both autocorrelated error and systematic trends is provided in Ramirez's and Crano's (2003) study of California's "three-strikes" law, which took effect in California in 1994. This law made a 25-year-to-life sentence mandatory for anyone convicted of a third major felony. Ramirez and Crano were interested in the law's effect. Do criminals really calculate the cost/benefit ratio before committing a crime? To test this possibility, they studied monthly crime rates 12 years before and 5 years after the law's implementation. Crimes are cyclical in nature—for example, in each year of the study, crime spiked in December. (We could speculate on the reasons for this, but this result certainly gives little comfort to those seeking peace on earth, good will toward men.) In addition, the data were obviously autocorrelated. Numbers of crimes committed in June were more closely correlated to those of May and July than to those of February and April. The statistical procedures made available by Box and Jenkins (1970) and Berry and Lewis-Beck (1986) supply the necessary corrections. The research provided an answer to the question, "Does the law work?," but the answer was nuanced, depending on the type of crime involved. When studying crimes of passion (e.g., violent physical assaults), the three-strikes law reduced the rate of crime over the long run, but it had no immediate impact. This result suggests that the law operated not as a deterrent, but rather that it took violent career criminals off the streets.[2] For nonviolent, "white-collar" crimes, however, the three-strikes law appeared to have both an immediate deterrent and a more long-term, incapacitating effect. That is, it appeared to cause an immediate and statistically significant decrease in white-collar crime, while at the same time incarcerating a proportion of those who made a living off such activities. Both effects cumulated, causing a dramatic decline in white-collar crime. When considering drug-related crimes, however, the law appeared to have no deterrent or incapacitating effect whatsoever.

Comparison Time-Series Design

Assuming that comparable statistical records are available across times and places, the **comparison time-series design** combines features of an interrupted time-series design and a comparison group design. If a social program is introduced in one location or institution but not in some other, preexisting differences between the treatment and comparison site make it difficult to interpret any posttreatment differences. However, if time-series data based on the same record-keeping system are available for both sites, and if both are subject to similar sources of cyclical and noncyclical fluctuations, then the time-series data from the comparison control group can serve as an additional baseline for evaluating differences in change in the experimental series. When the time series of two groups are roughly parallel in trend of scores prior to the introduction of the quasi-treatment (i.e., the intervention), but diverge significantly afterwards (as illustrated in Figure 10.6), many potential alternative explanations for the change in the latter series can be ruled out. As with any time-series design, statistical analyses of two groups via comparison time series can be complex (Berk, Hoffman, Maki, Rauma, & Wong, 1979; Berry & Lewis-Beck, 1986), but the logic of the design is straightforward and has been used to good avail in a number of evaluation settings.

A second method of forming comparisons for the interrupted time series is to include variables in the analysis that are parallel to the critical variables but which should not be affected by the interruption. For example, in Ramirez's and Crano's (2003) three-strikes study, data on minor crimes were available and were included in the analysis. These crimes should have been affected by the same extraneous variables as serious crimes (e.g., general economic conditions, social unrest, etc.), but were not affected by the enactment of the law. Thus, ideally, the law's passage would affect the rate of serious crime, but not misdemeanors. If differences in these crime rates occurred after

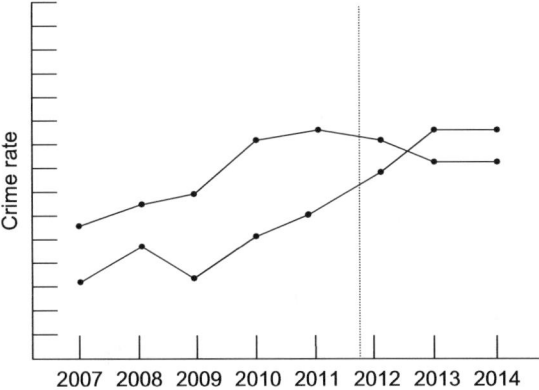

FIGURE 10.6 Comparison time-series data.

the introduction of the three-strikes law, in the appropriate direction, they would lend support to the efficacy of the law change on serious criminal behavior.[3]

Growth Curve Modeling

A **growth curve model** is conducted to determine the longitudinal trajectory or shape of observations for participants measured at multiple time points (Liu, Rovin, & Molenaar, 2012; Speer & Greenbaum, 1995). For example, after long-term unemployed individuals take part in a job-skills training program, a program evaluator may be interested in evaluating the efficacy of the intervention after participants are placed in a job. The evaluator assesses job performance each month for five months. Does the pattern of results show an incremental improvement month after month, with the highest performance scores found at month 5? Or do the trainees improve from the first to the second month, but then do the benefits stabilize and performance scores remain flat? Or, do trainees gradually improve in the first two months, with the highest score in month 3, but then gradually show a decline in the last months, back to the original baseline score? These patterns and many other types of growth patterns may be investigated with growth curve modeling. Although growth curves may be estimated with structural equation modeling, we will focus on the multilevel modeling variant.

In growth curve modeling, time points of measurement are nested within each participant. The hierarchical design of growth modeling is depicted in Figure 10.7. At first sight, this figure might appear completely counterintuitive, but it is logical once the reasoning is understood. If you were assessed on the same measure once a week for four weeks, these points of observations are

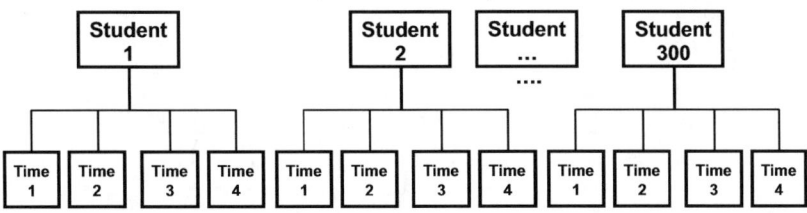

FIGURE 10.7 Growth curve model and its nested hierarchy: Measurement time points nested within each student.

nested within you. For another person, the times of measurement also are nested within him or her. Because multi-level models involve a nested design, the approach statistically controls for the clustering of scores in times across participants. This is a desirable feature, as the technique could be undertaken to estimate the growth pattern across time in the sample as a whole. Accounting for these person-to-person variations (e.g., demographic characteristics) via the intraclass correlation helps to statistically "remove" these individual differences so that detection of the underlying growth trajectory is not obscured (Review Chapter 9 for a more thorough treatment of multi-level modeling and the intraclass correlation).

To illustrate some instances of growth curve models, suppose that undergraduate students at your university are followed over four years, and their alcohol consumption is assessed. Growth curve analysis might show that number of drinks consumed per year increases with each passing year, with the highest rate of consumption during the senior year. A consistent incremental change from time point to time point is called a *linear trend* (Figure 10.8a). Another linear trend, illustrated in Figure 10.8b, shows a gradual linear decrement in alcohol consumption from year to year (This

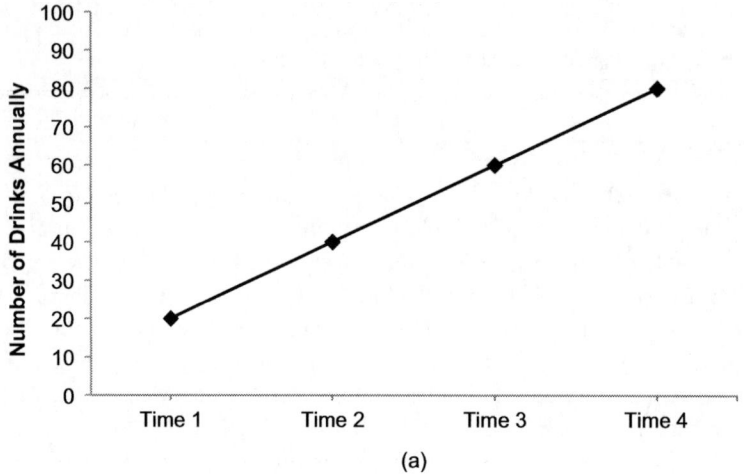

FIGURE 10.8a Growth curve models with linear trends.

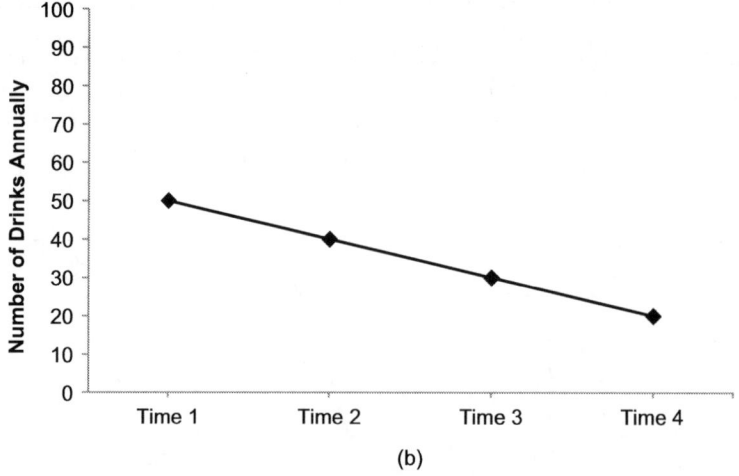

FIGURE 10.8b

second situation probably does not reflect reality at many universities). It also is possible for the trajectory to show a *quadratic trend,* as in Figure 10.9a. Here, drinking increases from the first to second year, stabilizes at the third year, and declines to initial rates of consumption in the fourth year of college. A possible rationale for this pattern is that students start taking upper division courses during their third year, and because these courses are more challenging they may now drink the same rate as their second year, so as to not be too inebriated during studying. The alcohol consumption level is back to its original rate in the senior year when students reduce their consumption, shifting their energy in an effort to graduate. Many other forms of growth trends are possible—for example, the *cubic trend* shown in Figure 10.9b.

Growth curve models also may be used to evaluate patterns of change across time as a function of different groups. Suppose the drinking patterns across four years for a sample at your university are compared to the drinking patterns across the same four years for another university that implemented a strict anti-alcohol policy. A growth curve for one group might resemble that of

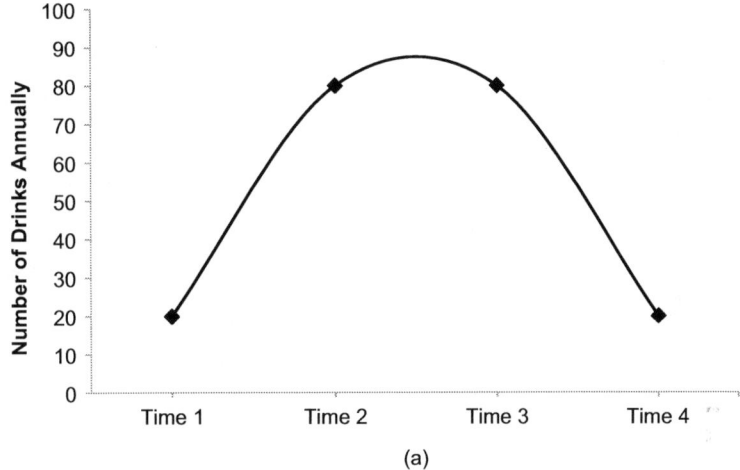

FIGURE 10.9a Growth curve models with other trend forms.

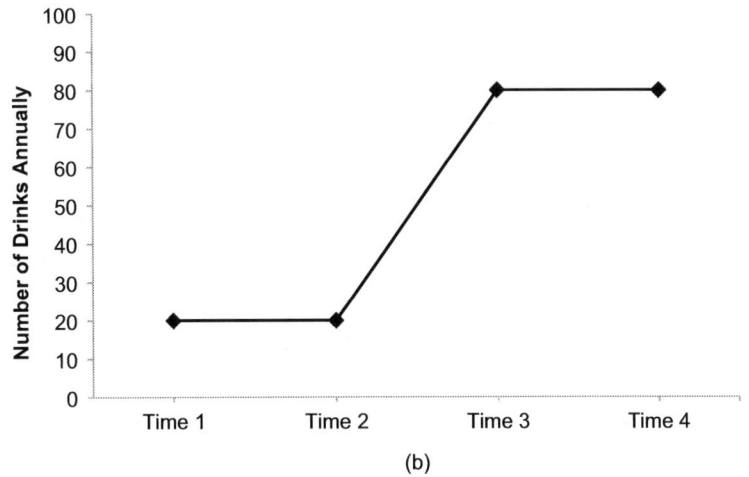

FIGURE 10.9b

Figure 10.9a, and a growth curve for the other group might resemble that of Figure 10.9b. It is possible to examine the pattern of change over time for each group, and also to determine if the shape of the trajectory is systematically different between the groups.

Regression-Discontinuity Design

The final quasi-experimental design to be described here is applicable to cases in which exposure to a treatment program is based on some clear selection principle. Unlike time-series designs, which may involve the observations across many time points for one or many comparison groups, the regression-discontinuity design involves comparing groups on either side of a cutoff point. The **regression-discontinuity design** (RD) is conducted to test the existence of some systematic relationship between a pretest selection variable, used for the purpose of placing participants in comparison groups, and a posttest measure of interest. If individuals are selected for inclusion in a special educational enrichment program on the basis of achievement test scores, for instance, we would expect their test scores (apart from any program effects) to be positively, linearly related to later measures of educational attainment. The RD design is used to determine if there is a discontinuity in scores between those immediately above and immediately below the cutoff for inclusion in the program, and if there are differences in the slopes of the regression lines on each side.

The RD design is quasi-experimental because it is meant to mimic a true experiment in which a group of participants at a cutoff point are randomly assigned to a treatment or a control condition. For example, suppose the State Department of Education has developed a program for children whose families fall below the poverty line established by the federal government. To test the effect of the program, the state might take those falling slightly above and slightly below the poverty line and *randomly assign* them to the program or control condition. The effect of the program then could be tested in a similar way to the pretest-posttest control group experimental design. Such a design might prove politically unfeasible, however, and the RD design provides a means of testing program effects without making assignments that are difficult to justify on any basis other than scientific utility.

In the regression-discontinuity approach, if selection into the special program is associated with a specific cutoff point on the selection variable, we can use those who fall immediately below the cutoff point as a comparison to those falling immediately above the cutoff. Although overall we would expect those below to perform differently (either much better or much worse) than those above, in the absence of a special treatment we would not expect any abrupt change in outcomes for those falling near one another on either side of the cutoff. If such a change did occur, we could take this as evidence of a treatment effect above and beyond the expected selection effect (Thistlethwaite & Campbell, 1960). This design is especially useful when scarce resources are used as interventions. Such a *regression-discontinuity* effect is illustrated in Figure 10.10 for the case of a positive (merit-based) selection factor. A full treatment of the assumptions and statistical analyses for this design is available in Reichardt and Henry (2012) and Hallberg, Wing, Wong, and Cook (2013).

The regression-discontinuity design is less common than comparison time-series designs in program evaluation settings, partly because assignment of participants to groups based on a criterion cutoff score is relatively rare, and partly because it requires extensive data collection for individuals across the full range of scores on the selection variable. However, when regression-discontinuity analyses are used, they often are focused on important, socially relevant issues. For example, using this approach researchers have investigated the effects of mandatory divorce counseling laws (Deluse, 1999), HIV prevention in West Africa (Arcand & Wouabe, 2010), targeted funding for

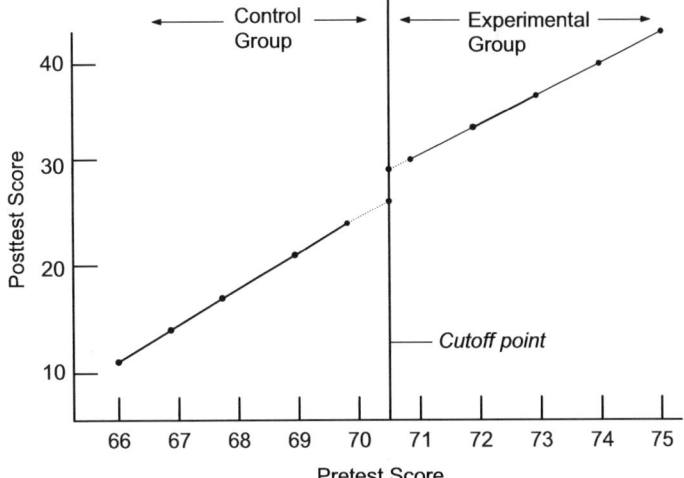

FIGURE 10.10 Regression-discontinuity design.

disadvantaged children (Henry, Fortner, & Thompson, 2010), programs for mathematically gifted African-American children (Robinson, Bradley, & Stanley, 1990), and the effects of being placed on the Dean's list on college students' later academic performance (Seaver & Quarton, 1976).

Regression-discontinuity is an interesting quasi-experimental design to consider, especially in contrast to true experimental designs. Whereas true experiments are based on randomization as the basis for assignment to different groups, the regression-discontinuity design is based on a *non-random* cutoff score. In either instance, strict application of the selection rule permits cause-effect conclusions to be drawn if the cutoff rule is strictly enforced. If it is not, the design's capacity for causal interpretation is forfeit. In addition, it is essential that the relationship between pretest and posttest is linear, or the interpretability of the ensuing results is severely compromised. The statistical power of analyses of the RD design also is low: Using RD analysis requires two to four times as many observations as experimental designs to attain the same degree of statistical power. Given these problems, the RD design obviously is not preferable to a randomized experiment, if the latter is possible. However, as a special case, the RD design does help to illustrate how research purposes can be adapted to policy-relevant conditions without significant loss of interpretability. In the appropriate circumstances, the design provides information that may prove extremely useful for policy-making purposes, and this same evaluation could be made of many of the other designs outlined by Campbell and Stanley (1963), Shadish et al. (2002), Bickman and Rog (2009), and other researchers who have discussed and developed quasi-experimental designs. These designs are ideally suited to circumstances of social or practical importance that do not admit to pure experiments.

Use of Archival Data in Longitudinal Research

Researchers rarely have sufficient lead time prior to the introduction of an intervention to obtain premeasures over an extended period specifically for the purposes of evaluation. Hence, the use of time-series quasi-experimental designs often depends on the availability of statistical records or other archival documents that have been kept for purposes other than research. Sometimes the only relevant and available historical materials are written records (newspaper summaries, case records, personal letters, etc.) that must be subject to *content analysis* to be useful as research data (the methods and purposes of content analyses are covered in Chapter 14). For present purposes we have dealt only with research based on the availability of quantitative records or statistical indices compiled by institutions or government agencies for various accounting purposes.

Fortunately North America and Europe have proven "statistics-happy" for much of their recent histories. In the U.S., for example, in addition to the constitutionally mandated census of the entire population every 10 years, which provides valuable demographic information on a regular basis, numerous federal agencies are charged with maintaining statistical databases of records of births and deaths, hospital admissions and other health records, various indices of economic activity, records of arrests, convictions and other indices of criminal activity, unemployment statistics, and the like. Parallel record-keeping goes on at state and local levels, which is important for evaluations of locally implemented social programs.

Use of statistical archives has a number of advantages, but also creates some disadvantages for research purposes. First, it limits the dependent measures or outcome variables that can be assessed to the type of information on which records happen to have been kept. Records kept for administrative purposes may or may not reflect the primary goals of the particular social program being evaluated. For instance, in evaluations of the criminal justice system, it is easier to obtain archival records on recidivism (re-arrests or re-imprisonment) than on program participants' more positive outcomes. In educational settings, information on achievement test results is much more likely to be available than are indicators of other types of positive student outcomes, such as social adjustment or moral development.

Another limitation imposed by reliance on archival records is the time interval covered by a given statistic, which may or may not be the unit of time ideal for research purposes. If statistics are accumulated on a daily basis, researchers have considerable flexibility to aggregate data over any time period they choose, though they must contend with the costs involved in compiling large amounts of data. On the other hand, if summary statistics have been maintained only on a yearly basis, the research will have to cover a long period for a sufficient number of data points to be available for purposes of statistical analyses.

Finally, a major worry with many archival studies is the possibility that the nature or method of record keeping has changed over time. Record-keeping systems can be altered in many ways, usually for administrative convenience. For one thing, the *criterion* for inclusion in the data file may be changed. Crime statistics, for instance, can be dramatically affected by changes in the activities or actions on which police are required to file reports. Records also may be altered in form or content, such as changes in categories of information or in times at which information is recorded. Sometimes, and this is especially relevant in medical research, new techniques of diagnosis will allow more certain or more rapid identification of diseases that could not always be clearly diagnosed before the new test. This change will produce data that suggests a rapid rise in the incidence of the disease. Sometimes the researcher will know enough about the diagnosis or record-keeping system to make conversions between different versions of the same information, but more often such changes render data noncomparable from one time to another. If changes in administrative record-keeping methods occur in close proximity to the introduction of a social program, the records may become useless as measures of program-induced changes.

On a positive note, use of archived data usually provides much broader swaths of the population than is possible in laboratory-oriented research. Often archival data is representative of large groups of the populace—cities, states, or the country. Being able to extrapolate one's results to the entire population of, say, adolescents across the country, or pensioners in Ohio, lends a certain value to the research enterprise. It helps offset the difficulties and restrictions that the quasi-experimental methods can impose on the researcher, and for some makes the trade-off worthwhile.

Conclusion

Quasi-experimental methods serve as a bridge between nonexperimental and experimental methods. The quasi-experimental approach allows us to study important issues and to make estimates of the strength of manipulated or naturally occurring "treatments." The confidence we can place in these estimates usually is not as great as that which we can derive from true experimental designs, which involve random assignment, but sometimes the issue is important enough that we are willing to pay this price to generate even rough estimates of the strength of relationships or the effectiveness of treatments. With sufficient thought and effort, quasi-experimental designs can produce important insights that, because of contextual constraints, might not have been researchable through the more standard experimental techniques. In this chapter, we have only scratched the surface of the variety of possible quasi-experimental designs. The chapter was meant to lay the groundwork. The elaboration of the many variations that can be implemented is a function of the reader's ingenuity, creativity, and motivation.

Questions for Discussion

1. Why are propensity scores better than post hoc matching? Isn't a propensity score just an aggregate of many matched characteristics? Would we obtain the same results if we used post hoc matching across 10 variables and if we created a propensity score for those 10 variables? Why or why not? Would pairing propensity scores that are not exactly equal be effectively the same as pairing two participants that are matched on 9 of 10 variables?
2. What kinds of research questions or contexts might lend themselves to the use of growth curve modeling? To the use of the regression-discontinuity design?
3. You are interested in knowing whether the particular way that personal trainers motivate the members of Gym XYZ is actually a good motivational technique (they all appear to follow the same sort of protocol), or whether it is the gym members who are innately motivated to exercise. How could you approach this research question from the perspective of a field experiment? How would this field experiment differ from a program evaluation of the same personal trainer motivational technique? Would the two research perspectives differ at all? Why or why not? As a research consultant for an evaluation firm, could you conduct a program evaluation exactly the same way as you would if you were conducting a field experiment? Why do we draw the distinction between experiments and evaluation?

Notes

1. Regressed scores are obtained by multiplying the pretest score, in standardized score form, by the value of the reliability coefficient (i.e., the test-retest correlation).
2. Criminologists suggest that 90% of all crimes are committed by 10% of the population. As such, incarcerating a "career criminal" (termed incapacitation) will have a disproportionate effect on crime rates, and the California law did just that.
3. This assumes, of course, that criminals knew which offenses would earn a strike and which would not, and were reasonably certain that a minor crime would not escalate into a serious felony (e.g., knocking over the clerk while exiting a convenience store might cause serious injury, thereby escalating the problem from petty theft to assault).

References

Andresen, M. A., & Boyd, N. (2010). A cost-benefit and cost-effectiveness analysis of Vancouver's supervised injection facility. *International Journal of Drug Policy, 21,* 70–76.

Arcand, J.-L., & Wouabe, E. D. (2010). Teacher training and HIV/AIDS prevention in West Africa: Regression discontinuity design evidence from the Cameroon. *Health Economics, 19* (supp. 1), 36–54.

Arceneaux, K. (2005). Using cluster randomized field experiments to study voting behavior. *Annals of the American Academy of Political and Social Science, 601,* 169–179.

Berk, R. A., Hoffman, D. M., Maki, J. E., Rauma, D., & Wong, H. (1979). Estimation procedures for pooled cross-sectional and time series data. *Evaluation Quarterly, 3,* 385–410.

Berry, W. D., & Lewis-Beck, M. S. (1986). *New tools for social scientists: Advances and applications in research methods.* Beverly Hills, CA: Sage.

Bickman, L., & Rog, D. J. (Eds.) (2009). *The Sage handbook of applied research methods.* Thousand Oaks, CA: Sage.

Boruch, R. (2012). Deploying randomized field experiments in the service of evidence-based crime policy. *Journal of Experimental Criminology, 8*(3), 331–341.

Box, G.E.P., & Jenkins, G. M. (1970). *Time series analysis: Forecasting and control.* San Francisco: Holden-Day.

Campbell, D. T. (1969). Reforms as experiments. *American Psychologist, 24,* 409–429.

Campbell, D. T., & Erlebacher, A. (1970). How regression in quasi-experimental evaluation can mistakenly make compensatory education look harmful. In J. Hellmuth (Ed.), *The disadvantaged child (Vol. 3): Compensatory education: A national debate* (pp. 185–210). New York: Brunner-Mazel.

Campbell, D. T., & Stanley, J. C. (1963). Experimental and quasi-experimental designs for research on teaching. In N. L. Gage (Ed.), *Handbook of research on teaching* (pp. 171–246). Boston: Houghton Mifflin.

Crano, W. D., Alvaro, E. M., & Siegel, J. T. (in press). The media campaign as a focal prevention strategy: A guide to their design, implementation, and evaluation. In L. M. Scheier (Ed.), *Handbook of drug prevention.* Washington, DC: American Psychological Association.

Crano, W. D., & Messé, L. A. (1985). Assessing and redressing comprehension artifacts in social intervention research. *Evaluation Review, 9,* 144–172.

Deluse, S. R. (1999). Mandatory divorce education: A program evaluation using a 'quasi-random' regression discontinuity design. *Dissertation Abstracts International: Section B: The Sciences & Engineering, 60,* 1349.

Donaldson, S. I. (2007). *Program theory-driven evaluation science: Strategies and applications.* Mahwah, NJ: Lawrence Erlbaum Associates Publishers.

Donaldson, S. I., Christie, C., & Mark, M. M. (2009). *What counts as credible evidence in applied research and evaluation practice?* Thousand Oaks, CA: Sage.

Donaldson, S. I., & Crano, W. D. (2011). Theory-driven evaluation science and applied social psychology: Exploring the intersection. In M. M. Mark, S. I. Donaldson & B. Campbell (Eds.), *Social psychology and evaluation* (pp. 140–161). New York: Guilford.

Donaldson, S. I., & Scriven, M. (Eds.) (2003). *Evaluating social programs and problems: Visions for the new millennium.* Mahwah, NJ: Erlbaum.

Galton, F. (1885). Regression towards mediocrity in hereditary stature. *Journal of the Anthropological Institute, 15,* 246–263.

Green, D. P., Aronow, P. M., Bergan, D. E., Greene, P., Paris, C., & Weinberger, B. I. (2011). Does knowledge of constitutional principles increase support for civil liberties? Results from a randomized field experiment. *The Journal of Politics, 73,* 463–476.

Hallberg, K., Wing, C., Wong, V., & Cook, T. D. (2013). Experimental design for causal inference: Clinical trials and regression discontinuity designs. In T. D. Little (Ed.), *The Oxford handbook of quantitative methods (Vol. 1): Foundations.* (pp. 223–236). New York, NY US: Oxford University Press.

Henry, G. T., Fortner, C. K., & Thompson, C. L. (2010). Targeted funding for educationally disadvantaged students: A regression discontinuity estimate of the impact on high school student achievement. *Educational Evaluation and Policy Analysis, 32,* 183–204.

Hovland, C. I., Lumsdaine, A. A., & Sheffield, F. D. (1949). *Experiments on mass communication.* Princeton, NJ: Princeton University Press.

Johnston, L. D., O'Malley, P. M., Bachman, J. G., & Schulenberg, J. E. (2013). *Monitoring the future national survey results on drug use, 1975–2012. Volume II: College students and adults ages 19–50.* Ann Arbor, MI: Institute for Social Research, University of Michigan.

Kershaw, D., & Fair, J. (1976). *The New Jersey income-maintenance experiment.* New York: Academic Press.

Krueger, A. B., & Zhu, P. (2004). Another look at the New York City school voucher experiment. *American Behavioral Scientist, 47,* 658–698.

Kuklinski, M. R., Briner, J. S., Hawkins, J. D., & Catalano, R. F. (2012). Cost-benefit analysis of communities that care outcomes at eighth grade. *Prevention Science, 13,* 150–161.

Lee, S., & Aos, S. (2011). Using cost–benefit analysis to understand the value of social interventions. *Research on Social Work Practice, 21,* 682–688.

Liu, S., Rovine, M. J., & Molenaar, P.C.M. (2012). Selecting a linear mixed model for longitudinal data: Repeated measures analysis of variance, covariance pattern model, and growth curve approaches. *Psychological Methods, 17,* 15–30.

McCain, L. J., & McCleary, R. (1979). The statistical analysis of the simple interrupted time-series quasi-experiment. In T. D. Cook & D. T. Campbell (Eds.), *Quasi-experimentation: Design and analysis issues for field settings* (pp. 233–293). Chicago: Rand McNally.

McDowell, D., McCleary, R., Meidinger, E., & Hay, R. (1980). *Interrupted time-series analysis.* Beverly Hills, CA: Sage.

McNemar, Q. (1940). A critical examination of the University of Iowa studies of environmental influences upon the I.Q. *Journal of Psychology Bulletin, 37,* 63–92.

O'Leary, A., Ambrose, T. K., Raffaelli, M., Maibach, E., Jemmott, L. S., Jemmott, J. B., III, Labouvie, E., & Celentano, D. (1998). Effects of an HIV risk reduction project on sexual risk behavior of low-income STD patients. *AIDS Education and Prevention, 10,* 483–492.

Orwin, R. G. (1997). Twenty-one years old and counting: The interrupted time series comes of age. In E. Chelimsky & W. R. Shadish (Eds.), *Evaluation for the 21st century: A handbook* (pp. 443–465). Thousand Oaks, CA: Sage.

Ramirez, J. R., & Crano, W. D. (2003). An interrupted time series analysis of California's three strikes law on instrumental, violent, minor, and drug-related crime: Deterrence and incapacitation. *Journal of Applied Social Psychology, 33,* 110–144.

Reichardt, C. S., & Henry, G. T. (2012). Regression-discontinuity designs. In H. Cooper, P. M. Camic, D. L. Long, A. T. Panter, D. Rindskopf & K. J. Sher (Eds.), *APA handbook of research methods in psychology, Vol. 2: Research designs: Quantitative, qualitative, neuropsychological, and biological* (pp. 511–526). Washington, DC: American Psychological Association.

Robinson, A., Bradley, R. H., & Stanley, T. D. (1990). Opportunity to achieve: Identifying mathematically gifted Black students. *Contemporary Educational Psychology, 15,* 1–12.

Rosenbaum, P. R., & Rubin, D. B. (1983). The central role of the propensity score in observational studies for causal effects. *Boimetrika, 70,* 41–55.

Salovey, P., & Williams-Piehota, P. (2004). Field experiments in social psychology: Message framing and the promotion of health protective behaviors. *American Behavioral Scientist, 47,* 488–505.

Scriven, M. (1967). The methodology of evaluation. In R. Tyler, R. Gagne & M. Scriven (Eds.), *Perspectives on curriculum evaluation* (pp. 39–89). Chicago: Rand McNally.

Seaver, W. B., & Quarton, R. J. (1976). Regression discontinuity analysis of dean's list effects. *Journal of Educational Psychology, 68,* 459–465.

Shadish, W. R., Cook, T. D., & Campbell, D. T. (2002). *Experimental and quasi-experimental designs for generalized causal inference.* Boston: Houghton Mifflin.

Speer, D. C., & Greenbaum, P. E. (1995). Five methods for computing significant individual client change and improvement rates: Support for an individual growth curve approach. *Journal of Counseling and Clinical Psychology, 63,* 1044–1048.

Struening, E. L., & Brewer, M. B. (Eds.) (1983). *Handbook of evaluation research* (university ed.). Beverly Hills, CA: Sage.

Thistlethwaite, D. L., & Campbell, D. T. (1960). Regression-discontinuity analysis: An alternative to the ex post facto experiment. *Journal of Educational Psychology, 51,* 309–317.

Thorndike, R. L. (1942). Regression fallacies in the matched groups experiment. *Psychometrika, 7,* 85–102.

PART III
Data Collecting Methods

11
SURVEY STUDIES
Design and Sampling

In some fundamental ways, survey research is different from the experimentally oriented methods that occupied our attention in the initial chapters of this text. In this chapter, the term *survey* refers to the process of polling, or surveying, some group of respondents with respect to topics of interest to the researcher—their attitudes, perceptions, intentions, behaviors, and so on. Surveys may involve mailed questionnaires, telephone interviews, face-to-face interviews, or even online pop-ups. Most survey research is intended to use the responses obtained to estimate the responses of a larger group or population. Therefore, a central concern in survey contexts is, "How well do the responses of a subset of individuals actually represent those of that population?" Generally, we are less concerned with issues of internal validity (i.e., is an experimental manipulation responsible for the obtained findings?), because surveys are primarily used for descriptive or non-experimental research studies. Although researchers are increasingly using surveys as a vehicle for experimental studies as well, the central goal of most survey research is to provide sample estimates of population values that are as accurate as possible. Most of the technical aspects of survey sampling have been developed in the service of this goal.

Selection vs. Assignment

To draw the distinction between experimental and survey research, it is useful to emphasize the differences between sampling of participant units and assignment of these units to conditions. Recall that in the sections of the text devoted to experimental design, we stressed the importance of random assignment of participants to conditions. In true experiments, we are concerned primarily with ensuring that participants are randomly assigned to the various conditions of the study and less concerned with the characteristics of the original population from which participants were drawn. The core requirement for random *assignment* is that each person participating in the study has the same chance of being assigned to a specific experimental or control condition as any other person. Random assignment is essential if the full power of experimental techniques to foster causal statements is to be realized.

Most researchers recognize that the generalizability of results is dependent on the features of the larger population pool from which the participants were drawn, but this consideration is secondary for most experimental research. For example, if participants used for a study were all students enrolled in an undergraduate course in the fall semester, then without replicating the study with demographically disparate participants it would be dangerous to generalize findings beyond that group. Of course, we often are not content to generalize to such a restricted population, but to go further in application involves some risk of overextending our results. This should not be interpreted as a criticism of experimentation, or of random assignment of individuals who were selected from restricted a population. Rather, it is intended to caution researchers not to overextend the boundaries of their findings. This observation also helps to draw a distinction between assignment and sample selection, where the methods used in obtaining participants are of central importance. *Sampling* participants is different from, and perhaps more fundamental than *assigning* participants. Sampling is not concerned with the rules that govern the placement (assignment of participants) into the treatment conditions of a study, but rather with the issue of how those particular people got into the study in the first place.

A research study begins by selecting (randomly or not) a sample of participants for investigation, and if an objective is to examine outcome differences between groups, these participants are assigned (randomly or not) to different study conditions. A random *sampling* procedure is necessary to achieve high external validity for generalization of results back to the population of interest, and random *assignment* of participants to different conditions is necessary to achieve high internal validity for making causal inferences. There are many forms of random (e.g., simple random sampling, stratified, multistage) sampling and nonrandom (e.g., convenience, snowball) sampling approaches that will be discussed in this chapter, but first some important preliminary issues will be considered.

Census or Sample Survey?

In the technical sampling literature, a distinction is made between a census and a sample survey. A **census** is an investigation involving all the potential units that could be included from the target population (the universe of interest). In comparison, a sample refers to a subset of eligible units in a population. In the United States, the government conducts a national census every decade to obtain demographic characteristics of every person living in the country. Census workers are responsible for going door to door to interview residents living in households, but to ensure comprehensive coverage of all members of the populace, homeless people and incarcerated prisoners also are surveyed. In most research, a sample is preferred to the use of the complete set of possible units because, *within some reasonable degree of sampling error,* the sample will approximate the results that would have been obtained had a complete census been taken. A sample is collected at a fraction of the cost associated with a complete enumeration of all population units.[1]

A census does not necessarily imply a massive number of all units, such as every person living in a particular nation or even on earth, but the intended population to which the researcher wishes to generalize the survey results. An investigator wishing to estimate the anxiety level of people suffering from malaria obviously is not concerned with the anxiety scores of everyone in the world. Instead, the targeted population would be individuals suffering from this particular disease. For a study examining grade point average held by teenagers living in Canada, the targeted population would be the teens living in that country, but if the researcher's purpose is to generalize to female teenagers attending a particular high school, with findings to be used by local school administrators, then logically the population of interest is female students of that age cohort attending that school.

Precision and Sampling Error

Social researchers' preference for surveys over a complete census is based on the understanding that a survey sample will reproduce the results of a census "within some reasonable degree of error." This understanding prompts consideration of an important issue in sampling, the estimate of precision. An *estimate* is a statistical value computed from members of a sample. It serves as an inference, with some degree of sampling error, of a population value. Examples of estimates include the mathematical mean of cigarettes smoked, self-esteem score, or widgets built; or the proportion of cigarette smokers, right-handers, or women in a population. The precision of an estimate is inversely related to the degree of **sampling error (standard error)**, or the expected *typical* discrepancy between the estimate calculated from a sample and the value that would be obtained if the entire targeted population (census) had been included in the study. Sampling error represents the discrepancy expected if many samples were randomly drawn from the same targeted population. Obviously, if all the population members were included, the concept of sampling error would not be applicable. Sampling error, which concerns the extent that a sample deviates from that of the population, should not be confused with measurement error.

Suppose we know that a particular high school contains a population of 1,500 students. The researcher is interested in the number of hours the typical student spends each academic quarter studying English composition. Figure 11.1 shows the distribution of sample means, which is the theoretical distribution of all possible randomly selected samples of a given sample size (in this case, 100), drawn from the same population. The figure shows that this population averaged 20 hours of studying per academic quarter. The distribution of sample means is found by calculating the standard error of the mean. In this case, the standard error is 3 hours.

Now, let's assume that two researchers each randomly draw a different sample of 100 students from this same high school. The first researcher obtains a mean estimate of 18 hours spent studying, the second researcher calculates an estimate of 20 hours. Because not every student from the targeted population was included in both of these samples, we expect fluctuations in mean estimates across the different samples due to chance. We also expect natural sampling variability between each of these two sample estimates and that of the actual population value. If a third investigator's sample found results showing 29 hours studying, the estimate would appear to be well beyond the difference of 2–3 hours that seems reasonable if only sampling error was involved. Estimates beyond a reasonable degree of sampling error suggests an unrepresentative error, or biased sample, which is unlikely to provide a precise sample estimate of the population value.

To provide a concrete example of the use of sampling and sampling error, suppose we have available a list of all of the 45,000 students who attend a large Midwestern university. We know that 20,000 of these students, our targeted population, live off campus and we wish to determine

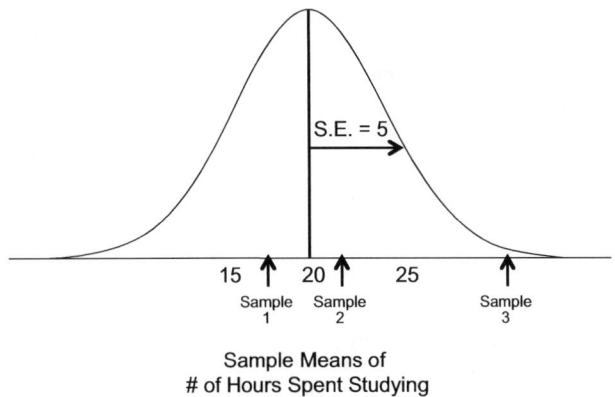

FIGURE 11.1 Distribution of sample means: 100 participants were randomly drawn for each sample.

TABLE 11.1 Textbook cost distribution of off-campus students.

Textbook Cost Category	Population 1	Sample 1	Population 2	Sample 2
$0–$25	600	36	0	0
$26–$50	900	47	0	0
$51–$75	980	56	0	0
$76–$100	2,840	149	4,000	220
$101–$125	3,700	183	6,000	290
$126–$150	3,800	177	7,000	315
$151–$175	2,800	129	3,000	175
$176–$200	1,520	72	0	0
$201–$225	1,220	58	0	0
$226–$250	1,000	55	0	0
> $250	640	38	0	0
Number of Students	20,000	1000	20,000	1,000
Mean Cost Per Student	$135.22	$134.00	$124.25	$124.12
Standard Deviation	57.25	59.60	24.34	25.40

the average textbook costs these students paid this semester. We have a list of these 20,000 students. This is known as the **sampling frame**, a listing of the population of interest from which members of a population are drawn and used as the sample for a study. In addition to the average textbook costs, we want to know something about the distribution of costs across this population. How could we perform this study? We could perform a census by contacting all 20,000 off-campus students to learn their textbook costs in the present semester. The mathematical average of these costs across the entire targeted population could then be computed, as shown in the "Population 1" column at the bottom of Table 11.1.

Contacting all 20,000 off-campus students of our hypothetical university might tax our research resources beyond the breaking point, however, and so instead we decide to sample only 1,000 of the total population. To do this, we use a table of random numbers (details of using such a table are discussed later in this chapter) to select 1,000 people from the off-campus housing list (our sampling frame) to be part of the sample, and we contact these individuals for our survey. Usually, we will not know the true population value (called the *population parameter*); however, we will be able to estimate the parameter from the from the sample results. The probable accuracy between the sample and population estimate is termed the *precision* of that estimate. We can estimate the precision of a sample mean by determining the sampling error, or standard error (S.E.), of the mean. A high sampling error reflects low precision, whereas high precision is reflected by a low sampling error. The precision of a simple random sample is estimated by the following formula:

$$S.E. = \sqrt{s^2/n},$$

where S.E. = the standard error of the estimated mean (the inverse of precision),
   s = the standard deviation of the sample, and
   n = the number of participants in the sample.

All three terms in the formula use information from the sample to infer population values.

Under some circumstances, it is useful to modify the standard error estimate by a factor known as the *finite population correction,* or fpc, as follows:

S.E. = $\sqrt{(1-f)\ s^2/n}$

where f = the sampling fraction, i.e., the proportion of the total population included in the sample.

The fpc is included in the calculation of the precision estimate to reflect the facts that in simple random sampling units are chosen without replacement, and that the population from which the sample is drawn is not infinite (as assumed in standard statistical theory). The fpc formula indicates that sampling without replacement results in greater precision than sampling with replacement. When the sampling fraction is small (say, less than 1 in 20), the effect of the fpc on the standard error is minor. This follows logically, because in situations involving a small sampling fraction, the likelihood of selecting the same respondent more than once (when sampling with replacement) is minimal, hence the sampling effect on the standard error is minimal. Thus, in practice, with small sampling fractions, the fpc value is negligible and rarely used.

In addition to the fpc, the formulas presented here contain two other clues about factors that influence the precision of an estimate. Notice that the size of the sample has much to do with the sampling error (or lack of precision of the estimate). In fact, the sample size, not the sampling fraction, plays the predominant role in determining precision. The precision formula clearly shows that as sample size increases, the standard error decreases. As a larger sample size is more reflective of the population, increasing the number of respondents will reduce the standard error of an estimate. However, the relationship is not one-to-one because it is the square root of the sample size that is entered in the formulas for the standard error. This indicates that if researchers wish to double the precision of an estimate (if s remains constant), they would have to quadruple the sample size. Because of this law of diminishing returns for increasing sample size to enhance precision, and considering the costs of participant recruitment, the majority of national studies (e.g., public opinion polls and national datasets) use samples of no more than 1,000 to 2,000 people to provide estimates of population values with reasonably high levels of precision.

The other important term required to calculate the formula for the standard error is the standard deviation, denoted by the term *s,* which represents the variability of the *individual* participant values in the sample. From Table 11.1, the mean and standard deviation of the sample parallel the corresponding values for the population. As population information is usually unknown, the sample estimates are used as an approximation of their respective population values. The larger this sample's standard deviation term, the greater the standard error of the mean. In other words, the more variable the spread of individual values used to compute the sample estimate (in our example, semester textbook costs) of the population, the greater the standard error of the sample mean, and, consequently, the lower the precision of the sample mean.

Consider Table 11.1 again. As shown here, the range of costs in "Population 1" is relatively wide. A random sample of 1,000 respondents drawn from this population produced results shown in the "Sample 1" column, where the standard deviation is $59.60. Now consider the distribution of students at another university, "Population 2." Such a set of restricted values might be obtained if all were made to select from a restricted range of courses. As can be seen in this example, the standard deviation of a sample (sample 2) of the respondents drawn from this population is much smaller than that of the sample of population 1. This is so because the variability of the true population values of population 2 are themselves smaller than those of the first. To take an extreme example, suppose that the population of off-campus students each paid exactly $200 for their semester's textbooks. In this instance, any sample size would provide an absolutely precise estimate of the population mean. A moment's reflection on the precision formulas will reveal why this is so. When values are the same for all units in a sample, there is, by definition, no variation in these values. The sample standard deviation would equal exactly zero, and upon solving the formula the standard error also would be zero. The results of any division of this term (no matter what the sample size, n) also would equal zero. Thus, the more restricted the sample values, the more precise the sample estimate, all other things being equal. Or, to put it another way, the smaller the standard deviation of the sample, the fewer respondents will be needed to obtain greater precision of estimate for the sample mean.

Random Sampling

Sampling can be classified as random or nonrandom (Henry, 1990). In **random sampling**, a random mechanism, at some point during the process, is used to obtain a sample intended to be representative of the underlying population. Random samples can be drawn in many ways, including simple random sampling, systematic sampling, stratified sampling, cluster sampling, and multistage sampling. Random sampling may involve randomly selecting members from a population, members within strata of a group, or sampling location clusters (e.g., neighborhoods in a city). Random sampling is also known as *probability sampling,* because the probabilities of a member of a population being included in the sample may be determined (at some point in the process), although probabilities of member selection may or may not be equal.

In **nonrandom sampling**, a nonrandom mechanism is used to obtain a sample from a population. Samples are gathered based on convenience, by snowball sampling or quota sampling approaches. Also known as *nonprobability sampling,* the probability that members are selected from a population cannot be determined, usually because a sampling frame listing of potential respondents or locations is unavailable. Any approach using random sampling will produce higher external validity than nonrandom approaches.

Random sampling is undertaken in the service of the fundamental goals of efficiency and economy. Efficiency refers to the attempt to balance considerations of cost with those of precision. One of the central preoccupations of many sampling approaches is to devise ways by which the precision of estimates can be enhanced without resorting to samples of unmanageable size, and to provide sample estimates of population values of high precision. Nonrandom sampling approaches have been developed in the service of economy, and are undertaken not to enhance the precision/cost ratio, but rather to reduce the expenses involved in sampling and data collection. We will consider examples of both random and nonrandom sampling on the pages that follow.

Simple Random Sampling

In **simple random sampling**, every member of the population in question has an equal (and nonzero) probability of being selected every time a unit is drawn for inclusion in the sample.[2] *Simple random sampling* should not be confused with the overarching term of *random sampling.* The probability of selection in simple random sampling is equal to the sampling fraction. It is calculated by dividing the number of units to be included in the sample by the total number of units in the population. Thus, in the examples of Table 11.1, the sampling fraction was 5%, because 1,000 of a possible 20,000 students were sampled. Sampling approaches of this type are called *epsem* designs, which stands for "equal probability of selection method." Simple random sampling, systematic sampling, and proportionate stratified sampling approaches are examples of epsem designs.

In creating and selecting a simple random sample, the researcher has a relatively restricted set of procedural options. In situations involving a small population, one can enter each of the population units on individual elements (slips of paper, discs, etc.), mix the elements well, and choose the number planned for the sample. Picking names out of a hat is an example of this process: If all the names are entered individually, on elements (e.g., slips of paper) of the same size, if the elements are mixed well, if the person doing the choosing does so without looking into the hat (or otherwise exerting an influence on the particular names that are chosen), and if sampling without replacement occurs, as the elements are not returned to the hat after being selected, we have a simple random sample. If any of these conditions are violated, the result is not a simple random sample.

In research situations in which the underlying population is large, such a process becomes unwieldy. Let's reconsider the example of Table 11.1. Obviously, using the "name-in-the-hat" approach would be unwise in this study. The sampling process would be so tedious that the research probably would never be completed (Imagine writing the names of 20,000 people on index cards, putting these into a (very large) hat, mixing them, and choosing 1,000 cards at random). In such cases, the use of a computer or a table of random numbers is highly recommended.[3]

The process begins with a determination of the required sample size. Guidelines for estimating sample size are presented later in this chapter. For present purposes, let us assume as in the example that we have decided upon a sample of 1,000 students from the total eligible population of 20,000. To choose the specific students who are to constitute our sample, we would number each of the names on our population list, from 00001 to 20000. This list is our sampling frame. Then, using a table of random numbers, we could select the first 1,000 different 5-place random numbers that corresponded with the numbers on the list of students. So, if we came upon the number 18921 when searching in our random number table, we would include the 18,921st student on the list in our sample; however, if a random number of 22430 was obtained, it would not be used to select a unit into the sample because there are only 20,000 eligible students on our frame (i.e., there is no student whose "ID number" corresponds to that from the random number table). When employing a random number table, it is good practice to pick a starting point at random each time the table is used. This helps to assure that the same investigator does not always make use of the same set of random numbers when selecting samples.

A table of random numbers may be found on this webpage: www.nist.gov/pml/wmd/pubs/upload/AppenB-HB133-05-Z.pdf. A more efficient approach is to use a computer to generate random numbers based on the number of population units to be sampled, as found on this webpage: http://graphpad.com/quickcalcs/randomN1.cfm. Many potentially useful approaches for drawing simple random samples have been suggested for reasons of ease in various sampling contexts, but if our recommendation were sought about the appropriate way of drawing a sample, it would be very simple: Use a random number table.

Systematic Sampling

An alternate means of choosing the students from our off-campus student list involves a technique known as systematic sampling. **Systematic sampling** requires sampling every predetermined nth member from a population. In this approach, as before, a specific sample size is determined. Then, the size of the sample is divided by the total eligible population to determine the sampling fraction. In our example, the sampling fraction was 1,000/20,000, or 1 in 20. A number between 1 and 20 is randomly chosen, and then every 20th person after that number is selected for the sample of 1,000. Thus, if we randomly chose the number 15 as our starting point, we would include in our sample the 15th, 35th, 55th, 75th, etc., student from the renters list. We would continue in this fashion until we had sampled exactly 1,000 students.

In some ways, systematic sampling resembles simple random sampling, because all of the units in the sampling frame *initially* have an equal chance of being selected (systematic sampling is an epsem method). It differs from simple random sampling because the probability of units being included in the sample is not equal. Thus, if the number 15 were randomly chosen as our starting point, the probability of the 16th student being included in the sample is zero, because our sampling interval is 20. However, the probability of students 15 and 35 both being included in the sample is 1/20, because if 15 is chosen (a 1 in 20 chance), then 35 is sure to be chosen as well. This technique is classified as a type of random sampling because the sampling begins with a random starting point.

Estimating the precision of a systematic sample is difficult unless we are willing to make some simplifying assumptions. In practice, it is generally assumed that if the listing of population members in the sampling frame is haphazard, or unsystematic, the resulting (systematic) sample approximates a simple random sample (and hence, the precision formulas presented earlier may be used). This generally is a safe assumption unless the members of the frame are ordered in a systematic or cyclical manner and the sampling interval coincides with the length of the cycle. For example, suppose a frame contained the names of all applicants for a marriage license. Suppose the names of the couples to be married are listed in order, with the woman's name always coming before the man's. If we used an odd number as our sampling interval, our sample would be more or less evenly represented by men and women. However, an even numbered interval would produce a sample consisting entirely of men, or of women, depending on our starting point. This kind of regularity is not what we seek in obtaining a representative sample. However, sampling frames with cyclical arrangements "are rarely met in practice, and situations in which they may occur are usually easily recognized" (Kalton, 1983, p. 19).

Stratification and Stratified Samples

Moser and Kalton (1972) made the important point that the definition of randomness refers to the means by which a sample is drawn, not to the outcome of this process, which yields the sample itself. Thus, on rare occasions it is conceivable that one could draw a random sample that, in fact, appeared to be anything but random. To return to our textbook cost example, suppose that one of our research issues concerned the question of whether student costs were associated with class standing. Do off-campus seniors, for example, typically pay more for books than off-campus sophomores? To answer this question, we would require that both seniors and sophomores be included in the sample. However, it is possible that even if there were a fair number of sophomores on our "off-campus" list, our sample might contain none. Such a chance event of highly imbalanced subsamples is extremely unlikely in a large sample, but if we were extraordinarily unlucky, it could occur, even if our sampling technique were flawless. Small sample sizes are more susceptible to this problem.

To ensure that an adequate number of participants are selected from each of the different subgroups of the population, survey researchers generally make use of a technique known as **stratified sampling**, in which the population is divided into theoretically meaningful or empirically important strata before members are randomly drawn from each stratum (or subpopulation) and used for the sample. Respondents then are randomly selected *from within each stratum,* and this permits prespecified subsample sizes for each stratum. The subsamples are later combined to yield the final sample. Two forms of stratified sampling are common, depending on the manner in which the sampling fraction is employed. Frequently, the same sampling fraction is used for each of the strata; in such a case, the result is called a *proportionate stratified (random) sample.* Sometimes a different sampling fraction is employed within each stratum; in this instance, the resulting sample is termed a *disproportionate stratified (random) sample.* Generally, research issues dictate whether a proportionate or disproportionate stratified sample will be drawn.

To provide an example of situations that would call for the use of proportionate or disproportionate stratified sampling, consider the following scenario. Suppose the Democratic governor wanted to raise the state income tax, but was concerned about the effect such an action might have on her political future. To obtain some prior information regarding the effect of such a move on her popularity, and the differential impact that such a proposal might have on a number of different "constituencies" that were important to her continued effectiveness, she commissions a survey to study the issue. Depending on the number and complexity of the populations (constituencies) of interest, this survey could take many forms, but let's begin with a simple case.

Suppose we wanted to determine the reaction to the tax hike from people of two obvious constituencies, registered Democrats and registered Republicans. To survey and ensure adequate coverage of both subpopulations, (1) the list of registered voters in the state (the sampling frame) could be divided into Democratic and Republican strata, (2) some sampling fraction (say, 1%) decided upon, (3) the appropriate number of people for the sample (in this case, 1% of the total number of registered Democratic and Republican voters) randomly chosen from the combined lists, and (4) the resulting sample polled.[4] Because the same sampling fraction is employed for both strata, the sample is a proportionate stratified *random sample* (i.e., an "epsem" design). Note that in this approach, the proportion of Democrats and Republicans is approximately the same in both the population and the sample. Thus, if Democratic voters constitute 65% of the population, 65% of the sample would consist of Democratic voters. Proportionate stratified random sampling can increase precision if the stratification variable makes a difference. If Republicans and Democrats react differently to the tax increase idea, their conflicting responses would be treated as error variance had political affiliation not been included as a stratifying variable. Stratifying accounts for the systematic differences associated with party affiliation.

In some instances, a proportionate sampling strategy does not provide a sufficient number of respondents within a stratum to allow for confident statistical analysis. For instance, if the governor wanted to analyze the data of the Republican voters on their own, a 1% sampling fraction of the 35% of the total population who registered as Republicans might not be sufficient to produce a stable estimate. In this instance, a sampling fraction greater than that used to choose Democrats could be used to sample Republicans. This would render the sample a disproportionate stratified sample.[5] The oversampling provides a greater number of respondents on which to base a surer estimate of the population value.

To expand the example, suppose the simple Democratic/Republican categorization was too gross for the governor's purposes, as a more fine-grained voter stratification was desired. To do this, Democrat and Republican voters could be further subdivided by sex and county. The resulting sample, formed by the combination of the selection variables—political party affiliation, sex, and county—using a constant or uniform sampling fraction (again, let us say, 1%), could be surveyed and their data analyzed. The findings would supply a more precise overall estimate of the state's electorate than the simpler approach, but it would be considerably more costly. The sampling operations of this example are diagrammed in Figure 11.2. Note that each stratum (e.g., county level) is made up of various substrata (e.g., county A, B, C). As in the previous example, given the use of the same sampling fraction or proportion from each subpopulation, the sample takes the form of a proportionate stratified random sample.

As noted, in some instances it is wise to employ different sampling fractions among strata. Suppose the governor feels that people of high socioeconomic status (SES) might have a disproportionate influence on the next election's outcome, so it is important that she knows what these affluent voters think of her tax hike idea. To determine this, we might have a different scenario in which the population is stratified according to SES and political party affiliation. (Voter registration lists do not provide SES information, but we might use a rough SES proxy based on voters' home addresses) The stratified subgroups from which the sample is to be drawn for county A might resemble that of Table 11.2. Here, the SES stratum consists of five substrata (upper, upper-middle,

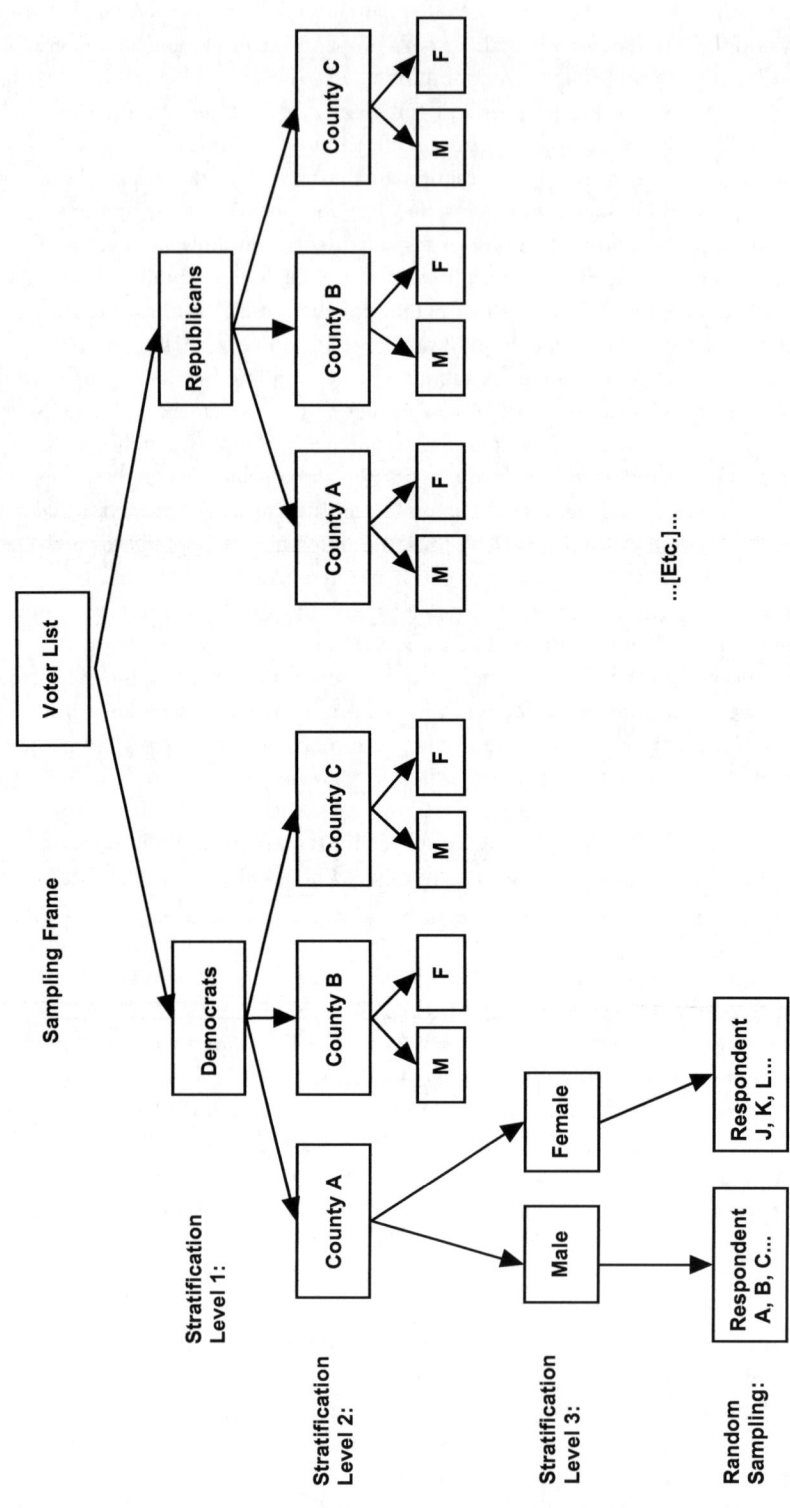

FIGURE 11.2 Schematic diagram of stratification sampling.

TABLE 11.2 State voter population in county A, stratified by party preference and socioeconomic status (SES).

SES	Democratic		Republican	
	Males	Females	Males	Females
Upper	800	1200	3000	1600
Upper-Middle	3000	3600	9000	8000
Middle	20000	28800	31900	19100
Lower-Middle	39000	41800	20000	22000
Lower	25000	24000	3000	4900

middle, lower-middle, or lower SES); the political party stratum consists of two substrata (Democrat or Republican).

As shown in Table 11.2, there are relatively few voters in county A at the upper end of the SES categorization. Yet we suspect that their opinions matter greatly, because these people tend to control the communications media and contribute the lion's share to political campaigns. Because the governor is interested in their reactions, we decide upon a disproportionate sampling strategy. We randomly sample 5% of the potential population in the upper SES categories (i.e., a sample of 100 Democrats—40 men and 60 women, and 230 Republicans—150 men and 80 women), 2.5% of those in the upper-middle strata (165 Democrats and 445 Republicans), and 0.5% of the respondents at the lower end of the income distribution. (As in proportionate stratified sampling, the actual sampling units—respondents, in this case—are chosen randomly, within the constraints imposed by the sampling fraction and the stratification rules.) This approach is called disproportionate stratified (random) sampling because the five subgroups formed by the SES stratification are not proportionately represented across the overall sample. The two highest SES groups are oversampled relative to the other three groups. It is important to note, however, that when the overall precision estimate is calculated, the sample is weighted so as to offset or compensate for the disproportionate oversampling of the two highest SES subgroups. In calculating the overall precision estimate, that is, responses are weighted to redress the imbalance of the sample in such a way as to statistically "remake" the sample into a proportionate stratified sample. The application of sampling weights is elaborated later in this chapter.

Why should the survey researcher bother to stratify? Earlier, we suggested that one compelling reason was to offset the possible selection of unusual or nonrepresentative group of respondents from a subpopulation. Although this nonrepresentativeness is possible, it is unlikely if members of a subpopulation are reasonably well represented in the population. More importantly, proportionate stratification helps ensure that the distribution of respondent units of each group in the sample is the same as that in the population, and this enhances the precision of our estimate. In other words, by ensuring that each of the subpopulations are adequately represented in our sample, we reduce sampling error in our estimates, because unaccounted variance that would have occurred as a result of the categorization variable are now accounted for.

Just as stratification by political party differences enhances the precision of our estimate, so too does stratification on the other factors employed in the examples presented. In general, it is true that the more stratification factors, the greater the precision of the subgroup estimates. In general, stratification adds to precision to the extent that the respondents of different strata characteristically respond differently on the issue under investigation. Thus, returning to our example, if the sample of men and women responded more or less identically to a tax increase proposal, then stratifying on sex would have little effect on precision—the stratification factor would not remove any source of variance. If they responded very differently, however, then stratification would positively affect precision of estimates. The trade-off bears consideration—stratification can be expensive and difficult, so to determine whether it is worth the costs involved, we should first decide whether or not the stratification factor is in some way related *systematically* to the variables under study.

Cluster Sampling

In many research contexts, the available sampling frame does not provide a list of all population members, but rather a location frame consisting of *places* in which population members might be found is available. For example, suppose we wished to sample the parents of public high school students in a large Midwestern city. We are interested in their feelings about the availability of advanced placement courses. The school board is reluctant to give us the list of names of the parents/guardians. Thus, we have no sampling frame, at least initially. We could proceed, nonetheless, by obtaining a detailed map of the city, which listed each block, and then by randomly sampling these natural clusters to use as the sampling frame. In **cluster sampling**, geographic locations (or clusters or segments) are randomly sampled, and all members from the clusters selected are used for the sample. In this method, the sampling frame is identified (say, all city blocks of houses), and from this population, specific clusters (city blocks, in this case) are chosen randomly. Once a cluster is chosen for inclusion in the sample, *all* members of the cluster are surveyed (in our example, all eligible parents of high schoolers within the chosen cluster, or block, would be surveyed). Cluster sampling is classified under the umbrella of random sampling because the clusters are randomly chosen, although all members within the selected clusters are then used for the sample.

Multistage Sampling

In **multistage sampling**, clusters of locations are sampled from a geographical sampling frame (as in cluster sampling), and then (unlike cluster sampling) units within each cluster are sampled as well. As the name of this approach suggests, the sampling process is extended to more than one stage or occasion. To return to our high school example, for a two-stage sample we divide the total city into blocks, and then randomly select some of these blocks for our sample. However, instead of including all members of the chosen blocks (i.e., cluster sampling), we randomly sample from within them. Thus, only members selected from each of the chosen clusters are used. This procedure can be extended to more stages. For example, in a national election survey, we might break the nation into counties, then census tracks, then blocks within the chosen census tracks, and, finally, households within the tracks, and specific voters within the household. Figure 11.3 illustrates the differences between cluster and multistage sampling. As presented in the figure, random sampling takes place exactly once in cluster sampling, with clusters being randomly selected, and all individuals within these selected locations are included. Multistage sampling involves two stages, and the random sampling takes place more than once, at the cluster level and again at the participant level of the selected clusters.

A potential distorting influence in cluster or multistage sampling is that clusters generally do not contain the same number of potential respondents. For instance, in our high school example, not all of the selected city blocks contain the same number of parents. This problem is exacerbated when the cluster sizes are of great variability, as would be the case when counties are used as the primary sampling units in a statewide or national sample, and individual households are the elements to be sampled. In such cases, potential respondents do not all have an equal probability of selection, and the precision of the resulting estimates is thereby jeopardized.

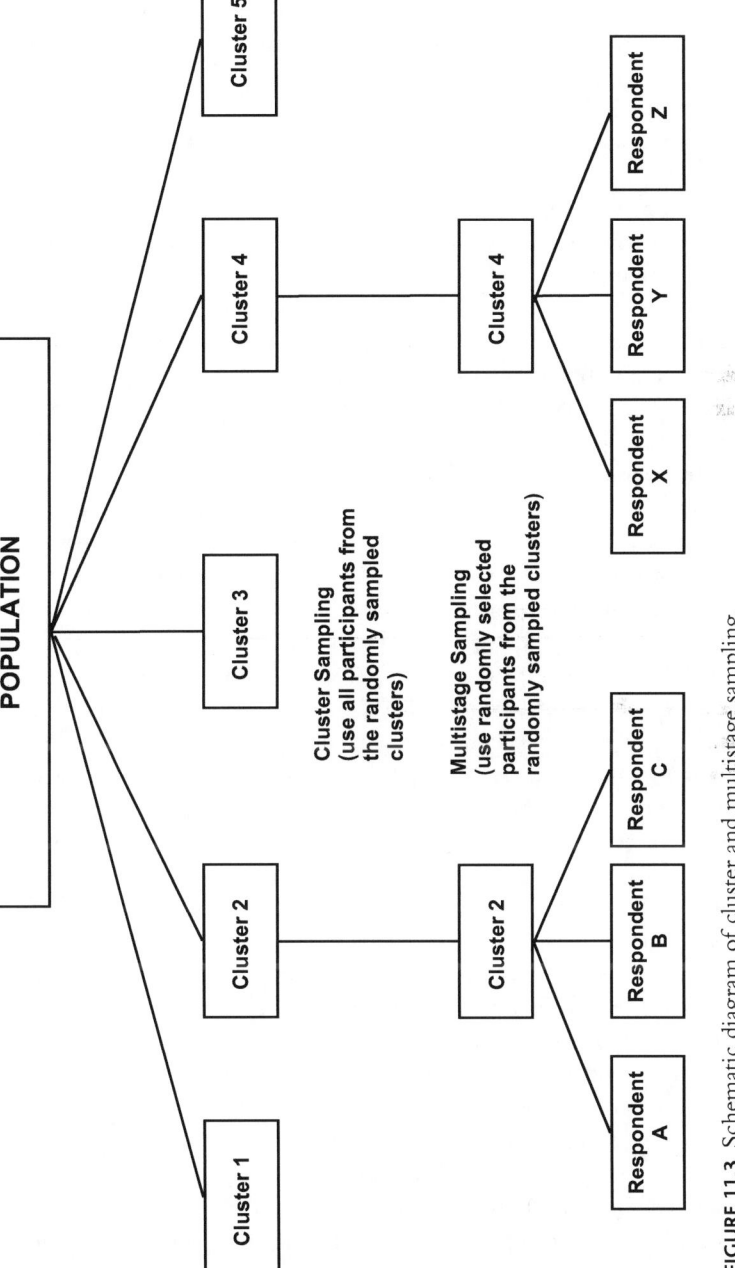

FIGURE 11.3 Schematic diagram of cluster and multistage sampling.

An approach known as *probability proportional to size sampling* (PPS) has been developed to solve this potential problem. Kalton (1983; also Levy & Lemeshow, 2008) has discussed the details of this technique; for our purposes, it is sufficient to understand that the PPS sampling approach ensures that the likelihood of selection in a cluster or multistage sample is the same for all potential sampling units (or respondents) no matter the size of the cluster from which they are drawn. Under such constraints, the sample is an epsem one, and the standard approaches for estimating precision may be used. Generally PPS sampling is preferred in cluster or multistage sampling designs.

Multistage sampling is particularly useful when the population to be studied is spread over a large geographic area. Suppose we wished to use face-to-face interviews to determine the proportion of a state's inhabitants who used some form of state-financed social service. Using a multistage sampling approach, we could use the state's natural segmentation into counties, and randomly select a given number of counties for the sample. Then, we could randomly select towns within each of the chosen counties, neighborhoods within the towns, and blocks within the neighborhoods. Then we could list the dwellings within the blocks, and (in the case of multistage sampling) sample individual respondents within the dwellings. Notice that by using this approach, there is no necessity for constructing a sampling frame of individuals, which in many instances would be prohibitively expensive, if not impossible. Instead, our interviewers need only learn the number of potential respondents within a household selected for sampling, and then select among respondents by some prespecified scheme. Some survey samplers, for example, use the "birthday" rule: The person whose birthday is closest to the date of the interview is chosen as the respondent. In research situations of this type, multistage sampling offers a practical alternative to simple (or stratified) random sampling, which requires a sampling frame of potential respondents before the initiation of the research. However, like cluster sampling, it does require a sampling frame of locations. The multistage sampling approach usually does not provide estimates that are as precise, and this is especially true if the clusters are homogeneous on the issues tapped in the survey.

To illustrate this point, suppose that the citizens of certain counties were impoverished relative to those of others (and hence, were more likely to make use of the social services offered by the state). If, by chance, these poorer counties were overrepresented in the sample, the survey would provide inaccurate estimates. A relative overabundance of poorer counties would suggest that more people statewide made use of the state's services than was actually the case, whereas the opposite (though equally erroneous) conclusion would be drawn if the richer counties were inadvertently overrepresented.

With cluster and multistage sampling approaches, the precision of the survey estimates thus depends on the distributional characteristics of the traits of interest. If the population clusters are relatively homogeneous on the issues that are central to the survey, with high heterogeneity between clusters, the results obtained through this method will be less precise than those obtained from a random sample of the same size. However, if the population clusters are relatively heterogeneous (i.e., if the individual clusters provide a representative picture of the overall population), multistage sampling will generate estimates as precise as simple random sampling of respondents. Notice that the heterogeneity of a sample has different implications for cluster and stratified sampling. With stratified sampling, increased heterogeneity within strata results in a *loss* of precision—the respondents (or sampling units) within strata ideally should be as similar as possible. With cluster or multistage sampling, however, increased heterogeneity within clusters results in *increased* precision.

The stratification of clusters in advance of selection is often employed to offset the homogeneity problem. Thus, counties can be stratified by population size, unemployment level, and so on, using statistics from the U.S. Census or Department of Labor. In the high school example, homerooms could be stratified by grade, male/female ratio, and proportion of students receiving free lunches.

By this pre-stratification process, we help ensure that clusters from different strata are represented approximately equally in the sample.

Two-phase sampling. In two-phase (or double) sampling, all respondents (who might have been chosen by any sampling method, such as simple random, cluster, or multistage sampling) complete the basic survey. Then, either concurrently or some time thereafter, additional information is sought from the previously selected respondents. In two-phase sampling, two (or more) surveys are conducted: The basic survey, in which all participate, and the auxiliary survey, which employs a specified subsample of the main sample. Two-phase sampling is useful and widely used. The United States Bureau of the Census, for example, has used two-phase sampling in its population counts for more than 40 years. In the census, standard data are collected from all households, but some households are randomly selected to be asked to provide considerably more information in the form of a more extensive survey.

Perhaps the most important use of two-phase sampling is in developing stratification factors. When the auxiliary data are collected subsequent to (rather than concurrent with) the basic survey information, the initial survey can be used to create stratification factors. Often in two-phase sampling, numerically rare groups that cannot be identified on the basis of readily available information are sought for study. On the basis of the information obtained in the first-phase sample, the sought-after group is identified and usually disproportionately oversampled, with a lesser sampling fraction being used for the remaining population. In this way, "rare" respondent groups can be identified in sufficient numbers to allow for their study.[6]

Panel Surveys

The "multi-survey" form of the multiphase sampling method must be distinguished from the panel survey, in which a prespecified sample of respondents (a panel) is surveyed repeatedly over time. In panel surveys, the respondent sample is not successively "whittled down" over the course of the sampling phases, as is characteristic of multiphase sampling. The purpose of the panel survey is to assess the individual changes that might occur in the knowledge, opinions, or perceptions of the respondent sample over the course of time. Panel surveys have proved especially useful in public opinion contexts, in which the performance of a political figure is monitored over time, in surveys of voter preference (e.g., Rahn, Krosnick, & Breuning, 1994), and adolescent drug use (e.g., Crano, Siegel, Alvaro, Lac, & Hemovich, 2008). See Blalock (1985) for a discussion of some of the applications and methodological difficulties that panel designs can involve. Given careful sampling, panel surveys can provide a sensitive index of the mood of the entire nation. Indeed, panel surveys have proved to be very powerful tools in predicting the shifting allegiances of the electorate and the consequences of such shifts on the outcomes of state and national elections.

Nonrandom Sampling

The probability sampling approaches discussed so far serve the primary goal of obtaining a sample intended to be optimally representative of a targeted population by using some form of random selection mechanism (Henry, 1990). Extending results from a specific sample to a broader population is not the primary concern when using nonrandom sampling. Usually in nonrandom sampling, participants are obtained in any way possible so that an adequate sample size and sufficient statistical power is achieved. Unlike random sampling strategies, some type of sampling frame is unavailable or unobtainable by the researcher. Thus, nonrandom sampling procedures sacrifice precision of estimates for the sake of reducing recruitment costs.

Although generalizability of results to the larger targeted population is typically uncertain with nonrandom approaches, data derived from such samples are more informative than had no information been collected at all. As part of the larger scientific enterprise, the hope is that the study results would be corroborated subsequently by other researchers, through cross-validation or replications using different (and perhaps better) samples with varying characteristics. Nonrandom samples are typical not only in the social sciences but also in life and medical sciences as well. For instance, in biomedical research a new antidepressant drug may be tested on a volunteer sample consisting of mostly older women. Based on this sample, the results might show that it is an effective drug, which meets FDA approval, and it is released into the market. The volunteer sample is likely not reflective of the typical health status and demographic characteristics of the larger population of people suffering from depression. But delaying the release of this drug to others who may benefit, simply for the sake of external validity, probably is unwise. After the drug has been on the market, other researchers might come along to evaluate whether its efficacy holds in other samples, such as young men and those with high cholesterol. These later studies may find that the antidepressant is effective for young men, but ineffective for those with high cholesterol.

To illustrate generalizability issues stemming from nonrandom sampling, suppose that you are hired by a large shopping mall to conduct a customer loyalty survey. Mall executives inform you that the targeted population is all customers who shop at this particular mall. As a sampling frame listing of all shoppers is unavailable, you administer the survey on a Sunday morning as people are passing through the food court. This sample would likely be biased in several ways. Most likely, the questionnaire is administered primarily to individuals who are flashing smiles, walking at a leisurely pace, and without screaming children—as they are less likely to decline. Because you collected responses on a Sunday morning, the sample might comprise less religious customers. Perhaps these customers may be more loyal and frequent customers than the typical shopper at this mall. Moreover, as the study was conducted near the food court, the sample may overrepresent shoppers with stronger appetites and those shopping at stores located in the area. Thus, the estimate of loyalty scores is likely to overestimate that of the typical shopper at this mall.

Clearly, nonrandom sampling methods are limited in external validity. However, they are widely used, particularly for non-experimental research where correlations between variables are of interest, so let us consider three approaches that are used commonly. They are convenience sampling, snowball sampling, and quota sampling.

Convenience Sampling

In **convenience sampling**, the sample consists of people most readily accessible or willing to be part in the study. Volunteers or students in introductory psychology course are commonly employed convenience samples. Convenience samples using undergraduate students are especially common in the social sciences. Undergraduate students are not representative of the population at large. They are not even representative of people their age, as those who attend college are characteristically different (e.g., IQ, SAT scores, socioeconomic status) from those who do not. Furthermore, the use of undergraduates at a particular school is unlikely to be representative of all college students in general. For example, students attending a private liberal arts college may differ in many respects from students attending public research universities. College student samples might not even be reflective of the student body, as freshman students may be overrepresented in introductory courses from which such samples typically are derived.

Despite the potential of the Internet as a tool to sample individuals from all walks of life, most research collected through this format also makes use of convenience samples. Even if everyone who visits a website is invited to participate in a brief survey, those who click on a link to comply with the request are more prone to be regular visitors of that particular website, have an interest in the particular survey topic, and tend to have more free time to participate.

Using a convenience sample, Hazan and Shaver (1987) examined interpersonal relationship styles with a quiz posted in a local newspaper, the *Rocky Mountain News*. The questions were printed in the Lifestyles section with a captivating headline, "Tell us about the love of your life." Readers were asked to choose which of three categorical descriptions best described their feelings about romantic love. The 620 respondents who mailed in responses were subsequently classified into one of the three categories of romantic attachment styles: 56% secure (i.e., comfortable with intimacy), 25% avoidant (e.g., disliked intimacy), and 19% anxious/ambivalent (worried about intimacy). The results of this convenience sample are unlikely to reflect the population of all people who have had a romantic relationship. It probably was not representative of newspaper readers in general, or even the readership of this local paper. As the headline concerned personal relationships and was posted in the Lifestyles section, it was not startling to find that more than two-thirds of the respondents were female. Convenience samples are suggestive, but far from definitive. Even so, since Hazan and Shaver's seminal study, other investigations examining the distribution of attachment styles, using different sources of recruitment and demographically different samples, have supported the findings from the original study. In fact, using a nationally representative sample, Mickelson, Kessler, and Shaver (1997) supported the original results and found that that the most common romantic attachment style was secure (59%), followed by avoidant (25%), and then anxious (11%).

Snowball Sampling

In **snowball sampling**, initially sampled participants are asked to contact and recruit others in their social network. These new recruits in turn are asked to invite additional members, and so forth. Those who personally know initially recruited individuals will have a greater likelihood of being included in the sample. Snowball sampling might be helpful if the researcher wishes to take a relatively hands-off recruitment approach, and might also be a valuable route to recruit individuals belonging to marginalized or hard-to-obtain groups. An investigation on posttraumatic stress disorder obtained a sizable sample of defectors from North Korea by first contacting South Korean welfare and vocational agencies and support groups (Chung & Seo, 2007). These initially recruited defectors were asked to invite other defectors they personally knew to be involved in the research. Snowball sampling also has been profitably used to investigate the connection between childhood traumas and suicide attempts using a beginning sample of homeless street youth (Hadland et al., 2012).

To induce participants to dig through their personal contacts and invite friends and families to serve in a research project, it is wise to offer financial incentives. A sample furnished through snowball sampling tends to yield a final sample of participants who are more similar to each other than would be expected by chance. Participants recruited through snowball sampling will tend to have acquaintances who tend to be personally alike (e.g., politically, racially, living in the same city, etc.) compared to typical members of the intended larger population. This makes sense, as we are more likely to be friends with people who are similar to us and are geographically closer.

Quota Sampling

In **quota sampling**, members are sampled nonrandomly until a predefined number of participants for each of a specified set of subgroups is achieved. It differs from stratified sampling, which requires a listing of all members from each subpopulation, and which is used to select members from each subsample. This ensures that an adequate number of people belonging to relatively rare subpopulations are included as part of the study, to yield more precise subsample estimates. As a list of all subpopulation members of the targeted population is not always obtainable, the researcher might resort to quota sampling.

In some types of quota sampling, quotas are set relative to a rough guess of the subgroup proportion in the population. In other types of quota sampling, a number is set to achieve sufficient statistical power for each of the subgroups. Using this latter approach, for example, a researcher using quota sampling might wish to test the average time it takes men and women to solve a Sudoku puzzle, with the targeted population being math professors. To recruit participants, the investigator stands outside the math department at several universities and solicits respondents. Quota sampling is used, as math professors are predominantly males. After a day of data collection, the researcher may have administered the puzzle task to 50 male math professors, but to only 10 female math professors. Thus, sampling comes to a halt *for men* as the quota has been satisfied, but recruitment continues for women until the number in that subgroup hits 50. In this scenario, the investigator is not concerned with female and male math professors proportional to the gender distribution of math professors in the targeted population, but rather the mean scores in terms of minutes to solve the puzzle as a function of gender. By setting a quota to ensure an adequate number of members of a limited or rare subgroup, the calculation of the subgroup estimates will be more stable.

More Sampling Issues

Sampling Frame

As has been noted throughout this chapter, some listing of the population must be available to obtain a representative sample of a population, and this listing is called the sampling frame. In simple random sampling the frame is a listing of all the individual population units (or respondents), whereas in cluster or multistage sampling the initial listing involves the clusters that contain all the population units (or respondents).

Two types of sampling frames are commonly employed, *sampling frames of people* and *sampling frames of locations*. The first of these consists of a listing of all of the individuals of a specified population—the students of a university, the list of registered voters of a county or precinct, all subscribers of a magazine, members of a professional organization, and so on. Such lists are convenient and can prove useful for sample selection. However, possible limitations of the list must be acknowledged. For example, suppose that we obtained a list of all of the subscribers to *Fortune Magazine*. Would it be legitimate to use this list as the sampling frame for a survey? Of course it would, if we were concerned with estimating characteristics, beliefs, or behaviors of this particular *population of subscribers*. It would be an inappropriate frame to represent the U.S. population, because the subscribers to this periodical are, on average, considerably wealthier and better educated than the typical citizen. The sampling frame needs to provide a complete coverage of the population to which inferences are to be made. Kish (1965) has provided an extended discussion of factors that influence the quality of sampling frames.

Less obvious are the biases associated with using telephone directories as our sampling frame, a convenient, though not entirely satisfactory, sampling tactic. First of all, Blumberg and Luke (2011) estimated that nearly 36% of American homes did not have a landline, and of those that did, approximately 25% of them had unlisted numbers. Thus, it is dangerous to assume that a sample based on names drawn randomly from a telephone directory is representative of the general population. Too many potential systematic differences (poverty, mobility, differential needs for privacy, latent paranoia, etc.) between those with and without telephones, and between listed and unlisted subscribers, make such a practice risky. The technique of random digit dialing, discussed later in this chapter, presents one way of offsetting the problem of unlisted telephone subscribers, but it does not address the possibility that people who have telephone landlines may be systematically different from those who do not.

A sampling frame of locations consists of using a detailed map of a specific physical environment—a city or town, a precinct, ward, or neighborhood. Cluster or multistage sampling is used with location sampling frames. Using maps to define the list of clusters in a sampling frame is common in surveys that seek to cover reasonably wide geographic areas. In general, however, although their use is more difficult and demanding than survey designs that employ population lists of people as the sampling frame, in many situations no adequate population list is available. Under these circumstances, maps become a useful sampling alternative.

Sample Size

The question of sample size must be addressed when developing a survey. How many respondents must we sample to attain reasonable precision when estimating population values? Before we can answer this question, we must answer a series of other questions, and once these issues are decided upon, the sample size more or less defines itself. As in all other areas of survey sampling, the decision regarding the size of the sample involves trade-offs, most of which concern the complementary issues of cost and precision.

It seems intuitively plausible that the size of the sampling fraction would be an important determinant of the adequacy of the sample. Such is not the case, however. When the underlying population is large, precise sample results can be obtained even when the sampling fraction is quite small. What matters most is the *absolute size* of the sample, rather than the size of the sample *relative to* the size of the population. A moment's reflection on the formula for the standard error of a simple random sample will show why this is so. This formula demonstrates that the size of the sample, not the sampling fraction, determines precision.

The first decision that must be made in determining the survey sample size concerns the amount of error we are willing to tolerate. The greater the precision desired, the larger the sample needed. Thus, if we wish to obtain extremely precise findings—results that will estimate underlying population values with a high degree of accuracy—it must be understood that we will need to sample more respondents. Cost and precision go hand in hand. Suppose we wish to estimate the proportion of the population of those who possess a specific trait or characteristic, or who hold a given belief or value. Having made the decision regarding the degree of precision necessary for our purposes, we must make a rough estimate of the proportion of the population that possess the trait or belief. For example, we might want to estimate the proportion of a city's electorate that would vote for the Democratic gubernatorial candidate. To estimate the necessary sample size with a defined degree of precision, we would first have to estimate this percentage. Suppose that prior elections, or recent, informal surveys indicated that Democratic candidates could be expected to garner approximately 58% of the vote in the city. Having decided upon the necessary precision, we could determine the necessary sample size for a simple random sample by the formula,

$$n = p(1 - p)/(S.E.)^2,$$

where n = the necessary sample size,
 p = the estimated proportion of the city's population who plan to vote Democratic, and
 S.E. = the sampling or standard error of the sample proportion (i.e., the amount of error we can tolerate).

Applying this formula, assuming a standard error of 5% as acceptable, would yield the following:

$$n = .58(.42)/.05^2, \text{ or, } n = 97+ \text{ respondents are necessary.}$$

It is unlikely in most contexts that a standard error of this magnitude would be acceptable—it results in a 95% confidence interval with a margin of error of +/− 5%.[7] This probability represents the margin of error around the estimate that includes the "true" percentage. In other words, we can be reasonably sure that the actual electoral results would fall within (plus or minus) 5 percentage points of our estimate. Doubling the standard error roughly provides the confidence interval around the estimate.

This example provides a useful point of contrast for later calculations. It is informative to manipulate the two crucial components in the equation to determine the effects of differing precision needs and the influence of the accuracy of the proportion in estimating the population value on sample size. Suppose that instead of a standard error of 5%, the governor decided that no more than a 2% standard error was acceptable. This is a more reasonable choice, as it results in a 95% confidence interval with a margin of error of +/− 2%. In this case, assuming the same 58% favorableness estimate, the size of the simple random sample necessary for greater precision in the sample estimate reflecting the population value would change from 97+ people to 610. That is, 610 respondents would be needed to arrive at an estimate with a 2% standard error, assuming that 58% of the population favored the Democrat party. If an even smaller standard error of 1% were sought, as might be desired in a close race, more than 2,400 respondents would have to be surveyed. Again, the interplay of recruitment cost and precision of estimate is obvious.

A word of caution is required at this point. The calculations of the size of a sample necessary to estimate a population parameter at a given level of precision will hold only if the sampling procedure itself is properly executed. If our basic sampling technique is flawed, then the number of respondents sampled will not matter much—the results of the sample will not accurately reflect population values. A classic example of this observation is provided in a real-life case history that many think set back the cause of survey research for many years. This case, an often-told example in elementary sampling courses, occurred in 1936. At that time a popular magazine, the *Literary Digest,* attempted a national poll to estimate who the electorate would choose as its next president, Franklin D. Roosevelt, the Democratic candidate running for his second term, or Alf Landon, the Republican nominee.

The results of the poll, printed in bold headlines at the beginning of the October 31, 1936, edition of the *Digest,* read:

Landon, 1,293,669; Roosevelt, 972,897
Final Returns in The Digest's Poll of Ten Million Voters

Obviously, the sample size used by the *Digest* was more than respectable—it consisted of more than ten million people! Yet, the *Digest's* estimate was not only wrong, it was laughably off base. Despite the *Digest's* prediction, Roosevelt ended up with 523 electoral votes to Landon's 3! As a result, the headlines of the November 14 *Digest* read,

WHAT WENT WRONG WITH THE POLLS?
None of the Straw Votes Got Exactly the Right Answer—Why?

What did go wrong? Obviously, we cannot fault the *Digest* on the basis of sample size. But just as obviously, the poll's results were disastrously off base. How did a respected magazine, which had conducted similar polls in the past with a high degree of success, make such a blunder? A brief review of the sampling procedures the *Digest* employed supplies some insight into these problems—and illustrate the fact that sample size is not sufficient to guarantee accuracy of population estimates.

To perform their survey, the *Literary Digest* used telephone books and its membership list as the sampling frame. From their list, the *Digest* randomly sampled a large number of potential respondents, and sent them a "ballot" that was to be returned by mail. In retrospect, there are two glaringly obvious problems with this procedure: First, in 1936, the proportion of the populace that owned telephones was not nearly as great as it is today. Those who did own phones were among the wealthy, a group that traditionally votes Republican. What's more, only 20% of the mailed ballots were returned. Again, there is evidence that suggests that more wealthy, better educated people would do so. (In fact, the *Digest*'s own past polling experience had demonstrated that this was the case.) As such, the *Digest*'s sample was fatally flawed—it grossly oversampled those who, on the basis of important demographic indicators, would be likely to vote for a Republican presidential candidate, and grossly under-sampled those who would likely vote Democratic. Under these circumstances, it is little wonder that the *Digest* predicted the Republican candidate would receive a landslide 57% of the vote when, in fact, he received only a fraction of this proportion. The kinds of errors made by the *Literary Digest* are the stuff of which sampling legends are made.

Nonresponse

Attributable at least in part to the *Literary Digest* fiasco is the problem of dropouts or nonrespondents. Because sampling theory is based on probability theory, the mathematics that underlies sampling inference assumes *perfect* response rates. Otherwise, sampling weights must be derived and applied to the estimates. As Moser and Kalton (1972, p. 166) observed, "The theory is based essentially on the textbook situation of 'urns and black and white balls', and, while in agricultural and industrial sampling the practical situation corresponds closely to its theoretical model, the social scientist is less fortunate. He has to sample from an urn in which some of the balls properly belonging to it happen not to be present at the time of selection, while others obstinately refuse to be taken from it."

Survey researchers have devised many ingenious methods to reduce nonresponse in data collection. In mail surveys, for example, cash incentives to participate and follow-ups sent to those who do not return the survey within a specified period of time have been shown to have a positive effect on the response rate (e.g., Church, 1993; Griffin et al., 2011; Trussel & Lavrakas, 2004). In addition, considerable care is exercised in developing questionnaires of reasonable length, in personalizing the survey for the respondent, in guaranteeing anonymity, etc. In general, these tactics seem to be effective in raising response rates (Heerwegh, Vanhove, Matthijs, & Loosveldt, 2005; Muñoz-Leiva, Sánchez-Fernández, Montoro-Ríos, & Ibáñez-Zapata, 2010).

In telephone and face-to-face interviews, we encounter problems somewhat different from those of the mail interview. In phone and face-to-face research, the researcher must distinguish "not-at-homes" (NAHs) from refusals. In the case of NAHs, survey researchers employ repeated attempts at different times of day to contact the potential respondent. With refusals, different tactics are used. More established survey research organizations employ people with the descriptive job title of "refusal converters" to attempt to persuade recalcitrant respondents. In general, in the typical phone survey or face-to-face interview, most attempts to reduce the refusal rate focus on the means to gain "entry" or to develop rapport (see Chapter 13, on interviewing, for an extended discussion of these issues). Many phone surveys, for example, attempt to induce respondents' compliance by presenting a set of nonthreatening, impersonal, and innocuous questions at the beginning of the survey. Having obtained the respondent's initial buy-in, the interviewer then moves on to less innocuous disclosures, which people often are reluctant to provide at the outset of an interview.

When the chosen methods to secure cooperation fail, as they sometimes do, survey analysts move to a different strategy, which involves the attempt to reduce the biasing impact of those who have been selected for the sample but who are not present at the time the interviewer tries to contact them, or who refuse to cooperate with specific requests for information when they are interviewed. It is important to realize that these attempts are not *solutions* to the nonresponse problem, but rather means of attempting to reduce its biasing effect on the survey estimates. Detailing the technical aspects of these approaches is beyond the mission of this chapter (Groves, 2006; Singer, 2006); however, some of the more common techniques conceptualize the response/nonresponse distinction as a category on which members of the population can be stratified. If the researcher can obtain some information about the nonrespondents and compare it with that of the "respondent" stratum, then estimates of the probable response of the nonrespondents can be developed.

Other approaches (e.g., Cochran, 1977) make no inferences about the probable responses of the nonrespondents, but rather determine what the outcome of the survey would be if all of the nonrespondents had answered one way or the other (e.g., the technique asks, for example, "What if, had they participated, *all* the nonrespondents said that they planned to vote for—or against—the incumbent?"). This approach allows the researcher to draw boundaries on the percentage of the total sample likely to vote for the incumbent. However, if the number of nonrespondents is sizeable, this range can be so great that the survey has no practical utility. There are many examples of correction approaches of this type available in the sampling literature—probably because the problem is so ubiquitous. The researcher interested in gaining the insights necessary to apply these solutions to his or her sampling problem, or to invent a solution that will work for a particular problem that might be encountered, is encouraged to consult this literature (e.g., Groves, 2006; Massey & Tourangeau, 2013), or to read later sections of this chapter devoted specifically to the issue of missing data and how to handle them.

Applying Weights to Datasets

Due to the planned or unplanned oversampling or under-sampling of particular types of individuals (e.g., men, women, Democrats, Hispanic-Americans, etc.) for a study, the researcher might obtain a final sample that is not representative of the population (Meier et al., 2013; Pfeffermann, 1996; Hahs-Vaughn & Lomax, 2006). Weights are applied to estimates to undo this nonrepresentative sampling. After the sample data are collected, weights are statistically derived to take the sampling design into account and to adjust for any remaining imbalances in proportions of various subgroups between the sample and targeted population. The most common type of weighting variable is called a *general sampling weight,* which is used to calibrate the demographic characteristics (e.g., age, gender, race, marital status, socioeconomic status) of the sample to a *known* population. Known population demographics are based on information obtained, for example, from the last U.S. Census or a previously conducted representative study. This demographic adjustment will yield statistical estimates that are more representative of the general population. Additional types of weights also may be used to rectify other types of sampling problems. Participant nonresponse or attrition occurs when members of an identifiable subgroup are underrepresented in the sample because they refuse to participate at rates different from other groups. For instance, data may indicate that sampled participants over the age of 65 have a higher likelihood of refusal, perhaps because they are more distrustful of interviewers. Underrepresentation can be offset by judicious use of sampling weights.

An example will illustrate the practical utility of sampling weights. A researcher uses a multistage sampling design for a public opinion poll about the President's job performance. However, the final sample produces disproportionally fewer Hispanic-American respondents than expected, based on data from the U.S. Census. Specifically, the sample shows that 12% of respondents are Hispanic, but the most recent census shows that Hispanics comprise 16% of the population. Although appearing to be a relatively minor discrepancy, statistical analyses without application of weights might supply misleading results. Based on the sample, if the estimate shows the President received an average job performance rating of 7.0 out of 10.0 (across all respondents regardless of race), the opinions of Hispanics will be underrepresented in this overall score. Possibly, Hispanics typically give a higher job approval rating of the President than that of other racial groups. Through application of a weighting variable, the proportion of this racial group in the sample could be calibrated to the known proportion. After weighting, the estimate might now reveal an overall sample estimate of 7.5 out of 10.0 for the President's job rating. Weighting the estimate by the proper population proportion ensures that Hispanics contributed 16% to the overall mean score, commensurate with their actual numbers in the population. Applying weights takes advantage of the complexities of the sampling design and yields greater precision of estimates, with stronger external validity.

Weights are often applied when researchers analyze data from large public data sets. A valuable resource containing a vast storehouse of searchable public datasets is the Inter-university Consortium for Political and Social Science Research (ICSPR): www.icpsr.umich.edu/. Collected from more than 130 countries, this is the largest repository of social science databases, containing more than 17,000 datasets across all disciplines in the social sciences. The corresponding manuals and documentation, which describe many of the sampling plans detailed in this chapter, can be downloaded from the website. Documentation also describes how to apply the weighting variables found in the datasets. Free statistical software that takes into account sampling weights to produce greater precision of estimates is WesVar, available from www.westat.com/Westat/expertise/information_systems/WesVar/wesvar_downloads.cfm.

Types of Survey Studies

Random Digit Dialing

Over the years, the use of the telephone as a data collection method for surveys has increased markedly. The technique of random digit dialing was developed for telephone survey sampling. Although telephone surveys have been used for many years (e.g., Cooper, 1964; Troldahl & Carter, 1964), they have recently received intense critical attention—and this attention, in turn, has resulted in the refinement and further development of the telephone method of data collection. Random digit dialing was developed to overcome the frame deficiency of unlisted numbers in the telephone directory. As was noted, about 25% of U.S. residential telephone subscribers are unlisted, and it has been estimated that in some large metropolitan areas as many as 50% of all residential phones are unlisted. Thus, using the telephone directory as a sampling frame can result in considerable bias, especially if those who choose not to list their phone numbers are in some ways systematically different from those who do (see Blumberg & Luke, 2011).

To overcome this limitation, survey researchers developed a number of ingenious solutions involving *random digit dialing* (RDD), some of which, unfortunately, have some rather major practical deficiencies. The simplest random digit dialing approach calls for the use of a random number generator to develop lists of telephone numbers. The ensuing numbers are the random sample of those to be called. The problem with this approach is that most of the numbers generated in this manner are not in use, are fax numbers, or are not assigned to residential dwellings. Glasser and Metzger (1972) estimated that fewer than 20% of randomly generated numbers result in usable responses. When 80% of a survey researcher's calls are futile, the costs of the study are intolerable.[8] An alternative scheme makes use of the list of all published numbers in combination with a randomization process. The option begins with the random selection of telephone numbers from the phone directory. Then, the last two digits of each of the chosen numbers are deleted and replaced by random numbers. This approach has the advantage of assuring the survey researcher that the numbers employed in the study are potentially in use, and this in turn dramatically increases the proportion of usable numbers, from approximately 20%, when purely random numbers are used, to approximately 50%. However, this approach has disadvantages because directory-listed prefixes may be biased in some way—and 50% is still an unacceptably high proportion of useless calls. Kunz and Fuchs (2012) have suggested ways of improving the odds of reaching eligible respondents using RDD, but the issue of nonresponse remains troublesome, especially given the practice of call screening.

Telephone vs. Face-to-Face Interviews

Use of telephones to conduct surveys was seen as an improvement over the "standard" model involving face-to-face interviews. The most obvious reason for the move to phone interviewing is obvious—phone surveys can result in substantial savings of interviewer time and research funds. In fact, many large-scale national surveys today are done by telephone—the costs of doing otherwise would be prohibitive for most organizations. From the minute of its first use, researchers have debated the validity of telephone surveys relative to the more standard model. In early attempts to validate the telephone survey approach, researchers compared their phone results with those obtained under the standard face-to-face conditions. If the results were similar, a vote was cast in favor of the telephone approach by virtue of its efficiency and cost savings. Differences between the two survey modes often were taken as evidence of the failure of the phone survey to produce valid results. This interpretation is based on assumptions that rely more on tradition (we've always done it this way) than logic. Consider a survey in which sensitive issues are the focus of inquiry— respondents' use of illegal drugs, other illegal acts, risky sexual practices, and so on. In which context is the researcher likely to gain an honest answer to the following question:

> How many times in the last year have you driven while intoxicated?

Arguably, a person speaking anonymously over the phone might be more willing to give an honest answer to this question (assuming the answer was more than never) than a respondent facing his or her questioner across the kitchen table. The quasi-anonymity of the phone conversation would seem to promote more honest answers to sensitive questions. Hoppe and her colleagues (2000) suggest that this intuition is correct, as do McAuliffe, Geller, LaBrie, Paletz, and Fournier (1998). Both studies revealed small differences in respondents' answers to questions in telephone vs. face-to-face interviews, and when differences occurred, they suggested that the more valid answers were obtained over the phone because higher rates of socially undesirable behaviors were reported. Boekeloo, Schamus, Simmens, and Cheng (1998) found higher rates of reporting for both drug abuse and sexual encounters in their sample of early teenagers using a telephone vs. face-to-face interview, and concluded that the telephone survey was an acceptable means of obtaining valid data. This conclusion was reinforced by research of Meyer and colleagues, who successfully sampled gay and lesbian respondents using brief screening interviews in RDD samples (Meyer & Colten, 1999; Meyer, Rossano, Ellis, & Bradford, 2002). Based on findings of this kind, Noble, Moon, and McVey (1998) touted the use of random digit dialing for large-scale policy research, and suggested that the technique produced results that did not appear less valid than those derived from more standard forms of interviewing. Greenfield, Midanik and Rogers (2000) agreed and suggested that the telephone survey approaches in general appeared to produce results similar to the more usual interview format. However, as Lavrakas (1993, 1998) suggested in his review of telephone survey methodology, caution should be exercised when using this approach. Because telephone service costs money, surveys making use of the phone, even random digit dialing surveys, systematically under-sample the poor, the undereducated, the disenfranchised, and people of modest educational accomplishment. On some issues, this underrepresentation may produce biased results, whereas on others, these sociodemographic variations may be inconsequential.

Research that acknowledges the response-rate difficulties now encountered in telephone interviewing has reconsidered use of address-based mail surveys (e.g., Link, Battaglia, Frankel, Osborne, & Mokdad, 2008). Whether phone, live face-to-face, or mail surveys ultimately provide the highest quality data is an evolving question, whose answer changes with every passing decade. At one point, the mail survey reigned supreme, then the face-to-face approach captured scientists' favor, and then the random digit dial model became popular. As discussed, these approaches have different strengths—economy, efficiency, likelihood of valid responses given the issue involved, etc.—but these strengths have evolved as time passed. The ultimate choice of technique will depend largely on available resources and the issues under study. The information presented to this point will allow a reasoned choice of method.

Answering Machines and Caller-ID

As phone answering machines and caller ID became an increasingly common feature of most homes, researchers worried that their telephone surveys would fall prey to nonresponse. People would screen calls, they reasoned, and when an unknown caller rang, they would not answer. If this response were common, the sampling design would be destroyed. Are answering machines and caller ID threats to survey research? Early research by Oldendick and Link (1994) investigated this question across nine random digit dial surveys and found that only 2–3% of households used answering machines to screen calls, and Xu, Bates, and Schweitzer (1993) found no differences in response rates for homes with or without answering machines. However, research suggests that call screening has become considerably more common. Tuckel and O'Neill (2002) found that "roughly two-thirds of Caller-ID subscribers . . . report screening either 'always' or 'most of the time'" (p. 30). Respondents with answering machines reported a slightly higher percentage, though some of these respondents also used caller ID. Leaving messages apparently does not enhance rates (Link & Mokdad, 2005), but providing minor incentives does (Homish & Leonard, 2009). Considering the characteristics of those who screen calls raises concerns. Oldendick and Link (1994) found that wealthy, white, educated, young city dwellers were most likely to screen calls. This consistency in demographic characteristics requires that researchers remain vigilant on this issue. Call screening is becoming increasingly frequent (Kempf & Remington, 2007), and if it remains consistently associated with demographic characteristics, survey researchers will face a difficult problem. Some attempts have been made to offset the problem (e.g., Callegaro, McCutcheon, & Ludwig, 2010), but there remains much to learn if the RDD approach is to provide representative data.

Internet Surveys

The development of computer-assisted self-administered interviews (CASAI) has made possible a new forum for survey research, namely, web-based and e-mail surveys. Instead of mailing self-administered questionnaires to potential respondents, respondents can be contacted by e-mail or through the web and directed to a site where they can complete a survey instrument online. This method of reaching a respondent sample has many advantages with respect to cost, time, and effort. The major problem with electronic surveying is sampling representativeness. In most cases, the sampling frame for a web-based survey is the population of people who have access to computers and feel comfortable using them regularly. In this sense, digital surveying approaches are in a similar position to that of telephone surveying in the 1950s, when many households still did not have telephone lines. Even though the number of households with computer access is large and increasing, it is still true that people who have Internet access are likely to be more affluent, more educated, and younger than the population at large. Furthermore, many web-based surveys are conducted on a volunteer basis. A general announcement of the availability of an opportunity to participate in a social survey is posted on popular websites, and interested respondents are instructed how to participate. Not surprisingly, the samples generated by such methods are highly self-selected and probably not typical of the population at large. The use of sites at which potential participants may learn of research opportunities (e.g., Amazon's Mechanical Turk, or the Social Psychology Network) offer even more opportunities for survey researchers, and findings suggest that data collected on these sites are comparable to those obtained in face-to-face research (Buhrmester, Kwang, & Gosling, 2011; Paolacci, Chandler, & Ipeirotis, 2010).

To implement probability-based random sampling for Internet surveys, some research organizations recruit panels of respondents by contacting individuals through standard RDD telephone survey sampling techniques. When potential respondents have been reached by telephone, they are invited to become part of a survey research panel and are provided with the necessary equipment to complete surveys online in exchange for their participation. For example, Knowledge Networks is one organization that has recruited a panel of nearly 100,000 potential respondents in this way and provides panel participants with Internet access via Web TVs. Once individuals are in the panel, they constitute a sampling frame for specific surveys. Random samples of the panel are drawn and are sent electronic messages instructing them to complete a survey on a specified site. This sampling method is initially costly in terms of recruitment and provision of hardware and Internet access, but it produces samples that are comparable in representativeness to those obtained by standard RDD telephone survey methods.

Missing Data

Each sampled person who chooses to participate in an investigation also must decide whether to answer a specific question or not. This creates a different type of nonresponse problem from that discussed earlier. Respondents sometimes answer a survey only partially, skipping over certain questions they do not want to answer. Missing values on a question bring into doubt the representativeness of the sample. Are the responses of those who answered a question representative of those who skipped it? Blank values are referred to as variable *missingness*. Although a variety of events may be responsible for missingness, especially problematic are sensitive questions concerning illegal activities, drug use, and sexual behavior.

Suppose a sizable number of sampled participants skipped an item that asked, "How many sexual partners have you had in your lifetime?" Any combination of these reasons are possible for respondents' failure to answer the question: (a) They had too many partners and were too embarrassed to disclose their high number; (b) They had too few partners and were embarrassed to disclose their low number; (c) They couldn't recall the exact number; (d) They didn't understand the question (e.g., what constituted a "sexual partner?"); or (e) Absolutely no systematic reason, as the skip was due to carelessness. Discovering the reasons underlying missing values is needed to deal with nonresponse bias. Classified according to the extent that nonresponse on one variable can be mathematically inferred from other measured variables, three types of missingness are possible: Missing completely at random, missing at random, and not missing at random (Buhi, Goodson, & Neilands, 2008; Roth, 1994; Schafer & Graham, 2002).

Missing completely at random (MCAR) occurs if the probability of missing responses in a variable is not explained by (or unrelated to) any other variable. Essentially, MCAR suggests that no rhyme or reason exists for why a question was skipped: Every person in the sample, that is, has an equal probability of responding or not responding to that question. Imagine taking an item with complete responses and then randomly deleting responses. The statistical estimate using all of the non-missing responses would be entirely sufficient to represent not only the missing responses but also all the responses had the entire sample answered the question. MCAR data might occur if, due to a printer malfunction, every other paper-and-pencil questionnaire accidentally omitted a particular question. The presumption, of course, is that no systematic difference exists in administration of the two versions to participants. MCAR requires attrition analyses to ensure that the probability of the variable containing missing values is unrelated (or uncorrelated) to any other variable. Suppose that 30% of all respondents did not answer the previous question about the number of lifetime sexual partners. If no systematic difference in variable nonresponse was shown as a function of gender—an equal percentage of males and females skipped the question—this is initial evidence for MCAR. However, this alone is not sufficient. To fully test MCAR requires that we examine the variable with missing values against all other items to ensure independence.

Missing at random (MAR) occurs if the probability of missingness in a variable is *not* random, but its missingness may be fully explained by the other measured variables in the dataset. Unfortunately, the "random" in MAR is a misnomer. It *does not* imply that the variable has an equal probability of whether respondents left the it blank, but that the missingness is manageable as other measured variables in the dataset are entirely sufficient to statistically account for and predict these empty values. Technically, the "random" refers to the deterministic notion that distributions of other variables could be used to probabilistically infer the missing values. Let's continue with the scenario that revealed 30% of participants did not respond to a question on lifetime sexual partners. Perhaps because of societal double standards in reporting, results might show that 50% of females but only 10% of males skipped this question. If the reason for the nonresponse is attributable entirely to the measured variable (e.g., respondents' sex), but not to any unmeasured variable(s) (e.g., social desirability, which was not assessed), then the requirement for MAR is satisfied.

Not missing at random (NMAR) occurs if a variable is not missing at random and its missingness is not explainable by the other measured variables in the dataset (but is explicable by other unmeasured variables). This is the least desirable form of nonresponse in the data, as it is impossible for missing values to be statistically deduced from other measured items in the dataset. NMAR implies that an unknown or unidentified event has caused the missing values. For instance, suppose the 30% of missing responses for the lifetime sexual partners question was attributable to participant social desirability bias. That is, 50% of those with high social desirability needs skipped the question, but only 10% of those low on social desirability needs skipped it. As this survey focused exclusively on questions concerning sexual behaviors, respondents' need for social desirability was never measured, but this was the actual underlying reason for the differential rate of nonresponses. Had the culprit of social desirability bias been measured and identified as the factor that caused differences in response rates, the missingness variable would be reclassified as MAR, and its values could be imputed.

To encourage higher response rates across questions, studies requiring a longer time commitment or interviews in people's homes usually offer some form of financial incentive. Another way to yield higher response rates is to assure confidentiality or anonymity at the onset of the investigation, so that sampled individuals will not avoid particular questions out of fear that their privacy might be jeopardized. Keep in mind that NMAR, MCAR, and MAR apply to single measure variables, so it is possible that a dataset may contain different variables each with different forms of missingness. In theory, the assumption of MCAR or MAR is not always tenable, as important but unidentified reasons exist as to why people might skip or decline a question. Both MCAR and MAR are instances of variable nonresponses said to be largely *ignorable,* a statistical term for a manageable situation, because these blank values could be logically inferred from other measured variables by statistical imputation. If the missing data in are assumed to be MCAR or MAR, the researcher may apply recent statistical software to automatically replace missing values with estimates deduced from the information of other variables in the dataset. The most acceptable missing value imputation techniques are maximum likelihood and multiple imputation (Schafer & Graham, 2002).

Conclusion

Surveys are a ubiquitous feature of everyday life. Their design, and the sampling rules that guide their application, have been developed over the years in social science. A central feature of such research is concerned with the rules that guide the sample of respondents. For many reasons, simple random samples are highly preferred, as their precision can be easily and reliably estimated. Simple random samples require a sampling frame and may be improved by stratifying the sampled group on the basis of theory-relevant variations. Cluster and multistage sampling, often found in large-scale studies of a population, are used when a sampling frame is unavailable. Nonrandom samples are often used, but their generalization to the underlying population is uncertain, and they are best used in hypothesis generation rather than hypothesis testing. Various tactics used to gather survey data—random digit dialing, face-to-face interviews, the Internet, etc.—are common. The construction of the measures used, of the actual questions to be posed in the survey, the manner in which they are delivered, and their general form and content were not considered in this chapter. In the next section, we devote five chapters to issues of this nature.

Questions for Discussion

1. What features distinguish proportionate stratified samples from disproportionate stratified samples? In which research contexts might one be preferred to the other?
2. If we want to conduct a representative national survey with approximately 2,000 respondents, with the goal of obtaining a relatively accurate idea of people's opinions regarding an important national issue, why might it be necessary to oversample certain groups? For the purposes of our survey, why would we want to find, for example, more Caucasian women who are in a committed same-sex relationship with children, compared to any other combinations of demographic characteristics? Why wouldn't we settle for a number of respondents who fit this group that is proportional to the size of the larger population (e.g., if 0.1% of people in the population fit this category, why would we want to recruit more than 2 respondents from our group of 2,000)?
3. You have been hired to predict the outcome of a statewide election. After running a superb survey, following all the rules, you tell your candidate that she has a 2-point lead on the opposition, and the precision of your estimate is +/− 3 points. She wants you to double the precision, so that your estimate is at +/− 1.5 points. Can you do it? If so, what are the cost and design implications of your attempt?

Notes

1. The United States census of the population is an incredibly costly endeavor, and in recent years sophisticated social scientists have argued that a sample would be a cheaper and reliable (though unconstitutional) alternative to the census. Others have argued against the sampling alternative. This chapter will illustrate the advantages and disadvantages of both positions.
2. An issue in the definition of *simple* random sampling is whether sampling is conducted with or without replacement. Following Kalton (1983, p. 10), we take this term to refer to sampling without replacement;

that is, once a unit is included in the sample, he, she, or it is not returned to the population, and thus cannot be chosen again. Sometimes the term simple random sampling without replacement is used to describe this form of sampling, and the term simple random sampling with replacement is used to describe the equivalent technique in which the units sampled at one draw is returned to the population before the next draw is made. In practice, almost all sampling is done without replacement.
3. Random number tables can be found in the appendix sections of most statistics textbooks, and today can be generated on most personal computers with almost any basic statistical software or Internet access.
4. Later in the chapter, we will discuss factors that help the survey researcher decide upon the number of units to employ in the sample. And in the chapters that follow this one, we discuss important considerations regarding the construction of the different types of measuring devices that can be employed in surveys.
5. The overweighting of Republicans could be undone in the statistical analysis of the data.
6. Although we have limited our discussion to a simple two-phase sampling process, the number of ancillary surveys that can be undertaken is limited only by cost considerations—and the patience of the respondents in the sample. When more than two sampling phases are used, the approach is termed multiphase sampling.
7. That is, the estimate is within 10% of the population percentage, with a 95% probability.
8. Jacoby, Young, and Watt (2008) also have commented on the ethical problems of missing data of this type in community level interventions.

References

Blalock, H. M. (1985). *Causal models in panel and experimental designs*. New York: Aldine.

Blumberg, S. J. & Luke, J. V. (December, 2011). *Wireless substitution: Early release of estimates from the National Health Interview Survey, January–June 2011*. National Center for Health Statistics. Retrieved from: www.cdc.gov/nchs/nhis.htm.

Boekeloo, B. O., Schamus, L. A., Simmens, S. J., & Cheng, T. L. (1998). Ability to measure sensitive adolescent behaviors via telephone. *American Journal of Preventive Medicine, 14,* 209–216.

Buhi, E. R., Goodson, P., & Neilands, T. B. (2008). Out of sight, not out of mind: Strategies of handling missing data. *American Journal of Health Behavior, 32,* 83–92.

Buhrmester, M., Kwang, T., & Gosling, S. D. (2011). Amazon's Mechanical Turk: A new source for inexpensive, yet high-quality data? *Perspectives on Psychological Science, 6,* 3–5.

Callegaro, M., McCutcheon, A. L., & Ludwig, J. (2010). Who's calling? The impact of caller ID on telephone survey response. *Field Methods, 22,* 175–191.

Chung, S., & Seo, J. (2007). A study on posttraumatic stress disorder among North Korean defectors and their social adjustment in South Korean. *Journal of Loss and Trauma, 12,* 365–382.

Church, A. H. (1993). Estimating the effect of incentives on mail survey response rates: A meta-analysis. *Public Opinion Quarterly, 57,* 62–79.

Cochran, W. G. (1977). *Sampling techniques*. New York: Wiley.

Cooper, S. L. (1964). Random sampling by telephone—An improved method. *Journal of Marketing Research, 1,* 45–48.

Crano, W. D., Siegel, J. T., Alvaro, E. M., Lac, A., & Hemovich, V. (2008). The at-risk adolescent marijuana nonuser: Expanding the standard distinction. *Prevention Science, 9,* 129–137.

Glasser, G. J., & Metzger, G. D. (1972). Random-digit dialing as a method of telephone sampling. *Journal of Marketing Research, 9,* 59–64.

Greenfield, T. K., Midanik, L. T., & Rogers, J. D. (2000). Effects of telephone versus face-to-face interview modes on reports of alcohol consumption. *Addiction, 95,* 277–284.

Griffin, J. M., Simon, A. B., Hulbert, H., Stevenson, J., Grill, J. P., Noorbaloochi, S., & Partin, M. R. (2011). A comparison of small monetary incentives to convert survey non-respondents: Randomized control trial. *BMC Medical Research Methodology, 11,* 81.

Groves, R. M. (2006). Nonresponse rates and nonresponse bias in household surveys. *Public Opinion Quarterly, 70,* 646–675.

Hadland, S. E, Marshall, B., Kerr, T., Qi, J., Montaner, J. S., & Wood, E. (2012). Suicide and history of childhood trauma among street youth. *Journal of Affective Disorders, 136,* 377–380.

Hahs-Vaughn, D. L., & Lomax, R. G. (2006). Utilization of sample weights in a single-level structural equation modelling. *The Journal of Experimental Education, 74,* 163–190.

Hazan, C. & Shaver, P. S. (1987). Romantic love conceptualized as an attachment process. *Journal of Personality and Social Psychology, 52,* 511–524.

Heerwegh, D., Vanhove, T., Matthijs, K., & Loosveldt, G. (2005). The effect of personalization on response rates and data quality in web surveys. *International Journal of Social Research Methodology: Theory & Practice, 8,* 85–99.

Henry, G. T. (1990). *Practical sampling.* Newbury Park, CA: Sage.

Homish, G. G., & Leonard, K. E. (2009). Testing methodologies to recruit adult drug-using couples. *Addictive Behaviors, 34,* 96–99.

Hoppe, M. J., Gillmore, M. R., Valadez, D. L., Civic, D., Hartway, J., & Morrison, D. M. (2000). The relative costs and benefits of telephone interviews versus self-administered diaries for daily data collection. *Evaluation Review, 24,* 102–116.

Jacoby, L. H., Young, B., & Watt, J. (2008). Public disclosure in research with exception from informed consent: The use of survey methods to assess its effectiveness. *Journal of Empirical Research on Human Research Ethics, 3,* 79–87.

Kalton, G. (1983). *Introduction to survey sampling.* Beverly Hills, CA: Sage.

Kempf, A. M., & Remington, P. L. (2007). New challenges for telephone survey research in the twenty-first century. *Annual Review of Public Health, 28,* 113–126.

Kish, L. A. (1965). *Survey sampling.* New York: Wiley.

Kunz, T., & Fuchs, M. (2012). Improving RDD cell phone samples: Evaluation of different pre-call validation methods. *Journal of Official Statistics, 28,* 373–394.

Lavrakas, P. J. (1993). Telephone survey methods: Sampling, selection, and supervision. *Applied social research methods series* (vol. 7, 2nd ed.). Newbury Park, CA: Sage.

Lavrakas, P. J. (1998). Methods for sampling and interviewing in telephone surveys. In L. Bickman, D. J. Rog & Debra J. (Eds.), *Handbook of applied social research methods* (pp. 429–472). Thousand Oaks, CA: Sage.

Levy, P. S., & Lemeshow, S. (2008). *Sampling of populations: Methods and applications.* New York: Wiley.

Link, M. W., Battaglia, M. P., Frankel, M. R., Osborn, L., & Mokdad, A. H. (2008). A comparison of address-based sampling (ABS) versus random-digit dialing (RDD) for general population surveys. *Public Opinion Quarterly, 72,* 6–27.

Link, M. W., & Mokdad, A. (2005). Leaving answering machine messages: Do they increase response rates for RDD Surveys? *International Journal of Public Opinion Research, 17,* 226–250.

Massey, D. S., & Tourangeau, R. (2013). New challenges to social measurement. *The Annals of the American Academy of Political and Social Science, 645,* 6–22.

McAuliffe, W. E., Geller, S., LaBrie, R., Paletz, S., & Fournier, E. (1998). Are telephone surveys suitable for studying substance abuse? Cost, administration, coverage and response rate issues. *Source Journal of Drug Issues, 28,* 455–481.

Meier, P. S., Meng, Y., Holmes, J., Baumberg, B., Purshouse, R., Hill-McManus, D., & Brennan, A. (2013). Adjusting for unrecorded consumption in survey and per capita sales data: Quantification of impact on gender- and age-specific alcohol-attributable fractions for oral and pharyngeal cancers in Great Britain. *Alcohol and Alcoholism, 48,* 241–249.

Meyer, I. H., & Colten, M. E. (1999). Sampling gay men: Random digit dialing versus sources in the gay community. *Journal of Homosexuality, 37,* 99–110.

Meyer, I. H., Rossano, L., Ellis, J. M., & Bradford, J. (2002). A brief telephone interview to identify lesbian and bisexual women in random digit dialing sampling. *Journal of Sex Research, 39,* 139–144.

Mickelson, K. D., Kessler, R. C., & Shaver, P. R. (1997). Adult attachment in a nationally representative sample, *Journal of Personality and Social Psychology, 73,* 1092–1106.

Moser, C. A., & Kalton, G. (1972). *Survey methods in social investigation* (2nd ed.). New York: Basic Books.

Muñoz-Leiva, F., Sánchez-Fernández, J., Montoro-Ríos, F., & Ibáñez-Zapata, J. Á. (2010). Improving the response rate and quality in web-based surveys through the personalization and frequency of reminder mailings. *Quality & Quantity: International Journal of Methodology, 44,* 1037–1052.

Noble, I., Moon, N., & McVey, D. (1998). 'Bringing it all back home'—Using RDD telephone methods for large-scale social policy and opinion research in the UK. *Journal of the Market Research Society, 40,* 93–120.

Oldendick, R. W., & Link, M. W. (1994). The answering machine generation: Who are they and what problem do they pose for survey research? *Public Opinion Quarterly. 58,* 264–273.

Paolacci, G., Chandler, J., & Ipeirotis, P. G. (2010). Running experiments on Amazon Mechanical Turk. *Judgment and Decision Making, 5,* 411–419.

Pfefferman, D. (1996). The use of sampling weights for survey data analysis. *Statistical Methods in Medical Research, 5,* 239–261.

Rahn, W. M., Krosnick, J. A., & Breuning, M. (1994). Rationalization and derivation processes in survey studies of political candidate evaluation. *American Journal of Political Science, 38,* 582–600.

Roth, P. L. (1994). Missing data: A conceptual review for applied psychologists. *Personnel Psychology, 47,* 537–560.

Schafer, J. L., & Graham, J. W. (2002). Missing data: Our view of the state of the art. *Psychological Methods, 7,* 147–177.

Singer, E. (2006). Introduction: Nonresponse bias in household surveys. *Public Opinion Quarterly, 70,* 637–645.

Troldahl, V. C., & Carter, R. E., Jr. (1964). Random selection of respondents within households in phone surveys. *Journal of Marketing Research, 1,* 71–76.

Trussel, N., & Lavrakas, P. J. (2004). The influence of incremental increases in token cash incentives on mail survey response. *Public Opinion Quarterly, 68,* 349–367.

Tuckel, P., & O'Neill, H. (2002). The vanishing respondent in telephone surveys. *Journal of Advertising Research, 42,* 26–48.

Xu, M., Bates, B. J., & Schweitzer, J. C. (1993). The impact of messages on survey participation in answering machine households. *Public Opinion Quarterly, 57*(2), 232–237.

12
SYSTEMATIC OBSERVATIONAL METHODS

In the previous section of this book, we were concerned with general strategies used in the design and implementation of different types of research. In the next seven chapters, we turn attention to methods of assessment and measurement used to collect the data that constitute the output of our research operations. We begin this section with a general consideration of systematic observational methods. This is an obvious and appropriate starting point, because all of the assessment or measurement techniques to be presented necessitate some form of systematic observation. Although all science is bound fundamentally to observation, the term "systematic observational methods" in our view has come to refer to a diverse set of techniques that are employed to study behavior that:

- (Usually) occurs outside the formal boundaries of the laboratory
- (Usually) is naturally instigated, i.e., does not make use of a controlled experimental treatment
- (Usually) places few restrictions on the allowable responses of the persons under observation
- (Usually) focuses on observable behaviors rather than internal, cognitive processes
- (Usually) entails a replicable system of codifying observed events

This last requirement for observational data allows other researchers to replicate the findings if the procedures detailed in the report are followed. It is this requirement that separates *systematic* observational techniques from other nonsystematic research approaches that may play a role in hypothesis generation or theory development, but that do not constitute formal data collection.

The first four bulleted points of our description of observational methods suggests both the range of research tactics that can be legitimately described as (systematically) observational, and the variations that characterize the various uses of this general approach to accumulate scientifically informative data. Systematic observation can and often has been used in the laboratory, where behaviors are highly constrained, but in this chapter we will focus our discussion principally on the use of observation in *natural* settings.

Three Aspects of Naturalism

The naturalistic character of data obtained through observational methods is the most valued feature of research of this type—it is the major reason why research is conducted outside the confines of the laboratory. In his discussion of the dimensions of field research, Tunnell (1977) observed that there was some confusion about how the naturalness of a research enterprise should be conceptualized. The criterion of *naturalness,* he observed, could be applied to the *behaviors* being studied, the *treatments* that are (or are not) applied, and the *setting* in which the research is conducted. Furthermore, these three facets could be combined in any number of ways, and these combinations would reflect the extent to which the total study could be judged as more or less naturalistic. At the extreme end of "unnaturalness," we have studies that constrain actions or require unnatural behaviors (i.e., actions that are not a usual part of a person's behavioral repertoire), make use of strong manipulations, and take place in unusual contexts. This set of descriptors provides a good summary depiction of many laboratory experiments. At the other end of the naturalness dimension, we have research that places no constraints on participants' behaviors, that does not impinge on the environment, and that occurs in natural settings. As seen from these examples, all scientific research, even experimental research, involves observation of a dependent variable. The behaviors, impingements, and settings on which the research is focused can vary widely, however, and Tunnell's (1977) system helps us situate research along the three dimensions of naturalness.

Natural Behavior

A primary goal of almost all observational research is to study natural behavior. As discussed (e.g., Chapter 7), impressive gains in generalizability can be realized if the behavior under study is naturally instigated and not made in response to the demands of the research situation or an experimenter. Behavior is considered natural to the extent that it is an existing part of the individual's response repertoire (i.e., it is not established to meet the specific demands of the study) and is unselfconscious (i.e., it is enacted without the actor's self-conscious awareness that he or she is the object of scientific scrutiny).

Many field studies represent attempts to transfer the control of the laboratory to naturalistic field settings and to study behavior that is generated by the participant, rather than to restrict the range of possible reactions specified in advance by the experimenter. In a clever field experiment, Moriarty (1975) induced individuals sunning themselves at a crowded beach to feel more or less responsible for the welfare of another by having a confederate ask a fellow sunbather to watch his radio while he went "to the boardwalk for a few minutes." Soon thereafter, another confederate approached the empty blanket, picked up the aforementioned radio, and, if not stopped by the "watchperson," ran off with it.

Participants' responses to the apparent theft of the property constituted the dependent measure. In this instance, participants' behaviors were naturalistic, that is, unconstrained and unselfconscious (in the sense that most probably did not think they were part of a psychological study). Their possible responses ranged from physically restraining the thief, following him, calling for help, leaving the scene, or ignoring the episode entirely. The naturalistic behavioral responses obtained in this research were used to study the relation between responsibility on pro-social behavior or bystander intervention, and the findings of this research were deemed by many to be more applicable to natural human behavior than those of earlier investigations that had been conducted in more artificial laboratory settings.[1] In the naturalistic approach emphasis is placed on examining people's observable behavior rather than beliefs and thoughts. Willems (1976, pp. 225–226) summarized this position well when he observed,

> To the ecologist, overt behavior simply is more important than many other psychological phenomena. For the ecologist, it is more important to know how parents treat their children than how they feel about being parents; more important to observe whether or not passersby help someone in need than what their beliefs are about altruism and kindness; more

important to note that a person harms someone else when given an opportunity than to know whether his self-concept is that of a considerate person. . . . It is not readily apparent to me how all of the data on how-it-looks, how-it-feels, and what-people-think-they-want will become translated into understanding . . . problems of long-term environmental adaptation and adjustment.

Willems's (1976) point is well taken, but it would be a mistake to overextend this view to a position that people's internal states are unknowable or uninteresting. As will be shown throughout this section, research methodologists have made giant strides in developing techniques to tap into cognitions, emotions, stereotypes, and other behavioral dispositions that guide overt actions and are sometimes not even recognized by their holders (see especially Chapter 16).

Natural Event

In Tunnell's (1977, p. 428) view, a natural treatment is a "naturally occurring, discrete event . . . that the subject would have experienced . . . with or without the presence of a researcher." By this definition, Moriarty's (1975) treatment (a staged theft of a radio) was not natural, because it required the researcher's active involvement. Although we are in general agreement with Tunnell's classification system, we find his natural treatment definition overly restrictive and inconsistent with the general intention of fostering more, and better, field research. In our view, a treatment (or an externally controlled or created event) can be considered natural, even if produced by the actions of an experimenter, if (1) it plausibly could have occurred without experimenter intervention, and (2) the participant is unaware of the fact that it did not. Thus, we would consider Moriarty's context and treatment "natural," even though it was introduced by the researcher and thus decidedly "unnatural." In our view, the experimental manipulation of the situation did not destroy its naturalness—the theft of people's belongings on public beaches does occur—and the participants' reactions suggest strongly that they did not suspect that they were involved in a scientific investigation.[2]

Natural Setting

Generally in the social sciences, a "naturalistic observational investigation" refers to a study that has been conducted outside the laboratory. Whether the researcher has intervened in the setting is irrelevant, so long as the research participants do not perceive it to have been established for research purposes. As in our discussion of natural treatments, respondents' perceptions of the setting, not the actions of the researcher, define the naturalness of the setting. In this sense, any setting can be considered natural if the respondent does not think it has been constructed for the purpose of research. Thus, a college classroom is a natural setting (at least for college students). Moriarty's beach scene is an obvious (good) example of a natural setting. It is reasonable to assume that people were unaware that the setting had been modified to allow for a systematic study of the effects of the specification of responsibility on helping behavior. The setting contributed to the credibility of the treatment. This last point bears emphasis; even though we might take great care in the development of our hypotheses, manipulations, measures, etc., it often is the case that we are lax in our choice of the setting in which our observation occurs. This is a mistake, because an ill-chosen setting can defeat even the most well-designed study by rendering data collection difficult or impossible (Weick, 1968, 1985).

It is important to understand that all three of the dimensions of naturalness that Tunnell has brought to our attention interact, and thus could produce a situation in which the observed responses are very different from those we expect. In a study similar to Moriarty's (1975), Howard and Crano (1974) staged a theft of another's books. In our terms, the treatment, setting, and behaviors were completely naturalistic. The (natural) settings for this research were the Michigan State University library, the student union, and a popular on-campus grille. The treatments (the behaviors of the victim and the thief) were well rehearsed and generated no suspicion. And, of course, the behaviors of the respondents in reacting to the theft were unconstrained. Even so, there was surprising (and unexpected) behavioral variation in the degree to which bystanders were willing to intervene (by stopping or identifying the book thief) in the three settings. Rather little help was provided to the victim in the library, more help was provided in the lounge, and the most help was provided in the grille. The authors reasoned that different norms dictated appropriate behavior in the settings and were responsible for the variations in helping that were observed. Such norms can powerfully influence behavior even when events call for a radical departure from the usual, or prescribed, forms of action. Though unexpected, these findings were more credible because of the naturalistic circumstances in which they were observed.

Whereas Tunnell's (1977) three-dimensional classification used to judge the extent that research is naturalistic can be useful, it is important to realize that a number of other features having to do with the design of the study will play a major role in determining the extent to which naturalness will be achieved. Two of the most important of these primary design considerations are the extent to which the observer is involved in the activities that are under investigation, and the type and form of coding system that is chosen to summarize the behaviors that are the focus of the study. These two factors lead to a series of more specific tactical considerations that guide the conduct of any given observational study, as will be seen in the sections that follow.

Observer Involvement in the Naturalistic Setting: The Participatory–Nonparticipatory Distinction

The degree to which an observer interacts with the individuals under study is one of the most important determinants of the procedures of the study, of the quality of the data that will be collected, and of the uses that can legitimately be made of the obtained results. Observer participation or interaction with the observed can vary tremendously, from complete engagement with those observed in the situation to removal in both time and space from those being studied. As the technique that calls for the greatest intimacy between observer and observed, **participatory observation (or participant observation)** is an "intense social interaction between researchers and participants in the milieu of the latter, during which time data, in the form of field notes, are unobtrusively and systematically collected" (Bogden, 1972, p. 3). The approach is one of the most widely used methods in sociology and cultural anthropology, and has long been viewed by many in these fields as an indispensable feature of these disciplines. Methods involving participatory observation have given rise to considerable controversy over the years, probably because the method allows the researcher so much freedom in defining his or her appropriate realm of action and demands so little systematization of the observation techniques that are employed. Indeed, Williamson and Karp (1977) observed that one of the most remarkable features of this approach was the *lack* of agreed-upon rules or standard operating procedures used to guide its use.

As might be expected, the venues and topics in which participant observation approaches have been employed are vast, ranging from studies of go-go dancers in the Philippines (Ratliff, 1999), to an end-of-life patient in the southern U.S. (Tulis, 2013), to communicative competence in an Inuit community in the Canadian Arctic (Collings, 2009), to midwifery in Ontario (Bourgeault, 2000), to communication in groups on the Internet (Polifroni, von Hippel, & Brewer, 2001). Given the diversity of potential applications, a good definition of this technique that encapsulates even a minority of participatory observation research is difficult to develop. DeWalt and DeWalt (2010) provided a good working definition of participatory observation as "a method in which a researcher takes part in the daily activities, rituals, interactions, and events of a group of people as one of the means of learning the implicit and tacit aspects of their life routines and their culture" (p. 1). The participatory observer, in other words, becomes a part of the everyday life of the observed, while also gathering data. The observer is a part of the context, and so almost inevitably affects the ongoing behavior. This feature of participatory observation is responsible for much of the controversy that surrounds the approach. It is an inevitability of the method, however—its greatest strength and simultaneously its greatest potential weakness—and we will return to this issue when discussing the relative advantages and disadvantages of participatory and nonparticipatory techniques.

The term participatory observation, then, broadly describes the general research process in which an observer observes from within the context he or she wishes to study. The observer passes as or becomes a member of a group and uses this insider status to gather information about it. Typically, participatory observation entails the simultaneous collection and analysis of data (Lofland, 1971), because in this technique the processes of hypothesis generation and hypothesis testing often occur almost simultaneously.

Gaining Entry

To make best use of the technique of participatory observation, the observer first must gain entrance into the group under study. A good example of some of the possible dangers and distortions involved in this entry process was provided by Festinger's, Reicken's, and Schachter's (1956) now classic study of the Seekers. Briefly, the Seekers were a cult that claimed to have had contact with extraterrestrial beings, the Guardians. These benevolent spacemen had informed the leader of the earthbound group that a major flood was soon to inundate the northern hemisphere. The Seekers believed the Guardians would eventually send these adherents a flying saucer at the last minute to transport them out of harm's way. Though the cult was not large, belief in the prophecy was strong among its members.

Festinger and his associates, not sharing the faith, decided that this group provided a good opportunity to study the effects of disconfirmation of a strong expectation on people's future behavior. The best way to accomplish this investigation, they reasoned, would be to observe the cult from the inside and thus obtain an intimate view of their proceedings. The Seekers were not a proselytizing group—membership was by invitation only. As the authors admitted, "our basic problems were . . . obtaining entree for a sufficient number of observers to provide the needed coverage of members' activities, and keeping at an absolute minimum any influence which these observers might have on the beliefs and actions of members of the group. We tried to be nondirective, sympathetic listeners, passive participants who were inquisitive and eager to learn whatever others might want to tell us" (Festinger et al., 1956, p. 237).

To gain entry into the group, members of Festinger's team hid their social science credentials, approached the Seekers and claimed "psychic experiences" of the type calculated to interest the members of the group. The experiences were constructed so that they could be interpreted in light of the Seekers' system of beliefs. The danger that these stories, necessitated by the membership selectivity of the Seekers, interfered with the natural equilibrium of the group was recognized: "Unhappily, [the ruse] had been too successful, for, in our effort to tailor a story to fit the beliefs of the members of the group, and thus gain their approval for our observers, we had done too well. We had unintentionally reinforced their beliefs that the Guardians were watching over humanity and were 'sending' chosen people for special instruction about the cataclysm and the belief system" (Festinger et al., 1956, p. 241). Given the nature of the entrance requirements, however, the observers had little choice but to fabricate psychic experiences to gain admittance to the group.

Unfortunately, the Seekers interpreted the stories concocted by new members as proof of the correctness of their beliefs. The actions of the researchers had the inadvertent effect of bolstering the Seekers' beliefs.

The necessary entry-gaining actions of Festinger's observers illustrate a point that should be recognized in all studies making use of participatory observer techniques: That is, in almost all closed groups, the problem of entry (of the investigator) assumes great importance. The actions the nonmember performs in gaining admittance to the group under investigation can powerfully affect the ongoing actions of the group and the quality of the data that are subsequently collected. Thus, in attempting to join a group for the purposes of participatory observation, the most unobtrusive means possible should be used so that the natural group situation remains so. Failing that, a detailed account of any possible interference resulting from the entry process should be included in descriptions of the research, as in Festinger's study. This description will not solve the interference problem, but it at least will alert the reader to possible distortions that might reside in the results.

A different approach to entry (and a different set of problems) is evident in Thorne's (1988) study of the draft resistance movement during the Vietnam War. Thorne first joined the antidraft movement, and later decided to use her experiences as a source of data for her thesis. To avoid deceiving her peers, Thorne discussed her plans, which were met with responses that ranged from "hostility to mild tolerance" (Thorne, 1988, p. 134). Whereas Thorne avoided deceiving those who shared her political convictions, her openness may have altered the fundamental nature of the interactions that ensued *after* she disclosed her research plans. By disclosing her intentions, she was able to maintain truthfulness to a much greater degree than the participatory observers of Festinger et al. (1956) could. It could be argued, however, that her disclosure affected the naturalness of the context just as strongly as Festinger's observers had.

These two extreme examples do not offer a clear solution to the problem of entry. Complete openness as to motive and approach is certainly more ethically defensible, but in no way does it solve the problem of the observer affecting the observed. Complete nondisclosure of techniques and motivation, as exemplified by Festinger et al. (1956), would appear to solve the problem of group members reacting unnaturally to one of their group; unfortunately, the manner in which observers gained entry, and the effects of their actions while in the group, can take a toll on the quality and credibility of the behavioral observations that are made.

Going Native

The entry problem is only one of the difficulties encountered when using participatory observation. Just as there is a large literature in anthropology, psychology, and sociology devoted to the solution of entry problems, so too have social scientists been concerned with the problem of "going native." Overidentification with the observed group tends to blind the observer to many relevant aspects of the total situation and draws attention to those events perceived to be of interest to the group, which may or may not be scientifically worthwhile. Given Thorne's (1988) identification with the draft resistance movement, one might question the quality of the data her research produced. Could she be an unbiased and nonjudgmental observer, given her political commitments?

A hypothetical example will help to illustrate this point. Suppose a pair of agnostic social scientists were interested in the patterns of interaction that occurred during prayer services of a Pentecostal sect; furthermore, during the course of observation of this church group, the researchers became so deeply impressed by the fervor of the members that they entered into the activities and eventually attained complete membership in the organization. Would their accounts of the group's activities and practices prove of interest? Possibly. A more difficult question concerns the scientific value of the work. Remember, the fact of the researchers' conversion does not necessarily diminish their scientific expertise. It is the manner in which this expertise is employed that gives cause for concern. Observer-bias problems aside, we must critically examine the phenomena on which our observers chose to focus attention. This is not to suggest that a researcher cannot become close to those he or she observes (see Mehan & Wood, 1975; Thorne, 1988), but rather that the ultimate purpose of the engagement—the systematic collection of reliable information—be kept in mind at all times. It is the overly complete identification with the group under study, failure to integrate new information with known information (a kind of scientific tunnel vision), and discounting of information that casts the group in a poor light and proves so troublesome when the observer "goes native."

Partial Participatory Observation and Nonparticipatory Observation

By restricting the degree of participatory observation in the situation under study, investigators can simultaneously control the problems both of entry and of going native. This solution has generated studies in which observers were, for the most part, unseen by the observed, their existence oftentimes not even suspected. The most extreme form of nonparticipatory observation is of the type directed toward *archival records,* in which events previously recorded are adopted by the scientist for study. Webb, Campbell, Schwartz, Sechrest, and Grove (1981) have demonstrated how such unlikely sources as tombstones, pottery shards, obituaries, a city's water pressure, newspaper headlines, library withdrawals, and even the U.S. Congressional Record have all been employed as useful sources in the search for social information. We discuss one form of this kind of analysis in Chapter 14.

Less remote from the actual events under consideration, and perhaps more common, are investigations of ongoing group or individual activity in which the observer is partially or totally concealed. Total concealment requires an observational setting of a high degree of structure. Because the observer must remain undetected, it is essential that the group under study remain within the setting in which the observer is concealed. Attempts at completely concealed, nonparticipant observation have resulted in a variety of research operations that are sometimes interesting, often amusing, and almost always ethically questionable. Henle's and Hubble's (1938) observers, for example, hid under beds in college dormitories to collect their data. This strategy is not recommended today. Less dangerous, but clearly questionable, was Carlson's, Cook's, and Stromberg's (1936) research in which observers eavesdropped on people's conversations in theater lobbies. The list could be extended indefinitely, but it is clear that concealed observation is usually an ethically questionable operation. Such research techniques should be considered only after all other options have proved fruitless (see Chapter 20).

Ethical considerations aside, in many situations concealment is impossible. Accordingly, social scientists have altered their research operations in such a way as to allow for partial participatory observation. The tactic of limited researcher participation, however, generates many difficult problems in its own right, as is illustrated by the number of techniques developed for their solution. Soskin and John (1963), for example, somehow convinced a married couple who were about to embark on a two-week vacation to wear small radio transmitters during the entire vacation period. In this way, the observers had a complete sound recording of the couple's interactions. Clearly, the volunteers in this study knew they were being observed. The degree of observer participation in their lives, however, was not nearly as great as it would have been if Soskin or John had accompanied the couple during their vacation, following them wherever they went, etc. As such, the degree of observer participation in this study was slightly less than complete and somewhat more than that occurring when total concealment is employed.[3]

A variant on this theme makes use of structured diaries and time sampling (DeLongis, Hemphill, & Lehman, 1992; Robinson & Goodbey, 1997; Leigh, 1993), in which respondents complete a set of questionnaires regarding their mood, their perceptions of interaction partners, thoughts, actions, etc., at time intervals specified by the researcher (say, daily, or at randomly determined intervals). Robinson and Goodbey (1997), for example, asked participants to monitor their time allocations (leisure vs. obligatory) over the course of the day, and Leigh (1993) had participants note their alcohol consumption and sexual activity at the end of each day. The "observations" made under these circumstances are of the self-report, retrospective variety, but the naturalism of the setting in which the data collection takes place, the natural behavior under study, the short duration between action and recording, and the natural events that occur place this approach among the naturalistic methods employing partial observer participation.

To avoid reliance on retrospective reports of behavior, researchers may use the **experience sampling method** (ESM), in which respondents carry a pager, text messaging device, computer tablet, or other electronic reminder device; when the device sounds, each respondent completes questions about what they are doing, thinking, feeling at that moment. Alternately, participants may be asked to complete a measure at a specified time (or times) each day. Usually, data are collected continually for days, weeks, and even months. If a cell phone is used, it usually is programmed to contact respondents once in every given block of time (say, once every two hours or every day), although a random time schedule may also be used (Kubey, Larson, & Csikszentmihalyi, 1996; Larson & Csikszentmihalyi, 1983). ESM uses a time-sampling technique intended to obtain slices of life events across people's everyday behaviors and activities. For instance, every time the electronic device goes off, college students might be instructed to write down the activity in which they were engaged and to rate its degree of pleasantness on a 10-point scale. After a month of data collection, researchers might find that across all the experiences of college students, collected throughout many time points, the average scores of certain types of activities (e.g., a meaningful conversation with a friend or a study date with a smart classmate) are much more pleasurable than others activities (e.g., taking out the trash or reading Beowulf). Because information was collected throughout the day, the events could be collapsed by time, with potential results revealing that college students tend to engage in the least pleasant activities in the morning upon waking up and to engage in more pleasurable activities as the day progressed.

The value of the ESM diary approach is that it "catches" respondents in their natural milieu, and thus allows the researcher to associate the outcomes of various natural events with respondents' subsequent moods, intentions, behaviors, etc. If data are drawn on a random schedule, they would appear less susceptible to the cyclical biases that might occur if the diaries were always completed at the same time of day for a month. If participants were simply asked to complete measures at the end of each night, they may exhibit a tendency to place a greater emphasis on temporally non-distant events, such as experiences occurring that evening, or they might be more susceptible to distortions in accurately recalling behaviors and mood states earlier that day. However, this daily approach to ESM is still less problematic then one-time surveys in which participants are asked to recall their attitudes and behaviors of the more distant past. Data collected from the ESM are usually estimated with multi-level models (see Chapter 9), The basic ESM study requires a two-level nested design: Measurements of experiences at the different time points are nested within each participant.

With sufficient creativity, the ESM and other diary methods can be used to study a variety of important issues. Larson, Csikszentmihalyi, and their colleagues, for example, used this method to document the negative effects of solitude on people's feelings, and the generally positive aftereffects of no longer being alone (Larson & Csikszentmihalyi, 1978, 1980; Larson, Csikszentmihalyi, & Graef, 1980). It is difficult to envision the means by which solitude could be studied credibly in a laboratory context. Nezlek, Wheeler, and Reis (1983) have employed a structured diary approach to study such issues as the initiation and personal control of social encounters. During a two-week period, their participants were instructed to record responses to questions asking about every social encounter lasting at least 10 minutes. These studies provide valuable real time insights into the effects that everyday events have on people's natural behaviors. As such, we these kinds of diary-based approaches have become increasingly popular (Reis & Gable, 2000).

In an interesting application, Peters and her colleagues used the ESM to study chronic pain (Peters et al., 2000). They reported no evidence of reactivity to the monitoring, and found differences in reported pain taken by the ESM and reports taken retrospectively. Klumb and Baltes (1999) have used the ESM to study the validity of retrospective reports in elderly people, and the approach has proved useful in this context as well. Findings derived from the ESM methodology, especially if integrated with other data obtained under different methodological auspices, have the potential to expand our understanding of social behavior. In general, approaches that combine more than one method of measurement bolster confidence in the validity of our results.

Another example of partial participatory observation is provided in studies of the patient-therapist relationship. In studies of this type, an observer (often a student in training) attends the therapeutic hour, but strictly as an observer—the observer does not interact in any way with either patient or therapist. A more common variant on this theme involves the filming of the therapeutic interaction for later study. Often, both therapist and patient know of the ongoing observation, but it is felt that this form of "participation" is less intrusive than that in which the observer is physically present. However, as might be expected, research indicates that people who know they are being watched tend to emit more socially desirable behaviors. Roberts and Renzaglia (1965), for example, showed that the mere presence of a microphone had a measurable effect on the behaviors of both patient and therapist. Zegiob, Arnold and Forehand (1975) found that people were more likely to play positively with children when being observed, and Samph (1969) observed more acts of altruism when people knew they were being watched than when they did not. These studies suggest that the mere fact of observation can bias the observational record. Despite this, today the use of audio or video recordings in social research is becoming increasingly common. These approaches have the advantage of allowing the researcher to examine and reexamine the behaviors of interest at a time of his or her choosing. The capability of "taking a second look" to resolve possible misinterpretation of the observations usually enhances the reliability of any behavioral coding. The point at which techniques of this sort fall on the participant-nonparticipant continuum depends on the obtrusiveness of the recording device. If participants are unaware of the observation, the research can be judged nonparticipatory observation by the investigator (if, perhaps, unethical); if respondents are aware of the taping, and the recording machinery is an obvious part of the setting, then as Roberts and Renzaglia (1965) demonstrated, the degree of observer interference can be as severe as it would have been had the observer been physically present.

A somewhat different form of participatory observation by researchers was suggested by Mahl (1964), who found voice frequencies below 500 cps to be a good indicator of people's emotional state, yet apparently not under conscious control. As such, respondents can know they are being observed, yet be unable to alter the particular behaviors under investigation. Along these same lines, in an earlier series of investigations, Ponder and Kennedy (1927) found the reduction of the period between eye blinks to be a good indicator of emotional excitement, if the respondent was in a situation in which gross physical movements were impossible or impractical (e.g., while sitting in the witness chair in a courtroom, while waiting for a golf opponent to sink or miss a putt, etc.). The eye blink response has been used as a general indicator of psychological stress; recent research suggests that victims of wartime-induced posttraumatic stress disorder show exaggerated eye blinking to startling stimuli (typically, bursts of white noise) (e.g., Morgan, Grillon, Southwick, Davis, & Charney, 1996).

Pupil dilation, too, has been found to provide some useful information about the internal state of the individual. Research by a number of investigators (e.g., Atwood & Howell, 1971; Hess, 1965;

Hess, Seltzer & Shlien, 1965) has suggested that pupil dilation, a response that people ordinarily do not monitor or attempt to control, provides a reasonable if indirect indication of interest (see Janisse, 1973, for a review of some of the pitfalls to be avoided when using this measure). Dabbs and Milun (1999) used pupil dilation as an indirect assessment device for measuring racial prejudice (as inferred from papillary responses indicating greater attention to people of a different race). Thus, this measure, like those making use of lower vocal frequencies or eye blink latencies would appear to provide the social scientist with a useful, if limited, assessment of the psychological state of a respondent. For present purposes, the important aspect of these measures is that they provide examples of indicators of people's internal states, over which they sometimes can—but usually do not—exert conscious control. As such, measures of this type sometimes are valued over the more direct approaches because they are less likely to be used by the respondent to misdirect the investigator.

Participatory Observation: When and Why

Given the problems of entry, of going native, and of observer interference in the natural actions of the group under investigation, to which studies employing observer participation are so susceptible, we might wonder why participatory observation would ever be used. Cicourel (1964) provided perhaps the best defense of this approach when he observed, "More intensive participation has the advantage of affording the observer a greater exposure to both the routine and the unusual activities of the group studied. The assumption is that the more intensive the participation on the part of the researcher, the 'richer' the data" (p. 44). The personal relationships that can form in participant observation research can materially influence the quality of the data that are collected. For this reason, participatory observers are urged to be friendly, nonthreatening, concerned with the group's welfare, etc. Indeed, there is a growing literature in the social sciences demonstrating Guba's (1980, p. 21) point: "Good guys get better data." The observer can best demonstrate friendliness, humanness, etc., with the respondents when he or she is in relatively frequent contact with them, i.e., in participatory observation research (see also Guba & Lincoln, 2008).

Becker (1958), reacting to the question of when participatory techniques should be used, responded as follows: "Sociologists usually use this method when they are especially interested in understanding a particular organization or substantive problem rather than demonstrating relations between abstractly defined variables. They attempt to make their research theoretically meaningful, but they assume that they do not know enough about the organization a priori to identify relevant problems and hypotheses and that they must discover these in the course of the research" (pp. 652–653).

If we accept Cicourel's and Becker's attempts at delineating the boundaries of this technique, then participatory research methods would seem to be most useful in situations of the exploratory, hypothesis-generating variety, in which great amounts of "rich," if not necessarily reliable, information are needed. The primary concern here is the accumulation of large amounts of data, not on the data's reliability or validity.[4] Once having identified a set of behaviors of interest, however, it follows that techniques involving far less observer participation should be favored. In this way, the potential interference that can be generated by the observer's presence in the group under investigation is circumvented. In Cicourel's (1964) view, the cost of this removal of the observer is calculated in terms of a loss of richness in the data; however, because behaviors for investigation in a hypothesis-testing study have already been chosen, and the observer is focusing on a strictly prescribed set of responses, the loss would seem inconsequential.

For the most part, the nonparticipatory methods are most deficient in those areas that call for greater observer participation. Generally, nonparticipatory techniques require the observer to conduct research in settings that restrict the mobility of the observed group, thus enabling the observer

260 Data Collecting Methods

to maintain isolation from the group and, at the same time, ensuring that the respondents remain within the observational setting. Restrictions of this type can be employed while simultaneously maintaining the naturalness of the observational settings, behaviors, and treatments.

At every point on the observer participation-to-nonparticipation dimension, there are advantages to be gained and dangers to be avoided. The careful investigator must assess the relative costs of one method in light of the advantages it offers. This assessment is dependent on many factors, most notably the amount of information one possesses about the issue under investigation, the availability of both settings and participants for observation, and the ethical propriety of the techniques that will be employed to capitalize on the advantages of the chosen approach.

Coding Observations

The observational researcher must not only decide on the degree to which he or she will participate in the observational study, but also how the actions and behaviors to be observed should be recorded and codified. Figure 12.1 presents a flowchart of the steps to be taken in developing a coding system to be use in observational research. Each of these steps will be considered in detail.

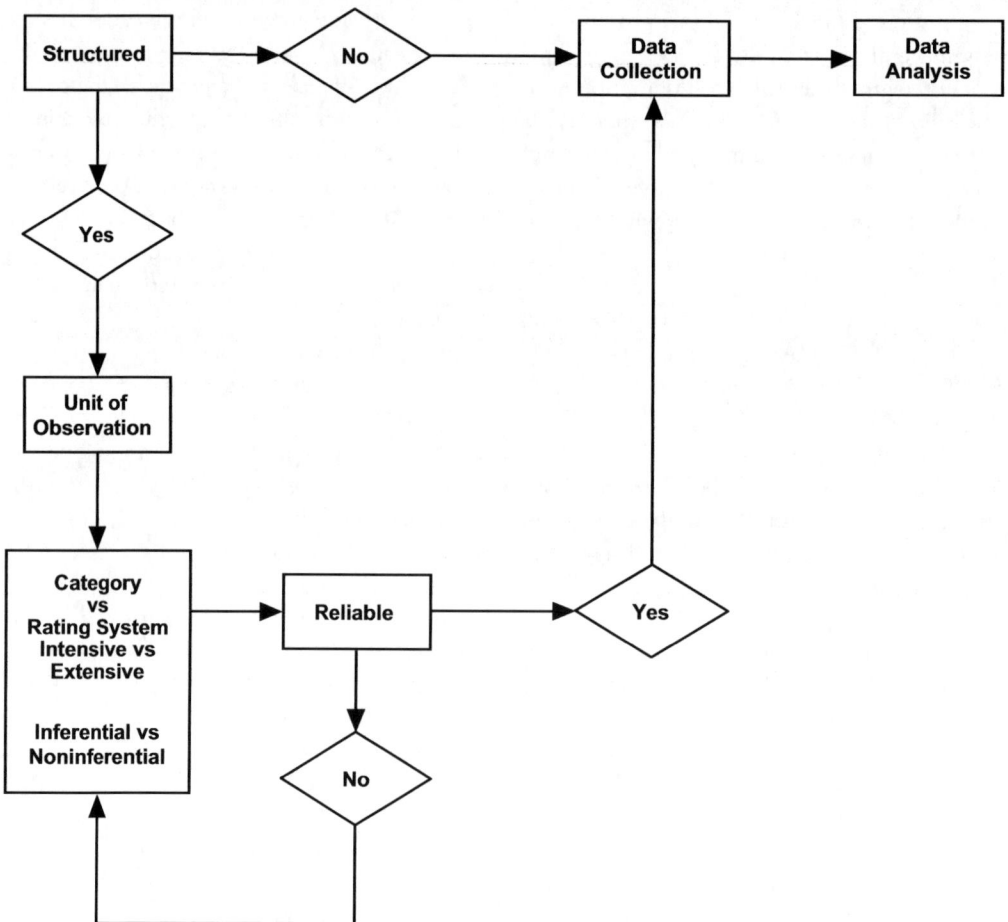

FIGURE 12.1 Steps in the development of a coding system.

The Structured-Nonstructured Dimension

The differing theoretical orientations and research training backgrounds of social scientists have resulted in wide variations in the degree of structure of the coding systems they use in observational research. At one extreme of this dimension are the proponents of complete systematization of procedures to collect the observational data. These researchers argue that structure must be imposed on the mass of input accruing to any observational study to investigate effectively any hypothesized relationship. Common in research of this type are coding systems that focus on a limited and explicit portion of the possible range of behaviors that occur. In this way, reliable ratings of specific behaviors thought to have some theoretical importance can be established.

Those favoring less structured observational techniques have argued against attempts to focus on a limited range of behaviors. The "constriction" of the observational field, they suggest, can result in a loss of valuable data that happen not to fall within the range of the chosen coding system. One of the most forceful and influential presentations on behalf of the nonstructured orientation is found in Glaser and Strauss's (1967) text, *The Discovery of Grounded Theory*. In this book, researchers are urged to enter the observational research setting with no prior theoretical preconceptions.[5] In **grounded theory**, the researcher is expected to start the study with no preconceptions so that theory is generated on the basis of the observations and is continually revised in light of new observations. The resulting "grounded" hypotheses, based on the actual data they are developed to address, are expected to prove more valid, or true to life, than those resulting from theoretical deductions that are not grounded in this manner (Strauss, 1991; Strauss & Corbin, 1997; Wertz et al., 2011). The initial attractiveness of this approach is great; however, Glaser and Strauss's (1967) method raises some important methodological issues, to which we now turn our attention.

Early Data Returns

A potential difficulty with the grounded theory approach is that conclusions based on initial observations inevitably influence the interpretation of subsequent observations—and this is the essence of the grounded theory approach. As mentioned earlier in this book, and in Rosenthal's (1966) volume on experimenter expectancy effects, the sequential analysis of "early data returns" represents a subtle but nonetheless real source of bias. In examining the effects of early data returns, for example, Rosenthal, Persinger, Vikan-Kline, and Fode (1963) arranged for each of eight naive students serving as experimenters to test two experimental confederates and then a group of naive participants. The student experimenters were informed about the directional hypothesis of the research. Half the experimenters obtained data from confederates (who followed a script), who always produced results consistent with experimenter expectations, whereas the other half of experimenters were confronted with confederates who provided results that disconfirmed the hypotheses. When examining the effect of this manipulation on the recorded responses of the naive participants that all experimenters later studied, Rosenthal et al. (1963) found that experimenters who had obtained the confirmatory data early in the investigation continued to report obtaining such patterns of data even when subsequently examining the naive participants who offered disconfirming results. Experimenters whose expectations were disconfirmed initially were less susceptible to this confirmation bias.

Clearly, the most obvious way to avoid this potential source of bias is to reserve detailed inspection of results until all the data are collected. This recommendation is contrary to the grounded theory approach because the technique calls for the continuous revision of both hypotheses and research direction as a function of the data as they are collected. The potential for observer bias would seem particularly high in the grounded theory approach.

Generalizability of Observations

In addition to the potential confirmation bias difficulties resulting from the sequential analysis of data, the manner in which nonstructured observations are collected also poses problems for the validity of the obtained results. The question of whether or not the "discovered" relationships are artifacts of the specific observational sample or represent meaningful, generalizable discoveries is difficult to address in research of this type. When an observer has no predetermined categories of behavior to attend to, those events that stand out in the specific research setting will be noticed (Borgida & Nisbett, 1977). These hyper-visible events, however, will not necessarily occur in different settings. Concentrating on the conspicuous occurrences of a given situation can compromise the comparability of the obtained findings with those gathered in different settings. As Weick (1985, p. 44) has observed, "Routine activity is the rule, but it seldom gets recorded." Bertrand Russell (1930) made essentially the same point when he observed that great people were great only infrequently—most of the time, their lives were relatively humdrum.

Consider the dilemma of observers who employ no prespecified observational system in their research. Literally hundreds of different behaviors occur in situations involving even very simple everyday activities. For example, suppose we were to observe the act of vacuuming—possible observable variables that constitute this simple chore ranges from the brand of vacuum used, the size of vacuum, the shagginess of the carpet, the color of the carpet, the amount of time the participant vacuums, whether a primarily forward or backward motion was used in handling the contraption, the amount of dirt collected in the dustbin, the sociodemographic characteristics of the person doing the vacuuming, and so forth. Can the observer make any clear assertions regarding the generality of the behaviors that are observed if no a priori coding procedure was established? Probably not, since any obtained patterns might be specific to the sample of behaviors noticed and chosen for observation. The problem of the situation-specific determination of what is observed or noticed is avoided when the investigator enters the research field with predetermined categories of behavior to guide and structure the observational activities.

It would be unwise to interpret this critique of no-structured methods as a general condemnation of this approach. Insofar as the focus of these methods is generating testable hypotheses, we have no objection to their use. Barton and Lazarsfeld (1969, p. 182) advanced this position even more strongly when they observed, "Research which has neither statistical weight nor experimental design, research based only on qualitative descriptions of a small number of cases, can nonetheless play the important role of suggesting possible relationships, causes, effects, and even dynamic processes. Indeed, it can be argued that only research which provides a wealth of miscellaneous, unplanned impressions and observations can play this role." It is when the theories or hypotheses suggested by such methods are accepted, without first having undergone the necessary verification process in more controlled settings, that the potential dangers of nonstructured observation become real. Nonstructured techniques are valuable in generating theories, but their use in hypothesis testing situations is always debatable.

Structured Methods: Category Systems

Whereas it might appear at first glance that nonstructured techniques provide a simple means of conducting research, this is decidedly not the case. The ability to extract significant aspects of group or individual behavior, to filter from the mass of input those relationships of potential theoretical importance, and to reconstruct from necessarily incomplete notes the pattern and flow of the observational record is acquired only after intensive commitment to research of this type (Hoare, Mills, & Francis, 2012). It was partly for this reason, and partly in response to the call for more quantitatively based research techniques, that social scientists reoriented their observational methods in the direction of greater structure. The most extreme point of this development is represented by research in which rating scales are used to quantify and summarize the actions of the person or group under study. Rather than begin at this extreme in our discussion of structured observational techniques, we will first direct our attention toward methods that make use of category systems. These techniques fall somewhere near the midpoint of the structured-ness dimension, between the completely open, nonstructured varieties of research at one extreme, and the severely constricted rating-scale approaches at the other.

Every category system represents an attempt to quantitatively summarize the qualitative behaviors that occur in the observational setting. In its most simplistic form, this approach might involve a simple count of the number of times specific types of events occur. A category is a specific description of a behavior, or other observable aspect, of a group or individual. A set of these descriptions, quite literally a checklist, constitutes a category system (or system of categories). Each of these categories represents the level of a variable being observed. Given a system of two or more categories, the observer's task is to note the number of times respondents' actions fall into one of the unique categories that constitute the variable. Categories of a variable should be mutually exclusive; an event coded as satisfying the demands for inclusion in a given category should not satisfy the demands of any other category. The question of the degree of intensity of occurrence is usually not a concern when category systems are used, unless different categories are defined by different intensities. Like a light switch (rather than a rheostat), the category is either "on" or "off."

The Unit of Observation

A recurring issue in research making use of category systems concerns the unit of behavior to be considered when categorizing a social act—that is, when does one behavior stop and another begin? The problem of unit definition has plagued social scientists for some time, probably first inviting the attention of early quantitative anthropologists (e.g., see Murdock, 1967; Murdock & White, 1969). The question then, as now, concerns the problem of the definition of the appropriate observable unit of study. For example, how is one to define and code a given culture? By geographical area: Should Russia be categorized as a Western or Eastern nation? By common language: Is British English categorically different from or the same as American English? By common leaders, beliefs, kinship terms, or inheritance rules? The unit problem in observational research, though at a level of somewhat less grand proportion than that encountered by quantitative anthropologists, nevertheless is troublesome.

In many cases, solutions for specific category systems have been made by defining the observable units with respect to the categories being employed. For example, in his analysis of small group interaction, Bales (1950) chose as the observable unit of behavior " . . . the smallest discriminable segment of verbal or nonverbal behavior to which the observer . . . can assign a classification" (p. 37). In other words, any act that could be classified was counted as a unit of behavior. In Leventhal's and Sharp's (1965) coding system of facial expressions, *time* determined the unit; for a given, prespecified period, observers coded the expressions of the forehead and brow, then the eyes, then the mouth, etc. Given the physical restrictions of Leventhal's and Sharp's observed group (women in labor) on whom this technique was employed, the time-determined unit offered a useful and unambiguous solution to the problem of the selection of the behavioral act for categorization. In observational studies of young children, however, the definition of an action by temporal criteria could invite catastrophe, because the mobility of such targets might be such that they were not available for observation when the time for observation occurred. Accordingly, many observers of children's behavior have used the child's attention span in defining the unit of observation. So as long as a child attends to a given object (be it another child, a teacher, a toy, etc.), this is a single unit of observation. When attention shifts to another object, this shift defines yet another observable "unit" for categorization. These examples represent the polar extremes of the determination of unit, from the objectively defined unit, time, to the respondent-defined unit, attention shift. A combination of both of these approaches could be used; for example, another study may define an observable unit as children focusing attention on an object or activity for at least 15 seconds before it may be defined as a codable unit.

There are some coding systems in which the respondents themselves define the unit. For example, DePaulo Kashy, Kirkendol, Wyer, and Epstein (1996) were interested in studying lying in naturalistic settings. Information on many variables on the topic was collected, including the types of lies told, why, to whom, and so on. The researchers asked their volunteers to keep a diary and to note all of their daily social interactions that lasted more than 10 minutes, as well all the lies they told during an interaction, no matter what its duration. As the researchers were aware of the challenges in narrowly defining to participants the features that precisely constituted a lie (e.g., whether a "little white lie" should be considered a lie), the participants were allowed to use their own personal judgment in defining the unit of lying—that is, they were to count as a lie any action they took intentionally that successfully misled another person. It is risky to allow participants to define the unit of analysis; some respondents, for example, might have minimized the reporting of their lying, in considering some forms of deception (e.g., lies that did not hurt anybody) to not really be lies, so as to appear more ethical or truthful. However, to adopt other unit-defining methods would be awkward, if not impossible, using the diary approach. Allowing the participant to define the unit was a conscious choice of the researchers that was dictated by the method.

As can be seen, there are many gradations of unit definition. There is no general rule to guide the researcher in choice of unit of observation, other than the rule of common sense and the objectives of the researcher. As in DePaulo et al. (1996), it often is the case that the observational context itself will suggest, if not completely dictate, the unit and the manner in which it is defined.

Time: When and How Long

An important general consideration in developing category systems concerns time. When using the temporal aspect of systematic observations, two general issues arise. The first of these has to do with the timing of observations. Some systems divide the behavioral stream in terms of temporal units. That is, over every time interval (say every 5, 10, or 20 seconds), a behavioral code is assigned to the individual or group under observation. In this approach, time defines the unit. Research of this form often is used to study recurring interdependencies between behaviors. In a study of young children's play behavior, for example, we might find that children's aggressive outbursts are often preceded by other children frustrating their desires.

A second way in which time is used in observational research is not as a segmenting system, but as a dependent measure, signifying the duration of a particular coded event. Returning to our children's example, we might code both the child's aggressive outburst *and its duration*. This form of measurement is becoming increasingly popular with modern video techniques, which impart a running time signature on the interaction record (Bakeman, 2000).

Category System Construction

Given the number of potential category systems, how can the investigator choose one over the others? Or, having considered the possible choices and rejected them all, what are the criteria the researcher should bear in mind in constructing his or her own category system? In the following paragraphs, we consider some important aspects of category-system construction.

Intensity-Extensity of Systems

Perhaps one of the most important questions the prospective category-system constructor must address concerns the degree of detail required of the observational data. Should the researcher pursue a general description of all broad events that occur in the observational setting, or, rather, concentrate intensively on a particular set of precisely defined actions or behaviors, to the exclusion of all others? Clearly, this answer will depend on the topic under investigation. Even with the same event, the level of observational scrutiny from intensive narrow detail (e.g., a smiling child with braces salivating over a cheeseburger dripping with sauce) to broad extensive coverage (e.g., a child eating lunch) might render a different picture of the results.

Making use of an extensive system, which aims for broad coverage (at the expense of fine detail), an investigator can enhance the likelihood that all potentially relevant events occurring within the observational period will at least have been noted, i.e., categorized. It usually is the case, however, that the more extensive the category system, the less complete are the recorded (or coded) details of any given event made by the observers. Thus, whereas the researcher making use of an extensive coding scheme might be able to describe the general outlines of the total behavioral patterns, it is unlikely that these data will convey much precise or nuanced information from any specific event.

Increased precision of description demands a constriction of observational focus. To describe an event intensively, the observer must ignore other, perhaps equally important, incidents that happen to occur simultaneously. For example, if coders are instructed to pay attention exclusively to faces in categorizing emotional expression (e.g., joy, anger, fear, or sadness), observations of body movements in general (e.g., aggressive or nonaggressive body stance) might be overlooked. If one is concerned about a specific behavior or set of behaviors, this loss of general, broad information might not be bothersome. However, observational specificity assumes considerable knowledge of the events of possible significance in the situation under investigation.

For example, suppose that we wished to study nonverbal communication among members of a specific adolescent gang. To accomplish this, we construct an elaborate coding scheme through which the changing facial expressions of the observed individuals can be intensively studied. The coding scheme is so detailed that categories are provided for even the subtlest facial nuances. However, if after months of pretesting the system, training coders, gaining entry into the gang, and so on, we discover that a major value of the gang members is the maintenance of a poker face at all costs, then our efforts will have been largely wasted. Here, all participant facial expressions will be coded as belonging to the same category (neutral expression) for that variable. A more extensive, less detail-specific system, such as coding for types of hand gang signs and types of overall body language, might not have been defeated by idiosyncratic norms of this type. Conversely, if we had already known about the major aspects of nonverbal communication within the gang, the use of a *general* extensive coding system could have proved extremely inefficient. An extensive category system in this example would provide not only much unnecessary, irrelevant data, but also would prohibit the investigator from intensively concentrating on the relevant behaviors.

There is an obvious trade-off involved, then, in the choice of intensive versus extensive category systems. The decision regarding the type of system to use should be based primarily on the relative amount of information the investigator possesses about the phenomenon of interest. In an exploratory study, intensive concentration on a very specific set of behaviors (e.g., nonverbal displays) is risky because the arbitrarily chosen indicators might convey little worthwhile information. This might arise if all the observations are coded into the same category, if the researcher has

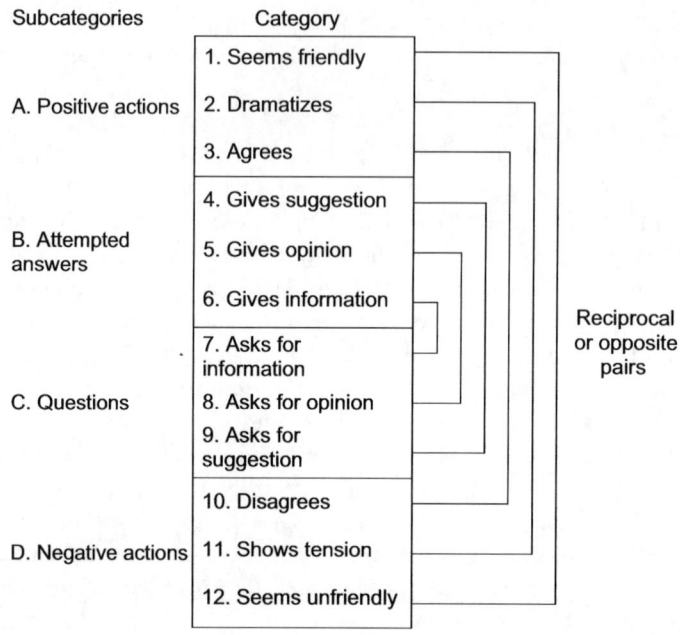

FIGURE 12.2 Categories of Bales's interaction process analysis: 1 variable with 12 categories.

difficulty in discerning and therefore distinguishing the observations (e.g., everyone appears to have a neutral expression). While concentrating on specific actions, other more important details can be neglected. When the boundaries of the phenomenon in question have been clearly delineated and such minor details in categories can be observationally discerned by the coders, the use of an intensive system that focuses specifically on the events known to be important is strongly suggested.

Most of the widely used category systems range between the extremes of complete coverage of all broad events and intense concentration on minute behavioral details. A good example of a fairly extensive (and widely used) category system, which is limited to the classification of interpersonal behavior, is provided by Bales's (1950, 1970) interaction process analysis (IPA), presented in Figure 12.2. (See Bales & Cohen, 1979 for extended discussions of this general approach, and Nam, Lyons, Hwang, & Kim, 2009, for an example of its application.) In this system, the 12 coding classifications represent a broad range of possible interactive behaviors that can occur between members of a small group.[6]

An example of a contrast to Bales's extensive system is Caldwell's (1968) model, which she dubbed APPROACH, a procedure for patterning responses of adults and children. Caldwell's 65-category coding scheme is more restrictive in the events observed and recorded. In this case (as in most other systems of this type), an intensive categorization system reflects the researcher's desire to provide a system that is sensitive enough to allow for very fine distinctions to be made between highly similar behaviors.

Number of Categories in the System

Apart from differing in terms of intensity/extensity of categories, the most striking contrast between the Bales and Caldwell systems is the difference in the absolute number of categories employed in each scheme. The choice of number of categories for the variable being studied is an important consideration in constructing or choosing a coding system. Generally, the more complex the behavior to be observed, the more simple the category system should be. The logic of this assertion becomes clear upon examination. Keep in mind that with all coding systems, decisions on the part of coders regarding the assignment (i.e., categorization) of any given action are a vital part of the research process. Furthermore, in the study of any complex set of behaviors, even the most intricate of systems will not be so complete as to handle every action that occurs. Thus, the combination of highly complex observational data and a large number of possible coding options (some of which require the observer to make extremely fine-grained judgments among coding alternatives) can result in an overload in the capacity of even the most experienced, well-trained coder.

Using fewer, broader categories will tend to transform the coders' function from one of split-second decision-making to that of more leisurely observation and categorization of events. In Figure 12.2, although 12 categories or levels may be coded for this variable, the researcher may choose to collapse and code into four categories instead (positive actions, attempted answers, questions, negative actions). Thus, instead of differentiating among the three types of positive actions (i.e., seems friendly, dramatizes, or agrees) as separate categories, such observations will be judged the same and simply coded as positive actions. Although this produces a much easier coding system for the observers, this will yield data insensitive to discriminating the various types of positive actions.

With the widespread use of electronic recording devices, some of these issues are less important than has previously been the case. Even so, despite the assistance of modern technology, it is still true that coders "burn out," so lessening the demands on them is a good long-term strategy. In much observational research, especially that conducted in settings that restrict respondents' movements (e.g., the research laboratory), videos of the critical interactions can be made, and these can be viewed as often as necessary to ensure a reliable coding of behaviors. In this way, complicated coding schemes can be used to study even complex behavior. Such a combination will call for considerable re-reviews of the video, but with a sufficiently motivated cadre of coders, such a process can result in a highly informative analysis.

Studying behavior of the more simple variety demands a more elaborate classification system to ensure that the subtle behavioral differences that do occur in the situation will be noticed. An example of the types of behaviors that can be examined through the use of a complex coding scheme is provided by Caldwell (1968), whose observers were to note the actions and reactions of individual children to their surroundings, a nursery school setting. In this setting, coders had ample time to determine which of the 65 APPROACH categories described the responses of the child they were observing. Using the same system to classify the responses of adults in a group discussion situation would have proved considerably more difficult, because the adult's actions would have been more subtle, exhibited greater purpose, and occurred with greater rapidity and frequency. In this instance, Bales's 12 categories of the IPA would be a more realistic and appropriate option, unless the group interaction was videotaped.

Increasing the Number of Categorical Variables

So far we have only discussed coding categories in single variable systems. It also is possible to categorize responses guided by several coding dimensions or variables. DePaulo et al. (1996) provide a good example of such an approach. In their research on lying, the researchers were interested in four different variables reflecting this behavior: The content of the lie, its reason, the type of lie, and the lie's referent. A schematic of this system is presented in Table 12.1. Researchers assigning categorical codes to the lies respondents mentioned in their diaries would code each lie according to each of the four variables of content, reason, type, and referent. Coding decisions for these

TABLE 12.1 Coding scheme of DePaulo et al. (1996): 4 variables.

Variable	Category
Content	1. Feelings 2. Accomplishments or Knowledge 3. Actions or Plans 4. Factors or Property
Reason	1. Protect Liar 2. Protect Other
Type	1. Total Falsehood 2. Exaggeration 3. Subtle (evasion or omission)
Referent	1. Liar Himself/Herself 2. Target of Lie 3. Another Person 4. Event or Object

four types of variables provides more information and thus more variables for subsequent analyses. After data collection, two or more variables might be evaluated in statistical tests to determine if a relationship or association exists. Results might show that lies typically classified as "feelings" for the content variable tended to also be classified as "protect liar" for the reason variable. The results would imply that lies to conceal actual feelings serve the social purpose of protecting the liar from emotional harm.

Assessing Category Use

As has been emphasized, constructing a useful coding system should involve careful consideration of the relationship between the coding system, the observational context, and the types of behaviors to be observed. To construct a coding scheme independent of some consideration of the settings in which it will be employed, and of the types of behaviors it will be used to classify, is foolhardy at best. Thus, we recommend that the practicality and utility of any given coding system under construction be regularly and systematically investigated. Arbitrarily selecting a coding system often results in superfluous categories or some classifications that should be broken down into smaller, more precise units of analysis. This is not meant as an argument to reinvent the wheel with each new study, but rather that the coding scheme should be compatible with the research purposes and terrain (see Bakeman & Casey, 1995, or Bakeman & Gottman, 1997, for more extended discussions of this issue).

In the initial phase of category construction, it is best to employ the planned system in a pilot test, to note the frequency with which the various categories of a variable are employed. In general, a good set of categories will be one in which all of the category levels are used relatively frequently and evenly. If a given category is consistently underused, it either should be broadened, to account for more of the behaviors that occur, or dropped as one of the levels of the variable. Conversely, a category whose frequency of usage is considerably greater than all of the others should be divided into more discriminating classifications. Category refinement of this nature should proceed until the distribution of descriptive classifications in the preliminary investigation is not extremely disproportionate. Only when this phase of the construction process is completed should the investigator consider using the system in a real research setting.

Inference

In addition to the potential problems that have been mentioned, the category system constructor is faced with a difficult decision when deciding upon the degree of inference the prospective system will require of coders. Should the classification system deal strictly with *observable events,* or, rather, require the coder to make some inferences regarding possible attitudes, motivations, or intentions of the participant under investigation? As psychological tendencies and states are not directly observable, information regarding these mental processes must be inferred from observable behaviors. If a coding variable is based solely on clearly observable behaviors, then the investigator need not be overly concerned about possible differences in interpretation of the same behavior by different observers. Such concrete, behavior-based category systems, however, often do not allow for the clear transmission of the "feeling" of the interaction. The subtle nuances of the observational situation are lost, often at cost to the interpretation and integration of the obtained results. Many years ago, Heyns and Zander (1953, p. 390) illustrated the choices confronting the scientist quite well:

> At the simpler (noninferential) extreme, [the observer] might develop categories such as "Shoves other children," "Calls other children names," "Asks for help,".... On the other hand, he may use such categories as "Shows hostility," "Demands submission," [etc.]. In the latter case the observers are looking at the same behavior but are making inferences concerning it.

When determining the inference level of categories, much depends on the degree to which the coding operations of the investigation are removed from the actual observational setting. If the research operations call for the concurrent observation and coding of behavior, then inferences regarding the motivation underlying the observed events can cause problems. Interpreting and coding a person's motives "on line" is difficult. Coding on line does not allow the coder the time to sit back and think about an actor's internal state. Inference-making is facilitated if the coding and categorization operations are being observed on video-recorded actions, however.

The predominant school of thought recommends that observational methods be applied only to directly observable events and behaviors. Many value the methodology of systematic observation precisely because it is largely inference free, although there might sometimes be disagreements among raters observing the same event. We appreciate this view. Indeed, keeping coder judgments of underlying, unobserved cognitions to a minimum is bound to facilitate the reliability of a coding scheme. On the other hand, inferences about the motives, beliefs, or emotions underlying a given behavior can sometimes be quite obvious. These inferential judgments add richness to the coding scheme, if they can be made reliably.

Interrater Reliability

A primary consideration in the construction of any observation coding system concerns the issue of the reliability of observers in coding the categories of a variable. As Geller (1955, p. 194) noted, "The fewer the categories, the more precise their definition, and the less inference required in making classifications, the greater will be the reliability of the data." Weick (1985, p. 38) outlined four types of comparisons that could be used in observational research to assess the extent of rating reliability:

> First, the ratings of two persons observing the same event would be correlated, a measure that would rule out the errors of change in the person and the environment. Next, the ratings of the same observer watching a similar event at two different times would be compared (this

would rule out errors of content sampling.) Then the agreement of two observers observing an event at two different times would be correlated. This measure ... would be expected to yield the lowest reliability of the four comparisons. Finally, the observations of a single observer watching a single event would be compared in a manner similar to odd–even item correlations in a test. This is a check on internal consistency or the extent to which the observer agrees with himself. If the category system is explicit and well defined, this measure of reliability would be expected to yield the highest correlation.

Assessing all four types of rating reliability for every variable in a study would be daunting. Doing so represents the gold standard in ensuring that the rating system is reliable, but most observational research normally assesses just one of these forms of reliability, usually interrater reliability of the same event in time.

In qualitative classification systems, nominal measurement scales are employed, with values that have no meaningful quantitative differentiation in terms of whether a higher value reflects a higher score. Examples of qualitatively coded variables include participant gender (male or female), race (White, Latino, Asian, Black), and whether the participant performed a particular action (yes or no). Another example of a qualitative rating system is presented in Table 12.1, which shows that for a particular observation, one of the four categorical levels (1 = feelings, 2 = accomplishments or knowledge, 3 = actions or plans, and 4 = facts or property) could be assigned for the content variable. The most fundamental question of interrater reliability is, "Do the ratings of two or more observers who have witnessed the same event(s) coincide to an acceptable degree?" By acceptable degree, we mean beyond that which would occur by chance. For example, if we have a system consisting of only two categories, and our two observers agree 60% of the time on this variable, should we be satisfied? Recognizing that agreement in such a system containing two categories would occur by chance 50% of the time, it is evident that a 60% intercoder agreement rate is not much to write home about.

Cohen's kappa is an index to assess the extent of agreement between two coders of a qualitative categorical variable while controlling for chance (Cohen, 1960, 1968). Kappa's value can range from .00 (no agreement whatsoever) to 1.0 (perfect agreement). Conceptually, the statistic is relatively straightforward. We begin with a matrix whose rows and columns reflect the various categories of the coding scheme. The rows represent the codings of observer A; the columns represent those of observer B. So for example, suppose we are using the category system that DePaulo et al. (1996) used to code lying, and we are focusing on the first dimension of their system, namely the content of the lie. We could develop an agreement matrix by listing all the codings made by two observers for the content variable, as in Table 12.2. Each coder separately indicated the core content identified in each of the 236 lies. The diagonal entries in the table represent the number of times the coders have overlapped (i.e., agree) on a given category. The non-diagonal elements represent disagreements. The greater the number of entries off the diagonal, the lower the kappa and the lower the interrater reliability of the coding system.

To calculate Cohen's Kappa (κ), we first need information on the proportion of intercoder agreement. This is calculated by summing the diagonal entries and dividing by the total number of observations. In our example,

$P_{agree} = (44 + 61 + 38 + 19)/236$, or $162/236$, or .686.

The index reveals that 68.6% of the observations of content overlap between the two coders. To find the proportion of interrater agreements expected by chance, we multiply each column total with its respective row total, and sum these products. This sum would then be divided by the

TABLE 12.2 Agreement matrix used in calculating Cohen's Kappa: 2 observers qualitatively coding 256 lies.

		Observer B				
	Category	1	2	3	4	Total
	1. Feelings	44	5	0	6	55
	2. Accomplishments	4	61	5	22	92
Observer A	3. Actions	2	5	38	0	45
	4. Facts	0	18	7	19	44
	Total	50	89	50	47	236

square of the total number of observations. In our example, this process would require the following calculations:

$$P_{chance} = [(50 * 55) + (89 * 92) + (50 * 45) + (47 * 44)]/236^2$$
$$= [(2750) + (8188) + (2250) + (2068)]/55696.$$

The end result of this series of calculations is 15256/55696, or .274 (27.4% of observations are due to chance agreement).

To determine Cohen's Kappa, we use the following formula:

$$K = \frac{P_{agree} - P_{chance}}{1 - P_{chance}}.$$

Plugging our values into this formula, this produces $K = .567$. The value is somewhat less than the proportion of intercoder agreement originally found ($P_{agree} = .686$), and reflects the adjustment made after ruling out chance agreements.[7] This is not a particularly strong result. Generally, observational researchers suggest that a Kappa greater than .75 is "excellent"; Kappas between .60 and .75 are "good," Kappas from .40 to .59 are "fair," and those less than .40 indicate a "poor" intercoder agreement (Fleiss, 1981).

The concordance matrix of Table 12.2 gives some indication of the source of the relatively low Kappa, and by extension, its solution. To improve the coding scheme, or the coder training, we scrutinize the off-diagonal entries. Are there cells off the diagonal that suggest an inordinate or unacceptable number of disagreements? In the hypothetical table presented here, it is clear that our two observers had most disagreement on the categorization of lies as involving either accomplishments (category 2) or facts (category 4), as these reveal the highest number of non-correspondences. This suggests that the researcher must clarify the operational definition of these two categories to the coders, combine or remove categories, or spend more time training coders about the categorical distinctions—or all three.

So far the discussion of interrater reliability has been limited to qualitative classifications between exactly two coders. **Fleiss' Kappa** (1971) index assesses the extent of agreement between two or more coders of a qualitative categorical variable while controlling for chance. Fleiss' Kappa ranges on a reliability index from 0 to 1.0, with the same cutoff criteria involving "excellent," "good,", "fair," and "poor" for Cohen's Kappa. With exactly two coders, it is acceptable to use Fleiss' Kappa to calculate interrater reliability, as the resultant value will be the same as Cohen's Kappa (except for rounding error).

Weick (1985) holds that the reliability of a coding system is a reflection of both the discriminability of the classifications that constitute the scheme and the efficacy of coder training. In the construction of category systems, interrater reliability is of major importance, because without it very little use can be made of the collected observations. For example, suppose in our research we have obtained the intercoder agreement matrix of Table 12.2. The level of agreement is not satisfactory, but which coder's observation is the more accurate? We have no way to answer this question. It is equally difficult to determine the cause of disagreement, that is, whether it is attributable to insufficient coder training or to the non-discriminability of some of the categories that constitute the coding system.

Enhancing coder agreement often calls for nothing more than practice. Given sufficient practice with a coding scheme, most coders can learn to employ reliably even the most complex of systems. Non-discriminability of categories, however, represents a more difficult problem. If a single unit of behavior can be logically classified through the use of two or more categories contained in the same coding variable, this gives rise to intercoder disagreements that augmented training will not resolve.[8] The appropriate response to problems of this type is to restructure categories to delineate more clearly the boundaries of each, by, for example, combing categories posing challenges in coder discrimination. This, in turn, calls for additional coder instruction and training, to determine whether the sought-for effectiveness in category differentiation has occurred.

All the previously mentioned aspects of system construction affect the reliability of the coding scheme. The interrater reliability of a coding variable will be enhanced if:

- The coding variable is extensive, rather than intensive.
- The unit of analysis is predefined by the observer, rather than based on some dynamic action of the observed.
- The coding variable consists of a small rather than large number of categories.
- Actions of the observed and classification by observers are not concurrent processes (i.e., audio or video devices are used to allow for careful review of the observational data).
- Only directly observable behaviors are assessed, so that little or no psychological inference is called for.

We do not mean to suggest that these considerations should always serve as the central criteria to determine how categories are constructed for each variable, but rather to call attention to the fact that some types of categorization are less susceptible to problems of interrater unreliability.

Structured Methods: Rating Scales

Sometimes the research is not concerned with classifying observed events into distinct qualitative categories, but rather with quantitatively rating observations in terms of frequency, amount, or duration. In its simplest form, a quantitative rating scale is an extension of a qualitative system, in which a coder classifies by evaluating the magnitude or intensity of a variable. Quantitative observations may be ordinal, interval, or ratio (Hallgren, 2012), with higher values representing greater quantities of the observed variable. Examples of quantitative coding variables include the amount of time (in seconds or minutes) that a lie was elaborated on. Another example is the frequency of the number of times that the same lie is told. To make inferences about non-directly observable psychological or attitudinal events, a coding variable might use quantitative ratings with end points to help guide judgments. For example, coders might be required to evaluate the persuasiveness of each lie, from 1 (very unconvincing) to 10 (very convincing). This additional aspect of coding often makes achieving interrater reliability more difficult and alters the way it is assessed.

The intraclass correlation (ICC) is an index of interrater reliability for two or more coders of a quantitative variable (Shrout & Fleiss, 1979). The ICC ranges from 0 to 1.0, with higher values

TABLE 12.3 Interrater scores used in calculating the ICC: Four observers quantitatively rating 15 lies.

Lie #	Observer A	Observer B	Observer C	Observer D
1	9	9	10	10
2	6	5	6	5
3	2	4	5	9
4	2	4	3	4
5	3	2	5	3
6	6	5	7	7
7	5	6	8	6
8	2	5	4	6
9	7	7	7	7
10	3	3	5	2
11	8	9	1	2
12	3	3	5	2
13	9	10	7	8
14	7	9	7	4
15	5	5	5	6

representing stronger interrater reliability for that variable. Recall from Chapter 9 that this is the same ICC that is used in analyses of multi-level modelling and has a similar logic: Observations are nested under each coder. In other words, each coder rates observations for all participants in a study. In this case, the ICC refers to the degree to which two or more coders' observations overlap.

Suppose that each of four observers independently provided a rating, based on the previously mentioned 10-point persuasiveness scale, for 15 lies. The judgments are shown in Table 12.3. The ICC would be used to provide an evaluation of the extent that observers' ratings are related. Unlike Cohen's Kappa and Fleiss' Kappa, both of which necessitate an exact correspondence in categorization among coders to be deemed a match, the ICC does not require identical scores from coders to yield a relatively acceptable index. Whereas qualitative rating scales are concerned with *absolute agreement* among raters (coded categories do or do not match), quantitative scales are more concerned with consistency or *relative agreement* among raters (the extent of the match among raters). A high ICC will be achieved if the pattern of rated scores assigned by a coder are relatively consistent and in the same direction as the scores for the other coder(s). Thus, if one coder's mean scores are consistently higher than another's, but their patterns of scores are highly similar, a strong ICC will be found.

Using the values shown in Table 12.3, the calculation of the ICC yields a respectable interrater reliability of .80. Although the statistical details are beyond the scope of the chapter, the ICC may be understood as the extent of correlation among the scores made by multiple raters. Let's try to understand how certain patterns of obtained scores may impact the value of the ICC. Inspecting Table 12.3, notice that for lie #1, the four coders did not assign precisely the same values. Although not identical, the ratings assigned for this lie will tend to contribute to a higher ICC because the relative agreement pattern shows that all four raters typically assigned higher scores. Conversely, lie #3 would contribute to a lower ICC because the categorizations across all four judges were erratic: Observer 1 gave a low score, observers 2 and 3 gave middling scores, and observer 4 gave a high score. In fact, if this particular lie were omitted from the analysis, the remaining 14 lies would yield a higher recomputed ICC of .84.

Researchers should understand the circumstances in which it is suitable to use the ICC versus Cohen's Kappa, versus Fleiss' Kappa, in assessing interrater reliability. If the quantitative ratings from

Table 12.3 were accidentally used to compute Fleiss' Kappa, which would yield an assessment of absolute coder correspondence for the 10 categories, that would yield an erroneously low and meaningless interrater reliability value.

Combining Quantitative and Qualitative Codings

Separate qualitative and quantitative coding variables may be integrated into the same observational study. By inclusion of multiple variables to assess and code all features and aspects of events, relationships and associations among variables could be profitably examined in advanced statistical analyses. Suppose that a researcher coded observations based on the qualitative variable of *reason for lying* (protecting the liar or protecting the other person) and also the quantitative variable of persuasiveness (using a 1 to 10 point scale) of that same lie. Suppose that this system was used by observers to code the lies, with both variables found to yield strong interrater reliabilities. After determining acceptable systematic agreement among raters, this then gives the investigator permission to go forward using these reliable variables in statistical analyses. A t test analysis might show that the persuasiveness score averaged 8.5 if the reason for the lie is to protect the liar, but a significantly lower average persuasiveness score of 4.0 is found if the reason concerned protecting others.

It also is feasible that a variable may be coded categorically, and then levels of the categories are coded quantitatively to provide additional information. Consider the plight of an observer making use of Bales's IPA in coding the behavior of an individual in a small group interaction. The observed participant's response to another person in the group must be classified through the use of one of the 12 IPA categories. In itself, this can be a difficult job. Suppose that the observer must determine qualitatively the proper classification of an action and also estimate quantitatively the intensity of the response. Having decided that an act by person A "seems friendly" (category 1) toward person B, the coder must then quantify whether this friendliness was 1 = *very low,* 2 = *somewhat low,* 3 = *average,* 4 = *somewhat high,* or 5 = *very high.* The result of this combined approach is that the complexity of the coders' task is greatly increased, because they must not only categorize but also rate the critical behaviors (in terms of intensity, magnitude, duration, etc.).

In opposition to these disadvantages stands the possibility of increasing the information value of the obtained results. Returning to Bales's IPA, suppose that given what you've mastered about observational coding, you travel back in time to the early days of the founding of the United States. You find yourself observing the members of the Constitutional Convention on 1787 in their deliberations on the Declaration of Independence. One member of the Congress, feeling great ambivalence over Jefferson's document, hesitantly states, "Yes, I suppose I can go along with this." You code this as an instance of category 3, "agrees." Another member, perhaps better understanding the historical significance of his actions, jumps up and screams, "I will stake my fortune and my life on this document!" This action also is coded as an instance of category 3. Clearly, these two acts are different, yet both receive the same score—the categorical (but quantity-free) IPA cannot denote even this obvious distinction in intensity. Through the inclusion of quantitative coding, such as an indication of the strength of the agreement from 1 (some agreement) to 5 (full agreement), differences of this type are not glossed over, and a more descriptive picture of the social interaction is conveyed.

Conclusion

In observational research, the degree of control placed on the allowable actions of the observer is wide-ranging. At the least controlled pole, we have the open, unconstrained methods of the early ethnographers; this approach to the accumulation of information is different from that of the highly structured, often ritualistic practices of today's experimentalists. We believe that the development of increasingly sophisticated methods to reduce the impact of the observer on the observed reflects the growth, evolution, and overall progress of the science of human behavior. Yet, as we suggested at the beginning of this chapter, it often is the case that the more elementary, basic, "foundation-building" observational techniques have been neglected in favor of the more "advanced" experimental ones. This can be a mistake. Schwartz and Jacobs (1979, p. 327) highlighted the importance of observational methods when they stated, "Ordinarily (in the experimental methods), one has a hypothesis, knows pretty well what it means, and wants to know if it is true. Here (in the observational methods), one has a hypothesis, is pretty sure that is true, and wants to know what it means (wants to know what is true.)."

Questions for Discussion

1. What is Cohen's Kappa? Why is it a better estimate of inter-judge agreement than a simple percentage of agreement measure?
2. Can a research laboratory (where participants would typically participate in psychological experiments) be an appropriate setting for naturalistic observation? In what situations might this be reasonable? Why would a researcher *want* to use a laboratory as the preferred setting to observe "natural" behavior? What would be an example of two studies where the only difference between them is that one used naturalistic observation to assess the dependent measure, and the other used an "unnatural" measure (e.g., written self-report) to assess the same dependent construct? Could you think of a situation in which participants are knowingly interacting with the experimenter in a laboratory setting, but the data being collected are still considered "natural behaviors?"
3. You are interested in understanding the group processes, member dynamics, and development of group norms among members of semi-closed societies (e.g., the Freemasons, Cannon Club members at Princeton University, etc.). You eventually gain access to a society of this type by posing as a member during one of their ceremonies, and collect extensive field notes. What are your ethical obligations as a researcher to the members of the society who have been the subject of your research? Does gaining access as a non-researcher mean that it is unnecessary to obtain informed consent before collecting data? Alternatively, does gaining access as a non-researcher mean that you are bound by the rules of the society that you "joined" (which probably means not secretly collecting data)? Ultimately, do researchers risk entering an ethical gray area when they gain access to an insular population under the guise of something other than observational research, where they do not obtain informed consent, and when they are not responsible for adhering to the group's rules and norms? Can such research be justified in terms of costs and potential benefits?

Notes

1. In Moriarty's (1975) study, 95% of those asked to watch the "victim's" belongings did intervene in the theft, whereas in a similar study that did not include a specific request, no one even tried to stop the staged theft of an expensive calculator in a college library (Austin, 1979).
2. Whether a study of this kind would be viewed today as ethically defensible is an open question. We discuss questions of this type in Chapter 20.
3. It is interesting to note that after the first day of observation, the couple's references to the materials in the study became extremely infrequent. This does not necessarily mean that the couple's behavior was unaffected by their participation in the study, however, but does suggest that awareness of observation decreases over time.

4. In fairness, it should be noted that Becker has found the participatory observational approach suitable for hypothesis- and theory-testing, but he indicated that this operation could legitimately occur only after a number of prior requirements were satisfied (also see Kidder, 1981).
5. The use of any coding scheme presupposes the existence of some hypothesis. If there were none, then the observer focusing on a certain restricted set of behaviors (which all coding schemes assume) would have no reasonable basis for doing so.
6. Note, however, that Bales's categories deal with the nature of the interaction, not its content.
7. A number of online programs are available to reduce the drudgery of calculating Kappa (e.g., http://vassarstats.net/kappa.html).
8. A good indication of non-discriminability of categories occurs when the same observer, reviewing the same behaviors (typically through the use of video recordings), assigns different scores from the first to the second observation. Results of this type suggest that the coding classifications cannot be employed with any degree of reliability.

References

Atwood, R. W., & Howell, R. J. (1971). Pupillometric and personality test score differences of female aggressing pedophiliacs and normals. *Psychonomic Science, 22,* 115–116.

Austin, W. G. (1979). Sex differences in bystander intervention in a theft. *Journal of Personality and Social Psychology, 37,* 2110–2120.

Bakeman, R. (2000). Behavioral observation and coding. In H. Reis & C. Judd (Eds.), *Handbook of research methods in social and personality psychology* (pp. 138–159). New York: Cambridge University Press.

Bakeman, R., & Casey, R. L. (1995). Analyzing family interaction: Taking time into account. *Journal of Family Psychology, 9,* 131–143.

Bakeman, R., & Gottman, J. M. (1997). *Observing interaction: An introduction to sequential analysis* (2nd ed.). New York: Cambridge University Press.

Bales, R. F. (1950). *Interaction process analysis.* Cambridge, MA: Addison-Wesley.

Bales, R. F. (1970). *Personality and interpersonal behavior.* New York: Holt, Rinehard, and Winston.

Bales, R. F., & Cohen, S. P. (1979). *SYMLOG: A system for multiple level observation of groups.* New York: Free Press.

Barton, A. H., & Lazarsfeld, P. H. (1969). Some functions of qualitative analysis in social research. In G. J. McCall & J. L. Simmonds (Eds.), *Issues in participant observation.* Reading, MA: Addison-Wesley.

Becker, H. S. (1958). Problems of inference and proof in participant observation. *American Sociological Review, 23,* 652–660.

Bogden, R. (1972). *Participant observation in organizational settings.* Syracuse, NY: Syracuse University Press.

Borgida, E., & Nisbett, R. F. (1977). The differential impact of abstract versus concrete information on decisions. *Journal of Applied Social Psychology, 7,* 258–271.

Bourgeault, I. L. (2000). Delivering the "new" Canadian midwifery: The impact on midwifery of integration into the Ontario health care system. *Sociology of Health and Illness, 22,* 172–196.

Caldwell, B. M. (1968). A new "approach" to behavioral ecology. In J. P. Hill (Ed.), *Minnesota symposia on child psychology* (vol. 2, pp. 74–108). Minneapolis, MN: University of Minnesota Press.

Carlson, J., Cook, S. W., & Stromberg, E. L. (1936). Sex differences in conversation. *Journal of Applied Psychology, 20,* 727–735.

Cicourel, A. V. (1964). *Method and measurement in sociology.* New York: Free Press of Glencoe.

Cohen, J. A. (1960). A coefficient of agreement for nominal scales. *Educational and Psychological Measurement, 20,* 37–46.

Cohen, J. A. (1968). Weighted kappa: Nominal scale agreement with provision for scaled disagreement or partial credit. *Psychological Bulletin, 70,* 213–220.

Collings, P. (2009). Participant observation and phased assertion as research strategies in the Canadian Arctic. *Field Methods, 21,* 133–153.

Dabbs, J. M., Jr., & Milun, R. (1999). Pupil dilation when viewing strangers: Can testosterone moderate prejudice? *Social Behavior and Personality, 27,* 297–302.

DeLongis, A., Hemphill, K. J., & Lehman, D. R. (1992). A structured diary methodology for the study of daily events. In F. B. Bryant, J. Edwards, R. S. Tindale, E. J. Posavac, L. Heath, E. Henderson & Y. Suarez-Balcazar (Eds.), *Methodological issues in applied social psychology* (pp. 83–109). New York: Plenum Press.

DePaulo, B. M., Kashy, D. A., Kirkendol, S. E., Wyer, M. M., & Epstein, J. A. (1996). Lying in everyday life. *Journal of Personality and Social Psychology, 70,* 979–995.

DeWalt, K. M., & DeWalt, B. R. (2010). *Participant observation: A guide for fieldworkers* (2 ed.). Plymouth, UK: AltaMira Press.

Festinger, L., Riecken, H. W., & Schachter, S. S. (1956). *When prophecy fails.* Minneapolis, MN: University of Minnesota Press.

Fleiss, J. L. (1971). Measuring nominal scale agreement among many raters. *Psychological Bulletin, 76,* 378–382.

Fleiss, J. L. (1981). *The design and analysis of clinical experiments.* New York: Wiley.

Geller, E. (1955). Systematic observation: A method in child study. *Harvard Educational Review, 25,* 179–195.

Glaser, B. G., & Strauss, A. L. (1967). *The discovery of grounded theory: Strategies for qualitative research.* Chicago: Aldine.

Guba, E. (1980). *The evaluator as instrument.* Unpublished manuscript, Indiana University, Bloomington, IN.

Guba, E. G., & Lincoln, Y. S. (2008). Paradigmatic controversies, contradictions, and emerging confluences. In N. K. Denzin & Y. S. Lincoln (Eds.), *The landscape of qualitative research* (3rd ed., pp. 255–286). Thousand Oaks, CA: Sage.

Hallgren, K. A. (2012). Computing inter-rater reliability for observational data: An overview and tutorial. *Tutorials in quantitative methods for psychology, 8,* 23–34.

Henle, M, & Hubbell, M. B. (1938). "Egocentricity" in adult conversation. *Journal of Social Psychology, 9,* 227–234.

Hess, E. H. (1965). Attitude and pupil size. *Scientific American, 212,* 46–54.

Hess, E. H., Seltzer, A. L., & Shlien, J. M. (1965). Pupil responses of hetero- and homosexual males to pictures of men and women: A pilot study. *Journal of Abnormal Psychology, 70,* 165–168.

Heyns, R. W., & Zander, A. F. (1953). Observation of group behavior. In L. Festinger & D. Katz (Eds.), *Research methods in the behavioral sciences.* New York: Holt, Rinehart, and Winston.

Hoare, K. J., Mills, J., & Francis, K. (2012). Sifting, sorting and saturating data in a grounded theory study of information use by practice nurses: A worked example. *International Journal of Nursing Practice, 18,* 582–588.

Howard, W. D., & Crano, W. D. (1974). Effects of sex, conversation, location, and size of observer group on bystander intervention in a high risk situation. *Sociometry, 66,* 255–261.

Janisse, M. P. (1973). Pupil size and affect: A critical review of the literature since 1960. *Canadian Psychologist, 14,* 311–329.

Kidder, L. H. (1981). Qualitative research and quasi-experimental frameworks. In M. B. Brewer & B. E. Collins (Eds.), *Scientific inquiry and the social sciences* (pp. 226–256). San Francisco: Jossey-Bass.

Klumb, P. L., & Baltes, M. M. (1999). Validity of retrospective time-use reports in old age. *Applied Cognitive Psychology, 13,* 527–539.

Kubey, R., Larson, R., & Csikszentmihalyi, M. (1996). Experience sampling method applications to communication research questions. *Journal of Communication, 46,* 99–120.

Larson, R., & Csikszentmihalyi, M. (1978). Experiential correlates of solitude in adolescence. *Journal of Personality, 46,* 677–693.

Larson, R., & Csikszentmihalyi, M. (1980). The significance of time alone in adolescent development. *Journal of Current Adolescent Medicine, 2,* 33–40.

Larson, R., & Csikszentmihalyi, M. (1983). The experience sampling method. In H. T. Reis (Ed.), *Naturalistic approaches to studying social interaction* (pp. 41–56). San Francisco: Jossey-Bass.

Larson, R., Csikszentmihalyi, M., & Graef, R. (1980). Mood variability and the psychosocial adjustment of adolescents. *Journal of Youth and Adolescence, 9,* 469–490.

Leigh, B. C. (1993). Alcohol consumption and sexual activity as reported with a diary technique. *Journal of Abnormal Psychology, 102,* 490–493.

Leventhal, H., & Sharp, E. (1965). Facial expressions as indicators of distress. In S. Tomkins & C. E. Izard (Eds.), *Affect, cognition, and personality* (pp. 296–318). New York: Springer.

Lofland, J. (1971). *Analyzing social settings: A guide to qualitative observation and analysis.* Belmont, CA: Wadsworth.

Mahl, G. F. (1964). Some observations about research on vocal behavior. *Disorders of Communication, 42,* 466–483.

Mehan, H., & Wood, H. (1975). *The reality of ethnomethodology.* New York: Wiley.

Morgan, C. A., III., Grillon, C., Southwick, S. M., Davis, M., & Charney, D. S. (1996). Exaggerated acoustic startle reflex in Gulf War veterans with posttraumatic stress disorder. *American Journal of Psychiatry, 153,* 64–68.

Moriarty, T. (1975). Crime, commitment, and the responsive bystander: Two field experiments. *Journal of Personality and Social Psychology, 31,* 370–376.

Murdock, G. P. (1967). Ethnographic atlas: A summary. *Ethnology, 6,* 109–236.

Murdock, G. P., & White, D. R. (1969). Standard cross-cultural sample. *Ethnology, 8,* 329–69.

Nam, C. S., Lyons, J. B., Hwang, H.-S., & Kim, S. (2009). The process of team communication in multicultural contexts: An empirical study using Bales' interaction process analysis (IPA). *International Journal of Industrial Ergonomics, 39,* 771–782.

Nezlek, J. B., Wheeler, L., & Reis, H. T. (1983). Studies of social participation. In H. T. Reis (Ed.), *Naturalistic approaches to studying social interaction* (pp. 57–75). San Francisco: Jossey-Bass.

Peters, M. L., Sorbi, J. J., Kruise, D. A., Kerssens, J. J., Verhaak, P.F.M., & Bensing, J. M. (2000). Electronic diary assessment of pain, disability, and psychological adaptation in patients differing in duration of pain. *Pain, 84,* 181–192.

Polifroni, M. A., von Hippel, W., & Brewer, M. B. (2001, May). *Nazis on the Web: Support for image theory in the Internet communications of white supremacists.* Paper presented at the annual meeting of the Midwestern Psychological Association, Chicago, IL.

Ponder, E., & Kennedy, W. P. (1927). On the act of blinking. *Quarterly Journal of Experimental Physiology, 18,* 89–110.

Ratliff, E. A. (1999). Women as "sex workers," men as "boyfriends": Shifting identities in Philippine go-go bars and their significance in STD/AIDS control. *Anthropology and Medicine, 6,* 79–101.

Reis, H. T., & Gable, S. L. (2000). Event-sampling and other methods for studying everyday experience. In H. T. Reis & C. M. Judd (Eds.), *Handbook of research methods in social and personality psychology* (pp. 190–222). New York: Cambridge University Press.

Roberts, R. R., & Renzaglia, G. A. (1965). The influence of tape recording on counseling. *Journal of Consulting Psychology, 12,* 10–16.

Robinson, J. P., & Goodbey, G. (1997). *Time for life: The surprising ways Americans use their time.* University Park, PA: Pennsylvania State University Press.

Rosenthal, R. (1966). *Experimenter effects in behavioral research.* New York, NY: Appleton-Century-Crofts.

Rosenthal, R., Persinger, G. W., Vikan-Kline, L., & Fode, K. L. (1963). The effect of early data returns on data subsequently obtained by outcome-biased experimenters. *Sociometry, 26,* 487–498.

Russell, B. (1930). *The conquest of happiness.* New York: Horace Liveright.

Samph, T. (1969). The role of the observer and his effects on teacher classroom behavior. Occasional Papers. Pontiac, MI: Oakland Schools.

Schwartz, H., & Jacobs, J. (1979). *Qualitative sociology: A method to the madness.* New York: Free Press.

Shrout, P. E., & Fleiss, J. L. (1979). Intraclass correlations: Uses in assessing rater reliability. *Psychological Bulletin, 86,* 420–428.

Soskin, W. F., & John, V. P. (1963). The study of spontaneous talk. In R. G. Barker (Ed.), *The stream of behavior* (pp. 228–281). New York: Appleton-Century-Crofts.

Strauss, A. (Ed.). (1991). *Creating sociological awareness: Collective images and symbolic representations.* New Brunswick, NJ: Transaction Publishers.

Strauss, A., & Corbin, J. (Eds.) (1997). *Grounded theory in practice.* Thousand Oaks, CA: Sage.

Thorne, B. (1988). Political activist as participant observer: Conflicts of commitment in a study of the draft resistance movement of the 1960s. In P. C. Higgins & J. M. Johnson (Eds.), *Personal sociology* (pp. 133–152). New York: Praeger.

Tullis, J. A. (2013). Participant observation at the end-of-life: Reflecting on tears. *Health Communication, 28,* 206–208.

Tunnell, G. B. (1977). Three dimensions of naturalness: An expanded definition of field research. *Psychological Bulletin, 84,* 426–437.

Webb, E. J., Campbell, D. T., Schwartz, R. D., Sechrest, L., & Grove, J. (1981). *Nonreactive measures in the social sciences.* Boston: Houghton-Mifflin.

Weick, K. E. (1968). Systematic observational methods. In G. Lindzey and E. Aronson (Eds.), *The handbook of social psychology, Vol. 2:, Research Methods* (2nd ed.). Reading, MA: Addison-Wesley.

Weick, K. E. (1985). Systematic observational methods. In G. Lindzey and E. Aronson (Eds.), *The handbook of social psychology* (3rd ed., (pp. 567–634)). Reading, MA: Addison-Wesley.

Wertz, F. J., Charmaz, K., McMullen, L., Josselson, R., Anderson, R., & McSpadden, E. (2011). *Five ways of doing qualitative analysis: Phenomenological psychology, grounded theory, discourse analysis, narrative research, and intuitive inquiry.* New York: Guilford Press.

Willems, E. P. (1976). Behavioral ecology, health, status, and health care: Applications to the rehabilitation setting. In I. A. Altman & J. F. Wohlwill (Eds.), *Human behavior and environment* (pp. 211–263). New York: Plenum.

Williamson, J., & Karp, D. (1977). *The research craft: An introduction to social science methods.* Boston: Little-Brown.

Zegiob, L. E., Arnold, S., & Forehand, R. (1975). An examination of observer effects in parent-child interactions. *Child Development, 46,* 509–512.

13
INTERVIEWING

The research **interview** is a data collection method in which participants verbally communicate information about their behavior, thoughts, or feelings in response to questions verbally posed by an interviewer. Unlike most of the observational methods discussed in the preceding chapter, interviews always involve some form of verbal interaction in which the investigator requests information from a respondent, and this feature distinguishes the technique from self-administered questionnaire methods (to be discussed in detail in Chapter 15) in which respondents may never interact with a researcher. The interactive process of the interview, and its dependence on verbal or linguistic responses, constitutes both its major strength and its major drawback as a method of social research.

It is almost always easier and less expensive to use written questionnaires than it is to expend the time and effort necessary to conduct interviews (Bartholomew, Henderson, & Marcia, 2000). Thus, it is important to consider the circumstances under which the interview method is most appropriate. Probably the most important basis for choosing the interview occurs when the research issue demands a personal, interactive, and verbal method of data collection. This might be the case, for instance, when highly sensitive information is sought, or when certain responses call for verbal probing for details that would be difficult to elicit using a self-report questionnaire format.

Interviews also might be required with special respondent populations who have challenges in comprehension of a questionnaire (e.g., young children, the elderly, and the illiterate). Further, if the problem of nonresponse poses a serious threat to external validity, it may be more likely that efforts to cultivate rapport with the interviewee via personal contact may achieve higher response rates than the more impersonal self-reported questionnaire approach.[1]

Modes of Administration: Face-to-Face and Telephone

Before beginning the discussion on designing and conducting interviews, it is important to note that interviews do not always entail face-to-face encounters between interviewer and respondent. *Telephone interviews* are extremely common and popular, with good reason. Not many years ago, however, researchers were warned to avoid telephone interviews because it was assumed that people would be less willing than in face-to-face encounters to be interviewed, and those who did agree to participate would be unwilling to give the interviewer more than 5 to 10 minutes of their time. Seminal research focused specifically on this concern indicates that it is much less problematic than originally thought. Groves and Kahn (1979), for example, found that participation rates in telephone interviews were only 5% less than those involving face-to-face encounters, and Bradburn and Sudman's (1979) data demonstrated somewhat higher response rates to telephone, as opposed to personal, interviews—at least in urban areas. In addition, Dillman's (1978) research revealed that the response rate in telephone interviews was approximately 15% greater than that of mail surveys. In terms of respondents' willingness to participate in extensive telephone interviews, implications are much the same as those drawn from the response rate research.[2] Research by Quinn, Gutek, and Walsh (1980), Dillman (1978), and Smith and Kluegel (1984) all indicate that once committed to the telephone interview, respondents are unlikely to disengage prematurely. Studies using telephone interviews lasting as long as an hour have been conducted with no appreciable dropout problem (Kluegel & Smith, 1982). Herman (1977) coupled face-to-face with telephone interviewing. An interviewer went to the homes of those who refused a telephone interview or who could not be reached via phone. She found that the quality of responses collected from phone interviewees was comparable to that obtained from face-to-face respondents, although the phone interviewees were less likely to disclose personal information (e.g., for whom they voted). These findings supporting the comparability of telephone and face-to-face approaches still hold today (Hajebi et al., 2012; Lee et al., 2008).

Despite the many advantages of the telephone approach, it is important to keep in mind some potential disadvantages. In a face-to-face interview, the interviewer is more likely to detect and correct confusion on the part of the respondent (Bartholemew et al., 2000). The face-to-face interviewer is more likely to be able to clarify issues and to realize that a question posed does not carry the intended implication. This is an especially important advantage in the initial research phases in which the interview schedule (the list of questions to be employed) is being developed. The telephone interview also does not allow for the use of visual aids; this can prove to be important if complex questions or lengthy response options are to be provided the interviewee. Finally, the telephone interview does not provide the researcher with visual contact with the respondent. This can prove troublesome in situations in which visual cues are used to replace a number of otherwise lengthy or overly personal questions. In health surveys, for instance, a cursory visual inspection of the physical status of the respondent often proves useful in identifying whether the person is malnourished. Similarly, the telephone approach would seem less than optimal in situations in which respondents' socioeconomic status is to be estimated by visual inspection of their neighborhood or dwelling. In these cases, the telephone interview is not necessarily less costly than the more personal face-to-face approach. No matter what form the mode of interviewing assumes (telephone or face-to-face), the principles that govern good interview technique are the same. In the pages that follow, we will present guidelines that should be followed when using this method.

Developing the Interview

The interview method can be used to study a range of issues, across widely diverse respondent samples. The methodological variations available in the choice of specific interview method, question format, and so on, are equally diverse. Nevertheless, there are a number of common features that all interview research shares, which reflect the decisions the investigator faces at one time or another in the design of any interview study (Figure 13.1). We focus on these "choice points" in the following discussion to provide a general framework within which all of the many and varied forms of interviews might be conceptualized.

Broadly, the strategic research procedures characteristic of all interview studies involve decisions concerning (1) the question content, (2) the interview format, (3) how the interview will be conducted, (4) the sample or population from which respondents will be chosen, and (5) the methods

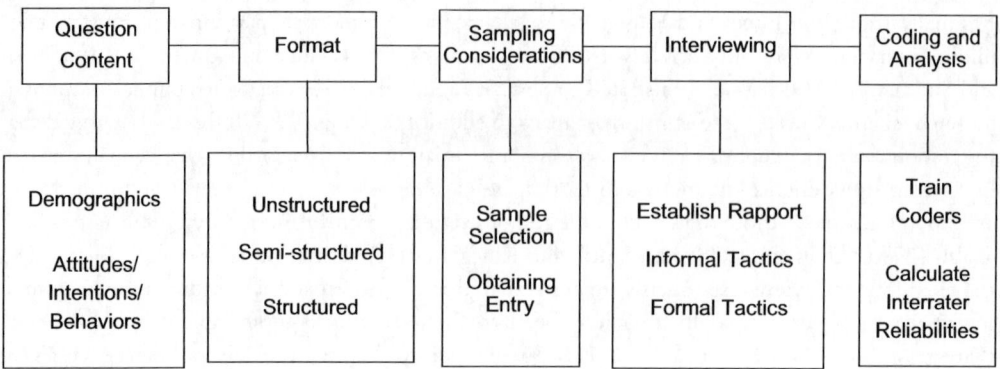

FIGURE 13.1 Steps in designing an interview investigation.

to be used in coding, aggregating, and analyzing respondents' answers. Earlier (Chapter 11) we dealt with considerations of sampling, and in the chapter that follows this one, we discuss the coding, aggregation, and analysis of verbal data. The task of the present chapter reduces to a consideration of the first three decisions.

Question Content

Although social scientists have become increasingly aware of the necessity for a systematic study of best practices for developing interview questions, there is surprisingly little in the way of research directed specifically toward this issue. Some (Dijkstra & van der Zouwen, 1982; Krosnick & Fabrigar, 1997, 2001; Rossi, Wright, & Anderson, 1983; Sudman, Bradburn, & Schwarz, 1996) do discuss some of the intricacies involved, but most of the advice seems to boil down to "use common sense" and "draw upon practical experience." This is undoubtedly sound advice, but it provides little direction for researchers in terms of specific item wording or format. Later in the chapter we discuss some of the factors that appear to affect the likelihood that people will interpret the meaning of a question properly, but for the moment it is sufficient to keep in mind a few simple but effective rules of thumb in question construction:

- Keep the items as brief as possible—the longer the item, the more likely it is to succumb to one or another of the problems listed below.
- Avoid subtle shadings—if you want to know about something, ask about it as directly as possible.
- Avoid double-barreled questions, i.e., questions that logically allow for two (possibly opposed) answers—"Do you like this year's Fords and Chryslers?"
- Use language the respondents understand (most people are not social scientists, so the jargon of the field is ill advised).
- If at all possible, pilot test the items on a small subsample of respondents drawn from the same population as the final sample.

The variety of issues that can be addressed in the interview represents one of the most appealing features of the methodology. This diversity, however, makes it difficult to categorize the types of questions that have been, and can be, used. Some researchers use a simple dichotomy to classify survey items—does the question focus on a public or a private action? Or, is the item concerned with *fact* or *opinion?* Experience suggests that these classifications are unnecessarily broad, and that the seeming simplicity of the categorization is more apparent than real. Schuman and Kalton (1985) suggested a more differentiated classification, which more sensitively describes the situations in which the interview might be used most profitably and the forms of information that might be sought through its use. We adopt their scheme with minor modifications.

Demographic Information

Questions concerned with descriptive personal characteristics of the respondent—age, religion, sex, race, income, etc., are perhaps the most common of all items used in interviews. In general, there is reason to believe that answers to questions of this type can be trusted, especially if the item is clear and precisely worded (e.g., Parry & Crossley, 1950; Weaver & Swanson, 1974). So, for example, it would be better to ask "date of birth" than "age" to determine the age of a respondent. The former is readily available in most people's memories, and is less likely to be distorted because of social desirability bias.

Two demographic variables that sometimes defy this observation (for rather different reasons) are race (ethnicity) and income. Given the subjective nature of race (even social demographers are hard put to provide an acceptable categorization system), and the even more subjective nature of ethnic origin in the United States, where the "melting pot" analogy is far more than symbolic, it is difficult to validate participants' responses to items of this type. Many view income as a private matter, and thus questions on this issue typically generate a relatively large (on the order of 5–10%) refusal rate. Nonresponse (or item refusal) is preferable to deliberate misreporting by a respondent, but it does cause problems in later analytic stages of the research, as refusal is usually treated as a missing response in an analysis. In addition, validity is cause for concern even with respondents willing to disclose personal income. For many, income varies as a function of the availability of overtime, seasonal fluctuations in worker demand, etc. In other instances, especially when total household income is at issue, systematic underreporting is likely because of income sources that typically are overlooked (e.g., interest, dividends, irregular or seasonal employment), producing a less than complete knowledge of household members' wages. Thus, estimates of income are likely to be imprecise.

With such problems, it is little wonder that some interview questions now seek less threatening information regarding the respondent's job, and then attempt to relate these answers to other items in extrapolating income or socioeconomic status (SES) from them (Cain & Treiman, 1981; Hodge, Siegel, & Rossi, 1964; Hollingshead, 1949). Given the near ubiquity of such items in almost all surveys, it is understandable why some researchers have recommended that a standardized set of demographic items be used in all interview research. We oppose such a recommendation because it represents a move in a direction away from the tailoring of questions to research objectives, a central tenet of good research design. For example, in examining socioeconomic status, the objective of one study might be to measure the concept using annual salary, whereas another study might seek a measure of total assets.[3]

Reconstruction From Memory

The interview is a practical means of investigating people's recall of past events. Some events having important social implications occur so rapidly or unexpectedly that researchers are unable to observe behavior at the time the events occur. Participants' recall of floods, blizzards, or riots are a few such occurrences that might provide valuable information for the social scientist. The investigation of less encompassing, but perhaps equally important past events at a personal level (e.g., marriage, births, promotions, etc.) also can be a rich source of information, but often they leave few accessible traces. By judicious use of the interview, such information becomes more available for research.

This is not to say that the data about past events obtained through interview techniques are perfectly trustworthy. Some events simply are not important enough to the respondent to remember. Consistent with this observation, Sudman (1980) has speculated that there are three important factors that influence fidelity of recall. They are:

- *Uniqueness of the event.* Did it stand out from other events? (e.g., most older Americans can remember exactly where they were, and what they were doing, when they learned that President John Kennedy had been shot).
- *Magnitude of the event.* Did it result in major economic or social costs or benefits? We're more likely to recall the day we won the $1 million lottery than the time we won $2 at the racetrack.
- *Long-term impact of the event.* Did it produce long-lasting consequences? Recall of an injury that led to amputation will be more memorable than one that, while equally serious, had consequences of limited duration.[4]

Although the specific event under study will have a major influence on the likelihood of recall accuracy, the nature and form of the questions employed in having participants reconstruct memories in interviews also can have a significant effect on accuracy. Cannel, Miller, and Oksenberg (1981) suggest that instructions that stress the importance of the interview topic positively affect the completeness of people's responses. Indeed, Cannel and associates sometimes go so far as to ask the respondent to sign an agreement acknowledging the importance of accuracy and completeness of answers.

Also effective in such situations is the use of longer, rather than shorter, questions. People tend to give longer and more complete answers to longer questions, even if the longer question is merely a multiple restatement of the shorter version (Ray & Webb, 1966). This is likely attributed to the implicit social norm of reciprocity: When you ask someone a wordy question, the other person will likely offer a wordier response. Although briefer questions are generally preferred, longer questions may be used when accuracy of recall is at stake. Finally, by reinforcing more complete answers, the interviewer can encourage respondents to provide more extensive, and presumably more accurate, responses. Although there is some danger that such reinforcement could bias participants' responses, if used judiciously this tactic appears capable of stimulating more complete answers without unduly influencing their content.

Attitudes, Intentions, and Behaviors

Interviews are commonly used to assess people's attitudes, intentions, and behaviors. We distinguish between these terms because an attitude is an evaluative belief about a person or thing ("How strongly do you agree or disagree with your Congressperson's vote on the Dream Act?"), which may or may not carry with it any behavioral implications, whereas an intention is an indication of a person's decision to act ("How much do you like exercise?" vs. "How many times do you plan on exercising in the coming month?"). The items tap types of beliefs that are conceptually different from behavior ("How many times did you exercise in the past month?"). In Chapter 15, we discuss the elements that must be considered in developing of attitude measures, and this information will not be repeated here.[5] However, Schuman and Kalton (1985) have identified two aspects of interview questions—constraint and specificity—that are particularly relevant to interviews in which people's attitudes, intentions, and behaviors are the focus of study.

Question specificity refers to how the question is phrased, implicating that minor changes of wording may have marked effects on people's responses. Rugg (1941), for example, found that only 25% of respondents in a national sample were willing to "allow speeches against democracy," but, when the question was put to a comparable sample in slightly modified form, Rugg found that 46% were against "forbidding" such speeches. Evidently, the different connotations of the words "forbid" and "(not) allow" produced these differences, even though the implications of the two questions were identical.

Question constraint refers to the response format and the options available for answering a question. *Open-ended questions* allow respondents to supply any relevant response ("What is your favorite way to exercise?"); *closed-ended questions* restrict the options that can be chosen in answering the question (Which is your favorite way to exercise? Running, aerobics, or lifting weights?). Respondents' answers are constrained by the available choices. A common constraint involves participants' choice of possible responses that do not include the "Don't Know" or "No Opinion" option. Of course, if a respondent spontaneously chooses one or the other of these "Don't Know" responses, it typically is recorded as such. It would be foolish to force an answer when the respondent indicates no knowledge of the topic. However, research by Schuman and Presser (1981) has demonstrated that the mere presence of an explicit "No Opinion" option has a strong effect on the proportion of respondents likely to answer in this manner. Questioning respondents under standard conditions about an obscure piece of legislation (the Agricultural Trade Act of 1978), the researchers found that two-thirds of their sample had "no opinion." When an explicit "No Opinion" option was made available to another, comparable respondent group, the proportion that chose this alternative rose to 90%.

Given this apparent effect of the "Don't Know" option, researchers should evaluate whether its use will increase or decrease the accuracy of the information obtained. If the issue involves factual information and the researcher judges that the respondent population includes many people have no knowledge of the issue at hand, then it is advisable to include this option (Bishop, Oldendick, Tuchfarber, & Bennett, 1980).[6] Conversely, if the measure is concerned with beliefs, attitudes, or values, and the researcher judges that most people do have opinions, which are not altogether firm, the "Don't Know" option should be avoided, as it can result in considerable underreporting of opinions (Krosnick et al., 2002). A good practice is to avoid disclosing to participants that there is a "Don't Know" option—and allow them to spontaneously offer this answer if indeed they do not possess an opinion about the matter. The "Don't Know" option is undesirable because such answers usually are treated as missing values in most statistical analyses. This compromises the statistical power in many statistical techniques, especially ones using listwise deletion, in which the *all* responses for the participant are discarded if he or she uses a "Don't Know" answer for just one of the items.

Sensitive Beliefs and Behaviors

Sometimes an investigation may be focused on behavior that is highly personal, secretive, or illegal. People engaging in such actions usually are unwilling to be observed when doing so; however, surprisingly, they often are quite willing to discuss their experiences, especially if they can be assured of anonymity or confidentiality. Kinsey, Pomeroy, and Martin's (1948) study of sexual practices in the United States, Schaps and Sanders's (1970) investigation of marijuana usage, and Bergen, Shults, Beck, and Qayad's (2012) investigation of self-reported drunken driving are examples of interviews focused on actions people would not like to be observed doing.

Considerable research has investigated the degree to which respondents underreport the extent of their involvement in private, embarrassing, or socially undesirable actions. The research on this issue is mixed. In some areas, research suggests the validity of self-reports of illicit activity. For example, considerable research suggests that with appropriate safeguards, adolescents' self-reports of drug use are trustworthy (Denis et al., 2012; Hornik & Orwin, 2012; Richter & Johnson, 2001; Smith, McCarthy, & Goldman, 1995). On the other hand, with less strenuous methods to guarantee truthful reporting, there seems to be a tendency for people to distort, or to fail to admit to, actions that are illegal or viewed with disapproval by the society at large. For example, married respondents underreport sexual infidelity (Andrews et al., 2008), their BMIs, especially if they are obese (Visscher, Viet, Kroesbergen, & Seidell, 2006), criminal recidivism (Kroner, Mills, & Morgan, 2007), use of cocaine and marijuana during the third trimester of pregnancy (Bessa et al., 2010), and past histories of sexually transmitted diseases (Hong, Fang, Zhou, Zhou, & Li 2011). Attempts to solve the underreporting problem typically take one of two forms. The simplest entails a concerted effort on the part of the investigator to secure respondents' commitment to the interview, to assure them that their answers will not be traceable, and to provide reinforcement and feedback over the course of the interaction (Cannell et al., 1981). In some circumstances involving sensitive items, the interviewer may make use of audio computer-assisted self-interview software (ACASI), in which questions are presented via computer, and the respondent answers using the keyboard. In this way, potentially embarrassing information need not be divulged to the interviewer. If the respondent believes the promise of anonymity, the likelihood of truthful responding is enhanced.

Interview Structure

Assume that after extensive consideration of a number of potentially employed alternatives, an investigator has decided to use the interview as his or her principal data-gathering device. What, then, are the available options? The answer to this question depends on the extent of information the researcher possesses about the phenomenon to be studied. If no hypotheses have been generated, and no questions have been decided upon, then unstructured interviewing should be used. However, if on the basis of theory or previous research a definite list of hypotheses about responses has been developed, then structured interviewing is appropriate Unstructured interviews may focus on a specific topic but do not have an a priori schedule of questions to collect specific types of information. Structured interviews are used to request information using a predetermined schedule of questions and to ensure that all questions are asked the same way and in the same order for all participants. Semi-structured interviews lie somewhere between completely unstructured and completely structured interviews.

The Unstructured Interview

The **unstructured interview (exploratory interview)** encourages freely generated questions by interviewers and responses by interviewees. It does not demand that specific types of information be collected. In unstructured interviews, neither the phrasing of the questions nor the allowable types of responses are constrained. There is no "interview roadmap" (structure) to guide the interviewer, whose queries are dictated by the dyadic verbal exchanges between respondent and interviewer and by the general subject matter of the research. It is the responsibility of the interviewer to pursue leads that appear promising or informative. The number of such leads that ultimately prove productive usually is a function of the technical skill of the interviewer and the extent to which he or she is versed in the topic under study. Thus, questions are generated on the spot by the interviewer. They are based on what participants previously expressed, and may be thought of as dynamic conversation between interviewer and respondent. The less structured the interview, the greater demands on the interviewer's competence.

The Semi-Structured Interview

In a **semi-structured interview (structured–nonscheduled interview)**, a set of predetermined topics must be covered, but it is up to the interviewer to decide how to ask the questions, which usually are tailored to each interviewee. This interview form is a compromise between the completely unstructured exploratory interview and the completely structured interview to be discussed next. The semi-structured interview imposes on the researcher the necessity of obtaining certain specified types of information (hence the term structured), but does not have an interview schedule specifying the manner in which the information is to be obtained. Suppose using a semi-structured interview, an interviewer wishes to obtain information about people's perceptions of same-sex marriage. During the interview, given that there is no schedule that dictates the way this issue is approached, one participant might be asked, "What are your feelings about same-sex marriage?"; a second respondent might be asked, "What are your opinions about people of the same sex getting married?"; a third interviewee may be asked, "Should people of the same sex be allowed to marry?" These questions represent different ways of requesting the same structured information about the topic of same sex marriage. The use of this technique is predicated on the assumption that some rough theoretical position has indicated the types of information useful for the purposes of the study. In a semi-structured interview, the task of the interviewer involves requesting specific types of information as decided prior to the interview. The means to be employed in completing the task are not.

As with the unstructured interview, the semi-structured interview is not used to best advantage in testing hypotheses, because the phrasing of questions varies from respondent to respondent, given that no fixed set of interview questions are used as a constraint. Semi-structured interviews require interviewers of considerable technical competence, because they must be able to guide and redirect respondents to the critical information, even though there is no schedule of prespecified questions to assist them in this task. Because the interviewer's work will consist of investigating prespecified types of information, he or she need not be overly sensitive to variation in responses that occur outside the topic boundaries initially established. This "narrow focus" relative to an unstructured interview can result in a loss of information, because the prespecified focus of the semi-structured interview constricts the research field. Although this constriction may result in a loss of wider knowledge about the topic, such techniques provide for a more intensive and focused investigation of the concepts and ideas thought to be most promising.

This is not to suggest that the scope of semi-structured interviews must be narrowly focused. The groundbreaking research program of Kinsey and his associates (1948) was accomplished primarily through interviews of the semi-structured variety. Kinsey understood that questions focused on various sexual practices would affect different respondents in different ways, and thus a standardized schedule was not indicated. The very sequence in which certain topics were introduced was varied accordingly, as these sample instructions indicate:

> For unmarried males, the sequence [should be] nocturnal emissions, masturbation, premarital petting, premarital intercourse with companions, intercourse with prostitutes, animal contacts, and the homosexual. For males who have never gone beyond the tenth grade in school, premarital intercourse can be discussed much earlier in the interview, because it is generally accepted at that social level; but masturbation needs to be approached more carefully if one is to get the truth from that group.
>
> (Kinsey et al., 1948, p. 48)

These interviews were structured insofar as interviewers were required to inquire about specific sexual habits, but they lacked a fixed schedule requiring a prescribed order of questioning or specific question wording. Had Kinsey's interviewers followed a prespecified interview schedule, they almost certainly would have alienated a portion of the respondent sample. The use of the semi-structured interview form is especially appropriate when the sample is diverse, and thus phrasing of the questions can be tailored to each individual. However, if the sample is characterized by a more homogeneous respondent group, or if the topics are anticipated to affect all respondents in the same way, then the use of a schedule for the interview is recommended.

The Structured Interview

In a **structured interview**, the interviewer requests specific types of information by asking the same list of questions in the same order for all interviewees, using a fixed schedule of questions. Considered the most systematic form of interview, the researcher is discouraged from deviating from the standardized script. Even if the participant provides an interesting response that might shed light on the topic, the interviewer is not allowed to pursue it, as the schedule of questioning must be the same for all respondents. Thus, a change in one word of the question is not permitted, as it might spur different responses from different participants. For this reason, structured interviews may be more challenging to conduct when participants are demographically diverse. The level of competence necessary to conduct a structured interview is less than that required for unstructured and semi-structured interviews, and this fact is reflected in interview costs savings (Schuman & Kalton, 1985). However, although the structured interview restricts deviations from the question script, it still calls for some technical expertise, because a poorly trained or unmotivated interviewer can sabotage even the most highly structured research project.

Open- and Closed-Ended Questions

Before proceeding with a detailed discussion of structured interviews, it is important to note a distinction between types of question constraint. Interviews may use a closed-ended question, in which the interviewer imposes a constraint on the possible options for responding. Interviews making use of this type of question are analogous to verbal multiple-choice tests—information is asked of a respondent, who is given a set of allowable answers from which to choose, e.g., "Are you a Catholic, Protestant, Jew, or Muslim?" If the possible range of options is not carefully considered, some (e.g., Buddhists and atheists) would be unable to choose among the options. An open-ended question without responses being constrained would be, "What is your religion?," allowing respondents freely to indicate any religion. Both questions seek the same information, but in the latter case, no constraint is placed on the allowable response, which must be coded subsequent to the interview.

The most obvious administrative difference between these approaches is that using open-ended questions can place greater demands on the interviewer, who must note the respondent's replies. At the analysis phase, more costs can be incurred, especially on questions allowing for wide-ranging replies, because with this form of question a system for classifying respondents' answers must be developed before analysis can proceed (see Chapter 14 on the use of content analysis techniques for this purpose). With the closed question format, the classification scheme is provided in advance. This simplifies the interviewer's job, in addition to reducing analysis costs. But there is more to it than this benefit.

The seemingly minor administrative differences between open- and closed-ended questions are associated with major differences in the types of issues that interviews making use of these two question forms typically are designed to address. The structured interview making use of closed-ended questions allows for the greatest degree of standardization in the interviewer-respondent interaction. As in an experiment, all respondents are provided with a standard set of interviewer-produced stimuli (questions), along with a set of allowable answers. Interview schedules involving the same list of standardized questions are used in situations in which the investigator possesses considerable prior knowledge about the phenomenon of interest, and the options are constrained. Given that such question types are systematized by having the interviewer phrase the same questions in the same order, this method provides greater control and generates a more standard research context.

The required standardization of questions and allowable responses characteristic of the structured-scheduled closed-ended interview can be accomplished only when the researcher's specification of a participant's potential range of responses is nearly complete. If the researcher unwisely uses questions constrained by only a few options without adequately defining the universe of potential responses, the data may prove unusable. Interview questions that give rise to very different reactions (sometimes called *self-stimulation effects*) can have a negative impact on standardization. If a question elicits heightened interest from 10% of the sample, for example, problems regarding the comparability of these data with that of the other 90% must be considered, unless there is some way of differentiating those who were interested in the question from those who were not. The solution to this problem lies in the proper specification of question phrasing, consideration of potential responses, and their anticipated effect on respondents. Such systematization to derive a set of standardized interview questions can be assured only after considerable preliminary research.

Self-stimulation effects are not the only problem that premature use of closed-ended questions can produce. Even more likely are problems brought about by answers that force the interview to abandon the preset schedule. To return to our earlier example, suppose that in reply to the question, "Are you Catholic, Protestant, Jew, or Muslim?," our respondent were to respond, "No." At this point, the closed schedule must be abandoned, because that response does not fit into the standardized scheme, and there is a good possibility that later questions, if contingent upon the response, are now palpably inappropriate. Before proceeding in this circumstance, therefore, the interviewer must seek clarification of the respondent's answer. If the respondent meant, "No, I am none of these, I am an atheist," then later questions regarding the intensity of one's religious convictions, attendance at church, synagogue, or mosque, etc., would be inappropriate. If, however, the respondent's reply upon further questioning were found to mean, "No, I am none of these—I am a Buddhist," then the questions that follow on the closed-ended question may be usable. The clarification process forced upon the interviewer at this juncture, however, destroys the comparability of this interview with that of the others for whom the closed format was adequate. As suggested, use of a closed interview schedule that is insufficient to capture the respondents' range of replies can destroy the utility of the obtained data.

A potential disadvantage of using closed-ended questions is that they do not allow the interviewer to respond to novel information that might arise but that is not a part of the rigidly prescribed schedule—the interviewer must "stick" to the script as it was written and cannot react to new information given by the respondent unless this can be done within the context of the follow-on questions. In such circumstances, interviewees often assume that the researcher is paying little heed to their replies, and under these conditions maintenance of rapport becomes difficult. Despite these shortcomings, the structured-scheduled interview using closed-questions is most likely to be employed in hypothesis testing contexts because of the problems of noncomparability inherent in all the other types of interview formats. Given the demanding requirements that must be met before the closed-ended question can be employed, it is appropriate to ask whether the ideal of a completely comparable interview situation for all respondents can ever be attained in practice. The answer to this query depends principally on the issue or issues on which the interview is focused.

In general, the greater the research constraint (in terms of both researcher and respondent behaviors), the more specific or circumscribed will be the obtained data. Thus, an interview using open-ended questions might result in considerably more information regarding a respondent's choice of not only a particular response option, but also of the reasons for this choice. If the researcher has correctly decided on a closed-question format, however, this supplemental information might provide relatively little in the way of new or useful data.

It might at first appear that supplemental information, explaining and qualifying a given response, would never prove superfluous to a researcher interested in the validity of his or her results, but this is not always correct, particularly when the closed schedule interview is most appropriate. Consider the case of the public opinion pollster hired to determine the chances of a candidate's election to the Presidency of the United States. The desired end product of this research, an accurate assessment of public opinion regarding the available options (i.e., candidates), is clearly specified. Ultimately, even in the most tightly contested race, the pollster's primary job is to predict the winner. Given these parameters, the only data of any importance to the successful completion of the research mission are respondents' indications of the candidate they will support with their votes in the general election. Reasons underlying these choices are irrelevant *within the boundaries of the research question* (i.e., Who will win the upcoming election?).

Conducting the Interview

We have described the unstructured interview, the semi-structured interview, and the structured interview as if the operations that characterized these techniques were mutually exclusive. In practice, there are elements of all three types in almost all research interviews. Like most ideals, the descriptions presented are rarely realized, primarily because of the inevitability of uncontrolled, informal behaviors of the interviewer that occur during the administration of the schedule of questions. Previous research (Marquis & Cannell, 1969) using tape recordings of interviewers' behaviors demonstrated wide variations in language, even when completely structured interviews with fixed schedules were used—and the most experienced interviewers appeared to be the major culprits. A videotaped recording of these same interviews undoubtedly would have revealed even greater variation among interviewers, whose changes in seating position and posture, smiles, nods of the head, changes in expression, and vocal intonation would also be readily apparent to respondents. And although the effects of these "paralinguistic" behaviors are not completely understood, it is clear that they can affect an interview's tone and progress.

The correspondence between the ideal, "pure interview forms" presented earlier and those actually arrived at in practice is a function of a number of variables, and we will consider some of the most important of these. However, it should be stressed that the apparent ubiquity of extraneous interviewer behaviors does not necessarily compromise the validity of the interview as a research tool. The so-called "extraneous" interviewer behaviors that are so apparent in any close inspection of almost any interview at times prove to be necessary adjuncts of this research technique. If an interviewer were to completely ignore the replies and nonverbal cues of the respondent, the sensitive person-to-person interaction that plays an important role in any interview would be destroyed, and the quality of the obtained data adversely affected. Researchers employing completely "nondirective" techniques can testify to this fact, for in their attempts to force the interviewee to guide and control the course of the interview often succeed only in destroying the rapport that they so diligently courted in the initial phases of the interaction. "Rapport," "interviewer-respondent interaction," and "respondent cooperation" are words and phrases emphasized in almost every interviewing handbook, but as yet, we have presented no indication of the ways and means of generating these states conducive to the interview process. The following section is designed to remedy this deficiency.

Obtaining Entry

An important task that should precede interview administration concerns the establishment of entry, or gaining permission to approach an individual or group of individuals for research purposes. Richardson, Dohrenwend, and Klein (1965) distinguished two qualitatively different types of entry situations—those in which a population is insulated from the interviewer by a gatekeeper, and those in which the respondents are not. Different approach strategies should be used in these different contexts.

Commonly, a "gatekeeper" protects the population of potential respondents. The gatekeeper is an individual who can affect the likelihood of a respondent's cooperating with the interviewer. Trying to skirt the gatekeeper can cause real problems and thus should be avoided. Those who doubt this should imagine the consequences they would experience if they attempted to interview elementary school children during their afternoon recess or play period without first having secured the gatekeeper's (i.e., the school authority, such as the school principal's) permission. In this situation, it is quite possible that if permission were not obtained beforehand, the only information one would gain would be an indication of the speed with which the police responded to the call of an agitated educator. Examples of populations secured by a gatekeeper are readily available: elementary and high schools, members of unions, fraternities and sororities, athletic teams, adolescent gangs, church attendees, rock and roll bands, etc.

The most obvious and direct strategy in gaining access to a protected group is to approach the person in control and state the aims and methods of the proposed research in a way that is understandable, nonthreatening, and accurate. It also is important to provide some rationale as to how participation can benefit the target group. This advice is complicated because the effective gatekeeper in many settings is not immediately obvious. For this reason, Richardson et al. (1965) suggest that the interviewer not press for an immediate entry decision. If the researcher has misidentified the gatekeeper (e.g., asking permission from a teacher when the school principal should have been contacted), but nevertheless has convinced this person of the importance of the research, it is possible that the "misidentified" individual might intercede on behalf of the research. Forcing a pseudo-gatekeeper into a premature decision more often than not results in an outright rejection or, in the case in which entry is (apparently) secured, a later reversal by the real gatekeeper. It might appear more difficult to study samples protected by a gatekeeper than to investigate individuals not shielded in this manner. This is not necessarily true; the gatekeeper's approval can legitimize the survey and encourage respondents' cooperation. In populations that have no gatekeeper, this potentially facilitative influence is not available.

Two techniques that have been shown to facilitate entry in non-gatekeeper samples are letters of introduction and the "foot-in-the-door" approach. There is some evidence to suggest that a prior letter that alerts the potential respondent that he or she will be contacted later to participate in a research survey helps to increase the rate of participation (Brunner & Carroll, 1969; Cartwright & Tucker, 1969). The foot-in-the-door technique is based on the idea that securing a person's cooperation with a very minor request, and reinforcing this cooperation, facilitates his or her later cooperation with a major one (Freedman & Fraser, 1966). In applying this finding, Groves and Magilavy (1981) asked respondents to participate in a very minimal survey (two questions), and informed them that they might be called later to participate in a larger survey. Those who participated in the minimal survey were significantly more willing to cooperate with the later request than those who had not. Other researchers (e.g., Bloom, McBride, Pollak, Schwartz-Bloom, & Lipkus, 2006; Souchet & Girandola, 2013) have used variations of the foot-in-the-door approach in difficult field contexts with good success.

After Entry

Introduction of Purpose

Assuming that the interviewer can at least get a foot in the door, there are a number of introductory procedures that seem to have a positive influence on the likelihood that a person will agree to cooperate. Cannell and Kahn (1968) recommend that the interviewer first provide a general description of the research project, then discuss the more specific research objectives, and finally outline the means of attaining these goals. Certainly the language the interviewer uses here will not be technical or scientifically rigid, nor is it likely that the initial introduction will be as extensive as that presented when seeking a gatekeeper's approval. Satisfying respondents' curiosity about the study and their role in the research process is both important and necessary if real cooperation is to be secured.

Method of Selection

Having informed the potential respondent of the general nature of the research, disclosing information about how people were selected for study should be provided. If a specific "protected" group is being studied, and the gatekeeper has granted approval, this fact should be made known. The reasons for selection of the particular group to which the respondent belongs also should be mentioned.

If respondents who are not buffered by a gatekeeper are studied, some information about the sampling procedures employed in their selection should be given. Certainly a treatise on sampling design is not being suggested, but rather some general information about the selection process should be mentioned, if such techniques were used. This step is sometimes skipped in the introductory phase of the interview, and this omission is unfortunate because respondents who are unsure about why they were "singled out" for the interview sometimes are less than completely candid in their answers. Interviewers who are transparent in describing the recruitment and sampling process invite participants to reciprocate by offering more transparent responses.

Agency

Cannell's and Kahn's (1968) third step in the introduction process consists of identifying the organization or agency under whose auspices the study is being conducted. This procedure is even more important today than when it was suggested originally. Many unethical sales organizations have employed pseudo-interviews to gain access to potential customers, and the public is more and more aware of the fact that persons asking for "a moment of your time to gather information on a very important issue" more often than not are salespersons masquerading as social scientists. The resulting skepticism adversely affects the good will of potential respondents toward legitimate investigators. If satisfactory credentials can be presented, however, this difficulty can be overcome.

Anonymity

Many people who are not trained in the methods of social research assume that all survey responses can be traced directly back to their source—they are unaware that most analyses employ response pooling procedures that aggregate answers over the entire sample (or subsample) to infer general trends. Accordingly, the confidentiality or anonymity of an interviewee's responses should be guaranteed, if possible. It is profitable in such circumstances to avoid collecting identifying information—e.g., asking for the participant's full name—and to explain how the data will be aggregated and analyzed.

A willingness on the part of the potential respondent to take part in the interview might become apparent before the introductory sequence has been complete. The process sketched here paints an unduly pessimistic picture, for individuals often are quite eager to be interviewed and need not be persuaded through a long and arduous introductory process. There are many rewards accruing to interview respondents—emotional satisfaction, being able to express their views on matters of personal importance, the pride of being chosen to participate in a scientific investigation, the possibility of having their responses affect policy—all these factors make life much easier for the interviewer. The question then arises, "If I have secured entry by step 2 of the introductory process, should I continue through the entire sequence?" We believe this should be done, because in addition to securing cooperation, the steps enhance rapport. Neglecting any of the suggested procedures can compromise interview quality.

Interviewer Characteristics: Establishing Rapport

Many factors other than those mentioned here can influence the interviewer's chances of gaining entry and establishing rapport with respondents. Some of these reside in the characteristics of the interviewer. Included among these factors are the interviewer's physical appearance, dress, race, accent, apparent socioeconomic status, and ethnic heritage. Whenever possible, it is wise to match the obvious demographic characteristics of the interviewer with those of the expected respondent sample, and many research firms try to do this. A complete matching is rarely possible, but there usually are some salient aspects that should be attended to. Research suggests the importance of matching the race of the interviewer with that of the respondent (e.g., Cotter, Cohen, & Coulter, 1982), especially with sensitive topics concerning racial issues. People seem more reluctant to voice racial dissatisfactions with interviewers who do not match their own racial group. Findings of this type have persisted over the years, especially with racially sensitive issues, and appear to hold for Black and White respondents alike (Hatchett & Schuman, 1975; Schuman & Hatchett, 1974).

In more long-term interactions, the researcher is well advised to attend closely to a match of other social characteristics that might be important to respondents. Although complete matching is rarely possible, there usually are some salient features of the respondents' lifestyles that are shared by the interviewer that could facilitate their interaction. A good example of this form of matching is provided in William Foote Whyte's (1955) investigation of adolescent gang members in "Cornerville." The openness of interviewee responses was facilitated greatly by Whyte's extensive knowledge of baseball facts, and his bowling skill (!), two interests his respondents shared avidly. If Whyte had approached his respondents as a Harvard researcher whose interests did not carry him beyond the walls of the sociology library, the classic *Street Corner Society* might never have been written.

In addition to a match on demographic and lifestyle characteristics, there are other personal characteristics of the interviewer that may influence the relationship between interviewer and respondent, including the interviewer's enthusiasm for the research, his or her professionalism, and his or her apparent interest and friendliness with the respondent. Many of these factors cannot be directly controlled, but depend on the availability and selection of experienced and well-trained interview personnel.

Informal Tactics

Initial Question Sequence

Earlier, we raised the possibility that question order could influence the responses obtained in an interview (also Chapter 15). How one answers an early question may have a powerful influence on how later questions are answered. In addition to these considerations, it is important to understand that early interview questions can play a role in establishing rapport. Accordingly, the least threatening, least demanding, most general, and most easily answered questions should be presented first. As Kinsey et al. (1948), suggested, this order may vary as a consequence of respondent characteristics. Later, once cooperation is assured and the confidence of the respondent in the integrity of the interviewer is established, more difficult, specific, and sensitive issues may be broached.[7]

Leading Questions

Most of the early manuals on interviewing technique sounded a common injunction against the use of "leading questions." A **leading question** is phrased in a way to suggest the expected answer or the premise that must be accepted to answer the question (see Table 13.1). Considering the effects of experimenter expectancy (Chapter 6) reinforces the apparent wisdom of this warning. Arguments by Richardson and colleagues (1965) suggest that the injunction needs some qualification, arguing that under some admittedly constrained research conditions the leading question could prove a useful and non-biasing feature of proper interviewer technique. First, however, we must distinguish between two categories of leading questions, which have been termed *expectations* and *premises*.

A leading question in expectation form is a query whose wording alerts the respondent to the answer expected by the interviewer: "You voted for Obama, didn't you?" is an example of a leading question based on an expectation. A better way to phrase this question is, "For whom did you vote?" Even with the modification, this question still requires the premise that the person voted, a faulty assumption if the interviews were conducted using a sample that also included nonvoters. The premise form of leading question contains within it one or more assumptions that must be accepted if the question is to be answered. "When did you stop beating your wife?" is a classic leading question based on a premise. It presupposes the premises that (1) the respondent was or is married, (2) that he or she did, at least once, beat his or her wife, and (3) that he or she has stopped doing so. The general injunction against leading questions of the premise variety concerns queries with unfounded premises. But there are times when the premises underlying such questions are well founded and so can prove useful. The wife-beating question, for example, would not appear particularly ill advised if asked of a respondent with a history of arrests for domestic abuse.

It is difficult to phrase questions to be completely free of premises. At the very least, a premise made in all interviews is that the respondent will communicate using a language the interviewer understands. Only when the premise is a completely uninformed guess would there appear to be much cause for alarm, not so much because of the potential for biased responses, but rather because it could compromise the interviewer-respondent relationship. Expectations and premises can be combined in the same question, with each varying in degree of strength. Of central importance

TABLE 13.1 An example of a leading question exchange.

Speaker	Response
Interviewer	Do you feel you have biases against people who suffer from mental illness?
Respondent	Of course not.
Interviewer	So you support the mental health clinic being established in your neighborhood
Respondent	Are you nuts? I wouldn't risk my children's welfare in that way.
Interviewer	How so?
Respondent	By having a bunch of crazy people running around the neighborhood day and night.

is the degree to which the expectation or premise is founded on the interviewer's anticipation of the respondent's likely answer. If an expectation is completely accurate (and very often, accuracy almost can be assumed, based on earlier answers obtained in the interview), then there is little danger of bias in making use of it. Leading questions based on information generated earlier in the interview often are used by researchers to maintain the attention of the respondent over the course of the interaction. Well-informed expectations and premises indicate that the interviewer has been attentive to the interviewee's responses (e.g., "As you just mentioned having beaten your wife, how many times have you done so?"). Thus, in some instances, using informed leading questions actually might improve rapport and respondent cooperation.

Although the proper use of leading questions depends on the interviewer's near certain knowledge of the respondent's likely answer, they need not always be used in anticipating the *correct* reply. A tactic used by experienced interviewers that sometimes pays dividends consists in deliberately missing the point of the respondent's remarks (e.g., if aware that the interviewee is unmarried, the interviewer might ask "How many times have you beaten your wife?"). This tactic can result in an extensive elaboration of an earlier position, assuming that the interviewer's "misinterpretation" is outrageous enough, and that the respondent is motivated to correct it (the participant might respond with, "No, you don't understand, I'm not married. And if I were, I would never beat my wife.") The danger here is that the misinterpretation is not wrong enough, or that the respondent is not sufficiently motivated to correct the errant impression. An apparent complete and total misunderstanding of an individual's opinion, however, often is sufficiently motivating to elicit an elaboration, especially if the issues at hand are important to the respondent.

The use of leading questions involving expectations and premises presupposes that rapport has been established, that the interviewer has a very good idea of the respondent's likely reaction, and that the question is either totally correct or blatantly incorrect. Deploying leading questions with partially correct premises or expectations might have an adverse effect on the interview. A final piece of advice has to do with the frequency of deliberately leading questions: Overuse of these devices demeans the intelligence and sophistication of respondents, and can cause premature withdrawal from the interview.

Direction

When requesting elaboration of information, should the interviewer force specific clarifications and amplifications using a directive approach, or be completely nondirective, thus enabling the respondent to offer the clarification and amplification? The question of the degree to which an interviewer should direct the answers of a respondent is primarily of relevance in nonstructured and semi-structured interviews, and the answer depends on the aims of the research. If in response to an inquiry, a respondent were to reply, "Yes, I think property taxes are much too high in this city," an interviewer using a direct approach might steer the respondent's attention by mentioning that property taxes support public schools to determine the interviewee's views toward tax reductions on these institutions in light of the earlier expressed opinion that taxes were too high. Or, using a nondirective approach, the interviewer might simply restate the respondent's position by saying, "You said that taxes are too high," with the expectation that the respondent would be forced to clarify the original statement in response to the interviewer's declaration (note that the inquiry is presented in declarative, rather than interrogative, form). To a nondirective prod of this type, the interviewee often will elaborate and defend the earlier position. Whether during this nondirective process the respondent eventually mentions the specific issue of interest (e.g., tax reduction effects on public schools) cannot be answered. This must be considered when gauging the appropriate degree of direction used. Nondirective approaches appear most useful in unstructured interviews, as their general purpose is to keep the researcher from imposing his or her own views about what is important in the situation under investigation.

Informal Interviewer Behaviors

As any experienced interviewer will testify, not all respondents are responsive. Merely asking a question does not guarantee a complete, understandable, and unambiguous response. In some cases, the fortunate interviewer is paired with an articulate person who fits the role of the perfect respondent; more often, even with the most cooperative of respondents, some prodding is required. The informal behaviors used to elicit an amplification or clarification of an unsatisfactory response, although relatively under-investigated, are of real importance. Moreover, they are a ubiquitous component of all interviews—they are a constant feature of interviewer behavior (see Bradburn et al., 1979; Cannell et al., 1981; Marquis & Cannell, 1969).

A common behavior (or, in this instance, *non-behavior*) used to elicit elaborated responses is *silence*. It is important to understand that an interview is a research context involving interpersonal communication, and thus is subject to the same informal norms as other, more mundane conversations. In most conversations, cessation of verbal behavior on the part of one individual is interpreted as a cue to the other to begin another verbal exchange. In this way, each communicator's response (or silence) acts as a stimulus to the other. An interviewer can make use of this reciprocity norm of interpersonal communication in the following manner: if a respondent's answer is inadequate, the interviewer can fail to react—i.e., fail to reinitiate the conversation. Noticing that the answer did not provoke a reaction by the interviewer, the interviewee often will elaborate or amplify the earlier response. Of course, this tactic can be overused to the discomfort of the respondent—silence is a central feature of "stress interviews" (Chapple, 1953)—but when used sparingly, interviewer silence or nonresponse can stimulate respondents to elaborate their answers, with little danger of biasing the obtained data.

Verbal And Nonverbal Reinforcement

A different tactic that sometimes is used involves reinforcement. Phrases like "good," "fine," "interesting," and the like sometimes are used to encourage interviewees to amplify or elaborate a response. By reacting to respondents in this way, the interviewer demonstrates interest in their answers. This can strengthen rapport and assure continued cooperation. Unfortunately, whereas these tactics are undeniably motivating for respondents, the question of *what* is being motivated in not completely obvious. The "verbal reinforcement" literature suggests that an individual will express an opinion consistent with those that have been reinforced earlier in the interview (Fennis & Stroebe, 2010; Olson & Kendrick, 2008). Thus, an interviewer's verbal reinforcement of a respondent for providing a complete or elaborated answer might be interpreted by the respondent as a reinforcement of the particular *content* of the reply. This could seriously affect subsequent answers. More subtle, but equally effective reinforcers made by the interviewer are smiles, nods of the head, "uh-huh's," etc. Actions of this type encourage the respondent, but their biasing effects may offset their utility.

Group Interviews and Focus Groups

In a **group interview**, the interviewer verbally requests information from more than one interviewee at the same time, but they are discouraged from interacting with each other. Interaction generally involves only interviewer and one interviewee (at a time). Group interviews are commonly employed as part of the hiring practice in organizations when there are many applicants for the same position. To whittle down the pool of applicants, interviews may be conducted with several candidates at the same time. Depending on the structure of the interview, there may be a predetermined order in which a person answers a question, followed by the next person who responds to the same question, and so forth. In other variations, the interviewer poses a question, and only participants who choose to answer do so. All the approaches for conducting proper one-to-one interviews—level of structure, whether a fixed schedule is used, participants sampling, and question wording—also apply to conducting group interviews.

A **focus group** involves a moderator who obtains information by encouraging verbal discussion and interaction about a focused topic among a group of participants. In the typical focus group study, participants are recruited based on some criterion (gender, occupation, interests) relevant to the purpose of the investigation (Breen, 2006; Koppelman & Bourjolly, 2001). To facilitate interaction, participants often are seated around a table facing one another, not the moderator, who serves as the arbitrator who facilitates the focused discussion. The conversations are audio- or videotaped for later transcription.

Unlike participants in group interviews, those in focus groups are encouraged to interact and exchange ideas with one another to stimulate greater depth of discussion and insights about a topic. Observation of verbal interactions among group members might produce insights about group values and norms. The group dynamic is intended to spur responses that would not have been obtained if social interaction were absent. A focus group is characterized by three features (Krueger & Casey 2009; Wyatt, Krauspkpof, & Davidson, 2008):

1. *Qualitative data.* Quantitative data usually are not collected in focus groups, as questions such as "What percentage of the time do you use a condom?" are more appropriate in a questionnaire or interview format. A better fit would involve the question, "Discuss some reasons why people might or might not use a condom."
2. *Homogeneous participant groups.* Generally, respondents in focus groups are drawn from groups sharing a critical feature. Examples might involve groups of respondents who have tested out a new consumer product, patients suffering from the same medical condition, former drug users, doctors who work the late shift in hospitals, expert chess players, and the like. A recommendation is that recruited participants should not know each other beforehand, as preexisting relationships and alliances will affect the group dynamic.
3. *Discussion of a focused topic.* The "focus" in focus group refers to a common stimulus or unifying topic that promotes the discussion, conversation, dialogue, or debate. In a structured focus group, appropriate if a scheduled list of questions must be addressed, the moderator asks participants to converse about a topic, and the moderator shifts the conversation to the next topic after obtaining sufficient responses. In unstructured focus groups, a general topic is presented, and participants are asked to converse freely about any aspect related to that topic. Here, participants dynamically drive the direction of the discussion topic.

Responses obtained in focus groups emerge not only from the interaction between the moderator and participants, but also from participants' interactions. Focus groups' norms and dynamics are dictated by the composition of their members, which influences the responses expressed by group members. This inherent feature is especially advantageous. It facilitates dialogue and disclosure on topics that require social support from similar others. For example, consider a focus group of adults who were formerly victims of child abuse. If one participant has the courage to share his or her experiences openly, this might foster greater willingness from others to self-disclose sensitive information. On the other hand, the group setting also might prove an obstacle for collecting data. For example, if the vast majority of group members openly express why they are pro-choice, the sole member who is not espousing this position may be susceptible to conformity pressure. To minimize this problem, the moderator should make it clear when setting the guidelines of discussion etiquette that the group is a safe environment in which everyone should express their opinions freely.

The moderator plays an important role in facilitating the conversation among participants. More vocal group members may monopolize the discussion, offering their opinions more frequently, while the quiet members may opt to contribute less or not at all. It is the moderator's responsibility to notice this and ask for the opinions of those who would rather be wallflowers ("How about you, what do you think?"). A good moderator requires the diplomatic skills to ensure that a single person does not "hog" the spotlight, or the data collected will be skewed toward the opinions of this particular member. It is challenging for the moderator to be sensitive to the responses of all participants and make sure all opinions are heard. For this reason, most focus group investigations involve a relatively manageable number (typically 6 to 12) of participants. An effective moderator should be highly trained on the topic to be able competently to address questions arising about the topic at hand. Also imperative are conflict resolution skills, so the moderator knows how to defuse tense situations, for example, when a member might constantly interrupt or make disparaging remarks about others' views.

Some focus groups have more than one moderator. An approach involving two moderators might be used if the moderators are trained to express opposite viewpoints to help stimulate participant discussion of the pros and cons of an issue. This approach also may encourage participants to contemplate the entire range of opinions surrounding an issue.

Not all focus group studies use a moderator. In these highly unstructured focus groups, after giving instructions regarding rules for engaging in the discussion and information about the topic, the moderator leaves the room for a given period of time. The hope is that the absence of the moderator offers participants greater autonomy in openly expressing their uncensored views. Discussions lacking a moderator may be monitored, but because un-moderated focus groups require the questionable assumptions that participants will be self-motivated to engage each other in conversation, not stray from the main topic, and cover all the topics within the allotted time, groups lacking a moderator are rarely conducted and generally not recommended.

Focus groups usually are used as pilot studies in the formative stages in a new line of research or to obtain preliminary evidence to learn about an understudied topic. The findings obtained in focus groups might be used to gain insights for a subsequent quantitative study. In scale development and validation research, focus groups are used to establish the content validity of a construct.

Conclusion

As we have shown, the interview method can take many forms and can be applied to a range of disparate issues. Its general utility is widely appreciated by researchers, which is reflected in its widespread use. The method is flexible and can be applied at almost any stage of the research process. Interviews usually are administered face-to-face or on the telephone, and are used to study people's reconstruction of past events or current beliefs or behavioral reports. Different interview structures are determined by the needs of the research and the planned uses of the resulting data. The chapter that follows presents information on the ways in which the verbal responses collected in an interview study can be distilled into useful social scientific data.

Questions for Discussion

1. Why might telephone or face-to-face interviews sometimes be a better method of administering a survey than, for instance, online or paper-and-pencil surveys?

2. When using a telephone interview, is it better to avoid leading questions more than you would in a face-to-face interview? For example, are leading questions, especially questions that are intentionally incorrect to instigate more detailed responses, at greater risk of being misinterpreted when participants cannot see the nonverbal cues you might be exhibiting or other indications that you are being attentive rather than bored and aloof? Does planning the mood and tone of your interview depend on whether you will be interviewing in person or over the phone (e.g., your use of sarcasm, humor, leading questions, vocal intonation)? Why or why not? Similarly, do open-ended questions, and unstructured and semi-structured interviews yield different responses, depending on whether the interview is conducted in person or by telephone? How might responses differ, and what would be the explanation for why they differ?
3. You are conducting a study of adolescent risk-taking behavior, which means most of your questions are going to involve sensitive information and questions that might make respondents uncomfortable (e.g., substance use, sexual behavior, delinquent activity). You do not want to ask irrelevant questions that waste participants' time in the beginning of your interview, but recognize that opening your interview with "how often have you used oxycodone" might be a little jarring for participants. Since you want to be as efficient as possible with your interview questions, can you use small talk with the participant prior to the interview, and an extended introduction to the study, to build rapport? Since you are the interviewer and they are the participants, are you essentially asking innocuous questions before the sensitive questions, except in this context you are not recording responses to the small talk? Does it matter what questions are asked if the goal is to build rapport with participants to increase their likelihood of responding honestly to sensitive questions?

Notes

1. Interviews, of course, are used in many contexts other than basic research data collection. The clinical interview is a valuable tool of diagnosis and treatment in mental health settings, and extensive participant interviews often accompany the debriefing phase of a laboratory experiment. However, these specialized uses of the in-depth interview technique are beyond the purview of this text. In the present chapter, we will focus on the use of the interview in the general context of survey research
2. Of course, these findings presume that the respondent can be reached by phone in the first place. Given that approximately 95% of American households have telephones, this form of contact has not been problematic, at least in industrialized nations. However, in recent years the increasing use of answering machines, voice mail, and caller ID to screen out incoming phone calls has made access to potential participants for phone interviews somewhat more difficult (see discussion of sampling issues in Chapter 11).
3. Those who would like an overview of commonly employed measures (to use in developing their own specific item set) would be well advised to consult Van Dusen and Zill (1975) and the report of the American Psychological Association's (APA) task force on socioeconomic status (APA, 2007).
4. These factors probably interact with the specific event outcome in determining accuracy of recall. We know that pleasant outcomes are more likely to be remembered, especially those that have occurred recently; thus, winning $5,000 in the lottery is probably more readily recalled than losing $500 in a poker game, not only because it is a more pleasant outcome but also because it has a more enduring impact (Cannell & Fowler, 1963; Turner & Martin, 1982).
5. It is important to note that the principles that govern the reliable (and valid) measurement of attitudes apply equally to the measurement of behavioral intentions.
6. If accuracy of response is absolutely essential, it is important that the respondent know that choosing the "Don't know" option is not tantamount to an admission of ignorance.
7. In employment interviews, some questions may not be asked (see www.eeoc.gov/laws/practices/index.cfm), and these prohibitions should be honored in general interview research as well.

References

American Psychological Association Task Force on Socioeconomic Status. (2007). *Report of the APA task force on socioeconomic status.* Washington, DC: American Psychological Association.

Andrews, P. W., Gangestad, S. W., Miller, G. F., Haselton, M. G., Thornhill, R., & Neale, M. C. (2008). Sex differences in detecting sexual infidelity: Results of a maximum likelihood method for analyzing the sensitivity of sex differences to underreporting. *Human Nature, 19,* 347–373.

Bartholomew, K., Henderson, A. J. Z., & Marcia, J. (2000). Coding semistructured interviews in social psychological research. In H. Reis & C. Judd (Eds.), *Handbook of research methods in social and personality psychology* (pp. 286–312). New York: Cambridge University Press.

Bergen, G., Shults, R. A., Beck, L. F., & Qayad, M. (2012). Self-reported alcohol-impaired driving in the U.S., 2006 and 2008. *American Journal of Preventive Medicine, 42,* 142–149.

Bessa, M. A., Mitsuhiro, S. S., Chalem, E., Barros, M. M., Guinsburg, R., & Laranjeira, R. (2010). Underreporting of use of cocaine and marijuana during the third trimester of gestation among pregnant adolescents. *Addictive Behaviors, 35,* 266–269.

Bishop, G. R., Oldendick, R. W., Tuchfarber, A. J., & Bennett, S. E. (1980). Pseudo-opinions on public affairs. *Public Opinion Quarterly, 44,* 198–209.

Bloom, P. N., McBride, C. M., Pollak, K. I., Schwartz-Bloom, R. D., & Lipkus, I. M. (2006). Recruiting teen smokers in shopping malls to a smoking-cessation program using the foot-in-the-door technique. *Journal of Applied Social Psychology, 36,* 1129–1144.

Bradburn, N. M., Sudman, S., Blair, E., Locander, W., Miles, C., Singer, E., & Stocking, C. (1979). *Improving interview method and questionnaire design.* San Francisco: Jossey-Bass.

Breen (2006). A practical guide to focus-group research. *Journal of Geography in Higher Education, 30,* 463–475.

Brunner, G. A., & Carroll, S. J., Jr. (1969). The effect of prior notification on the refusal rate in fixed address surveys. *Journal of Advertising, 9,* 440–453.

Cain, P. S., & Treiman, D. J. (1981). The dictionary of occupational titles as a source of occupational data. *American Sociological Review, 46,* 253–278.

Cannell, C. F., & Fowler, F. J. (1963). Comparison of a self-enumerative procedure and a personal interview: A validity study. *Public Opinion Quarterly, 27,* 250–264.

Cannell, C. F., & Kahn, R. L. (1968). Interviewing. In G. Lindzey & E. Aronson (Eds.), *The handbook of social psychology* (2nd ed., vol. 2., pp. 526–595). Reading, MA: Addison-Wesley.

Cannell, C. F., Miller, P. V., & Oksenberg, L. (1981). Research on interviewing techniques. In S. Leinhardt (Ed.), *Sociological methodology, 1981.* San Francisco: Jossey-Bass.

Cartwright, A., & Tucker, W. (1969). An experiment with an advance letter on an interview inquiry. *British Journal of Preventive Social Medicine, 23,* 241–243.

Chapple, E. D. (1953). The standard experimental (stress) interview as used in interaction chronograph investigations. *Human Organization, 12,* 23–32.

Cotter, P. R., Cohen, J., & Coulter, P. B. (1982). Race-of-interviewer effects in telephone interviews. *Public Opinion Quarterly, 46,* 278–284.

Denis, C., Fatséas, M., Beltran, V., Bonnet, C., Picard, S., Combourieu, I., . . . & Auriacombe, M. (2012). Validity of the self-reported drug use section of the Addiction Severity Index and associated factors used under naturalistic conditions. *Substance Use & Misuse, 47,* 356–363.

Dijkstra, W., & van der Zouwen, J., (Eds.) (1982). *Response behavior in the survey-interview.* New York: Academic Press.

Dillman, D. A. (1978). *Mail and telephone surveys.* New York: Wiley.

Fennis, B. M., & Stroebe, W. (2010). *The psychology of advertising.* New York: Psychology Press.

Freedman, J. L., & Fraser, S. C. (1966). Compliance without pressure: The foot-in-the-door technique. *Journal of Personality and Social Psychology, 4,* 195–202.

Groves, R. M., & Kahn, R. L. (1979). *Surveys by telephone.* New York: Academic Press.

Groves, R. M., & Magilavy, L. J. (1981). Increasing response rates to telephone surveys: A door in the face for the foot-in-the-door? *Public Opinion Quarterly, 45,* 346–358.

Hajebi, A., Motevalian, A., Amin-Esmaeili, M., Hefazi, M., Radgoodarzi, R., Rahimi-Movaghar, A., & Sharifi, V. (2012). Telephone versus face-to-face administration of the Structured Clinical Interview for Diagnostic and Statistical Manual of Mental Disorders, fourth edition, for diagnosis of psychotic disorders. *Comprehensive Psychiatry, 53,* 579–583.

Hatchett, S., & Schuman, H. (1975). White respondents and the race-of-interviewer effect. *Public Opinion Quarterly, 39,* 523–528.

Herman, J. B. (1977). Mixed-mode data collection: Telephone and personal interviewing. *Journal of Applied Psychology, 62,* 399–404.

Hodge, R. W., Siegel, P. M., & Rossi, P. H. (1964). Occupational prestige in the United States. *American Journal of Sociology, 70,* 286–302.

Hollingshead, A. de B. (1949). *Elmstown's youth, the impact of social classes on adolescents.* New York: Wiley.

Hong, Y., Fang, X., Zhou, Y., Zhao, R., & Li, X. (2011). Factors associated with sexually transmitted infection underreporting among female sex workers in China. *Journal of Women's Health, 20*(1), 129–136.

Hornik, R., & Orwin, R. (2012). Robert Hornik and Robert Orwin on Stephen Magura's "Failure of intervention or failure of evaluation: A meta-evaluation of the national youth anti-drug media campaign evaluation. *Substance Use & Misuse, 47,* 1436–1438.

Kinsey, A. C., Pomeroy, W. B., & Martin, C. E. (1948). *Sexual behavior in the human male.* Philadelphia: Saunders.

Kluegel, J. R., & Smith, E. R. (1982). Whites' beliefs about blacks' opportunity. *American Sociological Review, 47,* 518–532.

Koppelman, N. F., & Bourjolly, J. N. (2001). Conducting focus groups with women with severe psychiatric disabilities: A methodological overview. *Psychiatric Rehabilitation Journal, 25,* 142–151.

Kroner, D. G., Mills, J. F., & Morgan, R. D. (2007). Underreporting of crime-related content and the prediction of criminal recidivism among violent offenders. *Psychological Services, 4,* 85–95.

Krosnick, J. A., & Fabrigar, L. R. (1997). Designing rating scales for effective measurement in surveys. In L. E. Lyberg, P. Biemer, M. Collins & E. D. De Leeuw, *Survey measurement and process quality* (pp. 141–164). New York: Wiley

Krosnick, J. A., & Fabrigar, L. R. (2001). *Designing great questionnaires: Insights from psychology.* New York: Oxford University Press.

Krosnick, J. A., Holbrook, A., Berent, M. K., Carson, R. T., Hanemann, W. M., Kopp, R. J., . . . & Conaway, M. (2002). The impact of "no opinion" response options on data quality: Non-attitude reduction or an invitation to satisfice? *Public Opinion Quarterly, 66,* 371–403.

Krueger, R. A., & Casey, M. A. (2009). *Focus groups: A practical guide for applied research* (4th ed.). Thousand Oaks, CA: Sage Publications.

Lee, S., Tsang, A., Lau, L., Mak, A., Ng, K. L., & Chan, D.M.-L. (2008). Concordance between telephone survey classification and face-to-face structured clinical interview in the diagnosis of generalized anxiety disorder in Hong Kong. *Journal of Anxiety Disorders, 22,* 1403–1411.

Marquis, K. H., & Cannell, C. F. (1969). *A study of interviewer-respondent interaction in the urban employment survey.* Ann Arbor, MI: Survey Research Center, University of Michigan.

Olson, M. A., & Kendrick, R. V. (2008). Origins of attitudes. In W. D. Crano & R. Prislin (Eds.), *Attitudes and attitude change* (pp. 111–130). New York: Psychology Press.

Parry, H. J., & Crossley, H. M. (1950). Validity of responses to survey questions. *Public Opinion Quarterly, 14,* 61–80.

Quinn, R. P., Gutek, B. A., & Walsh, J. T. (1980). Telephone interviewing: A reappraisal and a field experiment. *Basic and Applied Social Psychology, 1,* 127–153.

Ray, M. L., & Webb, E. J. (1966). Speech duration effects in the Kennedy news conferences. *Science, 153,* 899–901.

Richardson, S. A., Dohrenwend, B. S., & Klein, D. (1965). *Interviewing: Its forms and functions.* New York: Basic Books.

Richter, L., & Johnson, P. B. (2001). Current methods of assessing substance use: A review of strengths, problems, and developments. *Journal of Drug Issues, 31,* 809–832.

Rossi, P. H., Wright, J. D., & Anderson, A. B. (Eds.) (1983). *Handbook of survey research.* New York: Academic Press.

Rugg, D. (1941). Experiments in wording questions: II. *Public Opinion Quarterly, 5,* 91–92.

Schaps, E., & Sanders, C. (1970). Purposes, patterns, and protection in a campus drug-using community. *Journal of Health and Social Behavior, 11,* 135–145.

Schuman, H., & Hatchett, S. (1974). *Black racial attitudes: Trends and complexities.* Ann Arbor, MI: Institute for Social Research, University of Michigan.

Schuman, H., & Kalton, G. (1985). Survey methods. In G. Lindzey & E. Aronson (Eds.) *The handbook of social psychology* (pp. 635–697). Reading, MA: Addison-Wesley.

Schuman, H., & Presser, S. (1981). *Questions and answers in attitude surveys: Experiments on question form, wording, and context.* New York: Academic Press.

Smith, E. R., & Kluegel, J. R. (1984). Beliefs and attitudes about women's opportunity. *Social Psychology Quarterly, 47,* 81–95.

Smith, G. T., McCarthy, D. M., & Goldman, M. S. (1995). Self-reported drinking and alcohol-related problems among early adolescents: Dimensionality and validity over 24 months. *Journal of Studies on Alcohol, 56,* 383–394.

Souchet, L., & Girandola, F. (2013). Double foot-in-the-door, social representations, and environment: application for energy savings. *Journal of Applied Social Psychology, 43,* 306–315.

Sudman, S. (1980). Reducing response errors in surveys. *Statistician, 29,* 237–273.

Sudman, S., Bradburn, N. M., & Schwarz, N. (1996). *Thinking about answers: The application of cognitive processes to survey methodology.* San Francisco: Jossey-Bass.

Turner, C. F., & Martin, E. (Eds.). (1982). *Surveys of subjective phenomena.* Cambridge, MA: Harvard University Press.

Van Dusen, R. A., & Zill, N. (Eds.) (1975). *Basic background items for U.S. household surveys.* Washington, DC: Center for Coordination of Research on Social Indicators, Social Science Research Council.

Visscher, T.L.S., Viet, A. L., Kroesbergen, H. T., & Seidell, J. C. (2006). Underreporting of BMI in adults and its effect on obesity prevalence estimations in the period 1998 to 2001. *Obesity, 14,* 2054–2063.

Weaver, C. N., & Swanson, C. L. (1974). Validity of reported date of birth, salary, and seniority. *Public Opinion Quarterly, 38,* 69–80.

Whyte, W. F. (1955). *Street corner society.* Chicago: University of Chicago Press.

Wyatt, T. H., Krauskopf, P. B., & Davidson, R. (2008). Using focus groups for program planning and evaluation. *Journal of School Nursing, 24,* 71–77.

14
CONTENT ANALYSIS

Content analysis refers to a diverse domain of techniques designed to explore and describe qualitative verbal, written, and multimedia communications in a systematic, objective, and quantitative manner. Raw information collected through methods such as observational research, interviews, and focus groups can be used as data in content analysis to make sense of the findings. Information from multimedia sources—images, photographs, newspapers, audio clips, television shows, billboard advertisements, and Internet websites can be profitably examined using content analysis (Finn & Dillon, 2007; Stemler, 2001; Neuendorf, 2011). In content analysis, the investigator systematically reviews qualitative unstructured data and classifies them according to themes, characteristics, and patterns considered to be meaningful in addressing research questions. These coded variables usually are then used in statistical analyses, which provide quantitative information on the obtained data.

The research challenge posed by sorting and interpreting voluminous amounts of unprocessed qualitative data is daunting. Almost every social investigation involves the study of some form of communicative behavior. Be aware that "communication" is broadly defined. It does not imply information exclusively stemming from text-based messages or person-to-person interactions. A variety of types of audiovisual communications also may be content analyzed. These include paintings (Are girls or boys more likely to be depicted in cooperative or competitive play?), movies (Do action movies generally portray Muslim characters as heroes or villains?), photographs (How physically attractive are photographs of females in women's fashion magazines compared to men's car magazines?), comic strips (How likely are different comic strips to use sarcasm, satire, or bathroom humor?) and websites (Does a relation exist between the mean number of lines people write in their Facebook and how many friends they have on the site?). An encompassing definition of content analysis that satisfies all social scientists is apparently not possible, as is evident by the following attempts:

> "Content analysis is a research technique for the objective, systematic, and quantitative description of the manifest content of communication" (Berelson, 1952, p. 18);
>
> "Content analysis . . . refer[s] to the objective, systematic, and quantitative description of any symbolic behavior" (Cartwright, 1953, p. 424);
>
> "Content analysis, while certainly a method of analysis, is more than that. It is . . . a method of observation. Instead of observing people's behavior directly, or asking them to respond to

scales, or interviewing them, the investigator takes the communications that people have produced and asks questions of the communications" (Kerlinger, 1964, p. 544);

"Content analysis is a technique used to extract desired information from a body of material (usually verbal) by systematically and objectively identifying specified characteristics of the material" (Smith, 2000, p. 314);

"Content analysis is a research technique for making replicable and valid inferences from data to their context" (Krippendorff, 1980, p. 21).

"Content analysis is the study of recorded human communications, such as books, websites, paintings, and laws" (Babbie, 2010, p. 530).

The diversity of these characterizations suggests that content analysis as a method defies any single simple definition. One important distinction signaled by these definitions should be considered, however. In the first definition, Berelson (1952) limits content analysis to *manifest* (directly observable) content; in the next to final definition, Krippendorff (1980) calls for the analyst to make replicable and valid *inferences* from the qualitative data. In conducting a content analysis of television shows featuring mother-daughter relationships, an evocative episode might depict a scene showing a mother screaming at her daughter for some reason. A study exclusively focused on the manifest content would simply code that the mother is screaming at her daughter, whereas a researcher opting to make inferences might code that the mother is being emotionally abusive by berating the daughter. The degree of inference that the researcher decides to make mirrors the debate evident in discussions of how to conduct observational research (see Chapter 12). Some researchers allow no inference—only observed events (or behaviors) are coded. Other researchers might instead make inferences about the motivations or intentions that appear to underlie the observed event. Inferences are thought to provide a richer, more meaningful picture of the event under study; this richness often is bought at the cost of lowered measurement reliability and validity.

Conducting a Content Analysis

Before describing ways content analyses are undertaken, a brief mention of some necessary considerations is in order. Recognizing the similarity between the research procedures used by the content analyst and those of observation and interviewing methods will facilitate the transfer of information between the two previous chapters and this one.

Overview of the Process

Before beginning a content analysis, the investigator must first determine whether the technique is compatible with the ultimate goal of the research. Figure 14.1 provides a roadmap of the kinds of decisions that must be made in the process of mounting a content analysis. An imperative question that should be addressed is whether or not there is a body of content that may be culled to provide (or that can yield) the data necessary to answer the research question. For example, it may be impossible to conduct a content analysis of how exorcisms have been performed in the past 500 years by the Vatican, because this information is unavailable or you are not granted access to these private records. However, let us assume that that this information source does exist. In that case, the researcher must set rules for gathering the evidence and, if necessary, decide on the means of sampling the information. After deciding on the sampling scheme, the next decision concerns the coding system to be employed. Should a category or rating system be used? Do either (or both) provide the sensitivity necessary to answer the questions that gave rise to the research project in the first place?

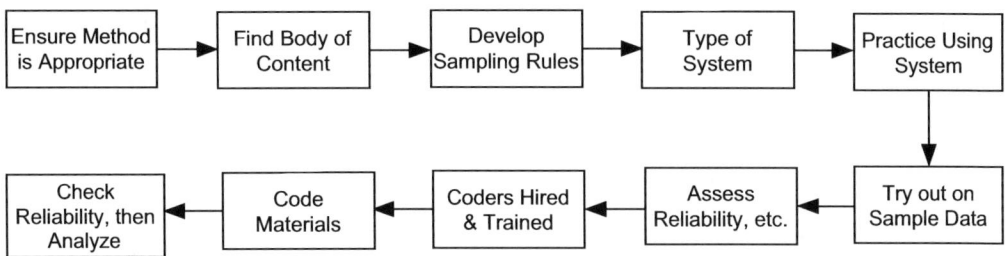

FIGURE 14.1 Steps in the process of developing a content analysis.

After deciding on the coding system, it is wise to test it on a sample of qualitative data. Researchers conduct "pilot studies" of this type to answer a simple question: Is the system workable? Can it be used reliably, and if so, does it promise to provide useful data? If not, the coding system should be modified. If yes, the researcher is ready to move on to the formal coding phase. In this next step, the content of interest is gathered, and the coders are trained and practice on this material. After reaching acceptable levels of interrater reliability, the critical communications are turned over to the coders. The coding may be done manually or by computer, but even computerized coding involves considerable human guidance. The data extracted from this process represent variables to be used in the statistical analysis and interpretation of the communications.

Coding Unit

A decision that must be made is whether to specify the procedures used in the coding system ahead of time or devise it during the coding process (Kondracki, Wellman, & Amundson, 2002). In **deductive content analysis**, the researcher determines the coding categories and units that will be the basis of the coding system prior to conducting the coding. This theory-driven strategy is based on hypotheses and models drawn from previous research on the topic, which specify the domains of content that are important to cull from the source data, and importantly, the purpose of the research. In **inductive content analysis**, the researcher allows coding categories and units to emerge empirically by continually revising and updating the coding system while in the midst of conducing the coding. This data-driven strategy might be used if there is little preexisting knowledge about the topic, so the researcher is required simultaneously to develop the coding scheme while coding. The inductive approach is akin to using unstructured exploratory interviewing or observational methods using grounded theory. When used in an exploratory fashion, the method can prove costly and cumbersome. It is probably more useful to establish a systematic coding scheme prior to peeking into the vast amount of qualitative data.

Once a coding scheme has been decided on, the investigator is faced with a series of decisions, and these decisions parallel those used in observational research. Consider the questions an observer must answer when attempting to categorize the behaviors of children in a nursery school setting. First, the researcher must decide when or what exactly should constitute the measurement unit for a variable. In observational research, time might be employed as the unit of behavior to be categorized (see Chapter 12). For example, whatever activity a child engages in for at least three minutes might be considered the unit of interest. For other coding variables, the attention or focus that a particular child directs toward another object (a toy, the teacher, another child) defines the unit. When the child's focus shifts from one object to another, this is taken to indicate a new unit to be categorized for that same variable. Similar decisions need to be made in defining the unit of text or material to be used in content analyses. Usually, however, a distinction is made between the **coding unit**, the specific variable to be classified in a content analysis, and the **context unit**, the embedded context within which the meaning is to be inferred in a content analysis. Sometimes these types of units are identical, but more often the coding unit (e.g., word) is analyzed within a prespecified block of material that constitutes the context unit (e.g., paragraph).

Words and Themes as Coding Units

As content analysis of text-based information is most popular in this form of research, most of the examples we discuss will involve this particular source of material, but such methods also could apply to the study of other types of communicative content. The coding unit might concern a word (a particular word of interest), a theme (an assertion, an idea, or a declaration captured in a single sentence or embedded across several sentences), the source of an item (e.g., a news story, editorial, Internet article, Twitter message, chat room message, or posting in an online message group), or a specific individual or personality type. Each coding unit represents a variable. From the standpoint of identifiability, the use of a word as the coding unit represents the simplest coding strategy for textual and auditory information, but the utility of investigations using such units is highly circumscribed. An interesting example of the use of the word as coding unit and doing a frequency count of that unit was provided by Mosteller and Wallace (1964). The investigators used content analytic techniques to determine the authorship of 12 *Federalist Papers* variously attributed either to James Madison or Alexander Hamilton. In a preliminary investigation of Madison's and Hamilton's *known* writings, Mosteller and Wallace identified 265 words that both men used, but with varying frequency. These known frequencies were compared with those of the same words appearing in the disputed papers. By this frequency-of-use comparison, Mosteller and Wallace's analysis suggested that Hamilton did not author the papers, and, furthermore, that Madison probably did.

Another coding unit is the *theme,* which represents underlying ideas, motifs, or views. Berelson (1952, p. 138) defined the theme as "a simple sentence . . . an assertion about a subject matter." Being of greater complexity than a single word, these units often provide more information than can be realized through the use of the word. Themes are more challenging to code, requiring thoughtfully reading and interpreting the text rather than performing a blind count of the number occurrences of a word. Themes entail greater research expense in terms of identification, construction, and classification of content. Consider the problem of the researcher attempting to categorize thematically newspaper editorials regarding attitudes toward Barak Obama's performance as president. The following sentence is found in an editorial: "Obama has demonstrated some remarkable blind spots in his handling of the health care reform issue; however, his handling of the economy was nothing short of superb, despite a recalcitrant Republican Congress." Can this sentence be judged as an expression of the writer's attitude toward Mr. Obama? Certainly. Is that attitude favorable or unfavorable? This is a more difficult question. To answer it, the researcher's first task is to decompose the sentence into more easily classified assertions or themes. Within this particular sentence, there are three such themes: 1) Obama was not adroit in his handling of health care reform; 2) He did a great job with the economy; 3) He did so despite a difficult Republican Congress. Only the first and second of two of these identified themes reflect the writer's attitude toward Obama. The first contains an unfavorable evaluation, but the second presents a more positive assessment. The final theme has nothing to do with the editorialist's attitude toward Obama (it is concerned with the opposing political party), and hence is discarded from consideration. How the researcher codes the first two parts of the sentence (and other coded themes concerned with President Obama) will determine the assessed attitude espoused in that particular editorial.

Although this sentence from an editorial piece was easily broken down into themes, not all content encountered is so amenable to analysis. In the case of more complex stimuli, judges often will disagree over the identification of themes and then about the meaning of themes that were identified. The more syntactically and linguistically complex the stimuli to be investigated, the more likely it is that such disagreements will be encountered. Interrater reliability should be used to evaluate the extent of such disagreements.

If coding problems of this type can be resolved, thematic analyses, or those making use of both themes *and* words as coding units, generally provide more information than analyses based on words alone. A good example of the combination of content units is found in the work of Stone and Hunt (1963), who attempted to determine whether they could discriminate between real and fabricated suicide notes through content analysis. To do so, they collected a group of real suicide notes from court records and asked 15 people, matched on general demographic characteristics with the victims of these suicides, to write suicide notes that could be perceived as real. Stone and Hunt (1963) were able to discriminate between the real and the simulated notes on the basis of three criteria. First, the real notes were more likely to contain references to concrete entities (persons, places, or things); second, real notes were more likely to use the word "love"; finally, fake notes were more likely to elaborate on thought processes or decisions about committing suicide.

The researchers arrived at these findings by counting the occurrences of these three themes and words in each of the notes, which yielded three coded variables that were subsequently used in statistical analyses. Subtracting the scores obtained on the first two variables from the third, Stone and Hunt (1963) were able to statistically discriminate between real and simulated suicide notes in 13 of 15 instances. To cross-validate their coding system, they then applied the same three criteria to another 18 notes, and correctly differentiated real from simulated suicide notes in 17 of 18 instances. This "hit ratio" was significantly better than that of independent raters who were not privy to the content coding scheme. The combination of word and theme as coding units in this study allowed for a more comprehensive extraction than that afforded by the use of the simpler (word) unit alone.

Use of context units. With the word as coding unit, interpretation problems are minimal, and analyses involving simple words as coding units generally involve only the *enumeration* of the occurrence of the word in the material under study. The context in which the word appears is irrelevant to the analysis. Word processors can be used to search and count the occurrence of specific words. With more complex coding units such as themes, some consideration of the context unit usually is required to allow confident interpretation of the meaning of the coding unit. For example, suppose an investigator were interested in studying a writer's attitudes toward communism, and encountered the following sentence (see Danielson, 1963, p. 188): "The communists are taking over the world bit by bit." How is this sentence to be judged? It is impossible to code for a theme without some knowledge of the context (the paragraph or passage) in which the sentence was embedded. If this quotation had appeared in a speech given by Vladimir Putin, it would undoubtedly be seen as a positive reference to communism. If, however, this sentence were part of a keynote address delivered by George W. Bush to the annual convention of the Daughters of the American Revolution, its implied evaluation of communism would be radically altered. In other words, the context of the theme is extremely important in judging its meaning. The context unit usually is prespecified. It defines "the largest division of context which may be consulted by a coder . . . to assign a score to a basic coding unit" (Danielson, 1963, p. 188). In text with deep embedded meanings, the coding units and context units that are used are seldom the same. The context unit, of course, can never be smaller than the coding unit: When the theme is used as the coding unit, its context unit usually entails more extensive amounts of text.

Limits may be placed on the size of the context unit (e.g., every sentence rather than every paragraph) for two purposes. The most important is to insure reliability. If coders were free to peruse as much or as little of the content as they desired in classifying a theme, differences between coders in amount of context surveyed might cause differences in evaluations. The second reason involves economy. Coders are expensive, and some limits must be imposed on the amount of time they are permitted to spend in the classification of a given theme.

Spatial and Temporal Coding Units

Two other types of units used in content analysis deserve brief mention. These include the **spatial unit**, which refers to measurement in terms geographical, geometric, and dimensional properties (e.g., inches of newspaper column, dimensions of magazine article, shape of a photograph), and the **temporal unit**, which refers to measurement in terms of properties of time (e.g., minutes of a television or radio broadcast, seconds of a conversation). Measures of this type often are used to study the degree of attention devoted in a medium for some specific type of information. For example, suppose one wished to investigate whether the president of Mexico was mentioned positively or negatively in front pages of a sample of North American newspapers. In this project, the front page of newspapers would constitute the *context unit,* and whether the President of Mexico is discussed in either a positive or negative light represents the *coding unit.* The *spatial unit* would be precise measures of space devoted to the discussion of the President. Because this is not audiovisual information stretching across time, *temporal units* are not pertinent. The kinds of studies that make use of spatial and temporal coding units are limited, as they tell nothing of the substantive attitudes expressed within the communication.

Spatial and temporal units are relatively uninformative of communication content, so they often are combined with other coding units. By coding for all four types of units, researchers have a greater variety of quantified variables for subsequent statistical analysis. Based on the content analyzed data, it would then be possible calculate the percentage of newspaper headings that mentioned the Mexican President in a positive versus negative light. Furthermore, one may also compute the statistical relationship between two or more of the variables: For example, when the President of Mexico is mentioned negatively, whether more paragraphs are devoted to him than when he is mentioned positively.[1]

Sampling

In content analysis, the term "sampling" does not accord with the traditional definitions, which involve selecting a subset of participants from a targeted population of people. Instead, sampling involves obtaining a reduced subset of elements from the targeted population of informational content (Neuendorf, 2011). A researcher, for example, might be interested in conducting a content analysis of racist websites hosted by hate groups. All such hate group websites would constitute the target population of relevant elements in the investigation, but because there are potentially thousands of these websites on the Internet, reviewing and content coding every one of these websites would be practically impossible. Depending on the desired degree of generalizability of findings, the researcher might select a random or nonrandom sampling approach to choose 10–20 sites for the content analysis.

Decisions concerning the way the sample of messages is chosen for content analysis are closely related to the analyst's choice of coding and context units. Such sampling usually involves several stages. In the first stage, the specific universe of content and of sources from which all data are to be drawn is identified. Depending on the research problem, the extensiveness of this universe can vary greatly. For example, before one could study the degree of attention American newspapers devote to recurrent turmoil in the Middle East, a number of sampling decisions would have to be made. First, the researcher must define the universe of possible sources. Should the sample be drawn from all possible newspapers published in the country? This limits the field somewhat, because there are many good papers originating in countries other than the U.S. Suppose the researcher decides to limit the sample further by studying only U.S. daily publications written in the English language. Should all such newspapers of this type (and there are many hundreds that meet these criteria) form the targeted population of sources? Perhaps, but this would mean that those dailies with circulations of 10,000 or less would be placed on par with papers whose readership numbers in the hundreds of thousands, even though the influence of the former on mass public opinion is certainly less than that of the large circulation daily. Because the number of papers with huge circulations is not great, a random sample would contain an overrepresentation of the smaller papers—at least in terms of actual readership. To avoid this problem, the researcher can further specify the universe by considering only those papers with circulations greater than 60,000.[2] From this targeted population of sources, the analyst might then randomly select a specific set of papers for the content analysis.

Source and Content Sampling

After deciding on the newspapers to be used, decisions then must be made about the extent of context to be investigated. Surely the researcher does not wish to read the entire edition of each paper in search of Middle East news items. Coding time considerations alone would prohibit such an approach. In response to this problem, the investigator may decide to sample only front-page news, ignoring the other sections of each newspaper. This would not seem to be a particularly bad choice, because the major news events of the day are almost invariably noted on the front pages of most newspapers. However, many newspapers reserve the second page for foreign news; thus, the investigator decides that the first and second pages will be searched for relevant articles about the Middle East.

The next question concerns the time period to be sampled. Is every possible edition of each sampled paper to be investigated? This will be difficult, because many of the papers in the sample will probably have been established many years ago. Suppose, then, that the investigator chooses to sample only those editions published during the years 2011 to 2014 inclusive. Of course, during this time period the sample dailies will have each published 1,460 issues (i.e., 4 (years) times 365 (days)). If the sample is composed of only 50 newspapers, the magnitude of the coding task (i.e., $50 \times 1{,}460 \times 2$, or 146,000 front and second pages to be investigated) is enormous. To meet this economically difficult situation, a final sampling strategy might be adopted. It involves sampling days of news copy. Rather than investigating every issue every day, each daily might be sampled every second, third, or fourth day. Or, better yet, within any given seven-day period, one, two, or three issues might be randomly selected from each newspaper. A schematic representation of the decision points that our hypothetical investigator encountered in generating this sample is presented in Figure 14.2. This figure illustrates an important distinction between two discrete types of sampling processes, source and content sampling. Decision points 1–4 are concerned primarily with the definition of the source sample from which units of content are to be drawn. Was the paper published in the United States? Was it an English-language paper? Was it a daily? Was its circulation greater than 60,000? All of these questions are concerned with the source of information. From the population fulfilling these requirements, a sample of specific news sources was drawn. The next phase is concerned with the sampling of content from within this chosen source sample. At this stage, coding and context units are sampled from each source and entered into the content analysis.

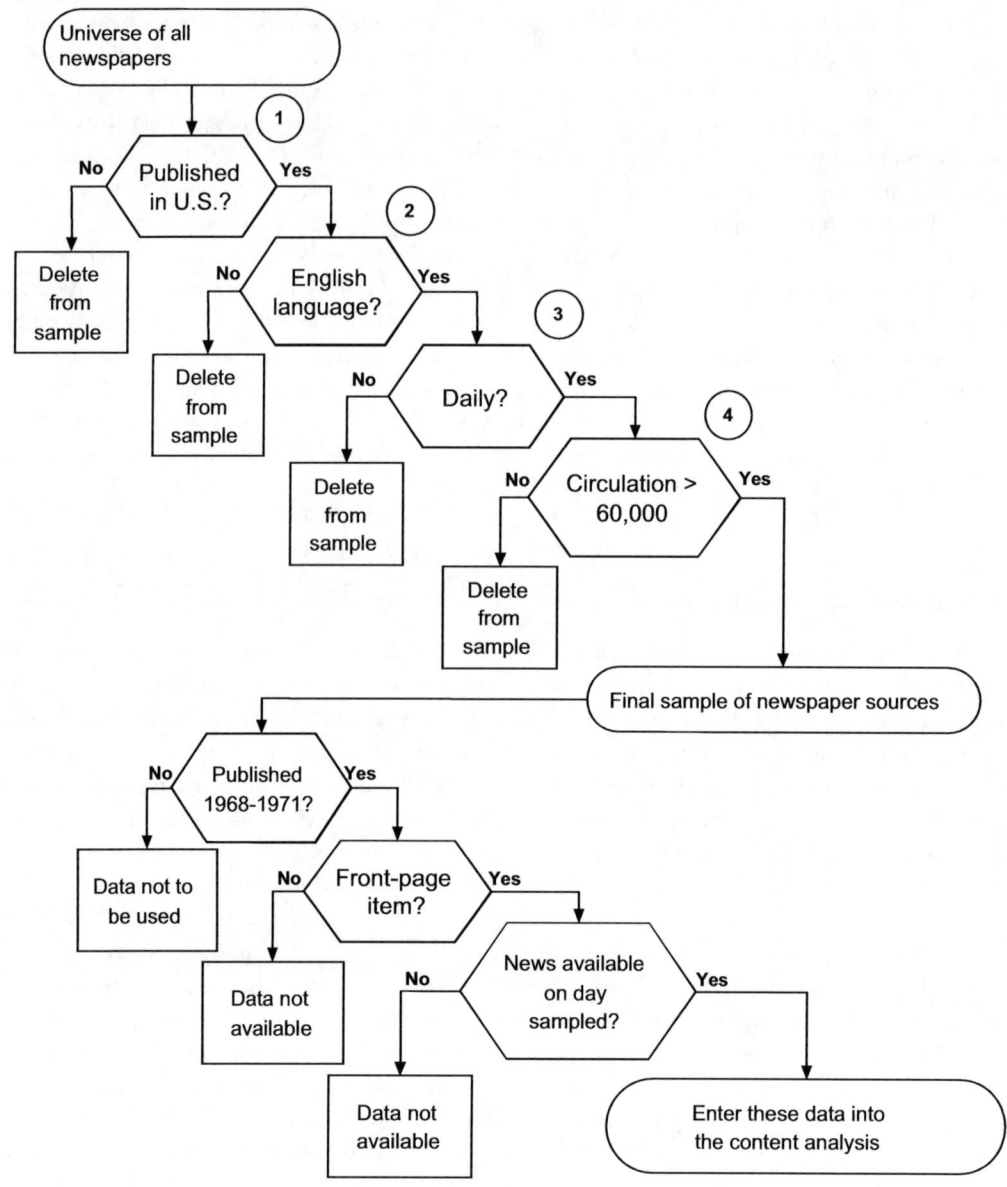

FIGURE 14.2 Schematic of decisions made in content sampling from a universe of newspapers.

The extensiveness of the particular content area from which messages are to be sampled, the coding and context units to be employed, the descriptive or inferential nature of the research—all of these considerations enter into the sampling decision. Not all content analyses involve a series of sampling decisions as extensive as those presented here. Consider, for example, the rather limited problem facing the investigator wishing to examine the physical qualities of the heroes of Hemingway's novels. The universe from which the content units are to be drawn, Hemingway's (seven) novels, is not extensive. In this instance, sampling within this targeted population of sources would tend to restrict unnecessarily the raw data on which the analysis is to be based. This point concerns the issue of generalizability, or external validity. Can the results be extended to his other writings that were not analyzed (short stories, poems, newspaper articles)? In content analysis, we are concerned with representativeness. If we draw a nonrepresentative sample of the content on which our analysis is based, it is likely that our results will not be representative of the more general universe of available content. A balance must be struck between efficiency and representativeness.

Often, an even more restricted selection of text, consisting of a single speech, message, or diary (see Goldman & Crano, 1976; White, 1947) sufficiently represents the population. In such instances, only this source is pursued in a content analysis. If a content analysis were performed on the literary style of books authored by Harper Lee, it would involve the only novel she ever wrote, *To Kill a Mockingbird*. Studies of this type are usually purely descriptive. The generalization based on the analysis of a single message usually is valid only when directed exclusively toward that particular message or communication source. To generalize to the targeted universe of communications, one must either analyze that universe or sample systematically from it and analyze the selected group of chosen messages. The more extensive the content universe, the more extensive should be the sample used in the analysis, if the generalization is to be trusted.[3] Thus, it would be foolhardy to attempt to make generalizations of a particular content analysis to all newspapers or all novels published over the last 10 years. Such an ambition would require the use of a nearly unmanageable sample of content and would prove to be of limited value even if accomplished, given the diversity and variability of the data that would be included in the sample.

Content Databases

The sampling process to obtain material for a content analysis is not always as difficult as it might seem on first consideration. Usually, an investigator does not have to locate years of newspaper hardcopies and then physically wade through each and every issue. Thanks to computerized databases and the Internet, today's social researcher has available a mass of data amenable for content analysis. Almost all of the world's important (i.e., heavily read) newspapers can be accessed online, and search and abstracting programs can be found with simple on-screen commands. Lexis-Nexis is probably the most well known of the newspaper archives. Among other things, it contains a huge database of newspaper reports and a powerful search function. For example, it contains the full text of every *New York Times, Washington Post,* and *Christian Science Monitor* article from 1980 onwards. The list could be extended almost indefinitely—the *Claremont (CA) Collage* has been abstracted by this service from September 1998, and the *Columbus Dispatch* from the first day of 1992. Lexis-Nexis is available online through many libraries. Broad searches could be conducted, with relevant results shown regardless of the newspaper sources. The search could be limited to specific newspapers, and further narrowed to specific publication dates.

Also available are electronic databases and Internet search engines containing archives of photographs, pictures, audio clips, musical expressions, videos, television episodes and other types of communication content that provide materials amenable to content analysis. Prior to these electronic search databases, content analytic research was limited by the investigator's patience in manually locating data. Now the limits have more to do with the researcher's creativity and motivation.

Coding Systems

To achieve scientific respectability, the coding procedures established in content analysis must be systematic. Documenting systematic procedures allows other researchers to replicate and extend the results of a particular content analysis study. One of the major ways of introducing systematization to this area is through the use of prespecified classification systems in the coding of content.

Rather than rely on the intuitive classification of communications, therefore, content analysts make use of coding schemes through which relevant dimensions of content are systematically identified and compared in some way. In Chapter 12, we presented an extensive section dealing with the choice and construction of coding systems in connection with observational methods. Those considerations apply as well in the case of content analysis. In observational methodology, categorizing the actions and behaviors of an individual or group occurring within the research situation is of primary interest. In content analysis, parallel aspects of the content of a communication are of central relevance. Generating a coding system is similar in both.

Many different coding systems have been employed by content analysts, studying almost every conceivable aspect of written, spoken, or pictorial communications. One of the major criticisms of this field, in fact, concerns its failure to generate mutually agreed-upon systems of coding through which diverse content could be investigated and compared across all types of content analysis projects. Researchers appear more intent on individually tailoring coding schemes to fit their particular research problems than on developing more generally employable techniques. Because the number of systems in the content analysis literature is so extensive, it is likely that an investigator willing to search through the appropriate journals will be able to obtain a "pre-used" coding system suitable for almost any research need. (In two bibliographic tours de force, Holsti (1969, p. 104–116) listed 13 pages of various category systems under the rather modest title of "Categories: Some Examples," and Smith (2000, p. 323), in a table labeled "Some Coding Systems Developed for Social Science Research," cited more than 21 systems used across 10 major topic areas (e.g., life-span development, moods and emotions, values, self, etc.). Investigators searching for an established category scheme should consult these sources.

A notable exception to the trend toward the generation of idiosyncratic coding schemes is found in computer analytic approaches, which, while restricted in some ways are nevertheless attractive to many.[4] Text analysis and character recognition software used for content analysis are listed in a review by Kondracki et al. (2002) and by Alexa and Zuell (2000), both of which describe previous research showing that human coders are susceptible to coding fatigue and inconsistency, whereas these problems do not occur when using content analysis software. Such programs are most helpful, however, for counting occurrences of words and simple themes. A feature of some of these programs is their capacity to account for synonyms when counting word occurrences, using an integrated thesaurus to perform frequency counts of an exact word only or selected synonyms of that word. Because such programs are functionally limited in extracting subtleties in embedded meanings when interpreting themes, problems may arise in accurately accounting for narrative structure or context. For example, text analysis software has problems differentiating among the usage of "mean" to refer to a nasty person, the arithmetic mean, living below one's means, or meaning to say something. For this and other reasons, after the software has performed the content analysis of the material, it is advisable to review and inspect output to ensure that the coding rules were followed as intended by the researcher.

The basic principles involved in all content analyses do not differ between computerized and manual approaches. To use computer software for content analysis, one must first understand how to do the job without a computer—to specify in advance the information to be sought, the rules to be applied to code the information and combine data, and so on. The coding rules must be clearly specified in either case. There is no question that the computer is extremely efficient and reliable, but it cannot generate coding rules for the investigator. To be a successful computer-content analyst, one must first become an effective non–computer–content analyst.

Statistical Analysis

After the raw qualitative material has been content-coded into manageable variables, the final step needed to facilitate interpretation of the rich data involves statistical analysis. Many content analysis studies simply report descriptive statistics, such as the percentage coded in each of the categories for a particular variable or the mean score on a rating scale. Other studies, in addition to offering descriptive information, also are designed to assess significant associations and relationships among the variables, thus allowing for a multivariate approach to understanding the patterns identified in the content.

Summary of the General Paradigm

Before providing a picture of the scope of use of this technique and the range of issues to which it has been addressed, a brief summary of the research paradigm commonly used in content analysis studies will be useful. Not surprisingly, the series of operations to be described coincide closely with those discussed in Chapter 12, which was focused on systematic observational techniques.

The scientific analysis of message content usually involves use of a prespecified coding system. The choice of coding system is best made on the basis of information relevant to the data to be categorized. In the case of a content analysis, this means that the researcher must become thoroughly familiar with the general body of content under consideration in advance of the choice or construction of a coding scheme. Only then is the investigator in a position to make an informed and reasoned decision regarding the most appropriate classificatory system. Closely bound to the choice of coding scheme are decisions regarding the appropriate units of analysis and the particular manner in which these units will be sampled from the larger universe of potential sources. Once coding scheme, units, and sampling rules have been decided upon, and coders trained, the content analysis can begin.

Coding messages is much like coding observed behaviors, except that the data under investigation are usually in written form.[5] As in all observational research, care must be taken to assure the reliability of the rules (or their application) used to categorize data. Krippendorff (1980) has distinguished among three approaches to reliability used in content analysis research. The most simple of these is concerned with *stability,* the extent to which the same coder assigns identical scores to the same content when he or she reviews it more than once in different sessions. Failure to obtain adequate "test-retest" reliability (stability) indicates intra-observer inconsistency; the analyst, that is, did not apply the coding criteria consistently from one session to the other, suggesting a lack of adequate coder training, or a coding system that is complicated or vague and thus impossible to employ in a consistent fashion. Stability of scoring is the minimal form of reliability and should not be the sole means of demonstrating the reliability of one's content analysis. This is because stability is dependent on the actions of a single coder, who might apply the coding rules consistently but in an idiosyncratic fashion. Different results might be obtained if another coder attempted to use the same rules.

A more stringent approach to reliability in content analysis is *reproducibility,* which reflects the extent to which the outcome of a specific coding process is the same when different coders analyze the same content. This approach is most commonly used in establishing the reliability of a coding scheme. Generally, it is termed "intercoder agreement" or "interrater reliability," because the correspondence between two (or more) coders' estimates of the same content is the measure of this form of reliability. When coding fails to generate reproducible results across judges, the failure can be attributed to intra-observer inconsistencies or inter-observer disagreements. Cohen's Kappa, Fleiss' Kappa, and the intraclass correlation are the recommended statistics to assess intercoder reliability. These procedures to assess interrater reliability were reviewed in Chapter 12.

Krippendorff (1980) defines the strictest form of reliability analysis as one that compares the accuracy with which a coding system reproduces, or compares to, some known standard. For example, in Stone's and Hunt's (1963) suicide note research presented earlier, the investigators knew which of the notes were real and which were fictitious.[6] To the extent that the coding system accurately reproduced this distinction, it was reliable (or accurate, as this form of reliability is termed). Accuracy can be weakened by intra-observer inconsistencies (poor stability), inter-observer disagreements (poor reproducibility), and the failure of the coding scheme to reflect the standard that is to be used in evaluating the content or construct of interest

In our terms, this last form of "reliability" is actually a validity operation, insofar as the investigation involves the correspondence between a predictor (the coded values) and an outcome (the behavior being predicted). It is a reliability operation in the sense that if intercoder reliability is deficient, the predictor will not adequately anticipate the outcome, but this same observation can be made of any measure. Unreliability of measures (or coding schemes) inevitably diminishes validity.

Once the reliability of the coding scheme has been established, the content analysis can proceed in accordance with the particular purposes of the research. If the study is one of simple description, the analyst will specify the decision rules used to assign a coding unit to a specific category and present the relative frequencies with which various categories were employed in coding a communication. Sometimes more than one source is analyzed, and the relative frequencies obtained between sources are compared. Schwab and Shneidman (1974), for example, examined various idiosyncrasies in logic that Kennedy and Nixon employed in their first two televised debates. On the basis of his classifications, the authors found that Nixon employed the communication strategies of "truth type confusion," "derogation," and "argumentum ad populism" more often than Kennedy, who instead concentrated on the "irrelevant premise" as his principal idiosyncrasy of reasoning in the debates.

When the aim of the analyst goes beyond that of simple description and thus requires drawing inferences from the content, the study's potential value is increased, but so is the possibility that faulty generalizations will be produced. Inferential content analysis can, of course, be undertaken legitimately, but should be attempted only after some means of testing the validity of inferences has been determined. Inferential content analyses make many more demands of the researcher than the descriptive variety, because they must not only describe content but also provide some statements regarding the motivations of the source responsible for the communication, and finally present some data bearing on the validity of these propositions. One can, for example, analyze and describe the various propaganda techniques employed by a politician engaged in a close race; whether on the basis of these findings the analyst is in a position to comment accurately on the personality structure of this source is an entirely different matter. A good example of this form of analysis was provided by Conway, Suedfeld, and Tetlock (2001) who, using content analytic techniques informed by strong theory, produced interesting research assessing the association of cognitive complexity of statesmen and their decisions to go to war.

Attempts by scientists to substantiate the inferences drawn on the basis of content analyses have taken a number of interesting turns. George (1959), for example, was able to check the goodness of the inferences of World War II propaganda analysts through a study of captured Nazi documents. Although this check was made years after the original analyses, George found the wartime content analysts' inferences accurate. Because of the need for external verification, the method of content analysis in and of itself is not best suited for testing hypotheses. Many of the arguments presented in opposition to the use of unstructured interviews (Chapter 13) apply here. Content analysis is, however, a superb technique for producing hypotheses, which, given the nature of their generation, often are supported in later research. The versatility of this method is such that it can be adapted to almost any type of communication (see Viney, 1983).

Representative Examples

Having discussed the general features of a content analysis, we can illustrate some of the many forms of this technique. Following the lead of Berelson (1954), Holsti (1968, 1969), and a host of others who have surveyed the literature on content analysis, we will describe research in accord with Lasswell, Lerner, and Pool's (1952, p. 12) classic questions used in the analysis of communications, "Who says what to whom, how, and with what effect."

Who Said It

Some of the most interesting studies employing content analysis have been conducted to examine the likely authorship of various documents. These studies take the form of the classic detective story, and sometimes are even more rewarding than the best of the genre. Earlier in this chapter, we discussed Mosteller and Wallace's (1964) examination of the probable authorship of 12 disputed *Federalist Papers*. In an investigation similar in form, Yule (1944) was able to point quite convincingly to the probable author of the classic *The Imitation of Christ*.

Biblical scholars, too, have used content analytic techniques extensively in attempting to settle questions of disputed authorship. While interesting, these studies do not always provide unambiguous results. For example, Morton (1963) identified seven elements of writing style that he felt would clearly distinguish among authors.[7] Using this system, he concluded that six different authors were responsible for the epistles traditionally ascribed to St. Paul, and challenged the orthodoxy of Christianity either to debunk his results or to revise their traditional views of the early church. The challenge was met by Ellison (1965), who, employing Morton's seven indicators "discovered" that James Joyce's *Ulysses* was written by five different authors, as discerned by passages that appear to be stylistically different in a content analysis, and that none of these individuals could have written *Portrait of the Artist as a Young Man*! The obvious failure of Morton's coding system in this particular case to identify the single authorship of *Ulysses* and *Portrait of the Artist* placed his contentions regarding the multiple authorship of the Pauline epistles in serious jeopardy.

What Was Said

Problems of validation are not nearly so pressing in studies directed toward answering the question, "What was said?" Investigations of this type typically are descriptive in nature and often attempt to generalize no farther than the messages on which they are based. As Holsti (1969, p. 43) noted, in this type of study, "the content data serve as a direct answer to the research question, rather than as indicators from which characteristics of the sources or audiences are to be inferred." Probably the bulk of content analytic studies conducted have focused on consideration of the question of "what was said." Berelson (1954, pp. 490–495) provided a classificatory system to study this question, and it is still useful. We will employ it loosely in examining this portion of the content analysis literature.

Trends

One of the most frequent aims of content analysis research has been the study of communication trends over time. Has the level of achievement motivation (McClelland, 1961) expressed in the stories included in children's primers changed during the last 50 years? Is the rate of politically inspired movies associated with economic conditions? Are the values and goals expressed in the movies today the same as those of 20 years ago? Is there greater self-disclosure of information on social network websites today than was evident in its early days? Questions of this sort are based on the assumption that the mass media act as a barometer of various aspects of the society they serve. Verification of this assumption is difficult, but the face validity of many of the studies undertaken with this general goal often is intriguing. Yakobson and Lasswell (1949), for example, studied the content of Russian May Day slogans from 1918–1943. During that period, political scientists had noted a gradual mellowing of revolutionary zeal on the part of the Soviets. Consistent with this observation, content analysis of slogans revealed that calls for universal revolutionary activities had steadily diminished and were replaced with an increased emphasis on nationalistic appeals. A result of this type, while relatively unconvincing when taken alone, proved compelling in conjunction with other, independently arrived at sources of information.

A different variety of trend-relevant content analysis is evident in work by Peterson, Seligman, and Vaillant (1988), who analyzed the optimism expressed by a group of Harvard seniors in a series of open-ended questionnaires. These responses were written in 1946. Thirty-five years later, the researchers analyzed the content of the writing and found a strong relation between pessimism and physical morbidity. Apparently, optimism and pessimism are associated with physical well-being.

Norms

Research related to the study of trends is evident in the use of content analysis to establish norms. In a representative example of this form of research, Ames and Riggio (1995) used content analytic techniques to score the responses of a large adolescent sample that had responded to Rotter's incomplete sentences personality test. The test was scored for evidence of psychological maladjustment, and the resulting findings, based on the large sample, were used in developing norms.

International Content Differences

One use of content analysis that is both interesting and common is the study of differences in communication content occurring between nations. Similarities or dissimilarities of between-nation content often are thought to reflect important aspects of the countries surveyed. Proving that content differences do in fact reflect underlying national differences calls for research operations beyond those of the usual content analytic variety. The descriptive data that studies of this type provide, however, can prove compelling, especially when presented in combination with other, known aspects of the nations under study.

Consider, for example, an investigation undertaken by Lewin (1947), in which he compared the literature of the Hitler Youth with that of the Boy Scouts of America. The major themes of both content samples stressed the value of physical fitness, discipline, and achievement. In the Hitler Youth literature, however, more emphasis was laid on national loyalty and racial pride, whereas the Boy Scout sample stressed generosity and imagination. In conjunction with experiences of World War II, this study provided support for a hypothesis regarding the child training practices that gave rise to the authoritarian Nazi.

Standards

Do news magazines fulfill their objectives of presenting a fair, unbiased discussion of public events? Do they meet the noble standards that the fifth estate has set for themselves? In an examination of the coverage afforded the major candidates in the 2008 and 2012 U.S. presidential elections, the Pew Research Center's Project for Excellence in Journalism found that the tone of the election coverage slightly favored the Democratic standard bearer over his opponents (www.people-press.org/files/legacy-pdf/9-25-12%20Press%20Release.pdf). In earlier research on treatment of Republican candidates for the presidency, Westley et al. (1963) found that *Time's, Newsweek's,* and *U.S.*

News and World Report's treatment of Republican leaders was only very slightly more favorable than that afforded the Democrats.

To Whom Was It Said

It is a truism among professional politicians that smart candidates will stress some issues to one audience while studiously avoiding these same issues with another. This is smart politics, but in days of immediate access to almost all features of public life, this strategy can be difficult to follow. In his bid for the presidency in 2012, for example, Romney told donors at a $50,000 per plate dinner that 47% of voters would chose Obama "no matter what" because they were people "dependent upon government, who believe that they are victims, who believe the government has a responsibility to care for them, who believe that they are entitled to health care, to food, to housing, to you-name-it . . . . These are people who pay no income tax . . . . I'll never convince them they should take personal responsibility and care for their lives." (see www.youtube.com/watch?v=MU9V6eOFO38). Can you imagine candidate Romney making that same statement to a group of unemployed job seekers or urban poor?

Content analysis can be used to provide empirical estimates of the extent to which communicators vary their messages as a function of audience. For example, John Foster Dulles, Secretary of State during the Eisenhower presidential administration, was the focus of two such investigations. Cohen (1957) and Holsti (1962) found clear evidence that the content of Dulles's communications was guided by a consideration of the audience for whom they were prepared. Similarly, Berkman (1963) found that advertising copy in *Life* and *Ebony* magazines was differentiated in terms of socioeconomic status of product users.

How Are the Facts Presented?

Investigations of this question generally focus on the form or style of the communication. Although the same information might be presented in two communications, one message might be considerably more influential than the other because of the way the facts were presented. Analysis of the way in which messages are structured constitutes the primary goal of investigations of the "how" variety.

Propaganda Analysis

Propaganda analysts have been particularly active in this area of research. Laswell (1927), for example, attempting to identify the reasons that underscored the British propagandists' success in World War I and the concomitant German failure, isolated four major goals that both sides attempted to realize. The first involved attempts to generate and maintain home front hostility toward the enemy, the second stressed preservation of friendly alliances, the third concerned attempts to secure the support of neutral countries, and the fourth focused on efforts to demoralize enemy soldiers and civilians. Because the propagandistic goals of the British and Germans were essentially the same—to gain an appreciation of the effectiveness of one side over the other—their communications had to be analyzed not in terms of what was said, but rather in terms of how it was said. A major reason for the British propagandists' success can be traced to the image of a beleaguered island nation they attempted to convey. The British pictured themselves as peace-loving islanders, forced to fight so that Western civilization might be saved from the barbarians. Their goal in the war was "to end all wars," and their methods were strictly humanitarian. German propagandists cited the need to extend Germanic *Kultur* as a justification for their war efforts. Humanitarianism was given short shrift, and British atrocities were rarely noted. Like their counterparts in the field, the German public relations staff was soundly defeated.

Stylistic Analysis

The analysis of propaganda does not exhaust the question of "How?" Considerable research focused on various aspects of literary or linguistic style has been conducted. Miles (1951), for example, attempted to describe in a quantitative fashion the differing stylistic patterns characteristic of distinct literary periods. Her analyses of poetic writings proved quite successful. Harvey (1953) attempted to discover the major distinguishing characteristics between best-selling novels and also-rans. Combining a number of content variables in a prediction equation, Harvey found that he could predict sales with better than 80% accuracy.

With What Effect?

The final general form of content analysis to be considered consists of investigations focused on the effects of a communication on its receivers. In other than the most highly restricted situations, potential problems of faulty generalization are acute in such studies. For example, sophisticated correlational analyses have been conducted to assess the association between coverage of championship heavyweight boxing matches in the media and subsequent increases in homicides in the U.S. (Phillips, 1983). Phillips (1982) also presented evidence based on archival records suggesting a link between the occurrence of suicide content in popular television soap operas and the frequency of actual suicides in the population at large. Vitaglione (2012) suggested communication effects could generalize beyond suicides, in research indicating that shortly after highly publicized NASCAR races aggressive driving accidents increased significantly.

Most investigations dealing with the effects of communications have sought more modest goals. Studies of the ease with which a communication can be comprehended by a reader (or group of readers) provide a good example of this type of restricted research. Many readability formulas have been devised and generally are based on sentence length and vocabulary difficulty (see, for example, Dale & Schall, 1948; Flesch, 1943). Usually in these studies communications judged by some formula to differ in readability are administered to research participants, whose comprehension is then tested. If patterns of participants' message comprehension are consistent with expert judgments of difficulty, the usefulness of the formula is supported.

One of the most common formulas used is the Flesch (1948) Reading Ease test, which assigns scores based on the average sentence length and the average number of syllables per word. The output of the formula ranges from 0 to 100. Scores ranging from 90 to 100 should be understood easily by the average third grader. Scores between 60 and 70 should be easily understood by eighth and ninth graders, and scores between 0 and 30 should be easily understood by college graduates. The readability score of the prior and present paragraph is 45.8, which should be easily understood by those whose educational attainment is at least at the twelfth grade. This test, and others like it, are widely used. Some states, for example, require insurance policies to be written at a level of difficulty similar to that of the indicated paragraphs.

All systems of this type are susceptible to the specialized or idiosyncratic use of language. Gertrude Stein's writing is characterized by short words and short sentences, but it is difficult to comprehend. The contextual qualities of her work, however, would confound almost all standard readability formulas by indicating that Stein's writings are easy to read. They are not.

Content Analyses on the Internet

The emergence of the Internet as a medium of communication has yielded ample opportunities for researchers to employ content analysis in their studies (e.g., Finn & Dillon, 2007; Lewis, Zamith, & Harmida, 2013). Sources that may be used include websites, social network profiles, online message groups, chat room conversations, Twitter messages or tweets, and the countless multimedia accessible through the click of a mouse. Although launched only in 2004 as a social networking utility for people to communicate with family members, friends, and coworkers, Facebook has been the subject of several content analytic studies. Extending previous research that evaluated text-based status updates, Hum and colleagues (2011) content analyzed the profile photos that people used in Facebook. The objective of the research was to understand how, through a mere picture, people represented their social identities online. The photos were drawn from profiles belonging to a convenience sample of undergraduate students who were Facebook friends of the researchers. Descriptive statistics computed from the coded variables revealed that the majority of photos depicted the user with no other individual, and typically did not show the person engaged in any form of physical activity. Most photos were found to be professionally appropriate, and gender differences did not emerge.

The Internet also could be used to furnish information on views and ideas promoted by fringe groups. Such content would normally be difficult to obtain if not for this relatively anonymous format of communication. Borzekowski, Schenk, Wilson, and Peebles (2010) evaluated websites that supported and endorsed eating disorders. After conducting a search using 15 related search terms, a relatively thorough list of 180 pro-eating disorder websites were included in the content analysis. The analysis showed that the vast majority (91%) of these sites were accessible to the public and did not require any special membership or password. Most of the websites presented content that was pro-anorexia (84%) and pro-bulimia (64%). Websites also were coded in terms of the types of tips offered to foster eating disorders, including dieting (74%), foods considered to be safe (68%), exercising (59%), purging (50%), pills and laxatives (49%), how to distract the self from eating (48%), how to hide the eating disorder (23%), and alternative medicines (22%). Statistical analyses were conducted with each of these variables, and the researchers judged (inferred) the danger or harm (low, medium, or high) of the website. The results suggested that the display of each of these tips was associated with greater perceived harm of the website.

Conclusion

The value of content analysis lies in its versatility. Issues that would be dangerous or impossible to research can be studied with this approach, using publicly available materials. The technique has been used to study almost all features of the communication process, from the disputed authorship of books and papers to the likely policy changes of authoritarian political regimes. Coding systems, machine- or human-based, are numerous and help to systematize data collection and analysis. Although content analytic methods are not ideal for hypothesis testing, they often are useful in developing the hypotheses that can be tested in more controlled contexts.

Questions for Discussion

1. What does it mean in content analysis to draw a representative sample? Why is it important? What kinds of questions can be answered by the various forms of content analysis?
2. You previously conducted an experiment that investigated the effects of having scantily clad men and women in advertisements on consumer behavior. Afterward, you realized you could

conduct a parallel study that examined the potential breadth of impact that this might have on the country's consumption of certain products. In other words, perhaps there are a sufficient number of half-naked models in advertisements that we have achieved a saturation point, or exposure to a greater number of ads (with models) for a particular product is directly proportional to the likelihood that a person will purchase that product. Could content analysis answer these questions—why or why not? What *could* content analysis tell us about the presence of barely dressed men and women in advertisements for different types of consumer products?

3. When can content analysis tell us more about a certain topic or phenomenon than other forms of analysis? Why? With content analysis, do researchers risk misinterpreting the original intent of the material they are analyzing, and is there any way to measure the likelihood of that risk? Is the original intent of material irrelevant, given that *interpretation* of the content is ultimately the content being analyzed? For example, if a political cartoon is meant to be satirical, but all readers (including your expert coders) interpret it literally, would the cartoon be coded in terms of its literal content or its intended content? And how would you know?

Notes

1. We note parenthetically that research by Markham and Stempel (1957) has demonstrated that the laborious and time consuming measurement process required in making use of spatial units often is unnecessary. These investigators found a strong positive relationship between the mere presence of an item (say, a foreign news story) and the number of column inches it occupied. Thus, rather than using spatial units or temporal units as measures of media attention, one might record the mere presence or absence of a selected content category within a series of predetermined context units. These frequencies often provide the same information as that gained through the use of spatial or temporal units, and can be gathered at significantly less expense.
2. More than 100 American daily newspapers satisfy this criterion.
3. In Chapter 11, we discuss techniques useful in drawing a survey sample; similar considerations may be applied in the case of content sampling.
4. An extensive discussion of computer-oriented techniques is beyond the scope of this text. The interested reader is directed to the following sources: Barry, 1998; Holsti, 1964; Miles & Huberman, 1994; Seidel, 1991; Stone, 2000; Stone, Dunphy, & Smith, 1966.
5. Some analyses are performed on verbal material, but the audio clips are usually printed before analysis is begun.
6. A mirror image of this type of analysis was performed by Hooker (1957), who asked a group of clinicians to content-analyze the projective test reactions of a group of men, some of whom were gay. The issue of the research was to determine if trained analysts could discriminate between homosexual and heterosexual men. At the time, homosexuality was considered a severe form of emotional unbalance. As Hooker expected, the clinicians were unable to distinguish the two groups. Their inability helped change medical opinion; ultimately, homosexuality was no longer considered a psychiatric disorder requiring treatment. We agree with these findings and their policy-related outcome; however, as methodologists, we are obliged to point out the fact that this study made its point by confirming the null hypothesis!
7. The stylistic indicators employed by Morton were sentence length, frequency of use of the words *and, but,* and *in,* frequency of use of definite articles, all forms of the verb to be, and use of the third-person pronoun.

References

Alexa, M., & Zuell, C. (2000). Text analysis software: Commonalities, differences, and limitations: The results of a review. *Quality and Quantity, 34,* 299–321.

Ames, P. C., & Riggio, R. E. (1995). Use of the Rotter Incomplete Sentences Blank with adolescent populations: Implications for determining maladjustment. *Journal of Personality Assessment, 64,* 159–167.

Babbie, E. R. (2010). *The practice of social research* (12th ed.). Belmont, CA: Wadsworth, Cengage Learning.

Barry, C. A. (1998). Choosing qualitative data analysis software: Atlas/ti and Nudist compared. *Sociological Research Online, 3.* www.socresonline.org.uk/socresonlint/3/3/4.html

Berelson, B. (1952). *Content analysis in communication research.* Glencoe, IL: Free Press.

Berelson, B. (1954). Content analysis. In G. Lindzey (Ed.), *Handbook of social psychology*. Reading, MA: Addison-Wesley.

Berkman, D. (1963). Advertising in *Ebony* and *Life*: Negro aspirations vs. reality. *Journalism Quarterly, 40,* 53–64.

Borzekowski, D. L., Schenk, S., Wilson, J. L, & Peebles, R. (2010). E-Ana and E-Mia: A content analysis of pro-eating disorder websites. *American Journal of Public Health, 100,* 1526–1544.

Cartwright, D. P. (1953). Analysis of qualitative material. In L. Festinger & D. Katz (Eds.), *Research methods in the behavioral sciences.* New York: Holt.

Cohen, B. D. (1957). *The political process and foreign policy: The making of the Japanese peace settlement.* Princeton, NJ: Princeton University Press.

Conway, L. G., III, Suedfeld, P., & Tetlock, P. E. (2001). Integrative complexity and political decisions that lead to war or peace. In D. J. Christie, R. V. Wagner & D.D.N. Winter (Eds.), *Peace, conflict, and violence: Peace psychology for the 21st century* (pp. 66–75). Upper Saddle River, NJ: Prentice Hall/Pearson Education.

Dale, E., & Schall, J. S. (1948). A formula for predicting readability. *Educational Research Bulletin, 27,* 11–20, 37–54.

Danielson, W. A. (1963). Content analysis in communication research. In R. O. Nafziger & D. M. White (Eds.), *Introduction to mass communications research* (pp. 180–206). Baton Rouge, LA: Louisiana State University Press.

Ellison, J. W. (1965). Computers and the testaments. In *Proceedings: Conference on computers for the humanities* (pp. 64–74). New Haven, CT.: Yale University Press.

Finn, J. & Dillon, C. (2007). Using personal ads and online self-help groups to teach content analysis in a research methods course. *Journal of Teaching in Social Work, 27,* 155–164.

Flesch, R. (1943). *Marks of readable style*. New York: Teachers College, Columbia University.

Flesch, R. (1948). A new readability yardstick. *Journal of Applied Psychology, 32,* 221–233.

George, A. L. (1959). *Propaganda analysis*. Evanston, IL; Row Peterson.

Goldman, R. M., & Crano, W. D. (1976). *Black Boy* and *Manchild in the Promised Land*: Content analysis in the study of value change over time. *Journal of Black Studies, 7,* 169–180.

Harvey, J. (1953). The content characteristics of best-selling novels. *Public Opinion Quarterly, 17,* 91–114.

Holsti, O. R. (1962). *The belief system and national images: John Foster Dulles and the Soviet Union.* (Unpublished doctoral dissertation.). Stanford University, Stanford, CA.

Holsti, O. R. (1964). An adaptation of the 'General Inquirer' for the systematic analysis of political documents. *Behavioral Science, 9,* 382–388.

Holsti, O. R. (1968). Content analysis. In G. Lindzey & E. Aronson (Eds.), *Handbook of social psychology* (pp. 596–692). Reading, MA: Addison-Wesley.

Holsti, O. R. (1969). *Content analysis for the social sciences and humanities.* Reading, MA: Addison-Wesley.

Hooker, E. (1957). The adjustment of the male overt homosexual. *Journal of Projective Techniques, 21,* 18–31.

Hum, N. J., Chamberlin, P. E., Hambright, B. L., Portwood, A. C, Schat, A. C., & Bevan, J. L. (2011). A picture is worth a thousand words: A content analysis of Facebook profile photographs. *Computers in Human Behavior, 27,* 1828–1833.

Kerlinger, F. N. (1964). *Foundations of behavioral research: Educational and psychological inquiry.* New York: Holt.

Kondracki, N. L. Wellman, N. S., & Amundson, D. R. (2002). Content analysis: review of methods and their applications in nutrition education. *Journal of Nutrition Education and Behavior, 34,* 224–230.

Krippendorff, K. (1980). *Content analysis: An introduction to its methodology*. Beverly Hills, CA.: Sage.

Lasswell, H. D. (1927). *Propaganda technique in the world war*. New York: Knopf.

Lasswell, H. D., Lerner, D., & Pool, I. de S. (1952). *The comparative study of symbols*. Stanford, CA: Stanford University Press.

Lewin, H. S. (1947). Hitler Youth and the Boy Scouts of America: A comparison of aims. *Human Relations, 1,* 206–227.

Lewis, S. C., Zamith, R., & Harmida, A. (2013). Content analysis in an era of big data: A hybrid approach to computational and manual methods. *Journal of Broadcasting and Electronic Media, 57,* 34–52.

Markham, J. W., & Stempel, G. H. (1957). Analysis of techniques in measuring press conference performance. *Journalism Quarterly, 34,* 187–190.

McClelland, D.C. (1961). *The achieving society*. Princeton, NJ: Princeton University Press.

Miles, J. (1951). *The continuity of English poetic language*. Berkeley, CA: University of California Press.

Miles, M. B., & Huberman, A. M. (1994). *Qualitative data analysis: An expanded sourcebook.* Thousand Oaks, CA: Sage.

Morton, A. Q. (1963). A computer challenges the church. *The Observer,* Nov. 3, 21.

Mosteller, F., & Wallace, D. L. (1964). *Inference and disputed authorship: The Federalist.* Reading, MA: Addison-Wesley.

Neuendorf, K. A. (2011). Content analysis—A methodological primer for gender research. *Sex Roles, 64,* 276–289.

Peterson, C., Seligman, M. E., & Vaillant, G. E. (1988). Pessimistic explanatory style is a risk factor for physical illness: A thirty-five-year longitudinal study. *Journal of Personality and Social Psychology, 55,* 23–27.

Phillips, D. P. (1982). The impact of fictional television stories on U.S. adult fatalities: New evidence of the effect of the mass media on violence. *American Journal of Sociology, 87,* 1340–1359.

Phillips, D. P. (1983). The impact of mass media violence on U.S. homicides. *American Sociological Review, 48,* 560–568.

Schwab, P., & Scneidman, J. L. (1974). *John F. Kennedy.* New York: Twayne Publishers.

Seidel, J. (1991). Method and madness in the application of computer technology to qualitative data analysis. In N. Fielding & R. M. Lee (Eds.), *Using computers in qualitative research* (pp. 107–116). London, GB: Sage.

Smith, C. P. (2000). Content analysis and narrative analysis. In H. T. Reis & C. M. Judd (Eds.), *Handbook of research in social and personality psychology* (pp. 313–335). Cambridge, UK: Cambridge University Press.

Stemler, S. (2001). An overview of content analysis. *Practical Assessment, Research & Evaluation, 7.* Retrieved from http://pareonline.net/getvn.asp?v=7&n=17.

Stone, P. J. (2000). Content analysis. In A. E. Kazdin (Ed.), *Encyclopedia of psychology, Vol. 2.* (pp. 291–292). Washington, DC: American Psychological Association.

Stone, P. J., Dunphy, D. C., & Smith, M. S. (1966). *The General Inquirer: A computer approach to content analysis.* Oxford, England: MIT Press.

Stone, P. J., & Hunt, E. B. (1963). A computer approach to content analysis using the general inquirer system. In E. C. Johnson (Ed.), *American Federation of Information Processing Societies, conference proceedings,* (pp. 241–256). Baltimore, MD: Association for Computing Machinery.

Viney, L. L. (1983). The assessment of psychological states through content analysis of verbal communications. *Psychological Bulletin, 94,* 542–563.

Vitaglione, G. D. (2012). Driving under the influence (of mass media): A four-year examination of NASCAR and West Virginia aggressive-driving accidents and injuries. *Journal of Applied Social Psychology, 42,* 488–505.

Westley, B. H., Higbie, C. E., Burke, T., Lippert, D. J., Maurer, L., & Stone, V. A. (1963). The news magazines and the 1960 conventions. *Journalism Quarterly, 40,* 525–531.

White, R. K. (1947). "Black Boy": A value analysis. *Journal of Abnormal and Social Psychology, 42,* 440–461.

Yakobson, S., & Lasswell, H. D. (1949). Trend: May Day slogans in Soviet Russia. In H. D. Lasswell, N. Leites, R. Fadner, J. M. Goldsen, A. Gray, I. L. Janis, A. Kaplan, D. Kaplan, A. Mintz, I. de S. Pool, & S. Yakobson (Eds.), *The language of politics: Studies in quantitative semantics* (pp. 233–297). New York: George Stewart.

Yule, G. U. (1944). *The statistical study of literary vocabulary.* London: Cambridge University Press.

15
QUESTIONNAIRE DESIGN AND SCALE CONSTRUCTION

Studying people's beliefs, attitudes, values, and personalities is a central research preoccupation of the social sciences. Typically, we use questionnaires or scales to measure these internal states or dispositions. Such measures rely on **self-report** by asking respondents to provide answers to a set of questions or scale items that inquire about their personal thoughts, feelings, or behaviors. Using these measures requires that we consider variations in responses among respondents as meaningful and not attributable to mere measurement error. In theory, all participants are expected to interpret stimuli (typically the questions or items used in a scale or questionnaire) identically. That is, a given scale item is assumed to mean the same thing to all participants, and differences in their responses to these hypothetically "identical" items are assumed to reflect real differences in their underlying dispositions.

Questionnaires

Two complementary approaches characterize attempts to establish measures to assess differences among people in their internal states or dispositions. For convenience, we will term the slightly less formal measures *questionnaires*, and the more rigorously designed measures *rating scales*. A **questionnaire** involves a single item to assess each construct, and typically is brief in length because participants are unwilling, unable, or unlikely to take part in a longer assessment. Nationally representative polls of voter sentiment or quality-of-life ratings often use measures (i.e., questionnaires) of this sort. A **rating scale** involves multiple items to assess each construct and typically is used by researchers with access to participants more willing to take part in a longer assessment. Questionnaire and scale construction are integral to many of the data collection methods discussed throughout this text, so it is important to have a good understanding of their strengths and weaknesses. We often do not have the luxury of length, and thus make use of questionnaires. That is, we are unable to use multiple items to tap a person's views of the same target—a person, event, or object. From earlier chapters, remember that the benefit of assessing a target with multiple items reflects our acknowledgement that a single item is insufficient to capture or triangulate a construct meaningfully. Sometimes the limitation is imposed because of time costs: When conducting a national survey, for example, adding even a single item can be prohibitively expensive, so we must be content with an item or two to assess people's thoughts and feelings on a given topic. In other cases, many concepts are under scrutiny, and to use multiple items to tap each of them would create an overly long instrument. Fears of participant fatigue, and the accompanying loss of data quality, motivate the use of a single item per concept. Some questionnaires are lengthy, measuring many concepts, but for our purposes we will consider the more typical brief questionnaire.

Questionnaires may be administered in the context of an interview study (Chapter 13) or in written form as a self-administered measure. There are no formal rules for questionnaire design, but considerable folk wisdom has grown around their construction, given the intense focus on such measuring instruments over the past 70 years in social science (see Fabrigar, Krosnick & McDougall, 2005; Krosnick & Fabrigar, 2001). We present some rules of thumb that are commonly adhered to. As will be seen, these rules will apply as well in the development of rating scales.

Wording Questions

The first rule is to determine what you want to know. The more direct the phrasing of the question, the more likely is its true meaning understood. Complicated questions are more likely to be misunderstood or misread and less likely to provide the sought-for information. To capture information on binge drinking, the question "How many times have you done it?" should first define binge drinking, then be precisely phrased as "How many times, if any, have you binged in the last (*week, month, year,* or *in your life*)?

A second rule of thumb is to use short, simple sentences containing a single grammatical clause, if possible and if needed, when developing queries. This rule helps avoid the use of a **double-barreled question**—a single item that asks more than one question at once. Asking "Do you think civil rights activists have gone too far and that the government should crack down on militant civil rights organizations in this country?" is an example of a double-barreled question. The problem with such questions, of course, is that it is not easy to know which of the multiple queries contained in the item the respondent is answering. This compound sentence should be rewritten as two questions: "Do you think civil rights activists have gone too far?" and "Do you think the government should crack down on militant civil rights organizations in this country?

Open-Ended Questions

A distinct advantage of questionnaires over scales is the capacity to use items with an open-ended response format. An open-ended item is one that poses a question but does not constrain the answer. The advantage of open-ended questions (e.g., "Who is your favorite mayoral candidate?") over close-ended ones (e.g., "Who is your favorite mayoral candidate: Smith, Jones, or Bradley?") is that the former does not force respondents to choose among a limited set of response options. If the respondent's answer to the questions posed here were "Johnson," the first would capture it, whereas the second would not. Visser, Krosnick, and Lavrakas (2000) have argued that open-ended questions are clearly preferable to closed questions in questionnaire construction contexts. However, whereas open-ended questions may tap respondents' views with greater fidelity than close-ended items, their added sensitivity comes with a cost, which involves developing methods of analyzing the free responses that the open items generate. In the mayoral example, analyzing the content of open-ended answers would not prove onerous. However, respondents must be able to recall their preferred choice, which may prove a disadvantage of an open-ended question. Without a prompt, some voters might be unable to recall their preferred candidates, but would be able to recognize and select that option if reminded with a close-ended multiple-choice format or a ballot.

Whenever the list of possible answers is relatively constrained and readily anticipated, coding answers becomes an almost mechanical task. So, for example, if we were to ask, "Who do you believe is responsible for California's energy problems?," informed respondents would most likely have a rather limited list of possibilities to draw from: The avaricious electric companies, unscrupulous politicians, careless consumers, and a few other nefarious eco-villains. However, if the issue is one that admits to a host of possible answers, e.g., "What should the U.S. do about global warming?," a coding scheme is necessary, and its development may prove costly. Whether the cost is tolerable depends in part on available resources, the complexity of the issue, and the number of topics being studied. In contexts in which the questionnaire contains many issues, each of which require constructing a coding scheme, the costs can be high. Sometimes, however, "open-ended questions seem to be worth the trouble they take to ask and the complexities in [their] analysis" (Visser et al., 2000, p. 238).

Question Ordering

In our discussion of interview methodology (Chapter 13), we stressed the importance of establishing rapport to help ensure the quality of the interaction and the truthfulness and completeness of the answers respondents provide the interviewer. In many self-report questionnaire studies, there is little, if any, opportunity to establish rapport. The items are posed by a more or less anonymous questioner, with little attempt at developing any relationship with the participant, or are presented on a printed page with a brief introduction of purpose. In circumstances like these, question order may become crucial. In questionnaire development, the analogue of the rapport-building process requires that the least threatening items be presented first. Only after the respondent has become comfortable with the research, and somewhat committed to it by virtue of answering a number of questions, should more personal or threatening questions be presented. For example, in research on adolescent drug use, nonthreatening queries are commonly presented before items assessing use of illegal substances are posed. This is the reason why demographic characteristics, which involve rather sensitive personal information (e.g., income, race/ethnicity), should be posed near the end of a questionnaire. Sometimes the ordering of items can keep a respondent in a study, and this is not a trivial concern.

Another issue related to question order has to do with the possibility that one's earlier answers may affect later ones. For example, suppose we were to ask, "Should freedom of speech be absolutely guaranteed in this country?" Most respondents would answer this question affirmatively. However, the affirmation of this fundamental human right might have ramifications on later answers having to do with the value of freedom—of thought, of expression, and of action. Affirming free speech probably inclines respondents to more liberal views on later items. However, suppose instead we were to ask, "Should hate speech be banned?" As before, a reasonable proportion of the respondent sample probably would answer this question affirmatively. In this case, later questions having to do with freedom of expression, thought, and action might be colored by this earlier response, but in a way opposite to that of the first example. The more liberal orientation induced in the first case might be attenuated, and this attenuation could have a discernible effect on later responses. The earlier items might "prime" the mindsets of participants when they respond to subsequent items (Sudman & Bradburn, 1982).

If questionnaire items were presented to all respondents in identical order, the problems cause by this early-item-influence could bias the research outcome. To combat it, some researchers recommend that questionnaire developers who fear the problem of influence from an early item counterbalance or randomize the order of questionable items across participants (see Rasinski, Lee, & Krishnamurty, 2012; Tourangeau, Rips, & Rasinski, 2000; Tourangeau & Rasinski, 1988).[1] For self-administered written questionnaires, varying question order entails generating multiple different versions of the questionnaire and randomly allocating versions to respondents. For questionnaires delivered by telephone interviewers, question ordering can be varied through the use of computer-assisted software preprogrammed to sequence the order of the items. This reordering should not involve the entire questionnaire. The least threatening questions, as noted, should appear first. However, within the entire questionnaire, the order of items that might be reactive should be counterbalanced or randomized across blocks of participants. Thus, if a questionnaire developer anticipates that answers to any of the six items dealing with a particular topic might mutually influence the other answers, the order of those items might be counterbalanced or randomized (Schuman & Presser, 1981; Standing & Shearson, 2010).

Dropout and the No-Opinion Response Format

We want to avoid losing respondents if possible. Whether respondent loss is attributable to a person's refusal to initiate the questionnaire or to complete it once begun, the loss of respondents represents, at a minimum, a threat to the generalizability of research results. Persuading potential respondents to take part in our research has been covered elsewhere (e.g., see Chapter 13). Here we are concerned with respondents who virtually drop out of the research by refusing to answer one or more questionnaire items. In these instances, many common statistical tests that apply listwise deletion will remove such respondents from the analysis.

A particularly difficult issue that affects the likelihood that a respondent will complete *all* items of a questionnaire is the inclusion or noninclusion of a "no opinion" (or "don't know") option. Some questionnaires allow respondents to indicate that they hold no opinion on an item (or don't know the answer to a question in a knowledge scale); others allow for a "neutral" response; still others do not provide a "middle-of-the-road" category, forcing respondents to take a stand (albeit, perhaps, a weak stand) on one side or another of the issue. Investigations of the effects of these variations in response format have been conducted for many years (Converse, 1964; Rubin, 1987), and there are good arguments on both sides regarding whether or not to include a no-response option. Respondents generally seem to prefer the no-opinion (or don't know) option (Beatty, Hermann, Puskar, & Kerwin, 1998; Lee & Kanazawa, 2000; Luskin & Bullock, 2011), but Krosnick and colleagues (2002) suggest that including a "no-response" option may encourage respondents to avoid the cognitive work involved in answering survey items, and thus discourage its use. Tourangeau, Cooper, and Conrad (2004) also have warned against the use of the option, insofar as it may affect respondents' interpretation of other available response options. In general, then, the advantages of allowing a middle option seem to be outweighed by the negative possibilities. In cases in which a good understanding of participants' feelings about a given issue is particularly critical, it is advisable to provide measures that allow for a clear interpretation of the meaning of the nonresponse option, if it is used. Wegener, Downing, Krosnick and Petty (1995) have suggested different measures that might help unravel the meaning of a "don't know" response, and we direct the interested reader to this work.

Constructing Rating Scales

The approach to creating effective items for questionnaires applies to scale development as well. Rating scales are formalized versions of questionnaires. The difference is that whereas a single item usually is used to represent each concept in a questionnaire, multiple items are used in creating scales. Because scales use multiple items to triangulate on, or to help define a concept, they are more appropriately used to measure attitudes, values, or personality dispositions, reflecting the view that people's attitudes or beliefs are not singularly defined.

When assessing individual differences on attitude or personality scales, each item often takes the form of a statement the participant is asked to endorse or reject. Louis Thurstone developed one such scaling approach, and although his model has been supplanted by more modern approaches, it forms the basis of many widely used scaling procedures today.

Thurstone's Method of Equal-Appearing Intervals

Developing rating scales to measure beliefs, opinions, and attitudes represents an important aspect of the history of social science research in the last century (Crano & Lac, 2012). First attempted by Thurstone (1928, 1931; Thurstone & Chave, 1929), attitude assessment has become one of the social sciences' most important and persistent preoccupations. In the typical Thurstone scale, respondents are asked to endorse the scale item or items with which they agree. Items are designed so that a single item, or a highly restricted range of items, should be endorsed by the respondent, and those that are more extreme or less extreme than the chosen alternative should be rejected. Items of this type have been termed *nonmonotone* (Coombs, 1950) or *noncumulative* (Stouffer, 1950), because it makes little sense to sum a respondent's scores over all items of the scale of this type. Agreement with one item does not imply an increased probability of agreement with any other item on the scale. In practice, it is difficult to develop scales of this type. Nunnally (1967) has persuasively illustrated this point by asking,

> . . . how could one find spelling words such that each would be correctly spelled only by persons in a narrow band of the attribute of spelling ability? An item that 'peaked' at the lower end of the scale would be one that is spelled correctly only by rather poor spellers. For an item that peaked in the middle . . . very few people with superior ability in spelling would give a correct response.
>
> (p. 69)

We encounter these difficulties when devising attitude scales based on Thurstone's model. Nonetheless, even though alternative models of scale construction are employed in most instances today, understanding Thurstone's approach is important as it forms the historical and logical basis for many of the more widespread alternatives.

Thurston's method of equal-appearing intervals is conducted in four phases. The first phrase in the scale construction process requires the researcher to generate many *potential* items, all of which appear at least initially to relate to the construct, object, or attribute of interest. A sufficient number of items should be developed to cover the complete range of the critical object. Items should be concise and worded in such a way that their meaning is clear. Double-barreled items should be avoided, as should items on which either complete acceptance or complete rejection by most members of the respondent sample might be expected.

In the second phase of the Thurstone scale construction process, a group of judges is recruited to develop the psychometric properties of the scale. Each judge independently estimates the degree of favorability or unfavorability expressed by each item toward the critical attitude object. Traditionally, an 11-point response format is used, with the end points bounded by the numbered phrases "1 (extremely favorable)" and "11 (extremely unfavorable)." Judges are instructed to disregard their own personal attitudes during item categorization and to try to ensure that the perceived distances in degree of favorability between contiguous points along the 11-point judgment dimension are approximately equal.

The third phase involves the selection of items for the final scale. Based on judges' ratings, the investigator determines the mean favorability rating for each item and its standard deviation. A large standard deviation is a danger signal, because it suggests that there is disagreement among judges with regard to the favorability of a given item. This result often occurs because of item ambiguity, violating a central assumption that each item should be interpreted identically by all judges. Thus, items exhibiting high standard deviations on judges' ratings should be discarded. From the pool of possibilities that remain, a reduced number of items (usually 11–22) are chosen to constitute the attitude scale. Items are chosen so that the scale values of the items derived from the judges' ratings cover the entire range of possible evaluations of the attitude object. In addition, items are chosen so that when they are arranged in ranked order with respect to mean values, approximately equal differences in intervals are maintained between the means of successive items, as implied by the name of the method.[2]

Administering the final set of items to participants is the fourth and final phase. We now move from the *scale construction* phases to the *scale administration* phase. In administering the scale, the researcher instructs participants to "indicate whether you agree or disagree with each item." Other variations of this response format employed in Thurston scales include answering "yes" or "no," or "true" or "false," to each item. The average value of the items chosen by a respondent is taken as that individual's attitude toward the object or issue under investigation. For example, consider the items in Table 15.1, which are drawn from Thurstone's and Chave's (1929) "Attitude Toward the Church Scale." These are the 12 statements that express the most unfavorable attitudes on the entire scale of the set of 45 items administered to participants. For illustrative purposes, we have presented these items in a manner different from that which a real respondent would experience.[3] The mean values the judges assigned to each item, for example, would not be presented to participants. In addition, instead of presenting them in a systematic order, as done here, items of different favorability ratings would have been mixed randomly. Respondents' mean scale value of the items each of them had endorsed would be their assigned score on Thurstone's "Attitude Toward the Church Scale."

TABLE 15.1 Twelve items from Thurston and Chave's (1929) "Attitudes Toward the Church Scale."

Item #	Item	Scale Value
1	I think the teaching of the church is altogether too superficial to have much social significance.	8.3
2	I feel the church is petty, always quarrelling over matters that have no interest or significance.	8.6
3	I respect any church-member's beliefs but I think it is all "bunk."	8.8
4	My experience is that the church is hopelessly out of date.	9.1
5	I think the church seeks to impose a lot of worn out dogmas and medieval superstitions.	9.2
6	I think the church is hundreds of years behind the times and cannot make a dent on modern life.	9.5
7	I think the church is a hindrance to religion for it still depends on magic, superstition, and myth.	9.6
8	The church represents shallowness, hypocrisy, and prejudice.	10.4
9	I regard the church as a static, crystallized institution and as such it is unwholesome and detrimental to society and the individual.	10.5
10	I think the church would be better off if churches were closed and the ministers set to some useful work.	10.5
11	I think the organized church is an enemy of science and truth.	10.7
12	I think the church is a parasite on society.	11.0

Reliability

A major common indicator of scale quality—internal consistency (Chapter 3)—is not a meaningful concept in the context of the Thurstone scale, because such measures make use of participants' overall responses to *all* items of a scale. In this case, we have information only on which items the respondent endorsed. However, test-retest methods of reliability estimation can be used to estimate a scale's temporal consistency reliability.

In addition to the fact that this scaling model forces the investigator to employ this more costly technique to estimate reliability, there are other methodological issues that should be considered when using this approach. For example, whether a judge can be sufficiently objective to disregard important personal feelings in evaluating the favorability of an attitude item is an open question. Hovland and Sherif (1952) found that judges' attitudes toward African-Americans had a strong influence on the manner in which they viewed the favorability of various items focused on racial prejudice. Items judged as being neutral by racially prejudiced judges were viewed as antagonistic to African-Americans by African-Americans and non-prejudiced White judges. On the other hand, Webb (1955) and Upshaw (1965) argued that although the absolute score assigned an item may vary as a function of judges' attitudes, the rank order of the items is maintained—i.e., the *relative* position of items remains unchanged no matter what the judges' attitudes—and thus the utility of Thurstone's stimulus scaling procedure in developing scales of individual differences is maintained. Though this issue is unresolved, there is little disagreement about the fact that constructing Thurstone scales is difficult and time-consuming, and furthermore, that such scales do not take advantages of available technological developments. In the sections that follow, we will discuss some of the more popular of the alternative models used in scaling differences among individuals.

Guttman's Scalogram

An early attempt to improve upon the Thurstone model was suggested by Louis Guttman (1944, 1947; Guttman & Suchman, 1947). The Guttman scalogram method makes use of the concept of *cumulative* or *monotone* items. With items of this type, the more favorable (or extreme) the respondent's attitude toward an object or issue, the higher (or more extreme) the individual's total attitude score. Results obtained from items from a monotone scale could be summed or averaged to derive a cumulative score of the construct or dimension being judged. Nunnally's (1967) earlier example of tests of spelling ability here is informative. Presumably, a child who could spell a difficult word would have little trouble with less difficult ones. Similarly, a child who had trouble spelling even easy words would find difficult ones next to impossible to spell correctly. The idea of a cumulative or monotonically increasing level of difficulty (or extremity of belief) underlies Guttman's approach. The hallmark of Guttman's method is that it presents participants with items of increasing extremity with regard to the issue under investigation. If the scale is of high quality, an individual who endorses an item at a given level of extremity (or favorability) also is expected to endorse all less extreme items. Under ideal conditions, knowledge of a participant's total score would enable the investigator to reproduce exactly the individual's pattern of responses. Consider the hypothetical scale of Table 15.2:

Items that make up the scale are arranged in a gradually ascending order, with item 5 being the most positive evaluation of (or attitude toward) public health care in the United States. If the scale is found to be reliable (or reproducible, to use Guttman's term), we would expect that those respondents who endorsed item 3 would also have endorsed items 1 and 2. Furthermore, the knowledge that a respondent endorsed two items should enable us to predict with a high degree of certainty

TABLE 15.2 Example of Guttman scalogram for "Scale of Attitudes Toward Public Health Care."

Item #	Item	Yes	No
1	A universal public health care plan might in the long run prove to be beneficial in America.		
2	It is probably a good idea that the U.S. begin a universal public health care plan.		
3	A universal public health care plan is in the best interests of the country.		
4	A universal public health care plan would be a very positive development in the United States.		
5	A universal public health care plan would be the best thing that has ever happened to people in the United States.		

that the chosen items were items 1 and 2 (that is, if the scale was highly reproducible). If an investigator can reconstruct the specific items a respondent checked by knowing the total number of items endorsed, the scale is said to possess a high *coefficient of reproducibility*. To determine the coefficient of reproducibility, the statistical expression of the extent to which participants' patterns of response can be inferred from their total scores, we need know the total number of responses generated by the total sample of respondents and the number of times participants' choices fell outside of the predicted pattern of responses (errors). To calculate this statistic, use the following formula:

Coefficient of Reproducibility = 1 − (Total Errors/Total Responses)

The scale construction procedures used in Guttman's system are all designed to result in a scale with a high coefficient of reproducibility. It often is erroneously assumed that a high coefficient value indicates a unidimensional scale. However, if the likelihood of endorsement (i.e., the "popularity" of an item) varies greatly from item to item, it is possible to obtain a high coefficient of reproducibility with items that have very little to do with one another. Imagine that the scale consisted of items on public health care policies as well as liberal political ideology. Generally, people who support universal public health care tend to hold more politically liberal views. This combination would result in a high coefficient of reproducibility, even though the items may tap separate constructs.

The difficulty involved in establishing a trustworthy (internally consistent) reliability coefficient for Guttman's scaling approach has resulted in its relative underutilization. Green (1956), Cliff (1977), and Kenny and Rubin (1977) have all discussed this issue, and have proposed alternate and generally more conservative methods of assessing the reproducibility of Guttman scales. Although these alternatives are improvements over the standard method, none as yet has gained widespread acceptance. As such, the tendency among many attitude researchers is to avoid Guttman's approach unless it is clearly suggested by the research operations. An exception to this general observation is found in the social distance measure devised by Bogardus (1959). This is still a popular measure, used to assess the extent of social distance people would be most comfortable maintaining between themselves and a representative member of some identified group (Catholic, Armenian, dockworker, etc.). In this scale, respondents are asked if they would accept a member of the identified group as visitors to their country, as citizens, neighbors, close personal friends, or as close relatives by marriage. Presumably those who were willing to accept a person from a specific social grouping as a close personal friend also would be willing to allow all lower levels of relationship—as a neighbor, a citizen, and a visitor to the country.

Often, the Guttman approach either does not lend itself so neatly to the demands of the research, or the research does not provide a means of validating the scale—i.e., of discerning whether the items that constitute the scale accurately represent the construct it is intended to assess. In circumstances such as these, alternate measurement models should be chosen.

Likert's Method of Summated Ratings

The model of scale construction designed by Rensis Likert (1932) is one of the two most popular approaches for generating reliable scales to examine differences among people. Compared to Thurstone's method of equal-appearing intervals, or Guttman's scalogram analysis, Likert's model proves not only more efficient in terms of time and resource expenditure, but also more effective in developing scales of high reliability (in terms of both internal consistency and temporal stability). Unlike Thurstone's or Guttman's methods, in which participants offer a binary response (e.g., yes or no) for each item, in Likert's method respondents indicate the degree or extent of agreement or disagreement to each item using a "multiple-choice" format. On each item, respondents pick one of (usually) five options indicating the extent to which they agree with the position espoused in the item. Response options commonly presented are "strongly agree," "agree," "neutral or undecided," "disagree," and "strongly disagree."

In a scale of attitudes toward the Army, for example, participants might be asked to respond to the statement, "The U.S. Army has been a positive force for peace throughout the world," through choosing one of these five response options. Presumably, a person with a favorable attitude toward the Army would "agree" or "strongly agree" with the statement, whereas an individual with a negative view of the Army would be more likely to endorse the "disagree" or "strongly disagree" option. If we assign values of 1 to 5 to these response options (with higher scores representing more positive attitudes), then a person's overall attitude toward a given issue or entity would be represented by the sum or mean of his or her responses over all the items on the scale.

The item employed here is an example of a *positively worded* statement, because choosing "agree" or "strongly agree" indicates a favorable attitude toward the object—in this instance, the Army. An unfavorably, or *negatively* worded item is one on which strong agreement indicates a strong negative attitude (and with these items, the scoring procedure is reversed, i.e., "strongly agree" is scored +1, whereas "strongly disagree" is given the score of +5). An example of an item that reverses the intent of the previous example might be, "The Army has had a harmful effect on world peace."

The summation or averaging process across items is used to calculate a composite scale score, which is an implicit recognition that any single item is at best a fallible representative of the underlying construct or attitude it is intended to represent. By combining a participant's responses over many such items, however, we hope to minimize the "noise" or measurement error that the imperfections of each item contribute to the overall score (especially if the items have different sources of measurement error), thereby arriving at a more internally reliable measure of the construct. If we consider each item in a "Likert scale" as a different operational definition of the attitude or construct it is intended to tap, then the logic of this scaling approach is consistent with the logic of multiple operationalization. We assume that all of the "operations" (i.e., items) will miss the mark to some extent (that is, no single item will perfectly capture the construct it is intended to represent), but we attempt to design items so that they miss the mark in different ways; thus, the resulting scale (i.e., the total or averaged score across all items) should provide a more sure identification of the construct of interest than any single item. If each item is susceptible to error, and if the error is random, then over a series of items the error should cancel, leaving only the reliable true score. The scale construction process developed by Likert is adopted to minimize effects of item-specific "irrelevancies" (error), and thereby arrive at the best operationalization (scale) of people's evaluations on any given issue (Crano, 2000).

The initial steps of scale development using this method resemble those of both Thurstone and Guttman. As in these earlier approaches, a large number of potential items are initially gathered, and obviously double-barreled, ambiguous, or confusing items are rewritten or discarded. At this point the similarity to earlier methods ends, for rather than searching for items that represent the entire continuum of the construct, the Likert model calls for creating items that are *moderately* favorable or unfavorable toward the attitude object under study. Because respondents indicate their *degree* of agreement using the response options for each item, generating items of widely varying degrees of favorability is unnecessary. The response format itself provides the respondent's indication of extremity. Given the scale construction procedures employed in developing Likert-type scales, the use of extreme items in the initial research phases would be a waste of effort, because the later scaling operations would almost certainly indicate that such items should be discarded. To examine the topic of parental attitudes toward spanking children as a form of discipline, for example, an appropriate item for the Likert technique would be, "Parents should consider spanking as a form of discipline," using options from 1 (strongly disagree) to 5 (strongly agree). Extreme items, such as "Parents have the right to beat their children," do not lend themselves to Likert's scaling approach.

After creating a number of items that appear to tap the construct of interest, and to do so unambiguously, the researcher administers the item set to a group of respondents. It is advisable to multiply the number of items by 10 when estimating the necessary number of respondents for this phase of the scale construction process; thus, the initial assessment process to determine the quality of a set of 20 items would call for the use of approximately 200 respondents.

After collecting participants' responses, the researcher may use either classical testing theory (e.g., item-total correlations) or more modern test approaches (e.g., confirmatory factor analysis and item response theory) to evaluate the psychometric properties of the scale (See Chapter 3 for a review of these approaches). For simplicity of illustration, the following example makes use of item-total correlations. Item scores are summed over each participant, thereby creating a total score for each. Then the complete matrix of intercorrelations between all pairs of items and between each item and the total score is calculated. Statistical software is used to compute a correlation matrix, which provides auxiliary information to allow for the calculation of coefficient alpha as an index of internal consistency (Chapter 3). Higher correlations generally yield a higher Cronbach's alpha. However, it is important to realize that Cronbach's alpha produces a higher coefficient as the correlation across items becomes stronger *and* as the number of items increases. Thus, using a large number of items in this initial scale construction phase will result in a strong alpha coefficient if the choice of items was at all reasonable.

The investigator's primary job at this point is to retain the items that form the best scale, and to discard items that correlate poorly with the rest of the scale. Coefficient alpha, an estimate of the internal consistency of the entire set of items, is not useful in an item-by-item analysis of this type. Of more practical utility is the investigation of each item's correlation with the total score, known as the item-total correlation (Chapter 3). As noted, the total score is conceptualized as the best estimate of the construct under investigation. However, because the total score is the outcome of many items, some of which probably are of low quality, it is far from a perfect representation of the underlying construct. To improve the precision of the scale, the investigator may discard the least fitting items; that is, those that do not correlate strongly with the total score. In developing the final scale, the researcher retains items having the highest item-total score correlations.

After having decided on the best items and discarded the worst ones, it is necessary to recalculate the item-total correlation using the "reduced set" of items, because the total composite score changes every time an item is discarded. If the initially strong correlations are maintained or improved, the investigator then should recalculate coefficient alpha on the reduced set to determine the degree of interrelatedness of items. An alpha coefficient of .75 or higher suggests that the scale is reasonably internally consistent. However, some "shrinkage" in the reliability coefficient must be expected when the item set is readministered to another group, because this scale construction process capitalizes on sample-specific variations (i.e., error). The extent of such attenuation or shrinkage is usually not severe unless the new sample is very different from that on which the scale was developed originally.

If coefficient alpha is weak (for example, if it falls short of an arbitrary value of .70), the internal consistency can be improved by the addition of more items that correlate positively with the original set and with the total score. This item-adding process can be continued until the desired level of reliability has been reached. It sometimes happens that a researcher has developed a multidimensional scale, which taps more than a single factor or subscale. This overall scale should consist of subscales that are somewhat correlated but that are conceptually distinct. When this is anticipated to occur, a factor analysis can be employed to illuminate the underlying factors representing the multidimensional scale.

Factor Analysis as an Aid to Scale Construction

Factor analytic techniques may be divided into two types. Exploratory factor analysis (EFA) is a statistical technique to assess the multidimensional structure of a scale if the researcher does not have hypotheses regarding the number and types of underlying factors that will emerge in the solution. Application of EFA identifies the subset of items that are most strongly correlated, with such items forming a factor, and can allow for (and identify) multiple factors.

Confirmatory factor analysis is a statistical technique to assess the multidimensional structure of a scale if the researcher has hypotheses regarding the number and types of underlying factors that will emerge in the solution. A hypothesis-based approach to factor analysis requires reviewing the relevant prior literature to make informed decisions about the how to phrase the items so as to represent each of the dimensions. In applications of CFA, the investigator must force or specify in software the proposed number of factors and test whether they fit the observed participant data. Only items that are hypothesized (without peeking at the collected data) to represent a factor should be allowed to load on that factor. Once the optimal items are retained, if the desire is to cross-validate the scale, it is then administered to a new set of participants. (See Chapter 3 for further description of these two forms of factor analysis.)

Osgood's Semantic Differential

Although Likert's approach represented an important technical advance over both the Thurstone and Guttman methods, it shares some of the liabilities of these procedures. All three scaling models, for example, require relatively major expenditures of time and effort in the scale construction process, and all three techniques require the development of a new set of items each time attitudes toward a new person or object are to be assessed. For these reasons, a technique pioneered by Osgood and his colleagues (Osgood, 1962; Osgood, Suci, & Tannenbaum, 1957; Snider & Osgood, 1969) has become popular as a standardized form of assessing attitudes towards objects and issues. The original development of this scaling model was stimulated by Osgood's attempts to determine the subjective meanings people attach to words or concepts. In Osgood's semantic differential scale, rather than asking respondents to respond to variations of statements concerning the concept under study (as in the Likert or Thurstone approaches, for example), the concept is presented directly and participants are instructed to react to it in the form of ratings on a number of bipolar adjectives, as in the illustration of Figure 15.1.[4]

Method of Summated Ratings (Likert)				
1. I think that my mother is a good person				
strongly agree (5)	agree (4)	neutral (3)	disagree (2)	strongly disagree (1)
2. My mother has a kind heart				
strongly agree (5)	agree (4)	neutral (3)	disagree (2)	strongly disagree (1)
3. I believe my mother is beautiful				
strongly agree (5)	agree (4)	neutral (3)	disagree (2)	strongly disagree (1)
4. My mother has a pleasant demeanor				
strongly agree (5)	agree (4)	neutral (3)	disagree (2)	strongly disagree (1)
5. I feel that my mother tries to be fair with people				
strongly agree (5)	agree (4)	neutral (3)	disagree (2)	strongly disagree (1)
Semantic Differential Scale (Osgood)				
My Mother				
1. Good (5)	(4)	(3)	(2)	Bad (1)
2. Kind (5)	(4)	(3)	(2)	Cruel (1)
3. Beautiful (5)	(4)	(3)	(2)	Ugly (1)
4. Pleasant (5)	(4)	(3)	(2)	Unpleasant (1)
5. Fair (5)	(4)	(3)	(2)	Unfair (1)

FIGURE 15.1 Construction of scales of "Attitudes Toward Mother" with Likert and Osgood models.

In semantic differential scales, a single stem indicating the construct to be judged is presented, followed by a set of adjectives pairs to be used in the judging process. In Likert scaling, different stems are used to describe the item to be evaluated, but the same response options (strongly agree, agree, etc.) are consistently used to capture responses. To illustrate these distinctions, suppose we constructed two scales to measure "Attitudes toward my mother" using the Likert and Osgood models. These scale types are contrasted in Figure 15.1. They each make use of 5 items, with each item anchored on 5-point options. With the Likert scale, it is necessary to generate a diverse list of statement stems, using the same "strongly agree" to "strongly disagree" options throughout. In contrast, using the semantic differential model simply requires presenting the construct, "my mother," followed by different bipolar adjectives (which, in essence, represent different items). An advantage of the semantic differential scaling model over Likert's is that options labels for just the bipolar ends (e.g., bad/good) are sufficient. Responses closer toward the middle reflect more neutral opinions on the continuum. Another advantage is that the variety of response anchors for this scale could later be reused to create other semantic differential scales. That is, the same set of response anchors in Figure 15.1 could subsequently be used to construct new rating scales to measure attitudes toward father, best friend, or even romantic partner. Another obvious advantage concerns time savings for participants and scale constructors. Even with the same number of items, a semantic differential scale will be shorter in length, easier to read, more difficult to misinterpret, and therefore completed more quickly by respondents than a Likert scale. From the scale constructor's perspective, the Osgood approach is considerably more efficient.

Many of the statistical analyses used to evaluate the properties of Likert scales are used in evaluating semantic differential scales. All the ratings made on any one item could be correlated with those made on each of the other items, and these data may be used in statistical analyses such as item-total correlations. The use of factor analysis will provide information regarding the extent to which various bipolar items are clustered and are independent from other items. Items that "load on the same factor," are highly interrelated with one another and are relatively weakly related with other items that do not load on their factor. It is assumed that items with different types of response options that cluster together are focusing on the same underlying psychological dimension or construct.

A number of studies have examined the dimensions of response options (see Osgood & Luria, 1954; Osgood et al., 1957; Snider & Osgood, 1969) with widely varying concepts being employed and with respondents from 26 different cultures around the world, and consistent findings have emerged—three factors or clusters of adjectives have been found consistently in studies of the semantic differential: (1) *Evaluation* or value of the object (e.g., good/bad), (2) *potency* or power of the object (e.g., strong/weak), (3) and activity or movement of the object (e.g., slow/fast). The adjective anchors involving evaluations tend to account for the most "meaning" or largest proportion of the factor variance in respondents' subjective interpretations of objects. Although it is most ideal to develop a semantic differential scale with items incorporating response anchors involving a mix of evaluation, potency, and activity, the exclusive use of evaluation anchors is common and sufficient for most research purposes. So, for example, to use semantic differential scales to measure people's attitudes toward public health care, we might employ the evaluative adjective pairs of Figure 15.2. A respondent's overall attitude in this case is defined as the sum or average of his or her scores over all 10 of the semantic differential evaluative items when rating the concept (public health care).

Item #		Public Health Care	
1	Good	:____:____:____:____:____:____:	Bad
2	Kind	:____:____:____:____:____:____:	Cruel
3	Beautiful	:____:____:____:____:____:____:	Ugly
4	Pleasant	:____:____:____:____:____:____:	Unpleasant
5	Fair	:____:____:____:____:____:____:	Unfair
6	Honest	:____:____:____:____:____:____:	Dishonest
7	Clean	:____:____:____:____:____:____:	Dirty
8	Valuable	:____:____:____:____:____:____:	Worthless
9	Positive	:____:____:____:____:____:____:	Negative
10	Wise	:____:____:____:____:____:____:	Foolish

FIGURE 15.2 Semantic differential items measuring "Attitudes Toward Public Health Care."

In this measurement approach, a respondent checks the point on each item that best indicates his or her degree of positivity or negativity toward the concept in question. It is common that other types of response anchors are interspersed among the critical evaluative items. Items with response formats connoting potency (e.g., strong-weak, rugged-delicate, large-small, hard-soft, heavy-light, etc.), and activity (e.g., active-passive, quick-slow, sharp-dull, excitable-calm, hot-cold) could be included, for example. However, typically in defining respondents' attitudes, only the responses on the evaluative items are summed. The summation process is identical to that involved in Likert scaling—and it involves the same assumptions, dangers, etc. Usually, 7-point response formats are used in semantic differential research, with higher scores used to connote positive views toward the object.

The semantic differential approach offers many practical advantages. Given the nature of the statistical process through which the various factors or "clusters" of items were developed, it is safe to assume that the internal consistency of such a measurement instrument will be high, an assumption that always should be verified. Investigations of the temporal stability of such instruments also have provided strong support for this measurement approach (e.g., Jenkins, Russel, & Suci, 1957; Osgood et al., 1957; Snider & Osgood 1969). The generality of the evaluative response as a major component of an individual's subjective reaction toward any object also is advantageous. The semantic differential technique apparently offers the researcher a ready-made attitude scale for assessing the beliefs and attitudes of almost any topic (see Osgood & Luria, 1954, 1976). As such, it offers a great practical advantage over the other forms of attitude assessment, all of which demand greater time expenditures in instrument development.

Response Formats

Care and common sense must be exercised when choosing the specific response categories for items used in a measurement instrument, because the specific attitude object under investigation could affect the meaning or appropriateness of the scales employed. For example, in a semantic differential measure the bipolar adjectives of fair-unfair appear appropriate if used to determine people's attitudes toward a justice of the U.S. Supreme Court; these same response anchors, however, would be less than optimal if the object of judgment were Ben & Jerry's Cherry Garcia ice cream. In this case, the use of an inappropriate response format introduces unnecessary error or imprecision in capturing participants' beliefs. To detect the presence of this problem (because, sometimes, inappropriate item stem and response anchors pairings are difficult to recognize), it is wise to calculate coefficient alpha and item-total correlations on all scales using semantic differential items. A strong coefficient of internal consistency and high item-total correlations indicate the items chosen to measure the attitude object are related to the overall composite.

In the Thurston and Guttman scale construction techniques, each item requires participants to select from a binary option (e.g., "yes or "no") to indicate their endorsement of an item. The Likert and Osgood techniques use more continuous response formats (e.g., "strongly agree" to "strongly disagree"). Technically, Likert and Osgood scale items use an ordinal response format; that is, the psychological distance between "strongly disagree" to "disagree" is not necessarily the same as the distance between "disagree" to neutral," or "neutral" to "agree." These response options have the feature of rank order, but not equal unit difference between response options. To satisfy the criterion for interval scaling, equal distances between any two adjacent response categories is required. It cannot be presumed in Likert or Osgood-type scales. Fortunately, research suggests it is acceptable to apply many parametric statistical techniques (based on the assumption of a normal distribution) to the outcomes of Likert and Osgood scaling procedures (Norman, 2010). Simulation research indicates that ordinal responses, especially if overall composites are used in the statistical analyses, approximate and satisfy distributional properties of a normal distribution.

Number of Response Options

Another response format issue requiring consideration concerns the number of response categories appropriate for an item. Items consisting of five and seven response categories are the most commonly encountered, but some researchers use a greater number (Wakita, Ueshima & Noguchi, 2012). Incorporating a greater number of response options can result in more gradations in responding, which may result in a more continuous assessment of a construct. Increasing the number of response categories thus may be beneficial in making the item more sensitive in discerning and differentiating smaller distinctions among participants. A tradeoff in the inclusion of a greater number of response options is the greater amount of time required to contemplate which of the many categories best corresponds to one's attitude toward an issue, and there is some question regarding respondents' capacities to make fine-grained distinctions in responding to attitude items. Although raising the number of response categories is beneficial, these advantages are relatively minor (Wakita et al., 2012). Malhotra, Krosnick, and Thomas (2009) have suggested that 7-point items offer the optimal level of discriminability.

Another factor affecting choice of response format is the extremity of end-point labels (Wyatt & Meyers, 1987). Research indicates that if the labels of the anchor points are less extreme (e.g. 5 = "mostly true" to 1 = "mostly false") rather than more extreme (5 = "completely true" to 1 = "completely false"), participants tended to select each of the possible options more equally. When using extreme adjectives for anchor labels, endpoints were rarely selected, with most responses distributed toward the middle, resulting in less variability in responses. Given that a practical scale should be effective in capturing a wide range of responses about an object, it is sound advice to avoid the use of extreme endpoint labels in most scales. However, it might be practical to use extreme labels in research domains on which people tend to have strong polarizing beliefs,

Use of Reversed Items

Another consideration concerns the choice of using or excluding reversed items. Many scales contain a mixture of positively and negatively phrased (or reversed) items. Reversed items are used to guard against the threat to measurement validity known as *acquiescence response bias,* the penchant for some individuals to agree to item statements regardless of content. Acquiescent responding could occur because of a personality disposition to be agreeable or the desire to please the investigator. The positively worded item of "Creative thinking promotes good decisions in my daily life," may be rephrased in the form of a negation of the positive statement, "Creative thinking does not promote good decisions in my daily life," or in the form of an opposing statement, "Creative thinking interferes with good decision making in my life." In computing the overall score, the reversed items should be scored in the opposite direction from the non-reversed items when using a response format of "strongly agree" to "strongly disagree." At face value, both statements appear to be nothing more than simple opposites, but item reversals produce greater misinterpretation, because such statements are more cognitively challenging to process and judge (Swain, Weathers & Niedrich, 2008; Weijters, Cabooter, & Schillewaert, 2010). Negatively worded item stems require greater capacity in working memory and greater focus to interpret, leaving less room for thought. Misunderstanding reversed items arises due to additional complexity in interpreting the meaning of the sentence when including the word "not." Heuristically, people tend to store beliefs in memory in the affirmative direction, not in terms of its negated counterpart. Furthermore, especially in lengthy scales, some participants may fail to attend to every single word in every statement, accidentally skipping over encounters with "not."

Investigators' desires to minimize participant acquiescence should be weighed against participant challenges in interpreting items correctly. Some research has suggested that scales should only use affirmative item stems, as the problems of interpretation introduced by reversals outweigh the problems attributed to acquiescence (Ebesutani, 2013). Although no definitive solution exists to simultaneously protect against acquiescence and cognitive load, a possibility is to keep the phrasing of all item stems in the affirmative direction, instead reversing the direction of response options for some items (Barnette, 2000). For example, create items with response options listed starting from the left with "strongly agree" to "strongly disagree," with the remaining items using reversed options listed from "strongly disagree" to "strongly agree." Afterward, all responses should be coded in the same direction, with higher values representing greater degree of that construct. Research has demonstrated that scales with a mix of items with reversals and non-reversals of option anchors yields similar Cronbach's alphas to scales containing all item stems and responses phrased in the same direction, and both strategies generate better reliability coefficients than scales containing a mixture of items with reversed and non-reversed stems. In their comparison of semantic differential and Likert-based measures, Friborg, Martinussen, and Rosenvinge (2006) found support for Osgood's approach, and suggested that its format avoided the acquiescence problem, both observations arguing in favor of the semantic differential scaling approach.

Conclusion

The systematic measurement of people's underlying beliefs, knowledge, attitudes, and values represents a major achievement of social science research. Owing to the imagination of our psychometric forebears and the technical virtuosity of those that followed, we have developed in the social sciences a set of techniques that allow us to peer into the thought processes of cooperative (and sometimes uncooperative) respondents. Scientifically grounded scaling approaches represent one of our field's greatest achievements. Properly applied, well-designed questionnaires and scales allow us some access to the thoughts and views of our respondents, and help us understand the views of the person or group under observation. Questionnaires and scales are powerful tools for applied and basic research. From scientific polling techniques to theory-testing research, behavioral researchers rely heavily on these self-report instruments as a versatile component of our methodological tool chest.

Questions for Discussion

1. What are some advantages and disadvantages of using open-ended vs. close-ended items?
2. What are the different types of factor analysis, and how can they assist with scale construction?
3. Your research advisor is hounding you for some data on people's attitudes toward the incumbent mayor, which you promised to deliver a while ago. The heat is on. You can choose to use an existing measure of reasonable (but not great) psychometric quality, or construct your own measure. Which route do you choose? Which scaling method would you use? Why?
4. It is fairly clear in research on attitudes that a neutral attitude (i.e., no opinion one way or the other) and an ambivalent attitude (i.e., equivalent positive and negative evaluations toward the same target) are different; however, how do we know whether a midpoint response (e.g., "4" on a 7-point scale, "0" on a -3 to $+3$ scale) is neutral for some people and ambivalent for others, particularly when there is no "ambivalent" response option? If space and time are an issue, is there any way to assess ambivalence without having separate items for positive and negative valence toward the target? Does any of this matter? Why or why not?

Notes

1. Some researchers even recommend that the order of response options be rotated (e.g., see Krosnick, 1991; Sudman, Bradburn, & Schwarz, 1996). This recommendation is made because of some evidence that suggests that people tend to ascribe more to the initial response options on written questionnaires and to later options on questionnaires that are read to them by an interviewer (Krosnick & Alwin, 1987; McClendon, 1991).
2. The equality of intervals separating the scale values of items is an important criterion of Thurstone's technique. If this requirement is met, it suggests that the scale may treated as being of interval, rather than ordinal, level.
3. Note that in this research higher values represented more negative attitudes.
4. Bipolar adjectives are logical opposites, or antonyms.

References

Barnette, J. J. (2000). Effects of stem and Likert response option reversals on survey internal consistency: If you feel the need, there is a better alternative to using these negatively worded stems. *Educational and Psychological Measurement, 60,* 361–370.

Beatty, P., Herrmann, D., Puskar, C., & Kerwin, J. (1998). 'Don't know' responses in surveys: Is what I know what you want to know and do I want you to know it? *Memory, 6*(4), 407–426.

Bogardus, E. S. (1959). *Social distance.* Los Angeles, CA: Antioch Press.

Cliff, N. (1977). A theory of consistency of ordering generalizable to tailored testing. *Psychometrika, 42,* 375–399.

Converse, P. E. (1964). The nature of belief systems in mass publics. In D. Apter (Ed.), *Ideology and discontent* (pp. 206–261). London: Free Press of Glencoe.

Coombs, C. H. (1950). Psychological scaling without a unit of measurement. *Psychological Review, 57,* 145–158.

Crano, W. D. (2000). The multitrait-multimethod matrix as synopsis and recapitulation of Campbell's views on the proper conduct of social inquiry. In L. Bickman (Ed.), *Research design: Donald Campbell's legacy* (Ch. 3, pp. 37–61). Beverly Hills, CA: Sage.

Crano, W. D., & Lac, A. (2012). The evolution of research methodologies in (social) psychology. In A. Kruglanski & W. Stroebe (Eds.), *Handbook of the history of social psychology* (pp. 159–174). New York: Psychology Press.

Ebesutani, C. K. (2013). *Evidence based assessment strategies for 'real world' clinical settings 73,* ProQuest Information & Learning, US. Retrieved from http://search.ebscohost.com/login.aspx?direct=true&db=psyh&AN=2013-99060-306&site=ehost-live&scope=site

Fabrigar, L. R., Krosnick, J. A., & MacDougall, B. L. (2005). Attitude measurement: Techniques for measuring the unobservable. In T. C. Brock & M. C. Green (Eds.), *Persuasion: Psychological insights and perspectives* (2nd ed., pp. 17–40). Thousand Oaks, CA: Sage.

Friborg, O., Martinussen, M., & Rosenvinge, J. H. (2006). Likert-based vs. semantic differential-based scorings of positive psychological constructs: A psychometric comparison of two versions of a scale measuring resilience. *Personality and Individual Differences, 40*(5), 873–884.

Green, B. F., Jr. (1956). A method of scaleogram analysis using summary statistics. *Psychometrika, 21,* 79–88.

Guttman, L. (1944). A basis for scaling qualitative data. *American Sociological Review, 9,* 139–150.

Guttman, L. (1947). The Cornell technique for scale and intensity analysis. *Educational and Psychological Measurement, 7,* 247–279.

Guttman, L., & Suchman, E. A. (1947). Intensity and zero point for attitude analysis. *American Sociological Review, 12,* 57–67.

Hovland, C. I., & Sherif, M. (1952). Judgmental phenomena and scales of attitude measurement: Item displacement in Thurstone scales. *Journal of Abnormal and Social Psychology, 42,* 215–239.

Jenkins, J. J., Russel, W. A., & Suci, G. J. (1957). An atlas of semantic profiles for 360 words. In *Studies on the role of language in behavior* (Technical Report No. 15). Minneapolis, MN: University of Minnesota.

Kenny, D. A., & Rubin, D.C. (1977). Estimating chance reproducibility in Guttman scaling. *Social Science Research, 6,* 188–196.

Krosnick, J. A. (1991). Response strategies for coping with the cognitive demands of attitude measures in surveys. *Applied Cognitive Psychology, 5,* 213–236.

Krosnick, J. A., & Alwin, D. F. (1987). An evaluation of a cognitive theory of response order effects in survey measurement. *Public Opinion Quarterly, 51*, 201–219.

Krosnick, J. A., & Fabrigar, L. R. (2001). *Designing great questionnaires: Insights from psychology.* New York: Oxford University Press.

Krosnick, J. A., Holbrook, A. L., Berent, M. K., Carson, R. T., Hanemann, W. M., Kopp, R. J., . . . & Conaway, M. (2002). The impact of 'no opinion' response options on data quality: Non-attitude reduction or an invitation to satisfice? *Public Opinion Quarterly, 66*(3), 371–403.

Lee, S.-G., & Kanazawa, Y. (2000). Handling 'don't know' survey responses: The case of Japanese voters on party support. *Behaviormetrika, 27*, 181–200.

Likert, R. (1932). A technique for the measurement of attitudes. *Archives of Psychology, 140*, 55.

Luskin, R. C., & Bullock, J. G. (2011). 'Don't know' means 'don't know': DK responses and the public's level of political knowledge. *The Journal of Politics, 73*, 547–557.

Malhotra, N., Krosnick, J. A., & Thomas, R. K. (2009). Optimal design of branching questions to measure bipolar constructs. *Public Opinion Quarterly, 73*(2), 304–324.

McClendon, M. J., (1991). Acquiescence and recency response-order effects in interview surveys. *Sociological Methods and Research, 20*, 60–103.

Norman, G. (2010). Likert scales, levels of measurement and the "laws" of statistics. *Advances in Health Science Education, 15*, 625–632.

Nunnally, J. C. (1967). *Psychometric theory.* New York: McGraw-Hill.

Osgood, C. E. (1962). Studies on the generality of affective meaning systems. *American Psychologist, 17*, 10–28.

Osgood, C. E., & Luria, Z. (1954). Applied analysis of a case of multiple personality using the semantic differential. *Journal of Abnormal and Social Psychology, 49*, 579–591.

Osgood, C. E., & Luria, Z. (1976). A postscript to "The three faces of Eve." *Journal of Abnormal Psychology, 85*, 276–286.

Osgood, C. E., Suci, D. J., & Tannenbaum, P. H. (1957). *The measurement of meaning.* Urbana, IL: University of Illinois Press.

Rasinski, K. A., Lee, L., & Krishnamurty, P. (2012). Question order effects. In H. Cooper, P. M. Camic, D. L. Long, A. T. Panter, D. Rindskopf & K. J. Sher (Eds.), *APA handbook of research methods in psychology, Vol. 1: Foundations, planning, measures, and psychometrics* (pp. 229–248). Washington, DC: American Psychological Association.

Rubin, D. B. (1987). *Multiple imputation for nonresponse in surveys.* New York: Wiley.

Schuman, H., & Presser, S. (1981). *Questions and answers in attitude surveys: Experiments on question form, wording, and context.* New York: Academic Press.

Snider, J. G., & Osgood, C. E. (Eds.) (1969). *Semantic differential technique.* Chicago: Aldine.

Standing, L. G., & Shearson, C. G. (2010). Does the order of questionnaire items change subjects' responses? An example involving a cheating survey. *North American Journal of Psychology, 12*, 603–614.

Stouffer, S. A. (Ed.) (1950). *Measurement and prediction.* Princeton, NJ: Princeton University Press.

Sudman, S., & Bradburn, N. M. (1982). *Asking questions: A practical guide to questionnaire design.* San Francisco: Jossey-Bass.

Sudman, S., Bradburn, N. M., & Schwarz, N. (1996). *Thinking about answers: The application of cognitive processes to survey methodology.* San Francisco: Jossey-Bass.

Swain, S. D., Weathers, D., & Neidrich, R. W. (2008). Assessing three sources of misresponse to reversed Likert items. *Journal of Marketing Research, 45*, 116–131.

Thurstone, L. L. (1928). Attitudes can be measured. *American Journal of Sociology, 33*, 529–554.

Thurstone, L. L. (1931). The measurement of attitudes. *Journal of Abnormal and Social Psychology, 26*, 249–269.

Thurstone, L. L., & Chave, E. L. (1929). *The measurement of attitudes.* Chicago: University of Chicago Press.

Tourangeau, R., Couper, M. P., & Conrad, F. (2004). Spacing, position, and order: Interpretive heuristics for visual features of survey questions. *Public Opinion Quarterly, 68*(3), 368–393.

Tourangeau, R., & Rasinski, K. A. (1988). Cognitive processes underlying context effects in attitude measurement. *Psychological Bulletin, 103*, 299–314.

Tourangeau, R., Rips, L. J., & Rasinski, K. (2000). *The psychology of survey response.* New York: Cambridge University Press.

Upshaw, H. S. (1965). The effects of variable perspectives on judgments of opinion statements for Thurstone scales: Equal appearing intervals. *Journal of Personality and Social Psychology, 2*, 60–69.

Visser, P. S., Krosnick, J. A., & Lavrakas, P. J. (2000). Survey research. In H. Reis & C. M. Judd (Eds.), *Handbook of research methods in social and personality psychology* (pp. 223–252). Cambridge: Cambridge University Press.

Wakita, T., Ueshima, N., & Noguchi, H. (2012). Psychological distance between categories in the Likert scale: Comparing different number of options. *Educational and Psychological Measurement, 72,* 533–546.

Webb, S. C. (1955). Scaling of attitudes by the method of equal-appearing intervals. *Journal of Social Psychology, 42,* 215–239.

Wegener, D. T., Downing, J., Krosnick, J. A., & Petty, R. E. (1995). Measures and manipulations of strength-related properties of attitudes: Current practice and future directions. In R. E. Petty & J. A. Krosnick (Eds.), *Attitude strength: Antecedents and consequences* (pp. 455–487). Hillsdale, NJ: Erlbaum.

Weijters, B., Cabooter, E., & Schillewaert, N. (2010). The effect of rating scale format on response styles: the number of response categories and response category labels. *International Journal of Research in Marketing, 27,* 236–247.

Wyatt, R. C., & Meyers, L. S. (1987). Psychometric properties of four 5-point Likert type response scales. *Educational and Psychological Measurement, 47,* 27–35.

16
INDIRECT AND IMPLICIT MEASURES OF COGNITION AND AFFECT

In social research, as in any other field of science, the use of the scientific method requires that our assertions be based on observable phenomena (see Chapter 1). Whatever inferences we wish to make about the causes and processes underlying social behavior must first be grounded in observations that can be recorded and replicated. Research that employs the experimental method involves manipulating some aspect of the physical or social environment, and then observing and recording some type of response of participants as the dependent variable. The observed response could be an overt behavior or action of some kind (e.g., stopping to give help, pressing a button to deliver an electric shock to another person, or choosing a gift). More often, however, the observed response is a written or oral report from a participant of his or her reactions to the situation, a judgment, or a decision. Similarly, in survey research involving interviews or questionnaires, the observations consist of respondents' self-reports of their behaviors, feelings, or beliefs. Because inner experiences—personal feelings and mental life—are not directly observable, social researchers must often rely on people's introspective reports of their private experiences to acquire data that are amenable to measurement and quantification.

In previous chapters we raised a number of issues and problems that must be considered in evaluating the validity of self-report measures as accurate assessments of respondents' true feelings and beliefs. When respondents are aware that they are participants in a scientific investigation, evaluation apprehension and social desirability concerns may lead them to adjust their responses to meet personal or social standards or expectations (see Chapter 7). Participants may be *unwilling* to report on their true feelings or reactions, particularly when embarrassing, sensitive, or politically charged issues are at stake. Even when respondents are willing to provide truthful and candid accounts, they may be *unable* to report accurately on their own inner feelings or mental states. In their classic research, Nisbett and Wilson (1977) argued and documented evidence showing that individuals do not always have conscious access to many of the mental processes that underlie their behaviors or decisions, at least not in a manner that they can verbalize and articulate.

Given the evidence that respondents often are either unwilling or unable to provide valid reports on certain aspects of their inner experiences or mental processes, exclusive reliance on introspective self-reports as our principal source of information about internal reactions is problematic. Fortunately, over the past few decades social researchers have developed an armory of new techniques and procedures for tapping the "inner world" of cognitive processes and affective experiences that do not rely on conscious self-report. The techniques that we describe in this chapter cannot fully replace self-report measures as a mainstay of social research, but they can augment more traditional techniques by providing different types of information that are not susceptible to the same motivational or capability limitations.

Indirect Measures

The scaling approaches discussed in Chapter 15 involve the *direct assessment* of respondents' expressed attitudes, preferences, judgments, knowledge, etc., because respondents are asked explicitly about these feelings or beliefs. Over the years, a number of techniques focused on the *indirect* assessment of attitudes have been developed. In indirect attitude assessment, "the investigator interprets the responses in terms of dimensions and categories different from those held in mind by the respondent while answering" (Kidder & Campbell, 1970, p. 336). Indirect approaches are used to reduce possible distortions that might come about when respondents answer questions in a socially desirable or normative manner to place themselves in a more favorable light. Many researchers feel that they can obtain more accurate evaluations by having respondents focus their attention on irrelevant but compelling features of the task. They hope that by using misdirection or assessing reactions of which people are unaware, their respondents will lower their defenses and present a more valid picture of their attitudes, beliefs, or judgments.

Many indirect techniques have been developed, with varying degrees of success (Dovidio & Fazio, 1992). Suppose, for example, that a researcher was interested in indirectly assessing respondents' attitudes toward labor unions, and decided to employ a **sentence completion task**, an indirect measurement in which a partial sentence is presented and participants are required to complete the sentence. In the instructions, the investigator might ask respondents to be "as creative as possible in completing the following sentence stems," among which would be the following:

> "The cost of living . . . "
> "The Teamsters have . . . "
> "My research methods course is . . . "
> "Unions are . . . "

Participants are to indicate the word or phrase that first comes to mind to complete each sentence. A presumption of the sentence completion approach is that the information most at the tip of the tongue or accessible in the mind of the participant will be offered as the response. If given the sentence stem of "My research methods course is . . .", students who answer "totally awesome" or "making my life complete" probably are enjoying the material more than students responding with "making me sweat, and not in a good way" or "preventing me from having an active social life." "Filler" items not of interest to the researcher often are included in such tasks to mask the intent of the study.

In addition to sentence completion tests, another approach is used to assess attitudes surreptitiously. The **thematic apperception test** is an indirect measurement in which the respondent views a deliberately ambiguous picture and then generates a story about the characters and scenario depicted in the picture. For instance, a drawing may depict two youths holding hands in a playground, but the drawing is sketched in such a way that participants will have to interpret the gender of each child, and whether they are holding hands because they are good friends, have a "crush" on each other, or are trying to avoid being punched by the other. The content of the respondent's story can be analyzed in terms of how the image is interpreted and the aspects of the image that most strongly drew the participant's focus. The intent of the measure is far from transparent, and thus the hope is that the method will allow the researcher to obtain more honest and unbiased answers than would more direct assessment methods.

Suedfeld, Guttieri, and Tetlock (2005; see also Suedfeld, Tetlock, & Streufert, 1992) have helped develop methods of coding the cognitive complexity (the capacity to integrate many different features of a complex issue to come to a meaningful synthesis) of political leaders, based on the leaders' own public statements. Expanding on a method developed by Schroder and his colleagues (e.g., Gardiner & Schroder, 1972; Schroder, Driver, & Streufert, 1967), this approach codes public pronouncements and attempts to develop insights into the depth and complexity of leaders' understanding of important issues. The approach has yielded interesting insights into the cognitive features of various leaders, typically in stressful circumstances. It obviously is indirect, in that the leaders probably did not assume that Suedfeld and his colleagues were tapping into their cognitive structures, sometimes years after they delivered their policy statements. Following Suedfeld's lead, Bligh and her colleagues have used archived speeches of major public figures to make inferences of their charismatic or leadership qualities (e.g., Bligh & Kohles, 2008; Bligh & Robinson, 2010; Seyranian & Bligh, 2008).

It must be acknowledged that these forms of assessment (the sentence completion, the TAT, the coding of the speeches of public figures) make considerable demands on the time and technical expertise of the investigator because the responses typically gathered in these methods do not lend themselves to easy scoring. Generally, coders must be trained to perform systematic content analyses of respondents' qualitative responses (Chapter 14). This training is labor intensive and time consuming. In addition, it is necessary that some estimates of the interrater reliability of the scoring procedure be developed (Chapter 12). If the interrater reliability level is unacceptable, the coding system must be revised or the coders retrained. Even with these challenges, however, indirect measures may provide valuable insights into processes that otherwise could not be studied. Despite the difficulties, and particularly in settings where unconscious motives might be involved, indirect approaches may be the most reasonable measurement method available. Under such circumstances, the difficulties involved in data acquisition and scoring must be considered part of the cost of admission.

Information Processing: Attention and Memory

Other methodologies for indirect assessment of attitudes and preferences rely on **implicit responses**, responses to stimuli that participants are not necessarily aware that they are making. Because many of these techniques for "getting inside the head" (Taylor & Fiske, 1981) have been adapted from procedures developed by cognitive scientists, they are often referred to collectively as "social cognition" methodologies, although many are intended to assess affect, emotions, and motives as well as cognitive processes.

Many of the techniques for assessing cognition derive from a general model of information processing that assumes that knowledge about the world and experiences is acquired and remembered through four stages or operations: *attention* (what information is attended to), *encoding* (how that information is understood and interpreted at the time of intake), *storage* (how information is retained in memory), and *retrieval* (what information is subsequently accessible in memory). Methodologically, these processes may be measured or documented by various techniques.

Measures of Attention

The information-processing model assumes that attention is a limited resource that is selectively distributed among the myriad of visual, auditory, and other sensory stimuli that bombard us at any point in time. Attention serves as a selective filter of the voluminous information that comes to us from the external world: We must first pay attention to information before it can be passed on to subsequent stages of memory. It is further assumed that the particular stimuli that capture and hold a person's attention are those that are most salient or important to the perceiver at the time. Thus, by measuring which inputs a person attends to when multiple stimuli are available, or measuring how long the person attends to particular stimuli compared to others, we have an indirect way of assessing what is important, interesting, or salient to that individual.

Visual Attention

The majority of research on attention (and hence, methods for assessing attention) focuses on the perception of visual information—either of actual events or displays of pictures, words, or other symbols. Measures of visual attention involve tracking direction and duration of eye gaze, i.e., when and how long the perceiver's eyes are fixated on a particular object or event presented in the visual field.[1] Atalay, Bodhur, and Rasolofoarison (2012), for example, assessed visual fixation patterns to analyze consumers' choices in horizontal displays of merchandise. Memory based methods failed to relate to choices, but eye gaze did. In another application, McArthur and Ginsberg (1981) used eye tracking to measure selective attention to specific individuals during an impression formation task.

Precise measurement of eye fixation patterns entails heavy technology and may require that participants hold their heads still in an apparatus so that their eye movements may be tracked and recorded across small distances. Computerized methods for producing visual displays and recording sequential eye movements are routinely used in visual research, but are generally less accessible or useful for social research. For purposes of social information processing, video recording participants' faces during social interactions or decision-making will usually provide sufficient information about location and duration of eye gaze to determine what is being attended to. Olson and Zanna (1979), for example, recorded participants' eye gaze while they inspected a pair of painting reproductions in a study of selective attention to preferred versus non-preferred objects. In this case, the measure of interest was how much time participants spent looking at the painting they had chosen compared to the alternative that was not chosen. Eye gaze proved to be a sensitive measure of selective allocation of visual attention and preference.

Interference as a Measure of Attention

Another way of assessing how much attention is being devoted to a particular stimulus is to determine whether the presence of a distracting stimulus interferes with attending to or processing a target stimulus. The well-known "Stroop effect" (Stroop, 1935) is an example of an interference-based measure of unintended attention. In this research paradigm, participants are presented with a series of words printed in various colors, and are instructed to not read the word but to identify aloud the color of ink in which each is printed. The relationship between the word and the ink color is varied. In *congruent trials,* each written word corresponds to the ink color (e.g., the word "green" printed in green ink.), so identification of ink color should be facilitated. In *incongruent trials,* the written word itself is a color different from the printed ink color (e.g., the word "red" printed in green ink), so the semantic meaning of the word interferes with the participant's ability to identify the ink color correctly. Thus, it takes longer to name the ink color on incongruent trials compared with trials in which the word is congruent with the ink color. This response interference is an indication that attending to the semantic meaning of the word is automatic and cannot be suppressed, even when instructed to identify the ink color instead.

The Stroop effect has been adapted as a general measure of automatic attention to semantic content (see Logan, 1980, and MacLeod, 1991, for reviews). Pratto and John (1991), for example, used the effect to study automatic attention to negative words. Respondents in this experiment were instructed to identify the colors in which words of personality traits were written. Some of the words referred to desirable traits (such as "honest") and others referred to undesirable, negative traits (e.g., "sadistic"). The delay in reaction time (or latency) to respond with the correct ink color was consistently longer when undesirable words were presented, suggesting that participants had difficulty ignoring the distracting effect of social stimuli with strong negative connotations.

Presented in Figure 16.1 is an illustration of a variant of the Stroop experiment, with the congruent and incongruent conditions on the left and right columns, respectively. Starting with one of the conditions, begin at the top and identify each shape aloud (rather than read the word) as fast as you can. If you make a mistake, try again until the shape is correctly identified. Proceed until you have reached the bottom. Then, identify each shape for the other condition. In the congruent condition, exhibiting correspondence between shapes and words, these shapes were likely identified at a relatively rapid rate. In the incongruent condition, as the shapes did not correspond with their semantic meanings, it should take longer to identify all the shapes. The delayed reaction time in the incongruent condition occurs due to reading—a process we have practiced all our lives and which therefore has become relatively automatic—in interfering with the ability to identify the shapes. Essentially, the conflicting processes of reading and shape identification simultaneously competed for our attention. The additional amount of time it requires to complete the incongruent condition over the congruent condition indicates the extent of interference.

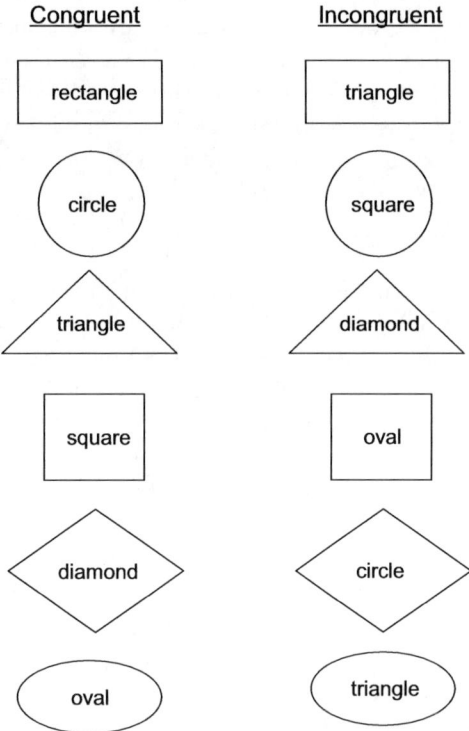

FIGURE 16.1 Stroop task using shape-word congruent and incongruent conditions.

Processing Time

A third method for assessing how important or significant particular information is to the perceiver is to measure the amount of time the individual spends viewing or contemplating the information before making a decision or judgment or moving on to another processing task. Duration of eye gaze is one measure of processing time, but more often this method is used when information is presented sequentially, as, for example, images are displayed successively or successive photographs or text are projected on a computer screen. If the participant is given control over the movement from one screen to the next, the amount of time spent viewing a particular screen provides a measure of processing time for that information.

As a measure of attention or interest, processing time is somewhat ambiguous because the measure is a combination of time spent encoding or interpreting the stimulus object (the second stage of information processing) as well as simply attending to it (first stage). Thus, the administration of more complex or ambiguous stimuli may engage longer processing time independent of their interest value. Nonetheless, the relative amount of time spent viewing each piece of information in a sequence often may provide useful information about the types of information that attract the most attention and cognitive effort. For instance, Fiske (1980) found that social stimuli (slides depicting social behaviors) that were rare, extreme, or negative elicited increased processing time. Similarly, Brewer, Dull, and Lui (1981) used looking time to demonstrate that information that is inconsistent with category stereotypes takes longer to process than information that is consistent with stereotypic expectancies.

Measures of Memory

The extent to which individuals can remember information or experiences provides significant clues regarding which information has been encoded and how it is stored in memory. In most social research employing memory as a dependent variable, the memory "test" is introduced unexpectedly and without advance warning to assess what is encoded and stored spontaneously when perceivers are not deliberately attempting to memorize information. Memory of stored information may be accessed in either of two ways: Recall or recognition. In a **recall measure**, the participant reports what he or she remembers about information that was previously presented. This task requires that the respondent first search and retrieve relevant material from memory, and then make the decision of whether or not the retrieved information is correct (i.e., that the person believes it was actually present on the occasion being recalled). Bypassing the search and retrieval stage, in a **recognition measure** the participant simply decides whether or not the material currently shown matches his or her memory of what was previously presented. The process of recall is considered more cognitively effortful and slower than the process of recognition, as recognition requires only familiarity with the previously exposed material.

An example of a test of recall is the open-ended question, "What is the capital of California?" In an attempt to answer the question, you would search your memory stores to retrieve this information and then decide if what you have in mind is the correct answer. A test of recognition is exemplified by a multiple-choice question; for example, "Which is the capital of California? (a) San Diego, (b) Los Angeles, (c) Sacramento, (d) Fresno." Having a sense of familiarity with this knowledge in the context of available options is sufficient for you to select the correct response. Recognition tasks are easier because it is only necessary to decide whether one of the presented options correctly matches what was stored previously in memory. Obviously, if you had never been exposed to the fact that the capital of California is Sacramento, this information would not be stored in memory, and recall and recognition responses would reflect random guesses.

Recall Measures

The typical paradigm for recall memory experiments involves an initial presentation of stimulus information, which may be anything from a list of words, a series of pictures, a written description or story, or a videotaped event. Usually the participant is given some cover story about why he or she is viewing the information (e.g., evaluating the writing style, forming an impression) that does not involve explicit instructions to remember the material being presented. After the presentation, some time is allowed to lapse, and then the participant is asked to report what they can remember of what was presented earlier.[2] With *free recall* tasks, participants are given no further instructions about what to search for in memory and are free to list anything that they think was presented earlier. In such a task, participants might be presented with a photograph of a supermarket aisle containing an array of products. After viewing the photograph, followed by removal of it and a delay, they might be instructed to freely recall as many of the products as possible. With *cued recall,* the participant is specifically instructed as to what type of information to retrieve (e.g., Were you shown any cereal products? What is the brand of the box of cookies? What were the products in the bottom row?). In either case, the participant provides a listing (either specific words or brief summaries) of each item he or she can recall from the earlier presentation.

Memory protocols produced from recall tests can be analyzed in a number of different ways, depending on what the researcher is hoping to learn from the content of the recalled material. The volume or quantity of memory (i.e., the number of different items listed) is sometimes used as a measure of the degree of attention and mental processing of the material presented earlier. A sparse listing of details suggests relatively little active processing of the stimulus materials, and greater volume suggests more processing. For this purpose, it does not necessarily matter whether the "recalled" information was actually presented or reflects the perceiver's own internal cognitions generated during the presentation stage (Petty & Cacioppo, 1986). For this reason, the sheer quantity of recall, without consideration of recall accuracy, is an imprecise measure of encoding that occurred during the original presentation, because we cannot know whether respondents are recording thoughts that they had at the time of the presentation or thoughts that were generated later, during the recall task itself.

More often researchers are interested in the degree of *accurate* recall represented in the memory protocol, i.e., whether or not the items participants listed match information actually presented at the earlier time. For this purpose, the recall lists must be evaluated and each item scored as correct or incorrect.[3] The final measure may then be the number of items correctly recalled (overall accuracy of recall), or the researcher may be interested in which items were more likely to be accurately recalled (compared to information forgotten or incorrectly recalled). Research on this topic has shown that people tend to have superior recall for items near the beginning (primacy effect) and end (recency effect) of a list of previously presented items.

Finally, the researcher may be interested not only in the items correctly recalled, but also in the content of errors as represented by the items in the recall list that do not match information actually presented. Such incorrect items are referred to as memory "intrusions" and provide clues as to how the original material was encoded and interpreted before being stored in memory. Unfortunately, intrusion errors in recall protocols provide a very imperfect indicator of encoding processes. First, participants often are very cautious about which items they report on a recall measure (assuming that they are being tested for accuracy), and so do not list items unless they are fairly confident that they actually appeared. As a consequence, the number of intrusions may be very small and unreliable as a measure of cognitive activity. Second, when intrusions do occur, we cannot tell whether they reflect cognitions that were generated at the time of the original presentation or simply bad "guesses" about information that cannot be recalled correctly.[4] For this reason, recognition measures usually are more appropriate for the study of memory errors than are recall measures.

Another method of analysis of recall protocols involves the researcher noting the *sequencing* of the items recalled, specifically which items are remembered first or later, and/or which items are recalled together. The former provides information about accessibility in memory (i.e., which information is recalled most easily and rapidly and which requires more search time and effort). The latter (measures of "clustering" in recall) provides information about how material has been *organized* in memory. Clustering measures are most often useful when information has been originally presented in some random or haphazard order but then appears in a different, more systematic order on the recall listings. Clustering measures are indices of the frequency with which items of the same "type" (or category) appear sequentially in the recall protocol compared to chance.[5] These indices are used to document the kinds of categorizations perceivers use to encode and organize incoming information in memory. For example, Hamilton, Katz, and Leirer (1980) used a measure of clustering in output of recall to show how behavioral information is organized in memory when perceivers are engaged in an impression formation task. In another social information processing study, Pryor and Ostrom (1981) used clustering measures to assess how incoming information about multiple persons in a social situation is processed and organized in memory. They found that when the persons were familiar individuals known to the perceiver, information was encoded and organized by individual person. But when the social stimuli were unfamiliar persons, memory was organized by behavioral categories rather than on a person-by-person basis.

Recognition Measures

As a test of the content of memory, recognition does not require the respondent to retrieve items from the memory store, but to identify whether the information currently shown was among the materials presented on a prior occasion. The difference between recall and recognition measures of memory parallels the difference between an essay exam and a multiple-choice exam (Taylor & Fiske, 1981). As with a good multiple-choice exam, the researcher using recognition methods must carefully design and select wrong answers ("foils") that will appear to be correct if the respondent's memory of the earlier material includes cognitions and assumptions that were not actually presented at the time. With recognition measures, the researcher's interest is primarily in the types of errors that are made, rather than in the accuracy of memory.

In general, there are two different kinds of recognition tasks. In one paradigm the respondent's task is to review each item presented by the researcher and indicate whether that item of information was or was not seen before by responding "old" or "new" (or "true," "false"). False recognitions (responding "old" to an item that was not present earlier) provide information about how the original materials were encoded and stored along with prior knowledge or inferences that the perceiver brought to bear at the time the information was received and processed. False recognition has been used to study the use of social category stereotypes in forming impressions of individual persons. For example, Cantor and Mischel (1977) demonstrated that participants misrecognized trait information that had not actually been presented if it was consistent with the personality type ("introvert" or "extravert") that had been attributed to the person described.

The second type of recognition measure involves assessing memory confusions. In this case, participants are given two or more options and asked to indicate which one corresponds to information presented in the original materials. An interesting application of the recognition confusion method is the who-said-what paradigm originally developed by Taylor, Fiske, Etcoff, and Ruderman (1978). In this paradigm, participants first view an audio-visual presentation of a discussion among a group of six persons. The content of the discussion is presented on an audio recording while a picture of the individual group member who is speaking is projected on a screen. Later in the session, the participant is shown an array of photos of the group members and a series of sentences that occurred during the discussion. For each sentence, the participant is to choose which specific group member made that particular statement. What is of interest here is which group members are confused with each other when an incorrect choice is made. In the original experiment using this method, Taylor and colleagues (1978) varied the composition of the discussion group to determine whether discussants were automatically categorized by sex or race while viewing the presentation. Consistent with the idea of automatic categorization, when the group consisted of three males and three females (or three Black and three White males), recognition errors were more likely to involve confusing one male with another male or one female with another female ("intra-category" errors) than misattributing a statement made by a female to a male or vice versa ("inter-category" errors). Like clustering measures in recall, recognition confusions are used to assess how persons are classified or categorized in memory, even if they are unaware of this categorization process.

Both types of recognition task suffer from one major disadvantage as measures of what has been encoded and stored in memory. Both accurate and false recognition can reflect information that was encoded at the time of presentation, but they also can reflect guessing or inferences made by respondents at the time the memory measure is taken—that is, memory may be constructed (or reconstructed) when the person is tested on what he or she remembers. More sophisticated methods of analyzing recognition and recall errors make use of signal detection models to decompose memory scores and to estimate the level of true recognition (Donaldson & Glathe, 1970).

Priming: Processing Without Awareness or Intent

Even though the memory measures discussed in the preceding section tap unintended memory, in the sense that participants are not aware at the time they receive information that they are going to be asked to remember it later, the memory tests themselves require active, conscious retrieval on the part of participants. As a consequence, these methods can assess only what participants are aware of experiencing and willing to report to the experimenter. Other social cognition methods have been developed that do not require such an active role on the part of respondents in order to tap cognitive processing and other internal mental states. Specifically, *priming* techniques are designed to assess automatic cognitive and affective processes that occur without awareness or intent.

The concept of priming was introduced in Chapter 6 and refers to the unintended influence that recent or recurrent experiences have on subsequent thoughts, feelings, and behavior (Bargh & Chartrand, 2000). The idea underlying priming techniques is that exposure to a priming stimulus creates a state of mental readiness or preparedness for perceiving and interpreting subsequent information. Priming effects reflect implicit memory processes that function independently of what can be consciously retrieved from memory. Because these processes occur automatically and without awareness, the priming effect has come to be utilized to tap implicit cognition and affect.

Concept Priming

Priming studies usually involve two phases: (a) A priming task involving participant exposure to a stimulus (independent variable), followed by (b) an outcome judgment task (dependent variable) to assess the influence of the prime on subsequent judgments. Priming methodology was first introduced to experimental social psychology in a set of studies conducted by Higgins, Rholes, and Jones (1977) that involved priming personality concepts and documenting effects on subsequent impression formation. The experimental procedures used by Higgins et al. (1977) are representative of the basic priming paradigm still used today. In the initial priming phase, participants performed a memorization task that exposed them to a set of words concerning either positive (e.g., "adventurous" and "independent") or negative (e.g., "reckless" and "irresponsible") personality traits. Then, in the subsequent judgment phase, the participants took part in what they believed to be a separate, unrelated task during which they were asked to read a story about a person named Donald who was described as engaging in behaviors such as sailing across the ocean alone and preferring to study by himself. The description was written as to be ambiguous, so that his behaviors could potentially be interpreted by participants in a relatively positive light (e.g., Donald is independent and adventurous) or in a negative way (e.g., Donald is reckless and irresponsible).

When participants were asked to report their impressions of Donald on a series of personality rating scales, those who previously had been exposed to words related to "adventurous" reported more positive impressions of Donald than did those who had been exposed to words related to "reckless" in the earlier task. This effect was obtained even though participants showed no awareness of the connection between the priming and judgment phases of the experiment.

Supraliminal Priming

The research paradigm used in the Higgins et al. (1977) experiment involved a conscious priming task. During the first phase participants were aware that they were viewing and processing words, even though they were unaware of the purposes of the word exposure. With such "supraliminal" priming, the participant is made fully aware of the priming stimuli, but not of the underlying concept that the stimuli are intended to make accessible. In a study, suppose that you were presented with the words "four," "legs," "sit," "seat." You are fully aware of these supraliminal words because they are presented explicitly on a page. The underlying emergent concept we sought to activate in your consciousness—but which probably was not completely obvious—is "chair."

Another frequently used supraliminal priming task is the "scrambled sentence task" (e.g., Srull & Wyer, 1979). With this technique participants are given a cover story that the study is designed to measure their language ability and their task is to make coherent, grammatical sentences out of each of a string of words. For example: "him was about worried she always," or, "is dependent on occasionally he them" should be unscrambled as "she was always worried about him" and "he is occasionally dependent on them." During the course of unscrambling the sentence priming task, the participant is exposed to words (e.g., "dependent," "worried") that are related to the concept that the researcher intends to activate (usually close synonyms). Later, the effect of the primed words on activating the concept is assessed on a subsequent impression formation or judgment task. Because the scrambled sentence task disguises the real purpose of the word presentation, participants are almost never aware that the earlier task has affected their subsequent judgment processes. Thus, supraliminal priming effects demonstrate how biases in person perception and decision-making can be invoked without participant awareness.

Subliminal Priming

Awareness of the prime can be reduced even further by techniques that present the priming stimuli in a way that perceivers are not even conscious of seeing them. "Subliminal" exposure is achieved by presenting the prime (usually a word or a picture) very briefly for a fraction of a second, and then immediately masking this stimulus trace with a supraliminally presented neutral or nonsense stimulus. Subliminal priming was first used in a social psychology experiment by Bargh and Pietromonaco (1982), who used subliminal presentation to replicate the earlier trait concept priming experiments of Higgins et al. (1977) and Srull and Wyer (1979).

The key to subliminal priming is determining a time or duration of exposure of the priming stimulus that is too short to be consciously recognized. Usually, the stimulus is projected by a tachistoscope (a device developed by perception researchers to project stimuli at very brief exposures) or on a computer screen, with the participant gazing at a fixation point (e.g., an asterisk) at the center of the screen. The duration of the prime is a matter of milliseconds, although how long the exposure can be and still remain below awareness depends on a number of factors, including where in the visual field the stimulus is projected. With *foveal* processing, the priming stimulus is presented at the fixation point (within 0–2 degrees of visual angle from the focal point of attention), a location at the center of the person's field of vision. With *parafoveal* processing, the prime is presented in the periphery or fringe of the visual field, at 3–6 degrees of visual angle from the focal point. Foveal presentation requires extremely short exposure time (on the order of 15 milliseconds) to be subliminal. Because parafoveal presentation is outside of the region of the focal point of attention, it allows for a somewhat longer duration (e.g., 60–120 milliseconds). However, it is somewhat more difficult to implement parafoveal presentations because the researcher has to ensure that the participant's overall field of view includes the field in which the peripheral stimulus is presented.

Regardless of where the priming stimulus is presented, it must be followed immediately by a subsequent presentation (in the same location) of a "masking" stimulus to prevent extended exposure in visual iconic memory.[6] A masking stimulus is a pattern with the same physical features as the prime. So, for example, if the priming stimulus is the word "PREGNANT," the subsequent masking pattern would be a meaningless string of letters ("XQFBZRMQ") that covers the location where the prime was presented. Participants who are subliminally exposed to this prime, intended to active a sexist mindset, might be susceptible in the outcome judgment phase to answer "yes" to the question "Are women less capable than men in management positions?"

Because subliminal exposure permits presenting primes without participants being consciously aware of the presented stimulus, there is no need to mislead them into believing that the stimulus exposure and judgment tasks are separate phases. Thus, the immediate effects of an activated concept on subsequent judgments or evaluations can be assessed. Subliminal priming has proved to be particularly useful for assessing the biasing effects of social stereotypes when perceivers are unaware that the stereotype has been subconsciously activated. Social category stereotypes have been primed by subliminal presentation of stereotype-related words (e.g., Devine, 1989; Devine, Forscher, Austin, & Cox, 2012) or photos of faces of outgroup category members (e.g., Bargh, Chen, & Burrows, 1996, Experiment 3).

Assessing Awareness

Regardless of whether supraliminal or subliminal priming techniques are used, it is important that the researcher determine that participants were truly unaware of the priming manipulation. Awareness matters, because if participants consciously recognize that there is a relationship between the presentation of the prime and the subsequent judgment task, they are likely to intentionally correct for the potential influences of the prime before making their responses in an attempt to appear unbiased. With supraliminal priming, the issue is whether participants become aware of the researcher's intent to activate certain constructs in the first task that may affect their judgments or behavior in the second task. To avoid awareness, it is important to camouflage the relation between the priming and judgment phases of the experiment as much as possible, including moving to different rooms or having different experimenters give instructions

Usually, manipulation checks for conscious awareness of the primes occur during an extensive debriefing session after the experiment is completed. Participants are probed for suspicions or knowledge of the intent of the experiment. This may be accomplished through the use of a "funneled debriefing" (e.g., see Chartrand & Bargh, 1996), a sequence of questions designed to elicit any suspicions or inferences that the participant may have made about the purpose of the experiment or the relationship between the priming task and the judgment task. When subliminal priming techniques are used, possible awareness of the prime presentations can be assessed by somewhat more objective means. The recommended procedure is to tell participants at the end of the experiment that they were exposed subliminally to some stimuli and ask them to try to guess the content of the presented stimuli. If they are unable to explicitly recall any of the words or images that were presented as primes, it is safe to assume that they were not consciously aware of the content of the material used in the priming exposure. An even more conservative procedure is to give participants a multiple-choice recognition test to see if they can identify the actual primes from among a set of distractor foils. (Because participants may correctly guess some of the correct answers by chance, it is best to compare their performance to that of a control group of respondents who have not actually been exposed to the subliminal stimuli. If the participants exposed to the priming stimuli are unable to guess more accurately than the controls, it is safe to assume that awareness was not a problem.)

Sequential Priming

Another variation on priming techniques is used to assess automatic associations between mental concepts. The idea behind sequential priming is that if one stimulus has become associated with some other concept, feeling, or behavior, then presentation of that stimulus will automatically activate (prime) those associations. In that case, if the prime and the association are presented sequentially, responding to the second (target) stimulus will be facilitated because of the prior preparation produced by the prime.

The basic structure of the sequential priming paradigm is as follows. On each trial, the prime stimulus (a word or a picture) is presented for a short duration (e.g., 150 milliseconds), then erased, and after a brief delay the target stimulus (outcome task) is presented and the participant makes a judgment about the target by pressing a key to indicate his or her response. The outcome measure of interest is the speed of reaction time to make a judgment of the target stimulus. If the target is connected with the prime in a person's memory, then responding to that target should be facilitated when the prime has been presented just before. Thus, if the response made by a participant is faster when the target (e.g., tangerine) is preceded by a relevant prime (e.g., orange) than when the same target is judged in the presence of an irrelevant prime (e.g., carpet), this indicates that the two concepts (orange and tangerine) are automatically associated in a person's memory. Because reaction times are measured in milliseconds, sequential priming requires the use of software programs with very precise timing recorders to detect minor (millisecond) differences in average speed of response.

Although the duration of presentation of the priming stimulus in the sequential priming paradigm is relatively short, it is a supraliminal exposure, and hence participants are consciously aware that they perceive it. For this reason, sequential priming requires some cover story that explains to participants why they are viewing the primes, even though their task is to respond only to the target stimuli. This may be done by telling participants that the study is about people's ability to perform two tasks simultaneously. On each trial, they are being asked to attend to and remember the first stimulus presented, while at the same time they are to make a judgment about the second (target) stimulus. In addition, the potential effects of awareness are minimized by limiting the amount of time for making a response. The window of time allowed between the onset of the prime presentation and the onset of the subsequent target presentation (the "stimulus onset asynchrony," or SOA) is kept short (usually no more than 300 milliseconds), so that there is no opportunity for conscious processing of the priming stimulus before a judgment about the target is called for. With such brief delays, only automatic (implicit) effects should be able to occur.

Lexical Decision Task

In one version of the sequential priming technique, the target stimulus is a string of letters, and the judgment that the participant is to make is to indicate as quickly as possible whether the string is an actual word or not. If the target is a word, this judgment is made more quickly when it is preceded by presentation of a prime concerning a related word or concept. For instance, when the prime is an overarching category label (e.g., "furniture"), target words representing members of that category (e.g., "chair") are recognized faster than target words that do not belong to the category (e.g., "bird") (Neely, 1977). Based on this principle, the lexical decision task can be used to assess automatic activation of stereotypic traits when the prime is a social category label or picture (e.g., Cunningham & Macrae, 2011; Macrae, Bodenhausen, & Milne, 1995).

Automatic Evaluation

The sequential priming technique was adapted for use in social psychology by Fazio and his colleagues to assess automatic attitudes or evaluative responses to social stimuli (Fazio, Sanbonmatsu, Powell, & Kardes, 1986). In Fazio's version of the paradigm, the priming stimuli are words or pictures of an attitude object, followed by target words that are evaluative adjectives (e.g., "delightful," "awful"). The respondent's task is to indicate as quickly as possible whether the target word has a good or bad connotation. If the prime automatically elicits an evaluative reaction of some kind, then the participant's evaluative response is expected to carry over to the judgment of the target. If the evaluative meaning of the target sufficiently matches that of the prime, responding should be facilitated. So, for instance, if the primed stimulus has a positive connotation (e.g., "party"), it should then speed up judgments of positive target adjectives (e.g., "good"). Conversely, a positive prime should slow down (inhibit) judgments of a subsequent negative target adjective (e.g., "bad"). Thus, the pattern of facilitation and inhibition of evaluative judgments of a target provides an indirect (implicit) measure of attitudes activated by the prime. Presentation of a positive prime will speed up responding to positive adjectives and slow down responding to negative ones. Presentation of a negative prime will speed up responses to subsequent negative judgments and inhibit positive judgments.

Fazio's automatic evaluation paradigm has been used specifically to measure implicit prejudices. For example, Fazio, Jackson, Dunton, and Williams (1995) used photos of White and Black faces as primes in the sequential priming task. Participants were instructed to attend to and remember the faces (for a later recognition test) while they were doing an adjective evaluation task (target stimuli). On some trials, positive or negative adjectives were preceded by a prime of a facial photo of a White person; on other trials the same adjectives were preceded by a prime of a photo of a Black person. Implicit prejudice is assessed by comparing (for each participant) the response times on trials with Black primes to those obtained on trials with White primes. Automatic negative attitudes toward Blacks are indicated when judgments of negative adjectives are faster following Black primes than following White primes. Conversely, automatic positive attitudes toward Whites are indicated when judgments of positive adjectives are slower for Black primes than White primes. Interestingly, individual differences in automatic evaluation were not correlated with explicit self-report measures of racial prejudice, suggesting that the priming task taps into evaluative reactions that people may be unwilling or unable to report directly.

Pronunciation Task

An alternative method for assessing implicit evaluation and other automatic associations replaces the judgment reaction time measure with a measure of time taken to pronounce the target word aloud. Again the idea is that if the target word has been activated by presentation of a preceding prime, the time it takes to recognize and speak the word will be shorter than in the absence of a relevant prime. Using the pronunciation task in a sequential priming paradigm, Bargh, Chaikin, Raymond, and Hymes (1996) demonstrated that automatic evaluation effects occur even when the task is not an evaluative one (pronunciation does not require the respondent to make an explicit good-bad judgment, as in the Fazio paradigm). In another interesting application of this method, Bargh, Raymond, Pryor, and Strack (1995) used the pronunciation task in a study of males who were identified as potential sexual harassers. Compared to other participants, they found that harassers showed significant facilitation of pronunciation of sexually related words when they had been primed by a situation of having power. This finding supported the hypothesis that sexual harassment is related to implicit associations between power and sex.

Issues Related to Use of Reaction Time Measures

All of the sequential priming techniques (as well as a number of other social cognition methods) rely on the analysis of reaction times as an indicator of automatic processes. Researchers making use of these methods need to be aware of some methodological issues in using reaction times as a dependent variable. Many factors other than the priming effects of interest can influence response latencies to particular target stimuli, including word length and word frequency. Thus, it is extremely important that these stimulus features be controlled for in making comparisons between priming conditions.

Reaction time measures also create some problems for data analysis purposes. First, the distribution of response times is typically positively skewed (in that very long reaction times occur occasionally but extremely short latencies are impossible). For this reason, various transformations of the reaction time measure (e.g., taking the square root, or the natural logarithm) may need to be used to normalize the distribution for purposes of analysis. Second, the researcher needs to be concerned about "outliers" in each participant's reaction time data—excessively long reaction times that indicate the respondent wasn't paying attention at the time of presentation of the target stimulus, or excessively short reaction times that reflect anticipatory responding before the target was actually processed. Such outliers should be removed from the data set before analyses are conducted. Typically, response times shorter than 300 milliseconds are trimmed as too fast to represent true responses (Bargh & Chartrand, 2000). In general, only very extreme outliers should be trimmed (e.g., reaction times that are more than three standard deviations above and below the mean reaction time), and care should be taken that deletions are equally distributed across the different priming conditions.

Other Measures of Automaticity

Sequential priming methods are designed to assess responses elicited spontaneously or automatically, without intent or effort on the part of the respondent. Most automatic responding is presumed to occur early in information processing; given additional time and cognitive effort, some automatic processes may be overridden or corrected by more thoughtful, deliberative cognitive processing (Conrey, Sherman, Gawronski, Hugenberg, & Groom, 2005; Payne, 2001)—hence the importance of short SOA in the sequential priming paradigm, as brief response times preclude the opportunity for deliberative processing. Alternative methods for assessing automatic responses rely on different strategies for reducing the influence of intentional processing.

Cognitive Busyness

Capacity for conscious processing can be limited by various techniques for creating cognitive overload, either presenting a lot of information very rapidly (e.g., Bargh & Thein, 1985), or occupying cognitive resources with a secondary task (what Gilbert, Pelham, and Krull (1988) referred to as "cognitive busyness"). A cognitive busyness manipulation might require participants to hold an eight-digit number in memory (distractor task) while they are engaging in a judgment task or while the stimulus information is being presented (the primary task: see Parker, Clarke, Moniz-Coo, & Gardiner, 2012). Gilbert and Osborne (1989) used this method to test a two-stage model of attribution processes. Participants in the experimental condition were given a string of numbers to remember throughout the entire time they were viewing a videotape of a woman engaging in a discussion with a stranger; participants in the control condition viewed the same tape without the secondary memory load task. After the video presentation, all were asked to make attributions about the causes of the actor's behavior. As predicted, participants in the cognitive overload condition gave more dispositional (e.g., personality) attributions than those in the control condition, who provided more situational explanations for the behavior. These findings were consistent with the theory that dispositional judgments occur automatically and effortlessly, whereas situational attributions require more deliberation and cognitive effort. In later studies, Gilbert and Hixon (1991) used a similar cognitive overload manipulation to assess automatic activation and use of social stereotypes in impression formation.

Response Interference Techniques

Responses that are automatically elicited can be expected to interfere with production of other responses that are incompatible with it. We have already mentioned the use of interference effects in connection with the Stroop color-naming task as a measure of automatic attention allocation. The Stroop effect demonstrates that performance of an instructed response can be inhibited when an incompatible automatic response is elicited by the stimulus. Thus the occurrence of such interference can be interpreted as an indication of automatic processing at work.

As another use of response interference as a measure of automatic processes, the **implicit association test (IAT)** assesses automatic associations between mental concepts by classifying and sorting items as quickly and accurately as possible into different categories (Greenwald, McGhee, and Schwartz, 1998). Administered using a computer, a stimulus (word, person's name, or picture) is presented in the center of the screen, and the respondent is instructed to press a key to indicate whether it is an exemplar of one of two broader categories The experiment is designed so that a phase involves making judgments using response pairings that are stereotypically congruent, and another phase in which response pairings are stereotypically incongruent.

An example of an IAT, with four trials in each of the congruent and incongruent conditions, is presented in Figure 16.2. In the congruent phase, the participant is instructed to press the right-hand key if the word shown at the center is either a Black name or has a negative connotation, and the left-hand key if it is either a White name or has a positive connotation. In the incongruent phase, the pairings are changed so that the right-hand key should be used if the word shown is either a White name or negative word and the left-hand key is used for either a Black name or positive word. If the anti-Black concepts are mentally connected in a person's memory, then trials where the response pairings are stereotypically congruent (e.g., Black/negative and White/positive)

Implicit Measures of Cognition and Affect 357

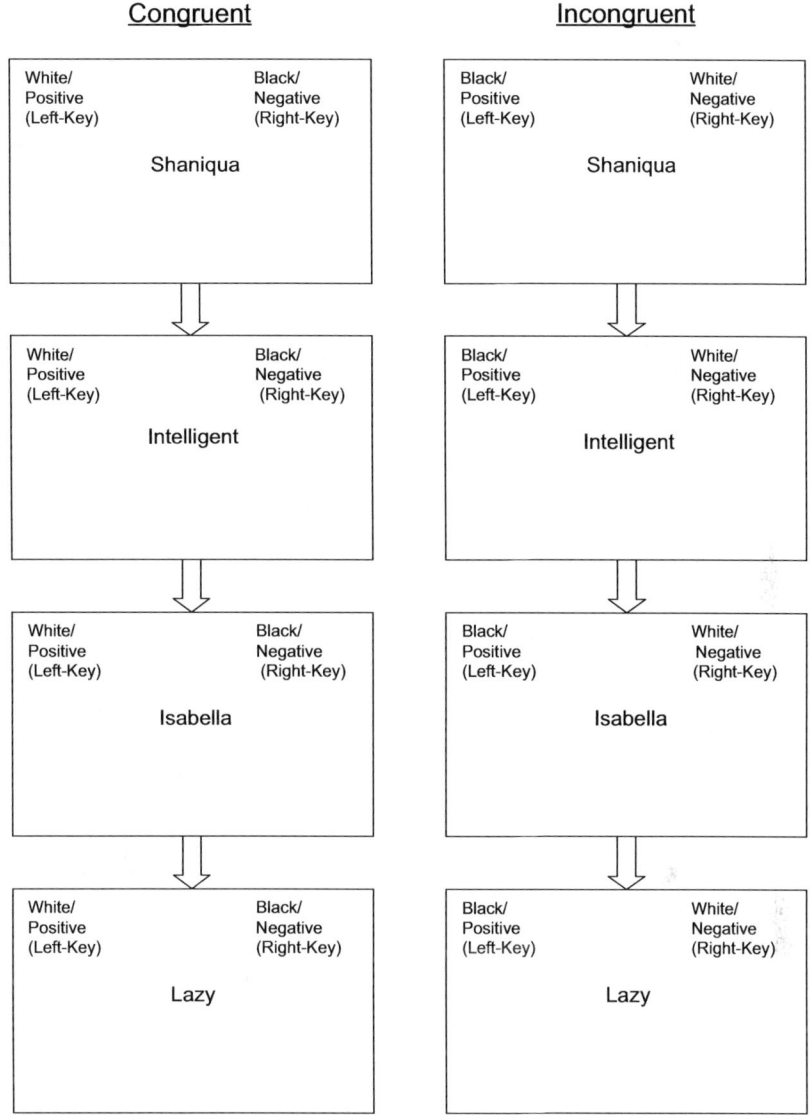

FIGURE 16.2 Screenshots of implicit association test for stereotypically congruent and incongruent conditions.

will have faster reaction times than trials in which the pairings are reversed and are stereotypically incongruent. That is, people with more implicit racial biases are expected to respond more quickly to trails consisting of response pairings that are consistent rather than inconsistent with racial stereotypes. Thus, the difference in speed of responding to the congruent over the incongruent trials is a measure of degree of implicit association between concepts represented in a person's memory. The IAT has been widely used in social psychological research to assess implicit prejudice (associations between social categories and evaluative words) and stereotype content (associations between social categories and stereotypic trait words).[7]

A quantitative review examined 126 previous studies that have assessed the degree of correspondence between IAT measures and the equivalent versions of self-report measures (Hoffmann,

Gawronski, Gschwendner, Le, & Schmitt, 2005). The average study reported a correlation of .24, suggesting that although explicit and implicit measures tended to positively coincide, other underlying mechanisms are responsible for making these measurement methods predominantly distinct. More recent research has raised the issue of the validity of the IAT; the predictive validity of this particular approach for behavior is not without its detractors (Oswald, Mitchell, Blanton, Jaccard, & Tetlock, 2013).

Social Psychophysiology: Physiological Traces of Affect and Cognitive Processing

The various priming techniques described in the preceding section have the advantage of tapping processes and subtle responses that may not be accessible to conscious awareness. However, they all share the disadvantage that the researcher must be concerned that participants not become aware of the true purpose of the priming manipulation, because awareness can influence the critical responses. Internal physiological responses are less susceptible to alteration by conscious awareness and thus provide the possibility for yet less reactive methods for assessing implicit, unintended responses.

The use of measures of physiological responses has a long history in social research, as seen in research designed to assess internal states such as interpersonal attraction, aversion, specific emotions, or stress. Most of these early investigations relied on unitary physiological measures such as respiration, pulse rate, finger temperature, and skin conductance (see Blascovich, Mendes, Hunter, Lickel, & Kowai-Bell, 2001; Guglielmi, 1999). Social researchers were relatively unsophisticated about underlying physiological processes, and as a consequence most of these early attempts did not result in valid or reliable assessments of the psychological states of interest. One major problem is that there is rarely, if ever, a simple one-to-one relationship between a single physiological response and some specific internal psychological state (Blascovich, 2000; Blascovich & McCall, 2013). The often-used Galvanic skin response (GSR), for instance, provides an indicator of general arousal, which may arise from any number of positive or negative states, including stress, excitement, aversion, or sexual desire. Changes in heart rate may signal physical exertion, attention, anticipation, or arousal, with relatively little differentiation when measured in isolation of other physiological responses.

Fortunately, recent advances in theory and methodology now allow for multivariate physiological assessments that are capable of distinguishing different motivational states, positive and negative affect, attention, and active cognitive processing. Because these indicators are potentially relevant to many phenomena of interest to social researchers, such as assessment of prejudice, social emotions, social stress, and interpersonal motives, the availability of sophisticated physiological measures has given rise to the subfield of "social psychophysiology" (Cacioppo & Petty, 1983) or "social neuroscience" (Cacioppo, Berntson, Ernst, & Ito, 2000; Norman, Hawkley, Luhmann, Cacioppo, & Berntson, 2013) designed to capitalize on these methods for understanding the interrelationships between psychological and physiological/neurological states. The downside of this development is that these techniques require expensive equipment, sophisticated programming, and more than superficial training in physiology, neuroscience, and complex statistical techniques to make good use of the available methods. Nonetheless, the capability for conducting experiments that include physiological measures is gradually expanding, and physiological methods are taking their place among our tools for assessing implicit cognition and feelings.

Most physiological measures used in social research involve noninvasive techniques, that is, ways of recording internal physiological responses from the surface of the body. Usually some form of electrophysiological recording is involved because various physiological events produce detectable electrical signals at the surface level (Blascovich, 2000). Depending on the location and type of recording, electrophysiological measures record signals of neural, cardiovascular, or endocrine system activity occurring in response to current situational inputs. In modern methods, it is the patterns of responses from multiple signals over time that serve as markers of specific psychophysiological states. Some examples of uses of these physiological measures in social research will be described in the following sections.

Cardiovascular Indices

Although heart rate alone is an inadequate marker of any specific arousal state, measures of heart rate in combination with other recordings of cardiac and vascular performance can differentiate different states of anticipation or stress (Blascovich & Kelsey, 1990). Tomaka, Blascovich, Kelsey, and Leitten (1993), for example, demonstrated that specific patterns of cardiovascular responses can distinguish between feelings of threat (a negative, avoidance state) versus challenge (a positive, approach state) as motivational states in anticipation of potentially difficult or stressful situations, such as performing difficult arithmetic problems or preparing for a public speech. Threat is marked by increased pituitary-adrenocortical activity (PAC), which is associated with negative physiological consequences of stress. A challenge response to the same situation, however, is marked by increased sympathetic-adrenomedullary activity (SAM), which is associated with benign states and improved performance (Dienstbier, 1989).

Tomaka and Blascovich (1994) validated the usefulness of this distinction for assessment of psychosocial processes by demonstrating that individuals with high beliefs in a just world (as measured by self-report questionnaire) showed a challenge response to a potentially stressful performance situation and performed better than individuals with low beliefs in a just world, who instead showed a threat response pattern to the same situation. In another study, Blascovich et al. (2001) found that White participants showed a predominance of threat response when assigned to work in a team task with a Black partner, compared to participants who showed a challenge response when working with a same-race partner.

Facial Measures of Affective States

One of the difficulties of many physiological indicators of arousal is that these measures do not distinguish between arousal due to positive affect or approach and negative affect or avoidance. Facial expressions, however, do vary in ways that correspond to specific positive or negative social emotions (Ekman, 1993). Ekman and Friesen (1978) developed and validated an elaborate facial action coding system (FACS) to assess various emotional states on the basis of detailed aspects of spontaneous facial expressions. Using this system, researchers can be trained to observe people's facial expressions to distinguish among the basic emotions of happiness, sadness, anger, fear, disgust, contempt, and surprise, which Ekman (2007) considered universal across cultures. This method of measuring internal states has a number of drawbacks, however. First, training to use the FACS is extensive and requires a considerable investment of time and effort. Second, although facial expressions are usually produced without conscious intention, it is possible to control and conceal facial responses if one makes an effort to do so. Thus, facial expression is not always a valid measure of implicit affect.

Facial Electromyograph

Although overt facial expressions are potentially controllable, individuals are not able to control the tiny, visually imperceptible movements of specific facial muscles that occur at the onset of an emotional or affective response to stimulus events. Thus, Cacioppo and his colleagues (e.g., Cacioppo & Petty, 1981; Cacioppo, Petty, Losch, & Kim, 1986) have recommended the use of facial electromyograms (EMG) specific to targeted facial muscles as physiological markers of positive and negative affective states. EMG measures focus in particular on specific muscles of the eyes and mouth associated with corrugator ("frown muscles") and zygomaticus ("smile muscles") activity. Electromyographic recordings obtained from electrodes distributed across areas of the face indicate that corrugator EMG activity increases and zygomaticus activity decreases during negative affect. Conversely, zygomaticus EMG increases and corrugator EMG decreases signal positive affect (Cacioppo et al., 1986). Interestingly, the EMG recordings successfully discriminate between different affective states even when judges observing videotapes of the participants' overt facial expressions are unable to identify whether the affect is positive or negative.

Vanman, Paul, Ito, and Miller (1997) made use of the diagnostic capability of EMG activity to assess implicit attitudes toward members of racial outgroups. In their experiments, White participants were shown slides of Black or White individuals and were asked to imagine themselves in a situation in which they were partnered with that individual in a cooperative task. On overt self-report ratings of the potential partners, respondents tended to show preferential ratings for Black targets. EMG facial measures, however, showed the opposite pattern, with more negativity exhibited toward Black partners.

Startle Eyeblink Reflex

Another minute facial muscle measure that may prove useful to index affective states is electromyograms specific to reflexive eyeblinks (Blascovich, 2000). The startle eyeblink response refers to the reflexive blinks that occur when individuals perceive an unexpected, relatively intense stimulus, such as a loud sound. The startle eyeblink reflex is negatively toned. Hence Lang and his colleagues (Lang, Bradley, & Cuthbert, 1990, 1992) have reasoned that the eyeblink response should be facilitated or enhanced if the perceiver is in a negative affective state and inhibited if the perceiver is experiencing ongoing positive affect. Subsequent research has demonstrated that the strength or intensity of the startle eyeblink reflex as measured by EMG activity is sensitive to affective states as predicted. Thus the eyeblink reflex may prove useful, as well as other EMG indices, as a measure of covert affect.

EMG techniques require sophisticated equipment and technology to implement and have the added disadvantage that participants must sit still (with electrodes planted on various parts of their faces) and minimize extraneous head movements while responses are being recorded. Thus the method is hardly unobtrusive, and the kinds of stimulus situations in which the technology can be used are limited to relatively passive viewing conditions such as presentations of slides or video displays. Nonetheless, EMG recordings have proved to be valid indicators of implicit affect that individuals may be unaware of—or unwilling to express overtly. EMG measures can be a useful tool for testing theories about activation and influences of nonconscious affect, even if their practical application may be limited.

Measures of Brain Activity

Indicators of cognitive and affective processing are also assessed in various noninvasive measures of brain activity. Again, these techniques require access to expensive and sophisticated equipment (much of it developed for medical research), but they are finding their way into social research applications. Neuroscientific or brain-imaging procedures to assess brain activity are classified into three major families: Transcranial magnetic stimulation, event-related potential, and functional

TABLE 16.1 Major neuroscientific methods.

Technique	Purpose	Measurement	Assumption
Transcranial Magnetic Stimulation (TMS)	Examine cause and effect between stimulation of a brain region and the consequent reaction.	Measures behavioral reaction due to magnetic field stimulation of a brain region. Data are considered experimental.	Brain processing invoked artificially by a magnetic field is the same as what naturally occurs.
Event-Related Potential (ERP)	Examine rapid changes in brain wave activity during mental operations.	Measures electrical activity in brain using electrodes placed on the scalp. Amplitudes and shapes of different varieties of brain waves may be examined. Data are considered correlational.	Brain processing is represented by greater electrical activity in brain.
Functional Magnetic Resonance Imaging (fMRI)	Examine and map brain regions active during mental operations.	Measures level of oxygen flow in the blood vessels of the brain. Data are considered correlational.	Brain processing is represented by greater oxygen flow in blood vessels.

magnetic resonance imaging (Quadflieg & Macrae, 2011). A summary description of the purpose of each neuroscience method, its system of measurement, and its assumptions are presented in Table 16.1. Although each neuroscience technique is tailored to address a general type of research question, it is possible to employ all three to study the same brain processes.

Brain Stimulation

In **transcranial magnetic stimulation** (TMS), external magnetic pulses are transmitted through the scalp to different brain regions to identify the part of the brain that produces a specific behavior. By sending magnetic pulses, neurons in these regions are excited from their resting state. Because a brain locale is stimulated with focused magnetic fields, the technique is primarily undertaken to determine the cause and effect relation between brain regions and behavioral responses. In one TMS study, Cattaneo, Mattavelli, Platania, and Papagno (2011) examined gender stereotyping. Two areas of the frontal cortex—the left dorsolateral and right anterior—had been implicated in prior research as related to stereotypical reactions. Magnetic waves were targeted to both these areas while participants performed an implicit association test regarding gender stereotypes. When these regions were stimulated, compared to when they were not, male participants exhibited greater anti-female biases on the IAT. Female participants did not exhibit a gender bias on the test. Generally in TMS research, the technique is coupled with the use of event-related potentials or functional magnetic resonance imaging to verify that that the targeted brain region was indeed stimulated after invoking the magnetic wave.

Brain Wave Measures

In research using techniques of **event-related potential** (ERP), electrodes attached to multiple regions of the scalp are used to measure rapid waves of electrical brain activity arising from the processing of information. An electrical storm of voltage fluctuations is generated while a participant is processing information. Examination of the amplitude of ERP is typically assessed with the procedure known as electroencephalography (EEG), with these terms used interchangeably in the literature. In typical ERP studies, participants are presented with a series of stimuli to process, and then various types of brainwave signals are gauged.

Use of ERP measures in social research include studies of hemispheric asymmetry (differential activation of the right or left hemispheres of the brain under different stimulus conditions or tasks) and computation of the patterns of EEG waveform that follow presentation of a stimulus. In both types of measures, the location and timing interval of differential brain activity is used to assess emotional responding, categorization, and evaluative reactions (Guglielmi, 1999). For example, Cacioppo and his colleagues (e.g., Cacioppo, Crites, Berntson, & Coles, 1993; Cacioppo, Crites, Gardner, & Berntson, 1994) have made use of one component of ERP—the late positive potential (LPP), which occurs approximately 300 milliseconds after onset of a stimulus—to assess implicit positive and negative evaluative reactions. The amplitude of the LPP is larger when a presented stimulus is unexpected or categorically distinct from previously presented stimuli. Thus, to measure whether a stimulus is reacted to negatively, participants are first presented with a series of (known) positive stimuli and then the target stimulus. If ERP amplitude increases significantly in response to the target, it is assumed that a shift to negative evaluation has been registered, even when respondents are unwilling (or unable) to report a negative evaluation overtly.

Neuroimaging

Advances in brain imaging techniques have seen widespread application in the field of cognitive neuroscience and are gradually finding application in social research as well. Regional cerebral blood flow, as measured by *positron emission tomography* (PET) has been used to investigate the relationship between regional brain activity and induction of various emotions, but different studies have produced discrepant findings about the regional differentiation of specific emotions (e.g., Lane, Reiman, Ahern, Schwartz, & Davidson, 1997; Robinson, 1995). PET scans also have been used to assess differences in processing of information relevant to the self and processing of information about others (Craik et al., 1999).

More recently, **functional magnetic resonance imaging** (fMRI), which measures the relative degree of oxygen flow through blood vessels in the brain, identifies which brain regions are implicated in various cognitive and emotional processing functions. Fluctuations in low and high oxygen flow throughout the brain as a result of information processing are detected by placing a participant in a magnetic resonance scanner. Software programs assist researchers by showing the degree of oxygenation in each brain sub-region. Unlike a PET scan, the methods of fMRI do not require participants to ingest some sort of radioactive biochemical substance to trace the movement of a chemical in the brain during mental processing. This is a main reason why fMRI has virtually supplanted PET scanning research. An assumption of fMRI is that a one-to-one correspondence exists between greater brain activity and greater oxygen flow in a locale. Although this correspondence is strong, as cerebral blood flow is indeed linked to brain oxygenation in those same areas, it is possible that processing of some types of information might not attain a sufficient threshold to be biologically detected and indicated in the form of oxygen flow.

Interpreting the results of fMRI output for social research requires a deep understanding of what activation of specific regions of the brain signifies. For example, one intriguing finding with potential social implications is fMRI evidence that processing faces of racial outgroup members generates more activity in the amygdale region of the brain than processing faces of ingroup members. Furthermore, White individuals whose amygdalas fired up the most also scored higher on two other measures of implicit attitudes toward Blacks (Phelps et al., 2000). This result was interpreted in light of other evidence that the amygdala is an area of the brain implicated in negative emotional reactions such as fear and anxiety. However, more recent research indicates that amygdala activation has many different processing implications and, more generally, signals the motivational importance of social stimuli (Van Bavel & Cunningham, 2010). Thus, although exploring the brain activity associated with social processing is generating a great deal of interest, we caution against expecting any simple one-to-one relationships between specific brain regions and complex cognitive and evaluative processes (Willingham & Dunn, 2003).

The output of all three families of brain imaging studies are subject to considerable statistical variation across measurement occasions within the same individual. A neutral stimulus (e.g. blank screen) is often used as a base assessment of random brain activity. This is necessary because the brain remains active even when a participant is not actively processing information or is distracted by random thoughts. Measurable difference in brain activity beyond that of the neutral stimulus may be attributed to processing of the stimulus (signal). A large signal relative to baseline indicates brain reaction and processing of the presented stimulus. Another strategy to rule out interference due to random brain noise is to repeatedly present the same stimulus in sequential trials to the same participant. The patterns of brain activity are then averaged across the multiple trials. The idea is that random noise should cancel out after averaging the many recordings of brain reactions. Brain imaging studies commonly use repeated-measures designs, with each participant serving in the control condition (neutral stimulus) as well as the in the treatment condition (target stimulus).

Statistical variations in brain activity also may fluctuate across people. Because participants arrive at the research laboratory with different preexisting memories and histories, even if viewing the same stimulus, different people might produce slightly different patterns of neuroactivation. Adding to this complexity is that more than one region of the brain could be activated when perceiving a stimulus. However, by conducting social neuroscience research that uses many participants who are presented with the same stimulus, it is possible to determine an "average" or typical pattern of neuroactivation.

Interpreting imaging patterns is still in early stages of development. A frequent question raised about neuroimaging research is the extent to which such studies have external validity or generalizability outside the laboratory (Quadflieg & Macrae, 2011). Given that this research modality typically requires participants to lie down in a still pose and in a confined space while neuroimaging instruments are recording brain activity, subtle head movements will inaccurately isolate the cortical region activated upon receipt of a stimulus. Obviously in natural, everyday situations, people usually are not physically or socially restricted in such unusual ways when processing social information. Furthermore, the types of stimulus and response tasks used in neuroscience methods are relatively artificial and systematically controlled through computer presentation. To illustrate the unusual social context of a brain-imaging study, a presented stimulus might involve a headshot of a person of the opposite sex. This unidirectional process of the participant observing and having a brain response to a static photograph of a head does not mirror the reality of interpersonal social exchanges, which typically include the brain functions of listening, speaking, and physical gesturing. Current technology primarily permits imaging instruments, which are computer intensive and bulky, to be conducted inside the confines of a laboratory. Thus, laboratory research using neuroimaging measurements is susceptible to many of the same advantages (e.g., systematic control of variables) and disadvantages (e.g., artificiality) of laboratory studies in general.

Conclusion

The social cognition methods reviewed in this chapter are intended primarily to assess implicit cognitions and feelings that respondents are unwilling or unable to report on more explicit measures of internal states. Measures of attention, processing time, memory, reaction time, and physiological responses provide a different perspective on mental processes than that provided by traditional self-report methods. When these different types of assessment all converge on the same diagnosis (as evidenced by strong correlations), we have impressive convergent validation of the construct under investigation. But as we have seen, implicit and explicit measures of internal states sometimes produce discrepant findings. Such differences in outcome raise the issue of which methods assess the "true" attitude, feeling, or cognitive process most accurately.

Possibly, discrepancies between explicit and implicit measures of attitudes, feelings, and beliefs reflect the fact that respondents are hiding or misrepresenting their true responses on overt self-report measures. In that case, implicit measures provide a more valid assessment of participants' actual thoughts and feelings, because these are less susceptible to intentional control or deception. And, indeed, it often is the case that discrepancies between implicit and explicit measures occur with respect to assessments of attitudes or beliefs that are undesirable or politically sensitive, such as racial prejudices, stereotyping, or negative emotional states. Another possibility for differences between responses on explicit and implicit responses is not because people deliberately misrepresent their conscious beliefs or feelings, but because their conscious attitudes are in actuality different from their subconscious responses. Explicit attitudes that derive from controlled cognitive processing may reflect what individuals consciously and intentionally believe and value, even though they may hold residues of more negative affective reactions and beliefs at the level of automatic, unintentional processes. In this case, explicit self-report measures may be more valid than implicit measures, if one presumes that most of social life is carried out under consciously controlled processing conditions.

Most researchers who use implicit measures do not contend that such measures are more valid than traditional self-report measures of respondents' true mental or affective states. Rather, most believe that implicit or automatic responses reflect underlying processes different from those assessed via explicit measures. The challenge is to determine which processes and outcomes are related to these implicit measures that are not predicted or accounted for by other methods of assessment. As we have discussed, automatic processes may be more likely to emerge when individuals are performing under cognitive overload or extreme time pressure. There is also evidence that implicit measures of automatic reactions predict subtle nonverbal behaviors in certain social situations better than do explicit measures. For example, in the study we described previously by Fazio et al. (1995) that used sequential priming to assess automatic racial prejudice, the reaction time assessment of automatic evaluation was not correlated with participants' scores on a self-report measure of racial attitudes. However, when participants interacted with a Black confederate of the experimenter after the attitude measurement session, subsequent ratings by the confederate of the participant's friendliness and interest during the interaction proved to be significantly correlated with the individual's evaluative bias in the priming task. Thus, the automatic evaluation measure did seem to successfully predict other subtle, nonverbal (and probably nonconscious) overt behavior. Other studies of the predictive validity of implicit measures such as this will be needed to better understand the relationship between implicit cognitive and affective processes and social behavior.

Questions for Discussion

1. Most measurement instruments (e.g., surveys and other self-report measures) are predicated on the assumption that people have access to their cognitive processes and are sufficiently aware of their psychological states to be able to report them accurately. However, research indicates that we might not always have access to our psychological processes, nor are we always able to accurately determine *why* we are currently feeling or acting a certain way. How might we assess the likelihood that prospective jury members will be racially biased when determining guilt

or innocence, when the jury members themselves do not think they are biased or prejudiced in any way? If you are a consultant for a jury selection firm, how could you estimate people's implicit bias toward certain racial or ethnic groups, particularly in the context of a courtroom (i.e., where using an IAT procedure is not feasible)?

2. Implicit and explicit or self-report measures of the same construct often correlate poorly, or moderately at best with each other. So are our implicit measures assessing the same construct as our explicit measures? Many studies have produced results in which implicit evaluations fluctuated while explicit evaluations remained stable, and vice versa, but does that mean that the different types of measures are assessing different features? Could it be that both types of measures *are* tapping the same construct, but tapping entirely different aspects of that construct? Is there any way we can determine whether this is true? How would you test the convergent and discriminant validity of an implicit measure? Would you expect one implicit measure to be more likely to correlate with another implicit measure than with an explicit measure? Why?

3. Tony suggests that almost all psychological processes can be measured using implicit or indirect techniques, but that we just haven't figured out how to measure some of them. Do you agree? For example, how might we assess the extent to which people identify with a social group or category using indirect or implicit measurements? How could we potentially measure "implicit" attachment style with one's parents without using behavioral observation? Would developing such techniques be worthwhile? What information might they tell us, especially if they correspond poorly with self-report or explicit assessments of the same constructs? How would we know whether the implicit construct we are measuring is "identification" or "attachment style" if the constructs were originally conceptualized in terms of explicit observation and self-report?

Notes

1. Actually, eye fixations shift three or four times a second within minute distances, even while attending to a single object. However, this level of precision is not appropriate for most social research purposes, where more gross assessments of direction of gaze are sufficient.
2. The time interval between presentation and recall can vary from just a few minutes to a matter of hours or days, depending on whether short-term or long-term memories are being assessed. When the recall measure is taken in the same session within minutes of the original presentation, participants are usually given some unrelated "filler" task to occupy their attention during the interval and prevent active rehearsal of the presented materials. When the recall measure occurs at some later time in a separate session, the researcher has less control over the intervening events and cannot know whether the participant has been thinking about or rehearsing the presentation during the lapsed period of time. However, because participants had not been instructed to remember what they experienced, it is generally assumed that such rehearsal is unlikely.
3. Different standards of accuracy may be applied depending on the type of material being recalled. When very specific items of information have been presented, an exact match may be required for correctness. However, when the information is more complex or ambiguous, items are often evaluated by the "gist" criterion. That is, an item is scored as correct if the coder judges that it captures the general idea of what was presented.
4. The same problem applies to interpretation of accurate responses, because we cannot know whether correct items represent actual memory of the presented materials or simply good "guesses." However, the more detailed and complex the information that has been presented and recalled, the less likely it is that guessing accounts for accuracy.
5. The two most commonly used clustering measures are the Stimulus Category Repetition index (SCR) developed by Bousfield and Bousfield (1966), and the Adjusted Ratio of Clustering (ARC) measure recommended by Roenker, Thompson, and Brown (1971). See Hamilton et al. (1980) and Ostrom, Pryor, and Simpson (1980) for discussions of the relative merits of each of these indices for social cognition research.

6. Unless the visual buffer is erased or overwritten, a visual image remains in short-term memory store even after the stimulus image has been removed from the visual field.
7. If the reader is interested in how the IAT is conducted, IAT tests of implicit associations to race, sexual orientation, gender, and age can be accessed on the Internet at https://implicit.harvard.edu/implicit/.

References

Atalay, A. S., Bodur, H. O., & Rasolofoarison, D. (2012). Shining in the center: Central gaze cascade effect on product choice. *Journal of Consumer Research, 39,* 848–866.

Bargh, J. A., Chaiken, S., Rayond, P., & Hymes, C. (1996). The automatic evaluation effect: Unconditionally automatic attitude activation with a pronunciation task. *Journal of Experimental Social Psychology, 32,* 185–210.

Bargh, J. A., & Chartrand, T. L. (2000). Studying the mind in the middle: A practical guide to priming and automaticity research. In H. Reis & C. Judd (Eds.), *Handbook of research methods in social and personality psychology* (pp. 253–285). New York: Cambridge University Press.

Bargh, J. A., Chen, M., & Burrows, L. (1996). Automaticity of social behavior: Direct effects of trait construct and stereotype activation on action. *Journal of Personality and Social Psychology, 71,* 230–244.

Bargh, J. A., & Pietromonaco, P. (1982). Automatic information processing and social perception: The influence of trait information presented outside of conscious awareness on impression formation. *Journal of Personality and Social Psychology, 43,* 437–449.

Bargh, J. A., Raymond, P., Pryor, J., & Strack, F. (1995). The attractiveness of the underling: An automatic power-sex association and its consequences for sexual harassment and aggression. *Journal of Personality and Social Psychology, 68,* 768–781.

Bargh, J. A., & Thein, R. D. (1985). Individual construct accessibility, person memory, and the recall–judgment link: The case of information overload. *Journal of Personality and Social Psychology, 49,* 1129–1146.

Blascovich, J. (2000). Using physiological indexes of psychological processes in social psychology. In H. Reis & C. Judd (Eds.), *Handbook of research methods in social and personality psychology* (pp. 117–137). New York: Cambridge University Press.

Blascovich, J., & , Kelsey, R. M. (1990). Using cardiovascular and electrodermal measures of arousal in social psychological research. In C Hendrick & M. Clark (Eds.), *Research methods in personality and social psychology* (pp. 45–73). Newbury Park, CA: Sage.

Blascovich, J., & McCall, C. (2013). Social influence in virtual environments. In K. E. Dill (Ed.), *The Oxford handbook of media psychology* (pp. 305–315). New York: Oxford University Press.

Blascovich, J., Mendes, W., Hunter, S., Lickel, B., & Kowai-Bell, N. (2001). Perceiver threat in social interactions with stigmatized others. *Journal of Personality and Social Psychology, 80,* 253–267.

Bligh, M. C., & Kohles, J. C. (2008). Negotiating gender role expectations: Rhetorical leadership and women in the US senate. *Leadership, 4,* 381–402.

Bligh, M. C., & Robinson, J. L. (2010). Was Gandhi "charismatic"? Exploring the rhetorical leadership of Mahatma Gandhi. *The Leadership Quarterly, 21,* 844–855.

Bousfield, A. K., & Bousfield, W. A. (1966). Measurement of clustering and sequential constancies in repeated free recall. *Psychological Reports, 19,* 935–942.

Brewer, M. B., Dull, V., & Lui, L. (1981). Perceptions of the elderly: Stereotypes as prototypes. *Journal of Personality and Social Psychology, 41,* 656–670.

Cacioppo, J. T., Berntson, G. G., Ernst, J. M., & Ito, T. A. (2000). Social neuroscience. In A. E. Kazdin (Ed.), *Encyclopedia of psychology, Vol. 7* (pp. 353–355). Washington, DC, and New York: American Psychological Association.

Cacioppo, J. T., Crites, S., Berntson, G., & Coles, M. (1993). If attitudes affect how stimuli are processed, should they not affect the event-related brain potential? *Psychological Science, 4,* 108–112.

Cacioppo, J. T., Crites, S., Gardner, W., & Berntson, G. (1994). Bioelectrical echoes from evaluative categorizations: I. A late positive brain potential that varies as a function of trait negativity and extremity. *Journal of Personality and Social Psychology, 67,* 115–125.

Cacioppo, J. T., & Petty, R. E. (1981). Electromyograms as measures of extent and affectivity of information processing. *American Psychologist, 36,* 441–456.

Cacioppo, J. T., & Petty, R. E. (Eds.) (1983). *Social psychophysiology: A sourcebook.* New York: Guilford.

Cacioppo, J. T., Petty, R. E., Losch, M, & Kim, H. (1986). Electromyographic activity over facial muscle regions can differentiate the valence and intensity of affective reactions. *Journal of Personality and Social Psychology, 50*, 20–268.

Cantor, N., & Mischel, W. (1977). Traits as prototypes: Effects on recognition memory. *Journal of Personality and Social Psychology, 35*, 38–48.

Cattaneo, Z., Mattavelli, G., Platania, E., & Papagno, C. (2011). The role of the prefrontal cortex in controlling gender-stereotypical associations: A TMS investigation. *Neuorimage, 56*, 1839–1846.

Chartrand, T. L., & Bargh, J. A. (1996). Automatic activation of impression formation and memorization goals: Nonconscious goal priming reproduces effects of explicit task instructions. *Journal of Personality and Social Psychology, 71*, 464–478.

Conrey, F., Sherman, J., Gawronski, B., Hugenberg, K., & Groom, C. (2005). Separating multiple processes in implicit social cognition: The Quad-Model of implicit task performance. *Journal of Personality and Social Psychology, 89*, 469–487.

Craik, F., Moroz, T., Moscovitch, M., Stuss, D., Winocur, G., Tulving, E., & Kapur, S. (1999). In search of the self: A positron emission tomography study. *Psychological Science, 10*, 26–34.

Cunningham, S. J., & Macrae, C. N. (2011). The colour of gender stereotyping. *British Journal of Psychology, 102*, 598–614.

Devine, P. G. (1989). Stereotypes and prejudice: Their automatic and controlled components. *Journal of Personality and Social Psychology, 56*, 680–690.

Devine, P. G., Forscher, P. S., Austin, A. J., & Cox, W.T.L. (2012). Long-term reduction in implicit race bias: A prejudice habit-breaking intervention. *Journal of Experimental Social Psychology, 48*(6), 1267–1278.

Dienstbier, R A. (1989). Arousal and physiological toughness: Implications for mental and physical health. *Psychological Review, 96*, 84–100.

Donaldson, W., & Glathe, H. (1970). Signal-detection analysis of recall and recognition memory. *Canadian Journal of Psychology, 24*, 42–56.

Dovidio, J. F., & Fazio, R. H. (1992). New technologies for the direct and indirect assessment of attitudes. In J. M. Tanur, (Ed.), *Questions about questions: Inquiries into the cognitive bases of surveys* (pp. 204–237). New York: Russell Sage Foundation.

Ekman, P. (1993). Facial expression of emotion. *American Psychologist, 48*, 384–392.

Ekman, P. (2007). *Emotions revealed* (2nd ed.). New York: Holt.

Ekman, P., & Friesen, W. V. (1978). *Facial action coding system: A technique for the measurement of facial movement.* Palo Alto, CA: Consulting Psychologists Press.

Fazio, R. H., Jackson, J. R. Dunton, B. C., & Williams, C. J. (1995). Variability in automatic activation as an unobtrusive measure of racial attitudes: A bona fide pipeline? *Journal of Personality and Social Psychology, 69*, 1013–1027.

Fazio, R. H., Sanbonmatsu, D. M., Powell, M. C., & Kardes, F. R. (1986). On the automatic activation of attitudes. *Journal of Personality and Social Psychology, 50*, 229–238.

Fiske, S. T. (1980). Attention and weight in person perception: The impact of extreme and negative behavior. *Journal of Personality and Social Psychology, 38*, 889–906.

Gardiner, G. S., & Schroder, H. M. (1972). Reliability and validity of the Paragraph Completion Test: Theoretical and empirical notes. *Psychological Reports, 31*, 959–962.

Gilbert, D. T., & Hixon, J. G. (1991). The trouble of thinking: Activation and application of stereotypic beliefs. *Journal of Personality and Social Psychology, 60*, 509–517.

Gilbert, D. T., & Osborne, R. E. (1989). Thinking backward: Some curable and incurable consequences of cognitive busyness. *Journal of Personality and Social Psychology, 57*, 940–949.

Gilbert, D. T., Pelham, B. W., & Krull, D. S. (1988). On cognitive busyness: When person perceivers meet persons perceived. *Journal of Personality and Social Psychology, 54*, 733–740.

Greenwald, A. G., McGhee, D. E., & Schwartz, J. (1998). Measuring individual differences in implicit cognition: The implicit association test. *Journal of Personality and Social Psychology, 74*, 1464–1480.

Guglielmi, R. S. (1999). Psychophysiological assessment of prejudice: Past research, current status, and future directions. *Personality and Social Psychology Review, 3*, 123–157.

Hamilton, D. L., Katz, L. B., & Leirer, V. O. (1980). Organizational processes in impression formation. In R. Hastie, T. Ostrom, E. Ebbesen, R. Wyer, D. Hamilton, & D. Carlston (Eds.), *Person memory: The cognitive basis of social perception* (pp. 121–153). Hillsdale, NJ: Lawrence Erlbaum.

Higgins, E. T., Rholes, W. S., & Jones, C. R. (1977). Category accessibility and impression formation. *Journal of Experimental Social Psychology, 13,* 141–154.

Hoffmann, W., Gawronski, B., Gschwendner, T., Le, H., & Schmitt, M. (2005). A meta-analysis on the correlation between implicit association test and explicit self-report measures. *Personality and Social Psychology Bulletin, 31,* 1369–1385.

Kidder, L. H., & Campbell, D. T. (1970). The indirect testing of social attitudes. In G. Summers (Ed.), *Attitude measurement* (pp. 333–385). Chicago: Rand-McNally.

Lane, R. D., Reiman, E., Ahern, G., Schwartz, G., & Davidson, R. (1997). Neuroanatomical correlates of happiness, sadness, and disgust. *American Journal of Psychiatry, 154,* 926–933.

Lang, P. J., Bradley, M. M., & Cuthbert, B. N. (1990). Emotion, attention, and the startle reflex. *Psychological Review, 97,* 377–395.

Lang, P. J., Bradley, M. M., & Cuthbert, B. N. (1992). A motivational analysis of emotion: Reflex-cortex connections. *Psychological Science, 3,* 44–49.

Logan, G. D. (1980). Attention and automaticity in Stroop and priming tasks: Theory and data. *Cognitive Psychology, 12*(4), 523–553.

MacLeod, C. (1991). Half a century of research on the Stroop effect: An integrative review. *Psychological Bulletin, 109,* 163–203.

Macrae, C. N., Bodenhausen, G. V., & Milne, A. B. (1995). The dissection of selection in person perception: Inhibitory processes in social stereotyping. *Journal of Personality and Social Psychology, 69,* 397–407.

McArthur, L. Z., & Ginsberg, E. (1981). Causal attribution to salient stimuli: An investigation of visual fixation mediators. *Personality and Social Psychology Bulletin, 7,* 547–553.

Neely, J. H. (1977). Semantic priming and retrieval from lexical memory: Roles of inhibitionless spreading activation and limited-capacity attention. *Journal of Experimental Psychology: General, 106,* 226–254.

Nisbett, R. E., & Wilson, T. D. (1977). Telling more than we can know: Verbal reports on mental processes. *Psychological Review, 84,* 231–259.

Norman, G. J., Hawkley, L. C., Luhmann, M., Cacioppo, J. T., & Berntson, G. G. (2013). Social neuroscience and the modern synthesis of social and biological levels of analysis. In D. D. Franks & J. H. Turner (Eds.), *Handbook of neurosociology* (pp. 67–81). New York: Springer Science + Business Media.

Olson, J., & Zanna, M. (1979). A new look at selective exposure. *Journal of Experimental Social Psychology, 15,* 1–15.

Ostrom, T. M., Pryor, J. B., & Simpson, D. D. (1981). The organization of social information. In E. T. Higgins, C. P. Herman, & M. Zanna (Eds.), *Social cognition: The Ontario Symposium* (vol. 1, pp. 3–38). Hillsdale, NJ: Lawrence Erlbaum.

Oswald, F. L., Mitchell, G., Blanton, H., Jaccard, J., & Tetlock, P. E. (2013). Predicting ethnic and racial discrimination: A meta-analysis of IAT criterion studies. *Journal of Personality and Social Psychology, 105,* 171–192.

Parker, S., Clarke, C., Moniz-Cook, E., & Gardiner, E. (2012). The influence of 'cognitive busyness' on causal attributions of challenging behaviour in dementia: A preliminary experimental study. *Aging & Mental Health, 16,* 836–844.

Payne, B. K. (2001). Prejudice and perception: The role of automatic and controlled processes in misperceiving a weapon. *Journal of Personality and Social Psychology, 81,* 181–192.

Petty, R. E., & Cacioppo, J. T. (1986). *Communication and persuasion: Central and peripheral routes to attitude change.* New York: Springer-Verlag.

Phelps, E. A., O'Connor, K. J., Cunningham, W. A., Funayama, E. S., Gatenby, J. C., Gore, J. C., & Banaji, M. R. (2000). Performance on indirect measures of race evaluation predicts amygdala activation. *Journal of Cognitive Neuroscience, 12,* 729–738.

Pratto, F., & John, O. P. (1991). Automatic vigilance: The attention-grabbing power of negative social information. *Journal of Personality and Social Psychology, 61,* 380–391.

Pryor, J. B., & Ostrom, T. M. (1981). The cognitive organization of social information: A converging-operations approach. *Journal of Personality and Social Psychology, 41,* 628–641.

Quadflieg, S., & Macrae, C. N. (2011). Stereotypes and stereotyping: What's the brain got to do with it? *European Review of Social Psychology, 22,* 215–273.

Robinson, R. G. (1995). Mapping brain activity associated with emotion. *American Journal of Psychiatry, 152,* 327–329.

Roenker, D. L., Thompson, C. P., & Brown, S. C. (1971). Comparison of measures for the estimation of clustering in free recall. *Psychological Bulletin, 76,* 45–48.

Schroder, H. M., Driver, M. J., & Streufert, S. S. (1967). *Human information processing.* New York: Holt, Rinehart & Winston.

Seyranian, V., & Bligh, M. C. (2008). Presidential charismatic leadership: Exploring the rhetoric of social change. *The Leadership Quarterly, 19,* 54–76.

Srull, T. K., & Wyer, R. S., Jr. (1979). The role of category accessibility in the interpretation of information about persons: Some determinants and implications. *Journal of Personality and Social Psychology, 37,* 1660–1672.

Stroop, J. R. (1935). Studies of interference in serial verbal reactions. *Journal of Experimental Psychology, 18,* 643–662.

Suedfeld, P., Guttieri, K., & Tetlock, P. E. (2005). Assessing integrative complexity at a distance: Archival analyses of thinking and decision making. In J. M. Post (Ed.), *The psychological assessment of political leaders: With profiles of Saddam Hussein and Bill Clinton* (pp. 246–270). Ann Arbor, MI: The University of Michigan Press.

Suedfeld, P., Tetlock, P. E., & Streufert, S. (1992). Conceptual/integrative complexity. In C. P. Smith, J. W. Atkinson, D. C. McClelland & J. Veroff (Eds.), *Motivation and personality: Handbook of thematic content analysis* (pp. 393–400). New York: Cambridge University Press.

Taylor, S. E., & Fiske, S. T. (1981). Getting inside the head: Methodologies for process analysis in attribution and social cognition. In J. Harvey, W. Ickes, & R. Kidd (Eds.), *New directions in attribution research* (vol. 3, pp. 459–524). Hillsdale, NJ: Erlbaum.

Taylor, S. E., Fiske, S. T., Etcoff, N., & Ruderman, A. (1978). The categorical and contextual bases of person memory and stereotyping. *Journal of Personality and Social Psychology, 36,* 778–793.

Tomaka, J., & Blascovich, J. (1994). Effects of justice beliefs on cognitive appraisal of and subjective, physiological, and behavioral responses to potential stress. *Journal of Personality and Social Psychology, 67,* 732–740.

Tomaka, J., Blascovich, J., Kelsey, R. M., & Leitten, C. L. (1993). Subjective, physiological, and behavioral effects of threat and challenge appraisal. *Journal of Personality and Social Psychology, 65,* 248–260.

Van Bavel, J. J., & Cunningham, W. A. (2010). A social neuroscience approach to self and social categorisation: A new look at an old issue. *European Review of Social Psychology, 21,* 237–284.

Vanman, E. J., Paul, B. Y., Ito, T. A., & Miller, N. (1997). The modern face of prejudice and structural features that moderate the effect of cooperation on affect. *Journal of Personality and Social Psychology, 73,* 941–959.

Willingham, D. T., & Dunn, E. W. (2003). What neuroimaging and brain localization can do, cannot do, and should not do for social psychology. *Journal of Personality and Social Psychology, 85,* 662–671.

17
SCALING STIMULI
Social Psychophysics

Developing and using scales of high utility, generality, and psychometric quality (i.e., of high reliability and validity) is a common part of the social researcher's job description. As discussed in Chapter 15, questionnaires and rating scales are constructed to measure differences among individuals. For example, a scale of attitudes toward nuclear energy, assessed with multiple items, has as its purpose the classification of individuals along a continuum, so that those with the highest scores are defined as most in favor of adopting nuclear energy, and those with the lowest scores as least in favor. Those scoring in the middle are considered intermediate on their attitudes toward this energy source. In this form of scaling, the items are used to compute a summary score for the purpose of arranging people at some point on the scale: All items are designed to tap the same construct, they are assumed to differ only in terms of measurement error. So on our attitudes toward nuclear energy scale, we assume that the questions (items) we pose to respondents, and that are used to create our summary score, all tap the same underlying construct (in this case, attitudes toward nuclear energy). Measures of this variety are called scales of differences among individuals, *or* scales of individual differences. Individual difference scales are the most common form of scale used in contemporary social research.

Though less common, we sometimes are concerned with perceived differences among a set of stimuli (i.e., to what extent stimulus 1 differs from stimulus 2 and 3), rather than differences among a set of respondents (i.e., to what extent person 1 differs from persons 2 and 3). Developing measurement scales that tap into perceived differences among stimuli (instead of differences between individuals) is called **stimulus scaling** (or *scales of stimulus differences*). As will be shown, creating stimulus scales calls for an approach and a set of assumptions that are quite different from those used in individual differences scaling.

The psychophysicists of 100 years ago attempted to bring the measurement logic of physics into the psychological laboratory—to borrow and apply the methods of measurement used in the physical sciences to the behavioral sciences. They were interested in developing measures of features for which no obvious metric existed (e.g., beauty, taste, preference for violent movies, etc.), and to do so with high degrees of reliability and validity. A central goal of their efforts was to produce measures that accurately represented the judgments of the sample on which the measure was based. It is for this reason that Dawes and Smith (1985, p. 515), referred to stimulus scales as "group attitude scales." The real utility of the stimulus scaling approaches is that they allow us to impose a metric on judgments for which no obvious "yardstick" exists. In the physical sciences, this issue usually does not arise—if we wish to know the weight of an object, we place it on a scale; if we wish to know the loudness of a sound, we use a decibel meter. But suppose we want to order a group of people's judgments of 10 paintings, from most to least beautiful, and to do so in a way that the distances between adjacent points on our "beauty" scale are approximately equal. Or, more prosaically, suppose we wanted to have a group of friends arrange 10 different brands of pizza from most to least delicious, along a "deliciousness" continuum that represented the group judgment and also provided a clear indication of the distances that separated one pizza from the others.

With these two sets of stimuli, no obvious physical yardstick exists. We do not have rulers with which we can unambiguously and with high consensus judge beauty or deliciousness. However, such scales can be developed. In building such a scale, any differences in people's orderings, which signify individual differences of opinion that could vary from person to person, are considered irrelevant. The statistical treatment of the data, collapsed across all respondents in the entire sample, reveals not only the relative popularity of each of the stimuli, but also their relative distances from one another, on a scale having interval properties (i.e., equal distances separate contiguous units across the entire continuum). In marketing research conducted by a pizza company, such findings might be profitably used in an effort to mimic the ingredients of the most popular brand, or to identify the closest competitors.

In stimulus scaling we are concerned principally with differences between stimuli (or items). As such, systematic variations among stimuli are considered meaningful and important—they are the focus of investigation and, as noted, variations in judgments among participants are considered the result of measurement error. This is an important distinction between stimulus scaling and individual differences scaling, and this bears reemphasis. In stimulus scaling, we assume that individual differences in perceptions and evaluations of the stimuli being judged are the result of error. Differences in respondents' judgments are not viewed as the result of meaningful differences among people. The opposite assumption is made in scaling individuals—that is, we assume that there are no differences among the stimuli (or items) that constitute the measurement instrument. Unless we learn otherwise, all items are assumed to tap the same underlying construct—belief, trait, attitude, intention; in scales of individual differences, variations between respondents are real and potentially meaningful. The differences in underlying assumptions between stimulus and individual differences scaling are important. They indicate that the two scaling approaches should be applied to different types of research problems, because they will produce different outcomes and different ways of arranging stimuli and people. Each type of scaling method is valuable in its own right, and each satisfies different research needs.

Scaling Stimuli

Although judgments of human respondents are used to construct scales of stimuli and scales of individual differences, the approaches require development of different measurement operations. A typical use of stimulus scaling techniques is found in marketing research, where a researcher may be interested in comparative evaluations of different products, brands, packages, etc. Another use is found in the political arena, where comparative evaluations of competing candidates or social policies might be under scrutiny, or in criminology, where the perceived seriousness of different types of crimes might be at issue.

Typically in stimulus scaling studies, respondents compare one stimulus against all the others along a specific dimension or quality, or judge stimuli in terms of their degree of similarity or dissimilarity. These comparisons are used to form a continuum, choice matrix, or perceptual map that represents the aggregate judgment of perceived stimuli of the entire respondent sample (Hout, Goldinger, & Ferguson, 2013).[1] This judgmental continuum provides a summary of participants' opinions regarding relative similarities of the objects in the stimulus set. Using this technique, we obtain an ordering of stimuli along the continuum, and, perhaps more importantly, the intervals along the continuum are equal—in other words, the procedure produces scales of equal unit interval quality.

In one of the classic stimulus scaling investigations, Louis Thurstone (1927) assessed the beliefs of 266 University of Chicago students regarding the seriousness of 19 different crimes. The crimes included, among others, arson, bootlegging, forgery, homicide, larceny, libel, perjury, rape, and smuggling.[2] Rather than ask the students to rate the seriousness of each crime on 10-point scales, Thurstone paired every crime with each of the others, and asked his participants simply to underline the more serious of the two for every comparison. So, on a given judgment, a participant might be asked to judge whether perjury or rape was the more serious crime. On the next judgment, the participant might judge the more serious of libel vs. bootlegging. Crano and Cooper (1973) have argued that such binary judgments often are more reliable and less demanding of respondents, compared to those that require fine-grained ratings or discriminations. It is for this reason, among others, that stimulus scaling approaches are sometimes preferred to other techniques of determining people's beliefs.

Interestingly, Thurstone's results revealed that his sample of university students (in 1927) considered crimes against persons (homicide, rape, kidnapping, assault) as being the most serious, just as students today probably would. Property offenses and victimless crimes (vagrancy, receiving stolen goods, etc.) fell into the less serious segment of the scale. Later replications of this study by Coombs (1967) and Borg (1988) produced results consistent with the early findings, though the researchers did find some deviations from the original study. For example, in Coombs's (1967) study, 369 University of Michigan students served as participants. They judged rape the most serious offense and homicide as the second most serious, whereas this ordering was reversed in Thurstone's (1927) original study. Coombs's research also disclosed that students of 1967 did not consider bootlegging nearly as serious as Thurstone's participants had, whereas seduction of a minor was considered more serious in the later sample. These variations between studies probably are attributable to changing attitudes over time, or with differences in the interpretation of various crime labels, and provide interesting insights into contemporary views of crime.[3]

Techniques for Stimulus Scaling

The Method of Pair Comparison Scaling

Of all the classic psychometric stimulus scaling techniques, two approaches—the method of pair comparison and the method of rank order—are most common in social research. In the method of **pair comparison scaling**, a set of stimuli is examined by presenting every possible pair of stimuli to each respondent, whose task is to choose whether they prefer one stimulus over the other with which it is paired on the basis of a quality or dimension (e.g., beauty, taste, sex appeal) stipulated by the researcher. This is the method Thurstone (1927) used in his study of the perceived seriousness of crimes. The choices are aggregated across all participants, and the analysis of the data provides a summary of the respondent group's order of preferences among stimuli.

To lend some degree of concreteness to this discussion, consider the following example. Suppose that we were interested in respondents' attitudes regarding relative differences in acting ability among six popular male actors. This *stimulus set* includes Brad Pitt, Tom Cruise, Johnny Depp, Leonardo DiCaprio, Morgan Freeman, and Anthony Hopkins.

Notice that we are not concerned that one respondent thinks that Hopkins is a better actor than Depp, whereas another has the opposite opinion. In stimulus scaling, we are concerned with how the stimuli (our six actors) are arranged along a continuum of acting ability by the total sample. Differences of opinion among the individuals who constitute the sample are not at issue. Indeed, as noted, these participant differences are considered a form of measurement error.

There is no obvious "acting ability" yardstick that we can use to order these actors, yet the task is far from impossible. Employing the method of pair comparison scaling, we would first assemble every possible pair of actors. In this case, this process would yield 15 non-repetitive pairs.[4] For example, Depp would be paired with Cruise, DiCaprio, Freeman, Hopkins, and Pitt; Cruise with DiCaprio, Freeman, Hopkins, and Pitt, and so on. Identical stimuli would not be paired (i.e., Depp would not be paired with Depp, as this is considered a repetitive pair). Then, each of the pairings would be presented to each respondent, with the instructions, "On each card, circle the better actor of each pair." To facilitate this task and to avoid problems that might occur if every participant received the same ordering of pairs, we might place each pair of names on index cards and randomly shuffle the cards prior to giving them to participants. The process of presentation and randomization of each pair can be facilitated with a computer. The entire deck of index-card stimuli might look like those of Figure 17.1.

Suppose we administered our set of 15 pair comparison cards to 100 volunteers. To summarize the obtained data, we could arrange respondents' judgments in a *choice matrix*, as in Table 17.1. In this matrix, the cell entries represent the number of respondents who chose the *column* stimulus over the *row* stimulus. So in Table 17.1, the data indicate that Depp was chosen over Cruise by 40 of 100 respondents (conversely, Cruise was chosen by 60 of 100 participants as a better actor than Depp). Freeman was chosen by an equal number of respondents when compared with Pitt. Although no pairing entailed Depp vs. Depp, it is standard to enter an equal probability of selection (e.g., 50) for the diagonal values of the matrix. The column mean gives a reasonable indication of the aggregate opinion regarding acting ability by the sample who judged the stimulus set. The mean data suggest that the respondents viewed DiCaprio and Pitt as fairly comparable and superior to Cruise and Depp; Hopkins and Freeman were judged the best of the lot, with Hopkins a clear favorite of the

FIGURE 17.1 Stimuli used in the pair comparison scaling study of actors. The instructions to the task might read, "On each card, circle the better actor of each pair."

TABLE 17.1 Similarity (or choice) matrix in a pair comparison scaling study of acting ability (n = 100).

Actor	Depp	Cruise	DiCaprio	Freeman	Hopkins	Pitt
Depp	50	60	55	50	70	60
Cruise	40	50	60	70	80	60
DiCaprio	45	40	50	60	60	45
Freeman	50	30	40	50	60	50
Hopkins	30	20	40	40	50	35
Pitt	40	40	55	50	65	50
Mean	42.5	40.0	50.0	53.3	63.3	50.0

sample. If this sample were drawn in such a manner as to make it representative of a population (say, of college students, members of the Motion Pictures Academy of Arts and Sciences, citizens of Monaco, etc.), we might generalize these results to the population from which they were drawn.

If we wanted to develop a comprehensive index of the respondents' choices that had the property of an *interval scale*, we would transform the choice matrix to a proportion matrix by dividing each frequency by the total number of respondents. Then, following Guilford (1954, pp. 154–177), we would perform a set of statistical operations on the data to determine if respondents' choices satisfied a set of necessary assumptions. The assumptions are focused on the issue of whether the aggregated data accurately reproduce the matrix of data from which they were calculated. If they do, the ordering of the stimuli are said to have equal-interval properties. That is, identical differences separating the stimuli are meaningful at all points of the scale. Thus, a .15 unit difference between stimuli falling at one end of the scale is the same as a .15 unit difference between stimuli falling at the opposite end of the scale. The scale, in other words, has the property of equal intervals.

For example, when using the method of pair comparisons, if the mean acting abilities of three actors were 60 for Actor A, 50 for Actor B and 40 for Actor C, then the researcher may be able to state that the extent that Actor A is a better actor over Actor B reflects the same difference in acting ability of actor B over actor C. We can infer more from equal-interval data than the mere order of the stimuli (as would be the case if an *ordinal scale* were formed).

Data *transitivity* is a central assumption of the scaling operations employed to transform respondents' preferences into a scale of equal interval quality. The transitivity of preferences must be satisfied if the researcher is to convert binary judgments of paired comparisons of data that are ordinal quality or higher.[5] Transitivity implies logical consistency in judgment, such that if a group of respondents feel that Hopkins is a better actor than Pitt, and Pitt better than Cruise, then they should judge Hopkins better than Cruise. Such a set of transitive judgments would be expressed as follows:

> If Hopkins is judged better than Pitt,
> and Pitt is judged better than Cruise,
> then Hopkins *should* be judged better than Cruise

It sometimes happens that a transitive relationship of this type is not obtained (e.g., in this example, Cruise might be judged better than Hopkins). Intransitive or logically inconsistent choices can be caused by many factors. For example, the stimuli might appear so similar on the choice dimension that respondents cannot differentiate them reliably. Judges who were wildly enthusiastic about all the actors, or hated all of them more or less equally, would be hard put to differentiate them in a transitive manner. Another possibility is that the scale along which respondents judge the stimuli is multidimensional. In our actor-rating example, it might be that an individual's choice of Cruise over Hopkins was dictated by sex appeal, whereas the choice of Hopkins over Pitt was based on difference in the actors' voice quality; Pitt might be favored over Cruise owing to his appearance in a new movie the respondent enjoyed very much, or by some complex interaction of the voice quality and sex appeal factors (see Tversky, 1969).

A sufficient number of unreliable or intransitive choices made by the sample will result in a data set that will not satisfy the minimum criteria of scale quality. That is, tests used to determine the reliability of the scale will indicate that the data upon which the scale is to be based are not sufficiently trustworthy to put any faith in the resulting scale (Mosteller, 1951). In this situation, the researcher is in a difficult position. It is clear that the scaling process has failed, but why it failed is uncertain. Some likely possibilities to investigate when seeking the source of the problem involve participants' familiarity with the stimulus dimension, the definitional specificity of the choice dimension, the differentiability of the stimuli, and the dimensionality or clarity of the choice dimension that is used to judge the stimuli.

Participants' familiarity with the stimuli being judged is the easiest issue to assess, but the hardest to offset. It sometimes happens that some fraction of the participant sample simply is unfamiliar with all the stimuli that are to be compared. For example, suppose that some of our participants did not know much about Brad Pitt, and could not remember what Anthony Hopkins looked like. They could not be expected to compare these actors reliably with others whom they could recall. Comparisons involving these unfamiliar stimulus objects well might prove unreliable, or intransitive, and thus spoil the overall scale.

Sometimes, the choice dimension is not specified clearly, or, if clearly specified, is not one that participants can use consistently. Returning again to our actor example, good acting involves many different qualities. If we are not specific about the particular quality or dimension we wish our sample to use in forming their evaluations, the complexity of the judgment dimension will defeat our attempts at developing a reliable measure. Thus, the researcher must provide clear instructions regarding the particular dimension to be used in judging the stimulus set.

The issue of specificity is related to the multidimensionality of the choice dimension the participants use in forming their judgments. We know that quality of acting can be differentiated along a number of different dimensions (e.g., quality of voice, dramatic expression, subtlety of body movements, etc.). If our participants were not provided clear and explicit guidelines regarding the dimension to judge the stimuli, and instead used one dimension in one comparison and another in a later comparison, there is a good possibility that the judgments will prove intransitive. The shift in dimensions used from one judgment to another will cause inconsistencies within a respondent. If a sufficient number of judgments (or judges) suffer from this problem, the scale will not be reliable.

The differentiability of the stimuli also can prove problematic in stimulus scale construction. For example, suppose we wanted to order the stimulus set of popular brands of beer along a dimension of tastiness. We ask our sample to judge among the following seven beers: Amstel, Beck's, Budweiser, Guinness, Heineken, Michelob, and Rolling Rock. Although all of our judges have experienced each brand at one time or another, some of them (not being connoisseurs of the art form) might not be able to distinguish among all, or many, of them. This is not necessarily the result of unfamiliarity. For some, it may be that the differences among the various beers simply are not detectable. In this case the scaling effort will fail. Indeed, it would fail even if the pair comparison study were run as a taste test—that is, if participants were given small glasses of beer to taste and compare, rather than trying to match taste with brand from memory (remember, with 7 stimuli, this would require 21 pair comparisons, or 42 small glasses of beer). If the beers were relatively indistinguishable—or even if two or three of them were—the researcher might find that the resulting choice matrix would not allow for development of a reliable measurement scale.

Another problem that can arise when we choose to use a pair comparison scaling approach comes about because of participant fatigue. Recall that N(N–1)/2 non-repeated pairs of combinations can be derived from N stimuli. Thus, if our research problem involved the judgment of 20 actors' ability, or 20 beers, each respondent would have had to make 190 comparisons. Distortion of results attributable to boredom, fatigue or, in the case of the beer example, intoxication, is possible in such situations and would produce a data set that probably would not result in a reliable stimulus scale. Some researchers reduce the complexity of the problem by not administering the complete set of all possible pairings to the entire sample. That is, participants judge a different subset of the pair comparisons. Statistical procedures are available to allow this form of pared-down comparative process, but presentation of the complete set of paired stimuli to all judges is preferable. Other researchers divide the task across multiple testing occasions. For example, half of all the item pairs are judged first, the remaining subset judged later. This, too, lightens participant load, but variations between test days may introduce unacceptable amounts of error into the process. The problem is best solved by using a relatively restricted number of stimuli which, when paired using all possible combinations, do not produce an overwhelming demand on participants' stamina.[6]

Lest we paint too gloomy a picture, we should recognize the positive features of the pair comparison scaling approach. Under appropriate circumstances, the method can produce an accurate and concise summary of a group's judgments, even when the dimension along which the judgments are made has no obvious physical metric. The "appropriate circumstances" involve a set of well-defined stimuli that are discriminable and familiar to the respondents and a unidimensional judgment rule that is precisely stipulated in the instructions. Furthermore, there should be a reasonable number of stimuli that does not overburden the stamina or cognitive capacities of respondents.

It should be understood that interval scale results do not allow for absolute judgments, or judgments that entail ratio-level data (e.g., this actor (or beer, or pizza) is twice good as the competition). Although Anthony Hopkins was rated tops in our hypothetical exercise, for instance, it is possible that in an absolute sense the majority of respondents consider him a very poor actor. Hopkins falling at the top of the scale does not necessarily imply that the respondents thought him a great, or even a good, actor—possibly, they simply found him less bad than the others in the comparison group. Only data of *ratio* quality provide a true zero-point, which in the present instance would allow us to determine whether the aggregate participant sample viewed the top-rated actor as good or bad. If a true zero point had been established (by other scaling methods), we could infer that actors falling above zero had been viewed positively by the sample; those below it were seen as bad actors. In addition, the presence of the true zero would allow us to determine the degree to which one stimulus exceeded another on the dimension used by the sample to differentiate the stimuli.[7]

The Method of Rank Order

In the method of **rank order scaling**, a set of stimuli is examined by having each respondent order all stimuli simultaneously along a choice dimension stipulated by the researcher. Rank order scaling is a comparative stimulus scaling technique that enables the researcher to avoid many of the problems inherent in the pair comparison scaling, while producing results that closely approximate that of the more laborious pair comparison method (Misra & Dutt, 1965). Modifying the previous example, we could present our six actors to participants and ask them to rank them in order of acting ability, with 1 representing the best actor and 6 representing the worst actor. If using index cards, the names of the six actors are individually written on different index cards. Then, participants merely sort the names from best to worst actor. From the data obtained in this simple operation, we could construct an equal-interval scale of participants' judgments (see Guilford, 1954, pp. 178–196, for a description of the statistical operations to be used). Notice that this technique avoids two potentially serious problems of the pair comparison scaling approach. First, because all objects of judgment are presented at once and the respondent simultaneously ranks them, judgmental intransitivity is impossible. If A is ranked over B, and B over C, then A must be ranked over C in the rank order approach. In addition, the method of rank order avoids some of the administrative drudgery of pair comparison scaling, especially when large numbers of stimuli are to be compared.

Recall that a total of 190 pair comparisons would be generated from a set of 20 stimuli. If the method of rank order were used, the task would be confined to the judgments involved in ordering only those 20. Thus, the technique appears to demand less of the respondents. Nonetheless, some prefer the pair comparison scaling approach in situations involving small numbers of stimuli (say, 10 or fewer). In these situations, participants' responses are thought to be more reliable than in a rank order task because only two objects of judgment are involved in any given pair comparison (cf. Crano & Cooper, 1973). Proponents of pair comparison scaling believe that the dimension along which stimuli are to be judged can be held in mind more faithfully when it need be applied in choices involving only two stimuli. In the rank order method, it could be argued that essentially all the stimuli are judged at once. On the other hand, if a large number (more than 20) items are in the stimulus set, even the rank-order method may be overly demanding for respondents, who may find it difficult to hold that many stimuli in mind at one time.

Aside from these distinctions, the methods of pair comparison and rank order scaling share noteworthy similarities. First, both methods are used to generate *comparative judgments* of a set of stimuli. That is, either scaling process provides information regarding relative differences between stimuli as judged by the participant sample, and these differences are arranged on a scale of equal intervals. Note that neither method provides information regarding the judges' *absolute* appraisal of the rated objects on a ratio scale.

Another important similarity between these two stimulus scaling methods concerns the assumptions regarding differences between participants' ratings. Because responses to stimulus objects are pooled across participants in both methods, differences between participants are considered irrelevant and therefore are ignored. Respondents are viewed as replicates, and differences among them are attributed to error or unreliability. In other words, by virtue of the way in which the data are assembled and combined, these approaches assume that all participants in a sample would produce the identical pattern of choices if their judgments were perfectly reliable. This assumption is necessary to justify the pooling of responses over participants. Fortunately, violations of this assumption can be tested (see Guilford, 1954; Torgerson, 1958), and if the violation is not too extreme, it can be offset.

Multidimensional Scaling Models

The scaling techniques we have discussed to this point are designed to develop unidimensional scales. Indeed, researchers working in this scaling tradition generally strive to achieve unidimensionality in their scales. If judges can slide from one dimension to another when comparing stimuli, the classic psychometric methods fail to produce reliable measures, and this is especially problematic in pair comparison scaling. Some investigators, however, have argued that unidimensional scales do not adequately reflect the complexity we commonly encounter in our everyday lives. Obviously, we can judge actors in terms of "acting ability," especially when that term is strictly defined for us. However, the single dimension that we forced participants to use in our study to judge the goodness or badness of acting ability probably grossly oversimplifies the complex judgment scheme that people use in reality. Scott (1968) recognized this fact when he argued that using a single dimension to construe a complex stimulus object (an actor, a beer, etc.) "is patently unrealistic if one

378 Data Collecting Methods

takes seriously the widely held psychological principle that any response is multiply determined" (p. 250). Arguments of this nature have proved persuasive to many, and multidimensional scaling approaches have become more widely used in the social sciences. An extended discussion of multidimensional scaling is beyond the scope of this book, and it is fair to say that multidimensional scaling approaches are not nearly as well developed as might be expected. Recall that Scott made his observations nearly 50 years ago. However, some general points, along with the preceding discussion of unidimensional approaches, should prove a useful introduction to these techniques.

Unfolding

Coombs (1964) supplied an appropriate point of transition between unidimensional and multidimensional scaling and between stimulus and individual difference scaling. In Coombs's **unfolding technique**, the preference order of a set of stimulus objects as well as a set of respondents are simultaneously determined along the same dimension stipulated by the researcher. In this sense, respondents are considered an additional set of "stimuli" to be ordered along a dimension. Coombs's unfolding technique thus bridges the two scaling traditions—stimulus scaling and individual difference scaling.

Consider the following example: Sam, Jenny, and Brian are at a point in their college careers when they must choose an academic major. For convenience, let us assume that these three students can choose among six different areas, and the rank ordering of their choices is as presented in Table 17.2.

Although their choices obviously are quite distinct, a single preference structure can be constructed that summarizes the inclinations of all three students toward each of the six possible academic majors, as ranked from 1st choice to 6th choice, as depicted in Figure 17.2. To determine whether the scale of Figure 17.2 adequately summarizes the ordered choices of our three students, consider the point at which Brian falls on the preference scale. In terms of scale distances, the major closest to Brian is theatre, then psychology, then chemistry, etc. Thus, Brian's placement on the scale accurately reproduces his preference rankings of Table 17.2. We could create a more graphic illustration of Brian's preferences by vertically "folding" the scale at his ideal point (i.e., the point at which he intersects the scale), with distances closer to this fold preferred over majors that are farther away—hence the term "unfolding technique" to describe Coombs' approach. Using distances from each student's ideal point as indicators of relative preferences, we are able to reconstruct exactly the preference rankings of each of the students as they were presented in Table 17.2. If seeking to examine individual differences, each student's position in the top half of Figure 17.2 should be contrasted: Sam and Brian, being more proximal, are more similar in their ranking sequence for majors than the rankings made by Jenny. Inspection of the location of the majors in lower half of the Figure 17.2 informs us that the majors of chemistry and physics, which are closer

TABLE 17.2 Three students and their ranked preferences on six academic majors.

Ranked Preference	Jenny	Sam	Brian
1	Chemistry	English Literature	Theatre
2	Physics	Psychology	Psychology
3	Theatre	Art	Chemistry
4	Psychology	Theatre	English Literature
5	English Literature	Chemistry	Physics
6	Art	Physics	Art

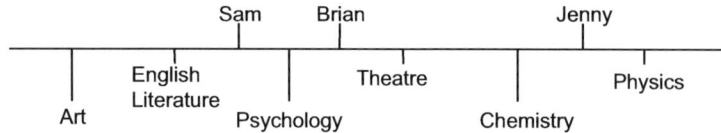

FIGURE 17.2 Underlying preference structure for three students and six majors.

in distance, tend to be more similar in the ordering sequence than to the majors of art or English literature. Thus, in the unfolding technique scaled data allows for the simultaneous evaluation of stimuli differences and individual differences. As Galanter (1966) observed, "By using this (unfolding) technique, we see . . . that although different people may exhibit different preferences . . . it may very well be the case that the differences in the revealed preferences conceal an underlying consistency in the preference structure" (p. 131).

The utility of the unfolding technique is enhanced if the dimension along which the preference stimuli are ordered is somehow identifiable. In the present example, we could hypothesize that the dimension that helped determine the ways the students arranged their preferences was the degree to which mathematical ability was required by each of the academic majors. If the school records of our three students showed that Jenny's mathematical aptitude test score exceeded that of Brian's, whose score was greater than Sam's, then our confidence in our description of the critical dimension would be enhanced, as would the utility of the scale.

A good research example of the use of the unfolding technique was provided by Poole (1981), who investigated the ratings that members of the U.S. Senate received from 26 special interest groups, which ranged from Americans for Democratic Action on the left to the National Taxpayers' Union on the right. Poole found that a single dimension, on which Senators were arranged in terms of their liberal or conservative leanings, accounted for nearly 80% of the variance in the special interest groups' ratings. What's more, Senators' votes on a number of crucial issues could be predicted on the basis of their relative standing on the liberal-conservative dimension that Poole derived. And the accuracy of these predictions surpassed that based on political party affiliation. As Dawes and Smith (1985, p. 529) observed, "Poole's results are striking. Not only does the unfolding technique yield a single dimension that fits the data well, but in addition, the results are in accord with intuitions about which congressional members are conservative or liberal—and can be used to predict crucial votes."

It is possible that the students' preferences could have been so diverse that a simple one-dimensional preference structure could not have been constructed in such a way that it accurately summarized all choices. For example, suppose that mathematical aptitude and verbal aptitude were the two factors that influenced each of the student's choices. In this case, the unfolding solution would have required two dimensions, and the students' ideal preference points would be located not on a single scale, but somewhere in the two-dimensional space described by mathematical aptitude and verbal aptitude.

Multidimensional Scaling Approaches

Many multidimensional scaling approaches have been developed over the years (e.g., see Carroll & Arabie, 1980; Coombs, Dawes, & Tversky, 1970; Guttman, 1968; Kruskal, 1964a, 1964b; Kruskal, Young, & Seery, 1977; Schiffman, Reynolds, & Young, 1981; Shepard, 1962a, 1962b; Shepard, Romney, & Nerlove, 1971; Torgerson, 1958). Usually, **multidimensional scaling** (MDS) relies on ratings of the degree of similarity or dissimilarity among pairs of stimuli, rather than binary judgments or ordering of preferences, to identify the number and types of dimensions that underlie a set of stimuli. In research designed to determine the factors or dimensions that underlie the raw data, factor analysis is appropriate for individual differences scaling, but MDS is used for scaling comparative ratings. Specifically, MDS requires the sample to assign similarity ratings for all possible pairs of the set of stimuli. Data in this format are not suitable for factor analysis.

In an interesting example of the use of multidimensional scaling, Wish, Deutsch, and Biener (1970) identified the number and types of dimensions people used when judging the similarity of various nations. To accomplish this, Wish and colleagues drew up a list of 21 nations and presented all possible pairs of these nations to each of 75 respondents, who were instructed to judge their degree of similarity (using a 9-point judgment scale). The degree of similarity between each pair of nations was calculated across respondents and entered into a similarity matrix, which would resemble that of the actor example presented in Table 17.1. Multidimensional analysis of these similarity judgments revealed that four dimensions largely determined respondents' judgments of nations: Political ideology, level of economic development, geography and population, and the culture and predominant race of the countries. Although the study simply instructed the sample to rate the degree of similarity for each nation pair, the analysis with MDS suggests that participants tended to apply these four dimensions when making their similarity judgments. It seems likely that most respondents were not aware that these dimensions had influenced their similarity-dissimilarity judgments of nations.

Earlier MDS research that instructed participants to rate the similarity of personality traits (stimuli) revealed two dimensions: Intelligence and sociality (Rosenberg, Nelson, & Vivekananthan, 1968). For example, the traits of "reliable" and "practical" were each perceived as high in both intellectual and sociality, but the traits of "boring" and "dishonesty" were each perceived as low in both features.

These dimensions—intelligence and sociality—are synonyms for competence and warmth respectively, two features used in the development of Fiske, Cuddy, and Glick's (2006) stereotype content model. Although these latter researchers did not use the pair comparison scaling approach to develop their central theoretical dimensions, MDS might be used to extend their line of research. For example, research using MDS may be conducted to evaluate the perceived similarity/dissimilarity of social groups. Suppose participants are presented with pairs of words depicting social groups (e.g. housewife and wealthy), and are instructed to assign a rating of 1 (extremely dissimilar) to 10 (extremely similar) to each pair. Analysis of the similarity ratings might reveal the emergence of competence and warmth, two dimensions that might underlie respondents' judgments, and which appear to Fiske and associates as intelligence and sociality.

Presented in Figure 17.3 are possible results of the *perceptual map* that might be found in a study of this type. Noting where the data points are situated, the illustration shows that northerners, lawyers, and wealthy people are perceived to be relatively high in competence; housewives, elderly, blind, and the homeless are low on the dimension. Furthermore, housewives, elderly, blind, southerners, and northerners are perceived as high in warmth, but the homeless, lawyers, and the wealthy people are not. Taking into consideration both dimensions, northerners are viewed as high in competence and warmth, but the homeless are considered low on both dimensions. Research on the stereotype content model suggests that when forming social impressions of others, we tend to classify on these two stimulus dimensions.

Alvaro and Crano (1997) used MDS to estimate the proximity of a set of attitudinal beliefs held by their participant sample. They presented a set of attitude items, and asked participants to estimate the likelihood that if they changed their attitude about one of the items, they would change

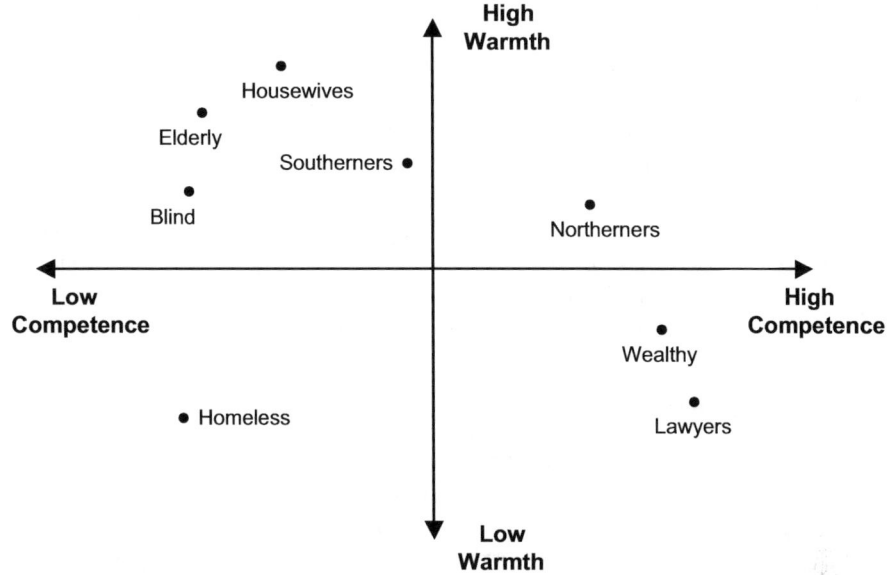

FIGURE 17.3 Multidimensional scaling on dimensions of competence and warmth.

their attitude on another. Following is an example of the format they used to investigate perceived similarities and difference among any pair of items.

> If you changed your mind regarding your position on HOMOSEXUALS IN THE MILITARY, what is the percentage likelihood that you would also change your position on ABORTION? Percentage = _____ (Note: percentages may range from 0–100%)

A higher percentage score indicated greater similarity between the two items. Participants' responses were used to create a matrix of similarities among all possible pairs of items. The MDS approach produces a map, or a picture, of the spatial relationships among all the stimuli that are presented. Alvaro and Crano's MDS analysis suggested the emergence of two dimensions of attitude objects in the similarity matrix.[8] For purposes of testing their theory of attitude change, Alvaro and Crano (1997) were searching for highly proximal attitude objects. So, as expected, the abortion item mapped very closely to the contraception item. Participants thought that if they were to change their attitude toward abortion, they also would change their attitude toward contraception. However, the MDS also revealed proximal attitude objects that participants did not think were related, and these were used in the design of a follow-up study that investigated ways in which a persuasive message about a specific attitude object affected a seemingly unrelated attitude object (see also Crano & Chen, 1998).

The MDS approach is a highly useful, if underused method in social research. Although underused, the approach has not been ignored completely. Some of the more intriguing uses of MDS in the social science literature involve studies of the ways in which Alzheimer's patients cluster common objects (e.g., instruments, animals, etc.), as compared with the mappings of elderly non-Alzheimer's patients (Ober & Shenaut, 1999), differences related to variations in music preferences (Tekman, 1998), adolescent functioning (Wardenaar et al., 2013) and risk behaviors (Dong & Ding, 2012), and factors that affect judgments of emotion in faces (Halberstadt & Niedenthal, 1997).

Conclusion

We consider the underuse of stimulus scaling methods in social science a missed opportunity. The techniques are based on classic psychophysical methods developed over many years and have proved robust and reliable. They provide relatively fine-grained dimensions underlying beliefs and preferences, and reveal how similar or dissimilar these items are on the identified dimensions. Recall that variations among participants are assumed to be a function of error. If sufficient disagreement exists, the stimulus scaling procedures will fail; that is, their statistical analysis will suggest that the summary "group attitude scale" is not trustworthy, but most often the approaches produce reliable summary information of interval-level quality. We hope this brief discussion of some of the more widely known techniques will encourage their more extensive use in social research.

Questions for Discussion

1. Why would researchers use pair comparison or rank order stimulus scaling? Besides applications to product preferences and consumer behavior, what information might stimulus scaling be able to give us that cannot be obtained with other, simpler investigative techniques? How do we conceptualize stimulus scaling techniques differently from other attitudinal assessments? In other words, what assumptions about the stimuli and participants differ between types of measurement techniques?
2. Why do you think multidimensional scaling has been underused? Is greater attention to MDS warranted? What is a possible example of a research question or issue that has been studied before, but that MDS may provide greater elaboration to about *how* and *why* a relationship between variables exists?
3. What do we mean by transitivity? Why is it important?
4. Rank order and stimulus scaling techniques share unique strengths and unique weaknesses relative to one another. What are some of them?

Notes

1. This combination of judgments across all respondents requires the earlier-noted assumption that respondents would all judge the stimuli identically were it not for measurement error. If this assumption were not made, it would not be logical to combine data in this way.
2. Some of the "crimes" Thurstone used in his study (e.g., abortion, adultery) would not be considered illegal today.
3. Borg (1988, p. 60) suggested that participants in Thurstone's (1927) sample might have read "seduction of a minor" as referring to "having sex with a girl under 21," whereas today's students might have read the same item as "molestation of a 3-year-old."
4. To calculate the number of pairs that will result from a given number of stimuli, use the following formula: $p = [n(n-1)]/2$, where p = number of pairs, and n = the number of stimuli. Thus, in our acting quality study, we would produce $[6 \times 5]/2$ pairs. Thurstone (1927) used 19 different crimes, and thus produced 171 pairs of stimuli.
5. Remember in Chapter 1 we stated that interval level measures require the properties of both ordered sequence and equal differences between measurement points on the construct.
6. Alternatively, pictorial approaches in which participants arrange all objects in two-dimensional space simultaneously also are available, but they will not be considered here (see Hout et al., 2013).
7. True zero refers to the fact that the property is completely absent (e.g., I lost 0.0 lbs. on my diet, or I have $0.00 in my wallet). Unlike physical constructs such as weight, "acting ability" is a psychological construct that does not really have a true zero-point (one can be a good, mediocre, or poor actor, but it does not make sense to talk of zero point of acting ability, or for an actor to have absolutely no acting ability—though we all might have witnessed performances in which this possibility came to mind.).
8. In MDS, if the mapping process is successful, the distances derived from the map will equal those found in the similarity matrix. Increasing the number of dimensions usually results in a better fit of map with matrix, but the trick is to scale the similarity matrix using as few dimensions as possible.

References

Alvaro, E. M., & Crano, W. D. (1997). Indirect minority influence: Evidence for leniency in source evaluation and counter-argumentation. *Journal of Personality and Social Psychology, 72,* 949–965.

Borg, I. (1988). Revisiting Thurstone's and Coombs' scales on the seriousness of crimes. *European Journal of Social Psychology, 18,* 53–61.

Carroll, J. B., & Arabie, P. (1980). Multi-dimensional scaling. *Annual Review of Psychology, 31,* 607–649.

Coombs, C. (1964). *A theory of data.* New York, NY: Wiley.

Coombs, C. H. (1967). Thurstone's measurement of social values revisited forty years later. *Journal of Personality and Social Psychology, 6,* 85–91.

Coombs, C. H., Dawes, R. M., & Tversky, A. (1970). *Mathematical psychology.* Englewood Cliffs, NJ: Prentice-Hall.

Crano, W. D., & Chen, X. (1998). The leniency contract and persistence of majority and minority influence. *Journal of Personality and Social Psychology, 74,* 1437–1450.

Crano, W. D., & Cooper, R. E. (1973). Examination of Newcomb's extension of structural balance theory. *Journal of Personality and Social Psychology, 27,* 344–353.

Dawes, R. M., & Smith, T. L. (1985). Attitude and opinion measurement. In G. Lindzey & E. Aronson (Eds.) *The handbook of social psychology* (pp. 509–566). Reading, MA: Addison-Wesley.

Dong, Y., & Ding, C. (2012). Adolescent risk behaviors: Studying typical and atypical individuals via multidimensional scaling profile analysis. *Journal of Adolescence, 35,* 197–205.

Fiske, S. T., Cuddy, A. J. C., & Glick, P. (2006). Universal dimensions of social cognition: Warmth and competence. *Trends in Cognitive Sciences, 11,* 77–83.

Galanter, E. (1966). *Textbook of elementary psychology.* San Francisco: Holden-Day.

Guilford, J. P. (1954). *Psychometric methods.* New York: McGraw-Hill.

Guttman, L. (1968). A general nonmetric technique for finding the smallest coordinate space for a configuration of points. *Psychometrika, 33,* 469–506.

Halberstadt, J. B., & Niedenthal, P. M. (1997). Emotional state and the use of stimulus dimensions in judgment. *Journal of Personality and Social Psychology, 72,* 1017–1033.

Hout, M. C., Goldinger, S. D., & Ferguson, R. W. (2013). The versatility of SpAM: A fast, efficient, spatial method of data collection for multidimensional scaling. *Journal of Experimental Psychology, General, 142,* 256–281.

Kruskall, J. B. (1964a). Multidimensional scaling: A numerical method. *Psychometrika, 29,* 1–27.

Kruskall, J. B. (1964b). Multidimensional scaling by optimizing goodness of fit to a nonmetric hypothesis. *Psychometrika, 29,* 115–129.

Kruskall, J. B., Young, F. W., & Seery, J. B. (1977). *How to use KYST 2: A very flexible program to do multidimensional scaling and unfolding.* Murray Hill, NJ: Bell Telephone Labs.

Misra, R. K., & Dutt, P. K. (1965). A comparative study of psychological scaling methods. *Journal of Psychological Research. 9,* 31–34.

Mosteller, F. (1951). Remarks on the method of paired comparisons: III. A test of significance for paired comparisons when equal standard deviations and equal correlations are assumed. *Psychometrika, 16,* 207–218.

Ober, B. A., & Shenaut, G. K. (1999). Well-organized conceptual domains in Alzheimer's disease. *Journal of the International Neuropsychological Society, 5,* 676–684.

Poole, K. T. (1981). Dimensions of interest group evaluation of the U.S. Senate, 1969–1978. *American Journal of Political Science, 25,* 41–54.

Rosenberg, S., Nelson, C., & Vivekananthan, P. S. (1968). A multidimensional approach to the structure of personality impressions. *Journal of Personality & Social Psychology, 9,* 283–294.

Schiffman, S. S., Reynolds, M. L., & Young, F. W. (1981). *Introduction to multidimensional scaling: Theory, methods, and applications.* Bingley, UK: Emerald Group Publishing.

Scott, W. A. (1968). Attitude measurement. In G. Lindzey & E. Aronson (Eds.) *Handbook of social psychology, Vol. 2. Research methods* (2nd ed., pp. 204–273). Reading, MA: Addison-Wesley.

Shepard, R. N. (1962a). The analysis of proximities: Multidimensional scaling with an unknown distance function. I. *Psychometrika, 27,* 125–140.

Shepard, R. N. (1962b). The analysis of proximities: Multidimensional scaling with an unknown distance function. II. *Psychometrika, 27,* 219–246.

Shepard, R. N., Romney, A. K., & Nerlove, S. (Eds.) (1971). *Multidimensional scaling: Theory and applications in the behavioral sciences.* New York: Academic Press.

Tekman, H. G. (1998). A multidimensional study of music preference judgments for excerpts of music. *Psychological Reports, 82,* 851–860.
Thurstone, L. L. (1927). Method of paired comparisons for social values. *Journal of Abnormal and Social Psychology, 21,* 384–400.
Torgerson, W. S. (1958). *Theory and methods of scaling.* New York: Wiley.
Tversky, A. (1969). Intransitivity of preferences. *Psychological Review, 76,* 31–48.
Wardenaar, K. J., Wigman, J.T.W., Lin, A., Killackey, E., Collip, D., Wood, S. J., . . . & Yung, A. R. (2013). Development and validation of a new measure of everyday adolescent functioning: The Multidimensional Adolescent Functioning Scale. *Journal of Adolescent Health, 52,* 195–200.
Wish, M., Deutsch, M., & Biener, L. (1970). Differences in conceptual structures of nations: An exploratory study. *Journal of Personality and Social Psychology, 16,* 361–373.

18
METHODS FOR ASSESSING DYADS AND GROUPS

The preceding chapters on measurement and social cognition dealt with methods for assessing characteristics and behaviors of individual persons. **Monadic variables** are characteristics of single persons (e.g., age). A person's attitude toward abortion, for instance, is considered monadic because it refers only to that particular individual's own attitude. In many areas of social science, however, we are concerned with persons who interact in dyads (pairs) or groups. In this case, we are not assessing properties of the individuals separately, but rather the nature, relationship, structure, process, or outcomes of the interacting group members as a unit. **Dyadic variables** are characteristics of the relationship between two persons or their combined outcomes (e.g., level of warmth of their interaction). **Group variables** refer to a characteristic of a set of three or more persons (e.g., total number of widgets created by a work team). In this chapter, we consider the assessment of group or dyadic variables. Measures of behaviors or attitudes of interacting persons are a special case because the assessments taken from each of the group members are *interdependent,* insofar as each group member's score is expected to be related to, or influenced by that of the other member(s).

Dyadic Designs

A common vocabulary is used to describe members in a dyadic design (Cook & Kenny, 2005; Kenny & Ledermann, 2010). The **actor** is the person who perceives, records, and provides information or a score regarding an interpersonal interaction with a partner in a dyad. The **partner** is the person with whom the actor is interacting during a particular dyadic exchange. Consider the following examples of three different studies of interacting dyads:

- Dyad 1: Tom & Peter
  (a) How much Tom likes Peter using a 1 to 10 point scale.
  (b) How much Peter likes Tom using a 1 to 10 point scale.
- Dyad 2: Dick and Paul
  (a) How many times Dick smiles when interacting with Paul.
  (b) How many times Paul smiles when interacting with Dick.
- Dyad 3: Harry and Mary
  (a) How intelligent Harry thinks Mary is.
  (b) How intelligent Mary thinks Harry is.

In each of these three dyadic interactions, for part (a), the actors are Tom, Dick, and Harry, with Peter, Paul, and Mary being their partners, respectively.[1] For part (b), the roles of actor and partner are reversed. The person who provides the observation or score for the measure is defined as the actor. Thus, if both members of a dyad provide scores, then both members serve as actors as well as partners to each other. The actor's score on a measure is influenced not only by the actor's own characteristics, but also by those of the particular partner as well. For instance, Tom's liking of Peter is in part a consequence of something about Tom (e.g., his attitudes and behaviors), but it also is influenced by characteristics of Peter (e.g., his attitudes and behavior) and by the nature of the relationship between the two of them. All three of these examples, then, involve dyadic designs, because they are concerned with *two persons and their interaction*.

Dyadic variables may be classified into three types (Kenny, Kashy, & Cook, 2006): within-dyad variables, between-dyad variables, and mixed variables. Examples of the three types are shown in Table 18.1 in a scenario involving brother-sister pairs. A *within-dyad variable* is one in which variations in scores are found within members of each dyad, but the same total score is shown from dyad to dyad. An example is a variable representing a game in which each brother and sister pair competed to see who could win the most of 10 marshmallows (Table 18.1). In this case, the total number of marshmallows is the same (10) for every dyad, but the distribution within dyads varies. A *between-dyad variable* is represented by a measure in which the same score is assigned to both members of the dyad, with variations in scores exhibited from dyad to dyad. Continuing with the brother-sister scenario, such a measure might involve how many toys each pair shares together at home (Table 18.1). Sharing is a relational concept, so the distinction between actor and partner is unnecessary, and members of each pair receive the same (dyadic) score. Other examples of between-dyad variables include the physical distance between members of the dyad, the amount of mutual gaze, and the frequency of simultaneous speech of each pair—the same value serves for both members of the dyad since it describes the pair as a unit.

In the final type of dyadic measure, a *mixed variable* exhibits variations in scores within-dyads and between-dyads. For example, both members of the brother-sister pair report on their personal attitudes toward their mother, using a rating scale from 1 to 10. In a mixed variable, obtained scores could differ within each brother-sister pair and across sibling pairs as well.

Dyadic research may vary in the methods used to assess characteristics of the dyads. If conducted as observational research, the investigator or coder might carefully watch the dyadic interaction and code for relevant variables. Behavioral observations could transpire in a systematically controlled laboratory setting or in a naturalistic setting. Using self-report measures to assess attitudes or feelings after the interaction, measures might concern the actor ("Rate how positively you feel about yourself") or the respective partner ("Rate how positively you feel about the other person"), or each person's assessment of the positivity of the interaction itself.

TABLE 18.1 Examples of the three types of dyadic variables in a sample of brother-sister pairs.

Pair	Within-Dyad Variable (# of marshmallows won out of 10)		Between-Dyad Variable (# of toys shared at home)		Mixed Variable (attitudes toward mother)	
	Brother	Sister	Brother	Sister	Brother	Sister
Dyad 1	6	4	3	3	7	3
Dyad 2	3	7	4	4	10	8
Dyad 3	4	6	6	6	8	9
Dyad 4	9	1	1	1	5	8
Dyad 5	5	5	8	8	2	2

Some studies might appear to be dyadic, but actually are not. An investigation is not considered dyadic if data are collected exclusively from only one member of the pair. This happens when one of the two persons interacting is a confederate or an accomplice of the experimenter. In studies involving confederates, there are multiple actors (participants), but usually only a single partner (the confederate). When each of the actors separately interacts with the same partner, the data from each actor can be considered monadic, particularly if the confederate's behavior has been scripted by the researcher.[2] For example, consider research that measures the degree of self-esteem reported by participants after a confederate expresses a degrading insult. In such a study, the confederate is constant across all dyads. As only one member of each dyad provides a score, it is not truly a dyadic design. In this chapter we will focus on the study of truly dyadic, not monadic, measures.

Deriving Dyadic and Group Level Variables

Some variables of dyadic or group properties involve assessments of the interacting members in a dyad or group. For instance, the level of interpersonal attraction between two persons may be scored by an observer who watches an interaction between the pair and then rates that interaction in terms of degree of warmth, engagement, and mutuality expressed by the pair. Similarly, group cohesion (the group-level counterpart to interpersonal attraction) can be rated by observers of group process considering the group as a whole, or the performance of a group on a collective task may be assessed by evaluating the overall group product independent of the contributions of individual members.

Sometimes overall scores for each dyad or group are derived from measures computed from each of the component members. The overall score is the sum or mean of the scores of the constituting members. For instance, the average attraction between Peter and Tom may be the mean (which is simply the sum divided by 2) of the degree of liking that Peter expresses for Tom and the liking that Tom expresses for Peter. At the group level, cohesion may be the mean of all of the group members' expressed liking for the group as a whole.

In other cases, the dyadic analysis is based on the degree of difference found between the ratings or behaviors of the paired members. For instance, attitude dissimilarity is usually measured as the degree of difference between the attitude expressed by person A of the pair and the attitude expressed by person B. The physical distance between two persons also is a dyadic variable, because it is based on the distance between the physical location of the individuals. For example, we might record how far apart two participants stand from each when they are having a conversation. At the group level, belief similarity or dissimilarity is assessed by some measure of the variability of the attitude scores of individual members. A smaller variability reflects greater similarity (consensus) among members.

Although dyadic variables may involve simple mean scores of the component members, group variables sometimes can be considerably more complex. For instance, designs containing multiple groups (to be discussed later in this chapter) require statistical procedures to assess the contribution of variables at the participant level and at the group level.

Dyadic and group level variables may be derived from individuals, but sometimes they are meaningful only at the level of the dyad or group. Group size provides a concrete example of what we mean here. Size is measured by counting individuals who compose the group—each individual contributes to this measure at the group level. However, size as a conceptual variable exists only as a property of each group, not in the individual bodies that constitute each group. Dyadic similarity is another example. Although individual A has an attitude that can be measured monadically, as does individual B, the distance between the attitudes of the members of the pair is a characteristic at the dyadic level and is not meaningful at the participant level.

Measuring Reciprocity or Mutuality

When working with dyadic variables, a number of issues arise that do not occur when working with monadic ones. When one has scores from both members of the dyad—so that each person serves as both actor and partner—it is possible that the two scores are correlated. The *degree of reciprocity* (or correspondence) is the extent that scores provided by both members to the same measure are correlated, and is usually of theoretical importance in dyadic research. Let us consider some examples:

- In a study of randomly paired couples (Walster, Aronson, Abrahams, & Rottman, 1966), the investigators were interested in discovering the degree of reciprocity of attraction between the individuals who constituted the dating couples. That is, they were studying to what extent the members of the pairs mutually liked or mutually disliked each other.
- Numerous theorists (e.g., Sprecher, Treger, & Wondra, 2013; Won-Doornink, 1979) have discussed the conditions that affect the degree of self-disclosure that occurs in two-person relationships. Of particular interest is whether disclosure from one person stimulates comparable disclosure from the other member of the pair. It is then theoretically useful to measure the degree of reciprocity in self-disclosure.
- Communication scientists have speculated that in communicative social interactions, one person will tend to be dominant and the other submissive. If we take the number of interruptions as a measure of domination, we may want to see if in dyads there is one person who interrupts the other repeatedly while the other rarely interrupts. In this case, the behavior is not reciprocated, but rather compensated, and the predicted correlation between measures is negative rather than positive.
- Social researchers might have people play laboratory games, such as the Prisoner's Dilemma (see Chapter 7). Of interest in such settings might be the degree of reciprocity between players. Thus, if one person is generally cooperative, is the other person cooperative too? And, conversely, if one person is competitive, is the other competitive?
- In studies that examine pairs of children interacting, one way to index the degree to which two children are engaging in a social interaction is to measure the degree of relationship between their number of utterances. If the two children are interacting, then there should be some level of correspondence in their number of utterances. If the young children were only speaking to themselves, the number of utterances of the two would be unrelated.

These illustrations demonstrate that it is essential for many research questions to be studied in such a manner to allow for the investigation of reciprocity. The measure of reciprocity depends upon whether the dyad is symmetric or asymmetric. In a **symmetric dyad**, the members of each pair are indistinguishable by a relevant feature, such as their respective role or status in the relationship. Examples of symmetric dyads are friends (friend X-friend X'), identical twins (twin A-twin A') or roommates (roommate X-roommate X'). In an **asymmetric dyad**, the members of each pair are distinguishable by a relevant feature, such as their respective role or status in the relationship. For instance, members of married heterosexual couples are distinguishable (husband-wife), as are teacher-student, parent-child, brother-sister, and boss-employee. In the roommate example, if we studied roommates who are of different genders (female roommate X-male roommate Y), the dyads would be considered asymmetric.

For asymmetric dyads, the degree of reciprocity can be measured by the Pearson correlation coefficient. So, for instance, to assess the degree to which members of a group of married couples agree on how satisfied they are with their marriage, one simply correlates the satisfaction expressed by the husbands with that of their respective wives. A stronger positive correlation signifies greater correspondence within couples—if the husband is satisfied, so is the wife, and vice versa.

For symmetric dyads there is no rule on how to compute such a correlation because there is no obvious way to identify one individual's score as the "X" variable and the other's as the "Y" variable. There are two common, yet faulty, solutions to this problem. The first is to find some way of distinguishing the two members of the dyad. For example, if the dyads are same-sex siblings, they can be distinguished by the relative age (younger-older) of each dyad's members. The second way is to distinguish the members within a dyad in some arbitrary fashion. For instance, one uses a coin flip to designate one individual as person 1 and the other as person 2, and repeating this process for each dyad pair in the sample. To measure reciprocity correlationally, we enter the score of person 1 as the X variable and that of person 2 as the Y variable, and compute the correlation between the scores.

For symmetric dyads, neither of these two approaches is ideal. The first, which calls for the discovery of a relevant variable by which to distinguish people, is not always feasible because there may be no reasonable characteristic to distinguish members of the dyad. The second approach, making use of an arbitrary (or relatively meaningless) rule to distinguish the member also is misguided because as will be shown, minor variations in who occupies each role can have an effect on the obtained results. The correct approach makes use of a specialized measure of association called the *intraclass correlation coefficient*. In symmetric dyads, we denote the two values reported by each indistinguishable member as X and X' and the mean of all scores as M. The number of dyads is n. The formula for the intraclass correlation is based on the following two quantities:

$$MS_B = \frac{2\left[\frac{\Sigma(X + X')}{2} - M\right]^2}{n - 1}$$

$$MS_W = \Sigma(X - X')^2 / 2n$$

The intraclass correlation is defined as:

$$r = \frac{MS_B - MS_w}{MS_B + MS_w}$$

For dyads, the intraclass correlation, like an ordinary correlation coefficient, ranges from -1 to $+1$, with zero indicating no relationship between the variables of interest. The intraclass correlation is the most appropriate as a measure of degree of correspondence in scores for members within symmetric dyads.

In Table 18.2 we present scores from eight pairs of college roommates as an example. The scores indicate the extent to which an individual trusts his or her roommate. The intraclass correlation for these pairs of roommates is .43, which indicates that the roommates reciprocated their trust in one another—that is, if one member of a pair had high trust in the other, it is likely that his or her roommate would indicate relatively high trust also. A standard Pearson correlation coefficient on the data of Table 18.2 would reveal a slightly different result ($r = .51$). However, as noted, the Pearson r is susceptible to variations in the placement of the data into variable X or X'; Thus, if the scores of pair A of the table were reversed, the Pearson r would be affected (now, $r = .48$), whereas the intraclass correlation would not. For this reason, the intraclass correlation is clearly preferable in analyzing symmetric dyads.

The Pearson correlation and the intraclass correlation are used to assess the correspondence between scores on one variable collected from each member of the dyad. The **actor-partner interdependence model** is a multivariate framework for examining two or more variables from

TABLE 18.2 Trust scores from eight pairs of college roommates.

Pair	Scores	
	Roommate X	Roommate X'
A	7	10
B	8	8
C	7	7
D	8	7
E	7	8
F	7	8
G	4	6
H	6	6

each member of the dyad to determine the correspondence and reciprocity of their interpersonal relationship (Cook & Kenny, 2005; Kenny & Ledermann, 2010). Typically, this framework is estimated using a multiple regression or a structural equation model (Chapter 9). Both statistical techniques enable the researcher to statistically control, and therefore disentangle, the unique and simultaneous contribution of members of a dyad.

Although using the actor-partner interdependence model to examine symmetric dyads is possible, a correction is necessary to account for the fact that members are statistically indistinguishable (Kenny & Ledermann, 2010). Applying the model to asymmetric dyads is more straightforward. Depicted in Figure 18.1 is the actor-partner interdependence model for a sample of married heterosexual couples. Both members of each husband-wife pair provide scores on at least two variables (attitudes and behaviors) assessed at two points in time. (Although the model may be estimated with cross-sectional data, longitudinal collection of data enables the unraveling of temporal events.) Assessed at the initial round are measures of attitudes (e.g., level of trust), and at the later round are the measures of behaviors (e.g., number of chores performed). The scores of husband-wife dyads are expected to be interdependent: It is reasonable to assume that because of their intertwined lives, the scores of each member will be affected by many of the same household events. Thus, their scores are allowed to be correlated at each measurement round. The predictive path weights (one-directional arrows) are partial correlations or beta weights, statistically controlling for the attitudinal

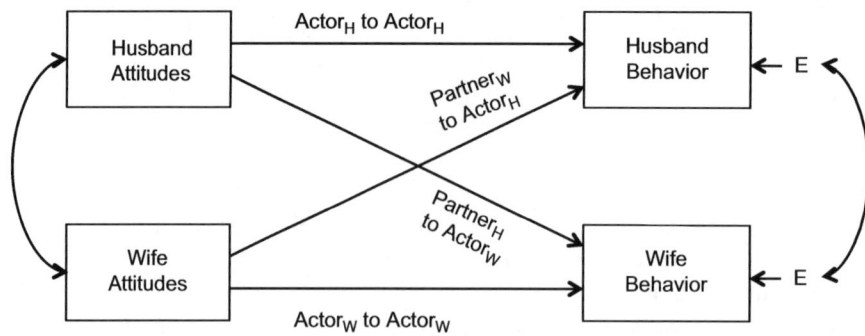

FIGURE 18.1 Actor-partner interdependence model.
Note: H = Husband, W = Wife

variables of both members. Thus, the husband's behavior is a simultaneous function of his own and his wife's attitudes. Likewise, the wife's behavior is simultaneously predicted by her own as well as her husband's attitudes. Given that both husband and wife provide scores, they are actors as well as partners to each other.

Designs to Study Group Structures

Round Robin Designs

One problem with dyadic measurements is that it often is difficult to distinguish monadic and dyadic components contributing to the derived score. For instance, the overall attraction between Tom and Harry (their mean ratings of each other) may tell us something about the nature of the relationship between the two of them—something that is unique to them as a specific dyad. However, the score at the dyadic level also reflects something about Tom and Harry as individuals. Perhaps Tom is the kind of person who expresses liking for everyone he meets. In that case, any dyad with Tom as a member would have a high attraction score, but this may be more a property of Tom than of the relationship with that particular partner. Even a physical distance score may be primarily determined by the behavior of one member. For example, Tom might have a dispositional tendency to stand in close proximity to all other people. When all we have is one dyad with Tom as a member, we cannot tease apart how much the overall attraction score is due to Tom alone and how much is a reflection of that particular dyad.

So far, we have assumed that each person under study is a member of one and only one dyad. If there is a total of 16 persons, as there was in the earlier example in Table 18.2, there would be a total of 8 dyads. If the researcher wants to examine the interaction of each member paired with each and every other member in a group, it is necessary to employ a more complicated design. A **round robin design** is used to examine multiple combinations of dyads in a group by creating all possible pairs of persons, with each member rating each and every member. For instance, consider the now classic research by Theodore Newcomb (1961), who studied a group of 17 men living in the same university house. He asked each of these college men to rate how much he liked each of the others. With 17 respondents, the total number of dyads that can be formed (to compare the liking of each actor for each potential partner in the group) is calculated by the formula $N \times (N-1)/2$, in this case, $17 \times 16/2$, or 136 dyads. Round robin designs are used infrequently in the social sciences, as they require all possible combinations of dyads. However, they are used on occasion. In research on interpersonal attraction, we have already mentioned that Newcomb used a round robin design. In their replication of Newcomb's (1961) study, Curry and Emerson (1970) used the same method. Round robin designs have also been used to study communication in monkeys (Miller, Caul, & Mirsky, 1967), intertribal relations in East Africa (Brewer & Campbell, 1976), and defense mechanisms in person perception (Campbell, Miller, Lubetsky, & O'Connell, 1964).

There are two major advantages of collecting data using a round robin design. First, one obtains many more observations from each participant without increasing the number of participants needed. This gain in the number of comparisons lends added power to the statistical analysis of the collected data. Second, with a round robin design one can determine how a person rates or responds generally to others, and how that same person is rated and responded to *by* others. It then is possible to describe the score of a given actor with a given partner as being a function of (a) the set of actors being studied, (b) how the actor responds in general, (c) how others respond in general to the partner, and (d) how the actor uniquely responds to that particular partner. Such an analysis of two-person relationships has been termed the Social Relations Model by Kenny and La Voie (1984) (see also Kashy & Kenny, 2000).

TABLE 18.3 Round robin design.

Actor (Person Doing the Rating)	Partner (Person Being Rated)					
	John	Paul	Mike	Bill	Dave	Phil
John		12	12	15	15	10
Paul	9		4	13	11	4
Mike	14	9		15	15	9
Bill	11	8	7		9	7
Dave	6	8	7	8		4
Phil	12	10	8	15	13	

Table 18.3 presents an illustration of a round robin design. The numbers in the table represent the liking scores (on a scale from 1 to 15) of six persons toward each other. The rows in the table are the actors (they are reporting the score), and the columns are the partner. Thus, all actors also serve as partners in pairings. So, for instance, the table indicates that John likes Paul (with a score of 12 on the liking scale), whereas Paul's liking for John is only 9. We have left blank the entries in which the same person is both actor and partner to signify that those numbers are not gathered (the study is focused on interpersonal liking and not how much participants like themselves).

By reading down each column of Table 18.3, we can see who is rated by the other members as being popular overall, and who is not. It appears that that the members typically perceived Bill as the most popular person (15 + 13 + 15 + 8 + 15 = 66) and Phil as the least popular (10 + 4 + 9 + 7 + 4 = 34). Reading across rows, we can see the person who generally likes the other members the most and the one who likes the other members the least. It appears that John tends to like his group members most (12 + 12 + 15 + 15 + 10 = 48), and that Dave likes them the least (6 + 8 + 7 + 8 + 4 = 33). We can view the general tendency to like (or dislike) others as a *response set*, a tendency to respond in a consistent fashion.

With a round robin design, it is possible to obtain a more refined measure of reciprocity than we can obtain from pair data. Consider what would happen if persons who were rated as popular in the group tended not to like the other persons in the group. If this were true, it would build a negative bias into the reciprocity correlation. For instance, for the data in Table 18.3, the intraclass correlation across the pairings of dyads is −.38. Once overall popularity and liking response sets are controlled, however, the correlation becomes .65. Thus, statistically controlling for and thereby removing the effects of popularity and the liking response set gives a more accurate estimate of the intraclass correlation. To measure reciprocity in attraction more validly, we need to subtract from each score the extent to which the actor likes the other group members in general, and the extent to which the partner is liked by the others.[3] The removal of popularity and the response set for liking provides a more valid measure of dyadic reciprocity in a round robin design (Kenny & La Voie, 1982).

Sociometric Analysis

A methodology similar to the round robin design can also be used to measure properties of groups such as cohesion and communication structure. Earlier we discussed the measurement of members' attraction toward all members in their group as a whole. In this context, measurement involves rating scales similar to those used to measure other social attitudes. A different approach to the measurement of attraction in group settings was developed in the 1930s by J. L. Moreno (1934), whose methods gradually became known as sociometry. **Sociometry** refers to the assessment of social acceptances and rejections of members in a given group by asking each member to indicate whether he or she likes or dislikes each of the other members in the group. For example, Clore, Bray, Itkin, and Murphy (1978) asked children in a summer camp to identify their best friends. They used these sociometric data to assess the degree to which children chose other children who were members of different ethnic groups.

In a sociometric design, there are two different kinds of choices that can be made by each member of a group. First, the participants can be asked to indicate whether or not they *accept* each of the group members. Examples of acceptance choices include liking, preferring to work with, preferring to be on the same team with, and the like. The second type of choice is *rejection*. Examples of rejection choices include disliking, rejection, and aversion of another member. The researcher can ask each participant to make choices regarding acceptances, rejections, or both, but in many studies only acceptance choices are required. In that case, the investigator has the option of defining the number of choices a person can make. For instance, it is common to ask all respondents to choose their three best friends in a group (an "acceptance" choice). Although it seems more natural not to place any restrictions on the number of choices the participant can make in this type of design, it is advisable to do so. If the number of choices is not set by the researcher, those who make many more choices than others in the group will have an inordinate influence on the resulting sociometric structures. We can represent participants' choices in what is called a *sociomatrix,* in which each individual in the group is represented by a row and a corresponding column, with his or her response recorded in the appropriate cell. In Table 18.4 we provide an example of a sociomatrix for a group of six. In this example (because the number of group members is relatively small), each person in the group is asked to respond about each of the other group members, with acceptance choices represented by a "+," rejection choices by a "–," and non-choices by a "0." Each cell in the matrix represents the response that the individual in the corresponding row made for the individual in the column.

A sociomatrix employs a round robin design because data are generated for all possible pairs in the group. Although the design is round robin, the data are of a different type. The data in a sociomatrix involve categorical responses of acceptance or rejection, whereas in the round robin example presented in Table 18.3, quantitative ratings are used to assess degree of acceptance-rejection.

There are a number of interesting questions that can be answered by analyzing the data of a sociomatrix (Terry, 2000). One type of question concerns whether the group is in *balance*. According to Heider's (1958) theory, if A likes B, and B likes C, then A also should like C. Measures of the degree of balance in a sociomatrix of N participants are given in Holland and Leinhardt (1978).

TABLE 18.4 Sociomatrix for a six-person group.

Person Doing the Choosing	*Person Being Chosen*					
	A	B	C	D	E	F
A		+	+	0	–	–
B	+		0	–	0	–
C	0	0		+	–	–
D	–	0	+		0	–
E	–	–	0	0		+
F	–	0	0	0	+	

Note: + indicates acceptance, - indicates rejection, 0 indicates non-choice

From a sociomatrix it also is possible to measure the popularity of individuals within the group. One needs simply to count the number of acceptances received by each person and subtract from this sum the number of rejections, if any. A person who receives a higher computed score is deemed more accepted by others. This simple computation strategy is valid when the number of choices to be made by each participant is set by the investigator. If respondents are free to choose (accept or reject) any number of other members, somewhat more complicated methods must be employed to assess popularity.

One can also determine from a sociomatrix the degree of reciprocity in the group. We begin by counting the number of pairs who reciprocate attraction (i.e., both members choose the other), and divide this quantity by the total number of pairs. The resulting number is the proportion of reciprocated pairs. This quantity should be compared to a baseline proportion of reciprocated pairs that would be expected if respondents' choices were completely random. One useful baseline index involves calculating the total number of choices actually made in the group, dividing this number by the total number of choices possible and squaring the resulting proportion. For example, if there were nine persons in a group, and each made three acceptances, the total number of acceptance choices made is 9×3, or 27, and the total number of pairs is 72 (9×8). The baseline proportion of reciprocal choices thus is $(27/72)^2$, or .141. That is, if the choices were being made without any mutuality, 14% of the pairings would turn out to be matched acceptances by chance. This baseline proportion would be compared to the actual number of reciprocated choices to determine the extent of reciprocation (beyond chance levels) in the group under study.

From a sociomatrix we also can detect the presence of *cliques* or subgroupings that exist with a group. Table 18.5 presents an example of a sociomatrix whose data were gathered by Sampson (1969) from monks in a Catholic monastery. Each of the 18 trainee monks was asked to state, using

TABLE 18.5 Acceptance choices among 18 monk trainees.

Monk Doing the Choosing	Monk Being Chosen																	
	A	B	C	D	E	F	G	H	I	J	K	L	M	N	O	P	Q	R
A		+	+		+													
B			+		+	+												
C		+					+	+										
D		+	+		+													
E		+		+		+												
F		+					+				+							
G			+	+	+													
H									+	+			+					
I								+			+				+			
J								+	+			+						
K								+	+				+					
L								+		+			+					
M									+	+				+				
N									+			+						
O		+										+						+
P															+		+	+
Q									+							+		+
R										+						+	+	

Note: + indicates acceptance

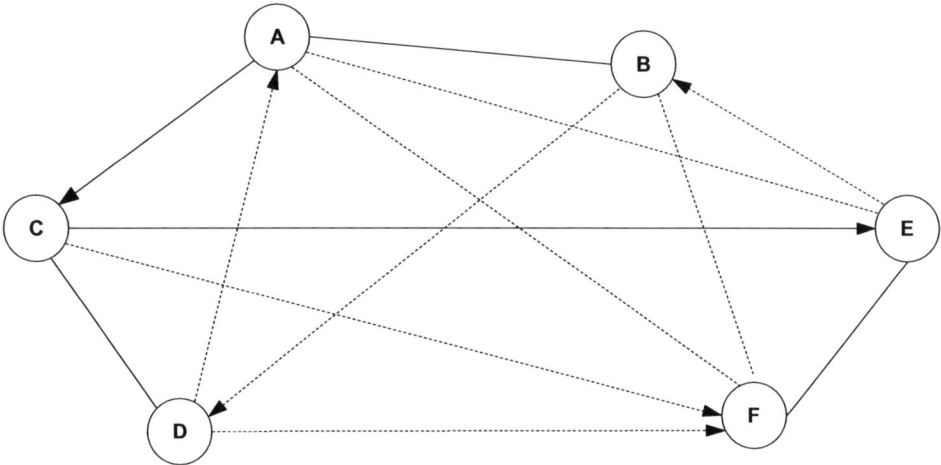

FIGURE 18.2 Sociogram of person relations presented in Table 18.4.

acceptance choices, which three other monks they liked the most. The matrix has been arranged to show the three clear subgroups that were formed. The subgroups are indicated in the table by boxes. Sampson labeled the first group (monks A through G) as the "traditionalists," the second group (monks H through N) as the "Young Turks," and the third group (monks O through R) as the "outcasts." These subgroupings were determined by a sociomatrix procedure called *block modeling* (White, Boorman, & Breiger, 1976). (Note that monk "A" is a loner in that no other monks choose him among their three most liked, but he is included in the first subgrouping because all of his choices fall in that traditionalist group.)

The sociomatrix can be drawn into a figure to indicate who likes (acceptance choice) whom, and who does not. Such a drawing is called a *sociogram*. If person A likes person B, the two are connected by a solid arrow going from A to B, and vice versa if the choice is reciprocated. If rejection choices are made, they too are indicated by directional arrows, but acceptance choices are indicated by a plus, and rejection by a minus. We have taken the sociomatrix in Table 18.4 and redrawn it as a sociogram in Figure 18.2. Sociograms are more useful than sociomatrices if the number of respondents is less than 10. If we were to draw a sociogram for the monastery study, the resulting diagram would be much too unwieldy to interpret.

Social Network Analysis

Sociometric analysis is concerned with the affective ties among members of a social group using acceptance and rejection choices. Social network analysis is a related methodology concerning the communication links or connections among units (individuals or organizations) in a social system. Like sociometry, **social network analysis** uses dyadic relations as the basic unit of analysis, with the resulting data organized into matrix representations. However, the two methodologies differ in a number of ways. Whereas sociometry is usually applied to studies of relatively small, bounded groups, social network analysis often involves large social systems where the member units may be organizations or political units as well as individuals. The basic measure in a sociometric analysis is the acceptance or rejection relationships among group members, but the basic measure in a network analysis is some index of connectedness, communication, or exchange among component members. The specific kind of linkage being studied depends on the researchers' objectives and interests, but some common measures are exchanges of information or commodities (i.e., trade relations), presence or absence of telecommunication links, shared memberships (e.g., overlapping boards of directors), kinship relations, or collaborative efforts (e.g., coauthored publications). Data regarding the existence of linkages may be obtained from self-report questionnaires or interviews with the actors (or organizational representatives), or from archival sources such as publication citation indices, trade records, or IRS reports.

As with sociometry, the raw data on linkages for a social network analysis are compiled into an $N \times N$ matrix (where N is the number of members).[4] When the linkage data are symmetrical (e.g., the presence of trade or kin relations), only the $N(N-1)/2$ elements below the diagonal in the matrix are needed for the database, but when measures are asymmetrical (e.g., A initiates communication with B, versus B with A), the full matrix is used. Measures derived from this matrix data can relate to individual units or the system as a whole (Knoke & Kuklinski, 1982; Scott, 1991; Wasserman & Faust, 1994) and statistical techniques often use advances in graph theory and other complex mathematical models (Robins, 2013). Measures reported by members include number of direct linkages to other units in the system, closeness (ease of interaction with others), and centrality. Other measures describe the nature of the linkages themselves, such as stability, symmetry, or strength. Finally, other analyses focus on characteristics of the network as a whole, such as measures of degree of connectedness (saturation), centralization, and other structural features. Because of the versatility of this methodology, it is used widely across the social science disciplines interested in the study of social systems as a whole, including sociology, communication science, anthropology, science and technology studies, and organizational science (e.g., see Abbott, Bettger, Hampton, & Kohler, 2012; Cillissen, 2009; Eveland & Kleinman, 2013; Meisel et al., 2013; Monge, 1987; Trotter, 2000).

Designs to Study Multiple Groups

The study of dyads or a single group is an essential feature of almost all of the social sciences. Also essential is the study of the behavior of many groups, each containing individual members. In round robin designs and sociometry, we have considered examining dyadic pairs of memberships in a single group. Now we shift attention to designs involving multiple groups. Studying variations across individuals each nested within different groups calls for a methodological perspective different from that adopted when investigating individuals within a single group.

Unit of Analysis in Nested Designs

The major design used by social scientists to study people interacting in groups and differences across the groups is known as multi-level modeling (MLM), which was discussed in Chapter 9. Usually in these designs, each person is a member of one and only one group. Consider a study of elementary school children in which the researcher has 300 students available to serve as participants. These children are found in 10 different classrooms in the school. Each student, of course, is a member of one classroom, and this raises a potential problem for the researcher, because the scores of participants who are the members of the same group usually are more similar than the scores of those who are members of different groups. This similarity of scores happens because of conformity, social norms, modeling, and other social influence factors that operate when members within the same group interact. Even when the members of a group do not interact with each other directly, they may be exposed to common experiences or events that have similar effects on all of them. For instance, students in the same classroom not only interact with each other, they also share a common teacher and a common environmental setting (e.g., same grade level, size of classroom) that may influence them all. Because of these shared social factors, the scores of people in the same group are likely to be interdependent, making the units statistically *nonindependent*. As will be seen, this nonindependence must be considered in the data analysis.

With data from the hierarchically nested design of this type (i.e., participants' scores are nested within classrooms), one can use either the person or the group as the unit of analysis. So in this classroom example, if person is the unit of analysis, correlations between variables and other statistics are computed for the sample of 300 persons. When the group is the unit of analysis, variables at the group level serve as the data in statistical analysis. In this case, the sample size would be 10, because 10 classrooms (groups) were used, and thus the group is the unit of analysis (vs. 300 if person was the unit).

When scores of members of the same group are statistically independent (e.g., students in the same classroom are not any more similar than they are to students of another classroom), then the individual can be used as the unit of analysis. This is desirable because it permits a more powerful statistical analysis of data, and statistically significant relations are more likely to be revealed if more, rather than fewer, units are employed in the analysis. However, if the scores of persons within each group are not statistically independent, then group analytic techniques such as hierarchical linear modeling should be used to simultaneously estimate effects at the grouping level (e.g., classrooms) and the participant level (students). (A general approach to the assessment of dependence in dyadic and group data is also given by Kenny et al., 2006; Sadler & Judd, 2001).

Other Group Designs

Used much less frequently than the hierarchical nested models in studying multiple groups are two types of designs for groups with small numbers of participants. In the *generations design,* one begins with a single group of a given size—say, three units, or actors. One makes the appropriate measurements on persons A, B, and C. Then person A is removed from the group and a new individual, Person D, is added. After measurements are taken, Person B is removed, and Person E is added. The process of removing a person and adding another is continued, and eventually the group consists of no original members. This design mimics in a laboratory the life and death replacements of cultures. The design was first used by Jacobs and Campbell (1961) to study the persistence of norms in groups. The researchers inserted a confederate into an original group of five persons, and the confederate influenced the group members to give a certain response. The confederate was then removed, a new (naive) participant took his place, and the behavior of the group was studied. Jacobs and Campbell were able to show that adherence to the norm set by the confederate was still evident many "generations" after the confederate and all the original group members had been removed from the group. Although used infrequently, the generations design can be used to answer some questions much more effectively than many of the more popular alternatives.

Another design that can be used in small group research is the *rotation design*. In the rotation design we begin with a set of, say, nine persons. Then each person is placed in a group with each other person once and only once. With nine persons and a group size of three, each person would serve in four different groups. So if we denote the persons as 1 through 9, we would have a total of 12 group combinations as depicted in Table 18.6.

At each time point, three different groups, labeled A, B, and C, are formed. No two persons are in the same group more than once. For instance, person 3 is in a group with persons 1 and 2 at time 1, with persons 4 and 8 at time 2, with persons 5 and 7 at time 3, and with persons 6 and 9 at time 4. The person is in a group with each of the eight others once and only once, thus satisfying

TABLE 18.6 The rotation design.

Group	Time			
	I	II	III	IV
A	P1, P2, P3	P1, P5, P9	P1, P6, P8	P1, P4, P7
B	P4, P5, P6	P2, P6, P7	P2, P4, P9	P2, P5, P8
C	P7, P8, P9	P3, P4, P8	P3, P5, P7	P3, P6, P9

Note: P = person

the requirements of the rotation design. Essentially, this is an extension of the round robin design from combinations of dyad pairings to combinations of group placement.

Barnlund (1962) used a rotation design to study whether the same person emerged as a leader, regardless of the group. He created groups of five people, and each person interacted in six sessions (corresponding to six time points). No two persons were in the same group more than once. At each of the six sessions, the groups worked on a different type of task: Artistic, construction, intellectual, coordination, literary, or social. Barnlund found that there was a fair degree of stability in leadership: Participants who sought a leadership role tended do so across sessions, regardless of the task. The rotation design, though used infrequently, can be used to examine the stability of a person's behavior across different groups and situations. Kenny and Hallmark (1992) have provided software for analysis of rotation designs.

Measuring Group Process and Outcomes

Most of the methods for assessing group level variables that we have discussed thus far involve measuring structural features of the grouping unit. Many of these measures can be obtained without actually observing the group in interaction, through reports from group members or from archival records. Many of the more interesting and challenging issues in the study of groups arise from attempts to code and quantify the processes of group interaction itself, as well as the group performance, decisions, or products that arise from those processes. The study of group interaction process is a topic of interest in a number of social and behavior science disciplines, including social psychology, communication sciences, administrative sciences, sociology, education, and clinical psychology (McGrath & Altermatt, 2001). As a consequence, the nature of such measures are as varied as the purposes and composition of groups themselves, so a complete cataloging of measures and data collection techniques is beyond the scope of this chapter (for overviews, see Kerr, Aronoff, & Messé, 2000; McGrath, 1984; McGrath & Altermatt, 2001). However, we can provide some discussion of the most common methodological issues and paradigms that arise in these types of studies.

Interaction Processes

Process measures are sometimes derived from retrospective reports and ratings by members within each group after interaction has taken place. However, most studies of group process involve observation of the actual interactions among group members as they unfold in real time—either through direct observation or by videotaping the group in process and then analyzing the video record. In Chapter 12, we considered the most well-known observational system for classifying and recording interactive behaviors within groups—Bales's (1950, 1970) Interaction Process Analysis (IPA). The

IPA and related observation systems (e.g., Borgatta & Crowther, 1965) provide a detailed record of what takes place during group interaction. Using the IPA generates categorical data representing the sequence of occurrence of interactive acts. Various methods of aggregating or summarizing the data from these records can be used to characterize the processes that have taken place in that group. For example, member contributions can be measured by aggregating each member's speaking turns during the group session and computing the proportion of total speaking turns for each.

Data from the IPA also permit quantitative summaries of the content of member contributions. For instance, Slater (1955) used IPA records to identify the roles that evolve among group members as they interact. He distinguished between two important types of functions that could be carried out by different group members—socio-emotional functions (behaviors that help to maintain good relationships among group members) and task functions (behaviors that contribute to getting the group's job done). Subsequent research on group effectiveness has used these two variables, as well as other role measures derived from IPA data, to assess how well specific groups are functioning (Forsyth, 1990).

The frequency data generated from interaction process analyses can be analyzed using various statistical techniques for analyzing categorical data, such as chi-square contingency analysis or log-linear and logit models (Argesti, 1996; Tian, 2013). However, the dynamic nature of group process often involves studying groups over time, which adds to the complexity of data analyses. In analyzing measures taken from the same interacting group at sequential points in time, we must take into account *serial dependence* among behaviors over time. Just as measures taken from members within the same group are nonindependent (i.e., correlated with each other), so, too, the set of behaviors in a group is to some extent dependent on the behaviors that occurred just prior to it. For example, a group containing competitive members will likely remain competitive when assessed again at a later time point. Sequential analyses (e.g., Gottman & Roy, 1990) are used to assess the degree of serial dependence in a data set. (See Chapter 10 for further discussion of time series analyses.)

Cognitive Processes in Groups

In addition to behavioral acts that can be observed during the course of interaction among members of a group, groups also have a cognitive life, i.e., the knowledge structures and information processing that are brought to bear to make group interaction and coordination possible. The study of group cognition has generated considerable interest in the social sciences (Theiner, 2013; Tindale, Meisenhelder, Dykema-Engblade, & Hogg, 2001; Wegner, Erber, & Raymond, 2004). For this purpose, novel methodologies have been developed to assess such things as how much and what information is shared among group members, how information is distributed, what group members know about each other's knowledge and skills, and what kind of "mental models" group members have about their task and structure.

The distribution of knowledge in a group may be analyzed by coding the contents of each member's knowledge prior to group interaction and assessing the degree of overlap between information held by one member and that of other members of the group (e.g., Kameda, Ohtsubo, & Takezawa, 1997). The degree of overlap in knowledge prior to interaction can be compared with that obtained after the group interaction. The amount of shared information that members have at the outset of the group process can also be experimentally manipulated, as in the *hidden profile technique* developed by Stasser and Titus (1985). In this paradigm, members of four-person groups are instructed to engage in discussion for the purpose of coming to a consensus in selecting the best of three political candidates. Before discussion begins, each of the members is given a different set of information (some positive, some negative) about each of the three candidates. Some of the information is given to all four members (shared knowledge), and other information is uniquely given to just one of the members (unshared knowledge). During the discussion, if members opt to verbally distribute all of the available information (shared + unshared), candidate A is clearly the best choice. However, no one individual member of the group is aware that doing so would be beneficial. Thus, the group's decision (to choose candidate A versus B or C) will reflect how much the unshared information is brought up and used in the group discussion. Using this paradigm, researchers have found that shared knowledge is more likely to be discussed than is unshared knowledge, and as a result, groups often miss the "hidden profile" of information and fail to choose the best candidate.

In addition to the knowledge and information that individual group members bring to a task, they also develop *metacognitions* as the group interacts across time (Hinsz, Tindale, & Vollrath, 1997). At the group level, metacognition refers to the knowledge members possess about the knowledge and skills of each of the other group members, sometimes called *transactive memory* (Ren & Argote, 2011; Wegner, 1987), and about their understanding of the collective goals of the group (sometimes called *shared mental models;* Klimoski & Mohammed, 1994). Tindale et al. (2001) provide a good illustration of group metacognition in their description of sports teams:

> For example, each of the nine members of a baseball team must have an understanding of the rules of the game and the roles for each player . . . for the team to work together. Thus, team players must have a mental model of the task (rules of the game) and the group (the roles of each player) . . . to play effectively. However, this knowledge must be shared among the members in order for it to aid in team effectiveness. Two players who have different models of how to react in a given situation could each behave in ways that would interfere with the other's behavior.
>
> (p. 18)

The importance of giving groups opportunity to develop shared mental models and transactive memory was demonstrated experimentally by Moreland, Argote, and Krishnan (1998). They found that when three-person groups were trained together (in a common session, without direct interaction among members) to perform a task of assembling a radio, they were subsequently able to perform the same task significantly better than groups who had been trained on the same task individually. Methods such as those used by Moreland and his colleagues are teaching group researchers a great deal about the role of shared cognition in group process and coordination.

Computer-Mediated Group Interaction

Another innovation in the study of small groups is found in research on computer-mediated communication, which provides new ways of recording interactive behaviors and group process, as well as new questions to be addressed by group researchers (Bazarova & Yuan, 2013). Computers can be used as a tool for accomplishing group tasks, as when group members work together at a single computer or work at different computers with shared access—a process known as "groupwork" (e.g., McGrath & Hollingshead, 1994; Olson, Olson, Storreston, & Carter, 1994). But most often computers are used by groups as a medium of communication among members who are not in face-to-face contact (e.g., Walther, 2012; Walther, Deandra, & Tong, 2010). Research comparing computer-mediated communication with face-to-face group interaction addresses interesting questions about the role of nonverbal cues in group process and interpersonal coordination, effects of status cues on rates of participation, and amount of information shared among group members (for reviews see Hollingshead & McGrath, 1995; Kiesler & Sproull, 1992). For example, the importance of paralinguistic and nonverbal communication to transactive memory in dyads was documented in experiments by Hollingshead (1998). In this research, dating couples worked together on a general knowledge test either through computer-mediated or face-to-face communication. Face-to-face couples performed significantly better than the computer-mediated couples, apparently because they were able to use nonverbal cues to assess which partner knew the correct answer. Couples who did not know each other prior to the experiment did not show this advantage, suggesting that the effective use of nonverbal information is part of a transactive memory that develops over time.

Computer-mediated groups also become more effective over time. In a longitudinal study comparing computer-mediated and face-to-face communication, Hollingshead, McGrath, and O'Connor (1993) examined task performance of work teams formed from an undergraduate psychology class, in which the task involved writing a joint paper on course materials. The work groups met weekly in 2-hour lab sessions over the course of 13 weeks. Results showed that the computer-mediated groups had poorer task performance than face-to-face groups initially, but after three weeks differences were no longer evidenced in the quality of papers produced by the two types of teams. Because of the role of learning in all forms of group process, the results of longitudinal studies of groups may show very different results from those obtained in cross-sectional studies at a single point in time.

Comparing Groups and Individual Performance

A long-standing issue in the study of groups is that of evaluating the "value-added" by having people work together in groups rather than as lone individuals. Some tasks clearly require the concerted effort of multiple individuals working together because the nature of the task itself is beyond the capabilities of any one person to accomplish (e.g., moving a very large and heavy structure, fighting an invading force, getting to the moon). For many intellectual or physical tasks, however, it is not always clear whether groups of persons working cooperatively together produce more or better products than could be attained by having individuals work separately and then pooling the output of their individual efforts. To address this question, social researchers have developed the method of comparing performance (or products) of a real, interactive group with the products of a **nominal group**, which is composed of the same number and types of people as the real groups, but the members work independently rather than in an interaction, and the group product is a combination of their individual performances or output.

One interesting example of the evaluation of group performance comes from the study of *brainstorming groups*. Brainstorming was initially developed by an advertising executive (Osborn, 1957) as a method for enhancing the generation of creative ideas through group interaction. The idea of a brainstorming group is that members throw out ideas in a freewheeling fashion, without evaluation or censure, building on ideas as they are generated. Based on the notion that interaction would both stimulate and inspire new ideas and combinations of ideas, Osborn made some very strong assumptions about the importance of group processes for creative output. For example, he claimed that "the average person can think up twice as many ideas when working with a group than when working alone" (Osborn, 1957, p. 229).

How has this claim held up to the results of systematic research? Alas for Osborn's credibility, the results of several reviews of studies comparing interacting brainstorm groups with similarly instructed nominal groups consistently show that real groups generally produce fewer and poorer quality ideas than nominal comparison groups (Diehl & Strobe, 1987; Mullen, Johnson, & Salas, 1991). Findings such as these have led group researchers to study the concept of *process loss*—those aspects of group interaction and coordination that inhibit or interfere with group production. For instance, in the case of brainstorming, the fact that group members must take turns talking may block production of ideas, and social psychological processes such as social comparison and evaluation apprehension may also be contributing factors to inhibit output (Stroebe & Diehl, 1994). By reducing some of these influences, "process gains" may override "process losses," producing conditions under which real groups outperform the nominal group (Dennis & Valacich, 1993).

Conclusion

The study of persons in dyads and groups allows for the testing of a number of important hypotheses that could not be tested otherwise. Hypotheses concerning reciprocity, interpersonal attraction, and similarity can be tested best with dyadic measures. To understand the processes that are actually operating in the study of groups and dyads, it is necessary to go beyond a naive and intuitive analysis of the data. Often we must take a score obtained from a dyad or group and partition it into component parts—at the individual, dyadic, and group level—to interpret its meaning accurately. Such a partitioning was illustrated in our discussion of the round robin design, the measurement of attraction, and the analysis of scores of interacting groups. We need to divide a score into components that reflect the different processes that operate at different levels and that contribute to an observed score. It might seem that all of the difficulties encountered when dealing with dyadic and group data diminish their attractiveness, which analyses conducted at the person level might avoid. We prefer to view these complications as interesting challenges that once confronted and conquered reveal fascinating and vital aspects of social interactions that could not be studied otherwise.

Questions for Discussion

1. Although round robin designs may not be used in social research very often, they may be usefully employed. Do you think there are other variables (besides liking and attraction) that would be usefully investigated in research with round robin designs (and that could not be obtained any other way)? For example, you may be interested in studying cohesion and leadership in work groups and find that certain types of people seem to be hubs of perceived similarity—that is, among different group member dyads, when each member felt similar to the *leader* of the group, they identified strongly with the group; however, each member did not feel so similar to other group members. Could this sort of information be obtained without a round robin design? What are other examples of creative uses for round robin designs?
2. What added benefit do we obtain from dyadic research designs that we do not get from individual participant designs? Is research of group processes distinct from research on dyadic processes? Why? What potentially relevant information do we lose when we include only one part of a larger group (e.g., one member of a dyad) in our sample? Should all group-related processes be studied with dyadic or group designs, assuming that any information collected from multiple members of the same group is likely to be nonindependent?
3. Almost all teams that have won the Super Bowl (the championship of the National Football Association) claim their success is based on the love of the players and coaches for one another. "We are family" is a common, if banal, refrain. Could you use a sociometric approach to test this claim? How?

Notes

1. The terms actor and partner correspond to responder and stimulus, respectively, in a dyadic situation. Although we will generally use the terms actor and partner here, other terms can be used. For instance, Cronbach (1955) used the terms *judge* and *target,* and Swann (1984) uses the terms *perceiver* and *target*. In research on nonverbal communication, the terms *receiver* and *sender* as well as *decoder* and *encoder* correspond to actor and partner. We prefer the terms actor and partner because they are not specific to any one area of research.

2. Interactions that are computer mediated (such as real or simulated "chat rooms") lend themselves to this type of design. The partner in a computerized interaction is often a simulated creation of the experimenter, in which case the interest is in the behavior or responses of the single participant who is reacting to a pre-programmed stimulus person (e.g., Crano & Hannula-Bral, 1994). Sometimes, however, the researcher is studying real online interactions between two or more actual persons (e.g., McKenna & Bargh, 2000). In this case, the measurements would be dyadic or group-level variables.
3. We cannot take a simple average across rows to measure the response or a simple average across columns to measure popularity. More complicated methods are required, because the person does not interact with himself or herself (Kenny, Lord, & Garg, 1984; Warner, Kenny, & Stoto, 1979).
4. When the number of actors in a system is very large (as often is the case) network analyses require access to very large computer facilities.

References

Abbott, K. M., Bettger, J., Hampton, K., & Kohler, H. (2012). Exploring the use of social network analysis to measure social integration among older adults in assisted living. *Family & Community Health: The Journal Of Health Promotion & Maintenance, 35,* 322–333.

Argesti, A. (1996). *An introduction to categorical data analysis.* New York: Wiley.

Bales, R. F. (1950). *Interaction process analysis.* Cambridge: Addison-Wesley.

Bales, R. F. (1970). *Personality and interpersonal behavior.* New York: Holt, Rinehard, and Winston.

Barnlund, D. C. (1962). Consistency of emergent leadership with changing tasks and members. *Speech Monographs, 29,* 45–52.

Bazarova, N. N., & Yuan, Y. (2013). Expertise recognition and influence in intercultural groups: Differences between face-to-face and computer-mediated communication. *Journal of Computer-Mediated Communication, 18,* 437–453.

Borgatta, E. F., & Crowther, B. (1965). *A workbook for the study of social interaction processes.* Chicago: Rand-McNally.

Brewer, M. B., & Campbell, D. T. (1976). *Ethnocentrism and intergroup attitudes: East African evidence.* Beverly Hills, CA: Sage.

Campbell, D. T., Miller, N., Lubetsky, J., & O'Connell, E. J. (1964). Varieties of projection in trait attribution. *Psychological Monographs, 78* (entire issue 592).

Cillissen, A.H.N. (2009). Sociometric methods. In K. H. Rubin, W. H. Bukowski, & B. Laursen (Eds.), *Handbook of peer interactions, relationships, and groups* (pp. 82–99). New York: Guilford.

Clore, G. L., Bray, R. M., Itkin, S. M., & Murphey, P. (1978). Interracial attitudes and behavior at summer camp. *Journal of Personality and Social Psychology, 36,* 107–116.

Cook, W. L, & Kenny, D. A. (2005). The actor-partner interdependence model—A model of bidirectional effects in developmental studies. *International Journal of Behavioral Development, 20,* 101–109.

Crano, W. D., & Hannula-Bral, K. A. (1994). Context/categorization model of social influence: Minority and majority influence in the formation of a novel response norm. *Journal of Experimental Social Psychology, 30,* 247–276.

Cronbach, L. J. (1955). Processes affecting scores on "understanding of others" and "assumed similarity." *Psychological Bulletin, 52,* 177–193.

Curry, T. J., & Emerson, R. M. (1970). Balance theory: A theory of interpersonal attraction? *Sociometry, 33,* 216–238.

Dennis, A. R., & Valacich, J. S. (1993). Computer brainstorms: More heads are better than one. *Journal of Applied Psychology, 78,* 531–537.

Diehl, M., & Stroebe, W. (1987). Productivity loss in brainstorming groups: Toward the solution of a riddle. *Journal of Personality and Social Psychology, 53,* 497–509.

Eveland, W. R., & Kleinman, S. B. (2013). Comparing general and political discussion networks within voluntary organizations using social network analysis. *Political Behavior, 35,* 65–87.

Forsyth, D. R. (1990). *Group dynamics* (2nd ed.). Pacific Grove, CA: Brooks/Cole.

Gottman, J. M., & Roy, A. K. (1990). *Sequential analysis: A guide for behavioral researchers.* New York: Cambridge University Press.

Heider, F. (1958). *The psychology of interpersonal relations.* New York: Wiley.

Hinsz, V. B., Tindale, R. S., & Vollrath, D. A. (1997). The emerging conceptualization of groups as information processors. *Psychological Bulletin, 121,* 43–64.

Holland, P. W., & Leinhardt, S. (1978). An omnibus test for social structure using triads. *Sociological Methods and Research, 7,* 227–256.

Hollingshead, A. B. (1998). Retrieval processes in transactive memory systems. *Journal of Personality Social Psychology, 74,* 659–671.

Hollingshead, A. B. & McGrath, J. E. (1995). Computer-assisted groups: A critical review of the empirical research. In R. Guzzo & E. Salas (Eds.), *Team effectiveness and decision making in organizations* (pp. 46–78). San Francisco: Jossey-Bass.

Hollingshead, A. B., McGrath, J. E., & O'Connor, K. M. (1993). Group task performance and communication technology: A longitudinal study of computer-mediated versus face-to-face work groups. *Small Group Research, 24,* 307–333.

Jacobs, R. C., & Campbell, D. T. (1961). The perpetuation of an arbitrary tradition through several generations of laboratory microculture. *Journal of Abnormal and Social Psychology, 62,* 649–658.

Kameda, T., Ohtsubo, Y., & Takezawa, M. (1997). Centrality in sociocognitive network and social influence: An illustration in a group decision-making context. *Journal of Personality and Social Psychology, 73,* 296–309.

Kashy, D. A., & Kenny, D. A. (2000). The analysis of data from dyads and groups. In H. Reis & C. Judd (Eds.), *Handbook of research methods in social and personality psychology* (pp. 451–477). New York: Cambridge University Press.

Kenny, D. A., & Hallmark, B. W. (1992). Rotation designs in leadership research. *The Leadership Quarterly, 3,* 25–41.

Kenny, D. A., Kashy, D. A., & Cook, W. L. (2006). *Dyadic data analysis.* New York: Guilford Press.

Kenny, D. A., & La Voie, L. (1982). Reciprocity of attraction: A confirmed hypothesis. *Social Psychology Quarterly, 45,* 54–58.

Kenny, D. A., & La Voie, L. (1984). The social relations model. *Advances in Experimental Social Psychology, 18,* 142–182.

Kenny, D. A., & Ledermann, T. (2010). Detecting, measuring and testing dyadic patterns in the actor-partner interdependence model. *Journal of Family Psychology, 24,* 359–366.

Kenny, D. A., Lord, R., & Garg, S. (1984). *A social relations model for peer ratings.* Unpublished manuscript, University of Connecticut, Storrs, CT.

Kerr, N. L., Aronoff, J., & Messé, L. A. (2000). Methods of group research. In H. Reis & C. Judd (Eds.), *Handbook of research methods in social and personality psychology* (pp. 160–189). New York: Cambridge University Press.

Kiesler, S., & Sproull, L. (1992). Group decision making and technology. *Organizational Behavior and Human Decision Processes, 52,* 96–123.

Klimoski, R., & Mohammed, S. (1994). Team mental model: Construct or metaphor? *Journal of Management, 20,* 403–437.

Knoke, D., & Kuklinski, J. H. (1982). *Network analysis.* Beverly Hills, CA: Sage.

McGrath, J. E. (1984). *Groups: Interaction and performance.* Englewood Cliffs, NJ: Prentice-Hall.

McGrath, J. E., & Altermatt, T. W. (2001). Observation and analysis of group interaction over time: Some methodological and strategic choices. In M. Hogg & R. S. Tindale (Eds.), *Blackwell handbook of social psychology: Group processes* (pp. 525–573). Oxford, UK: Blackwell.

McGrath, J. E., & Hollingshead, A. B. (1994). *Groups interacting with technology.* Thousand Oaks, CA: Sage.

McKenna, K., & Bargh, J. A. (2000). Plan 9 from Cyberspace: The implications of the Internet for personality and social psychology. *Personality and Social Psychology Review, 4,* 57–75.

Meisel, M. K., Clifton, A. D., MacKillop, J., Miller, J. D., Campbell, W., & Goodie, A. S. (2013). Egocentric social network analysis of pathological gambling. *Addiction, 108,* 584–591.

Miller, R. E., Caul, W. F., & Mirsky, I. A. (1967). Communication between feral and socially isolated monkeys. *Journal of Personality and Social Psychology, 3,* 231–239.

Monge, P. R. (1987). The network level of analysis. In C. R. Berger & S. H. Chaffee (Eds.), *Handbook of communication science* (pp. 239–270). Newbury Park, CA: Sage.

Moreland, R. L., Argote, L., & Krishman, R. (1998). Training people to work in groups. In R. S. Tindale, L. Heath, J. Edwards, E. Posavac, F. Bryant, Y. Suarez-Balcazar, E. Henderson-King, & J. Myers (Eds.), *Social psychological applications to social issues: Applications of theory and research on groups* (vol. 4, pp. 37–60). New York: Plenum Press.

Moreno, J. L., (1934). Who shall survive? *Nervous and Mental Disease Monograph, No. 58.*

Mullen, B., Johnson, C., & Salas, E. (1991). Productivity loss in brainstorming groups: A meta-analytic integration. *Basic and Applied Social Psychology, 12,* 3–24.

Newcomb, T. M. (1961). *The acquaintance process.* New York: Holt, Rinehart, & Winston.

Olson, J. S., Olson, G., Storreston, M., & Carter, M. (1994). Groupwork close up: A comparison of the group design process with and without a simple group editor. *ACM Transactions on Information Systems, 11,* 321–348.

Osborn, A. F. (1957). *Applied imagination.* New York: Scribners.

Ren, Y., & Argote, L. (2011). Transactive memory systems 1985–2010: An integrative framework of key dimensions, antecedents, and consequences. *The Academy of Management Annals, 5*(1), 189–229.

Robins, G. (2013). A tutorial on methods for the modeling and analysis of social network data. *Journal of Mathematical Psychology, 57,* 261–274.

Sadler, M. S., & Judd, C. M. (2001). Overcoming dependent data: A guide to the analysis of group data. In M. Hogg & R. S. Tindale (Eds.), *Blackwell handbook of social psychology: Group processes* (pp. 497–524). Oxford, UK: Blackwell.

Sampson, F. (1969). *Crisis in the cloister* (Unpublished doctoral dissertation). Cornell University, Department of Sociology, Ithaca, NY.

Scott, J. (1991). *Social network analysis: A handbook.* London: Sage.

Slater, P. E. (1955). Role differentiation in small groups. *American Sociological Review, 20,* 300–310.

Sprecher, S., Treger, S., & Wondra, J. D. (2013). Effects of self-disclosure role on liking, closeness, and other impressions in get acquainted interactions. *Journal of Social and Personal Relationships, 30,* 497–514.

Stasser, G., & Titus, W. (1985). Pooling of unshared information in group decision making: Biased information sampling during discussion. *Journal of Personality and Social Psychology, 53,* 81–93.

Stroebe, W., & Diehl, M. (1994). Why groups are less effective than their members: On productivity losses in idea-generating groups. In W. Stroebe & M. Hewstone (Eds.) *European Review of Social Psychology* (vol. 5, pp. 271–303). London: Wiley.

Swann, W. B. (1984). The quest for accuracy in person perception: A matter of pragmatics. *Psychological Review, 91,* 457–477.

Terry, R. (2000). Recent advances in measurement theory and the use of sociometric techniques. In A.H.N. Cillessen, & W. Bukowski (Eds.), *Recent advances in the measurement of acceptance and rejection in the peer system* (pp. 27–53). San Francisco: Jossey-Bass.

Theiner, G. (2013). Transactive memory systems: A mechanistic analysis of emergent group memory. *Review of Philosophy and Psychology, 4,* 65–89.

Tian, G.-L. (2013). Incomplete categorical data design: *Non-randomized response techniques for sensitive questions in surveys.* Hoboken, NJ: Taylor & Francis.

Tindale, R. S., Meisenhelder, H. M., Dykema-Engblade, A., & Hogg, M. A. (2001). In M. Hogg & R. S. Tindale (Eds.), *Blackwell handbook of social psychology: Group processes* (pp. 1–30). Oxford, UK: Blackwell.

Trotter, R. T., II. (2000). Ethnography and network analysis: The study of social context in cultures and society. In G. L. Albrecht & R. Fitzpatrick (Eds.), *The handbook of social studies in health and medicine* (pp. 210–229). London: Sage.

Walster, E., Aronson, V., Abrahams, D., & Rottman, L. (1966). Importance of physical attractiveness in dating behavior. *Journal of Personality and Social Psychology, 5,* 508.

Walther, J. B. (2012). Interaction through technological lenses: Computer-mediated communication and language. *Journal of Language and Social Psychology, 31,* 397–414.

Walther, J. B., Deandrea, D. C., & Tong, S. (2010). Computer-mediated communication versus vocal communication and the attenuation of pre-interaction impressions. *Media Psychology, 13,* 364–386.

Warner, R. M., Kenny, D. A., & Stoto, M. (1979). A new round robin analysis of variance for social interaction data. *Journal of Personality and Social Psychology, 37,* 1742–1757.

Wasserman, S. & Faust, K. (1994). *Social network analysis: Methods and applications.* New York: Cambridge University Press.

Wegner, D. M. (1987). Transactive memory: A contemporary analysis of the group mind. In B. Mullen & G. Goethals (Eds.), *Theories of group behavior* (pp. 185–208). New York: Springer-Verlag.

Wegner, D. M., Erber, R., & Raymond, P. (1991). Transactive memory in close relationships. *Journal of Personality and Social Psychology, 61,* 923–929.

Wegner, D. M., Erber, R., & Raymond, P. (2004). Transactive memory in close relationships. In H. T. Reis, C. E. Rusbult (Eds.), *Close relationships: Key readings* (pp. 269–279). Philadelphia: Taylor & Francis.

White, H., Boorman, S., & Breiger, R. (1976). Social structure from multiple networks, I: Block models of roles and positions. *American Journal of Sociology, 81,* 730–779.

Won-Doornink, M. J. (1979). On getting to know you: The association between stage of a relationship and reciprocity of self-disclosure. *Journal of Personality and Social Psychology, 15,* 229–241.

PART IV
Concluding Perspectives

19

SYNTHESIZING RESEARCH RESULTS

Meta-Analysis

All sciences progress by the gradual accretion of knowledge. Although surely inspired, Einstein's classic formula relating energy to a function of mass and velocity was not drawn out of thin air. His creative insight was based on a synthesis and extension of the available knowledge of the time (Clark, 1971; Kuhn, 1970). Over the years, social scientists have relied on a similar process of intuition and integration of the prior research literature to develop new insights, which sometimes lead to the accumulation of yet more knowledge. A **primary study** is an original study reporting on the results of analysis of data collected from a sample of participants (e.g., a journal article, research report, dissertation). It serves as the principle unit of empirical knowledge. All the chapters in the textbook up to this point have described strategies for designing and conducting primary studies. To the extent that the existing literature on a phenomenon is accurate and we have comprehensively collected these primary studies, we can develop an understanding of the structure of interrelationships that underlie the obtained results. Current knowledge is the foundation of future discoveries.

Traditionally, this constructive process of integrating knowledge was based on a **narrative review**, a qualitative approach for summarizing and interpreting primary studies that have addressed the same research question (Johnson & Eagly, 2000). The time-honored integrative process of narrative review has been supplemented in recent years by the development of methods of *quantitative reviews* or *syntheses*. The most widespread type is **meta-analysis**, a quantitative approach for summarizing and interpreting primary studies that have addressed the same research question. Meta-analytic procedures allow for the quantitative assessment of the relationship among constructs that reflect a specific phenomenon. Although the traditional narrative review has served us well, its critics suggest that it is prone to shortcomings, including (a) the failure to review the existing knowledge base comprehensively[1], (b) the lack of clearly stated rules for inclusion or exclusion of studies, and (c) the failure to use statistical metrics to combine findings across studies objectively. A systematic and objective meta-analysis is intended to avoid all of these problems and thereby develops a more comprehensive understanding of relationships among variables. The ultimate goal of meta-analysis is to construct a secure foundation on which to build a knowledge base using preexisting research.

Meta-analytic techniques require a thorough understanding of the research literature on a given topic, good intuition and creativity, and a dogged patience in locating and coding eligible primary studies. A meta-analysis, through quantitatively combining primary studies with varying measurement idiosyncrasies, offers a clearer path to understanding the true strength of relation between variables than does nonquantitative narrative review.

As a method of combining empirical studies, meta-analysis had its beginnings many years ago, but the advent of the technique was spurred by the refinement of more formalized statistics that now are used commonly (Cooper, 1979; Rosenthal, 1979; Rosenthal & Rubin, 1982).[2] Over this time period, important and thought-provoking syntheses have been published, and they have helped popularize this general approach (e.g., see Cooper, 1979, 2009; Eagly, Ashmore, Makhijani, & Longo, 1991; Eagly, Karau, & Makhijani, 1995; Heikkilä et al., 2013; Lac & Crano, 2009; Quon & McGrath, 2013; Wood, Lundgren, Ouellette, Busceme, & Blackstone, 1994). The shift from narrative reviews to meta-analysis was not always welcomed with open arms. Early on, many admitted in principle that meta-analysis could be a useful technique if its technical issues could be resolved, but even then doubted its necessity. We believe that meta-analysis offers a means of addressing research problems that the more traditional narrative reviews cannot. It represents yet another valuable tool for the social scientist, particularly when primary research on a phenomenon has been investigated using different methods, an approach to research that we have championed throughout this book. In effect, meta-analysis provides a way of assessing *construct validity* and *external validity* by pooling primary investigations that address the same hypothesis and which may involve different methods of design and measurement. Social science in general appears to share this evaluation. More than 7,000 meta-analyses have been published on issues of importance to social and medical science.

A simple example will help illustrate the role that meta-analysis can play in interpreting findings from methodological variants of studies examining the same underlying hypothesis. Suppose a researcher were interested in reviewing the relation between physical attractiveness (independent variable) and liking (dependent variable) in the literature. Immediately two relevant primary studies are located in the literature. Researchers in the first study hypothesized that an attractive rather than an unattractive target would be rated more positively by participants. To test this idea, the researcher showed manipulated pictures of an attractive or unattractive person and randomly assigned a large number of participants to each of these picture conditions. Participants were asked to rate the photograph using semantic differential items whose positive poles were pleasant, good, kind, thoughtful, and nice. The ratings on these measures were internally consistent, so the researcher combined them to compute an overall "liking" score. Statistical analysis disclosed that the physically attractive targets were rated significantly more positively than the unattractive targets (at $p < .05$). The researcher concluded that the results confirmed the hypothesis: Attractive targets stimulate significantly greater liking than unattractive targets.

Suppose another primary study instead involves a field experiment in which the manipulation involves a confederate who is dressed to look either very attractive or very unattractive. In this study, the confederate individually approached strangers (participants) in a shopping mall and asked to borrow their cellular phone. The dependent measure of liking was operationally defined as participants' latency of response in honoring the confederate's request. The study used a small sample size, and analysis of latencies suggested that the attractive and unattractive requester did not yield a statistically significant difference as a function of the confederate's attractiveness ($p > .05$).

What conclusion could a reader draw from these two studies? Is there a relation between physical attractiveness and liking, as suggested in the significant first study, or is this effect an artifact of the laboratory setting? Or, is the second study that produced a statistically nonsignificant result evidence that attractiveness does not increase liking, or is such a null finding due to lack of statistical power, or a poor operational definition of the liking variable (number of seconds participants took to lend their cellular phone)? We find ourselves in a quandary because the two studies produced different conclusions about the connection between attractiveness and liking, at least as we can infer on the basis of the statistical significance of the results. The problem with comparing studies on this basis is that statistical significance is affected by a host of methodological and statistical factors that do not necessarily reflect upon the validity of the proposed relationship, such as sample size or the reliability of measures. With all else being equal, a study containing a larger sample size is more likely to achieve statistical significance as it yields more stable estimates. Thus, probability values obtained are *not* directly comparable between studies, because they indicate *statistical significance,* not *practical significance.* To compare studies properly requires a common metric to express the size of the effect obtained in each of the two studies. This is the basic insight and contribution of meta-analysis—to convert the statistical tests of primary studies that address the same hypothesis into a common metric, and then to aggregate these studies to obtain an overall effect size estimate.

Stages in the Meta-Analysis Process

When operationally different but conceptually similar studies produce similar results (or produce results similar in terms of the sizes of their effects), our confidence in both the external and construct validity of our findings is enhanced. However, as our attractiveness example suggests, when results appear to differ among studies, it may be difficult to identify the source(s) of the discrepancy. Fluctuations in results obtained among studies that assess the same research hypothesis could stem from differences involving settings, participant samples, and operational definition of variables, to name a few of the methodological differences that characterize studies. When many studies of the same relationship or phenomenon have been conducted, it is possible to use meta-analysis not only to compute an overall effect, but also to sort out and identify the sources of variation in results across studies and thereby develop a deeper understanding of an underlying relationship. The particular steps in the meta-analysis may vary from synthesis to synthesis, but the procedures to be followed are the same.

Understand the Literature

The first step, as in any other approach to reviewing research literature, requires that we have a good understanding of the scientific studies that have been conducted on the phenomenon chosen for the meta-analysis. Techniques of meta-analysis are most effective when they are focused on a hypothesized relationship between (usually two) variables that can be specified with a high degree of precision. We begin with a specific hypothesis linking an independent variable with a dependent variable, or we specify a relationship between predictor and criterion variables if correlational methodology was the primary method used in past studies to investigate the relation On the basis of theory and prior research, the starting point is always the simple A—B relationship, whether causal or correlational. (It is possible to synthesize interrelations involving three or more variables using an extension of the basic two-variable idea.) Returning to our example, we assume that physical attractiveness elicits more liking—people respond more positively to attractive versus unattractive others. This cause-effect hypothesis relating two variables is an ideal candidate for meta-analysis.

A basic requirement is that there be sufficient past research on the relationship of interest. If there are few studies of the particular relationship to be aggregated, it is not likely that a synthesis will produce persuasive results. In general, a meta-analysis requires a relatively large number of existing studies that all examine the same critical relationship before the method's true power as an integrative force can be realized. Thus, meta-analysis requires that we have a good grasp of the literature and what has been done previously, to have some general idea about the pertinent studies that have been conducted on the critical relationship. To plunge into the meta-analysis before developing a strong command of the literature is foolhardy. Meta-analysis is labor intensive. To realize halfway through the project that some important studies have been overlooked, or that the basic relationship under study has not been specified correctly, usually results in a great loss of time and effort.

Study Inclusion and Exclusion Criteria

The importance of specifying a hypothesized relationship clearly becomes apparent in this phase, which entails choosing potential primary studies to be included in the meta-analysis. To choose studies, the researcher must decide on the search criteria to be used to determine the relevance of a particular study. The issue of how broadly or narrowly to define the relationship or constructs being investigated affects this choice. Problems may be framed at different levels of specificity or abstractness. A meta-analytic review of the effectiveness of a particular form of a one-to-one psychotherapy on reducing the depression symptom of oversleeping may prove too narrow, but a synthesis of the overall effectiveness of all types psychotherapeutic interventions on reducing all forms of mental illness is too broad. A review of the effect of cooperative tasks on interracial relations is more concrete and focused than a review of the effects of tasks on intergroup relations in general.

Choosing appropriate primary studies for inclusion or exclusion involves two distinct processes. The first requires a *tentative* specification of inclusion rules; that is, which studies of the critical relationship will be included in the synthesis and which will be excluded.[3] Studies are included if they meet a specific criterion, or set of criteria. For example, if a meta-analyst wishes to estimate the strength of the causal relationship between the chosen independent and dependent variable, then studies that made use of experimental methodology will be included in the meta-analysis. The meta-analyst might offer the rationale that correlational studies were excluded because that they cannot unambiguously support causal interpretations. Or, the meta-analyst may wish to summarize only studies published after a certain date, using the rationale that an important theoretical development did not emerge until after that point. If there are defensible theoretical reasons for these qualifications, the meta-analyst is fully justified in choice of criteria. A word of caution is in order, however; sometimes overly narrow inclusion criteria can overlook important information in studies. For example, in a meta-analysis of studies reporting gender differences in terms of perceived quality of life, Wood, Rhodes and Whelan (1989) found that men reported higher life-quality in studies published after 1978, whereas women reported a better quality of life in studies published before that date. This difference cannot be interpreted causally, of course, because cohort variations are not the result of systematic manipulation. However, Wood's and colleagues' (1989) results provide considerable grist for the speculative mill. If only studies published after 1978 were included and the timing of studies had not been coded, this meta-analytic result could not have emerged.

Published meta-analyses in the social sciences range from those that include as few as 8 (e.g., Packer, 2008) to 30 independent studies (e.g., Williams, Haertel, Haertel, & Walberg, 1982) to those containing more than 300 studies (e.g., Smith & Glass, 1977; Rosenthal & Rubin, 1978). In general, the number of primary studies available for consolidation varies as a function of the number of existing studies that have been conducted in that area, the search skills of the meta-analyst, and the inclusion specificity of the constructs being examined.

Returning to our attractiveness-liking example, we might incorporate only studies that manipulated the independent variable of attractiveness using photographs. In terms of the dependent variable, we might include only studies that have operationally defined liking in terms of attitude scales. More broadly, we might also include studies that operationally defined liking in terms of observable behaviors such as actions, donations, and eye contact. The decision about the allowable breadth of the constructs must be made in terms of the goals of the study and the number of studies available for analysis. In some cases, a very constricted operational definition of a variable will be chosen, because this range is specifically relevant to a theoretical aspect of the relationship to be meta-analyzed. In other circumstances, range will be constricted because there are not enough studies available to support a broader analytic inclusion approach. For example, we may narrowly define the liking variable in terms of observable behavior (e.g. seconds of eye contact).

Or, conversely, liking may be more broadly defined by a variety of measures, ranging from self-reports to behavioral indications of liking, including eye contact duration. More studies will be available with the less constricted definition, but we must be satisfied that the different measures are triangulating on the same construct.

There is some debate about the inclusion or exclusion of studies on the basis of quality. Some have suggested that studies that do not meet some common methodological standard (e.g., no control group, no manipulation check information, poor reliability of measures, etc.) should be excluded (e.g., Greenwald & Russell, 1991; Kraemer, Gardner, Brooks, & Yesavage, 1998). We believe, however, that meta-analysts generally should not exclude studies that meet substantive inclusion criteria, even those that are methodologically suspect. If the study meets the selection rules, it probably is wise not to go over the individual investigations and decide that some are to be excluded from the sample because they do not meet some high standard of methodological requirements. In our view, rather than including studies on the basis of methodological purity, a more promising approach entails rating the methodological rigor of each study, and then entering this rating as a potential moderator variable whose effect on the hypothesized relationship may be assessed in the meta-analysis. Such an assessment may show, for example, that only methodologically weak studies exhibit the postulated relationship. This result could prove useful and interesting, and would not be available if the weak studies were excluded a priori from the analysis. Assessing the role of a study-level moderator in a meta-analysis is elaborated later on.

Locating Primary Studies

After deciding on the inclusion rules, the researcher must gather every possible study that meets the criteria. This process can be accomplished with considerably more ease than it could a few short years ago. Computerized database literature searches in the social sciences are now possible by using sources such as those available in the Social Science Citation Index (Social SciSearch), Web of Science, the Education Resources Information Center (ERIC), Psychological Abstracts, PsycINFO, PubMed, Google Scholar, Sociological Abstracts, and Comprehensive Dissertation Abstracts. These bibliographic sources are available electronically at university libraries and are online for ease of access. One need only enter the appropriate search terms (usually one or more variants and synonyms of the critical variables of the meta-analysis), and the entire published literature can be searched. (The American Psychological Association's PsycINFO database, for example, contains studies dating back to the 1880s, and the Dissertation Abstracts database extends back to 1861.) Of course, social scientists are notorious for coining their own terms, so it is wise to employ search terms and criteria broadly and to survey the archives exhaustively for potentially relevant primary research. Campbell (1963), for example, listed more than 75 synonyms used in the literature to refer to the general concept that laypeople would identify as attitude or opinion. Thus, if we wished to conduct a meta-analysis on the effect of self-interest on attitudes, it would be shortsighted to search only for studies that combine the terms self-interest and attitude. Other synonyms for the attitude construct—opinion, belief, value, acquired behavioral disposition, etc.—would also be useful if combined with attitude importance, vested interest, outcome involvement, or commitment to represent self-interest. We know the appropriate search terms by being familiar with the research literature, and then learning more about the literature as we search it. An effective meta-analysis is meant to provide an accurate picture of a literature. If the literature search is deficient—if it does not produce the necessary raw materials for examination—the synthesis will be not be representative of that literature.

Another way of using the electronic databases is through descendancy and ascendancy search for eligible studies (Cooper, 2009). In **descendancy searching**, an important early and relevant primary study is identified and used as the starting point to search for all chronologically later studies (descendants) that have cited it. By an important study, we mean one that is clearly focused on a construct that is part of the hypothesized relationship in the meta-analysis. This study is widely recognized as definitive, or as a classic in the field. Usually, there is relatively good consensus surrounding such studies, and if more than one is available, all should be used to obtain additional studies in descendancy searching. Conversely, it also is practical to consider **ascendency searching**, in which the reference list of a recent and relevant primary study is consulted to perform a backward search to find chronologically earlier relevant studies (ancestors). These located primary studies, in turn, can be used for further backward literature searches, and the process is continued until all relevant studies are found.

Some of the literature sources listed here are important because they include unpublished studies. The ERIC database, for example, contains a large store of papers presented at major scientific conferences. Unpublished studies, such as student projects, may be located in popular Internet search engines (e.g., Google or Yahoo). Such papers are not published in a journal for various reasons, and the information would be lost were it not for the Internet. Unpublished research is important to include in meta-analyses, because we know that scientific journals are biased toward publishing primary studies showing significant results. Indeed, it is rare for a journal to publish a study containing results that are statistically nonsignificant. A number of comparative reviews have demonstrated that published studies tend to show larger effects than unpublished ones. Smith and Glass (1977), for example, examined the standardized effect size obtained in 375 studies of the effectiveness of psychotherapy on recovery outcomes and found that primary studies published in books and journals had effect sizes that averaged between .7 and .8, while dissertation studies averaged .6 and other unpublished studies only .5. If the goal of the meta-analyst is to describe the *universe* of studies that deal with a specific relationship, then this bias in the published research toward statistically significant studies could prove misleading. In the worst of all possible worlds, we might be seeing only the 5% of published primary studies that, by chance, satisfied the $p < .05$ level of statistical significance (Greenwald, 1975).

Publication bias occurs when primary studies are not published for some systematic reason, usually because results were not found to be statistically significant. This is known as the **file drawer problem** (Bradley & Gupta, 1997; Rosenthal, 1979, 1991), which is the tendency for unpublished studies to be tucked away in file drawers and therefore ignored in a meta-analysis, resulting in a synthesis not representative of the research that has been conducted. The extent that publication bias creates a problem for any meta-analysis may never be known fully. However, Rosenthal (1979, 1991) suggested a resolution to the problem that allows us to estimate the extent to which it may be an issue in a particular meta-analysis. This approach involves calculating the number of nonsignificant studies with null results (i.e., effect size of zero) that would have to exist "in the file drawers" before the statistically significant overall effect obtained from the meta-analysis of included studies would no longer be significant at the $p < .05$ level. The size of this number of unpublished studies helps us evaluate the seriousness of the threat to conclusions drawn from the meta-analysis. If the number of additional studies that would have to exist is very large before the observed relation is rendered nonsignificant, then it is not likely that studies "in the file drawer" would compromise the conclusions we reach on the basis of the available evidence. But if only a few additional studies with null results would reduce our obtained effects to the edge of statistical nonsignificance, we would have to regard the file drawer problem as a potential threat to the interpretation of the meta-analysis.

Computing Effect Sizes

If we are satisfied that our literature search procedures have succeeded in producing an archive of all (or most) studies relevant to our interests, we are ready to begin the computational phase of the meta-analysis. In this stage, we convert the test statistics reported in each primary study to the same effect size metric. An **effect size** serves as standardized metric of practical significance, or magnitude of relationship between two variables, and is the unit of analysis in a meta-analysis. To synthesize a selection of literature, we need to convert the statistical results of primary studies to the same standardized metric. Calculating effect sizes often is made difficult by studies that fail to provide the necessary statistics in the published paper to enable the conversion. As we have noted, the effect size computation serves as a statistical indicator of the strength of a given relationship between critical variables in a primary study. The paper reporting the original research must present results in terms of statistics (e.g., means and standard deviations, t test, F-test, χ^2 test) to allow conversion to an effect size in the meta-analysis. Once the results across a set of primary studies are transformed into effect sizes so they are all on the same metric, the magnitude of the effect from one study can be compared or combined with the effects from the other relevant studies.[4]

Three major families of metrics are commonly used to represent effect size (Borenstein, Hedges, Higgins, & Rothstein, 2009; Cooper, 2009). *Cohen's d,* or the standardized difference between two means, should be used as an indicator of effect size if the relation involves a binary variable and a quantitative variable. It is meaningful for non-experimental studies comparing differences in means between two groups on an outcome (e.g., the extent that males and females differ on level of self-esteem scores). It also is appropriate for primary research involving experimental designs to determine whether and to what extent two conditions of an independent variable yield different mean scores on the dependent variable. The formula for Cohen's *d* is:

$$\text{Cohen's } d = \frac{M_2 - M_1}{SD}$$

The difference in means is computed between the two groups—M_2 (e.g., treatment) compared to M_1 (e.g., control)—and is then divided by its pooled standard deviation. It is necessary to divide the difference by the standard deviation, as this takes into account the variation in scores within each primary study. So Cohen's *d* reflects both the size of the difference between two means and the amount of overlap between distributions of scores in the two conditions. Three general patterns of Cohen's *d* are possible, as diagrammed in Figure 19.1. If the result is shown to be in the hypothesized direction, with the treatment group (2) scoring higher than the control group (1), Cohen's *d* results in a positive value (Figure 19.1a). Two other possibilities could occur if results do not support the researcher's hypothesis. If the means of the two groups are about the same, the formula will yield a value of Cohen's *d* close to 0 (Figure 19.1b). If the results reveal that the control group (1) scored better that the experimental group (2) (opposite to that hypothesized), Cohen's *d* will be a negative value (Figure 19.1c). Thus, for our meta-analysis of attraction to liking, a Cohen's *d* is calculated for each of the primary studies to signify the difference in substantive effect between the attractive and unattractive conditions on liking scores. These 10 primary studies are displayed in Table 19.1 and will serve as the guiding scenario to detail the steps of a meta-analysis for the rest of the chapter. Eight studies show an effect size in the direction of the meta-analytic hypothesis, but the remaining two studies obtained results in the opposite direction

The *odds ratio* is most meaningfully interpreted as an effect size metric for studies that examine the relationship between two binary variables. For instance, it could serve as an indicator of practical significance in a non-experimental study comparing males and females on the outcome variable of whether they are marijuana users or not. Or it could be calculated for an experimental investigation comparing treatment and control groups on a dependent variable represented by two levels.

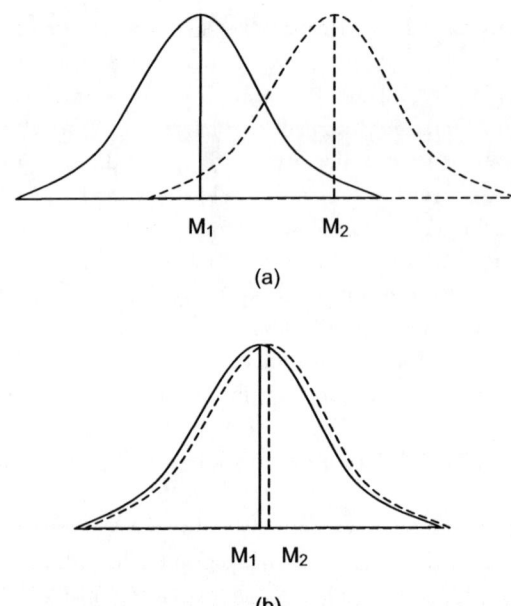

FIGURE 19.1 Examples of Cohen's d to indicate standardized difference in means between two groups.

TABLE 19.1 Hypothetical effect sizes (Cohen's d) of 10 primary studies.

Study #	First Author	Effect Size
1	Van Damme	−.15
2	Weaver	−.05
3	Stallone	.28
4	Jovovich	.35
5	Chan	.35
6	Grier	.37
7	Schwarzenegger	.56*
8	Yeoh	.59*
9	Snipes	.65*
10	Li	.89*

*$p < .05$

The odds ratio is less commonly reported as an effect size in social science studies, but is common in biomedical studies that examine binary outcomes of success or failure (e.g., survival or death, healthy or unhealthy).

The *correlation* is the most meaningful effect size metric for studies that examine a relationship in which both variables are quantitative. Used in non-experimental designs, the correlation is not only a type of statistical test, but it also serves as an indicator of effect size. It could be used to gauge the practical magnitude in a non-experimental study—for example, the covariation between an intelligence test and brain weight. Because the Pearson correlation coefficient is restricted to values ranging from −1.00 to 1.00, it should be corrected for skew, especially if coefficients are near either extreme ends, using *Fisher's Zr correction*, before aggregating studies in a meta-analysis (Cooper, 2009; see Hays, 1994). Although most of us are familiar with the correlation variant involving two quantitative variables, the correlation family actually consists of three types: (a) *Pearson correlation*, for assessing the relationship involving two quantitative variables, (b) *Point-biserial correlation*, for assessing the relationship involving a binary variable and a quantitative variable, and (c) *phi*, for assessing the relationship involving two binary variables. In fact, these three types of correlations may be combined in a meta-analysis. Given these advantageous properties, Rosenthal (1991) recommended the correlation as the preferred choice in a meta-analysis, especially if the hypothesis varies widely in terms of whether variables were originally measured using a binary or continuous quantitative metric.

These indices indicate the strength of a relationship, independent of the sample size of each study, and therefore allow comparison and aggregation of studies that might have used varying numbers of participants. Additional formulas for effect size conversion are beyond the scope of this book. Good sources for this information are Johnson and Eagly (2000), Feingold (1995), Hedges and Friedman (1993), Hunter and Schmidt (2004), and Borenstein et al. (2009).

Summary Effect

Once effect sizes are calculated for all primary studies, they are aggregated. This produces a **summary effect**, an overall effect size across the primary studies, that may be estimated using an unweighted, fixed-effect, or random-effects model. In our attractiveness to liking meta-analysis example, the weight of each effect size using each of these three weighting procedures is presented in Table 19.2. Studies 1 to 9 each contain 100 participants, while study 10 is represented by 1,000 participants. In an **unweighted model**, the effect sizes of primary studies are mathematically averaged, without taking into consideration the sample size of each study, to calculate the summary effect. In this scenario (Table 19.2), using the unweighted technique to combine studies, the summary effect is .38. In an unweighted model, the 10 studies, regardless of sample size, will each contribute 10% to the summary effect. Thus, investigations of 100 or 1,000 participants play an equal role in the estimation of the summary effect. Generally, this is not a justifiable practice, given that primary studies with larger samples contain more representative samples and yield more stable effect size estimates.

A weighted technique, therefore, is recommended for aggregating effect sizes in meta-analyses (Borenstein et al., 2009; Hedges & Olkin, 1985; Hunter & Schmidt, 2004). In a **fixed-effect model**, the effect sizes of primary studies with larger sample sizes are weighted more heavily to calculate the summary effect. It is most appropriate if the distribution of effect sizes is presumed to be homogeneous, As shown in Table 19.2, studies 1 to 9 each contains 100 participants, and therefore each plays a lesser role (5.3% to 5.6% each) to study 10 with 1,000 participants, which has a dominating weight (50.8%) in estimating the summary effect. Notice that the summary effect, .61, has been pulled disproportionately upward by the dominant contribution of study 10. This

TABLE 19.2 Estimating summary effects (Cohen's d): Unweighted, fixed-effect, and random-effects models.

Study #	Effect Size	N	Percent Weighted Contribution to Summary Effect		
			Unweighted Model	Fixed-Effect Model	Random-Effects Model
1	−.15	100	10.0%	5.6%	9.8%
2	−.05	100	10.0%	5.6%	9.8%
3	.28	100	10.0%	5.5%	9.8%
4	.35	100	10.0%	5.5%	9.8%
5	.35	100	10.0%	5.5%	9.8%
6	.37	100	10.0%	5.5%	9.7%
7	.56	100	10.0%	5.4%	9.7%
8	.59	100	10.0%	5.4%	9.7%
9	.65	100	10.0%	5.3%	9.7%
10	.89	1000	10.0%	50.8%	12.4%
	Summary Effect (Total N = 1900):		.38 ($p < .05$)	.61 ($p < .05$)	.40 ($p < .05$)

is not an ideal situation, because a study with a very large sample size relative to that of the other studies will overpower estimation of the summary effect. A fixed-effect model assumes that a single "fixed population" of studies, addressing the same hypothesis, underlies the effect size distribution. Consequently, the major disadvantage of a fixed effect model is that the distribution of effect sizes is expected to be largely homogeneous, with the meta-analysis findings only generalizable to the primary studies that were part of the synthesis.

In a **random-effects model**, effect sizes of primary studies are weighted as a compromise between sample size and number of primary studies to calculate the summary effect. It is the most appropriate estimation technique if the distribution of effect sizes is presumed to be heterogeneous. Let's examine the random-effects model of Table 19.2. Studies 1 to 9 with smaller sample sizes will each have a smaller contribution (9.7% to 9.8% each), but study 10, containing the large sample, has a slightly larger contribution (12.4%), to the summary effect. The study with a large sample size therefore would not drastically dwarf the contribution of the other studies. The summary effect calculated for the random-effects model is .40. The random-effects model assumes many "random populations" of studies addressing the same hypothesis, which are represented in the distribution of effect sizes. Because the effect sizes are expected to be heterogeneous, the meta-analytic findings may be generalized to the population of studies that were not even collected as part of the current meta-analysis. This is the primary advantage of the random-effects model. In theory and in practice, random-effects models should be the preferred choice over fixed-effect and unweighted models (Borenstein et al., 2009; Hedges & Vevea, 1998). Typically, a random-effects model is an accurate reflection of how research is actually conducted in the literature. Because an underlying relationship between two conceptual variables is usually investigated in methodologically different ways by different researchers, the meta-analyst must often cope with more heterogeneous effect sizes across studies, and this counsels the use of the random-effects model.

Heterogeneity and Moderators

The interpretation of summary effects should take into account the extent of homogeneity or heterogeneity of the distribution of effect sizes across the primary studies. When effect sizes are approximately similar in magnitude, primarily differing in sampling error, the distribution is said to be homogeneous. If this was indeed found, then the meta-analyst should compute the summary effect using a fixed-effect model. The extent of effect size dispersion in a meta-analysis is visually presented as a *stem and leaf display*. A hypothetical example is illustrated in Figure 19.2, where effects sizes for 10 studies are arrayed in a display where effect sizes are organized by first and second decimal places. Figure 19.2 shows a largely homogeneous set of effect sizes ranging from .34 to .45.

On other hand, the more dispersed the effect sizes of the primary studies over and above sampling error, the greater the heterogeneity. Heterogeneity of effect sizes is attributed to study variations in methodology and measurements in examining the same research hypothesis. An example of a heterogeneous distribution of effect sizes involves our 10 primary studies that examine the attractiveness to liking connection, as graphed using a stem and leaf display in Figure 19.3. Although the spread of effect sizes differs in Figures 19.2 and 19.3, both distributions are computed to have the same exact summary effect of .40. Obviously, the effect sizes from one primary study to another will not be exactly identical. Some random variation among the effect sizes is to be expected. However, if there is dispersion in effect sizes among the studies above and beyond that expected from sampling error, pointing to a random-effects model, the results cannot be regarded as homogeneous across the compiled primary studies. Heterogeneity in the strength and direction of effect sizes may provide important insights into potential study-level moderators. Moderators should be tested to determine what qualifies or changes the strength of the hypothesized A to B summary effect. Ideally, potential moderator variables should be determined in advance, on the basis of theory or empirically based hunches, but even post hoc moderators can prove enlightening.

When the effect sizes are heterogeneous, the meta-analysis should code for and evaluate the possibility of study-level moderators. We might want to qualify our meta-analytic hypothesis regarding attractiveness and liking, for example, by postulating that the relationship is stronger when people of the opposite sex are involved, or that the effect will be stronger when men are the actors and women the attractors, etc. Including such study-level moderating variables in the meta-analysis has

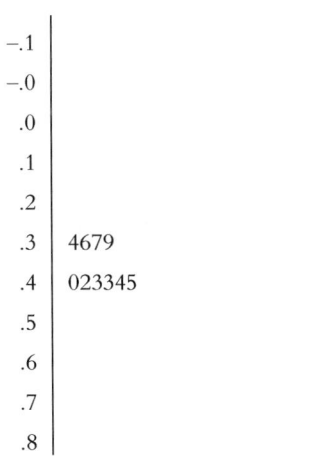

FIGURE 19.2 Stem and leaf display: Homogeneous distribution of effect sizes.

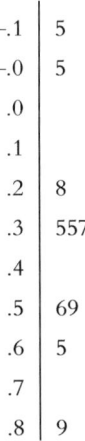

FIGURE 19.3 Stem and leaf display: Heterogeneous distribution of effect sizes (from values in Tables 19.1 and 19.2).

paid dividends when competing theorists have specified factors that impinge on the fundamental relationship under study (see Bond & Titus, 1983; Wood et al., 1994). In a meta-analysis, the more broadly we conceptualize the constructs, the more we will be dealing with study-to-study differences that involve conceptual rather than exact replications. It also is true that more broadly defined constructs are more likely to reveal meaningful differences among studies that are systematically different in terms of effect size—that is, the more likely we are to discover study-level moderators that affect the strength of the hypothesized relationship. A broadly defined construct will require that we break studies down by theoretically relevant levels of sub-studies to evaluate potential moderators. Meta-analysis is not useful for synthesizing small sets of studies that differ widely in methods and operationalizations of constructs (Cook & Leviton, 1980).

Study-level moderators may be classified into three varieties. *Methodological moderators* include methods factors, such as whether the study was conducted in a field or lab setting, whether self-report or behavioral measures were used, and whether the experimental design involved within- or between-group comparisons. *Demographic moderators* coded at the study level include the sample's average age (young, middle-aged, or older adults), socioeconomic status (wealthy or poor), and type of sample (undergraduate students or a representative sample from the population). *Theoretical moderators* involve studies that used different operational definitions to define the same construct, and the context under which the relationship was assessed (see Pillemer & Light, 1980, and Wood et al., 1994, for illustrations). Once potential moderator variables have been proposed, each study in the analysis is coded on each of these characteristics (i.e., whether the characteristic is present or absent in the operations or procedures, or the level that was present). The effects of the presence or absence of these moderators, or their level, are then examined to determine whether the variable can explain the heterogeneity among the effect sizes of the different studies that constitute the meta-analysis.

The effect of the moderator on the hypothesized A to B relationship can be tested in one of two ways. The first technique involves dividing the total set of studies into subsets that differ on the characteristic in question, to determine whether the summary effect computed within the subsets differ significantly from each other (Rosenthal & Rubin, 1982). To illustrate this approach, consider the hypothetical data in Table 19.3, which represent the hypothetical results of 3 moderators that were coded for in each of the 10 studies used in our attractiveness to liking meta-analysis. In each study, moderator variables pertaining to gender of the sample (females only, mixed, or males only) and type of manipulation (photographs, confederate, or other) are coded. We suspect that both moderator variables are responsible for effect size fluctuations in the studies used in the meta-analysis.

To statistically determine whether gender moderated the overall summary effect, we compute the summary effect for the three studies of female participants and compare this effect size to the summary effect for the three studies of male participants. Analyses show that the studies containing females revealed a weak connection between attractiveness and perceptions of liking ($d = .03$, ns), but this link was relatively strong in the male samples ($d = .60$, $p < .05$). A test of contrast between these values reveals that the attraction to liking relationship is significantly stronger in studies that contained male participants. This result implicates gender as a moderator in helping to explicate some of the heterogeneity across studies. Now conducting moderation analysis for the type of manipulation, we find a relationship for the three studies using manipulations of photographs ($d = .52, p < .05$), as well as for the two studies using manipulations of confederates ($d = .48$, $p < .05$). However, this nonsignificant difference indicates that type of manipulation did not account for heterogeneity in the dispersion of effect sizes.

A second method for assessing the contribution of a potential moderator variable to account for the variability in effect magnitude across studies is to enter the coded moderator variable into a meta-correlation or meta-regression, using each study's effect size as the dependent measure (Glass, 1978; Smith & Glass, 1980). Here, each study serves as the unit in the analysis. (In traditional

TABLE 19.3 Coding for three moderator variables.

Study #	Effect Size	Moderator 1: Gender of Sample	Moderator 2: Type of Manipulation	Moderator 3: Average Age of Sample
1	−.15	Females Only	Other	20
2	−.05	Females Only	Other	28
3	.28	Females Only	Other	33
4	.35	Mixed	Other	25
5	.35	Mixed	Photographs	24
6	.37	Males	Confederates	35
7	.56	Males Only	Photographs	33
8	.59	Males Only	Confederates	38
9	.65	Males Only	Photographs	45
10	.89	Mixed	Other	55

multiple regression, each participant serves as the unit of analysis.) Meta-regression is most appropriate when the moderator variable under consideration is defined quantitatively. For an example of this method, consider again that the meta-analyst also coded for the quantitative moderator of average age of participants in each sample, as shown in Table 19.3. As before, there is significant variation among studies in effect sizes from study to study. However, if one correlates this moderator with the effect size, it will yield a positive meta-correlation, significantly larger than zero (Chapter 9 discusses the interpretation of correlations). This suggests that there is a moderating effect of age of sample that differs across studies and tends to increase as the age of participants in a sample gets older. This particular finding would suggest that as people grow older, they may become more susceptible to liking people who are more attractive. Without considering this moderator factor, the overall meta-analysis would not paint a clear picture of variables that help to qualify the hypothesized A to B relationship.

Interpreting the meaning of the dispersion of effects in a meta-analysis is in part determined by the pattern of results obtained. If the summary effect is small and not statistically significant, it is important to determine that the null finding is not a result of a heterogeneous data set with positive and negative effect sizes canceling each other. If we have highly disparate effect sizes in the model, it is important to determine whether a study-level moderator might help to statistically explain the varying distribution of effect size across investigations. Finding potential moderators should be facilitated by theory regarding the variables involved in the hypothesized relation. However, sometimes a moderator might be suggested only after examining the pattern of effects. It should be recognized that serendipitous findings of this type are post hoc, and should be interpreted accordingly in a tentative fashion.

To show why this is so, suppose a researcher were to conduct a meta-analysis on prior research investigating the relation between fundamental attribution error (the tendency of observers to explain others' behavior in terms of personal, rather than situational, factors) and judgment behaviors (Ross, 1977; Gilbert & Malone, 1995). If a competent review of the literature were done, the meta-analyst might find that the effect sizes varied considerably from study to study, and the summary effect suggested no relation between the constructs ($r = 0$). Based on this summary effect alone, we would conclude that the fundamental attribution error does not impinge upon behavior. However, being in close touch with the data, the meta-analyst might realize that almost all the positive effect sizes are found in research conducted in Western cultures (the U.S., Europe, Australia), whereas the effect size is near zero and sometimes reversed in non-Western cultures

(China, Japan, etc.; see Choi, Nisbett, & Norenzayan, 1999; Fiske, Kitayama, Markus, & Nisbett, 1998). Testing Western vs. non-Western culture of (study) origin as a moderator of the link from fundamental attribution error to behavior, the meta-analysis may disclose results that clarified an apparent inconsistency among results in the area. This meta-analytic result should be used as the basis for hypotheses regarding how cultural variations in studies may qualify attributional biases on judgments. Interpreting serendipitous findings must always be undertaken with caution, however, irrespective of their intuitive appeal and the methodological source of their discovery (Kerr, 1998).

Interpreting the Meta-Analysis

Some meta-analyses might find a distribution of mean effect size indices that is not notably heterogeneous, but still the produces nonsignificant results. The hypothesized effects appear to be too weak to matter. Before jumping to this conclusion, it is important to be sure that the statistical power of the meta-analysis is sufficient. The statistical power afforded to detect whether a summary effect is significant is dependent on both the number of studies and the number of participants in each of the studies. If too few studies each containing small samples are used, the likelihood of discovering a reliable summary effect is minimized. Because results are pooled across many studies, however, sample sizes tend to be aggregated in most meta-analyses. This pooling results in greater statistical power than any single primary study in that area of research. Thus, meta-analysis is ideal for synthesizing areas of primary research typified by small samples.

Effect sizes often are interpreted as small, medium, or large as a function of the strength of relationship between two variables. Cohen (1988) and Rosnow and Rosenthal (1996) provide recommended values and computational advice for calculating and interpreting effect size magnitude for primary studies and summary effects. These recommendations are displayed in Table 19.4. This table provides a convenient shorthand guideline for describing the practical strength of a relationship. It should be understood that these represent rough guidelines of strength that should not to be rigidly interpreted. A major reason is that effect sizes are not meaningful when comparisons are made across widely different domains of research. A small effect for a drug treatment that reduces the risk of a debilitating disease or saves lives is more practically desirable than a large effect obtained in a treatment designed to improve people's bond with their pet cat. Thus, interpreting effect sizes is most meaningful when the meta-analyst considers both the context (What are the consequences of the findings?) and knowledge contribution (What insights are afforded to help understand this line of research?) (Ellis, 2010).

Even apparently small effect sizes discovered in a meta-analysis should not be dismissed lightly. Rosenthal and Rubin (1982) have proposed a method of interpreting effect size in terms of differences in positive or negative outcomes that are found between the treatment groups that form the basis of the meta-analysis. Applying their *binomial effect size display* (BESD) to interpret the summary effect provides graphic evidence of the practical importance of a relationship between two variables. The display is especially informative for a meta-analysis that yields, at cursory inspection, a small summary effect.

TABLE 19.4 Effect size guidelines.

Interpretation of Practical Effect	Cohen's d	Odds Ratio	r
Small	.20	1.50	.10
Medium	.50	2.50	.30
Large	.80	4.00	.50

	Attractive	Unattractive	
Liking	60	40	100
Not liking	40	60	100
	100	100	200

FIGURE 19.4 Binomial effect size display: Summary effect $r = .20$.

Continuing with our meta-analysis of attractiveness to liking, the summary effect we obtained using the random-effects model was Cohen's $d = .40$ (Table 19.2). For the purpose of creating a BESD, this value must first be converted to the correlation coefficient. Applying a formula to convert between effect sizes, the computation yields a summary $r = .20$. The BESD for this overall effect is shown in Figure 19.4. The BESD requires the hypothetical assumption that the entire meta-analysis could be represented and summarized by a total of 200 participants. Furthermore, each row and column must add up to 100 participants. To create a BESD for our summary $r = .20$, simply remove the decimal place, which yields 20. Then insert numbers for each of the four cells so that cells in each row or column are separated by exactly 20 (Figure 19.4). The BESD for our meta-analysis should be interpreted as follows. For participants receiving the attractive condition (rather than the unattractive condition), there will be a 20% greater difference in liking (rather than not liking). This display is a visually helpful device to highlight the practical importance of the summary effect, especially if it is presented to a general audience.

Suppose, in a different example, that a meta-analyst is interested in the hypothesis that manipulated message source (ingroup or outgroup) will have an impact on participants' ratings of persuasive effectiveness. The researcher gathers studies that investigate this relation. The results suggest that ingroup sources tend to be more persuasive than outgroup sources, but the summary effect size is small ($r = .10$) according to Cohen's guidelines. Rather than becoming discouraged, the meta-analyst turns to the BESD and calculates the difference between persuasive success and failure as a function of the manipulated sources. It reveals that the persuasive effect is 10% higher when the source of persuasion is ingroup (rather than outgroup). A marketing executive might find this result to be a very important argument for targeting messages on the basis of source-audience similarity. Even though the effect is not large statistically, in practical terms it is well worth considering.

Narrative Reviews vs. Vote Counting vs. Meta-Analysis

Conclusions of the research literature drawn from the quantitative meta-analysis may yield different conclusions from the more traditional narrative reviews. Prior to the advent of meta-analysis and its techniques, attempts were made to make traditional narrative reviews more quantitative. Known as **vote counting**, it is a method of literature review that involves counting and comparing the number of primary studies that are statistically significant or not (Cooper, Hedges, & Valentine 2009). For example, a vote counter may identify 10 studies that investigate a particular hypothesis, and then determine whether each one is statistically significant at $p < .05$. If the majority of the studies are statistically significant (e.g., 6 studies significant, but 4 studies nonsignificant), then the vote counter concludes that the relationship is supported. If vote counting reveals that the majority of the studies are nonsignificant (e.g., 4 studies significant, but 6 studies nonsignificant), then one concludes that the relationship does not exist. A major problem with vote counting is that a decision of whether a theoretical link is tenable is usually made on the basis of such borderline votes.

We have argued that direct comparison of probability values of primary studies is generally not a wise course, but the vote counting approach is completely dependent on such black-and-white cutoffs. The problem with vote counting is twofold. First, probability values between different studies are not directly comparable, as was noted. Second, perhaps more importantly, this approach loses considerable information as the magnitude of effect and its direction is completely ignored. Vote counting relies strictly on the dichotomous distinction of study significance or nonsignificance, whereas the overall effect obtained in a meta-analysis is more nuanced and accurate than those based on mere tabulation of supportive or non-supportive study outcomes (Cooper & Rosenthal, 1980).

To illustrate the differences in conclusions that might be drawn from meta-analytic vs. vote counting, consider again the data in Tables 19.1, 19.2, and 19.3. In the first table, only 4 of 10 studies reported statistically significant effects, although most of the studies had outcomes in the same, positive direction. In this scenario, our vote counting analysis would have led us to conclude erroneously that no relationship existed between attractiveness and liking. Conversely, the results of the meta-analysis showed a significant summary effect, with a value that indicates the magnitude of the relation. The difference in conclusion stems from accumulating the sample sizes from all the studies and the use of effect sizes in meta-analysis to estimate the strength of effects. In a meta-analysis, even studies with small or nonsignificant effect sizes add information about the general direction of the obtained summary effect. This added information often is important in clarifying the strength and direction of relationship between constructs.

Conclusion

Meta-analysis has much to offer in quantitatively consolidating and synthesizing research on a given topic. It promises to facilitate the growth and development of the social science enterprise, and as such should become a normal practice in our field. This is not to suggest that meta-analysis should supplant primary data collection, or even narrative reviews. Meta-analysis obviously cannot supplant primary research because original data are the fundamental inputs of the meta-analysis. Among other things, primary research produces data for inclusion in future meta-analyses, whereas the conclusions drawn from a meta-analysis foster and inform subsequent primary research.

Clearly, meta-analysis should—and will—play a larger role in the research enterprise in social science. Its advantages of empirical consolidation are too great to ignore, despite the painstaking efforts that such analyses entail and the lingering debates surrounding the most ideal methods of data gathering and effect size calculation. Even so, these advantages do not replace good qualitative reviews of the literature. Narrative reviews complement and enrich the interpretation of quantitative data summaries. The two approaches of reviewing the literature are best used in combination. Particularly where there are substantial variations in effects obtained across studies examining the same hypothesis, a careful consideration of moderators examining theoretical, demographic, and methodological differences among the studies included in a meta-analysis is essential for drawing meaningful conclusions. Such an examination is part and parcel of both qualitative and quantitative reviews.

Questions for Discussion

1. Is there ever a situation where a fixed-effect model is preferable to a random-effects model? That is, if in a meta-analysis one study has an exceptionally large sample, a fixed-effect model will weight the large sample very heavily, under the assumption that a larger sample is more

likely to approximate the "actual" effect size of the relationship we are interested in. If there is no evidence that the study with the largest sample also used the most reliable and valid assessment of the variables of interest, why should that one study be weighted disproportionately compared to other studies with smaller samples? Given this information, shouldn't researchers always use random-effects models for meta-analyses? Why?
2. What would you consider reasonable when attempting to find *all* possible studies to be included in your meta-analysis? Should you contact original authors if you find a relevant study but the article does not include enough information to compute an effect size? Would you only include studies that provide effect sizes in their articles, or at least enough information to compute them? What if there are several studies that appear to support your hypothesized relationship between variables, and you decide to contact the original authors to obtain effect size data from them. Would you also need to contact the original authors for an equivalent number of studies that do not support your hypotheses and do not provide effect sizes?
3. What is the file drawer problem? Suppose you find a very strong meta-analytic result. Should you worry about it? What if the result is just moderate? Or small? What determines the potential severity of the problem?

Notes

1. Of course, it is not fair to blame the narrative method for reviewers' failures to perform complete literature searches. However, the tradition of the narrative method does not necessarily call for complete surveying, which often produces a biased review.
2. Stigler (1986) finds evidence of rudimentary quantitative synthesis in the 1800s; Thorndike (1933) provides a somewhat more contemporary example.
3. The specification is tentative because as the meta-analysis progresses, the rules may be changed to account better for the available data.
4. If the necessary effect sizes cannot be extracted from published versions of otherwise relevant studies, they sometimes can be obtained from the researcher directly; however, this is not always possible or practical. If many of the relevant studies do not contain adequate statistical information, the researcher may have to resort to rudimentary procedures, such as combining exact probability values of statistical tests (Rosenthal, 1978; Rosenthal & Rubin, 1979). This does not provide nearly as much information about the magnitude and variability of effects, but it does use somewhat more information than vote counting techniques.

References

Bond, C. F., Jr., & Titus, L. J. (1983). Social facilitation: A meta-analysis of 241 studies. *Psychological Bulletin, 94,* 265–292.
Borenstein, M., Hedges, L. V., Higgins, J. P., & Rothstein, H. R. (2009). Introduction to meta-analysis. Chichester, UK: Wiley.
Bradley, M. T., & Gupta, R. D. (1997). Estimating the effect of the file drawer problem in meta-analysis. *Perceptual and Motor Skills, 85,* 719–722.
Campbell, D. T. (1963). Social attitudes and other acquired behavioral dispositions. In S. Koch (Ed.), *Psychology: A study of a science, Vol. 6: Investigations of man as socius.* New York: McGraw-Hill.
Choi, I., Nisbett, R. E., & Norenzayan, A. (1999). Causal attribution across cultures: Variation and universality. *Psychological Bulletin, 125,* 47–63.
Clark, R. D. (1971). *Einstein: The life and times.* New York: World Publishing.
Cohen, J. A. (1988). *Statistical power analysis for the behavioral sciences* (2nd ed.). Hillsdale, NJ: Erlbaum.
Cook, T. D., & Leviton, L. C. (1980). Reviewing the literature: A comparison of traditional methods with meta-analysis. *Journal of Personality, 48,* 449–472.
Cooper, H. M. (1979). Statistically combining independent studies: A meta-analysis of sex differences in conformity research. *Journal of Personality and Social Psychology, 37*(1), 131–146.

Cooper. H. M. (2009). *Research synthesis and meta-analysis: A step-by-step approach* (4th ed.). Los Angeles: Sage Publications.

Cooper, H. M., Hedges, L. V., & Valentine, J. C. (Eds.). (2009). *The handbook of research synthesis and meta-analysis* (2nd ed.). New York: Russell Sage Foundation.

Cooper, H. M., & Rosenthal, R. (1980). Statistical versus traditional procedures for summarizing research findings. *Psychological Bulletin, 87,* 442–449.

Eagly, A. H., Ashmore, R. D., Makhijani, M. G., & Longo, L. C. (1991). What is beautiful is good, but . . . : A meta-analytic review of research on the physical attractiveness stereotype. *Psychological Bulletin, 110,* 109–128.

Eagly, A. H., Karau, S., & Makhijani, M. G. (1995). Gender and the effectiveness of leaders: A meta-analysis. *Psychological Bulletin, 117,* 125–145.

Ellis, P. D. (2010). *The essential guide to effect sizes: Statistical power, meta-analysis, and the interpretation of research results.* Cambridge, UK: Cambridge University Press.

Feingold, A. (1995). The additive effects of differences in central tendency and variability in comparisons between groups. *American Psychologist, 50,* 5–13.

Fiske, A. P., Kitayama, S., Markus, H. R., & Nisbett, R. E. (1998). The cultural matrix of social psychology. In D. Gilbert, S. Fiske & G. Lindzey (Eds.), *The handbook of social psychology, Vol. 2* (pp. 915–971). New York: Oxford Press.

Gilbert, D. T., & Malone, P. S. (1995). The correspondence bias. *Psychological Bulletin, 117,* 21–38.

Glass, G. V. (1978). Integrating findings: The meta-analysis of research. *Review of Research in Education, 5,* 351–379.

Greenwald, A. G. (1975). Consequences of prejudice against the null hypothesis. *Psychological Bulletin, 82,* 1–20.

Greenwald, S., & Russell, R. I. (1991). Assessing rationales for inclusiveness in meta-analytic samples. *Psychotherapy Research, 1,* 17–24.

Hays, W. L. (1994). *Statistics (5th ed.).* Orlando, FL: Harcourt Brace College Publishers.

Hedges, L. V., & Friedman, L. (1993). Computing gender differences in the tails of distributions: The consequences of differences in tail size, effect size, and variance ratio. *Review of Educational Research, 63,* 110–112.

Hedges, L. V., & Olkin, I. (1985). *Statistical methods for meta-analysis.* Orlando, FL: Academic Press.

Hedges, L. V., & Vevea, J. L. (1998). Fixed- and random-effects models in meta-analysis. *Psychological Methods, 3,* 486–504.

Heikkilä, K., Nyberg, S. T., Theorell, T., Fransson, E. I., Alfredsson, L., Bjorner, J. B., . . . & Kivimäki, M. (2013). Work stress and risk of cancer: Meta-analysis of 5700 incident cancer events in 116 000 European men and women. *BMJ: British Medical Journal, 346,* f165.

Hunter, J. E., & Schmidt, F. L. (2004). *Methods of meta-analysis: Correcting error and bias in research findings* (2nd ed.). Thousand Oaks, CA: Sage.

Johnson B. T., & Eagly, A. H. (2000). Quantitative synthesis of social psychological research. In H. Reis & C. Judd (Eds.), *Handbook of research methods in social and personality psychology* (pp. 496–528). New York: Cambridge University Press.

Kerr, N. L. (1998). HARKing: Hypothesizing after the results are known. *Personality and Social Psychology Review, 2,* 196–217.

Kraemer, H. C., Gardner, C., Brooks, J. O. III, & Yesavage, J. A. (1998). Advantages of excluding underpowered studies in meta-analysis: Inclusionist versus exclusionist viewpoints. *Psychological Methods, 3,* 23–31.

Kuhn, T. S. (1970) *The structure of scientific revolutions* (2nd ed.). Chicago: University of Chicago Press (1st ed., 1962).

Lac, A., & Crano, W. D. (2009). Monitoring matters: Meta-analytic review reveals the reliable linkage of parental monitoring with adolescent marijuana use. *Perspectives on Psychological Science, 4,* 578–586.

Packer, D. J. (2008) Identifying systematic disobedience in Milgram's obedience experiments. *Perspectives on Psychological Science, 3,* 301–304.

Pillemer, D. B., & Light, R. J. (1980). How to use research evidence from many studies. *Harvard Educational Review, 50,* 176–195.

Quon, E. C., & McGrath, J. J. (2013). Subjective socioeconomic status and adolescent health: A meta-analysis. *Health Psychology, 33,* 433–447.

Rosenthal, R. (1978). Combining results of independent studies. *Psychological Bulletin, 85,* 185–193.

Rosenthal, R. (1979). The "file drawer problem" and tolerance for null results. *Psychological Bulletin, 86,* 638–641.

Rosenthal, R. (1991). Meta-analytic procedures for social research. Newbury Park, CA: Sage.

Rosenthal, R., & Rubin, D. B. (1978). Interpersonal expectancy effects: The first 345 studies. *Behavioral and Brain Sciences, 1,* 377–415.

Rosenthal, R., & Rubin, D. B. (1979). Comparing significance levels of independent studies. *Psychological Bulletin, 86*(5), 1165–1168.

Rosenthal, R., & Rubin, D. B. (1982). Comparing effect sizes of independent studies. *Psychological Bulletin, 92,* 500–504.

Rosnow, R. L., & Rosenthal, R. (1996). Computing contrasts, effect sizes, and counternulls on other people's published data: General procedures for research consumers. *Psychological Methods, 1*(4), 331–340.

Ross, L. (1977). The intuitive scientist and his shortcomings. In L. Berkowitz (Ed.), *Advances in experimental social psychology, 10,* 174–221. New York: Academic Press.

Smith, M. L., & Glass, G. V. (1977). Meta-analysis of psychotherapy outcome studies. *American Psychologist, 32,* 752–760.

Smith, M. L., & Glass, G. V. (1980). Meta-analysis of research on class size and its relationship to attitudes and instruction. *American Educational Research Journal, 17*(4), 419–433.

Stigler, S. M. (1986). *History of statistics: The measurement of uncertainty before 1900.* Cambridge, MA: Harvard University Press.

Thorndike, R. L. (1933). The effect of the interval between test and retest on the constancy of the IQ. *Journal of Educational Psychology, 25,* 543–549.

Williams, P. A., Haertel, E. H., Haertel, G. D., & Walberg, H. J. (1982). The impact of leisure-time television on school learning: A research synthesis. *American Educational Research Journal, 19,* 19–50.

Wood, W., Lundgren, S., Ouellette, J. A., Busceme, S., & Blackstone, T. (1994). Minority influence: A meta-analytic review of social influence processes. *Psychological Bulletin, 115,* 323–345.

Wood, W., Rhodes, N., & Whelan, M. (1989). Sex differences in positive well-being: A consideration of emotional style and marital status. *Psychological Bulletin, 106,* 249–264.

20
SOCIAL RESPONSIBILITY AND ETHICS IN SOCIAL RESEARCH

The social sciences share with all scientific endeavors the need to balance scientific zeal with other values that derive from the social context in which all scientific work takes place. To some extent the scientific ideal of objectivity inevitably conflicts with humanistic values, and all scientists must at some time come to grips with this conflict. The issue, however, is particularly acute for social scientists because the focus of their research is the behavior of other human beings, and thus not only the goals of research but the very process of data collection is subject to value conflicts. In this chapter we consider first those ethical issues that are related specifically to research with human respondents; we then focus on the more general issues of concern to all scientists in their choice of research problem and strategy of data reporting.

Ethics of Research Practices

Because the subject matter of the social scientist is human behavior and the processes responsible for behavior, it is inevitable that scientific interests might conflict with values placed on the rights of individuals to privacy and self-determination. The guidelines for behavioral and social research set by research societies such as the American Psychological Association's Committee on Ethical Standards (American Psychological Association, 2002; see also Knapp, 2011), and the President's Panel on Privacy and Behavioral Research (Surgeon General's directive, 1967) stress the necessity for **informed consent**, a process in which potential participants are informed about what participation in the study will involve so that they can make an informed decision about whether or not to engage in the research. Doing so emphasizes that participation should be voluntary. It is recognized that many phenomena could not be researched at all if this ideal were met fully, and that the rights of participants must be weighed against the potential significance of the research problem. Resnick and Schwartz (1973), for example, demonstrated in a verbal conditioning experiment that providing a complete description of methods and hypotheses to participants eliminated the phenomenon they were attempting to investigate.

In studies where full information cannot be provided to participants, the panel report recommends that "consent be based on trust in the qualified investigator and the integrity of the research institution." Thus, the ethical code does not provide absolute standards that relieve the scientist of important value judgments. Rather, judgments as to the relative importance of research programs and researchers' responsibilities for the welfare of their participants are the fundamental bases of research ethics.

Deception in the Laboratory

When research is conducted in the laboratory, there is seldom any doubt concerning participants' knowledge that they are the subjects of scientific investigation. The extent to which participation is fully voluntary is debatable, given the social and institutional pressures to take part in research that are sometimes involved. But generally, due to the artificial setup, participants in laboratory studies at least *know* that they are taking part in a research study. Beyond that, however, the information provided to participants in laboratory investigations is usually minimal to foster research purposes, and sometimes is intentionally misleading.

As we emphasized in Chapter 6, for the goal of measuring reactions that are as natural as possible, the methodological strategy of most laboratory research is directed toward motivating participants to behave spontaneously and therefore not self-consciously while involved in the conditions of the study. To this end research procedures might be presented and justified in the guise of an elaborate "cover story" designed to manage the participant's perception of the research setting and conceal the true purpose of the study. Thus, the researcher often goes beyond merely withholding information from the participant to deliberate misrepresentation of the details of his or her participation. The importance of this form of control in experimental research has been discussed in previous chapters of this book. Yet such deception is undeniably in violation of values of interpersonal trust and respect.

To what extent this violation is justified in the service of scientific goals and the potential advancement of human welfare is a matter of considerable controversy. Some critics have argued that deception is never justified and should not be permitted in the interests of social research (Ortmann & Hertwig, 1997). Most researchers take a more moderate view, recognizing that there is an inevitable trade-off between the values of complete honesty in informed consent and the potential value of what can be learned from the research itself. Just as the "white lie" is regarded as acceptable when used in the service of good manners, a minimal amount of deception may be tolerated in the service of obtaining trustworthy research data. However, there is some debate over whether behavioral scientists have exceeded this acceptable threshold of deception in their research.

For some years the practice of deception in laboratory experiments was accepted with equanimity by most experimenters. However, an article by Herbert Kelman (1967) reflected a growing concern with the widespread, and apparently unquestioned, use of deception in research in social research. Kelman's article called into question this practice on both ethical and practical grounds. Ethically, he argued, any deception violated implicit norms of respect in the interpersonal relationship that forms between experimenter and research participant. In addition, the practice might have serious methodological implications as participants become less naive and widespread suspiciousness begins to influence the outcomes of all human research. To offset these problems, Kelman recommended that social scientists (a) reduce unnecessary use of deception, (b) explore ways of counteracting or minimizing the negative consequences stemming from deception, and (c) use alternative methods, such as role-playing or simulation techniques, which substitute active participation for deception, with participants being fully informed of the purpose of the study.

Experimentation with these alternative methodologies has been attempted, but the results are mixed at best (see Chapter 6), and it remains uncertain whether the results of a role-playing simulation can be interpreted in the same way as those obtained under the real experimental conditions. Thus, the general consensus in the research community is that some level of deception sometimes is necessary to create realistic conditions for testing research hypotheses, but that such deception needs to be justified in light of the purpose and potential importance of the research question being studied. As Rosenthal (1994) put it, "The behavioral researcher whose study may have a good chance of reducing violence or racism or sexism, but who refuses to do the study simply because it involves deception, has not solved an ethical problem but only traded one for another" (p. 129). The various disciplines within the social sciences vary in the degree of tolerance for deception that is normative, with most fields of psychology accepting the practice of deception in experimental research under certain circumstances, whereas the field of behavioral economics rejects the need for deception in experimental studies under any circumstances.

Deception and Participant Well-Being

Apart from the issue of the relationship between experimenter and participant, the ethical acceptability of some deception experiments has been challenged on the grounds that the situations set up by the experimenter sometimes place research participants in a position of psychological distress or other discomfort. This potentially violates the other major canon of ethical research—to "do no harm" to those who participate. The extent to which such potential distress to participants is tolerable in the name of scientific research also is a matter of debate. As usual, the extremes are fairly well established—the risk of permanent physical or psychological harm without informed consent by the human participant is never permissible. However, consensus as to the acceptability of temporary or reversible psychological distress is more difficult to achieve. The Asch (1956) line judgment studies, for example, which provided the paradigm for much research on social conformity, clearly placed the naive participant in a position of psychological distress in weighing the evidence of one's own perceptions against the peer pressure of judgments made by presumably sincere fellow students (who actually were confederates). Most researchers seem to agree that the potential contribution of this line of research and the transitory nature of the psychological discomfort involved justified its undertaking.

The studies of destructive obedience conducted by Milgram (1974), on the other hand, have aroused considerably more variability in reaction. The design of Milgram's research on blind obedience to an authority figure, which has been mentioned previously in this textbook, involved deceiving participants into believing that they were administering a series of escalating electrical shocks to a fellow participant (actually this confederate was not really receiving any shocks), while being pressured by the experimenter to continue the procedure. In initial reports of the results of this research, Milgram himself gave detailed illustrations of evidence of psychological stress on the part of those participants who continued in the experiment. He observed that one such participant " . . . within 20 minutes . . . was reduced to a twitching, stuttering wreck, who was rapidly approaching a point of nervous collapse" (Milgram, 1963, p. 377).

As a consequence of these rather dramatic depictions of participant distress, the publication of Milgram's initial experiments was met with much critical reaction (e.g., Baumrind, 1964). Milgram's (1964) response to this criticism emphasized the significance of the research, particularly with regard to the unexpectedly high percentage of people who were willing to obey. He noted that great care had been exercised in post-experimental information sessions to assure that participants suffered no long-term psychological damage. Milgram also suggested that the vehemence of the critical response to his research may have been largely a function of the nature of his findings: Many participants were willing to shock the innocent victim all the way to the maximum voltage level. If more participants had behaved in a humane and independent fashion and refused to administer shocks at high voltage levels, the same research procedures might not have come under such intense attack. If so, it would seem that it was not so much the use of deception that was being criticized—the cover story disguised it is a learning study, with a shock to be delivered every time the victim made a mistake in word memorization—but the way participants reacted to the situation. Yet those very results—unexpected as they were—are what made the experiments so valuable to social science.

Debriefing: Explaining the Study to Participants at the End

Debate over the ethical acceptability of Milgram's experiments has revealed that whereas social scientists disagree about the frequency and extent that the use of deception should be tolerated, much research involving deception has been deemed permissible. Where deception is seen as necessary to the exploration of some research questions, attention turns to the best method of counteracting the negative implications of its use. For this purpose, considerable emphasis has been given to the importance of the **debriefing**, a session following participation in a study in which the participants are informed of the true purpose of the research. Kelman (1967) placed enough value on such debriefing procedures to regard their inclusion in the experimental design as an "inviolate" rule. Milgram's (1964) justification of his research procedures relied heavily on his use of extensive debriefing sessions during which participants were reassured about the nature of their responses and encouraged to express their reactions in what was essentially a psychotherapeutic setting.

When such attention is devoted to the content and handling of debriefing sessions, this may serve not only to "undeceive" the participants (and thereby relieve the researcher's pangs of conscience) but also to enrich the participant's own experience in terms of understanding human behavior and the nature of social research. However, we must caution against considering the debriefing session as a panacea for all ethical aches and pains of social research. Some research suggests that when used routinely or handled perfunctorily, debriefing procedures can cause more harm than good (Holmes, 1976a, 1976b; Ross, Lepper, & Hubbard, 1975; Walster, Berscheid, Abrahams, & Aronson, 1967).

Many researchers warn that routine debriefing may produce widespread suspicion and potential dishonesty among populations frequently tapped for participation in psychological research. Some research has been directed toward this issue, the results of which are interesting, though not entirely consistent. Brock and Becker (1966) exposed participants to one experiment followed by no debriefing, partial debriefing, or complete debriefing, and then tested the same participants again in a subsequent deception experiment. No differential reactions to the second experiment were obtained except when a strong deception clue was made available through a common element in the two experiments. Results revealed that only the completely debriefed participants, as classified in the first experiment, reacted with suspicion to the second experiment. On the other hand, Silverman, Shulman, and Wiesenthal (1970) compared students who participated in an experiment with deception to others who participated in an experiment without deception. Subsequently, significant differences in responses to a series of psychological tests emerged between these two conditions. Examination of these differences indicated that the previously deceived participants, in an effort to correct for a deceived self-image, responded with more favorable self-presentation biases than did the non-deceived participants.

The preceding two studies involved students who had participated in only one experiment prior to testing. Other studies have investigated the effects of multiple participations on attitudes and behavior related to behavioral research. Holmes (1967) found that the more research experience participants had, the more favorable were their attitudes toward psychological experiments, and the more they intended to cooperate in future research. Holmes's study, however, did not take into account the extent to which his participants had experienced deception in the studies in which they had served. A more direct test of the effects of frequent deception was provided by Smith and Richardson (1983), who tested the attitudes of more than 400 research participants who had served in a variety of experiments over the course of an academic quarter. They found that participants who had been in deception experiments evaluated their research experience more positively than those who had not been deceived, and that debriefing appeared to eliminate the negative feelings of those who felt they had been harmed by deceptive practices. Those who had participated in experiments using deception reported that they received better debriefing, enjoyed their experiences more, received greater educational benefits from the research, and were more satisfied with the research program than those who had not been involved in experiments with deception.[1] We speculate that some of these variations might be a function of differences between the types of experiments that made use of deception and those that do not. Often, deception-based studies are inherently interesting—they involve complex decision-making, arguing against a strong counter-attitudinal communication, making judgments about people and social events, and so on. Those that do not involve deception might require participants to memorize long lists of nonsense syllables, to respond as rapidly as possible to randomly presented visual stimuli, to decide which two of three tones are most similar, etc. These types of studies often are ethically pristine, but they might not be very enjoyable for participants.

With effective debriefing, the negative aspects of the deception studies might be offset, leading to more positive evaluation of the research experience on the part of participants. This requires, however, that the debriefing be conducted in such a way and with enough thought and effort that participants leave feeling that they have learned something by the experience and that their time has not been wasted.

Effective debriefing also is important in gaining participants' commitment to the purposes of the research and their agreement not to tell potential future participants about the deception employed. As a result of communication among members of a research participant "pool," the effects of debriefing-generated suspicion may extend beyond those who actually have participated in deception experiments. Weubben (1965) provided some indication of the extent of such intersubject "contamination" by finding that of 113 participants who had agreed to secrecy following an experimental debriefing session, 72 revealed the nature of the research to other potential participants. Reviews of deception research (Striker, 1967; Striker, Messick, & Jackson, 1967) indicate that there is inadequate assessment of such prior knowledge or suspicion on the part of participants and that the implications for the internal validity of laboratory experiments are still not well understood. Because of this, badly done debriefings—those that do not succeed in gaining participants' confidence, trust, and cooperation—can potentially harm the scientific enterprise.

Apart from these methodological considerations, debriefing may not always be effective in counteracting the lingering negative effects of certain kinds of deception manipulations after participation in the study. Walster et al. (1967) reported that for highly concerned participants, even lengthy debriefings were not successful in removing reactions to false information feedback regarding personal adequacy. Ross et al. (1975), too, found that the effects of deception sometimes were exceptionally difficult to offset. Particularly when the experimental manipulation involved providing false information of some kind about the participant's personality, competence, or self-esteem, an extensive form of debriefing known as "process debriefing" (Ross et al., 1975) may be required. Process debriefing entails discussing with participants how the deception may have temporarily influenced their own self-perceptions and the processes by which these effects might occur. Previous research has shown that this type of systematic debriefing is more successful in eliminating any lingering effects of the deception than a standard debriefing in which participants are simply told that the information was untrue but without discussion of process (Ross et al., 1975). Another technique for enhancing the effectiveness of debriefing is to show participants all of the experimental conditions so they can see how the information they had received was just one version of the experiment to which they had randomly been assigned. For instance, if participants had been given false feedback that their test performance was negative, they could be shown what the positive feedback condition looked like (and perhaps asked to imagine how they would have reacted to that feedback), to make more apparent how arbitrary the feedback had been.

Ethical Issues in Non-Laboratory Research

Although much of the debate about the ethical implications of deception focuses on laboratory experimentation, research conducted outside the laboratory often raises a host of other ethical issues and concerns. In addition to issues related to consent to participate, researchers also must consider issues of privacy and confidentiality when research data are collected in field settings. Because a major advantage of field research, from a scientific standpoint, is the possibility of obtaining samples of behavior under naturally occurring conditions, it frequently is advantageous to conduct such studies under conditions in which the nature of the research is disguised. Thus, the participants may not only be deceived about the purpose of the research, but may even be unaware that they are the subject of research in the first place. The use of "unobtrusive" measures (Webb, Campbell, Schwartz, Sechrest, & Grove, 1981) highlights this strategy, but even more traditional methods of data collection, such as the interview or questionnaire, are frequently presented in such a way as to disguise their true purpose.

Some scientists regard the practice of concealed observation or response elicitation as acceptable as long as it is limited to essentially "public" behaviors or settings normally open to public observation. Campbell (1969), for instance, provided a review of settings and behaviors for which disguised research strategies have been employed, including studies ranging from pedestrian violations of traffic signals (Lefkowitz, Blake, & Mouton, 1955), to mailing of "lost letters" (Milgram, 1969), interpersonal interaction in employment offices (Rokeach & Mezei, 1966), arranged encounters between strangers in public streets (Feldman, 1968), fund collection (Bryan & Test, 1967), and door-to-door solicitation (Freedman & Fraser, 1966). All of these involve behaviors that Campbell regarded as falling within the "public domain" and thus not requiring permission from participants nor subsequent debriefing. However, there remains the question of subjective definitions of what constitute "public" behaviors, particularly in settings where social norms lead to the expectation of anonymity in public places. Some social scientists (e.g., Miller, 1966) regard any form of unaware participation in research as an intolerable invasion of the individual's right to privacy. Although some settings may readily allow for interpersonal observation by the researcher, if individuals in these settings do not normally expect to be observed (or, rather, expect not to be), the issue of privacy remains. A case in point is provided in the research of Middlemist, Knowles, and Matter (1976), who studied the effects of "spatial invasion" in a men's bathroom by secretly observing participants' behavior at a urinal.

As field studies using an experimental design involve some intervention on the part of the researcher in determining the stimulus conditions to which the unaware participants are exposed, ethical considerations about hidden observation are further complicated by concern over such manipulations. Examples of experimentation in field settings include systematic manipulation of the content of applicant resumes sent to prospective employers (Schwartz & Skolnick, 1962), differential behavior on the part of salesmen toward customers (Brock, 1965) or customers toward salesmen (Jung, 1959; Schaps, 1972), varied content of requests for a dime from passing strangers (Latané, 1970), and the apparent condition of the victim of a feigned collapse in a New York subway train (Piliavin, Rodin, & Piliavin, 1969). To varying degrees, these all fall within a "normal range" of human experiences in public places, the only difference being their systematic manipulation by the researcher. Yet collecting data about people's behaviors in these situations clearly violates the spirit of "informed consent," especially when researchers decide it is best not to debrief those who have been observed, even after the fact.

Privacy on the Internet

The advent of the Internet as a venue for social research creates a new wrinkle in the continuing issue of what constitutes "private" behavior or invasion of privacy. In addition to archival records of communications that are exchanged through various web-based interest groups and online forums, researchers are more and more often becoming involved as "participatory observers" in such message groups. Currently, the prevailing philosophy is that preexisting content on the Internet constitutes "public domain" and therefore can be observed and recorded without obtaining consent, although there is an expectation that information about identity of the senders should be protected. However, if an Internet study is designed for the purpose of collecting new data from participants (e.g., survey questionnaires and Internet experiments), informed consent should be electronically obtained from participants. This type of informed consent form is usually represented as the first web page that potential participants encounter in an online study. The use of the Internet for research purposes remains a matter of public debate, in part due to the National Security Agency spying scandal (Black, 2013) that blew up after the disclosure of massive surveillance of citizens' email and phone conversations. More protections of privacy of such communications may ensue in the future.

Protecting Confidentiality of Data

One justification that researchers use for keeping participants uninformed about their inclusion in a field study is that the data collected from such sources are essentially anonymous, with no possibility of personally identifying the persons who provided the responses. Of course, if video or other recording techniques are used that preserve identifying information about the participants, the data are not anonymous and participants should be given the right to consent whether their data will be used. However, when data are recorded without any identifying information of any kind, any invasion of privacy is temporary and confidentiality of the data is insured in the long run.

Even when research is not disguised, avoiding recording of individual identifying information to maintain confidentiality of data is a good idea (Fisher & Vacanti-Shova, 2012). Assuring participants of the confidentiality of their responses is not simply for their benefit but can also increase the likelihood that they will be open and honest in their responses (Blanck, Bellack, Rosnow, Rotheram-Borus, & Schooler, 1992; Boruch & Cecil, 1979). An experiment conducted by Esposito, Agard, and Rosnow (1984) compared responses on a personality test given by participants who had been assured that their responses would be "strictly confidential" to those given by participants who had not been given such assurances. Those in the confidentiality condition provided data that were less influenced by social desirability biases than those in the control condition. This effect was obtained even though participants recorded their names on the tests that they took.

Protecting confidentiality is relatively easy when no identifying information (such as names, social security numbers, etc.) is recorded with the collection of data from individual participants. In many cases, however, participants' names or other identifying features are recorded for various reasons, and under those circumstances protection of confidentiality can present legal or ethical dilemmas for researchers (Blanck et al., 1992). This can occur when the research involves sensitive information (e.g., testing for HIV) or potentially illegal or dangerous behavior (e.g., child abuse), where reporting to partners or authorities may be seen as an ethical or legal responsibility. Research data in situations such as these are subject to subpoena, and researchers have sometimes been put into a painful conflict between their ethical responsibilities to research participants and their legal obligations. For research on some sensitive topics in the United States, it is possible to obtain a "certificate of confidentiality" from the Public Health Service (Sieber, 1992) that protects participant information from subpoena, but most research involving human participants is not protected in this way.

Datasets and Archival Research

Related to the general issues of invasion of privacy and confidentiality is the debate over creation of various national datasets for research purposes. Many datasets available online, and those distributed by reputable organizations, have removed personally identifying information about the participants. Such datasets may be obtained from the Pew Research Center, Census Bureau, Internal Revenue Service, Social Security Administration, and other agencies.

Longitudinal research might require that data records be kept about individual respondents, but these methods do not necessarily require that those individuals be personally identifiable. Systematic controls to screen researchers who wish to be granted access to data are designed to protect individual privacy and are not necessarily inconsistent with research aims. In their review of the potential benefits and risks associated with the creation of a national data center, Sawyer and Schecter (1968) proposed several standards of operation that would provide safeguards for privacy for participants who may be identified in a dataset. Among their major suggestions are the following:

- Only objective information be included in dataset,
- Individuals be given the right to review their files for accuracy, and to have errors corrected,
- Research analyses be restricted to random samples,
- Files of individuals be identified only by code numbers, with access to personal identification strictly restricted, and
- Security precautions be instituted for screening data users and access to the types of information

These last two suggestions are related to the fact that some identification of participant records might be required for adding new information to existing records longitudinally, or for producing a file for review at the participant's own request. To restrict access to the translation between a unique identifying number (e.g., a random number given to each participant) and personal identification (e.g., participant's full name), some sort of "linking" system (involving a mediating step between access to a particular file and connection between file number and person's name), should be employed. An example is that developed by the American Council on Education (Astin & Boruch, 1970). Creating linking systems of this kind can be expensive, but such costs balance the scientific usefulness of large data banks against the risks to individual privacy.

The Regulatory Context of Research Involving Human Participants

Our preceding discussion of ethical dilemmas is intended to convey the idea that there are no simple, absolute rules for deciding whether a particular research practice or method is ethical or not. Rather, considerable judgment is involved in weighing the potential value of the research against potential stress or other costs to research participants. Except for obviously dangerous or damaging actions on the part of the researcher, ethical decision-making involves a cost-benefit analysis rather than the promulgation of absolute strictures and rules. Much of the responsibility for making this assessment falls on the individual scientist, but an individual researcher alone is not always the best judge of what is valuable and necessary research and what is potentially harmful to participants. In fact, there is good evidence that biases enter into scientists' assessments of the utility of their own research (Kimmel, 1991). For that reason, the conduct of research that meets reasonable ethical standards and procedures is not just a matter of personal judgment—it is the law.[2]

Almost all social and behavioral research in the United States that is supported by federal funds or conducted in educational or research institutions that receive federal funding (of any kind) is subject to federal regulations regarding the conduct of research involving human participants. The primary directive is 45CFR46 in the Code of Federal Regulations, known as the "Common Rule." The code (last revised in 1991; for an up to date summary, see www.hhs.gov/ohrp/humansubjects/guidance/45cfr46.html) stipulates certain principles for protecting the welfare and dignity of human participants in research and prescribes policies and procedures that are required of institutions in which such research is conducted. The code has been continually scrutinized over the years, and in 2013 a committee of the National Research Council, The Committee on the Common Rule for the Protection of Human Subjects in Research in the Behavioral and Social Sciences, was actively meeting to consider changes to the regulations governing human research. As mentioned in Chapter 6 in connection with the initial planning stages of any research study, failure to comply with the procedures dictated by federal regulations can have dire consequences not only for the individual researcher involved, but for the whole institution in which he or she works.

Institutional Review Boards

Much of the responsibility for complying with federal regulations is delegated to the institutions (e.g., universities) in which the research is conducted. Every institution in which federally funded research is carried out is required to set up an **institutional review board** (IRB), a committee that evaluates, approves, and monitors all research projects in an institution with respect to ethical requirements and practices. The IRB is appointed by the university administration, but with certain requirements for representation by members of the community and legal experts, as well as scientists from departments across the institution. Before any program of research is begun, it is the principal investigator's responsibility to submit a complete description of the proposed research purposes and procedures to the IRB for review. Based on the information provided by the investigator, the members of the IRB evaluate the potential costs and risks to participants in the research as well as the potential benefits of the research if it is conducted as planned. A schematic representation of the IRB review process as it is practiced in most research universities is provided in Figure 20.1.

If the research described appears to meet ethical standards as set by the IRB committee, approval will be given to the investigator to conduct the research as described. Approvals are granted for a maximum of 12 months; if the research has not been completed within that time, the project must be resubmitted for continuing approval. If the IRB does not feel that the researcher has provided sufficient information to assess the potential risks of conducting the study, or if the proposed procedures do not appear to be fully justified, the proposal will be sent back to the investigator with contingencies or changes that must be made before the research can be approved. In the majority of cases, the review process ultimately results in a project that can be approved for implementation. But on occasion, the IRB can and will refuse to allow certain research studies to be done because they are deemed to be unethical or excessively risky.

Although many scientists regard the IRB review process as cumbersome and time-consuming, most recognize that it is now a standard part of the design and conduct of research involving human participants. Low-risk research that does not involve deception or issues of confidentiality usually can be handled by expedited review. But in other circumstances, most notably those involving potential danger, deception, or blatant manipulation of one form or another, the internal review committee serves a valuable function by requiring the researcher to defend the legitimacy of the research, the necessity for the questionable practices, and the cost-benefit analysis involved in conducting the investigation.

An important feature of the institutional review group is that it typically does not consist solely of the researcher's colleagues—many of whom, perhaps, have planned or conducted research similar to that under consideration—but rather of a group of impartial individuals, scientists and laypersons alike, whose primary goal is the protection of participants' rights. As such, the institutional review committee is not "too close to the forest to see the trees." This body often can alert conscientious investigators to a potential problem that neither they nor their colleagues had noticed, simply

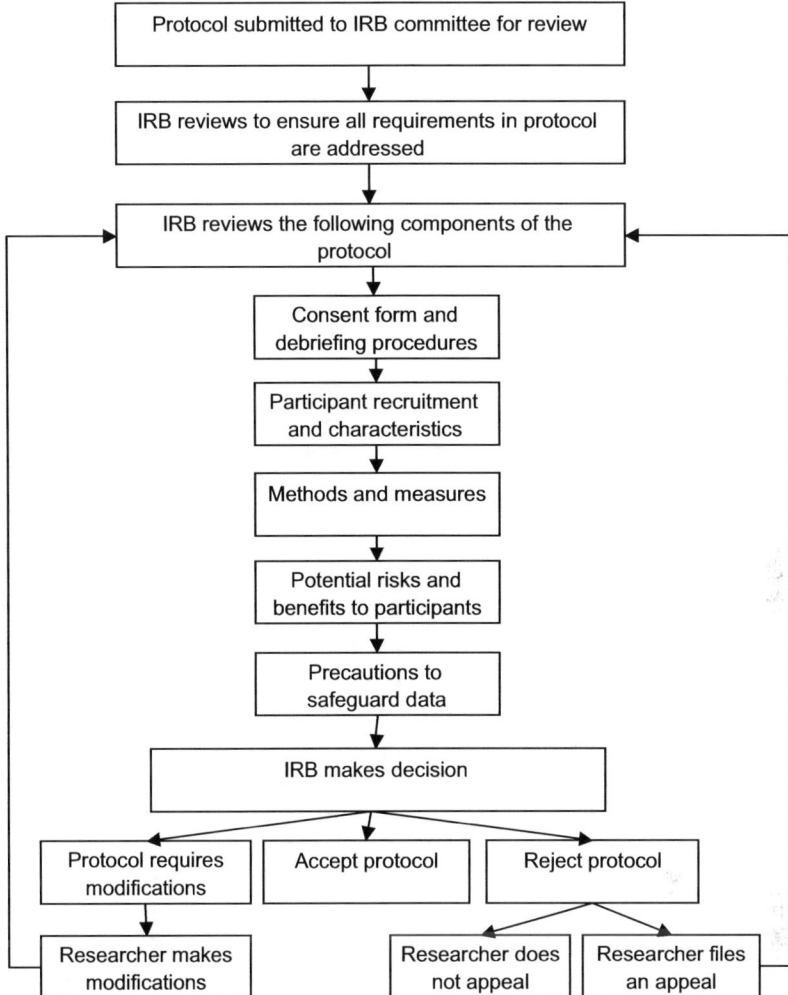

FIGURE 20.1 Process of IRB review.

because they were too involved with the technical and theoretical details of the research problem to notice the threats to participants' rights that the research might entail. When it works well, the IRB review process plays an important role in assuring ethical responsibility in contemporary social research.

Codes of Ethics

Although clearance by the local IRB is a mandatory aspect of research that involves human participants, this review procedure does not absolve researchers from further responsibility for the ethical conduct of their research. In addition to the procedures dictated by federal regulations, behavioral researchers also are subject to codes of ethics promulgated by scientific societies such as the National Academy of Sciences (1995) and the American Psychological Association (1983, 1985, 1992, 2002; Knapp, 2011) in the United States. Such codes and principles provide guidelines for scientists in the planning, design, and execution of research studies. However, rules can always be circumvented, and even a formal code will be ineffective unless sanctioned by social support reflected in editorial policies of professional journals, funding decisions of foundations and federal agencies, and other sources of professional recognition. Thus, it is our view that the best guarantee of continued concern over ethical standards is the frequent airing of ethical issues in a way that ensures exposure to each new generation of researchers.

Methodology as Ethics

Some social scientists draw a sharp distinction between ethical and methodological issues in the design and conduct of behavioral research, but others think that ethics and methodology are inextricably intertwined. Rosenthal and Rosnow (1984), for instance, promote the philosophy that sound research design is an *ethical imperative* as well as a scientific ideal. Taking into account that participants' time, effort, and resources are involved in the conduct of any social research, they argue that researchers are ethically obligated to do only research that meets high standards of quality to ensure that results are valid and that the research has not been a waste of participants' time. Rosenthal (1994) has gone so far as to suggest that IRBs should evaluate the methodological quality of research proposals as part of the cost-benefit analysis in their decisions about the ethicality of proposed research projects. Critics of this proposal (e.g., Parkinson, 1994; Sears, 1994) argue that ethical concerns and evaluation of the scientific merits of projects should be kept separate because they involve different expertise and different types of standards.

We are sympathetic to the general idea that the participants' investment of time and effort in research studies should be a factor in evaluating the costs of conducting research and that there is some ethical obligation to be reasonably sure that the research project is worth doing before such costs should be incurred. However, we also agree that IRBs should not be in the business of evaluating the methodological quality of research proposals, beyond some very general evaluations of the justification for the project and the qualifications of the principal investigators. As we hope the previous chapters in this book have conveyed, the criteria for good methodology are neither static nor absolute. Multiple methodological approaches are needed to meet different criteria and purposes of research, so no one study is likely simultaneously to possess high internal validity, construct validity, and external validity. Rather than IRBs reviewing a study based strictly on methods to be undertaken, the value of a particular research project must be evaluated in terms of the contribution it will make to a *body* of research employing various methods, rather than as an isolated enterprise. One responsibility of the social science methodologist lies in the development of recommendations that contribute to a balanced approach to scientific advance. In one sense, this guideline refers to promoting the use of diverse research strategies and methods of assessment, as has been advocated throughout this text. In a broader sense, however, this responsibility extends to one of precluding an overly narrow and rigid interpretation of a method of science to the exclusion of other forms of inquiry.

Ethics of Data Reporting

One arena in which ethical principles and scientific ideals converge is the prescription to report results of research and the methods by which they were obtained honestly and completely. Sadly, in all branches of science there are cases in which out-and-out fabrication of findings has been uncovered. A number of notorious instances of fraud committed in research have been discovered across disciplines, ranging from plagiarism to falsification of data (Broad & Wade, 1982; Stroebe, Postmes, & Spears, 2012). Although sanctions varied, for a good number of these individuals their researcher career came to a complete end after the discovery of scientific misconduct. Mechanisms that have been recommended to help identify fraudulent studies include whistleblowers who work in these laboratories, the peer-review process of journals, and replication studies to ascertain whether results obtained from a program of research could be confirmed.

Cases involving fraudulent data clearly violate both scientific and moral principles. However, there are other areas of reporting where the boundaries between ethical and unethical practice are not so clear-cut. Selective reporting of some results of a study and not others often occurs, and data from some participants are dropped from analyses if they are suspect in some way. Such practices can be justified to reduce unnecessary error in understanding and interpreting results of a scientific study, but these practices can be abused if used to distort the findings in the direction of reporting only what the researcher had hoped to demonstrate. To avoid such abuses, researchers need to use systematic criteria of dropping data from their analyses and to be scrupulous about reporting how these criteria were applied.

Researchers are expected to be honest about reporting results that do not support their hypotheses *as well as* results that do support their predictions. In addition, researchers need to be honest about what their hypotheses were in the first place. Quite often, the results of a research study are somewhat unexpected. This should be valued as part of the research enterprise—if we only got expected results, there would be some question about whether there was any need to undertake the research in the first place! When unexpected findings are obtained, we usually can generate explanations post hoc about why things came out that way. This is a valuable part of the research process—post hoc explanations become hypotheses for new research. However, in a research report, it is important to distinguish between interpretations of findings that are made after the fact and hypotheses that were made before the study began. Post-hoc explanations that are reported as if they had been hypothesized beforehand are a practice that Norbert Kerr has labeled "HARKing"—*Hypothesizing After the Results are Known* (Kerr, 1998). In the long run, this practice could compromise the foundation of social research by increasing the prevalence of studies containing results with Type I errors in the literature (Simmons, Nelson, & Simonsohn, 2011).

In light of these concerns, scientific societies and journal editors in the social sciences have been reconsidering some of the data reporting practices in their disciplines and establishing new norms and guidelines to encourage more complete and open reporting. In 2014, the Association of Psychological Science, for example, announced new guidelines for submissions of research articles to its flagship journal *Psychological Science* (see www.psychologicalscience.org/index.php/publications/journals/psychological_science/ps-submissions). Among the new requirements is a checklist of research disclosure statements that are intended to enhance the reporting of methods. At the time manuscripts are submitted for consideration for publication in the journal, submitting authors must confirm the following for each study reported in the manuscript:

- that all excluded observations and the reasons for exclusion have been reported in the Methods section
- that all independent variables or manipulations have been reported
- that all dependent variables or measures that were analyzed for the research study have been reported
- that information on how the final sample size for each study was determined has been reported

These new requirements have been implemented to encourage open reporting and to ensure that full and honest disclosure of all aspects of a research study does not detract from the chances that a manuscript will be accepted for publication.

Ethical Issues Related to the Products of Scientific Research

The development and use of atomic power in the 1940s quite effectively exploded the myth that scientific research is immune from considerations of morality and social values. Since that time, scientists have had to come to grips with the issues of moral responsibility for the potential applications of their research discoveries. Some resolve this issue by rejecting all responsibility, claiming that scientific knowledge is essentially neutral, potentially serving good or evil depending upon decisions outside the scientist's control. Others feel that if scientists are in a reasonable position to foresee the immediate applications of their research efforts, then they must accept responsibility for the consequences of their continuing in that line of research.

This issue becomes most acute when the factor of research sponsorship is considered. When a research project is financed wholly or in part by some governmental or private agency, the researcher sometimes is obligated to report results directly—perhaps exclusively—to that agency. In such cases the purposes of the sponsoring agency will clearly determine at least the immediate application of information or technical developments derived from that research, and the scientist can hardly deny foreknowledge of such applications, whatever other potential uses the discovery may have. Given the growing costs of research in the physical and social sciences, more and more projects must rely on sources of funding other than those provided by such presumably impartial agencies as universities, and more and more scientists are facing a choice between abandoning a particular line of research or conducting it under the auspices of some private agency with special interests.

With respect to the long-range goal of social research—understanding human behavior in social settings—every researcher must be aware that as such knowledge accumulates, the potential for using it as a means of gaining control over other people also increases. Thus, the ethical considerations of any researcher in this area must include who will be privy to this knowledge in the long run, and what are the chances that it will come under the exclusive control of one segment of the social system (Kelman, 1968, 1972). Of more immediate concern is the current usage of information collected, or techniques developed, in the course of social research. For example, in research devoted to diagnosing antisocial attitudes or problematic personalities, various "disguised" or "projective" techniques have been developed, which purportedly assess the trait of interest under the guise of measuring something else. What is the responsibility of the designers of these techniques when they are used by corporate personnel officers to weed out unsuspecting employees with potential anti-management values or attitudes? Or, alternatively, what is the responsibility of the researcher whose correlational study of social and attitudinal factors linked to student radicalism is used by university admissions officers to develop screening criteria for rejecting applicants?

The issue of social responsibility is made even more complex when one realizes that the conclusions to be drawn from research results or psychological tests often are grossly misperceived by naive analysts. In the preceding example, for instance, the users of disguised tests or screening criteria might be largely unaware of the high degree of error (i.e., potential misclassification) evidenced in such selection devices when applied to individuals. Similar issues are raised with respect to research yielding controversial results that reveal differences (e.g., in intelligence or personality variables) between different ethnic or racial groups. Because the ethnic variable is inextricably confounded with cultural and socioeconomic factors in contemporary Western society, the source of such differences in terms of genetic or cultural factors cannot be determined unambiguously, so researchers should report such results in a highly qualified fashion. However, there is no guarantee that other persons might not use the reported results to serve as justification for discriminatory practices based on the premise of innate differences between ethnic or racial groups.

Such potential misrepresentation of ambiguous research results has led some social scientists to suggest that a moratorium be declared on research involving race differences—either that such research not be conducted or that differences, if found, not be reported. Some scientists are horrified at the implication derived from this suggestion, that research data should be withheld on the basis of subjective moral judgments of individual researchers, whereas others take the more extreme position, that because scientists may vary considerably in what they consider ethically reprehensible or desirable, some kind of scientific commission should be formed to determine the distribution of research efforts and results.

Conclusion

After reviewing these various policy suggestions, we have come to the position that the ethical dilemmas faced by the scientist-researcher cannot be solved entirely by any centralized decision-making body, which may place restrictions on the kind of research that can be undertaken or on the reporting of research outcomes. Rather, we feel that public interests will be served best by programs that actively promote alternative lines of research and competing theoretical (or philosophical) positions. To this end, we offer three suggestions:

1. That research programs that currently rely on exclusive sources of support instead be multiply sponsored, or receive support from a combined scientific research fund supported by budget allotments from several different agencies,
2. That to the maximum extent possible, all research reports, techniques, and summaries be made available for public distribution,
3. That emphasis be given to the social responsibility of individual scientists or groups of scientists to educate the public on the nature of their research results in ways that will enhance understanding of both the conclusions and the qualifications and limitations that must be placed on the generalization of those conclusions.

In this view, scientists would be encouraged to resist associating with research programs that prevent public access to scientific data and, similarly, to avoid placing the stamp of scientific respectability on research that is seriously flawed owing to methodological difficulties, or whose limitations are not clearly specified. These suggestions reflect our conviction that researchers who arm themselves with the mastery of diverse methods, and apply this knowledge as active producers and consumers of open information, are equipped with the best weapons against the misuse of scientific data or instrumentation.

Questions for Discussion

1. You conducted a study that investigated whether people's moral beliefs made them more likely to engage in helping behavior when a person is in need; therefore, you measured behavioral intent (i.e., *how likely would you be to help a person in this situation*). In providing informed consent, participants were informed that they would be completing a survey that asked about their general beliefs and how they think they would respond in certain situations. After completing those items, participants were told that the study was finished and they were thanked for their time. After the ostensible completion of the study, as participants left the laboratory building, they all encountered a confederate in need of help. Participants' helping or not, and in what way, was recorded as the participants' final data point.

Can you use this behavioral measure in your analyses (the way the scenario is currently described)? Why? Since participants' actions occurred in a public place (outside the laboratory building), do they need to provide informed consent, or is it considered "in the public domain?" Does the informed consent participants initially provided include permission to use their behavior as data in your research? If your answers to any of these questions is "no," what could you do to make that behavioral data useable?
2. You conducted a longitudinal study of teenagers' alcohol and substance use behaviors, including self-reports on their use of illicit drugs. On the informed consent form, you acknowledged (both in writing and verbally to each participant) that there was always a remote possibility that the information they provide could be seen, intentionally or unintentionally, by people who are not involved with the research project—e.g., if there was a fire in the laboratory building, and rather than burn participants' responses, all of your paper-and-pencil data was strewn across the grounds outside the building. Because it was a longitudinal study, you had a record of participants' names and their corresponding ID numbers, but kept that record in a separate locked file cabinet in a different part of the lab relative to participants' data. However, after the fire, the document with participants' names and ID numbers fell in the same place as participants' data. Then, before you could collect all of the documents, some were stolen, including the document with the names and IDs, along with some participants' data. Should you contact those participants to tell them what happened? Or should you just hope that there are no catastrophic consequences for those participants? What else could or should you do? What are your ethical obligations to participants?
3. Currently, some countries do not require IRB approval before you can conduct research with human participants, nor do these countries have any sort of review entities that are equivalent to an Institutional Review Board. At a recent conference, a fellow researcher suggested you consider conducting research in one such country (e.g., Methodia [a fictional country used for the sake of argument]), to avoid the overly burdensome and excessive red tape of your institution's IRB. Technically, this would not violate federal guidelines for participant protections if you did not represent yourself as a member of your home institution—so you decide to do it. What are the ethical implications of such a practice? Is what you are doing ethical? Why or why not? How might this impact the process and integrity of conducting research in the U.S. and at your home institution, both for yourself and for other researchers?

Notes

1. They also, however, were somewhat more likely than non-deceived subjects to doubt the trustworthiness of psychologists!
2. Throughout this chapter we are describing regulations and procedures for ethics review that are based on federal laws and guidelines in the United States. The regulatory environment for the conduct of research with human participants varies from country to country, although many countries have adopted procedures that are modelled after those in the U.S. Each researcher, of course, is responsible for knowing the legal requirements in any country where they (or their collaborators) are conducting studies.

References

American Psychological Association. (1983). *Ethical principles in the conduct of research with human participants.* Washington, DC: Author.
American Psychological Association. (1985). *Standards for educational and psychological testing.* Washington, DC: Author.
American Psychological Association (1992). Ethical principles of psychologists and code of conduct. *American Psychologists, 47,* 1597–1611.

American Psychological Association (2002). *Ethical principles of psychologists and code of conduct.* Washington, DC: Author.

Asch, S. E. (1956). Studies of independence and conformity: A minority of one against a unanimous majority. *Psychological Monographs, 70*(9) (whole no. 416).

Astin, A. W., & Boruch, R. F. (1970). A "link" system for assuring confidentiality of research data in longitudinal studies. *American Educational Research Journal, 7,* 615–624.

Baumrind, D. (1964). Some thoughts on ethics of research: After reading Milgram's "Behavioral study of obedience." *American Psychologist, 19,* 421–423.

Black, I. (2013, June 10). NSA spying scandal: what we have learned. *The Guardian.* Retrieved from www.theguardian.com/world/2013/jun/10/nsa-spying-scandal-what-we-have-learned.

Blanck, P., Bellack, A., Rosnow, R., Rotheram-Borus, M. J., & Schooler, N. (1992). Scientific rewards and conflicts of ethical choices in human subjects research. *American Psychologist, 47.* 959–965.

Boruch, R. F., & Cecil, J. S. (1979). *Assuring the confidentiality of research data.* Philadelphia: University of Pennsylvania Press.

Broad, W., & Wade, N. (1982). *Betrayers of the truth.* New York: Simon and Schuster.

Brock, T. C. (1965). Communicator-recipient similarity and decision change. *Journal of Personality and Social Psychology, 1,* 6506–6554.

Brock, T. C., & Becker, L. A. (1966). "Debriefing" and susceptibility to subsequent experimental manipulations. *Journal of Experimental Social Psychology, 2,* 314–323.

Bryan, J. H., & Test, M. A. (1967). Models of helping: naturalistic studies in aiding behavior. *Journal of Personality and Social Psychology, 6,* 400–407.

Campbell, D. T. (1969). Prospective and control. In R. Rosenthal & R. L. Rosnow (Eds.), *Artifact in behavioral research.* New York: Academic Press.

Esposito, J. L., Agard, E., & Rosnow, R. L. (1984). Can confidentiality of data pay off? *Personality and Individual Differences, 5,* 477–480.

Feldman, R. E. (1968). Response to compatriot and foreigner who seek assistance. *Journal of Personality and Social Psychology, 10,* 202–214.

Fisher, C. B., & Vacanti-Shova, K. (2012). The responsible conduct of psychological research: An overview of ethical principles, APA Ethics Code standards, and federal regulations. In S. J. Knapp, M. C. Gottlieb, M. M. Handelsman & L. D. VandeCreek (Eds.), *APA handbook of ethics in psychology, Vol. 2: Practice, teaching, and research* (pp. 335–369). Washington, DC: American Psychological Association.

Freedman, J. L., & Fraser, S. C. (1966). Compliance without pressure: The foot-in-the-door technique. *Journal of Personality and Social Psychology, 4,* 195–202.

Holmes, D. S. (1967). Amount of experience in experiments as a determinant of performance in later experiments. *Journal of Personality and Social Psychology, 7,* 403–407.

Holmes, D. S. (1976a). Debriefing after psychological experiments: I. Effectiveness of postdeception dehoaxing. *American Psychologist, 31,* 858–867.

Holmes, D. S. (1976b). Debriefing after psychological experiments: II. Effectiveness of postdeception desensitizing. *American Psychologist, 31,* 868–875.

Jung, A. F. (1959). Price variations among automobile dealers in Chicago, Illinois. *Journal of Business, 32,* 315–326.

Kelman, H. C. (1967). Human use of human subjects: The problem of deception in social psychological experiments. *Psychological Bulletin, 67,* 1–11.

Kelman, H. C. (1968). *A time to speak: On human values and social research.* San Francisco: Jossey-Bass.

Kelman, H. C. (1972). The rights of the subject in social research: An analysis in terms of relative power and legitimacy. *American Psychologist, 27,* 989–1016.

Kerr, N. L. (1998). HARKing: Hypothesizing after the results are known. *Personality and Social Psychology Review, 2,* 196–217.

Kimmel, A. J. (1991). Predictable biases in the ethical decision making of American psychologists. *American Psychologist, 46,* 786–788.

Knapp, S. J. (2011). *APA handbook of ethics in psychology.* Washington, DC: American Psychological Association.

Latané, B. (1970). Field studies of altruistic compliance. *Representative Research in Social Psychology, 1,* 49–61.

Lefkowitz, M., Blake, R. R., & Mouton, J. S. (1955). Status factors in pedestrian violation of traffic signals. *Journal of Abnormal and Social Psychology, 51,* 704–706.

Middlemist, R., Knowles, E., & Matter, C. F. (1976). Personal space invasions in the lavatory. *Journal of Personality and Social Psychology, 33,* 541–546.
Milgram, S. (1963). Behavioral study of obedience. *Journal of Abnormal and Social Psychology, 67,* 371–378.
Milgram, S. (1964). Issues in the study of obedience: A reply to Baumrind. *American Psychologist, 19,* 848–852.
Milgram, S. (1969). The lost-letter technique. *Psychology Today, 3,* 30–33, 66–68.
Milgram, S. (1974). *Obedience to authority.* New York: Harper & Row.
Miller, S. E. (1966). Psychology experiments without subjects' consent. *Science, 152,* 15.
National Academy of Sciences. (1995). *On being a scientist: Responsible conduct in research.* Washington, DC: National Academy Press.
Ortmann, A., & Hertwig, R. (1997). Is deception acceptable? *American Psychologist, 52,* 746–747.
Parkinson, S. (1994). Scientific or ethical quality? *Psychological Science, 5,* 137–138.
Piliavin, I. M., Rodin, J., & Piliavin, J. A. (1969). Good Samaritanism: An underground phenomenon? *Journal of Personality and Social Psychology, 13,* 289–299.
Resnick, J. H., & Schwartz, T. (1973). Ethical standards as an independent variable in psychological research. *American Psychologist, 28,* 134–139.
Rokeach, M., & Mezei, L. (1966). Race and shared belief as factors in social choice. *Science, 151,* 167–172.
Rosenthal, R. (1994). Science and ethics in conducting, analyzing, and reporting psychological research. *Psychological Science, 5,* 127–133.
Rosenthal, R., & Rosnow, R. L. (1984). Applying Hamlet's question to the ethical conduct of research. *American Psychologist, 39,* 561–563.
Ross, L., Lepper, M. R., & Hubbard, M. (1975). Perseverance in self-perception and social perception: Biased attributional processes in the debriefing paradigm. *Journal of Personality and Social Psychology, 32,* 880–892.
Sawyer, J., & Schecter, H. (1968). Computers, privacy, and the national data center: The responsibility of social scientists. *American Psychologist, 23,* 810–818.
Schaps, E. (1972). Cost, dependency, and helping. *Journal of Personality and Social Psychology, 21,* 74–78.
Schwartz, R. D., & Skolnick, J. H. (1962). Two studies of legal stigma. *Social Problems, 10,* 133–142.
Sears, D. O. (1994). On separating church and lab. *Psychological Science, 5,* 237–239.
Sieber, J. E. (1992). *Planning ethically responsible research.* Newbury Park, CA: Sage.
Silverman, I., Shulman, A. D., & Wiesenthal, D. L. (1970). Effects of deceiving and debriefing psychological subjects on performance in later experiments. *Journal of Personality and Social Psychology, 14,* 203–12.
Simmons, J. P., Nelson, L. D., & Simonsohn, U. (2011). False-positive psychology: Undisclosed flexibility in data collection and analysis allows presenting anything as significant. *Psychological Science, 22,* 1359–1366.
Smith, S. S., & Richardson, D. (1983). Amelioration of deception and harm in psychological research: The important role of debriefing. *Journal of Personality and Social Psychology, 44,* 1075–1082.
Striker, L. J. (1967). The true deceiver. *Psychological Bulletin, 68,* 13–20.
Striker, L. J., Messick, S., & Jackson, D. N. (1967). Suspicion of deception: Implications for conformity research. *Journal of Personality and Social Psychology, 4,* 379–389.
Stroebe, W., Postmes, T., & Spears, R. (2012). Scientific misconduct and the myth of self-correction in science. *Perspectives on Psychological Science. 7,* 670–688.
Surgeon General's directives on human experimentation. (1967). *American Psychologist, 22,* 350–359.
Walster, E., Berscheid, E., Abrahams, D., & Aronson, E. (1967). Effectiveness of debriefing following deception experiments. *Journal of Personality and Social Psychology, 4,* 371–380.
Webb, E. J., Campbell, D. T., Schwartz, R. D., Sechrest, L., & Grove, J. (1981). *Nonreactive measures in the social sciences.* Boston: Houghton-Mifflin.
Weubben, P. L. (1965). Honesty of subjects and birth order. *Journal of Personality and Social Psychology, 5,* 350–352.

GLOSSARY

Actor   A person who perceives, records, and provides information or a score regarding the interpersonal interaction with a partner in a dyad.

Actor-partner interdependence model   A multivariate framework for examining two or more variables from each member of a dyad to determine the correspondence and reciprocity of features of their interpersonal relationship (love, trust, etc.).

Analogue experiment   In these studies, participants respond directly to a specially constructed situation that has been designed to reproduce or mimic selected features of a real-world situation.

Apprehensive participants   These participants are concerned that the experimenter will use their performance to evaluate their abilities, personality, social adjustment, etc., and react accordingly in the study.

Artifact   An artificial or spurious finding, a "pseudo-effect" that results inevitably from the properties of the measuring instrument or from the method of data collection employed.

Ascendency searching   The reference list of a recent and relevant primary study is consulted to perform a backward search to find chronologically earlier relevant studies (ancestors).

Asymmetric dyad   In these dyads, members are distinguishable by a relevant feature, such as their respective role or status in the relationship.

Autocorrelated errors   Measurement errors that occur if random events that affect the measure obtained at one time carry over and are correlated with measurements taken at temporally adjacent points in time.

Bidirectional causation   A relationship in which changes in A produce changes in B and, in addition, changes in B produce changes in A.

Census   A survey or enumeration involving all the potential units of a target population (the universe of interest).

Cluster sampling   In this form of sampling, geographic locations (or clusters or segments) are randomly sampled, and all members of the clusters selected are used in the sample.

Coding unit The specific variable to be classified in a content analysis.

Coefficient of determination The squared value of the Pearson correlation (r^2). It represents the proportion of variance shared between two (correlated) variables.

Cohen's kappa An index used to assess the extent of agreement between two coders of a qualitative categorical variable, which controls for chance agreement.

Comparison time-series design A design method that combines features of interrupted time-series and comparison-group designs.

Complete counterbalancing Used to control for treatment order effects. Sequencing of treatments involves every combination of treatment orderings, and each participant is randomly assigned to one of the sequences.

Conceptual hypothesis A prediction about relationships involving the theoretical constructs. It guides the purpose of a research study.

Conceptual replication An attempt to reproduce the results of a previous study by using different operational definitions to represent the same theoretical constructs.

Concurrent validity The extent to which a measure is related to, or explains, a relevant criterion behavior, with both variables assessed at the same occasion.

Confederate An actor or accomplice used by a researcher to pretend to be just another participant in a study.

Confirmatory factor analysis A statistical technique to assess the multidimensional structure of a scale. Used when the researcher has hypotheses regarding the number and types of underlying factors that will emerge in the analytic solution. It requires the researcher to begin with hypotheses precisely stipulating the number of potential factors, which items should load on (or correlate with) which factors, and how the factors should be correlated.

Confound A confound is a type of extraneous variable in which its effect, and that of the independent variable on the dependent variable cannot be separated, thereby posing a threat to internal validity.

Content analysis A diverse domain of techniques designed to explore and describe qualitative verbal, written, and multimedia communications in a systematic, objective, and quantitative manner.

Content validity An estimate of the extent that a measure adequately represents (or samples) the complete range or breadth of a construct under consideration.

Context unit In content analysis, this is the embedded context within which the meaning of a coding unit is to be inferred.

Convenience sampling In this weak form of sampling, the respondent sample consists of people most readily accessible or willing to be part of a study.

Convergent validity An estimate of the relationship between measures of constructs that are theoretically related.

Criterion validity The extent that a measure is related to, or predicts, a target outcome or criterion, usually a behavior.

Cronbach's alpha   An index of the internal consistency (reliability) of a set of items in a scale. It is a hypothetical value that would be obtained if all of the items that could constitute a given scale were available and randomly combined across a large number of tests of equal size.

Debriefing   A session following participation in a study, in which all are informed of the true purpose of the research.

Deductive content analysis   In this method, the researcher determines the coding categories and units that will be the basis of the coding system used in the analysis prior to conducting the coding.

Demand characteristics   The totality of all social cues communicated in a laboratory not attributable to the manipulation, including those emanating from the experimenter and the laboratory setting, which alter and therefore place a demand on participants' responses.

Dependent variable   A measured outcome or consequence, not manipulated by the researcher, and expected to be influenced by (or dependent upon) manipulation of the independent variable in an experiment.

Descendancy searching   In descendancy searching, an important early and relevant primary study is identified and used as the starting point to search for all chronologically later studies (descendants) that have cited it.

Discriminant validity   The extent that measures of constructs that are theoretically unrelated are independent of one another.

Double-barreled question   A single item that asks more than one question at the same time.

Double-blind procedures   A method in which both the participants and the researcher responsible for administering a study are made unaware of the treatment condition to which participants were assigned.

Dyadic variables   Characteristics or features of a relationship between the two persons, or their combined outcomes (e.g., level of warmth of their interaction, trust, etc.).

Ecological validity   An issue of external validity, involving the extent to which an effect occurs under conditions that are typical or representative in the population.

Effect size   A standardized metric of practical significance, it indicates the magnitude of relationship between two variables. It is the unit of analysis in meta-analytic research.

Endogenous variable   A variable explained by a determinant or predictor variable or variables, as postulated in a structural equation model.

Environmental manipulation   These treatments entail the systematic manipulation of some aspect of the physical setting.

Event-related potential   Electrodes attached to multiple regions of the scalp are used to measure these rapid waves of electrical brain activity that arise during the processing of information.

Exact replication   An attempt to reproduce the results of a previous study by using the same procedures, particularly the same operationalizations, to represent the same constructs.

Exogenous variable   A variable not explained by a determinant or predictor, as postulated in a structural equation model.

Experience sampling method In this technique, respondents carry a pager, text-messaging device, computer tablet, or other electronic reminder device to respond to researcher-produced questions about where they are and what they are doing, thinking, or feeling at that moment.

Experimental methods Techniques of inferring causal relations, in which participants' actions are limited or in some way constrained by the controlled manipulation of variables determined by the researcher.

Experimental realism The degree that an experiment has a real impact on participants during a study. Experimental arrangements of high realism induce participants to attend carefully to the task requirements.

Exploratory factor analysis A statistical technique to assess the multidimensional structure of a scale if the researcher does not have hypotheses regarding the number and types of underlying factors that will emerge in the scale's analysis.

External validity The extent of generalizability or certainty that results can be applied to other respondent groups, different settings, and different ways of operationalizing the conceptual variables.

Face validity A weak method of inferring validity based on superficial impressions regarding the extent that a measure appears to capture a construct.

Factorial design These designs involve combining levels of one independent variable with levels of all other independent variable(s), to expand the number of conditions in an experimental design.

Faithful participants Research participants willing to cooperate fully with almost any demand by the experimenter. They follow instructions scrupulously and ignore any suspicions they might have regarding the true purpose of the study.

Feasibility studies Studies conducted on a small scale to determine if the program as planned can be delivered effectively, given the existing constraints.

Field study Research conducted outside the laboratory; participants are studied in their own naturalistic environment or context.

File drawer problem Unpublished studies often are tucked away in file drawers and therefore ignored in a meta-analysis because they are not published. This results in a meta-analytic synthesis that is not representative of all the research that has been conducted, and that is positively biased.

Fixed-effect model In this meta-analysis approach, effect sizes of primary studies with larger sample sizes are weighted more heavily when the summary effect is calculated.

Fleiss' Kappa An index used to assess the extent of agreement between two or more coders of a qualitative categorical variable while controlling for chance.

Focus group A qualitative method in which groups of (usually 5–8) respondents provide information to a moderator who encourages verbal discussion and interaction about a focused topic of research interest.

Functional magnetic resonance imaging (fMRI) This is a measure of the relative degree of oxygen flow through blood vessels in the brain. It is used to identify which brain regions are implicated in various cognitive and emotional processing functions.

Good participants These respondents attempt to determine the experimenter's hypotheses and to confirm them.

Goodness of fit An overall index of how well all the computed estimates of a relationship in the model successfully reproduce the underlying matrix of correlations among the variables.

Grounded theory A method of generating theory on the basis of the observations. The theory is continually revised in light of new observations. The researcher is expected to start the process with no theoretical preconceptions.

Group interview In this method, an interviewer verbally requests information from more than one interviewee at the same time, but they are discouraged from interacting with each other.

Group variables The characteristics or variable features of a set of three or more persons (e.g., the age of the participants in a group, the total number of widgets created by a work team, etc.).

Growth curve model An analysis conducted to determine the longitudinal trajectory or shape of observations for participants measured at multiple time points.

Implicit association test An unobtrusive measure that assesses automatic associations between mental concepts by requiring participants to make classification judgments by sorting items as quickly and accurately as possible into different categories.

Implicit responses A person's responses to or evaluations of stimuli, biased by internal judgments of which they are not necessarily aware.

Independent variable A feature or characteristic manipulated independently of its natural sources of covariation to produce different conditions in an experimental study.

Inductive content analysis In this method, the researcher allows coding categories and units to emerge empirically by continually revising and updating the coding system while in the midst of the coding process.

Informed consent An informational process by which potential participants are told what participation in a study will involve, so that they can make a reasoned decision about whether or not to engage in the research.

Institutional review board (IRB) A committee that evaluates, approves, and monitors all research projects in an institution with respect to ethical requirements and practices.

Instructional manipulation A treatment that involves modification of the description of the purposes and procedures that participants encounter in a study.

Instrumentation error A threat to internal validity, in which scores are affected by changes in the properties of the measurement instrument, rather than as an outcome of exposure to different levels of a treatment.

Interaction effect An outcome that is evident when the effect of an independent variable on a dependent variable is altered or moderated by variations in the level of other independent variable(s), while controlling for the interacting variables' main effects.

Internal validity Indicates the extent that inferences of causation can be made about the obtained relationship between an independent variable and a dependent variable.

Interrupted time-series design A method in which the relative degree of change that occurs after a quasi-experimental treatment is examined by comparing observations across a series of time points prior to the treatment with observations taken at time points occurring after it.

Interval scale A measure in which higher scores represent increasingly greater levels of a construct (e.g., weight, height, religiousness). In such measures, equal distances in numbers reflect equal gradations in the critical variable across all levels of the measurement scale.

Interview A data collection method in which participants verbally communicate information about their behavior, thoughts, or feelings in response to questions verbally posed by an interviewer.

Intraclass correlation (ICC) An index of interrater reliability for two or more coders of a quantitative variable used to assess the extent to which participants have more homogeneous scores within higher-order grouping units relative to variability of participant scores across all groupings in a multi-level model.

Involuntary participants These subjects feel that they have been coerced to spend their time in an experimental investigation and consider it unjustifiable; therefore, they may vent their displeasure by actively attempting to ruin the study.

Item response theory A technique used to determine how each item in a scale operates in terms of difficulty, discrimination, and guessing to determine the overall score.

Latent factor A characteristic or construct not directly measured or observed, but which underlies responses on a measurement scale.

Latent structural equation model The result of the integration of confirmatory factor analysis and path analysis.

Leading question Questions phrased in a way to suggest the expected answer; they involve a premise that must be accepted to answer the question (e.g., "When did you stop abusing your wife?" presupposes that the individual at one time was abusive).

Main effect Occurs when overall mean differences are observed on a dependent measure as a function of one independent variable, while all levels of other independent variables are held constant.

Manipulation check A question or series of questions asked of participants to determine if they noticed the manipulation that was delivered in the experiment.

Measurement construct validity The overall validity of the measure with respect to the theoretical construct of interest is termed measurement construct validity.

Median split A process in which participants are divided at the "middlemost" score, with 50% of participants falling above and 50% falling below the split.

Mediator A third variable that serves as intermediary, to help explicate the chain of processes in a causal relationship.

Meta-analysis A quantitative approach used to summarize and facilitate interpreting primary studies that have all addressed the same research question.

Missing at random (MAR) This type of missing data occurs when the probability of missingness in a variable is not random, but may be fully explained by the other measured variables in the dataset.

Missing completely at random (MCAR) This type of missing data occurs if the probability of missing responses in a variable is not explained by (or is unrelated to) any other variable in the study.

Moderator A third variable that can either augment or block the cause-effect relationship between variables.

Monadic variables These involve characteristics of single persons (e.g., age, religiosity, IQ).

Mortality A threat to internal validity that occurs when selection procedures, treatment differences, or issues result in different proportions of participants dropping out of a study.

Multidimensional scaling A method that relies on ratings of the degree of similarity or dissimilarity among pairs of stimuli rather than binary judgments or ordering of preferences to identify the number and types of dimensions that underlie the stimulus set.

Multi-level modeling A statistical technique used to estimate the relationships of predictor(s) to a criterion, if the design involves a nested hierarchy of units.

Multiple operationalization An orientation that recognizes that no single operation or measurement provides sufficient information to define a theoretical concept, so the construct is measured through several techniques or operations.

Multiple regression An extension of the Pearson correlation, it is used to estimate the relationships of multiple predictors to a criterion.

Multistage sampling In this method, clusters of locations are sampled from a geographical sampling frame (as in cluster sampling), and then (unlike cluster sampling), units within each cluster are sampled as well.

Multitrait-multimethod matrix A validation technique in which multiple measures are used to assess the extent of association of theoretically related, but different, constructs, over and above the association that might come about simply because of shared measurement methods.

Mundane realism The degree to which various features of an experiment—instructions, treatments, and measurement operations—mirror real-world events that participants might encounter in their day-to-day experiences, rather than laboratory-specific operations.

Narrative review A qualitative approach for summarizing and interpreting primary studies that have addressed the same research question It resembles a meta-analysis without the statistics.

Needs assessment A method used to judge the extent of an existing social problem and to determine whether a program or intervention is required to remediate it.

Negative participants Research respondents unhappy with their participation, who seek to understand the experimenter's hypotheses so that they might sabotage the study.

Nominal group A collection of individuals composed of the same number and types of people as a real group, but whose members work independently and do not interact. The group product thus is a combination of individual performances or outputs.

Nominal scale A measure requiring only that different numbers be assigned to observations, so they may be differentiated.

Noncausal covariation A relationship in which changes in A are accompanied by changes in B, because both A and B are determined by changes in another variable, C.

Nonexperimental methods In this form of research, no variables are manipulated, but the relationships of naturally occurring variables are measured.

Nonrandom sampling In this form of selection, a nonrandom mechanism is used to obtain a sample from a population.

Nonvoluntary participants These participants unknowingly enter into an experiment situation and are unaware that they are part of a study until informed after the completion of the study. In some research, these individuals are never informed of their participation.

Not missing at random (NMAR) This form of missing-ness is said to be obtained if a variable is not missing at random, and its missing-ness is not explainable by the other measured variables in the dataset, but if it is explicable by other unmeasured variables.

Observed score The score obtained on a measurement instrument.

Operationalization The process of translating an abstract theoretical construct or concept into a concrete specification of procedures and measures, so that it may be observed, recorded, and replicated.

Ordinal scale A measure in which the ordering of number labels corresponds to the rank ordering of observations along some dimension.

Pair comparison scaling A stimulus scaling technique in which all possible pairs of stimuli are judged by respondents along some choice dimension (e.g., beauty, taste, sex appeal) stipulated by the researcher.

Parallel-forms reliability A measure of internal consistency assessed by devising two separate item sets intended to assess the same underlying construct, administered to the same participants at the same time, with degree of relatedness calculated.

Partial counterbalancing A compromise to complete counterbalancing that uses a Latin square design to account for the fact that it may be cumbersome to assign participants to every possible sequence of treatment orderings.

Participatory observation (participant observation) A method that involves intense social interaction between researchers and participants in the latter's milieu, during which time data, in the form of field notes, are unobtrusively and systematically collected.

Partner A person with whom an actor relates during a dyadic exchange.

Path model A type of structural equation model in which predictive relationships involving only measured variables are estimated.

Pearson product-moment correlation A statistic used to determine the extent of linear relationship between two variables, that is, the extent that variation in one measure is accompanied consistently by unidirectional variation in the other.

Placebo effect An outcome that occurs as a function of participants' beliefs in the efficacy of a treatment, rather than the active effect of treatment itself.

Posttest-only control group design An experimental design in which only a posttest, but no pretest, is given to randomly assigned participants in control and experimental groups.

Predictive validity The extent that a measure is related to or explains a relevant criterion outcome that typically is assessed on a subsequent occasion.

Pretest sensitization This threat to external validity occurs when participants in the experimental group are unduly sensitive to the treatment to which they are exposed as a function of prior exposure to the pretest.

Pretest-posttest control group design An experimental design in which both a pretest and posttest are given to participants randomly assigned to control or experimental groups.

Primary study An original study reporting the results of analyses of data collected from a sample of participants (e.g., a journal article, research report, dissertation).

Priming manipulation A treatment that induces a particular mindset or mental state of readiness in participants.

Program development A mechanism to provide initial feedback to program designers that can lead to revisions or alterations in program materials, design, and procedures before the intervention is implemented on a larger and more costly scale.

Program efficacy studies Research conducted on a small scale to determine whether the expected effects from the planned intervention occur as anticipated.

Program evaluation The application of social science methodology by program evaluators to assess social programs or interventions.

Program evaluator The person responsible for evaluating and assessing the many aspects and stages of a program or intervention.

Propensity score This represents the conditional probability of an individual's membership in one group (e.g., the experimental group) over another (e.g., the control group), given the pattern of that person's responses on the covariates used in the score's development.

Propensity score matching A statistical technique that uses complex statistical procedures, statistically matching participants on as many covariates as can be specified by the researcher to determine differences between comparison groups or to create roughly comparable groups to be used in lieu of random assignment.

Publication bias Refers to journal editors that publish only statistically significant results or findings in accord with the scientific zeitgeist of the time.

Quasi-experimental methods Variants of experimental methods that do not involve random assignment, but, as in experiments, participants are exposed to some form of variable manipulation imposed (or investigated) by the researcher.

Question constraint A question format in which allowable answers are prespecified.

Question specificity Reflects the manner in which the question is phrased, acknowledging the fact that minor changes of wording may have marked effects on respondents' answers.

Questionnaire An instrument that typically involves a single item to assess each construct under study; it typically is brief because participants are unwilling, unable, or unlikely to take part in a longer assessment.

Quota sampling In this method, respondents are sampled nonrandomly until a predefined number of participants for each of a specified set of (e.g., racial, ethnic, religious) subgroups is achieved.

Random assignment An allocation approach that requires that all persons available for a particular research study be able to participate in either the experimental or the control group, and that only chance determines the group to which any individual is assigned.

Random error A factor affecting scores in a study that is attributed to chance events that tend to artificially widen the variability or spread of observed scores in a nonsystematic way.

Random sampling In this form of selection, a random mechanism is used to obtain a sample intended to be representative of the underlying population.

Random selection A form of creating a pool of potential research participants that requires that chance determine the selection of participants for a study, thereby helping to assure the generalizability of results from the sample to the entire population of relevant persons.

Random-effects model In this meta-analysis approach, effect sizes of primary studies are weighted as a compromise between sample size and number of primary studies used to calculate the summary effect.

Rank order scaling This method involves respondents' ordering a set of stimuli along some dimension stipulated by the researcher.

Rating scale An instrument that makes use of multiple items to assess each construct and typically is used by researchers with access to participants willing to take part in lengthy assessments.

Ratio scale The highest level of measurement, involving equal unit differences between adjacent numbers along all areas of a scale (as in interval scales) and a meaningful absolute-zero point.

Recall measure A participant's report of recollection of information previously presented.

Recognition measure A measure of a participant's memory of whether or not test material was presented previously.

Regression-discontinuity design A quasi-experimental method conducted to test the existence of some systematic relationship between a pretest selection variable, used to place participants along some continuum (e.g., achievement, poverty), and a posttest measure of interest (e.g., school grades, job seeking).

Relevance An issue of external validity, it has to do with the question of whether an effect obtained in a study is pertinent to events or phenomena that actually occur in the real world.

Reliability The consistency with which a measurement instrument assesses a given construct.

Repeated-measures design A statistical design in which the same participants are repeatedly measured on the dependent variable, usually after more than one exposure to treatments.

Research hypothesis The empirical specification of a conceptual hypothesis, and a testable directional prediction about specific relationships in a study.

Research question A non-directional question about specific relationships in a study; this is less precise than a hypothesis, insofar as it merely queries the possibility of a relation, rather than specifying its direction or valence.

Robustness An issue of external validity concerned with the extent an effect obtained in one laboratory can be replicated in another laboratory with different participants, operationalizations of the critical construct, and researchers.

Role-playing simulation A method in which participants are instructed to actively imagine that they are actors in a specified real-world situation and to respond as they believe they would in that context.

Round robin design A method used to examine multiple combinations of dyads in a group by creating all possible pairs of persons, with each member rating each and every other member.

Sampling error (standard error) The expected typical discrepancy between the estimates calculated from a sample and the value that would be obtained if the entire targeted population (census) had been included in the study.

Sampling frame A complete listing of the population from which members of a sample are drawn and used.

Scientific method A general approach for acquiring knowledge using systematic and objective methods to understand a phenomenon, which involves logic and data-checking feedback on the validity of results.

Selection error A threat to internal validity that may occur if nonrandom processes are used to choose research participants and to assign them to experimental and control groups.

Selection-based interactions If participants were nonrandomly selected to serve in the various comparison groups of a study, they may experience differences in history, maturation, testing, etc., which may produce differences in the final measurement, thus threatening internal validity.

Self-report A method n which respondents provide answers to a set of questions or scale items that inquire about their personal thoughts, feelings, or behaviors.

Semi-structured interview (structured-nonscheduled interview) An interview schedule in which a set of predetermined topics must be covered, but no specific questions are prescribed.

Sentence completion task An indirect measurement tool in which a partial sentence is presented to participants, who are required to complete the sentence.

Simple random sampling A sampling technique in which every member of the population in question has an equal (and nonzero) probability of being selected every time a unit is drawn for inclusion in a sample.

Snowball sampling A sampling technique in which initially sampled respondents contact and recruit others in their social network for participation in the research.

Social manipulation An experimental treatment involving the delivery of scripted actions of another human being, usually a confederate working for the experimenter.

Social network analysis A method using dyadic relations as the basic unit of analysis, with the resulting data organized into matrix representations.

Sociometry The assessment of social acceptances and rejections of members in a given group; each member indicates likes or dislikes each of the other members in the group.

Solomon four-group design An investigative approach combining posttest-only and pretest-posttest control group true experimental designs to test the main effects of treatments, including pretest effects and the interaction of treatments with the presence/absence of the pretest.

Spatial unit A measurement in which geographical, geometric, and dimensional properties (e.g., inches of newspaper column, dimensions of magazine article, shape of a photograph) are used as the units of analysis.

Split-half reliability A test of internal consistency reliability assessed by randomly dividing a scale into two sets containing an equal number of items, both administered to the same respondents simultaneously, with a test of relatedness calculated between these two summed scores.

Statistical power The probability of obtaining a statistical significant effect, if indeed that effect truly exists; dependent on the strength of the relation between variables, the complexity of the study design, and the number of observations (participants).

Statistical regression The tendency of extreme scores to regress to the mean of the distribution from which they were obtained. A threat to internal validity that arises as a function of measurement error coupled with the selection of participants on the basis of extreme scores.

Statistical significance A measure of the probability of obtaining an observed effect by chance, a threat to internal validity.

Stimulus manipulation An alteration of theoretically implicated visual or verbal material in an experimental or quasi-experimental design.

Stimulus scaling Stimulus scales are measurement instruments designed to tap perceived differences among stimuli, rather than differences among individuals.

Stratified sampling A technique in which a population of interest is divided into theoretically meaningful or empirically important strata; members are randomly drawn from each stratum (or subpopulation) and used in the sample.

Structural equation model A statistical technique that overcomes the limitations of a multiple regression analysis by allowing the researcher to estimate and test the strength of relationships among multiple predictors and multiple criterion variables.

Structured interview A method in which a fixed list of questions is administered in the same order to all interviewees.

Summary effect The overall effect size across the primary studies of a meta-analysis; this may be estimated using an unweighted, fixed-effect, or random-effects model.

Summative evaluation A test conducted to assess whether a fully implemented program had an effect on the problem it was designed to address.

Symmetric dyad In these two-person groups, members of each pair are indistinguishable by any theoretically relevant features, such as their respective role or status in the relationship.

Systematic error (bias) Consistent error in measures that tend to artificially inflate or deflate observed scores.

Systematic sampling This form of sampling requires sampling every predetermined nth member from a population, after randomly choosing some starting point for the sampling process.

Temporal unit A measurement based on properties of time (e.g., minutes of a television or radio broadcast, seconds of a conversation).

Test-retest reliability A method of reliability testing assessed by administering a scale to the same participants twice, at different times. The degree of relatedness calculated between two administrations provides a measure of the test's stability.

Thematic apperception test An indirect measurement in which respondents view a deliberately ambiguous picture and then generate a story about the characters and scenario depicted.

Theory A formulation based on observations and insights, consisting of a series of tentative premises about ideas and concepts that lay the foundation for empirical research about a phenomenon.

Transcranial magnetic stimulation A technique by which external magnetic pulses are transmitted through the scalp to different brain regions to identify the part of the brain that is active when a specific thought or behavior is enacted.

True score The replicable feature of a concept that is being measured.

Unfolding technique A method to ascertain the dimensions responsible for the preferences of a group of respondents to a set of judgment stimuli.

Unidirectional causation A relationship in which changes in A produces subsequent changes in B, but changes in B do not influence A.

Unstructured interview (exploratory interview) A technique that encourages freely generated questions by interviewers and responses by interviewees; best used in the exploratory research phase.

Unweighted model A method in which effect sizes of primary studies are mathematically averaged to calculate the summary effect, without taking into consideration the sample size of each study.

Validity The degree of relationship, or the overlap, between a measurement instrument and the construct it is intended to assess.

Variable A characteristic or attribute that may differ, and that is the basic unit of observation and measurement in a study.

Voluntary participants Respondents in a study who are aware that they are under investigation, but who have made a conscious decision that the possible benefits involved outweigh the costs (measured in terms of time spent, privacy invaded, etc.) of being in the study.

Vote counting A literature review method that involves counting and comparing the number of primary studies that are statistically significant, or that support one explanation or another.

SUGGESTED ADDITIONAL READINGS

Chapter 1: Basic Concepts

Barki, H. (2004). Conceptualizing the construct of interpersonal conflict. *International Journal of Conflict Management, 15,* 216–244.

Campbell, J. P., Daft, R. L., & Hulin, C. L. (1982). *What to study: Generating and developing research questions.* Beverly Hills, CA: Sage.

Greenwald, A. G., Pratkanis, A. R., Leippe, M. R., & Baumgardner, M. H. (1986). Under what conditions does theory obstruct research progress? *Psychological Review, 93,* 216–229.

Lippke, S., & Ziegelman, J. P. (2008). Theory-based health behavior change: Developing, testing, and applying theories for evidence-based interventions. *Applied Psychology: An International Review, 57,* 698–716.

McGuire, W. J. (1997). Creative hypothesis generating in psychology: Some useful heuristics. *Annual Review of Psychology, 48,* 1–30.

Nisbett, R. E., & Wilson, T. D. (1977). Telling more than we can know: Verbal reports on mental processes. *Psychological Review, 84,* 231–259.

Wicker, A. (1989). Substantive theorizing. *American Journal of Community Psychology, 17,* 531–547.

Chapter 2: Internal and External Validity

Abelson, R. P. (1997). On the surprising longevity of flogged horses: Why there is a case for the significance test. *Psychological Science, 8,* 12–15.

Baron, R. M., & Kenny, D. A. (1986). The moderator-mediator variable distinction in social psychological research: Conceptual, strategic, and statistical considerations. *Journal of Personality and Social Psychology, 51,* 1173–1182.

Cohen, J. (1994). The earth is round ($p < .05$). *American Psychologist, 49,* 997–1003.

Cortina, J. M., & Dunlap, W. P. (1997). On the logic and purpose of significance testing. *Psychological Methods, 2,* 161–172.

Hallahan, M., & Rosenthal, R. (1996). Statistical power: Concepts, procedures, and applications. *Behaviour Research and Therapy, 34,* 489–499.

Hayes, A. F. (2013). *Introduction to mediation, moderation, and conditional process analysis.* New York: Guilford.

Hunter, J. E. (1997). Needed: A ban on the significance test. *Psychological Science, 8,* 3–7.

Schmidt, F. L. (1996) Statistical significance testing and cumulative knowledge in psychology: Implications for training of researchers. *Psychological Methods, 1,* 115–129.

Chapter 3: Measurement Reliability

de Champlain, A. F. (2010). A primer on classical test theory and item response theory for assessments in medical education. *Medical Education, 44,* 109–117.

DeShon, R. P. (1998). A cautionary note on measurement error corrections in structural equation models. *Psychological Methods, 4,* 412–423.

Fan, X. (1998). Item response theory and classical test theory: An empirical comparison of their item/person statistics. *Educational and Psychological Measurement, 58,* 357–381.

Muchinsky, P. M. (1996). The correction for attenuation. *Educational and Psychological Measurement, 56,* 63–75.

Reid, C. A., Kolakowsky-Hayner, S. A., Lewis, A. N., & Armstrong, A. J. (2007). Modern psychometric methodology: Applications of item response theory. *Rehabilitation Counseling Bulletin, 50,* 177–188.

Shevlin, M., Miles, J.N.V., Davies, M.N.O., & Walker, D. S. (2000). Coefficient alpha: A useful indicator of reliability? *Personality and Individual Differences, 28,* 229–237.

Chapter 4: Measurement Validity

Brewer, M. B., & Crano, W. D. (2014). Research design and issues of validity. In H. Reis & C. Judd (Eds.), *Handbook of research methods in social and personality psychology* (2nd ed., pp. 11–26). Cambridge, MA: Cambridge University Press.

Campbell, D. T., & Fiske, D. W. (1959). Convergent and discriminant validation by the multitrait-multimethod matrix. *Psychological Bulletin, 56,* 81–105.

Crano, W. D. (2000). The multitrait-multimethod matrix as synopsis and recapitulation of Campbell's views on the proper conduct of social inquiry. In L. Bickman (Ed.), *Research design: Donald Campbell's legacy* (Ch. 3, pp. 37–61). Beverly Hills, CA: Sage.

Eid, M., & Nussbeck, F. W. (2009). The multitrait-multimethod matrix at 50! *Methodology: European Journal of Research Methods for the Behavioral and Social Sciences, 5*(3), 71.

Höfling, V., Schermelleh-Engel, K., & Moosbrugger, H. (2009). Analyzing multitrait-multimethod data: A comparison of three approaches. *Methodology: European Journal of Research Methods for the Behavioral and Social Sciences, 5,* 99–111.

Weijters, B., Geuens, M., & Schillewaert, N. (2010). The individual consistency of acquiescence and extreme response style in self-report questionnaires. *Applied Psychological Measurement, 34,* 105–121.

Chapter 5: Designing Experiments: Variations on the Basics

Campbell, D. T., & Stanley, J. C. (1966). *Experimental and quasi-experimental designs for research.* Chicago: Rand-McNally.

Lana, R. E. (1959). Pretest-treatment interaction effects in attitude studies. *Psychological Bulletin, 56,* 293–300.

Rosnow, R. L., & Suls, J. M. (1970). Reactive effects of pretesting in attitude research. *Journal of Personality and Social Psychology, 15,* 338–343.

Smith, E. R. (2014). Research design. In H. Reis & C. Judd (Eds.), *Handbook of research methods in social and personality psychology* (2nd ed., pp. 27–48). New York: Cambridge University Press.

Solomon, R. L. (1949). An extension of control group design. *Psychological Bulletin, 46,* 137–150.

Winer, B. J., Brown, D. R., & Michels, K. M. (1991). *Statistical principles in experimental design.* New York: McGraw-Hill.

Chapter 6: Constructing Laboratory Experiments

Cronkite, R. C. (1980). Social psychological simulations: An alternative to experiments? *Social Psychology Quarterly, 43,* 199–216.

Fowler, S. M., & Pusch, M. D. (2010). Intercultural simulation games: A review (of the United States and beyond). *Simulation & Gaming, 41,* 94–115.

Greenwood, J. D. (1983). Role-playing as an experimental strategy in social psychology. *European Journal of Social Psychology, 13,* 235–254.

Kerr, N. L., & Bray, R. M. (2005). Simulation, realism, and the study of the jury. In N. Brewer & K. D. Williams (Eds.), *Psychology and law: An empirical perspective* (pp. 322–364). New York: Guilford.

McQueen, A., & Klein, W. M. (2006). Experimental manipulations of self-affirmation: A systematic review. *Self and Identity, 5,* 289–354.

Milgram, S. (1963). Behavioral study of obedience. *Journal of Abnormal and Social Psychology, 67,* 371–378.

Miller, A. G. (1972). Role playing: An alternative to deception? A review of the evidence. *American Psychologist, 27,* 623–636.

Mixon, D. (1972). Instead of deception. *Journal for the Theory of Social Behavior, 2,* 145–177.

Schultz, D. (1969). The human subject in psychological research. *Psychological Bulletin, 72,* 214–228.

Chapter 7: External Validity of Laboratory Experiments

Berkowitz, L., & Donnerstein, E. (1982). External validity is more than skin deep: Some answers to criticisms of laboratory experiments. *American Psychologist, 37,* 245–257.

Carlston, D. E., & Cohen, J. L. (1980). A closer examination of subject roles. *Journal of Personality and Social Psychology, 38,* 857–870.

Eastwick, P. W., Hunt, L. L., & Neff, L. A. (2013). External validity, why art thou externally valid? Recent studies of attraction provide three theoretical answers. *Social and Personality Psychology Compass, 7,* 275–288.

Henrich, J., Heine, S. J, & Norenzayan, A. (2010). The weirdest people in the world? *Behavioral and Brain Sciences, 33,* 61–135.

Mook, D. G. (1983). In defense of external invalidity. *American Psychologist, 4,* 379–387.

Orne, M. (1962). On the social psychology of the psychological experiment. *American Psychologist, 17,* 776–783.

Orne, M., & Scheibe, K. (1964). The contribution of nondeprivation factors in the production of sensory deprivation effects: The psychology of the "panic button." *Journal of Abnormal and Social Psychology, 68,* 3–12.

Parsons, H. M. (1978). What caused the Hawthorne effect? A scientific detective story. *Administration and Society, 10,* 259–283.

Chapter 8: Conducting Experiments Outside the Laboratory

Anderson C. A., Lindsay, J. J., & Bushman, B. J. (1999). Research in the psychological laboratory: Truth or triviality? *Current Directions in Psychological Science, 8,* 3–9.

Bargh, J. A., & McKenna, K. Y. A. (2004). The Internet and social life. *Annual Review of Psychology, 55,* 573–590.

Buhrmester, M., Kwang, T., & Gosling, S. D. (2011). Amazon's Mechanical Turk: A new source for inexpensive, yet high-quality data? *Perspectives on Psychological Science, 6,* 3–5.

Gosling, S. D., Vazire, S., Srivastava, S., & John, O. P. (2004). Should we trust web-based studies? A comparative analysis of six preconceptions about Internet questionnaires. *American Psychologist, 59,* 93–104.

McGraw, K. O., Tew, M. D., & Williams, J. E. (2000). The integrity of web-delivered experiments: Can you trust the data? *Psychological Science, 11,* 502–506.

Skitka, L. J., & Saris, E. (2006). The Internet as psychological laboratory. *Annual Review of Psychology, 57,* 529–555.

Chapter 9: Nonexperimental Research: Correlational Design and Analyses

Anderson, J. C., & Gerbing, D. W. (1988). Structural equation modeling in practice. A review and recommended two-step approach. *Psychological Bulletin, 103,* 411–423.

Buhi, E. R., Goodson, P., & Neilands, T. B. (2007). Structural equation modeling: A primer for health behavior researchers. *American Journal of Behavioral Health, 31,* 74–85.

Crano, W. D., & Mendoza, J. L. (1987). Maternal factors that influence children's positive behavior: Demonstration of a structural equation analysis of selected data from the Berkeley Growth Study. *Child Development, 58,* 38–48.

Kahn, J. H. (2011). Multilevel modeling: Overview and applications to research in counseling psychology. *Journal of Counseling Psychology, 58,* 257–271.

Li, S. D. (2011). Testing mediation using multiple regression and structural equation modeling analyses in secondary data. *Evaluation Review, 35,* 240–268.

MacCallum, R. C., Zhang, S., Preacher, K. J., & Rucker, D. D. (2002). On the practice of dichotomization of quantitative variables. *Psychological Methods, 7,* 19–40.

Zhao, X., Lynch, J. G., & Chen, Q. (2010). Reconsidering Baron and Kenny: Myths and truths about mediation analysis. *Journal of Consumer Research, 37,* 197–206

Chapter 10: Quasi-Experiments and Evaluation Research

Cook, T. D., & Shadish, W. R. (1994). Social experiments: Some developments over the past fifteen years. *Annual Review of Psychology. 45,* 545–580.

Cook T. D., & Campbell, D. T. (1979). *Quasi-experimentation: Design and analysis issues for field settings.* Chicago: Rand-McNally.

Donaldson, S. I., Christie, C., & Mark, M. M. (2009). *What counts as credible evidence in applied research and evaluation practice?* Thousand Oaks: Sage.

Krueger, A. B., & Zhu, P. (2004). Another look at the New York City school voucher experiment. *American Behavioral Scientist, 47,* 658–698

Rosenbaum, P. R., & Rubin, D. B. (2002). The central role of the propensity score in observational studies for causal effects. *Biometrika, 70,* 41–55.

Speer, D. C., & Greenbaum, P. E. (1995). Five methods for computing significant individual client change and improvement rates: Support for an individual growth curve approach. *Journal of Counseling and Clinical Psychology, 63,* 1044–1048.

Thistlethwaite, D. L., & Campbell, D. T. (1960). Regression-discontinuity analysis: An alternative to the ex post facto experiment. *Journal of Educational Psychology, 51,* 309–317.

Chapter 11: Survey Studies: Design and Sampling

Buhi, E. R., Goodson, P., & Neilands, T. B. (2008). Out of sight, not out of mind: Strategies of handling missing data. *American Journal of Health Behavior, 32,* 83–92.

Dillman, D. A. (2007). *Mail and Internet surveys.* Hoboken, NJ: Wiley.

Groves, R. M. (2006). Nonresponse rates and nonresponse bias in household surveys. *Public Opinion Quarterly, 70,* 646–675.

Hoppe, M. J., Gillmore, M. R., Valadez, D. L., Civic, D., Hartway, J., & Morrison, D. M. (2000). The relative costs and benefits of telephone interviews versus self-administered diaries for daily data collection. *Evaluation Review, 24,* 102–116.

Kalton, G. (1983). *Introduction to survey sampling.* Beverly Hills, CA: Sage.

Pfefferman, D. (1996). The use of sampling weights for survey data analysis. *Statistical Methods in Medical Research, 5,* 239–261.

Schafer, J. L., & Graham, J. W. (2002). Missing data: Our view of the state of the art. *Psychological Methods, 7,* 147–177.

Singer, E. (2006). Introduction: Nonresponse bias in household surveys. *Public Opinion Quarterly, 70,* 637–645.

Chapter 12: Systematic Observational Methods

Hallgren, K. A. (2012). Computing inter-rater reliability for observational data: An overview and tutorial. *Tutorials in Quantitative Methods for Psychology, 8,* 23–34.

Kubey, R., Larson, R., & Csikszentmihalyi, M. (1996). Experience sampling method applications to communication research questions. *Journal of Communication, 46,* 99–120.

McGraw, K. O., & Wong, S. P. (1996). Forming inferences about some intraclass correlation coefficients. *Psychological Methods, 1,* 30–46.

Shrout, P. E., & Fleiss, J. L. (1979). Intraclass correlations: Uses in assessing rater reliability. *Psychological Bulletin, 86,* 420–428.

Tunnell, G. B. (1977). Three dimensions of naturalness: An expanded definition of field research. *Psychological Bulletin, 84,* 426–437.

Weick, K. E. (1985). Systematic observational methods. In G. Lindzey & E. Aronson (Eds.), *The handbook of social psychology* (3rd ed., pp. 567–634). Reading, MA: Addison-Wesley.

Chapter 13: Interviewing

Becker, H. S. (1953). Field methods and techniques: A note on interviewing tactics. *Human Organization, 12,* 31–32.

Bradburn, N. M., Sudman, S., & Wansink, B. (2004). *Asking questions: The definitive guide to questionnaire design—For market research, political polls, and social and health questionnaires* (Revised ed.). San Francisco: Jossey-Bass.

Breen (2006). A practical guide to focus-group research. *Journal of Geography in Higher Education, 30,* 463–475.

Koppelman, N. F., & Bourjolly, J. N. (2001). Conducting focus groups with women with severe psychiatric disabilities: A methodological overview. *Psychiatric Rehabilitation Journal, 25,* 142–151.

Freedman, J. L., & Fraser, S. C. (1966). Compliance without pressure: The foot-in-the-door technique. *Journal of Personality and Social Psychology, 4,* 195–202.

Sudman, S., Bradburn, N. M., & Schwarz, N. (1996). *Thinking about answers: The application of cognitive processes to survey methodology.* San Francisco: Jossey-Bass.

Wyatt, T. H., Krauskopf, P. B., & Davidson, R. (2008). Using focus groups for program planning and evaluation. *Journal of School Nursing, 24,* 71–77.

Chapter 14: Content Analysis

Ames, P. C., & Riggio, R. E. (1995). Use of the Rotter Incomplete Sentences Blank with adolescent populations: Implications for determining maladjustment. *Journal of Personality Assessment, 64,* 159–167.

Finn, J., & Dillon, C. (2007). Using personal ads and online self-help groups to teach content analysis in a research methods course. *Journal of Teaching in Social Work, 27,* 155–164.

Kondracki, N. L., Wellman, N. S., & Amundson, D. R. (2002). Content analysis: Review of methods and their applications in nutrition education. *Journal of Nutrition Education and Behavior, 34,* 224–230.

Neuendorf, K. A. (2011). Content analysis—A methodological primer for gender research. *Sex Roles, 64,* 276–289.

Peterson, C., Seligman, M. E., & Valliant, G. E. (1988). Pessimistic explanatory style is a risk factor for physical illness: A 35-year longitudinal study. *Journal of Personality and Social Psychology, 55,* 23–27.

Stemler, S. (2001). An overview of content analysis. *Practical Assessment, Research & Evaluation, 7.* Retrieved from http://pareonline.net/getvn.asp?v=7&n=17

Chapter 15: Questionnaire Design and Scale Construction

Barnette, J. J. (2000). Effects of stem and Likert response option reversals on survey internal consistency: If you feel the need, there is a better alternative to using these negatively worded stems. *Educational and Psychological Measurement, 60,* 361–370.

Borg, I. (1988). Revisiting Thurstone's and Coombs' scales on the seriousness of crimes. *European Journal of Social Psychology, 18,* 53–61.

Friborg, O., Martinussen, M., & Rosenvinge, J. H. (2006). Likert-based vs. semantic differential-based scorings of positive psychological constructs: A psychometric comparison of two versions of a scale measuring resilience. *Personality and Individual Differences, 40,* 873–884.

Luskin, R. C., & Bullock, J. G. (2011). "Don't know" means "don't know": DK responses and the public's level of political knowledge. *The Journal of Politics, 73,* 547–557.

Norman, G. (2010). Likert scales, levels of measurement and the "laws" of statistics. *Advances in Health Science Education, 15,* 625–632.

Osgood, C. E., & Luria, Z. (1954). Applied analysis of a case of multiple personality using the semantic differential. *Journal of Abnormal and Social Psychology, 49,* 579–591.

Thurstone, L. L. (1931). The measurement of attitudes. *Journal of Abnormal and Social Psychology, 26,* 249–269.

Chapter 16: Indirect and Implicit Measures of Cognition and Affect

Cunningham, S. J., & Macrae, C. N. (2011). The colour of gender stereotyping. *British Journal of Psychology, 102,* 598–614.

Devine, P. G. (1989). Stereotypes and prejudice: Their automatic and controlled components. *Journal of Personality and Social Psychology, 56,* 680–690.

Gilbert, D. T., Pelham, B. W., & Krull, D. S. (1988). On cognitive busyness: When person perceivers meet persons perceived. *Journal of Personality and Social Psychology, 54,* 733–740.

Greenwald, A. G., McGhee, D. E., & Schwartz, J. (1998). Measuring individual differences in implicit cognition: The implicit association test. *Journal of Personality and Social Psychology, 74,* 1464–1480.

Hoffmann, W., Gawronski, B., Gschwendner, T., Le, H., & Schmitt, M. (2005). A meta-analysis on the correlation between implicit association test and explicit self-report measures. *Personality and Social Psychology Bulletin, 31,* 1369–1385.

Nisbett, R. E., & Wilson, T. D. (1977). Telling more than we can know: Verbal reports on mental processes. *Psychological Review, 84,* 231–259.

Olson, M. A., & Fazio, R. H. (2008). Implicit and explicit measures of attitudes: The perspective of the MODE model. In R. E. Petty, R. H. Fazio, & P. Briñol (Eds.), *Attitudes: Insights from the new implicit measures* (pp. 19–63). New York: Psychology Press.

Quadflieg, S., & Mccrae, C. N. (2011). Stereotypes and stereotyping: What's the brain got to do with it? *European Review of Social Psychology, 22,* 215–273.

Chapter 17: Scaling Stimuli: Social Psychophysics

Borg, I. (1988). Revisiting Thurstone's and Coombs' scales on the seriousness of crimes. *European Journal of Social Psychology, 18,* 53–61.

Carroll, J. B., & Arabie, P. (1980). Multi-dimensional scaling. *Annual Review of Psychology, 31,* 607–649.

Halberstadt, J. B., & Niedenthal, P. M. (1997). Emotional state and the use of stimulus dimensions in judgment. *Journal of Personality and Social Psychology, 72,* 1017–1033.

Misra, R. K., & Dutt, P. K. (1965). A comparative study of psychological scaling methods. *Journal of Psychological Research. 9,* 31–34.

Priester, J. R., & Petty, R. E. (2001). Extending the bases of subjective attitudinal ambivalence: Interpersonal and intrapersonal antecedents of evaluative tension. *Journal of Personality and Social Psychology, 80,* 19–34.

Snider, J. G., & Osgood, C. E. (Eds.) (1969). *Semantic differential technique.* Chicago: Aldine.

Tourangeau, R., & Rasinski, K. A. (1988). Cognitive processes underlying context effects in attitude measurement. *Psychological Bulletin, 103,* 299–314.

Chapter 18: Methods for Assessing Dyads and Groups

Hinsz, V. B., Tindale, R. S., & Vollrath, D. A. (1997). The emerging conceptualization of groups as information processors. *Psychological Bulletin, 121,* 43–64.

Kenny, D. A., & Judd, C. (1996). A general procedure for the estimation of interdependence. *Psychological Bulletin, 119,* 138–148.

Kenny, D. A., Kashy, D. A., & Cook, W. L. (2006). *Dyadic data analysis.* New York: Guilford Press.

Kenny, D. A., & Lederman, T. (2010). Detecting, measuring and testing dyadic patterns in the actor-partner interdependence model. *Journal of Family Psychology, 24,* 359–366.

McGrath, J. E., & Altermatt, T. W. (2001). Observation and analysis of group interaction over time: Some methodological and strategic choices. In M. Hogg & R. S. Tindale (Eds.), *Blackwell handbook of social psychology: Group processes* (pp. 525–573). Oxford, UK: Blackwell.

Robins, G. (2013). A tutorial on methods for the modeling and analysis of social network data. *Journal of Mathematical Psychology, 57,* 261–274.

Chapter 19: Synthesizing Research Results: Meta-Analysis

Cooper. H. M. (2009). *Research synthesis and meta-analysis: A step-by-step approach* (4th ed.). Los Angeles: Sage.

Hall, J. A., & Rosenthal, R. (1991). Testing for moderator variables in meta-analysis: Issues and methods. *Communication Monographs, 58,* 437–448.

Hedges, L. V., & Vevea, J. L. (1998). Fixed- and random-effects models in meta-analysis. *Psychological Methods, 3,* 486–504.

Lac, A. (2014). A primer for using meta-analysis to consolidate research. *Substance Use & Misuse, 49,* 1–5.

Smith, M. L., & Glass, G. V. (1977). Meta-analysis of psychotherapy outcome studies. *American Psychologist, 32,* 752–760.

Rosenthal, R. (1979). The file drawer problem. *Psychological Bulletin, 86,* 638–641.

Rosenthal, R. (1991). Meta analysis: A review. *Psychosomatic Medicine, 53,* 247–271.

Chapter 20: Social Responsibility and Ethics in Social Research

Kerr, N. L. (1998). HARKing: Hypothesizing after the results are known. *Personality and Social Psychology Review, 2,* 196–217.

Kimmel, A. J. (1991). Predictable biases in the ethical decision making of American psychologists. *American Psychologist, 46,* 786–788.

Martinson, B. C., Anderson, M. S., & de Vries, R. (2005). Scientists behaving badly. *Nature, 435,* 737–738.

Rosenthal, R. (1994). Science and ethics in conducting, analyzing, and reporting psychological research. *Psychological Science, 5,* 127–134.

Rosnow, R. L. (1997). Hedgehogs, foxes, and the evolving social contract in psychological science: Ethical challenges and methodological opportunities. *Psychological Methods, 2,* 345–356.

Sales, B. D., & Folkman, S. (Eds.). (2000). *Ethics in research with human participants.* Washington, DC: American Psychological Association.

AUTHOR INDEX

Abbott, K. M. 396
Abelson, R. P. 43, 113, 121n4
Abrahams, D. 388, 431
Adair, J. G. 129, 132
Adobor, H. 114
Adorno, T. W. 77
Agard, E. 434
Agnew, N. M. 29
Aksoy, O. 4
Alabastro, A. 148
Alexa, M. 312
Alger, C. 116
Allison, S. T. 119
Altemeyer, B. 77
Altermatt, T. W. 398
Alvaro, E. M. 89, 108, 202, 233, 380, 381
American Psychological Association 52, 299n3, 437; Committee on Ethical Standards 428; PsycINFO 413
Ames, P. C. 316
Amin-Esmaeili, M. 281
Amundson, D. R. 312
Anderson, A. B. 282
Anderson, C. A. 8, 143
Anderson, R. 261
Andrews, P. W. 286
Antona, M. 114
Arabie, P. 379
Argesti, A. 399
Argote, L. 400
Aristotle 3, 4, 5
Armstrong, A. J. 58, 61
Arnold, S. 258
Aronoff, J. 398
Aronson, E. 30, 39, 40, 105, 108, 112, 137, 431
Aronson, V. 388
Asch, S. E. 105, 106, 114, 430
Ashmore, R. D. 126, 410

Aspinwall, L. 149
Atalay, A. S. 345
Auriacombe, M. 286
Austin, A. J. 352
Austin, J. 68
Austin, W. G. 275n1

Babbie, E. R. 304
Bales, R. F. 263, 266, 267, 274, 276n6, 398
Ballard, J. 149
Baltes, M. M. 258
Banks, W. C. 114
Bargh, J. A. 108, 128, 129, 154, 350, 351, 352, 353, 355, 356, 403n2
Barnlund, D. C., 398
Baron, R. A. 7, 8
Baron, R. M. 24, 25, 175
Baron, R. S. 151
Barros, M. M. 286
Barry, C. A. 320n4
Barsilou, L. 108
Bartholomew, K. 280, 281
Barton, A. H., 262
Bazarova, N. N. 400
Beck, L. F. 285, 275
Becker, H. S. 259, 276n4
Becker, L. A. 431
Bedian, A. G. 54, 55
Beecher, H. K. 131
Bell, P. A. 7
Beltran, V. 286
Bem, D. J. 114
Bennett, S. E. 285
Ben-Porath, Y. S. 66
Bentler, P. M. 180
Berelson, B. 303, 304, 306, 314, 315
Berenson, J. 144
Berenson, R. 144

Berent, M. K. 285
Bergen, G. 285
Berkman, D. 317
Berkowitz, L. 105, 137
Bernard, A. 114
Berry, W. D. 206
Bessa, M. A. 286
Bettger, J. 396
Beuckalaer, A. D. 155
Bhaskar, R. 5
Bickman, L. 31, 211
Biener, L. 380
Bird, A. 15
Birnbaum, M. H. 151, 152, 154
Bishop, G. R. 285
Bizumic, B. 77
Blair, E. 281, 282, 296
Blake, E. L. 116
Blake, R. R. 433
Blalock, H. M. 233
Blascovich, J. 358, 359, 360
Bligh, M. C. 344
Block, J. 77
Bloom, P. N. 291
Blumberg, H. H. 15
Blumberg, S. J. 236, 241
Bodur, H. O. 345
Boekeloo, B. O. 242
Bogardus, E. S. 330
Bollen, K. A. 55
Bommel, P. 114
Bonnet, C. 286
Boorman, S. 395
Borenstein, M. 417
Borg, I. 372, 382n3
Borgatta, E. F. 399
Borsboom, D. 53
Borzekowski, D. L. 319
Bourjolly, J. N. 297
Bousfield, A. K. 365n5
Bousfield, W. A. 365n5
Bousquet, F. 114
Box, G.E.P. 206
Bradburn, N. M. 281, 282, 296, 325, 339n1
Brady, J. 149
Bray, R. M. 393
Breen, R. L. 297
Breiger, R. 395
Brewer, M. B. 23, 30, 105, 107, 108, 112, 119, 135, 137, 145, 170, 186, 253, 347, 391
Broadfoot, A. A. 53
Brock, T. C. 431
Brody, R. A. 116
Brown, S. C. 365n5
Brown, T. A. 55, 56
Brunner, G. A. 291
Brunswik, E. 136, 137
Bryant, F. B. 66, 67
Bryant, J. 40

Buchanan, T. 151
Buckhart, B. R. 66
Buhrmester, M. 151, 153, 244
Burger, G. 9
Burgoon, M. 51, 89
Burrows, L. 128, 352
Bush, George W. 307
Bushman, B. J. 143
Byrne, D.: *The Attraction Paradigm* 175

Cacioppo, J. T. 109, 136, 137, 348, 358, 360, 362
Cain, P. S. 283
Caldwell, B. M. 266, 267
Campbell, D. T. 11, 22, 27, 32, 39, 65, 69, 70, 71, 73, 74, 77, 83, 126, 170, 186, 190, 195, 197, 210, 211, 256, 343, 391, 397, 413, 433
Campbell, J. P. 9–10
Campbell, W. 396
Cannell, C. F. 286, 290, 292, 296, 299
Cantor, N. 349
Carlopio, J. 129
Carlsmith, J. M. 108, 112, 114
Carlson, J. 256
Carlston, D. E. 129
Carroll, J. B. 379
Carroll, S. J., Jr. 291
Carson, R. T. 285
Carter, M. 400
Carter, R. E., Jr. 241
Carter, T. J. 105, 121n3
Cartwright, A. 291
Cartwright, D. P. 303
Casey, M. A. 297
Casey, R. L. 268
Cattaneo, Z. 361
Cattell, R. B. 51
Caul, W. F. 391
Chabris, C. F. 154
Chaikin, S. 355
Chalem, E. 286
Chan, D. M.-L. 281
Chang, L. 73
Chapman, L. J. 77
Chapple, E. D. 296
Charles, E. P. 54
Charmaz, K. 261
Chatterjee, G. 154
Chave, E. L. 328
Chen, M. 128, 352
Chen, Q. 175
Chen, X. 381
Cheng, K. 144
Cheng, T. L. 242
Cheung, C. 150
Chico, E. 77
Choi, W. 150
Chu, V. 151
Cialdini, R. B. 9, 147
Cicourel, A. V. 259

Cillissen, A.H.N. 396
Clark, J. C. 114
Clark, M. S. 126
Clark, R. D. 409
Clarke, C. 356
Cliff, N. 330
Clifton, A. D. 396
Clore, G. L. 75, 393
Coaley, K. 58
Cohen, A. R. 114
Cohen, B. D. 317
Cohen, J. 28, 293
Cohen, J. A. 102, 121n1, 270, 271, 273, 313, 415, 422, 423
Cohen, J. L. 129
Cohen, S. P. 266
Collins, B. E. 8
Collins, M. A. 149
Collip, D. 381
Combourieu, I. 286
Conaway, M. 285
Condon, J. W. 175
Condon, L. 77
Connelly, B. S. 73
Conolley, E. S. 114
Conrad, F. 326
Conway, L. G., III 314
Cook, S. W. 256
Cook, T. D. 39, 65, 129, 190, 210, 211, 420
Cook, W. L. 385, 386, 390, 397
Coombs, C. 378
Coombs, C. H. 327, 372, 379
Cooper, H. M. 326, 410, 413, 415, 423, 424
Cooper, J. 107
Cooper, M. P. 326
Cooper, R. E. 372
Cooper, S. L. 241
Corbin, J. 261
Cotter, P. R. 293
Coulter, P. B. 293
Crano, W. D. 9, 12, 30, 51, 68, 74, 76, 107, 108, 128, 135, 148, 170, 175, 182, 183, 186, 190, 202, 206, 233, 253, 311, 327, 332, 372, 377, 380, 381, 403n2, 410
Cronbach, L. J. 35, 49, 52, 53, 54, 55, 62n2, 125, 174, 332, 338, 402n1
Crossley, H. M. 283
Crow, W. J. 116
Crowther, B. 399
Crutchfield, R. F. 106
Csikszentmihalyi, M. 257
Cuddy, A. 109
Cuddy, A.J.C. 380
Cunningham, S. J. 354, 363
Cunningham, W. A. 363
Curry, T. J. 391

Dabbs, J. M., Jr. 259
Daft, R. L. 9

Dalal, R. 143
Daneshfar, A. 114
Darley, J. M. 104, 118
Davidson, R. 297, 362
Davies, M.N.O. 56
Dawes, R. M. 370, 379
Dawson, E. J. 51
Day, D. V. 54, 55
Deandrea, D. C. 400
DeAngelo, L. 58, 62
de Ayala, R. J. 58
de Champlain, A. F. 57
DeMars, C. 57, 58, 62n4
Denis, C. 286
Dennis, A. R. 402
DePaulo, B. M. 264, 267, 270
DeShon, R. P. 53, 54
Deters, F. G. 150
Deutsch, M. 380
DeVellis, R. B. 56, 65
DeWall, C. N. 8
Diehl, M. 401
Dijkstra, W. 282
Dillard, J. P. 9
Dillman, D. A. 281
Ding, C. 381
Dohrenwend, B. S. 291
Donaldson, S. I. 30, 186, 187, 350
Dong, Y. 381
Donnerstein, E. 137
Dovidio, J. 119, 343
Downing, J. 326
Druckman, D. 116
Duchaine, B. C. 154
Duckitt, J. 77
Dulles, John Foster 316
Dull, V. 347
Dunn, E. W. 363
Dunton, B. C. 354
Dutt, P. K. 376
Dykema-Engblade, A. 399
Dyslin, C. J. 86

Eagly, A. H. 126, 409, 410, 417
Earleywine, M. 8
Eid, M. 73
Einstein, Albert 409
Eisenberg, N. 9
Eisenhower, Dwight D. 317
Ekman, P. 359
Ellison, J. W. 315
Embretson, S. E. 53
Emerson, R. M. 391
Epstein, J. A. 264
Epstein, J. S. 132
Erber, R. 399
Erlebacher, A. 197
Esposito, J. L. 434
Estes, W. K. 43n4

Etcoff, N. 349
Evans, D. C. 151
Eveland, W. R. 396

Fabrigar, L. R. 4, 282, 324
Fan, X. 53, 62, 167
Fang, X. 286
Fatséas, M. 286
Faust, K. 396
Fazio, R. H. 343, 354, 355, 364
Feingold, A. 417
Fennis, B. M. 296
Ferguson, M. J. 105
Ferguson, R. W. 371
Ferrando, P. J. 77
Festinger, L. 8, 112, 114, 254–5
Fiske, A. P. 422
Fiske, D. W. 70, 71, 73, 74
Fiske, S. T. 344, 347, 349, 380
Fleck, R. A. 114
Fleiss, J. L. 271, 272, 273, 274, 313
Flesch, R. 318
Flora, C. 37
Fode, K. L. 131, 132, 261
Forehand, R. 258
Forgas, J. P. 144
Forsman, L. 77
Forsyth, D. R. 399
Fournier, E. 242
Fowler, F. J. 299n4
Fowler, S. M. 114
Fraser, S. C. 146, 433, 291
Freedman, J. L. 114, 146, 291, 433
Freeman, S. 147
Frenkel-Brunswik, E. 77
Freud, Sigmund 9
Friborg, O. 338
Friedman, L. 417
Friesen, W. V. 359
Frohlich, P. F. 8

Gaertner, S. L. 119
Galanter, E. 379
Galtier, F. 114
Galton, Francis 190, 191
Gamson, W. A. 114
Gangestad, S. W. 286
García, D. J. 151
García, D. M. 151
Garcia-Margues, T. 4
Gardner, C. 413
Gardner, W. L. 107, 108, 362
Garg, S. 403n3
Geeza, A. A. 73
Geller, E. 242, 269
Genovese, Kitty 118
George, A. L. 314
Gerard, H. B. 40, 114
Gergen, K. J. 125

Germine, L. 154
Geuens, M. 78
Gilbert, D. T. 356
Ginsberg, E. 345
Girandola, F. 291
Glaser, B. G.: *The Discovery of Grounded Theory* 261
Glass, G. V. 149, 412, 414, 420
Glasser, G. J. 241
Gleser, G. C. 52
Glick, P. 380
Goldinger, S. D. 371
Goldman, M. S. 286
Goldman, R. M. 311
Gonsalkorale, K. 150
Goodbey, G. 257
Goodie, A. S. 396
Gosling, S. D. 149, 151, 153, 154, 244
Gottman, J. M. 268, 399
Graham, J. 151
Graham, J. W. 246
Graham, L. 149
Grandpre, J. 89
Green, B. F., Jr. 330
Greenberg, A. 126
Greene, D. 4
Greenfield, T. K. 242
Greenwald, A. G. 18, 356, 414
Greenwald, S. 413
Greenwood, J. D. 113
Grove, J. 256
Groves, R. M. 240, 281, 291
Guba, E. 259
Guetzkow, H. 116
Guilford, J. P. 374, 376, 377
Guinsburg, R. 286
Gulliksen, H. 45
Gutek, B. A. 281
Guttieri, K. 344
Guttman, L. 329–32, 333, 336, 379
Gynther, M. D. 66

Hajebi, A. 281
Halberg, K. 210
Halberstadt, J. B. 381
Hallahan, M. 27
Hallmark, B. W. 398
Hamilton, Alexander 306
Hamilton, D. L. 349, 365n5
Hampton, K. 396
Hanemann, W. M. 285
Haney, C. 114
Hannula-Bral, K. A. 403n2
Harris, M. J. 132, 131
Harvey, J. 318
Haselton, M. G. 286
Hassin, R. R. 105
Hastie, R. 121n4
Hatchett, S. 293
Hayes, A. F. 24, 175, 176, 183n6

Hazan, C. 235
Hedges, L. V. 417
Heider, F. 393
Heine, S. J. 126
Heled, E. 77
Henard, D. J. 57
Henderson, A. J. Z. 280, 281
Henle, M. 256
Henrich, J. 126
Henry, G. T. 210
Herman, J. B. 281, 326
Heyns, R. W. 269
Higgins, E. T. 350, 351
Hinsz, V. B. 400
Hixon, J. G. 356
Hodge, R. W. 283
Höfling, V. 73
Hofstede, G. J. 114
Hogg, M. A. 148, 399
Hol, A. M. 61
Holbrook, A. 285
Holland, P. W. 393
Hollingshead, A. de B. 283, 400, 401
Holmes, D. S. 431
Holsti, O. R. 312, 314, 315, 317
Hong, Y. 286
Hooker, E. 320n6
Hoppe, M. J. 242
Hornik, R. 286
Horowitz, I. L. 114
Horvitz, D. C.
Horwich, P. 15
House, P. 4
Hout, M. C. 371, 382n6
Hovanitz, C. 66
Hovland, C. I. 329
Howard, W. D. 252
Hulin, C. L. 9
Hunt, E. B. 307, 313
Hunter, J. E. 43n4, 54, 417
Hunter, S. 358
Hymes, C. 355

Inzlicht, M. 109
Isen, A. M. 145
Isenberg, D. J. 15
Itkin, S. M. 393
Ito, T. A. 358, 360
Iyer, R. 151

Jaccard, J. 6, 358
Jackson, D. N. 77, 432
Jackson, J. R. 354
Jacobs, J. 275
Jacobs, R. C. 397
Jacobson, L. 131
Jacoby, J. 6, 247n8
Jaffe, D. A. 114
Jastro, J. 131

John, O. P. 153, 345–6
John, V. P. 256
Johnson, B. T. 409, 417
Johnson, C. 401
Johnson, J. E. 149
Johnson, K. M. 151
Johnson, P. B. 286
Johnston, L. D. 187
Jones, C. R. 350
Jones, S. 152
Josselson, R. 261
Joyce, James: *Ulysses* 315
Judd, C. M. 397

Kahn, J. H. 170
Kahn, R. L. 281, 292
Kahneman, D. 4
Kalton, G. 226, 232, 239, 246n2, 283, 284, 288
Kameda, T. 399
Karp, D. 253
Kashy, D. A. 264, 386, 391, 397
Kawakami, K. 109
Kelloway, E. K. 54, 55
Kelman, H. C. 113, 429, 431, 440
Kelsey, R. M. 359
Kendrick, R. V. 296
Kennedy, J. L. 38
Kennedy, John F. 284, 314
Kennedy, W. P. 258
Kenny, D. A. 4, 24, 25, 175, 177, 330, 385, 386, 390, 391, 392, 397, 398, 403n3
Kenworthy, J. B. 8
Kerr, N. L. 398, 422, 439
Kerr, T. 235
Kessler, R. C. 235
Kiesler, S. 149, 154, 400
Killackey, E. 381
Kinsey, A. C. 285, 287, 288, 294
Kirkendol, S. E. 264
Kish, L. A. 236
Klein, D. 291
Klein, R. D. 114
Kleinman, S. B. 396
Klimoski, R. 400
Kluegel, J. R. 281
Klumb, P. L. 258
Knoke, D. 396
Kohler, H. 396
Kolakowsky-Hayner, S. A. 58, 61
Kommer, D. 75
Kondracki, N. L. 312
Kopp, R. J. 285
Koppelman, N. F. 297
Krambeck, H.-J. 119
Kramer, R. M. 119
Krantz, D. S. 149
Krantz, J. H. 143
Krauskopf, P. B. 297
Krauss, S. W. 77

Kraut, R. 154
Krauth-Gruber, S. 108
Krippendorff, K. 304, 313
Krishman, R. 400
Kroesbergen, H. T. 286
Kroner, D. G. 286
Krosnick, J. A. 4, 233, 282, 285, 324, 326, 337, 339n1
Krueger, A. B. 190
Krueger, R. A. 297
Kruskall, J. B. 379
Kuder, G. E. 62n2
Kuhn, T. S. 5, 15, 409
Kuklinski, J. H. 188, 396
Kulik, J. 144
Kwang, T. 151, 244

LaBrie, R. 242
Lac, A. 9, 148, 233, 327, 410
Lachenmeyer, C. W. 43n3
Lana, R. E. 99n2
Lane, R. D. 362
Lang, A. 8
Lang, P. J. 360
Langer, E. J. 147, 148, 154
Laranjeira, R. 286
Larson, R. 257
Lasswell, H. D. 315, 316, 317
Latané, B. 104, 118, 433
Lau, L. 281
La Voie, L. 391, 392
Lavrakas, P. J. 242, 324
Lawson, R. 131
Lazarsfeld, P. H. 262
Lebo, H. 154
Ledermann, T. 385, 390
Lee, Harper: *To Kill a Mockingbird* 311
Lee, S. 188, 281, 325, 326
Leigh, B. C. 257
Leinhardt, S. 393
Leitten, C. L. 359
Lemay, E. P., Jr. 126
LePage, A. 105
Lerner, D. 315
Leventhal, H. 149, 263
Levy, L. 106
Levy, P. S. 232
Lewin, H. S. 316
Lewis, A. N. 58, 61
Lewis, S. C. 319
Lewis-Beck, M. S. 206
Li, X. 286
Lievens, F. 155
Likert, R. 331–6, 338
Lin, A. 381
Lindsay, R.C.L. 129, 143
Link, M. W. 243
Lipkus, I. M. 291
Lippke, S. 5
Locander, W. 281, 282, 296
Longo, L. C. 126, 410

Lord, C. G. 106
Lord, R. 403n3
Lubetsky, J. 391
Luce, R. D. 115
Lui, L. 119, 347
Luke, J. V. 236
Lundmark, M. 154

Macedo, J. 119
MacKillop, J. 396
Madison, James 306
Magilavy, L. J. 291
Mahl, G. F. 258
Mak, A. 281
Makhijani, M. G. 126, 410
Malhotra, N. 337
Manicas, P. T. 5
Mann, J. 119
Marcia, J. 280, 281
Marcoulides, G. A. 46
Markham, J. W. 320n1
Marks, G. 4
Marotzke, J. 119
Marquis, K. H. 290, 296
Martin, C. E. 285, 287, 288, 294
Martin, E. 299n4
Martin, L. 108
Martinussen, M. 338
Masling, J. 129
Mathewson, G. 40
Mattavelli, G. 361
McArthur, L. Z. 345
McAuliffe, W. E. 242
McBride, C. M. 291
McCain, John 105
McCarthy, D. M. 286
McDonald, D. 116
McGrath, J. E. 398, 400, 401, 410
McGuire, W. J. 6, 9, 96
McKenna, K.Y.A. 154, 403n2
McMullen, L. 261
McSpadden, E. 261
McWhorter, S. K. 86
Mehl, M. R. 150
Meisel, M. K. 396
Meisenhelder, H. M. 399
Mellenbergh, G. J. 53, 61
Merrill, L. L. 86
Messé, L. A. 190, 398
Messick, D. M. 119
Messick, S. 64, 77, 432
Meston, C. M. 8
Metzger, G. D. 241
Mickelson, K. D. 235
Midanik, L. T. 242
Miles, A. 151
Miles, C. 281, 282, 296
Miles, J.N.V. 56, 318
Miles, M. B. 320n4
Milgram, Stanley 114, 130–1, 136, 430, 431, 433

Milinski, M. 119
Miller, A. G. 114
Miller, G. F. 286
Miller, J. D. 396
Miller, N. 4, 8, 20, 119, 360, 391
Miller, P. V. 284, 286
Miller, R. E. 391
Miller, S. E. 433
Mills, J. 39, 40, 262, 286
Mills, R. T. 149
Milne, A. B. 354
Milner, J. S. 86
Milun, R. 259
Miron, D. 40
Mirsky, I. A. 391
Mischel, W. 349
Misra, R. K. 376
Mitchell, G. 358
Mitchell, R. C. 285
Mitsuhiro, S. S. 286
Mixon, D. 113
Mohammed, S. 400
Moll, A. 131
Monge, P. R. 396
Mook, D. G. 30, 137, 138
Moore, B. 144
Moosbrugger, H. 73
Moreland, R. L. 400
Moreno, J. L. 392–3
Morgan, C. A., III 258
Morgan, R. D. 286
Moriarty, T. 251, 252–3, 275n1
Morton, A. Q. 315, 320n7
Moser, C. A. 226, 239
Mosteller, F. 306, 315, 375
Motevalian, A. 281
Muchinsky, P. M. 54
Mukophadhyah, T. 154
Mullen, B. 401
Murff, E. J. T. 114
Murphy, P. 393
Murrell, A. 119

Nadolny, D. 109
Nakayama, K. 154
Nanda, H. 52
National Academy of Sciences 437
Neale, M. C. 286
Nelson, C. 380, 439
Nerlove, S. 379
Newcomb, T. M. 391
Nezlek, J. B. 257
Ng, K. L. 281
Niedenthal, P. M. 108, 381
Nisbett, R. E. 109, 368, 422
Nisbett, R. F. 262, 342
Noel, R. 116
Norenzayan, A. 126, 422
Nunnally, J. C. 49, 64, 76, 327, 329
Nussbeck, F. W. 73

Obama, Barack 105, 294, 306, 317
Ober, B. A. 381
O'Connell, E. J. 391
O'Connor, K. M. 401
Ohtsubo, Y. 399
Oksenberg, L. 284, 286
Oldendick, R. W. 243, 285
Olson, G. 400
Olson, J. 345
Olson, J. S. 400
Olson, M. A. 296
Orne, M. 129, 130
Orwin, R. 205, 286
Osborn, A. F. 401
Osborn, L. 243
Osborne, R. E. 356
Osgood, C. E. 333–5, 336, 338
Ostrom, T. M. 349, 365n5

Paletz, S. 242
Papagno, C. 361
Parker, S. D. 145
Parry, H. J. 283
Patel, N. 108
Patterson, J. R. 76
Patterson, V. 154
Paul, B. Y. 360
Peebles, R. 319
Persinger, G. W. 261
Peterson, C. 316
Petty, R. E. 4, 108, 136, 137, 326, 348, 358, 360
Phillips, D. P. 318
Phills, C. 109
Piaget, Jean 9
Picard, S. 286
Pickett, C. L. 107
Pierce, A. H. 129
Pietromonaco, P.
Pike, S. W. 29
Piliavin, I. M. 143, 433
Piliavin, J. A. 143, 433
Platania, E. 361
Pollak, K. I. 291
Pomeroy, W. B. 285, 287, 288, 294
Ponder, E. 258
Pool, I. de S. 315
Poole, K. T. 379
Poortinga, Y. H. 77
Popper, K. R. 5
Pratto, F. 345–6
Presser, S. 285, 326
Pryor, J. B. 349, 355, 365n5
Pusch, M. D. 114

Qayad, M. 285
Quinn, R. P. 281
Quist, R. M. 148

Radgoodarzi, R. 281
Rahimi-Movaghar, A. 281

Raiffa, N. 115
Rajaratnam, N. 52
Ramirez, J. R. 206
Rapkin, D. P. 116
Raser, J. R. 116, 117
Rasolofoarison, D. 345
Rast, D. E., III 148
Rau, T. J. 86
Ray, M. L. 284
Raykov, T. 46
Raymond, P. 355, 399
Read, S. J. 8
Reed, C. F. 131
Reed, F. A. 119
Rees, M. B. 77
Reichardt, C. S. 210
Reid, C. A. 58, 61
Reips, U. D. 151, 155
Reis, H. 257
Ren, Y. 400
Renzaglia, G. A. 258
Resnick, J. H. 428
Reynolds, M. L. 379
Rhodes, N. 96, 412
Rholes, W. S. 350
Richardson, D. 431
Richardson, J. T. 77
Richardson, M. W. 62n2
Richardson, S. A. 291, 294
Richter, L. 286
Riecken, H. W. 8
Riggio, R. E. 316
Roberts, R. R. 258
Robins, G. 396
Robinson, A. 211
Robinson, J. L. 344
Robinson, J. P. 256, 257
Robinson, R. G. 362
Rodin, J. 143, 148, 433
Roenker, D. L. 365n5
Rog, D. J. 31, 211
Rogers, J. D. 242
Romney, Mitt 317, 379
Roosevelt, Franklin D. 238
Rorer, L. G. 77
Rosenberg, M. J. 113
Rosenberg, S. 380
Rosenthal, R. 27, 35, 127, 131, 132, 261, 410, 412, 414, 417, 420, 422, 424, 425n4, 429, 438
Rosenvinge, J. H. 338
Rosnow, R. L. 99n2, 127, 422, 427, 434, 438
Rosnow, R. W. 35, 127
Ross, L. 4, 421, 432
Rossi, P. H. 282, 283
Rothschild, B. H. 114
Rottman, L. 388
Roy, A. K. 399
Rubin, D. B. 132, 200, 410, 420, 422, 425n4
Rubin, D. C. 326, 330

Ruderman, A. 349
Rugg, D. 285
Russell, B. 262

Sadler, M. S. 397
Saenz, D. S. 106
Salas, E. 401
Samph, T. 258
Sampson, F. 394–5
Sanders, C. 285
Sanna, L. J. 4
Saris, E. 152
Sawyer, J. 435
Schachter, S. S. 8, 254
Schamus, L. A. 242
Schaps, E. 285, 433
Schenk S. 319
Scher, J. 149
Schermelleh-Engel, K. 73
Schiffman, S. S. 379
Schillewaert, N. 78
Schlenker, B. R. 125
Schleris, W. 154
Schmidt, F. L. 54, 417
Schmitt, M. 358
Schmitt, N. 74
Shults, R. A. 285
Schultz, D. 113
Schuman, H. 283, 284, 285, 288, 293, 326
Schwab, P. 314
Schwartz, G.
Schwartz, H. 275
Schwartz, J. 291, 356, 362, 414
Schwartz, R. D. 256, 433
Schwartz, T. 428
Schwartz-Bloom, R. D. 291
Schwarz, N. 4, 75, 282, 339n1
Scott, W. A. 377, 378, 396
Scullen, S. E. 73
Sears, D. O. 40, 126, 143, 438
Sechrest, L. 256
Secord, P. F. 5
Seery, J. B. 379
Seidell, J. C. 286
Seligman, M. E. 316
Seyranian, V. 344
Shadish, W. R. 39, 190, 211
Sharifi, V. 281
Sharkness, J. 58, 62
Sharp, E. 263
Shaver, P. R. 235
Shenaut, G. K. 381
Shepard, R. N. 379
Shevlin, M. 56
Shneidman, 314
Shrout, P. E. 272
Shulman, A. D. 431
Shults, R. A. 285
Sidney, R. 116
Siegel, J. T. 9, 108, 202, 233

Siegel, P. M. 283
Siegman, C. R. 77
Sigelman, L. 148
Silva, P. P. 4
Silverman, I. 431
Simmens, S. J. 242
Simonsohn, U. 132, 329
Singer, J. 149, 240, 281, 282, 296
Sivacek, J. M. 107, 128
Skitka, L. 152
Slater, P. E. 399
Sloan, L. R. 147
Slovic, P. 4
Smith, C. P. 304, 312
Smith, E. R. 29, 281
Smith, G. T. 286
Smith, M. L. 412, 414, 420
Smith, M. S. 320n4
Smith, S. S. 431
Smith, S. T. 114
Smith, T. L. 370, 379
Smoker, P. 116
Snow, R. 35
Solomon, R. L. 85–6, 89–91, 99
Sommerfeld, R. D. 119
Soskin, W. F. 256
Souchet, L. 291
Spearman, C. 54
Spencer, J. R. 145
Spinner, B. 129
Sprecher, S. 388
Sproull, L. S. 400
Srivastava, S. 153
Srull, T. K. 351
Stambaugh, R. J. 114
Stander, V. A. 86
Stanley, J. C. 22, 27, 32, 83, 126, 190, 195, 211
Starkey, B. A. 116
Stasser, G. 121n4, 399
Stein, Gertrude 318
Stempel, G. H. 320n1
Stepper, S. 108
Stevens, S. S. 13
Stocking, C. 281, 282, 296
Stoll, R. J. 116, 154
Stone, P. J. 307
Stoner, J. A. 15
Storreston, M. 400
Stoto, M. 403n3
Strack, F. 75, 108, 355
Strand, J. R. 116
Strauss, A. L.: *The Discovery of Grounded Theory* 261
Streufert, S. 165, 344
Stroebe, W. 296, 401, 438
Strohmetz, D. B. 129
Stromberg, E. L. 256
Stroop, J. R. 345–6, 356
Stults, D. M. 74
Sudman, S. 281, 282, 284, 296, 325, 339n1

Suedfeld, P. 314, 344
Suls, J. M. 99n2
Swann, W. B. 402n1
Swanson, C. L. 283

Tabi, E. 109
Takezawa, M. 399
Taylor, S. E. 149, 349, 344, 350
Tekman, H. G. 381
Terry, R. 393
Tetlock, P. E. 165, 314
Theiner, G. 399
Thomas, R. K. 337, 340
Thompson, C. P. 149, 211, 365n5
Thomsen, C. J. 86
Thorne, B. 243, 255, 256
Thornhill, R. 286
Thurstone, Louis 14, 326–9, 331, 332, 333, 339n2, 372, 382n2–4
Tian, G.-L. 399
Tindale, R. S. 399, 400
Titus, W. 399, 420
Tomaka, J. 359
Tong, S. 400
Torgerson, W. S. 377, 379
Torres, M. 119
Tourangeau, R. 240, 325, 326
Treger, S. 388
Treiman, D. J. 283
Trochim, W. 35
Trotter, R. T., II 396
Tsang, A. 281
Tuchfarber, A. J. 285
Tucker, W. 291
Tunnell, G. B. 250–1, 252, 253
Turkle, S. 154
Turner, C. F. 299n4
Tversky, A. 4, 375, 379

Underwood, B. 144
Uphoff, H. F. 38

Vaillant, G. E. 316
Vaisey, S. 151
Valacich, J. S. 402
Van Bavel, J. J. 363
van der Zouwen, J. 282
Van Dusen, R. A. 299n3
van Heerden, J. 53
van Herk, H. 77
Vanman, E. J. 360
Vazire, S. 153
Verhallen, T.M.M. 77
Viet, A. L. 286
Vikan-Kline, L. 261
Visscher, T.L.S. 286
Visser, P. S. 324, 325
Vitaglione, G. D. 318
Vivekananthan, P. S. 380
Vollrath, D. A. 400

Voloudakis, M. 89
von Hippel, W. 150, 253
Vorst, H.C.M. 61

Wagner, D. 75
Walker, D. S. 56
Wallace, D. L. 306, 315
Wallach, L. 125
Wallach, M. A. 125
Walsh, J. T. 281
Walster, E. 176, 388, 431, 432
Walther, J. B. 400
Wang, Z. 8
Wardenaar, K. J. 381
Warner, R. M. 403n3
Wasserman, S. 396
Watt, J. 247n8
Weaver, C. N. 283
Webb, E. J. 147, 148, 256, 284, 433
Webb, S. C. 329
Webber, S. J. 129, 132
Weesie, J. 4
Wegener, D. T. 4, 326
Wegner, D. M. 399, 400
Weick, K. E. 252, 262, 269, 271
Weijters, B. 78, 337
Wellman, N. S. 305, 312
Wells, G. L. 108
Wenzel, G. 144
Wertz, F. J. 261
West, T. V. 4, 183n5
Weubben, P. L. 432
Wheeler, L. 257
Wheeler, S. R. 68
Whelan, M. 412
White, D. R. 263
White, H. 395
White, R. K. 311
Whyte, William Foote: *Street Corner Society* 293
Wiesenthal, D. L. 431
Wigman, J.T.W. 381
Wilhelmy, R. A. 114
Wilke, H. 119
Willems, E. P. 251–2
Williams, C. J. 354
Williams, K. D. 150, 151
Williams, P. A. 412
Williamson, J. 253
Williams-Piehota, P. 190

Willingham, D. T. 363
Wilmer, J. B. 154
Wilson, D. 144
Wilson, G. D. 76
Wilson, J. L. 319
Wilson, R. 149, 150
Wilson, T. D. 9, 30, 105, 109, 112, 137, 342
Winer, B. J. 99n4
Wing, C. 210
Winkielman, P. 108
Wish, M. 380
Witt, P. N. 131
Wojcik, S. P. 151
Won-Doornink, M. J. 388
Wondra, J. D. 388
Wong, V. 206, 210
Wood, E. 235
Wood, H. 256
Wood, S. J. 381
Wood, W. 96, 410, 412, 420
Wright, J. D. 282
Wyatt, R. C. 337
Wyatt, T. H. 297
Wyer, M. M. 264
Wyer, R. S., Jr. 351

Xu, Y. 114 243

Yakobson, S. 316
Young, B. 247n8, 379
Young, F. W. 379
Yuan, Y. 400
Yule, G. U. 315

Zander, A. F. 269
Zanna, M. P. 107, 345
Zegiob, L. E. 258
Zemke, P. 119
Zentall, T. R. 8
Zhao, R. 286
Zhao, X. 175
Zhou, Y. 286
Zickar, M. J. 53
Zill, N. 299n3
Zillman, D. 8
Zimbardo, Philip 114
Zimmerman, D. W. 53
Zinnes, D. A. 116
Zuell, C. 312

SUBJECT INDEX

ACASI 286
acquiesence 76–7, 128, 338; response bias 77, 337
actor 8
actor-partner interdependence model 389–90
alpha *see* coefficient alpha
American Psychological Association: Committee on Ethical Standards 428
analogue experiments 117–20; collective decisions 118; individuals 118
answering machines and caller-ID 243
applied research: vs. basic research 30–1
apprehensive participants 129
archival data 211–12; *see also* content analysis
artifact 191; threats to internal validity 74–8, 337
ascendancy searching 414
asymmetric dyad 388, 390
attention, measures of 344–7; interference 345–6; processing time 347; visual 345
attenuation 54, 165, 176, 325, 333
attitude scales *see* rating scales
attrition *see* participant loss
audio computer-assisted self-interview software 286
autocorrelated errors 205, 206
automatic evaluation 354, 355, 364
automaticity 355–8; cognitive busyness 356; response interference techniques 356–8

Balance of Power (game) 116
balance theory 113
bargaining games 114
basic research 3–21; science and daily life 4–5; theories and hypotheses 5–6; vs. applied research 30–1
between-dyad variables 386
bias: experimenter *see* experimenter expectancy; observer 38, 133, 256, 261; publication 414; response 77, 337
bidirectional causation 24

binomial effect size display (BESD) 422–3
bipolar adjectives 333, 334, 336, 339n4
blind procedures 133–4; double blind 131, 133, 135
blocked designs 94–6; *see also* factorial design
blocking variable 94, 95, 98
brain stimulation 361
brainstorming groups 401
brain wave measures 361–2

California F Scale 77
cardiovascular indices 359
category systems 262–72; assessing use 268; construction 264–72; intensity-extensity 265–6; interference 269; interrater reliability 269–72; number of categories 266–7; time 264; unit of observation 263–4; variables 267–8; *see also* coding observations
causal direction 24
causation 23–5, 36, 164, 168; bidirectional 24; moderators and mediators of relationships 24–5; noncausal covariation 24, 42n2; reciprocal 177; third-variable 24; unidirectional 24; vs. covariation 24, 42n2
census 220, 221, 222, 230, 233; *see also* U.S. Bureau of the Census; U.S. Census
ceteris paribus 38
change, assessment of 190–5; regression artifacts 190–1
choice matrix 373, 374, 375; pair comparison scaling 372–6; prisoner's dilemma 115
classical test theory 45–53, 54, 56, 58, 62, 64, 73; assessing reliability 48–53; observed score 45–6, 47, 48, 52, 53, 54, 73, 164, 192, 402; random error 46; systematic error 46; true score 46
closed-ended questions 285, 288, 289
cluster sampling 224, 230, 236, 237, 246; *see also* multistage sampling
clustering 336, 349, 350, 365n5

code of ethics 437–8; *see also* ethical standards; ethics
coding observations 260–74; category systems 262–72; combining quantitative and qualitative 274; early data returns 261–2; grounded theory 261, 305; interrater reliability 269–72; number of categories 266–7; rating scales 272–4; structured-nonstructured dimension 261; units 263–4; variables 267–8; *see also* Cohen's Kappa; Fleiss' Kappa; intraclass correlation
coding unit 306, 314; spatial and temporal 308; words and themes 306–8
coefficient alpha 49–50, 55, 332, 333, 336
coefficient of determination 162, 166, 183n3, 193
cognitive busyness 356
cognitive dissonance 8, 156
Cohen's Kappa 270–1, 273
comparison group design 31, 195–200, 203, 206
comparison time-series design 206–7, 210
complete counterbalancing 97
computer-assisted self-administered interviewing 243
computer-mediated group interaction 400–1
computer simulations 121n4
concept priming 350–3; assessing awareness 352–3; subliminal 351–2; supraliminal 351
conceptual hypothesis 5, 6
conceptual replication 40, 138, 142, 149, 150
concurrent validity 67, 68
condition replicability 41
confederate 8, 47, 104, 106, 129, 130, 143, 150, 251, 261, 364, 387, 397, 410, 420, 430
confidentiality: data 434
confirmatory factor analysis 55, 56, 177, 178, 333
conflicting findings 8
confound 31–2, 96, 97, 103, 104, 142, 159, 167, 169, 171, 195, 200, 202, 318, 440; *see also* artifact
construct validity 65, 70, 71, 138, 142, 151, 410, 411; conceptual replication 138, 142, 149, 150; known groups method 68, 69; meta-analysis 409–11; multitrait-multimethod matrix 70–1, 73–4
contemporary test theory 53–61; factor analysis 54–7; item response theory 57–61; latent factors and correction for unreliability 53–4
content analysis 303–22; coding systems 311–12; coding unit 305–8; effects analysis 318–19; propaganda analysis 317–18; facts presentation 317–18; Internet 319; representative examples 314–15; sampling 308–11; statistical analysis 312–13; stylistic analysis 318; summary of general paradigm 313–14; to whom was it said 317; what was said 315–17; who said it 315; *see also* coding unit; context unit; deductive content analysis; inductive content analysis
content databases 311
content validity 66, 69, 298
context unit 306, 307–8, 320n1
control group 33, 84, 85, 90, 91, 97, 99n2; *see also* experimental design
convenience sampling 234–5

convergent validity 68–9, 70, 73, 151, 364
correction for attenuation 54
correlational analyses 167, 318
correlation and simple regression 161–5; accuracy of linear prediction 163–4; common variance 162–3; zero correlation 164–5
correlation coefficient 161, 162, 164, 165, 193, 388, 389, 417, 423
correlational research 159–84; causal analysis 23–5, 36, 164, 168; curvilinear relations 161; linear correlation 161, 164; nonlinear relationships 161; partial correlation 169, 170, 172, 176, 390; *see also* prediction; regression
cost-benefit analysis 188, 438
counterbalanced ordering 97
covariance: analysis 203
cover story 351, 353, 429, 430
criterion 53, 164, 170, 171, 182, 212, 251, 297; multiple regression 166–7, 169, 170, 171, 172, 175, 182, 194, 361; predictive validity 67, 68, 70, 358, 364
criterion validity 66–7, 70
criterion variable 26, 28, 163, 164, 166, 167, 171, 172, 411
Cronbach's alpha 49, 50, 53, 54, 55, 62n2, 332, 338
crowdsourcing 41; websites 153

debriefing 103, 299n1, 352, 431–2; funneled debriefing 353; process debriefing 432
deception: in the laboratory 429; and participant well-being 430
deductive content analysis 305
demand characteristics 133, 144
dependent variable 26, 27, 31, 32, 33, 34, 35, 48, 83, 85, 87, 89, 90, 92, 94, 95, 96, 97, 103, 104, 105, 107, 110, 111, 112, 113, 114, 136, 142, 143, 146, 148, 153, 159, 160, 350, 355, 410, 412, 415, 439; assessing in field settings 146–7, 251, 342; measurement validity 148, 200; memory 347
descendancy searching 413–14
diaries: structures 256, 257; use in research 267
direct effects 175–7, 180
discriminant validity 69–70, 74; combining with convergent validity 70–1
discrimination parameter 58
disguised field experiment 440
disproportionate stratified random sampling 226–7, 229
disturbance terms 179–80
double-barreled question 282, 324, 327
double-blind procedures 131, 133, 135
dyadic measures 385–406; group level variables 87–91; measuring reciprocity or mutuality 388–9
dyadic variables 385, 386, 387, 388

early data returns 261
EARTH (Exploring Alternative Realpolitik Theses) 116
ecological validity 136–7

EEG 362
effect size 103, 411, 414, 419–23, 424, 425n4; calculation 414–17; heterogeneity
electroencephalography *see* EEG
EMG *see* facial electromyograph
endogenous variables 174–5
entry 254–5, 291; after entry 292–3
environmental manipulation 104–5, 152
epsem designs 224
EQS 180
equal appearing intervals 327–9, 331
error rate 38; Type I 28, 29, 48, 439; Type II 28, 29, 48, 89, 102; *see also* bias; random error
ESP 38
ethical standards 428, 435, 436, 438
ethics: data reporting 438–9; deception and participant well-being 430; deception in the laboratory 429–30; issues related to the products of scientific research 440–1; methodology as 438; research practices 428–35; *see also* informed consent
event-related potential 361–2
exact replication 142, 420
excitation transfer 8
exogenous variable 174, 175
expectancy effects 131–2, 135, 261; early data returns 261
experience sampling method (ESM) 257–8
experimental design 83–100; basic variations 83–6; blocked designs 94–6; expanding the number of experimental treatments 86–94; factorial designs 87–90; interaction effects 90–4; posttest-only control group 85; pretest-posttest control group 33, 84, 85, 90, 91, 97, 99n2; repeated-measures designs and counterbalancing 96–8; Solomon four-group design 85–6, 89–90
experimental manipulations 104–9; environmental 104–5; instructional 107–8; priming 108–9; social 105–7; stimulus 105
experimental methods 22, 26, 27, 43n3, 101, 141, 181, 182, 213, 275, 342; *see also* quasi-experimental methods
experimental realism 112, 117, 120, 131
experimenter expectancy 139n2, 261, 294; and bias 131–5
experiments outside the laboratory 141–58; field experiment 143–9; Internet as a site for experimental research 149–55; research settings and issues of validity 142–3
exploratory factor analysis 55, 333
external validity: basics issues of 39–41; definition 27; and internal validity 22–44; of laboratory experiments 125–40; *see also* ecological validity; generalizability; relevance; robustness
extreme-response sets 76

face-to-face interviews 232, 239, 242–3, 244, 280–1, 400–1
face validity 65–6, 315
facial action coding (FACS) 359

facial electromyograph 359–60
factor analysis 54–7, 61, 333, 335, 380; confirmatory 177, 178, 333; exploratory 333
factorial design 87–90, 95, 98, 99n4; creating the design 87–8; example 89–90; factor independence 88–9; mixed 160; treatment interaction effects 89
faithful participants 129
false consensus effect 5
feasibility studies 187
Federalist Papers 306, 315
field experiments 143–9; application 149; control over independent variable 143–5; dependent variables 146–7; random assignment 145–6; unobtrusive measures 147–9
field research: vs laboratory research 29–30; *see also* field experiments; observational methods
field study 141, 434
file-drawer problem 414
fixed-effect model 417, 418, 419
Fleiss' Kappa 271, 273–4, 313
focus groups 66, 297, 298, 303
foot-in-the-door technique 146, 291
free recall 348
functional magnetic resonance imaging (fMRI) 361, 362

galvanic skin response 358
gatekeeper 291, 292
generalizability 40–1; across participants 126–31; across people 40–1; across settings 40–1; *see also* external validity
generalizability theory 52
general sampling weight 240–1
generations design 397
going native 255–6
goodness of fit 16, 181
good participants 129, 132
GPower 102
grounded theory 261, 305
group interview 296–7
group level analysis 396–8; nested design 170, 171, 172, 208, 257, 396–7
group level variables 387, 398, 403n2
group performance 401
group process measures 398–402
group variables 385, 387
growth curve model 207–10
guessing parameter 58–9, 60, 61
Guttman's scalogram 329–31

hang together 49, 55
HARKing 439
heterogeneity 232, 419, 420
hidden profile technique 399, 400
hidden third factor 167–8
hierarchically nested design 397
hypotheses: conceptual hypothesis 5, 6; research hypothesis 5, 9, 117, 127, 130, 134, 149, 155, 411, 419, 429
hypothesis generation 6–9, 134, 246, 250, 254

identification 181; under-identified model 181; just-identified 181
The Imitation of Christ 315
implicit association test (IAT) 356, 357–8, 361
implicit measures 108, 128, 354, 358, 364
implicit responses 344, 364
independent variable 26, 27, 31, 32, 34, 39, 48, 86, 87, 88–9, 90, 91–2, 94, 95, 96, 97, 98, 102, 103, 104, 105, 106, 111, 113, 118, 136, 142, 143, 159, 160, 166, 185, 189, 350, 410, 411, 412, 415, 439; control over 143–5
indirect effects 175, 176; *see also* mediator variables
indirect measures 343–4; *see also* sentence completion test; thematic apperception test
individual performance 401
inductive content analysis 305
information processing measures 344–50; attention 344–7; memory 347–50; processing time
informed consent 102, 428, 429, 430, 433, 434, 441, 442
institutional review boards (IRB) 103, 152, 436–7
instructional manipulation 104, 107–8, 111, 134
instrumentation effects 33, 38
instrumentation error 32
interaction effects 40, 90–4; forms 92–4; moderator variables 94; treatment 89
interaction process analysis 266, 267, 274, 398–9
interdependence model 389, 390
internal consistency 49–51; *see also* Cronbach's alpha; split-half reliability
internal validity: definition 27; and external validity 22–44; basic issues 31–9; causation 23–5; distinguishing 27–31; participant loss 36–4; phases of research 25–7; random assignment and experimental control 33–6; *see also* validity
International Processes Simulation 116
Inter-Nation Simulation 116
Internet: conducting experiments online 150–1; experimental research 149–55; methodological concerns 151–2; misconceptions about research 153–5; online studies 152–3; privacy 433–4; research 153–5; research on social network activity 150
Internet surveys 243–4
interrupted time-series design 203, 206
interval scale 14, 336, 374, 376
interviewer characteristics 293
interviews 280–302; administration 280–5; after entry 292–3; attitudes, intentions, and behaviors 284–5; conducting 290; demographic information 283; direction 295–6; face-to-face 242–3; group 296–8; informal tactics 293–4; leading questions 294–5; obtaining entry 291; open- and closed-ended questions 288–90; question content; reconstruction from memory 283–4; semi-structured 287–8; sensitive beliefs and behaviors 285–6; structure 286; structured 288; telephone vs. face-to-face 242–3, 280–1; unstructured 286; verbal and nonverbal reinforcement 296; *see also*

closed-ended questions; focus groups; gatekeeper; group interview; leading question; open-ended questions; question constraint; question content; question specificity; self-stimulation effects
intraclass correlation 171, 208, 272–3, 313, 389, 392
introspectionism 9
involuntary participants 127–8, 129
IRB *see* institutional review boards
item response theory 57–61; parameters of item characteristic curves 58–60; simultaneously estimating all three parameters 60–1
item-reversal 77

judgment experiments 105
just-identified 181

Kappa *see* Cohen's Kappa
Knowledge Networks 244

laboratory environment: set up 103
laboratory experiments, constructing 101–24; manipulation checks 109–10; participant pool selection 101; prepare materials 102–3; randomization procedures 110–1; realism 111–12; sample size 102; set up laboratory environment 103–4; social simulations and analogue experiments 112–20; submit plan to IRB 103; types of experimental manipulations 104–9
laboratory research 143, 144, 145, 151, 429; neuroimaging measurements 363; vs. field research 29–30
language: difficulty 76
latency *see* reaction time measures
latent factor 53–4, 55, 56–7, 58, 61, 62, 178–80
latent structural equation model 177–80
latent variables 61
law of large numbers 34, 94
leading question 294–5, 299
lexical decision task 354
Lexis-Nexis 311
Likert scale 331–6, 338
linear prediction: accuracy 163–4, 175
linear relationships 161–2, 163, 164, 183n3
linear trend 208–9
LISREL 180
literature: database 413–14, 415; understand 411
longitudinal research 211–12, 435

main effects 88, 89–92, 94
manipulation checks 109–10
matching: post hoc 195, 200; propensity score 200–3; *see also* regression artifacts
maturation effects 32, 33
measurement construct validity 65
measurement error 46, 53, 55, 56, 73, 164, 167, 177–8, 179, 221, 323, 331, 370, 371, 373, 382n1
measurement model 45, 178, 179
measurement reliability 45–63, 151, 304; classical test theory 45–53; contemporary test theory 53–61

measurement validity 64–80, 148; assessment 151; threats 74–8, 337; types 65–74
median split 57, 160, 183n1
mediators 24–5, 175, 176; multiple 183n6
mediator variables 25
memory measures 347–50; recall 348–9; recognition 349–50
meta-analysis 409–11; interpreting 422–4; locating primary studies 413–14; stages 411–22; study inclusion and exclusion criteria 412–13; understand the literature 411
Minnesota Multiphasic Personality Inventory (MMPI) 66, 77
missing at random (MAR) 245, 246
missing completely at random (MCAR) 244–5, 246
missing data 244–6; missing at random (MAR) 245, 246; missing completely at random (MCAR) 244–5, 246; not missing at random (NMAR) 245
mixed design mixed factorial design 95, 160; *see also* blocked design
moderators 24, 25, 136, 298, 421, 424; demographic 420; study-level, 419 420; theoretical 420
moderator variables 24–5, 96, 297–9, 413, 424; heterogeneity 419–22; interaction effects 94
monadic variables 385
Monitoring the Future 186–7
monotone items 329
mood effects 75
mortality 32, 36
MTMM *see* multitrait-multimethod matrix
multidimensional scaling 377–81; unfolding 378–9
multi-level modeling 170–2, 208, 396
multiple operationalization 12–13, 17, 70, 149, 331
multiple regression 166–7, 169, 170, 171, 172, 175, 182, 194, 361
multistage sampling 230–3, 236, 237, 240, 246; panel surveys 233; stratified 226–30, 232, 235
multitrait-multimethod matrix (MTMM) 70–1; evaluating results 73–4
mundane realism 112, 131, 137

narrative review 409, 410; vs. vote counting vs. meta-analysis 423–4
National Merit Scholarships 22
National Research Council 436
National Security Agency 434
naturalism 250–3; behavior 251–2; event 242; setting 252–3
natural randomization 145
needs assessment 186–7
negative participants 129
nested design 170, 171, 172, 208, 257, 396–7
nested variable 171
neuroimaging 362–3
nominal groups 401, 402
nominal scale 13
noncausal covariation 24
nonexperimental methods 22, 182

nonexperimental research 159–84; analyzing and interpreting 160–6; multi-level models 170–2; multiple regression 166–7; structural equation models 172–81; uses and misuses of correlational analysis 167–70
nonindependence: data 397
non-laboratory research: ethical issues 432–3
nonlinear relationships 161
nonmonotone items 327
nonprobability sampling 224
nonrandom sampling 233–6; convenience 234–5; quota 235–6; snowball 235
nonresponse: surveys 239–40
nonvoluntary participants 128–9
not missing at random 245
null hypothesis 28, 43n5, 89, 151, 320n7

observational methods 250–79; coding 260–74; concealed; naturalism 50–3; participatory-nonparticipatory distinction 253–60; participatory 253–4
observed score 45–6, 47, 48, 52, 53, 54, 73, 164, 192, 402
observer bias 38, 133, 256, 261
odds ratio 415, 417
online experiments 150–1
online studies 152–3
open-ended questions 285, 288, 290, 324–5, 347
operationalization 9–13, 19, 142, 145, 332, 420; definitions 10; generalizability 39; imperfections 11–12; measurement 45 64; multiple 12–13, 17, 70, 149, 331; variable 104
order effects *see* question ordering; repeated measures
ordinal scale 13–14, 374
Osgood's semantic differential 333–6
overt behavior 42n2, 111–12, 251, 342, 364

pair comparison scaling 372–6, 377, 380
panel survey 233
parafoveal processing 352
parallel forms reliability 52
partial correlations 169–70, 172, 176
partial counterbalancing 97–8
participant loss 36–7
participant roles 129–31; apprehensive participants 129; faithful participants 129; good participants 129; negative participants 129
participants: awareness 126–7; restriction of populations 126; voluntary 127
participant selection 101; randomization procedures 110–11
participant well-being 430
participatory observation 253–60; gaining entry 254–5; going native 255–6; partial 256–9; when and why 259–60
partner 385
path models 174–7; mediation 175–6; multiple mediation 176–7; recursive vs. nonrecursive models 177

Pearson product-moment correlation 161
Pew Research Center 435; Project for Excellence in Journalism 316
phantom construct 12, 56
phases of research 25–7; *see also* dependent variable; independent variable
placebo effect 131
population parameters 222, 238
Portrait of the Artist as a Young Man 315
post hoc matching 195, 200
posttest-only control group 85
potency 335, 336
power: statistical 28, 89, 102, 211, 233, 236, 285, 410, 422
practice effect 33
precision: and sampling error 220–4
prediction: vs. hypothesis-testing 168–9; *see also* correlation and simple regression, accuracy of linear prediction; linear prediction
predictive error 167, 174, 178, 179, 182
predictive validity 67, 68, 70, 358, 364
predictor variable 25, 26, 40, 163, 164, 166, 168, 173, 182, 183n5
President's Panel on Privacy and Behavioral Research 428
pretest-posttest control group design 31, 32, 33, 83–5, 97, 210; regression and matching 195
pretest sensitization 33, 84, 85, 90, 91, 97, 99n2
primary study 409, 410, 413, 414, 415, 419, 422
priming manipulation 104, 108–9, 352, 358
priming techniques 350–8; assessing awareness 352–3; concept 350–3; subliminal 351–2; sequential 353–5; supraliminal 351
prisoner's dilemma 115
Prisoner's Dilemma Game 116, 119, 120
privacy: invasion 127, 433; Internet 433–4
probability-based random 244
probability sampling 224, 233
processing time 347
product-moment correlation 161
program development 187
program efficacy 187, 188
program evaluation 186, 188, 195; confusion between process and outcome 189; political context 188–9; separation of roles 189; special characteristics 188–9
program evaluator 186, 189, 200, 207
program feasibility 187
propaganda analysis 314, 317–18
propensity score 200
propensity score matching 200–3
pronunciation task 355
proportionate stratified random sampling 224, 226, 227, 229
PsychExperiments 151
psychophysiological measures *see* cardiovascular indices 359; facial electromyograph 359–60; neuroimaging 362–3

publication bias 414
public behavior 433

quadratic trend 209
quasi-experimental methods 22, 84, 189–95, 212, 213; regression artifact and reliability 191–4; regression artifacts and assessment of change 190–5; statistical control of regression artifacts 194–5
quasi-experiments: comparison group 31, 195–200, 203, 206; pretest-posttest 31, 32, 33, 83–5, 97, 210; regression-discontinuity 210–11
question constraint 285, 288
question content 282–3
questionnaires 323–41; dropout and no-opinion response format 326; open-ended questions 324–5; question order 325–6; question wording 324; response formats; *see also* double-barreled question; Guttman's scalogram; rating scales; Thurstone scales
question ordering 325–6
question specificity 285
quota sampling 224, 236

random assignment 22, 38, 41, 83, 85, 88, 94–5, 96, 110–11, 185, 189, 190, 219–20; experimental control 33–6; field settings 145–6
random digit dialing 236, 241–2
random-effects model 417, 418, 423
random error 45, 46, 47, 48, 53, 54, 56, 192, 194, 196
random numbers 241, 242; table 110, 222, 225
random sampling 220, 224, 230; simple 224–5, 226, 232, 236, 246n2; stratified 226–7, 229, 232, 235
random selection 41, 233, 241
rank order scaling 376, 377
Rasch model 58
rating scales 76, 263, 272–4, 323, 324, 370, 386, 392; constructing 326–7, 335
ratio scale 14, 377
reaction time measures 355
realism: in an experiment 111–12; experimental 112, 117, 120, 131; mundane 112, 120, 131, 137
recall measures 347, 348–9, 365n2
reciprocity 174, 175–7, 388–90, 392, 394, 402
recognition measure 347, 349–50
regression 161–5; linear 163, 164; multiple 166–7, 169, 170, 171, 172, 175, 182, 194, 361; statistical 32
regression artifacts: assessment of change 190–1; matching 195–200; reliability 191–4; statistical control 194–5
regression-discontinuity design 210–11
regression line 163
reinforcement, verbal and nonverbal 296
relevance 137
reliability: assessing 48–53; Cronbach's alpha 49, 50, 53, 54, 55, 62n2, 332, 338; definition 45; internal consistency 49–51; regression artifacts 191–4; split-half 49; temporal stability 51–3

repeated measures definition 96; designs and counterbalancing 96–8
research hypothesis 5, 9, 117, 127, 130, 134, 149, 155, 411, 419, 429
research question 5, 159, 303, 304, 315, 361, 388, 409, 429; deception 431
research settings: and issues of validity 142–3
response formats 336–8; number of response options 337; use of reversed items 337–8
robustness 40, 41, 135–6, 137, 138
role-playing simulations 113–17; active 114; bargaining and negotiation games 114–16; international relations 116; passive 113–14; as research 116–17
round robin designs 391–3, 398

sample size 102, 151, 223, 237–9
sampling 220–4, 308–9; answering machines and caller-ID 243; cluster 224, 230, 236, 237, 246; multistage 230–3, 236, 237, 240, 246; probability-based random 244; random 220, 224, 230; simple random 224–5, 226, 232, 236, 246n2; source and content 309–11; stratified 226–7, 229, 232, 235; survey 220; two-stage 230; see also sample size
sampling error 28, 220–3, 419
sampling fraction 223, 224, 225, 226, 227, 229, 237
sampling frame 222, 224, 225–6, 227, 230, 232, 233, 234, 236–7
scaling: Guttman scalogram analysis 329–31; Likert method of summated ratings 331–6, 338; method of rank order 376–7; multidimensional 377–81; Osgood's semantic differential 333–6; pair comparison 372, 373, 376–7, 380; stimuli 370–84; Thurstone's method of equal-appearing intervals 14, 326–9, 331, 332, 333, 336, 339n2, 372, 382nn2–3; unfolding technique 378–9
scalogram analysis 331
scatterplots 161, 162, 163, 164, 183n2
scientific method 3–4, 5, 6, 10, 26, 342
scrambled sentence task 351
selection-based interaction 32
selection bias 36, 171, 191, 195
selection error 32
self-consciousness effects 127
self-report 71, 75, 109, 146, 148, 159, 257, 286, 323, 325, 342, 343, 364, 396, 413, 420
self-selection 35, 144, 145
self-stimulation effects 289
semantic differential 333–6, 338, 410
semi-structured interviews 286, 287–8
sentence completion test 343
sequential priming 353–5; automatic evaluation 354; issues related to use of reaction time measures 355; lexical decision task 354; pronunciation task 355
sham operation 38
shrinkage 167, 333
simple random sampling 224–5, 226, 232, 236, 246n2

simulation research 113, 116, 117, 121n4
snowball sampling 224, 235
social cognition 344, 350, 355, 363, 365n5, 385; see also implicit measures
social desirability 75–6
social manipulation 104, 105–7
social network analysis 150
social psychophysics see stimulus scaling
social psychophysiology 358–63; brain activity 360–1; cardiovascular indices 359; facial measures of affective states 359–60
social network analysis 395–6
social relations model 491
social responsibility and ethics in social research 428–44; ethical issues related to the products of scientific research 440–1; ethics of data reporting 438–9; ethics of research practices 428–35; regulatory context of research involving human participants 435–8
social simulations: and analogue experiments 112–20; role-playing 113–17
sociogram 395
sociomatrix 393–5
sociometric analysis 392–5
sociometry 393
Solomon four-group design 85–6; example 89–90
spatial unit 308, 320n1
split-half reliability 49
sponsorship of research 440
spurious relationship 24, 191
stages of research 411–22
standard error 221, 223–4, 237–8
startle eyeblink reflex 360
statistical analysis 312–13
statistical conclusion validity 27–9
statistical power 28, 89, 102, 211, 233, 236, 285, 410, 422
statistical regression 32; see also artifact
stimulus manipulation 104, 105, 111
stimulus scaling 370–84; techniques 372–6
stratified sampling 226–7, 229, 232, 235
statistical significance 28–9, 43n4, 46, 48, 102, 410–11, 414
stratified sampling 226–30, 232, 235
Stroop effect 345–6, 356
structural equation models 172–81, 182; fit 180–1; identification 181; path model 174–7
structured interview 288
subliminal priming 351–2
subscales 55, 77, 333
summary effect 417–18, 419, 420, 421, 422–3, 424; fixed-effect model 417, 418, 419; random-effects model 417, 418, 419, 423; unweighted model 417, 418
summated ratings 331–6
summative evaluation 188
survey research; answering machines and caller-ID 243; Internet 243–4; missing data 244–6; nonrandom sampling 233–6; random digit dialing

241–2; random sampling 224–33; selection vs assignment 219–49; telephone vs. face-to-face interviews 242–3; types 241–4; *see also* interviews; sampling
symmetric dyad 388, 389, 390
synthesis 149, 344, 409, 411, 412, 413, 414, 418, 425n2; quantitative *see* meta-analysis
systematic error 45, 46, 47, 48, 56, 192
systematic sampling 225–6

TAT 344
telephone interviews 243, 280–1
temporal stability 51–3; parallel forms reliability 52; test-retest reliability 51, 52, 191, 193, 195, 313
temporal unit 264, 308, 320n1
test-retest reliability 51, 52, 191, 193, 195, 313
thematic apperception test 343
theory 5–8; generating a hypothesis 6–9; and hypotheses 5–6; operation to measurement scales 13–15; role of in research 15–18; *see also* operationalization
Theory of Reasoned Action 178
threats *see* artifact, threats to internal validity; measurement validity, threats; validity, threats to experiments
Thurstone scales 14, 326–9, 331, 332, 333, 336, 339n2, 372, 382nn2–3; reliability 329
time-series design 203–6; archival data; autocorrelated errors 205, 206; comparison 206–7, 210; interrupted 203, 206; prewhitening 205
transcranial magnetic stimulation 361
translation 6, 10, 45, 435
treatment *see* manipulation checks
trial-and-error approach 26
triangulation 12, 70; *see also* multiple operationalization
true experiment 35, 83, 96, 110, 185, 189, 190, 210, 211, 213, 219
true score 45–8, 53, 54, 64, 74, 169, 191–7, 331
two-phase sampling 233, 247n6
two-stage sampling 230
Type I error 28, 29, 48, 439
Type II error 28, 29, 48, 89, 102

under-identified model 181
unfolding technique 378–9
unidirectional causation 24
unintentional processes 38, 43n6, 84, 132, 254, 364
unit of analysis 92, 99n1, 264, 272, 395, 415, 421; nested designs 396–7
unmeasured variables 34, 245
unobtrusive measures 147–8, 149; ethics 433
UN Security Council 116
unstructured interviews 286, 287
unweighted model 417, 418
U.S. Bureau of the Census 233, 435
U.S. Census 232, 240, 246n1

validity: concurrent 67, 68; construct 65, 70, 71, 138, 142, 151, 410, 411; content 66, 69, 298; convergent 68–9, 70, 73, 151, 364; criterion 66–7, 70; definition 45; ecological 136–7; external 22–44; face 65–6, 315; internal 22–44; measurement 64–80, 148, 200; operationalizations: predictive 67, 68, 70, 358, 364; statistical conclusion 27–9; threat to experiments 74–8, 337; *see also* construct validity
variable: between-dyad variables 386; blocking 94, 95, 98; category systems 267–8; coding observations 267–8; criterion 26, 28, 163, 164, 166, 167, 171, 172, 411; dependent 26, 27, 31, 32, 33, 34, 35, 48, 83, 85, 87, 89, 90, 92, 94, 95, 96, 97, 103, 104, 105, 107, 110, 111, 112, 113, 114, 136, 142, 143, 146, 148, 153, 159, 160, 350, 355, 410, 412, 415, 439; definition 10; group level 87–91; independent variable 26, 27, 31, 32, 34, 39, 48, 86, 87, 88–9, 90, 91–2, 94, 95, 96, 97, 98, 102, 103, 104, 105, 106, 111, 113, 118, 136, 142, 143, 159, 160, 166, 185, 189, 350, 410, 411, 412, 415, 439; moderator 24–5, 94, 96, 297–9, 413, 424; monadic 385; nested 171
verification 5, 25–6, 43n3, 262, 314, 315
voluntary participants 103, 127, 129
vote counting 423–4, 425n4

within-dyad variables 386
within-subject designs *see* repeated measures
World Wide Web *see* Internet